BEST PLACES®
SOUTHERN
CALIFORNIA

BEST PLACES®
SOUTHERN
CALIFORNIA

Edited by
ERIKA LENKERT

EDITION 1

SASQUATCH BOOKS
SEATTLE

Printed in the United States of America
Distributed in Canada by Raincoast Books Ltd.

First edition
02 01 00 99   5 4 3 2 1

ISBN: 1-57061-181-5
ISSN: 1524-9255

Series editor: Kate Rogers
Cover and interior design: Nancy Gellos
Maps: GreenEye Design

SPECIAL SALES

BEST PLACES® guidebooks are available at special discounts on bulk purchases for corporate, club, or organization sales promotions, premiums, and gifts. Special editions, including personalized covers, excerpts of existing guides, and corporate imprints, can be created in large quantities for specific needs. For more information, contact your local bookseller or Special Sales, BEST PLACES® Guidebooks, 615 Second Avenue, Suite 260, Seattle, Washington 98104, 800/775-0817.

SASQUATCH BOOKS
615 Second Avenue
Seattle, WA 98104
206/467-4300
books@SasquatchBooks.com
www.SasquatchBooks.com

CONTENTS

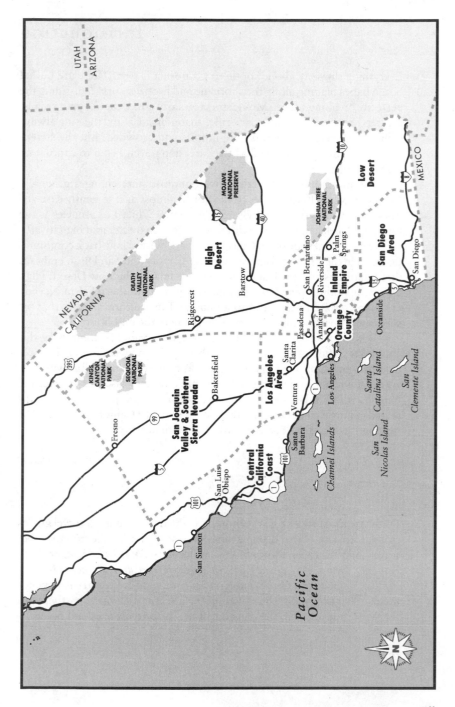

Introduction

Everything they say about Southern California is true. There are buffed beach babes blading along the shoreline and bronzed surf studs riding the perfectly breaking waves. Movie stars regularly cruise the shopping malls, theaters, and restaurants. Cars rule, materialism is in, the sun always shines, and, yes, the freeways are infinite and crowded. But the stereotypes, delightfully confirmed as they are, don't even begin to capture all that is Southern California.

The lower half of America's westernmost state changes gradually from its vastly different sister to the north, almost as if to gently ease visitors into the contrary lifestyles to the south. While Los Angeles is the undisputed celebrity county, with in-your-face character and big-city attitude, the Central California Coast's cooler clime and laid-back communities revel in their pastoral charm. Orange County and San Diego embrace that famously casual SoCal living, whereas inland, the Low Desert, High Desert, Inland Empire, San Joaquin Valley, and Southern Sierra Nevada are characterized by deserts, mountains, and agricultural terrains that are surprisingly earthy and relaxed in both landscape and lifestyle.

With such distinct geographic and cultural varieties comprising this enormous section of the state, it's possible to have many unique experiences over the course of one month, one week, or even one day. But wherever you visit when touring the region, you are bound to discover why for the millions who live here—including me, a well-traveled journalist who was reared in northern-biased San Francisco—Southern California is one of the most intriguing, diverse, and captivating destinations on earth.

—*Erika Lenkert*

Editor **ERIKA LENKERT** has authored or edited more than 15 travel guides to California and other destinations. She also shares her passion for food, travel, and lifestyles through articles for *Los Angeles Magazine, Bon Appétit, Travel & Leisure, InStyle,* Sidewalk, *Entertainment Tonight Online, Bride's,* and *California Homes.* Although Erika currently spends much of her time in San Francisco as the director of content partnerships for WineShopper.com, she considers L.A. the best place to call home.

Acknowlegments and Contributors

I've never been married. But given what I've heard about the over-whelming tasks required in planning the "Big Day," it's not a stretch to say that creating the first edition of *Southern California Best Places* was as intense, detail-oriented, time-consuming, and frustrating as planning a wedding. The location wasn't a particular oceanfront bluff with a tent overlooking the Pacific, but rather hundreds of dining and lodging establishments all over Southern California. The vows that were spoken were not of love, but more along the lines of "Kate (my editor), I faithfully do promise to send this chapter to you by next week." And while meddling families surrounding the grand occasion usually become horror stories, the people who gave their two cents at my party are the reason I can say: "Enjoy this incredible book, and explore the best of a larger-than-life, candidly colorful, and completely unique part of the world." After all the hard work that's gone into creating this tome to Southern California's finest, it's time for my honeymoon. . . . But not before thanking the bound-lessly talented contributors who brought this book to life. If you see them around, please throw some rice their way.

Native Angeleno, antique hound, and pop history enthusiast, **STEPHANIE AVNET YATES** offers her insight into pleasures found along the Central California Coast and in portions of Los Angeles. An experienced travel writer and guidebook author, she believes California is best seen from behind the wheel of a little red convertible.

Freelance writer **PETER JENSEN**, who navigates you through the desert areas, Inland Empire, San Joaquin Valley, and Sierra Nevada, lives in Del Mar, California. Jensen contributes regularly to *Sunset, This Old House, Coastal Living,* and *San Diego Home/Garden* and is the author of several books regarding travel destinations in the West.

HART MONROE is a freelance writer and filmmaker who lives quite happily—despite the smog, traffic, and constant parade of itinerant weirdos—on the cusp of Hollywood, with her four fantastic felines and Dewey, the Wonderdog. She shares the joys and curiosities of touring La-La Land and parts of Orange County.

Los Angeles resident **BONNIE STEELE** explores the unsung wonders of the Los Angeles valleys, as well as Fresno and portions of the city proper. She is the editor of *Valley Magazine,* a regional lifestyle magazine based in the San Fernando Valley, and *L.A. Brides,* a publication for area brides-to-be. She also contributes to such Web sites as Los Angeles Side-walk and has co-authored a guide to her hometown.

MARIBETH MELLIN, a contributor and former travel editor for *San Diego Magazine,* shares her insight into San Diego hotels and restaurants.

She is the author of several travel books on California and Latin America, and recently received the prestigious Pluma de Plata prize for writing about Mexico. She is also the editor of this book's companion guide, *San Diego Best Places*.

CHRIS RUBIN, the Los Angeles correspondent for *Travel & Leisure*, also contributes to publications from *Saveur* and *Bon Appétit* to *Wallpaper* * and *Wine & Spirits*. A native of the City of Angels, he highlights here his favorite Los Angeles hotspots.

MERRILL SHINDLER can be heard weekends talking about food on CBS Radio and is also the editor of the *Zagat Survey* in Los Angeles. His sense of humor and insider knowledge grace many of the restaurant reviews for our Los Angeles area.

MARAEL JOHNSON is an award-winning freelance travel writer who has authored or contributed to numerous guidebooks, including one she is currently writing on Los Angeles. She was raised in Southern California and proves her familiarity with the region by describing San Diego's attractions.

HELEN STOREY moved to the United States from London almost 20 years ago, and in that time, she has been a clothing designer, a decorative fresco painter, and a boutique owner. But it's as a freelance writer that she really shines, including contributions to *Los Angeles Magazine* and *Time Out New York*. For Best Places®, Helen introduces us to Santa Barbara and Montecito's finest.

GRETCHEN KURZ has been a journalist for more than 20 years and currently specializes in covering wine, food, and restaurant topics. A California native, Gretchen can often be found dining around on behalf of KIEV-AM radio, *Zagat Survey*, Sidewalk.com, and others. She will dive through flames for a great Zinfandel or any dish involving white truffles.

ELLEN CLARK, a native Southern Californian born in Pasadena, is an award-winning photojournalist who ventured to less-traveled areas of Los Angeles for this book. Her magazine, book, and newspaper assignments have taken her around the world from Timbuktu and West Africa to, in this case, such places as Downey, California.

Avid surfer and Southern California native **SANDOW BIRK** is a visual artist living and working in Los Angeles. His writing has appeared in *Surfer, Surfing, Juxtapoz,* and *Schwing* magazines, as well as in sidebars throughout these pages.

Special thanks are also in order for Kate Rogers, my abundantly patient, skilled, and encouraging series editor, managing editor Joan Gregory, and Gabriella Leone, Catherine Maxwell, David Hill, and Faith Winthrop, whose tireless and thorough research was critical in completing this guide.

—*Erika Lenkert*

About Best Places® Guidebooks

People trust us. BEST PLACES® guidebooks, which have been published continuously since 1975, represent one of the most respected regional travel series in the country. Each guide is written completely independently: no advertisers, no sponsors, no favors. Our reviewers know their territory, work incognito, and seek out the very best a city or region has to offer. Because we accept no free meals, accommodations, or other complimentary services, we are able to provide tough, candid reports about places that have rested too long on their laurels, and to delight in new places that deserve recognition. We describe the true strengths, foibles, and unique characteristics of each establishment listed.

Southern California Best Places is written by and for locals, and is therefore coveted by travelers. It's written for people who live here and who enjoy exploring the region's bounty and its out-of-the-way places of high character and individualism. It is these very characteristics that make *Southern California Best Places* ideal for tourists, too. The best places in and around the region are the ones that denizens favor: independently owned establishments of good value, touched with local history, run by lively individuals, and graced with natural beauty. With this first edition of *Southern California Best Places*, travelers will find the information they need: where to go and when, what to order, which rooms to request (and which to avoid), where the best music, art, nightlife, shopping, and other attractions are, and how to find the region's hidden secrets.

We're so sure you'll be satisfied with our guide, we guarantee it.

NOTE: *The reviews in this edition are based on information available at press time and are subject to change. Readers are advised that places listed may have closed or changed management, and, thus, may no longer be recommended by this series. The editors welcome information conveyed by users of this book. A report form is provided at the end of the book, and feedback is also welcome via email: books@ SasquatchBooks.com.*

How to Use This Book

This book is divided into eight major regions, encompassing San Simeon, Fresno, and Kings Canyon, and all destinations south to the Mexican border. All evaluations are based on numerous reports from local and traveling inspectors. BEST PLACES' reporters do not identify themselves when they review an establishment, and they accept no free meals, accommodations, or any other services. Final judgments are made by the editors. Every place featured in this book is recommended.

STAR RATINGS Restaurants and lodgings are rated on a scale of zero to four stars (with half stars in between), based on uniqueness, loyalty of local clientele, performance measured against the establishment's goals, excellence of cooking, cleanliness, value, and professionalism of service. Reviews are listed alphabetically, and every place is recommended.

★★★★ The very best in the region

★★★ Distinguished; many outstanding features

★★ Excellent; some wonderful qualities

★ A good place

NO STARS Worth knowing about, if nearby

UNRATED New or undergoing major changes

(For more on how we rate places, see the BEST PLACES' Star Ratings box, below.)

PRICE RANGE Prices for lodgings are based on peak season rates for one night's lodging for two people (i.e., double occupancy). Off-season rates vary but can sometimes be significantly less. Prices for restaurants are based primarily on dinner for two, including dessert, tax, and tip. Call ahead to verify, as all prices are subject to change.

$$$$ Very expensive (more than $200 for one night's lodging for two)

$$$ Expensive (more than $100 for dinner for two; between $150 and $200 for one night's lodgings for two)

$$ Moderate (between $40 and $100 for dinner for two; between $100 and $150 for one night's lodging for two)

$ Inexpensive (less than $40 for dinner for two; less than $100 for one night's lodgings for two)

ACCESS AND INFORMATION At the beginning of each chapter, you'll find general guidelines about how to get to a particular region and what types of transportation are available, as well as basic sources for any additional tourist information you might need. Also check individual town listings for specifics about visiting those places.

THREE-DAY TOURS In every chapter, we've included a quick-reference, three-day itinerary designed for travelers with a short amount of time. Perfect for weekend getaways, these tours outline the highlights of a region or town; each of the establishments or attractions that appear in boldface within the tour are discussed in further detail elsewhere in the chapter.

BEST PLACES® STAR RATINGS

Any travel guide that rates establishments is inherently subjective—and BEST PLACES® is no exception. We rely on our professional experience, yes, but also on a gut feeling. And, occasionally, we even give in to a soft spot for a favorite neighborhood hangout. Our star-rating system is not simply a AAA-checklist; it's judgmental, critical, sometimes fickle, and highly personal. And unlike most other travel guides, we pay our own way and accept no freebies: no free meals or accommodations, no advertisers, no sponsors, no favors.

For each new edition, we send local food and travel experts out to review restaurants and lodgings anonymously, and then to rate them on a scale of zero to four, based on uniqueness, loyalty of local clientele, performance measured against the establishment's goals, excellence of cooking, cleanliness, value, and professionalism of service. That doesn't mean a one-star establishment isn't worth dining or sleeping at—far from it. When we say that *all* the places listed in our books are recommended, we mean it. That one-star pizza joint may be just the ticket for the end of a whirlwind day of shopping with the kids. But if you're planning something more special, the star ratings can help you choose an eatery or hotel that will wow your new clients or be a stunning, romantic place to celebrate an anniversary or impress a first date.

We award four-star ratings sparingly, reserving them for what we consider truly the best. And once an establishment has earned our highest rating, everyone's expectations seem to rise. Readers often write us letters specifically to point out the faults in four-star establishments. With changes in chefs, management, styles, and trends, it's always easier to get knocked off the pedestal than to ascend it. Three-star establishments, on the other hand, seem to generate healthy praise. They exhibit outstanding qualities, and we get lots of love letters about them. The difference between two and three stars can sometimes be a very fine line. Two-star establishments are doing a good, solid job and gaining attention, while one-star places are often dependable spots that have been around forever.

The restaurants and lodgings described in *Southern California Best Places* have earned their stars from hard work and good service (and good food). They're proud to be included in this book—look for our BEST PLACES® sticker in their windows. And we're proud to honor them in this, the first edition of *Southern California Best Places*.

ADDRESSES AND PHONE NUMBERS Every attempt has been made to provide accurate information on an establishment's location and phone number. But it's always a good idea to call ahead and confirm. For establishments with two or more locations, we try to provide information on the original or most recommended branches.

AREA CODES Many area codes in Southern California are undergoing major changes. We have provided the most up-to-date area code information available at press time. If you have trouble reaching an establishment, however, call the operator for assistance, as its area code may have changed.

CHECKS AND CREDIT CARDS Most establishments that accept checks also require a major credit card for identification. Note that some places accept only local checks. Credit cards are abbreviated in this book as follows: American Express (AE); Carte Blanche (CB); Diners Club (DC); Discover (DIS); Japanese credit card (JCB); MasterCard (MC); Visa (V).

EMAIL AND WEB SITE ADDRESSES With the understanding that more people are using email and the internet to access information and to plan trips, BEST PLACES° has included email and Web site addresses for establishments, where available. Please note that the World Wide Web is a fluid and evolving medium, and that Web pages are often "under construction" or, as with all time-sensitive information, may no longer be valid.

MAPS AND DIRECTIONS Each chapter in the book begins with a regional map that shows the general area being covered. Throughout the book, basic directions are provided with each entry. Whenever possible, call ahead to confirm hours and location.

HELPFUL ICONS Watch for these quick-reference symbols throughout the book:

 FAMILY FUN Family-oriented places that are great for kids—fun, easy, not too expensive, and accustomed to dealing with young ones.

 GOOD VALUE While not necessarily cheap, these places offer you the best value for your dollars—a good deal within the context of the region.

 ROMANTIC These spots offer candlelight, atmosphere, intimacy, or other romantic qualities—kisses and proposals are encouraged!

 UNIQUELY SOUTHERN CALIFORNIA These are places that are unique and special to La-La Land and beyond, such as a restaurant owned by a beloved local chef or a tourist attraction recognized around the globe.

 Appears after listings for establishments that have wheelchair-accessible facilities.

INDEXES All restaurants, lodgings, town names, and major tourist attractions are listed alphabetically in the back of the book. Restaurants for the Los Angeles Area and San Diego County chapters are also listed by location in separate indexes at the end of this book.

READER REPORTS At the end of the book is a report form. We receive hundreds of reports from readers suggesting new places or agreeing or disagreeing with our assessments. They greatly help in our evaluations, and we encourage you to respond.

MONEY-BACK GUARANTEE See "We Stand by Our Reviews" at the end of this book.

LOS ANGELES AREA

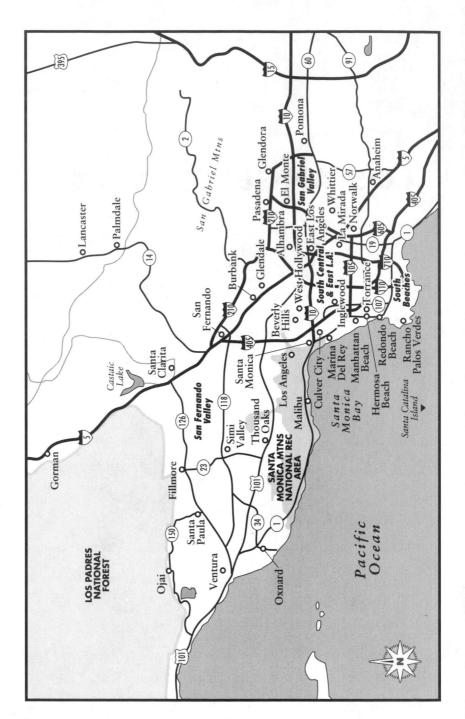

LOS ANGELES AREA

Los Angeles has been called La-La Land, Tinseltown, and "Nashville with a tan." For decades the city has been fodder for stand-up comics and talk show hosts. They've cracked wise about L.A.'s no-jacket-required atmosphere and about how everyone who lives here has a stack of headshots in their desk drawer and a screenplay in the hopper. Even Angelenos themselves seem to have a love-hate relationship with their city. They curse the smog and the traffic, and complain because it's almost impossible to get around without a car or find a place to park it if you have one. They whine about the price of buying a home, and they grumble that instead of being a real city Los Angeles is a confusing jumble of disparate and self-contained communities sharing nothing but a nodding acquaintance and a clogged freeway system.

On the other hand, Angelenos enjoy their city because it is the uncontested entertainment capital of the world and the bandleader of pop culture. There are more things to do and see here—scattered over a greater variety of locales—than in any other metropolis anywhere on the planet. Many in Los Angeles are proud that more than 80 languages are spoken in this United Nations of a town and that there are lively ethnic enclaves at every turn. Los Angeles also has a local arts and culture scene that, in its edgy vibrancy, is quickly surpassing New York's. But what's the real draw?

The perpetually summery weather, which makes it possible to shoot movies year-round; the wide range of topography—mountains, rugged canyons, deserts, the blue Pacific nudging miles of incomparable coastline—which convinced turn-of-the-century filmmakers to migrate from the East Coast and establish their nascent companies here. Los Angeles remains wrapped in film industry magic and mythos so potent that even hardened denizens starting an hour-and-a-half commute on a warm afternoon in January feel a thrill of excitement when they spot a movie company filming up the street, or see Mel Gibson strolling through Beverly Hills, or realize the woman on the corner stool in Starbuck's lapping a latte is Meryl Streep. They temporarily forget that Los Angeles is strung out like a jack-o-lantern's ragged teeth, with an overabundance of ugly strip malls and urban decay cramming the spaces in between; that it's full of industry, a working town, not as polished as its sister to the north or as venerable as its rival back east. But as the sun dissolves in a Technicolor tangerine puddle over the aquamarine sea, they remember for a moment that smog only makes the sunsets better.

ACCESS AND INFORMATION

Traveling to and from **LOS ANGELES INTERNATIONAL AIRPORT** is a snap when you call one of the major **SHUTTLE SERVICES**, such as Super-Shuttle (323/775-6600) or Prime Time (800/733-8267). Don't be surprised when the shuttle companies insist on picking you up two or three hours before your departure time, because traffic will undoubtedly be sluggish at best, and LAX is often mobbed. **TAXIS** are in abundance and cost a flat rate of $26.50 from the airport to downtown.

PARKING in Los Angeles is sometimes problematic, but not as challenging as in New York or San Francisco. Since this town is committed to car culture, valet parking is available practically everywhere, and it's relatively inexpensive at around $3.50 a pop. Most of the city's meters have one- or two-hour time limits, and the meter maids are zealous. Meanwhile, in many parts of the city—Santa Monica and certain sections of West Hollywood, for example—parking is by residential permit only or restricted in one way or another (especially during rush hours). Read every sign carefully and stay within the guidelines; tickets and towing are such a part of life here that they're practically a rite of passage for new arrivals.

The major hotels and most of the shopping malls have taxi stands, but cabs don't cruise in Los Angeles the way they do in Manhattan, so it's best to phone for one in advance.

The **MTA (METROPOLITAN TRANSPORTATION AUTHORITY,** 800/266-6883) runs the buses. There aren't enough of them, and they're usually behind schedule, so incorporate extra time into your plans to allow for that. The MTA has three lines: Red operates within the city; Blue heads north and south from downtown Los Angeles to "north" Long Beach; and Green travels east to west along the outer areas of Norwalk and the South Bay. MTA also runs the new MetroRail—what there is of it, and that doesn't go much of anywhere yet in metropolitan L.A. **AMTRAK** (800/USA-RAIL) trains arrive and depart from downtown's exquisite Spanish Revival–style **UNION STATION** (800 N Alameda; 213/624-0171), and **GREYHOUND** (800/731-2222) can be caught downtown at 1716 E 7th St; 213/262-1514.

Visitors to Los Angeles certainly appreciate that when making vacation plans they usually don't need to factor in the **WEATHER**. Angelenos appreciate it, too. That's why they grumble so much when the mercury dips a bit in the winter months, or when the hot **SANTA ANA WINDS** intermittently blow from August through October. The **RAINY SEASON** occurs from January to March, but in non–El Niño years it doesn't rain very much. Compared to what's happening in the rest of the country during those months, the City of Angels is still a paradise, and winter is when Angelenos appreciate their city most. There is, however, a phenomenon in Los Angeles called **JUNE GLOOM**: Because the marine layer

LOS ANGELES AREA THREE-DAY TOUR

DAY ONE: A day in the heart of old Hollywood. Indulge in flannel cakes and Golden Era atmosphere at **Musso & Frank's Grill,** then spend the morning gazing at the stars on the **Hollywood Walk of Fame,** and check out the stars' prints in the courtyard of **Mann's Chinese Theatre.** Visit the nearby **Hollywood Entertainment Museum** and **Hollywood History Museum.** Some of these experiences are cheesy, but they're something you gotta do once in your life. Lunch at **Off Vine,** then explore the wonders of **Griffith Park** in time to watch the sun set beyond the city from the Griffith Park Observatory parking lot. Stop for an apéritif at **Yamashiro,** then head down the hill to dine at Hollywood's renowned **Patina,** where you're likely to see some of Hollywood's living legends as you indulge in celebrity chef Joachim Splichal's provocative fare. Catch a late flick at **Laemmle's Sunset 5.** Finish off the evening with a drink at the sexy **SkyBar.**

DAY TWO: A chic L.A. day. Have breakfast on the bougainvillea-draped patio at the **Hotel Bel-Air,** then head to Beverly Hills for a morning of browsing the **Rodeo Drive** shops. After reinvigorating yourself with lunch at **Spago,** jump in the car and follow curvy **Mulholland Drive** above the hills and stunning homes, winding your way to an afternoon at the **Getty Museum at the Getty Center** (provided you've secured a parking reservation). Return in time for dinner at celebrity-filled **Mr. Chow,** and wind up the evening with a nightcap at the **Beverly Hills Hotel's Polo Lounge.**

DAY THREE: Beach Life. If you aren't a registered guest, at least eat breakfast at the lovely **Shutters on the Beach.** From here walk to the **Santa Monica Pier** and take a ride on the antique carousel, then make a shopping stop at touristy **Third Street Promenade.** Rent in-line skates or a bicycle and follow the **beachfront path** south to **Venice Beach** (about a half-mile jaunt along the 26-mile path). Return to your car and drive north on the Pacific Coast Highway for an afternoon at **Zuma Beach** in **Malibu.** Have a picnic lunch on the beach, then spend some time soaking up the sun. End your coastal day with dinner at Malibu's **Granita.**

of air is heavier during this month, the sun often doesn't appear before noon. Still, the **AVERAGE TEMPERATURE** during the summer is about 80 degrees, and about 70 degrees in the winter. If you're traveling to L.A., bring a jacket or a sweater no matter what the season, because most evenings are cool.

The Los Angeles freeway system isn't the only thing clogged by traffic these days. With fax machines and Internet connections, the phone system is under strain too. To remedy this, the phone companies have assigned more **AREA CODES** and reorganized existing ones. Downtown's prefix remains 213, while everything west of it to Beverly Hills is now classified as 323. Beverly Hills to the beach towns of Marina del Rey and up to Malibu remain 310, although as of April 1999 an additional code—424—was added and is now being assigned to new accounts. Calling these additional area codes doesn't necessarily mean you're placing a toll call, but it's best to check with the operator to make sure.

The people at the downtown office of the **LOS ANGELES CONVENTION AND VISITOR INFORMATION BUREAU** (685 S Figueroa Street, between Wilshire Boulevard and Seventh Street; 213/624-7300; www. lacb.com) are friendly and anxious to be of assistance. Their hours are 8:30am to 5pm, Monday through Saturday. There's a **HOLLYWOOD OFFICE** too, with the same hours and phone number (6541 Hollywood Boulevard near Cahuenga Boulevard; 213/236-2331). For a full schedule of sports or arts and culture events, call the **VISITOR HOTLINE**, 213/689-8822. You can hear the recorded information in Japanese, French, German, or Spanish. By calling 800/CATCH-LA you can arrange for a packet of information to be mailed to you. The **WEST HOLLYWOOD CONVENTION CENTER AND VISITORS BUREAU** is located in the Pacific Design Center (8687 Melrose Avenue, Suite M-25; 310/289-2525) and is open 8:30am to 5:30pm Monday through Friday. The **BEVERLY HILLS CHAMBER OF COMMERCE AND VISITORS BUREAU** (239 S Beverly Drive; 310/248-1000) is open weekdays 8:30am to 5pm. The **SANTA MONICA VISITORS CENTER** (1400 Ocean Avenue; 310/393-7593; www.santamonica.com) is open from 10am to 4pm in the winter, 10am to 5pm during the summer. They're closed on major holidays and during inclement weather.

Los Angeles

The magic of Los Angeles lies not in any one particular site or attraction, but rather in just being here, absorbing its diverse and overwhelming atmosphere. Celluloid City's distinct neighborhoods and glorious beaches are clipped together like a film that showcases individual vignettes; drive (and you must drive) ten minutes in any direction and the venue changes dramatically and immediately, which means you can submerge yourself in real-life versiouns of *Baywatch, Scenes from the Class Struggle in Beverly Hills, Melrose Place,* or *Swingers*—with less than a gallon of gas.

HOLLYWOOD AND WEST HOLLYWOOD

Hollywood is more a state of mind than a glamorous destination, but most visitors feel inclined to find that out for themselves. That said, there are a few worthy Tinseltown excursions. Along the gritty length of **HOLLYWOOD BOULEVARD**, remnants of the Golden Age are crammed in between kitschy souvenir shops and fronted by dubious-looking loiterers.

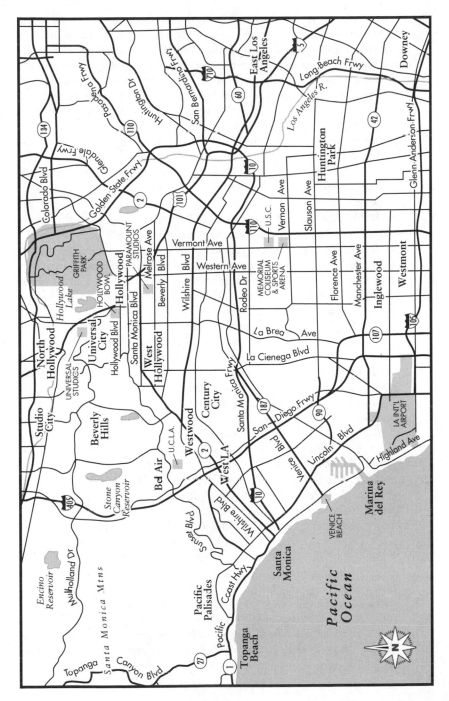

However, one genuine attraction is the **HOLLYWOOD WALK OF FAME**, which runs along Hollywood Boulevard between La Brea Avenue and Vine Street, and then along Vine down to Sunset Boulevard. Along "The Walk," the names of luminaries and super-luminaries in the film, radio, and television industries are commemorated by stars set in the polished mauve granite sidewalk. Another favorite is **MANN'S CHINESE THEATRE** (formerly Grauman's; 6925 Hollywood Boulevard, near Sycamore Avenue; 323/464-8186), where visitors may still match their hands and feet to the cement casts in the courtyard belonging to greats such as Clark Gable, Humphrey Bogart, Marilyn Monroe, Joan Crawford, Kirk and Michael Douglas, and Mel Gibson. Mann will soon have even more famous company when the upcoming home to the Academy Awards, the Academy Theater and mall complex, is completed (it's scheduled to open in 2000). However, Mann's merits alone make it a visit-worthy beacon of authentic Hollywoodness surrounded by a sea of schlock. The theater, with its murals, sparkling chandeliers, and carved-wood accents, was the site of countless Hollywood premieres in decades past; it remains pristine and is one of the most enjoyable spots in town to catch a flick. The **EL CAPITAN THEATER** (across Hollywood Boulevard at 6838; 323/467-7674) is another of the grand old movie palaces, almost as famous as Grauman's/Mann's, and it's been recently restored to its original grandeur.

Some budgetary corners were obviously cut at the new and interactive **HOLLYWOOD ENTERTAINMENT MUSEUM** (7021 Hollywood Boulevard; 323/465-7900), but it does give visitors an education in pre- and post-production phases of movie and television filming. Visitors can "foley" (add sound effects to) and edit pieces of film and video, enjoy make-up demonstrations, view an extensive collection of props and costumes, and sprawl in the captain's chair on the bridge of the starship *Enterprise*. Across the street from the museum, the recently reconstituted grand old **HOLLYWOOD ROOSEVELT HOTEL** (7000 Hollywood Boulevard; 323/466-7000) still reigns supreme at the corner of Sycamore Avenue. The open and airy upstairs gallery is lined with Hollywood yesteryear photos. L.A.'s latest historical attraction, the **HOLLYWOOD HISTORY MUSEUM** (1660 N Hollywood Boulevard; 323/464-7776) is scheduled to open in late 1999. Located in the elegant Deco Max Factor building, it's devoted to the preservation and veneration of the film industry. Its four-story, 45,000-square-foot facility holds a Smithsonian-like collection of film memorabilia representing all eras and genres. A more current exploration of the film world is available with a tour of **PARAMOUNT STUDIOS** (5555 Melrose Avenue; 323/956-1777). To the north and visible from all unobstructed mountain vistas, the **"HOLLYWOOD" SIGN** is perhaps the town's most recognized landmark.

The community of **WEST HOLLYWOOD** stretches east to west from Fairfax Avenue to Robertson Boulevard and north to south from Sunset Boulevard to Melrose Avenue. The area along Santa Monica Boulevard and just north and south of it is sometimes referred to as "Boys Town" because it's packed with bars, restaurants, cafes, and shops that cater to Los Angeles's gay scene. Architecture mavens may want to stop at the **PACIFIC DESIGN CENTER** (8687 Melrose Avenue at San Vicente Boulevard; 310/657-0800), near the border of Beverly Hills. Within this massive complex, constructed of brilliant green and blue glass, reside shops—many open to the public—full of the latest trends in home furnishings and design. The infamous **SUNSET STRIP** extends east to west along Sunset Boulevard from approximately La Cienega Boulevard to Robertson Boulevard. The shops are très chic and ultra-expensive. The numerous **OUTDOOR CAFES** are great for people-watching and star-sighting, and a lot of the club scene is located here.

BEVERLY HILLS, CENTURY CITY, AND WESTWOOD

West of West Hollywood is **BEVERLY HILLS**, a city jammed with fantastic places to eat and shop, but one of its most appealing activities is the 90-minute **BEVERLY HILLS ARTS AND ARCHITECTURE TROLLEY** tour (Saturdays, May through December, $5 adults, $1 children under 12). The I. M. Pei–designed Creative Artists Associates (CAA) building with its lobby Lichtenstein, the venerated PaceWildenstein and Gagosian galleries, as well as other important art and architecture sites in the area are stops along the way; 310/285-2438. The tour concludes at the **MUSEUM OF TELEVISION & RADIO** (465 N Beverly Drive; 310/786-1000), which offers special screenings and exhibitions; it also boasts a collection of over 90,000 radio and television shows that may be heard or viewed on audio and video monitors in private carrels on the second floor.

West of Beverly Hills along Santa Monica Boulevard is **CENTURY CITY**, with its enormous hotels, magnificent theaters, towering office complexes, and the **CENTURY CITY SHOPPING CENTER** (see Shopping, below), which is the premier mall in the city. Further west, the **UNIVERSITY OF CALIFORNIA, LOS ANGELES (UCLA)** is in the charming community of Westwood. Any visit to the campus must include a stop at the handsome, Romanesque-style, red-brick **FOWLER MUSEUM OF CULTURAL HISTORY** (310/825-4361; www.fmch.ucla.edu). The museum possesses a permanent display of cultural objects from the world over. In recent years, it has hosted the intriguing and highly popular "Scene of the Crime" and "Voodoo" exhibitions. Featuring sculpture by artists such as Rodin, Calder, and Hepworth, the **FRANKLIN MURPHY SCULPTURE GARDEN** is near the Fowler and well worth the extra steps. To find the **ARMAND HAMMER MUSEUM OF ART AND CULTURAL CENTER** (10899

Wilshire Boulevard; 310/443-7000), leave the UCLA campus via West-wood Boulevard and travel south to Wilshire Boulevard; the Hammer Museum is on the left. The most extraordinary feature of the museum, which opened in 1990, is its extensive collection of works by Honoré Daumier.

South of Beverly Hills, Westwood, and Century City in the Rancho Park area is the remarkable **MUSEUM OF TOLERANCE & SIMON WIESEN-THAL CENTER FOR HOLOCAUST STUDIES** (9786 Pico Boulevard, at Roxbury Drive; 310/553-8403; www.wiesenthal.com/mot/index.html), where visitors interactively explore the history of racism and the Holo-caust. The community of West Los Angeles is home to the **MUSEUM OF JURASSIC TECHNOLOGY** (9341 Venice Boulevard near Robertson Boule-vard; 310/836-6131; www.mjt.com), a peculiar collection of what the curator and staff—all kidding aside—refer to as "natural" displays. The establishment is an ingenious hoax that takes itself utterly seriously, but it's also a crucial stopover for anyone with a sense of humor and a taste for the astonishing.

SANTA MONICA

Santa Monica's **BERGAMOT STATION** (2525 Michigan Avenue; 310/829-5854), formerly a trolley stop, is a one-stop gallery crawl with more than 40 of L.A.'s most notable galleries clustered around the Santa Monica Museum of Art (see Museums, below). The **MUSEUM OF FLYING** (2772 Donald Douglas Loop N, off Rose Avenue; 310/392-8822) at the Santa Monica Airport features models of a DC-3 and a Spitfire. There's a very pleasant area for picnicking adjacent to the museum.

It's wonderful to stroll Santa Monica's **MAIN STREET** shops and restaurants; however, the nearby **THIRD STREET PROMENADE**, stretching three blocks from Broadway to Wilshire, with its street performers, splendid variety of trendy shops and eateries, farmers markets, outdoor setting, and carnival atmosphere, is seducing even the diehards away from the previously favored shopping mecca. Kids prefer meandering through **PACIFIC PARK** (380 Santa Monica Pier, at the foot of Colorado Boulevard off Ocean Avenue; 310/260-8744), located on the **SANTA MONICA PIER**. L.A.'s newest amusement park is a manageable size, with 11 child-friendly rides (as well as the respectable West Coaster for adults, which will excite a heart-stopping ripple or two), an arcade, unspectacular restaurants, and a captivating antique carousel that has been completely restored.

Also at the Santa Monica Pier is the interactive **UCLA OCEAN DIS-COVERY CENTER** (1600 Ocean Front Walk; 310/393-6149), which opened in 1997 and is the place where scrutinizing itty-bitty ocean critters in the microscope lab is the order of the day. The activity in the shark and ray tanks is absorbing, and so is the tidal pool display.

BEACHES

The **BEACHES** in Los Angeles are some of the best in the world, and the beaches in Malibu are the best in L.A. The **MALIBU SURFING BEACH** near the Malibu Pier—Beach Boys country—is the most famous one. Members of the neoprene-and-sun-streaked-hair crowd travel here from the world over to hang ten on breakers that sometimes measure 11 feet high. The most beautiful Malibu beach, however, is **ZUMA**, which is also known for having the cleanest water. **SANTA MONICA** and **VENICE BEACHES** are the most popular in Los Angeles, although during the summer months it's hard to find parking and even the stiff sea breeze can't dispel the miasma of Coppertone. Of the two, Venice is the more fun, and that's because of **VENICE WALK**, a low-rent version of the Third Street Promenade and in its own way just as satisfying. In summer it's mobbed with tourists and, admittedly, a lot of locals, who come to enjoy the musicians and other performers, scope out the stalls, shops, and cafes, and mingle with the freaks and scantily clad Rollerbladers.

DOWNTOWN

On the other side of town, both in style and location, is downtown Los Angeles's bustling **GRAND CENTRAL PUBLIC MARKET** (bounded by Third and Fourth Streets and Broadway and Hill Avenues; 213/624-2378). The market consists of an amazing square-block collection of stalls and stands full of produce, meats, fish, fowl, and multiethnic fast food, open daily from 9am to 6pm. Nearby is the ornate **BRADBURY BUILDING** (304 S Broadway Avenue), Los Angeles's oldest commercial building, built in 1893 and one of the true marvels of Los Angeles architecture. Another worthy landmark, the **BILTMORE HOTEL** (506 S Grand Avenue; 213/624-1011), built in 1923, had a face-lift a few years ago and is looking extremely well for her age. The Crystal Ballroom and the new lobby—a blend of Spanish rococo and Italian Renaissance—are wonders to behold. **ANGELS FLIGHT** (Fourth and Hill Streets), a funicular opened in 1901 to convey the rich to their Bunker Hill homes and recently restored to its former glory, offers a spectacular city view as the mini-railcar climbs to the pinnacle of Hill Street. A visit to downtown Los Angeles wouldn't be complete without a stop at **EL PUEBLO DE LOS ANGELES AT OLVERA STREET** to explore what the city was like when it was still a village, circa 1781. In the same locale are the **PICO HOUSE HOTEL** and **PLAZA CHURCH** (circa 1822), as well as the **AVILA ADOBE** house (circa 1818); 10 E Olvera Street; 213/623-2489. For those who want a more extensive and organized taste of historic downtown Los Angeles, **L.A. CONSERVANCY TOURS** (213/623-2489), led by very kindly and knowledgeable folk, offer a number of itineraries including "Marble Masterpieces" and Little Tokyo.

LITTLE TOKYO is located between First and Second Streets and Los Angeles and San Pedro Streets, surrounding the New Otani Hotel. Within its boundaries is the **JAPANESE-AMERICAN CULTURAL CENTER** (244 S San Pedro Street; 213/628-2725), which offers rotating exhibitions and occasionally presents performances by Japan's Grand Kabuki Theatre group. **OLD CHINATOWN,** located along Broadway Avenue and Hill Street north of First Street, has a wide array of shops and restaurants, but it's comparatively small and caters less to tourists and more to its Chinese-American residents.

GRIFFITH PARK, stretching from the L.A. to the San Fernando Valley and located between downtown and Hollywood, features the **GRIFFITH PARK OBSERVATORY AND PLANETARIUM,** which was immortalized in the James Dean flick *Rebel Without a Cause.* The Observatory offers star shows and information on just about every astronomical subject, while the Laserium presents light shows six nights a week. (Located at 2800 E Observatory Road; Laserium: 818/997-3624; Observatory: 323/664-1191.) Also within the park's boundaries are two other gems. The **GENE AUTRY MUSEUM OF WESTERN HERITAGE** (4700 Western Heritage Way; 323/667-2000; www.autrymuseum.org) preserves both the mythology and the history of the Old West within its seven themed galleries. The **LOS ANGELES ZOO** (5333 Zoo Drive; 323/644-4200) is now home to 2,000 creatures existing in simulated natural habitats, 78 endangered species among them.

MUSEUMS

The art collection isn't yet quite as grand as the brand-new, Richard Meier–designed, dazzling white travertine-and-glass buildings that house it, but director John Walsh of the **GETTY MUSEUM AT THE GETTY CENTER** (1200 Getty Center Drive, just west of the San Diego Freeway, Brentwood; 310/440-7300; www.getty.edu) promises he's working to remedy that. Meantime, the galleries, which opened in 1997, display what is there to its best advantage with their electronically controlled skylights. To visit this art enclave on 110 acres of high and rocky chaparral with a 360-degree view of the Los Angeles basin, the Pacific, and the Santa Monica Mountains, reservations must be made well (months) in advance. (The reservations are for parking only ($5); the museum itself is free.) However, it is possible to gain admittance without a reservation—only if you arrive by a mode of transportation other than car. It's a brief tram ride from the parking area to the plaza, where visitors enter the museum complex, composed of five galleries, an excellent gift shop, and remarkable outdoor gardens. Illuminated manuscripts, drawings, sculpture, decorative arts, and photographs are displayed on the first levels, paintings occupy the second.

The **SKIRBALL CULTURAL CENTER** (2701 Sepulveda Boulevard; 310/440-4500), in its new mountain location, is just a short distance from the Getty Center. The Moshe Safdie–designed complex has a chopped-from-rock feel and, like Meier's design for the Getty Center, achieves a beautiful cohesion between landscape and architecture. The center incorporates performance and conference facilities and a cafe, as well as an extensive and stimulating collection of historic art and artifacts tracing the Jewish experience. Youngsters will enjoy the chance to participate in the practice archaeological dig in the Discovery Center.

The recently redesigned façade of glass brick and marble at the **LOS ANGELES COUNTY MUSEUM OF ART (LACMA)** (5905 Wilshire Boulevard near Fairfax Avenue; 323/857-6000; www.lacma.org) is an enormous improvement over the old eyesore '60s version. LACMA's permanent collections include pre-Columbian Mexican art, an expansive silver collection, mosaics, Indian and Southeast Asian Art, and American and European paintings and sculpture. Curators are putting in extra effort to make LACMA cutting edge; with the recent Picasso and van Gogh shows, they're achieving their goal. There's now a new experimental gallery for children, the gift shop is one of the best of its kind in the metropolitan area, and on Friday nights there're often live jazz, blues, or classical music, a wine bar, and elegant eats under the portico.

LACMA may be the most imposing, but it's only one of several occupants of Museum Row. The **PAVILION FOR JAPANESE ART** (323/857-6000), with its fabulous permanent collection of paper art, pottery, kimonos, and much more, as well as the **GEORGE C. PAGE MUSEUM OF LA BREA DISCOVERIES** (323/934-PAGE; www.tarpits.org), with its tar pits and 650 species of plants and animals, are just behind LACMA. A few blocks away, heaven awaits car aficionados at the **PETERSEN AUTOMOTIVE MUSEUM** (6060 Wilshire Boulevard, east of Fairfax Avenue; 323/930-CARS; www.petersen.org). In historically authentic displays, the fins and fenders of Cords, Caddies, and almost any other fantasy-based make and model gleam as they did when they first rolled off the assembly line.

Angelenos adore downtown's **MUSEUM OF CONTEMPORARY ART (MOCA)** (250 S Grand Avenue, between Second and Third Streets; 213/626-6222; www.moca.org). Designed by the innovative Arata Isozaki and opened in 1986, the spacious and skylit galleries house a good permanent collection including works by Jackson Pollock, Robert Rauschenberg, Piet Mondrian, Andy Warhol, and the photographer Max Yavno. MOCA also presents a consistently impressive roster of fascinating traveling exhibitions, installations, and performance art. **THE GEFFEN (TEMPORARY) CONTEMPORARY AT MOCA** (152 N Central Avenue; 213/626-6222), in Little Tokyo (see Downtown, above), is no less beloved, which is why, after a Frank Gehry overhaul, the former police warehouse reopened its doors. The TC, as the Temporary Contemporary is affectionately known, is charmingly located across from the LAPD horse barn, where members of the mounted force can often be seen grooming their trusty steeds.

On the other side of town the **SANTA MONICA MUSEUM OF ART (SMMOA)** (2525 Michigan Avenue, west of Barrington Avenue, Santa Monica; 310/586-6488) has moved from its original location on Main Street and is now an integral part of the Bergamot Station art complex (see Santa Monica, above). The museum has no permanent collection of its own, but in the new 10,000-square-foot space, the long tradition of presenting mercurial and edgy exhibitions, multimedia installations, and performance art will continue.

SHOPPING

Designer brands reign on fabled **RODEO DRIVE** in Beverly Hills, between Santa Monica Boulevard and Wilshire Boulevard, where all the right labels are represented within a three-block stretch. Elite department stores can be found here, too, such as Barneys New York (9570 Wilshire Boulevard; 310/276-4400), Saks Fifth Avenue (9600 Wilshire Boulevard; 310/275-4211), and Neiman-Marcus (9700 Wilshire Boulevard; 310/550-5900). Inland, still-trendy **MELROSE AVENUE,** between Robertson Boulevard and La Brea Avenue, features frocks and accoutrements for the young and painfully fashionable. However, ultrachic **RON HERMAN FRED SEGAL** (8100 Melrose Avenue at Crescent Heights Boulevard; 323/651-4129) is still the number-one retail outlet if you want to bump into real Hollywood royalty. A more mature and scattered version of trendy Melrose is nearby **LA BREA AVENUE,** where an interesting explosion of antique shops and vintage clothing stores line the avenue from Melrose Avenue to Wilshire Boulevard. Los Angeles's **THIRD STREET** (not to be confused with Santa Monica's Third Street Promenade) has several wonderful gift stores within a few blocks east of La Cienega Boulevard. Worthy stops include **FREE HAND** (8413 W Third Street, between Orlando Avenue and La Cienega Boulevard; 323/655-2607) and **NEW STONE AGE** (8407 W Third Street, between Orlando Avenue and La Cienega Boulevard; 323/658-5969), which both carry unusual pottery and jewelry, and **ZIPPER** (8316 W Third Street, between Orlando and Sweetzer Avenues; 323/951-0620), a top choice for affordable retro and modern gifts and housewares. The **BEVERLY CENTER** (8500 Beverly Boulevard, at La Cienega Boulevard; 310/854-0070) is a multilevel mall complete with Bloomingdales, Macy's, boutiques, a food court, and a multiplex movie theater. **ROBERTSON BOULEVARD** between Melrose Avenue and Third Street is the place to stroll designer boutiques and fashionable furniture stores. **CENTURY CITY SHOPPING CENTER**, one of L.A.'s first malls and completely outdoors, is a world of its own, with an excellent food court, a multiplex movie theater, and a superb selection of shops, including a **METROPOLITAN MUSEUM OF ART STORE** (10250 Santa Monica Boulevard, between Century Park W and Avenue of the Stars; 310/553-5300; 310/552-0905). Santa Monica's **MONTANA AVENUE** offers elite—and complete—shopping to match its clientele. **SANTA MONICA PLACE** mall (310/394-1049), a whirlwind of major department stores (Robinsons-May and Macy's) and specialty shops, is bounded by Second Street, Broadway, Fourth Street, and Colorado Avenue. The mall's front yard is the **THIRD STREET PROMENADE**, a carnival of shops, tourist-oriented restaurants, movie theaters, and street performances.

Los Angeles has a wealth of great bookstores, and **BOOK SOUP** (8818 Sunset Boulevard at Holloway Drive; 310/659-3110) is foremost among them. Despite its chaotic appearance when you first come through the door and become overwhelmed by the cornucopia of fiction, travel, memoirs, cookbooks, magazines, special-interest fiction, and nonfiction—and by hordes of customers bumping into each other in the narrow aisles—there's a method to this madness. Thousands of culinary titles stock the small storefront of **COOK'S LIBRARY** (8373 W Third Street, between King's Road and Orlando Avenue; 323/655-3141). The **BODHI TREE** (8585 Melrose Avenue at Westbourne Drive; 310/659-1733) caters to New Agers, stocking volumes on holistic medicine, philosophy, astrology, alchemy, and the occult. **DUTTON'S BOOKS** (11975 San Vicente Boulevard, between Bundy Drive and Montana Avenue, Brentwood; 310/476-6263) offers an excellent collection of used and reference books as well as the latest fiction. **HENNESSY & ENGALLS ART & ARCHITEC-TURE BOOKS** (1254 Third Street Promenade, Santa Monica; 310/458-9074) has amassed one of the finest selections of art and architecture books in the country. They're well known for their sales and remainder tables and at any one time there may be as many as 4,000 titles on sale. **KOMA BOOKSTORE**'s (1764 N Vermont Avenue, above Hollywood Boulevard; 323/665-0956) specialty is "subversive" literature, with topics ranging from anal sex to bomb-making, and they have a catalogue, too. At **SAMUEL FRENCH** (7623 Sunset Boulevard at Stanley Avenue; 323/876-0570), an institution for actors in Los Angeles, every play that's ever been published is neatly arranged in alphabetical order on the floor-to-ceiling shelves. There's also a trove of publications on filmmaking, directing, how to prepare for auditions, and how to secure an agent, as well as film and music industry directories that many people in the area consider to be as sacred as the Bible.

PERFORMING ARTS

BASS TICKETMASTER (323/381-2000) offers tickets to almost every concert, performance, and event in town, including, during the high holidays, passes to the larger and more popular synagogues. A few venues, such as the Mark Taper Forum (see Theater and Comedy, below), offer day-of-performance or two-hours-before-performance half-price tickets, but you must appear in person to pay for them.

MUSIC: Founded in 1919 and now under the auspices of the brilliant and engaging director Esa-Pekka Salonen, the **LOS ANGELES PHILHAR-MONIC** (323/850-2000; www.laphil.org) is one of the world's most acclaimed orchestras. During their 26- to 30-week winter program, which opens each October, they're in residence at the Los Angeles County Music Center's Dorothy Chandler Pavilion (135 N Grand Avenue, near West Temple Street; 213/972-7211). During their 12-week summer season, the Philharmonic plays under the stars at the spectacular Hollywood Bowl (2301 N Highland Avenue, north of Hollywood Boulevard, south of the Hollywood Freeway; 323/850-2000). The Philharmonic's repertoire includes critically acclaimed interpretations of the classics, as well as the cutting-edge **GREEN UMBRELLA CONCERTS** performed by their New Music Group. During the winter season, the Philharmonic's renowned **CELEBRITY RECITAL SERIES** is incorporated into the program at the Dorothy Chandler. During summer, these recitals become the **VIRTUOSO SERIES** and a component of the program at the Hollywood Bowl. Summer is also the time to enjoy the Philharmonic's **CHAMBER ORCHESTRA** for its season at the historic, open-air John Anson Ford Theater (2580 Cahuenga Boulevard, east of Franklin Avenue; 323/461-3673). There isn't a seat in the house more than 100 feet from the stage, and it's also the venue for an eclectic variety of other music and dance programs. Pre-performance picnicking at the Hollywood Bowl and the John Anson Ford Theater is a beloved Los Angeles ritual. In 2002, when construction of the new **WALT DISNEY CONCERT HALL** (adjacent to downtown's Music Center) is scheduled for completion, the Philharmonic will leave the Dorothy Chandler Pavilion and take up residence there. The new facility, with a seating capacity of more than 2,300, is a Frank Gehry & Associates design and is, itself, a symphony of stainless steel panels, bearing an alarming resemblance to a series of toppling drive-in movie screens. In the most stunning example of philanthropic largesse the world of performing arts has ever encountered, the Disney family is footing the hundred-million dollar (and still counting) tab to make this tribute to Walt Disney a reality.

The Dorothy Chandler Pavilion is also where the **LOS ANGELES OPERA** (213/972-8001; www.laopera.org) resides. The company, which has traditionally included a large stable of young talent, debuted in 1986 with the world's foremost tenor, Placido Domingo, as the lead in Verdi's *Otello*. In 1995 Domingo assumed the position of artistic director and principal guest conductor, and he still functions frequently as both a performer and a conductor. The season, which begins in October, includes standards as well as rarely staged works. Peter Hemmings, who served a long tenure as managing director of the London Symphony Orchestra, is the company's general director. In December 1998, the company premiered Tobias Picker's *Fantastic Mr. Fox*.

The final resident of the Dorothy Chandler Pavilion is the country's number one professional chorus, the **LOS ANGELES MASTER CHORALE** (213/626-0624). Their repertoire ranges from classical to Broadway to pop. They occasionally perform at the Hollywood Bowl and often accompany the Philharmonic.

The recently restored and renovated Deco revival **WILTERN THEATER** (3790 Wilshire Boulevard at Western Avenue; 213/380-5005) presents a diverse program of performances, which have included the Dance Troupe of Lyon, Harry Connick Jr., and Yo-Yo Ma. Other terrific venues for enjoying an extensive array of performances include the **GREEK THEATER** (2700 N Vermont Avenue in Griffith Park; 323/665-1927); the **UNIVERSAL AMPHITHEATER** (100 Universal City Plaza near Lankershim Boulevard, Universal Studios; 818/622-4440); the **UCLA CENTER FOR THE PERFORMING ARTS** (Royce Hall, 405 Hilgard Avenue on the UCLA campus in Westwood; 310/825-4401); the **SHRINE AUDITORIUM** (665 W Jefferson Boulevard west of S Figueroa; 213/749-5123); and the **SANTA MONICA CIVIC AUDITORIUM** (1855 Main Street at Pico Boulevard in Santa Monica; 310/393-9961).

DANCE: Los Angeles doesn't have a resident ballet company like San Francisco or New York, but check out the schedules for the Wiltern Theater, the Music Center, and Grand Performances; all present dance events by small local or touring companies.

THEATER AND COMEDY: The **AHMANSON THEATER** and the **MARK TAPER FORUM** (www.taperahmanson.com) combine with the **DOROTHY CHANDLER PAVILION** (see Music, above) to form downtown's Los Angeles Music Center trinity. The incomparable Gordon Davidson is artistic director for both. The Ahmanson Theater was recently renovated to improve sight lines, enhance acoustics, and move the mezzanine closer to the stage. With its 2,600-seat capacity, it has been—since 1967—home to grand and glitzy musicals, revivals, and dramas such as Wendy Wasserstein's *The Heidi Chronicles, Phantom of the Opera*, 11 plays by Neil Simon and, more recently, *Rent, Fosse*, and *Titanic*. More than 50 productions at the Ahmanson have received prestigious and coveted Los Angeles Drama Critics Circle Awards. The Ahmanson uses the James A. Doolittle Theater (1615 N Vine Street, north of Sunset Boulevard;

323/462-6666) as an annex for mounting smaller productions like Yasmina Reza's *Art*, starring Alan Alda. The thrust stage at the Mark Taper Forum is only one of the reasons this little jewel is just about the most popular and certainly the best place in L.A. to see theatrical productions. Since its inception more than 30 years ago, the Taper has presented consistently knockout productions of dramatic and comedic plays. The Taper is now viewed as an Off-Broadway venue since many of the plays originally produced here have moved to Broadway, where they've garnered both commercial success and critical acclaim. Two—*The Kentucky Cycle* and *Angels in America*—have received Pulitzer Prizes. The SHUBERT THEATER (2020 Avenue of the Stars at Constellation Boulevard, Century City; 800/447-7400; www.shubert.com), which more than any other theater in Los Angeles feels like one of the big Broadway theatrical houses, best accommodates larger productions. *Ragtime* is among its recent successes. The GEFFEN PLAYHOUSE (10880 Le Conte Avenue, near Westwood Boulevard; 310/208-5454) in Westwood near UCLA mounts a diverse selection of productions, which in previous years has included Sir Ian McKellen's *Acting Shakespeare* and Steve Martin's *Picasso at the Lapin Agile*.

Richard Pryor got his start at THE COMEDY STORE (8433 W Sunset Boulevard, a block east of La Cienega, West Hollywood; 323/656-6225); so did Jim Carrey, Rosanne Barr, and David Letterman. Pauly Shore's mom, Mitzi, is the owner/proprietor. They all come back now and then and join the new talent. THE LAUGH FACTORY (8001 Sunset Boulevard at Crescent Heights Boulevard, Los Angeles; 323/656-1336) is another Sunset venue that often showcases big-name performers. The wildly outrageous Groundlings troupe, appearing regularly at the GROUNDLINGS THEATRE (7307 Melrose Avenue, near Poinsettia Place, Los Angeles; 323/934-4747) is one of the best improv groups in the city. Alumni include Jon Lovitz, Phil Hartman, Julia Sweeney, and Pee Wee Herman. THE IMPROV (8162 Melrose Avenue, west of Crescent Heights Boulevard, Los Angeles; 323/651-2583) is extremely popular and usually packed. Occasionally, one the bigger names in the comedy pantheon drops in to check out the new competition, or to test the yuk power of new material.

FILM: The AFI (American Film Institute) LOS ANGELES INTERNATIONAL FILM FESTIVAL (323/856-7600), which runs for two weeks every October, is the best and the biggest of the Los Angeles celluloid celebrations. Its focus is broad and multicultural, and it premieres the work of many emerging directors. The SANTA MONICA FILM FESTIVAL (1328 Montana Avenue, Santa Monica; 310/823-3323) is ongoing, presenting 12 monthly series of broad-spectrum independent films. Screenings occur on the third Thursday of the month, usually at the Aero Theater. The LOS

ANGELES INDEPENDENT FILM FESTIVAL (323/937-9155), which highlights the works of independent filmmakers, begins the third week of April at Los Angeles's Laemmle's Sunset 5 and other theaters around Hollywood. **OUTFEST: THE LOS ANGELES GAY AND LESBIAN FILM FESTIVAL** runs for 10 days in mid-July and features films by, about, and for gays and lesbians. Their main venue is the Directors Guild of America (DGA) theater, at 7920 Sunset Boulevard, Los Angeles, two blocks west of Fairfax Avenue; contact 323/960-9200 or www.outfest.org. Also screening at the DGA each April is the **CITY OF LIGHTS/CITY OF ANGELS FILM FESTIVAL** presenting a selection of French-language films (310/289-2000).

The **NUART THEATER** (11272 Santa Monica Boulevard, between Sepulveda Boulevard and Sawtelle Avenue, Santa Monica; 310/478-6379) is L.A.'s best art house, offering screenings of the work of dare-to-be-different filmmakers, as well as cult classics such as *Eraserhead* and *The Rocky Horror Picture Show.* Other excellent art-film venues include American Cinematheque, which specializes in retrospectives, tributes, and infrequently screened films at Hollywood's newly restored historic Egyptian Theater (6712 N Highland Avenue, Hollywood; 323/466-3456); Laemmle's Sunset 5 (8000 Sunset Boulevard, at Crescent Heights Boulevard, Los Angeles; 323/848-3500); Laemmle's Music Hall (9036 Wilshire Boulevard near Doheny Drive, Beverly Hills; 310/274-6869); The Royal (11523 Santa Monica Boulevard, five blocks west of the San Diego Freeway (405), West Los Angeles; 310/477-5581); and the Samuel Goldwyn Theaters at the Westside Pavilion shopping mall (10800 Pico Boulevard at Westwood Boulevard, Rancho Park; 310/475-0202). To find out where the movie you want to see is currently playing and to charge tickets, call the Los Angeles Times MovieFone, 777-FILM; the number works within all the region's area codes.

NIGHTLIFE

BARS: A lot of negative things that can be said about the City of Angels, but no one has ever complained about a shortage of fabulous watering holes. If you plan to make a night of it with a rambling pub crawl, a car is a must, and so is a designated driver because the DUI laws are strict in these parts and the LAPD deals harshly with offenders. Also bear in mind that where there are cocktails, there's the singles scene—often young enough to make you wonder whether this town really is composed of nothing but twenty-somethings.

In the Silver Lake–Los Feliz area, the warm and pleasantly shabby atmosphere at **AKBAR** (4356 Sunset Boulevard, near Fountain Avenue; 323/665-6810) is a good place to go on cold nights. It's mostly populated by the area's arty crowd of all sexual persuasions, and if you appreciate Britpop and electronica, the jukebox is awesome. As the name suggests, tiki style still dominates at **TIKI-TI** (4427 Sunset Boulevard, near Fountain Avenue, Los Feliz; 323/669-9381). The tropical drinks are served in coconut shells, and wearing an aloha shirt isn't unforgivable. **THE DERBY** (4500 Los Feliz Boulevard, near Hillhurst Avenue, Los Feliz; 323/663-8979) caters to swinging Gen-Xers mixed with some of the town's hottest veteran dancers. It's swanky, with private booths; there's usually live swing music on Wednesdays and Fridays, and swing dance lessons are available. What can be said about **THE DRESDEN ROOM** (1760 N Vermont Avenue, north of Hollywood Boulevard, Los Feliz; 323/665-4294), where Marty and Elayne Roberts still perform their '60s lounge act? The mixed crowd at the bar is usually five deep, and that speaks for itself. The **GOOD LUCK BAR** (1514 Hillhurst Avenue, north of Hollywood Boulevard, Los Feliz; 323/666-3524) is a favorite of the trendy and famous and their relatives. The **THREE CLUBS** (1123 N Vine Street, north of Santa Monica Boulevard, Hollywood; 323/462-6441) is smart and super-trendy. It has a dress code and a doorman to assure that everyone honors the requisite hipness. **THE ROOM** (1626 N Cahuenga Boulevard, north of Sunset Boulevard, Hollywood; 323/462-7196) is tough to find but worth the trouble once you've negotiated the ratty alley where it's hiding. The interior is sexy, the jukebox is solid, and the DJ spins an eclectic variety of music. The **LAVA LOUNGE** (1533 N La Brea Avenue, north of Sunset Boulevard, Los Angeles; 323/876-6612) is a groovy favorite tucked into an aging strip mall. Inside, hipsters rock to blues and surf. On the cusp of Hollywood, the funky **FORMOSA CAFE** (7156 Santa Monica Boulevard at Formosa Avenue; 323/850-9050) remains as popular now as it was 50 years ago with the Hollywood and celebrity set, young and old. **MOLLY MALONE'S** (575 S Fairfax Avenue, north of Wilshire Boulevard, Los Angeles; 323/935-1577) is cozy and intimate during the week. Weekends it jumps because there's a dance floor and live bands.

Bars with a view are generally more refined than the town's favored Hollywood haunts. The fearfully fashionable **360°** (6290 Sunset Boulevard at Vine Street, Hollywood; 323/871-2995) restaurant/lounge falls into that category. The stunning Japanese design of **YAMASHIRO** (1999 N Sycamore; 323/466-5125), at the crest of the Hollywood Hills, pales only in comparison to its city views. The **SKYBAR** (8440 W Sunset Boulevard, West Hollywood; 323/848-6025) at the oh-so-trendy Mondrian Hotel is very good for star-gazing—both the astral kind and celebs—if you can get past the doorman (or slip into the bar through the hotel before 8pm). The newly-hip-and-already-on-its-way-down **FENIX** (8538 Sunset Boulevard near La Cienega Boulevard, West Hollywood; 323/848-6677) at the Argyle offers the same city views with less haute hoopla.

The perennially cool **WHISKEY BAR** (1200 N Alta Loma Road at Sunset Boulevard, West Hollywood; 310/657-0611) in the Sunset Marquis

Hotel & Villas has no view, but is known as the Strip's less-self-conscious be-seen cocktail lounge. **BAR MARMONT**'s (8171 W Sunset Boulevard, west of Crescent Heights Boulevard, West Hollywood; 323/650-0575) retro-glamorous decor almost justifies the hefty cost of a cocktail. Cross into the boundaries of Beverly Hills and the cocktail scene becomes instantly more refined. Such is the case at hotel lounges such as **THE FOUR SEASONS** (300 S Doheny Drive at Burton Way; 310/273-2222) and the **REGENT BEVERLY WILSHIRE** (9500 Wilshire Boulevard at Rodeo Drive; 310/275-5200). **NIC'S AND THE MARTINI LOUNGE** (453 N Cañon Drive, north of Brighton Way; 310/550-5707) is a popular spot for martinis infused with spiced fruits.

On the Westside in Santa Monica, **REBECCA'S** (101 Broadway Avenue, at the corner of Ocean Boulevard; 310/306-6266), with its marine-flavored, ultramodern decor, is a favorite with the art gallery set; and **CHEZ JAY** (1657 Ocean Avenue; 310/395-1741), with its dark interior and the vintage tunes blaring from the box, attracts a large crowd of Santa Monica regulars. In Marina del Rey, the singles mecca of Los Angeles, **BAJA CANTINA** (311 E Washington Boulevard; 310/821-2252) is certainly doing its part to keep the singles scene alive. The place is usually packed with sun-tanned hard bodies talking fast and munching tortilla chips.

Downtown, check out the **GRAND AVENUE SPORTS BAR** in the Biltmore Hotel (506 S Grand Avenue; 213/612-1532) or **ENGINE COMPANY NO. 28**, in a converted 1912 firehouse (644 S Figueroa; 213/624-6996).

CLUBS: Los Angeles is at its best after dark, with many exciting dance and/or music clubs to choose from. In addition to the entries provided here, check out L.A.'s free publications *LA Weekly* and *New Times* (available at cafes, bars, and markets), or the Calendar section of the *Los Angeles Times,* for the complete word on what's happening in L.A.'s frenetic and fluid club scene. The heaviest concentration of clubs is in Hollywood and adjacent areas, so it's easy to hit more than one in an evening. The **CRUSH BAR** (1734 N Cahuenga Boulevard, north of Hollywood Boulevard, Hollywood; 323/463-SOUL) features '60s Motown and '70s and '80s chart-toppers. **THE PALACE** (1735 N Vine Street, above Hollywood Boulevard, Hollywood; 323/462-3000), in an old movie theater, has been pulling in hipsters of all ages for years with DJs spinning techno, house, and hip-hop and frequent concerts as well. **CIRCUS** (323/462-1291), which is usually called the Big Top, and **ARENA** (323-462-0714) share the same address (6655 Santa Monica Boulevard, two blocks east of Highland Avenue, Hollywood), have multiple dance floors, and offer a broad variety of salsa, techno, disco, and hip-hop. Both cater to both the straight and the gay crowds. The **CATALINA BAR & GRILL** (1640 N Cahuenga Boulevard, Hollywood; 323/466-2210) is a classy joint in the old sense of the phrase and one of the best places in the city for straight-ahead jazz. Many of the greats—Shirley Horne, Miles, and Ella, to name only a few—have put in an appearance or two at this one. Jennifer Lopez, Jimmy Smits, and other celebrity owners celebrate Latin music and dance at the CONGA ROOM (5364 Wilshire Boulevard, Los Angeles; 323/938-1696). The HOUSE OF BLUES (8430 Sunset Boulevard, West Hollywood; 323/848-5100), with its hydraulic stage, kitschy Louisiana ambience, and nightly first-rate jazz, rock, hip-hop, and blues acts, is hard to beat. The ROXY (9009 W Sunset Boulevard, West Hollywood; 310/276-2222) and the WHISKEY A-GO-GO (8901 Sunset Boulevard, West Hollywood; 310/652-4202) are cornerstones along the Sunset Strip. Both preview up-and-comers and new music by the seasoned. The JAZZ BAKERY (3233 Helms Avenue, behind Venice Boulevard, Los Angeles; 310/271-9039) is located around back of the old Helms Bakery, now the Antique Guild. The sound system is excellent and it's another great spot for straight-ahead jazz from big names and new talent. MCCABE'S (3101 Pico Boulevard, Santa Monica; 310/828-4403 or 310/828-4497) has a 150-seat theater where everyone who's anyone has played, and many of them pop back in to make surprise appearances and deliver acoustic performances. The most interesting and intense entrant in the Los Angeles jazz scene is the WORLD STAGE (4344 Degnan Boulevard, in the Crenshaw area; 323/293-2451). Thursday nights there are improv jams, and you might see a Marsalis brother playing next to today's nobody. It's not the best neighborhood, but there's safety in numbers, so go with a group. If Charlie Parker were still alive this is where he would hang. The MAYAN (1038 S Hill Street, between Olympic and 11th Streets; 213/746-4287), in the old Mayan vaudeville palace downtown, offers dance music as eclectic as its patrons.

PARKS

GRIFFITH PARK (2800 E Observatory Road; 323/664-1191), adjacent to Hollywood, is L.A.'s answer to New York's Central Park. Located in the lovely and rugged Los Feliz Hills, it's the ideal spot for a picnic or hike. The parking lot of the Griffith Park Observatory and Planetarium (see Downtown, above) is the preferred spot from which to scan the city's vast landscape (smog permitting). Griffith Park's northern hills are crisscrossed with more than 250 miles of bridle paths; horses can be rented from the Los Angeles Equestrian Center (480 Riverside Drive; 818/840-8401), or the Bar S Stables (1850 Riverside Drive; 818/242-8443). One of the dinner rides departing from SUNSET RANCH HOLLYWOOD STABLE (3400 N Beachwood Canyon Drive; 323/469-5450), sauntering through a section of the park and concluding at the Mexican restaurant Viva Fresh in Burbank, is a wonderful way to spend an evening.

SPANISH ROOTS AND CHICANO CULTURE

When Mexican philosopher Octavio Paz described Los Angeles, he wrote: "At first sight, the visitor is surprised not only by the purity of the sky and the ugliness of the dispersed and ostentatious buildings, but also by the city's vaguely Mexican atmosphere, which cannot be captured in words or concepts." Paz's perspective is not surprising, since from its earliest days as a sleepy pueblo founded by Spanish missionaries through its 20th-century explosion into bustling mega-metropolis, the area has maintained a Latin American flavor distinct from that of other American cities.

While that unique flavor has always seasoned the City of Angels with a subtle and spicy zest, after the World War II the influx of Latin American immigrants swelled, the undercurrent of Hispanic culture underwent a renaissance, and the Latin community further evolved its uniquely Southern Californian culture. Mexican and other Latino immigrants became lost between two worlds—not blending completely into "white" North American culture, yet simultaneously ostracized by their countrymen for not being "real" Mexicans. Gradually, they came to embrace both American and Latin cultures and to blend them together in a new sensibility: Chicano Culture.

As Chicano labor movements grew more vocal and visible in the 1970s, a sense of pride in their roots grew, and Chicanos (Americans born of Mexican parents) began to develop their own styles of dress, of speech, and of music—which frequently centered around such values as the strong family ties typical of their homeland but also embraced such Angeleno values as love of the automobile. These new styles blended into a subculture all its own, finally earning respect from both Mexicans and Americans.

The emergence of Norteño and Banda music, both of which incorporate elements of American country western and traditional Mexican music styles, has signaled the Chicano culture's emergence from the shadows. A huge success in Mexico, as epitomized by the late pop star Selena, these popular musical styles signaled the first time that cultural trends started by immigrants had trickled back home to alter the culture of the homeland.

As you travel through Southern California, notice the exaggerated sense of color to be found in Hispanic neighborhoods and throughout the city. Hear the soft cadences of Spanish spoken in the streets, smell the scents of Latin American cooking, and marvel at the wildly decorated "low-rider" cars on the roads beside you. For Los Angeles, once a sleepy Mexican town and now home to more than seven million Latinos, has not forgotten its roots—it has only modernized them.

RUNYON CANYON PARK (2000 N Fuller Avenue, at the dead end; 213/485-5111) is something of a surprise to visitors and to Angelenos alike. Once you're inside the iron gates, hiking up any of several serpentine mountain trails that commence about 50 yards beyond, it's a different world. Coyote and rattler sightings are common, the silence is soothing, the view from Inspiration Point at the summit is unparalleled, and all this is just a few blocks north of frantic Sunset Boulevard. With over 180 acres of grounds, a polo field, hiking trails, and ideal picnicking spots, WILL ROGERS STATE HISTORIC PARK (1501 Will Rogers State Park Road, off Sunset Boulevard; 310/454-8212) is an easy pastoral escape at the cost of $6 per car. PALISADES PARK (Ocean Avenue between Colorado Avenue and Adelaide Drive), a slim stretch of grass and palm trees fronting the Pacific Ocean, is a prime spot for watching the sunset, jogging, or taking in the sea air. The ethereal oasis known as the SELF-REALIZATION LAKE SHRINE (17190 Sunset Boulevard, before Sunset Boulevard dead-ends at the Pacific Ocean; 310/454-4114) hints that this town does have a sense of spirituality. The Buddhist cosmopolitan retreat, with its Zen lake, bridges, pastoral expanses, and meditators, is one of the city's most soothing and beautiful parks.

SPECTATOR SPORTS

Los Angeles may presently lack an NFL team, but there are two of almost everything else. The LAKERS basketball team and the KINGS hockey team previously played at the Great Western Forum in Inglewood but relocated to the brand-new downtown Staples Center (adjoining the Los Angeles Convention Center) in 1999. Tickets for both are available from BASS Ticketmaster (323/381-2000). The LOS ANGELES CLIPPERS (213/748-8000) basketball team are also scheduled to play at the new center. The LOS ANGELES DODGERS play at Dodger Stadium near Chinatown; for ticket information call 323/224-1491.

FESTIVALS

Los Angeles exploits any excuse for a party and hosts a variety of fairs, tournaments, shows, and festivals throughout the year. In January there's the annual AUTO SHOW (213/741-1151) at the L.A. Convention Center; a raucous celebration of Chinese New Year that consists of a street carnival and the GOLDEN DRAGON PARADE (Chinese Chamber of Commerce; 213/617-0396); and JAPANESE NEW YEAR (213/628-2725) in Little Tokyo, in which part of the revelry includes a seemingly endless line dance that winds through the area's shops as a good-luck blessing. The ACADEMY AWARDS (310/247-3000) are televised early in April. During the weekend before Easter, there's the ANNUAL BLESSING OF THE ANIMALS (213/625-5045) on Olvera Street, downtown. The best place for

EASTER SUNRISE SERVICES (323/850-2000) is the Hollywood Bowl. In May, there's the **LOS ANGELES/CALIFORNIA SCIENCE FAIR** (213/744-7400) at the California Science Center, where fanciful inventions abound, and the **CINCO DE MAYO** (213/625-5045) celebration on Olvera Street, celebrating Mexico's defeat of the French, is a guaranteed blast, although parking is problematic. The **VENICE ART WALK** (310/392-WALK), one of L.A.'s most enjoyable events, commences at Westminster Elementary School (1010 Abbott Kinney Boulevard), and you will have the opportunity to sample the fare of L.A.'s finest chef's while touring the studios of more than 50 artists. The **PLAYBOY JAZZ FESTIVAL** (213/850-2000) at the Hollywood Bowl in June offers an excellent lineup of jazz greats and emerging jazz artists. In August, enjoy **NISEI WEEK** (213/687-7193) in Little Tokyo and rejoice in everything Japanese. In October, celebrate **HALLOWEEN** in West Hollywood—L.A.'s answer to New Orleans' Mardi Gras and Halloween in the East Village. In November, the best way to celebrate **DÍA DE LOS MUERTOS** (Day of the Dead, November 1) are the parades and other festivities on Olvera Street; 213/628-7833. November is also the occasion for the **"VIVE LE BEAUJOLAIS" WINE FESTIVAL** (323/651-4741) at the Pacific Design Center. It's hosted by the French-American Chamber of Commerce, chichi, and quite enjoyable. The **HOLLYWOOD CHRISTMAS PARADE** (213/469-8311) takes place the Sunday after Thanksgiving. Attending it is a good way to inaugurate the holiday season. In December, you may want to visit **ART EXPO** (213/741-1151) at the Los Angeles Convention Center to enjoy acres—literally—of art in every medium by prominent, emerging, and unknown U.S. artists. Dress warmly for the **CHRISTMAS BOAT PARADE** (310/821-7614) in Marina del Rey, which usually occurs the two weekends before Christmas. **LAS POSADAS** (213/623-5045) on Olvera Street is a nightly Christmas celebration that includes a traditional candlelight march. One of the most beloved holiday traditions in the Southland is the annual **LOS ANGELES COUNTY HOLIDAY MUSIC PROGRAM** (213/972-7211) Christmas Eve day. It happens downtown in the Dorothy Chandler Pavilion (see Music, above) at the Music Center, and it's free.

RESTAURANTS

Ago / ★★☆

8478 MELROSE AVE, WEST HOLLYWOOD; 323/655-6333

With Robert De Niro, Ridley Scott, Miramax's Weinstein brothers, and other heavy hitters backing this super-trendy Italian restaurant, it's no surprise that it's an "industry" hangout. In fact, the stylish split-level dining room, with its open kitchen, brick wood-burning oven, and sleek bar, offers the perfect balance of visible yet intimate dining—a plus for the high-profile crowd who like a little of both. But executive chef (and partner) Agostino Sciandri, formerly of Toscana, and his inventive Italian cuisine are what truly make this restaurant a culinary favorite. While Sciandri's fare melds influences from Tuscany, Emilia-Romagna, and Liguria, his straightforward execution is sublime in such recent dishes as baby artichoke salad drizzled with olive oil and topped with shaved Parmesan cheese and walnuts, or veal wrapped with fontina cheese and asparagus on a mound of creamy mashed potatoes. And the man knows how to do risotto; the wild mushroom variation is respectfully al dente and pure heaven with every forkful. But the linguine with veal ragù, spaghetti with scampi and pumpkin flowers, and grilled salmon topped with a smart lemon-caper sauce are also good enough to ease the pain of the sure-to-be-hefty dinner bill. To end the evening, indulge in the creamy tiramisu. *$$$; AE, DC, DIS, MC, V; no checks; lunch Mon–Fri, dinner every day; full bar; reservations recommended; at La Cienega Blvd.* &

Alto Palato / ★★

755 N LA CIENEGA BLVD, WEST HOLLYWOOD; 310/657-9271

While this modern trattoria's high ceilings, colorful artwork, and sleek two-level design are in keeping with the neighborhood's fashionable art galleries and boutique furniture stores, the cuisine at Alto Palato is strictly classic Italian. Chef Paolo Monti delivers some of the best pizza this side of Rome; try one slice of his crisp, thin-crusted, wood-fired pies and you'll be a believer. Purists love the Margherita pizza's zesty sauce, fresh tomatoes, and smoke-infused crust; or the Siciliana, topped with grilled zucchini and the perfect amount of smoked mozzarella. There's life beyond designer pizza, though, and it comes in such dishes as lasagne à la Napoleon, a garlicky vegetable tart, and tender lamb shanks bathed in a fragrant red wine sauce. If the chef offers the special of thinly sliced filet of beef sautéed with arugula and garnished with white asparagus, order it; it always triggers praises throughout the dining room. *$$; AE, DC, MC, V; no checks; lunch Fri, dinner every day; full bar; reservations recommended; between Melrose Ave and Santa Monica Blvd.* &

Arnie Morton's of Chicago / ★★★

435 S LA CIENEGA BLVD, WEST HOLLYWOOD; 310/246-1501

Morton's is generally considered to be the best steak house in Chicago, and in the realm of all things carnivorous, the L.A. outpost of the national chain is equally reputed. The kitchen of namesake Arnie Morton, father of Hard Rock owner Peter Morton, serves truly outstanding cuts of meat—along with expertly prepared cocktails and appropriately paired wines in a masculine (leather, brass, wood) setting. But perhaps the most enjoyable aspect of a red-meat rendezvous here (aside from the dinner itself) is the waitstaff's four-minute presentation, during which they wheel out a cart teeming with Saran-wrapped cuts of beef and explain each one and its optional preparations. (Usually, perhaps for the heck of it, there's a lobster there too.) The overwhelming— and unintentionally humorous—display falls somewhere between a flight attendant's safety instructions and a QVC sales pitch. Invariably, though, the end result is an excellent huge cut of beef, perfectly prepared; it's served with heaping portions of spuds, spinach, and corn. Expect to pay handsomely for the honor of inhaling all this protein, and to leave very well fed. *$$$; AE, MC, V; local checks only; dinner only, every day; full bar; reservations recommended; 1 long block north of Wilshire Blvd.* &

Authentic Cafe / ★★☆

7605 BEVERLY BLVD, LOS ANGELES; 323/939-4626

Chef Roger Hayot's highly eclectic American-Southwestern-Chinese cafe is a casual and colorful eatery with a line waiting outside day in and day out. In fact, when the restaurant doubled in size, the line became even longer, and with good reason: Hayot serves large portions of very good food at very low prices. This is also a fine spot for people-watching, meeting, and greeting, as diners compare notes concerning the tamales versus the dumplings, powerfully spicy tortilla soup versus down-home chicken pot pie, and tortilla-crusted chicken versus jerked pork chops. Weekend brunch sidesteps the same old stuff with such in-demand entrees as *chilaquiles* (scrambled eggs, cheese, chiles, and tortillas) and the knockout grilled chicken salad. *$; AE, MC, V; no checks; lunch, dinner every day; beer and wine; reservations not accepted; north side of Beverly Blvd east of Fairfax Ave.* &

The Beach House / ★★☆

100 W CHANNEL ROAD, PACIFIC PALISADES; 310/454-8299

If you're not fortunate enough to have a friend who has great dinner parties at his beach house, dining at this casually elegant eatery is the next best thing. Restaurateur Liz Utter, former co-owner of La Cachette, has created a cozy, romantic room across from the beach with white walls, plenty of flickering candles, and wood shutters separating the dining room from the bustling bar area. While playful seaside fare is on the menu here—from jumbo bowls of clam and mussel steamers and seafood chowder to barbecued baby back ribs and a fresh cod bouillabaisse-style fish pot—a selection of more complex American-style dishes is offered as well. Starters like the warm tomato tart with goat cheese and fresh herbs and the flaky wild mushroom turnover score big points, as do such entrees as a flavorful ginger-crusted salmon served on a bed of lentils, and pan-seared boneless brook trout with a zesty lemongrass *nage*. Desserts like warm fruit cobblers and jumbo ice cream sundaes take comfort food to new heights. While you can't ogle views of the Pacific from The Beach House, the staff of bronzed Adonises who look like they surf (and audition) by day is scenery enough. *$$$; AE, DC, DIS, MC, V; no checks; dinner Tues–Sun; full bar; reservations required; at Pacific Coast Highway.* &

The Belvedere / ★★★

9882 SANTA MONICA BLVD, BEVERLY HILLS; 310/788-2306

The Belvedere at the Peninsula Beverly Hills Hotel, under executive chef Bill Bracken, draws locals and guests alike with its lovely, formal setting and colorful and creative cuisine of the California-Asian persuasion. The dining room is where power players come to breakfast on everything from homemade granola and oatmeal brûlée to a lobster-and-avocado frittata with charred tomato salsa. At lunch and dinner in the elegant, European-style room, Bracken offers eclectic dishes, from a curry-scented bisque of butternut squash and lobster to potato-crusted Chilean sea bass in an orange reduction with fresh dill. Yet while swordfish, salmon, and beef medallions are available in appealing preparations, Bracken doesn't forget the simple pleasures: his menu also includes a half-pound Angus beef burger, complete with grilled onions and Tillamook cheddar. Patio seating allows diners to enjoy the property's lushly land-scaped grounds—and is much in demand by smokers who can't get used to the California law prohibiting smoking in restaurants and bars. *$$$; AE, DC, DIS, MC, V; no checks; breakfast, lunch, dinner every day; reservations recommended; pbh@peninsula.com; between Wilshire Blvd and Lasky Dr.* &

Border Grill / ★★☆

1445 4TH ST, SANTA MONICA; 310/451-1655

Owned and operated by Susan Feniger and Mary Sue Milliken, the nationally famous duo known as the Too Hot Tamales on their Food Network television program, Border Grill is large, colorful, and loud—and has some of the best Latin food north of the border. Feniger and Milliken began with a tiny version of Border Grill on Melrose in 1985, and then moved on to the larger City Restaurant before opening in 1990 this much larger Border Grill, which reflects their love of all things Latin.

Architect Josh Schweitzer (Milliken's husband) designed the playful space to match their creative cuisine. There's a daily fresh ceviche, green corn tamales, and plantain empanadas among the appetizers. Signature entrees include the *pescado veracruzano*—tender sea bass in a broth laden with rice, olives, and herbs; and sautéed rock shrimp with toasted ancho chiles, slivered garlic, and seared greens. One delight all diners can look forward to is the array of zesty salsas, which are accompanied by chips. The bar is well stocked with top tequilas, as well as an exotic, smoky mescal called Encantado, and boasts an attractive social scene. *$$; AE, DC, DIS, MC, V; no checks; lunch Tues–Sun, dinner every day; full bar; reservations recommended; mail@bordergrill.com; www.border grill.com; between Broadway and Santa Monica Blvd.* &

Boxer / ★★★

7615 W BEVERLY BLVD, LOS ANGELES; 323/932-6178

Boxer's interior may be minimalist as a bento box, but the atmosphere is warm, flavors are lively, and prices are reasonable—enough so that avid fans describe it as a slice of San Francisco in the City of Fallen Angels. The cooking is California Quirky, with a cast of characters in the kitchen that's changed with some regularity over the years. The latest chef is Philip Dubois (formerly of Vida). As a graduate of the Fred Eric School of Anything Goes, Dubois has cut back on his menu puns (although his Cobb salad is called Cobble Cobble), but his culinary eccentricity is still intact in cutting-edge dishes like peppered ahi with a celery-root purée and candied kumquats, furikaki-crusted striped bass in soy cream sauce, and applewood-bacon-wrapped venison in mole sauce on a bed of *spaetzle*—a dish that manages to be American, Mexican, and German all at the same time. Adding to Boxer's charm is its wine list, which consists of your going to their wine shop next door to pick out a worthy—and reasonably priced—vintage. (There's no corkage fee if your wine's from their shop, Bicentennial 13.) Boxer also happens to be the finest kosher restaurant around—an attractive attribute for residents of this largely Jewish neighborhood. *$$; AE, MC, V; no checks; dinner Tues–Sun; wine available next door; reservations recommended on weekends; north side of Beverly Blvd east of Fairfax Ave.* &

Cafe Del Rey / ★★

4451 ADMIRALTY WAY, MARINA DEL REY; 310/823-6395

This marina-front restaurant has long been one of the prime reasons to head this far southwest for lunch or dinner. Executive chef Katsuo "Naga" Nagasawa's flavorful and creative fusion-style cuisine, which incorporates French, Italian, and Pacific Rim elements, is far more adventurous than other nearby options. Seafood is always a safe bet, where dishes like kung pao sausage seafood sound stranger than they taste. The tuna sashimi salad is a study in contrasting textures, with tender raw tuna, crisp strips of wonton, shredded cucumber, baby greens, and a tart dressing of *yuzu* (a Japanese citrus fruit). The honey-cured Peking duck is roasted three times, slowly and at different temperatures, and served with a raisin-and-plum-wine sauce, mango chutney, and coriander-laced pancakes. Desserts are particularly noteworthy. The glassed-in wine display room strongly hints that wine is an important part of Cafe Del Rey's appeal, but the monthly "winemaker dinners" and an impressive wine list—over 300 bottles—prove it. The bar also offers an unusually large and changing list of wines by the glass. Sunday brunch is packed, but getting a table is worth the effort. *$$$; AE, DIS, MC, V; no checks; lunch, dinner every day, brunch Sun; full bar; reservations recommended; between Mindanao and Via Marina.* &

Cafe Pinot / ★★☆

700 W 5TH ST, LOS ANGELES; 213/239-6500
Joachim Splichal's downtown outpost brings life to an otherwise dead-after-dark neighborhood with this spin-off of Pinot Bistro in Sherman Oaks. Situated right next to the downtown Public Library, this shoebox atrium restaurant has an upward view of downtown's shining towers and a patio view of the library's garden. The food is Splichal lite, which is to say that his eccentric, delicious *Mitteleuropa*/California cooking carries somewhat more earthly prices here. Expect a Splichalian menu that might include a savory warm leek and chanterelle tartlet (with caramelized onions—the man loves caramelized onions), a superbly seasoned warm herbed goat cheese on frisée and mâche, warm spinach salad with duck confit, silky oyster soup, rich seared loin of venison with sweet-potato hash, and moist, sage-infused rotisserie chicken with braised salsify. *$$; AE, MC, V; no checks; lunch Mon–Fri, dinner every day; full bar; reservations recommended; at S Flower St.* &

Campanile / ★★★★

624 S LA BREA AVE, LOS ANGELES; 323/938-1447
With owners/chefs Mark Peel and Nancy Silverton in control since its 1989 opening, Campanile continues to be one of L.A.'s finest restaurants. The Mediterranean-Romanesque 1920s building, once owned by Charlie Chaplin, is a delight in itself with its bell tower, high ceilings, casual bar, and a spacious divided dining room that make it an ideal venue for the rustic California-Mediterranean cuisine served by an unpretentious but professional staff. Campanile is famous for its excellently prepared fresh food, which includes a revered porterhouse dusted with cracked pepper as well as such specials as roasted monkfish wrapped in tomato, basil, and pancetta and served with roasted-tomato sauce and lentils, or cedar-smoked Scottish salmon with a ragout of sprouted legumes and romesco. But their creative pasta dishes, the addictive crisp flattened chicken with garlic-lemon confit and parsnip potatoes, and the absolutely knockout

lineup of grilled cheese sandwiches (Thursday nights) are equally awe-inspiring. With a wine list the size of Madonna's not-so-little black book, making a choice can be tough but rewarding; the list showcases selections from California, Italy, Spain, and France and features small wine producers from around the world. This is one place where it would be criminal to leave without at least sampling a dessert. Mom's apple pie is not some polished, artsy presentation, but a rough-hewn, baseball-sized individual pie filled with sweet and tart apple, surrounded by a pool of rich caramel sauce and a puddle of homemade applesauce, with Scotch caramel ice cream. Silverton's La Brea Bakery next door, known for single-handedly revolutionizing Los Angeles's bread scene, provides the bread for the restaurant. *$$$; AE, DC, DIS, MC, V; no checks; lunch Mon–Fri, dinner Mon–Sat, brunch Sat–Sun; full bar; reservations recommended; between Wilshire Blvd and 6th St.* &

Chaya Brasserie / ★★☆
Chaya Venice / ★★☆

8741 ALDEN DR, WEST HOLLYWOOD; 310/859-8833
110 NAVY ST (AT MAIN ST), VENICE; 310/396-1179
Wear black and expect to see celebrities at this California-French bistro/brasserie with Japanese touches, which was opened by a venerable restaurant family from Tokyo. Inside the warehouselike setting you'll find some of the most creative grill food around. Though the menu shifts with the seasons, chefs Shigefumi Tachibe and Masaru Morimoto have certain classic preparations that travel from menu to menu: seaweed salad with ginger-soy rice wine vinaigrette, Hawaiian tuna tartare, Cantonese chicken rolls, Chinese duck and mango salad, pan-fried shrimp with mashed potatoes, sesame-crusted whitefish, grilled Moroccan lamb chops, and sliced roasted venison with black peppercorn sauce. The menu at their sister restaurant, Chaya Venice, has more Japanese influence (due largely to its sushi bar) and is a choice spot for Santa Monica's handsome crowd. *$$; AE, MC, V; no checks; lunch Mon–Fri, dinner every day; full bar; reservations recommended; at Robertson Blvd.* &

Chez Mimi / ★★

246 26TH ST, SANTA MONICA; 310/393-0558
Named for owner Micheline Hebert, whose nickname is Mimi, this is one of the sweetest, most romantic new places in town. The former chef/owner of Chez Hélène, in both its Venice and Beverly Hills incarnations, Hebert moved to Santa Monica for her latest endeavor, a country French restaurant. Chez Mimi is spread over three cottages, each with its own fireplace, and lots of courtyard space for al fresco dining on temperate coastal nights—definitely the best, and most romantic, way to go here. Cuisine matches the decor: rustic French, with bouillabaisse and leg of lamb among the best main courses. And because Hebert hails from

31

Montreal, she prepares a few Quebecois specialties as well, like *tourtiere*—a hearty, spicy meat pie—and *chomeur,* an upside-down cake with caramel and raspberry. Her tarte tatin was honored as the best in town by a local French-language magazine. Service, mostly by French-accented waiters, is excellent, and the wine list is strong in both French and California selections. Whether you sit inside or out, you'll feel like you're dining in the countryside. *$$$; AE, DC, DIS, MC, V; no checks; lunch Tues–Sat, dinner Tues–Sun, brunch Sun; full bar; reservations recommended; south of San Vicente Blvd. at Montana Ave.* &

Chinois on Main / ★★★

2709 MAIN ST, SANTA MONICA; 310/392-9025

Although Wolfgang Puck's first foray into fusion occurred more that 15 years ago in this kitchen, the superstar chef's Chinois still rates as one of the best restaurants in town. Puck's wife, Barbara Lazaroff, did the dining room decor, as she has at most of his places, and this one's particularly fun and over the top, virtually exploding with color and huge floral displays. While the menu constantly evolves as new chefs rotate through the kitchen, some of the earliest creations are still the best: the whole sizzling catfish stuffed with ginger and topped with ponzu sauce and chicken salad of Napa cabbage, baby lettuce, chicken, and fried wonton skins in a Chinese mustard vinaigrette, sauteed foie gras with marinated and grilled pineapple, and Shanghai lobster with spicy ginger sauce and crispy spinach among the entrees, and an assortment of mini crème brûlées for dessert. Grab one of the seats at the kitchen counter in the back and watch the chefs work their magic, or stake out one of the tables along the front windows. But whatever you do, don't expect quiet conversation; acoustics here are as loud as the decor. *$$$; AE, DC, DIS, MC, V; no checks; lunch Wed–Fri, dinner every day; full bar; reservations required; between Hill and Ashland Sts.* &

Cicada / ★★

617 S OLIVE ST, LOS ANGELES; 323/655-5559

Stephanie Taupin was doing fine with Cicada in its original West Hollywood location when the magnificent space that had been Rex in the landmark Oviatt Building became available. Taupin moved across town, setting up shop in what had long ago been an elegant haberdashery. By adding gold leaf to the ceiling—all 15,000 square feet of it—she gave a warm glow to the beautiful space, both upstairs and down. The room is indeed the star, from the spectacular split staircase to the glass cabinets filled with prized wine and spirits. The food from executive chef Michael Shaheen's kitchen is Northern Italian, from ravioli filled with portobello mushrooms and spinach and ricotta gnocchi with diced chicken breast to a grilled, on-the-bone filet mignon served on penne with a barolo reduction. Fulvio Beltrami oversees the substantial wine list, split almost evenly between California and Italy, and diners should seek his counsel with confidence on lesser-known Italian bottles as well as after-dinner grappas. *$$$; AE, DC, MC, V; no checks; lunch Mon–Fri, dinner Mon–Sat; full bar; reservations recommended; between 6th and 7th Sts.* ⅃

Citrus / ★★☆

6703 MELROSE AVE, LOS ANGELES; 323/857-0034

Despite founding chef Michel Richard's decamping for the East Coast to open more of his casual Citronelle restaurants, and chef Alain Giraud moving over to Lavande at the Loews Santa Monica Hotel, Citrus remains one of the preferred California-French restaurants in Los Angeles. The large room is filled with tables topped with umbrellas, most of which have a view of the glass-fronted kitchen and a team of fanatically attuned cooks working their wonders. For lunch, the industry dish of choice is salad, or perhaps grilled fish. Come dinner, though, executive chef Daniel Rossi pulls out the stops with such contemporary renditions as grilled foie gras, a shiitake mushroom tart with garlic cream, peppered seared ahi tuna with a spicy *diable* sauce, and beef tenderloin bourguignonne, along with a high level of desserts inspired by master pastry chef Richard, who did, after all, train under Gaston Lenôtre. Try the crunchy napoleon of slow-baked caramelized phyllo with slices of crème brûlée and a butterscotch sauce and you'll dream about it for years to come. *$$; AE, MC, V; no checks; lunch Mon–Fri, dinner every day; full bar; reservations recommended; west of Highland Ave.* ⅃

Crustacean / ★★

9646 LITTLE SANTA MONICA BLVD, BEVERLY HILLS; 310/205-8990

Crustacean, in true Hollywood fashion, comes with its own subtitle: "Euro-Asian Cuisine." The owners, three generations of women, are Vietnamese, but this is not traditional Vietnamese cooking or even standard Asian fusion. It is the personal cuisine of Helene An, who was reared in a Hanoi culture that was both Vietnamese and French. Her affluent family's three chefs—French, Vietnamese, and Chinese—taught her how to cook, and the results are yours for the tasting at this nostalgic, camera-ready rendition of '30s colonial Hanoi. The dramatic entrance brings you past a floor-to-ceiling aquarium into the bar, where another aquarium beneath the floor, 80 feet long and filled with brightly colored koi, is the glass-topped pathway winding into the dining room. Seafood may well be the best way to go here, from lemongrass–scented Asian bouillabaisse and lobster in tamarind sauce to whole roasted Dungeness crab with garlic sauce. House specialties, such as An's giant tiger prawns and fantastically potent garlic noodles, are created in the "secret kitchen," a separate area where recipes are kept under wraps by allowing only family members access. *$$$; AE, DC, MC, V; no checks; lunch Mon–Fri, dinner Mon–Sat; full bar; reservations recommended; between Rodeo Dr and Roxbury Dr.* ⅃

33

Dan Tana's / ★★

9071 SANTA MONICA BLVD, WEST HOLLYWOOD; 310/275-9444
Dan Tana's remains one of L.A.'s most favored Italian restaurants, still going strong halfway through its fourth decade. At a restaurant so steeped in tradition, it's not surprising that chef Matte Mustac has been in the kitchen for nearly 30 years. But with the exception of a classic caesar salad, a superb steak, and some decent veal, food isn't the thing at Tana's as much as the New York speakeasy atmosphere, which attracts a celebrity-heavy clientele out for an old-fashioned meal and a good time. Chianti bottles hang in groups of three from the high ceiling, and basketball jerseys from former Los Angeles Lakers Magic Johnson and Vlade Divac, framed and autographed, hang on the walls. The bar is packed and noisy, and there's always a wait for a table. Service is professional—more than a few of the waiters have been here nearly since opening day—if a bit rushed. Don't leave without sharing a rich, creamy tiramisu. *$$$; AE, DC, DIS, MC, V; local checks only; dinner every day; full bar; reservations required; between Doheny Dr and Robertson Blvd.* &

Dar Maghreb / ★★

7651 SUNSET BLVD, WEST HOLLYWOOD; 323/876-7651
The name means "Moroccan house," and dining here is very much like being invited into the home of a wealthy Moroccan. Pass through the strikingly ornate and massive brass doors with intricate Islamic designs and the host, clad in a *djellaba*, the traditional robelike garment of the region, greets you as you enter. It's an opulent setting, complete with atrium and fountain; long, narrow dining rooms with high ceilings; and belly dancers undulating through the restaurant. Salmon, *m'choui* (lamb shoulder), and duck are often available as specials, but generally there's only one choice—a six-course prix-fixe dinner, which, unless you protest, is to be eaten with your fingers (water bowls provided). Highlights include *b'stilla*—a pastry shell filled with a mix of chicken, almonds, and scrambled eggs, topped with powdered sugar and cinnamon—and lemon chicken with olives. *$$$; DIS, MC, V; no checks; dinner every day; full bar; reservations recommended; between Fairfax and La Brea Aves.* &

Diaghilev / ★★★

1020 N SAN VICENTE BLVD, WEST HOLLYWOOD; 310/854-1111
When a special occasion calls for a big night out, make a reservation at this elegant eatery in the Wyndham Bel Age, which is named after famed Russian dancer Serge de Diaghilev. Gracious Dimitri Dimitrov will greet you like a long-lost relative and whisk you through the ornate dining room to your table adorned with fine china and stemware. As piano and harp music plays in the background, you and your companions might opt to

get in the opulent mood with a taste of caviar and a shot of fine vodka while you decide what to select from the Franco-Russian menu. Start with a rendition of borscht, made either with red or yellow beets and served with flaky pirozhki, or a traditional Russian appetizer like the beef-and-rice-stuffed cabbage rolls, then move on to such main courses as chicken Kiev with black truffles and a rich port wine suace, or a sautéed fillet of sturgeon with caviar. While an evening at this exquisite establishment can be spendy, it offers a refined dining experience not often found in Los Angeles. *$$$; AE, DC, DIS, JCB, MC, V; no checks; dinner Tues–Sat; full bar; reservation required; just south of Sunset Blvd.* &

The Dining Room at the Regent Beverly Wilshire / ★★☆

9500 WILSHIRE BLVD, BEVERLY HILLS; 310/274-8179
Beverly Hills native J. P. Amateau spends his free time exploring ethnic restaurants and markets looking for new ideas for his California/ Provençal menu, which is served in a very formal setting. As a result of these forays, Amateau offers an unusually large selection of nightly specials in addition to his regular dishes. He has a wonderful way with meats and, unlike many hotel chefs, is not fussy in his presentations. The focus is on creating delicious food served simply on attractive china. Service is attentive and professional, never overly familiar. Standouts include pan-roasted Sonoma foie gras atop a bed of arugula on a disc of toasted brioche and paired with sun-dried cherries and plump blackberries, and oven-roasted Colorado lamb chops in a rich bourbon sauce and accompanied by a mini sauté pan of fennel-laced mashed potatoes. The Dining Room features an unusually nice, adventurous, and reasonably priced wine list; for deep-pocketed connoisseurs, there's an impressive "Reserve" section. Every Friday and Saturday evening, there's dancing to live music from a first-rate trio. *$$$; AE, DC, DIS, JCB, MC, V; no checks; breakfast every day, lunch, dinner Mon–Sat; full bar; reservations recommended; www.fourseasons.com; between Rodeo Dr and El Camino Rd.* &

Flora Kitchen / ★

460 S LA BREA AVE, LOS ANGELES; 323/931-9900
Rivaling the enticing aromas streaming from the kitchen of this bright little cafe are the floral scents wafting in from the adjoining Rita Flora flower shop. Patrons can actually chow down on healthful salads and sandwiches among the sweet-smelling flowers or eat in the main cafe, which boasts a deli-style glass case chock-full of homemade salads— from penne with grilled vegetables to Tuscan beans with ahi. Wherever you stake out a table, Flora Kitchen serves up some downright yummy fare, like salads, homemade soups, panini sandwiches, plump crab cakes, and hearty lasagne. The artsy Mediterranean-style cafe is also a great

breakfast spot, where you can bring a good book and linger over a monster-sized cappuccino and fresh-baked scones. When breakfast is done, the antique shops and boutiques of La Brea Avenue are the lure just up the street. *$; MC, V; no checks; breakfast, lunch, dinner Mon–Sat; beer and wine; reservations not necessary; just north of Wilshire Blvd.* &

Four Oaks / ★★☆

2181 N BEVERLY GLEN BLVD, LOS ANGELES; 310/470-2265

Four Oaks is one of Los Angeles's most unabashedly romantic restaurants. Pass the parking lot, where twinkle lights spread into the trees in every direction, glance through the kitchen windows, where the staff labors over some of the best modern French-California cooking in Southern California, walk through the door, and just like that, you're in Provence—especially if you opt for the sylvan pleasures of the outdoor patio. Dishes are of exceptional focus and clarity: flavors are never hidden away beneath excessive sauces and flummery. Such is the case with the perfect duck breast carpaccio with horseradish and Parmesan; the heavenly traditional house-smoked salmon with capers and crème fraîche; the delectable basil-crusted halibut; the pepper-roasted duck; and the garlic-grilled lamb chops. This is a restaurant to which you don't want to take your cousin Mort from East Aardvark; it's the place to go with that special someone whom you want to dazzle with your wit and your taste. Sometimes, it even works. *$$; AE, MC, V; no checks; lunch Tues–Sat, dinner every day, brunch Sun; full bar; reservations required; about 2 miles north of Sunset Blvd.* &

Gardens / ★★☆

300 S DOHENY DR, LOS ANGELES; 310/273-2222

While breakfast here is power dining at its most cell-phone-wieldingly stereotypical, Gardens is also a top choice for a low-key dinner, with chef Carrie Nahabedian in the kitchen, excellent service in the dining room, and one of the most tranquil casual-meets-formal atmospheres in town. Nahabedian, who previously worked with Charlie Trotter, has long since established her own style, emphasizing light seasonal dishes with strong, clean flavors. Her forest mushroom soup comes accompanied by a wild mushroom fritter. She pairs seared foie gras with Arkansas black apples, cranberry compote, and Calvados sauce on one seasonal appetizer, while combining sea scallops with a salad of spinach, basil, and artichoke in orange essence in another. She tosses Russian caviar into a tartare of salmon and ahi, and uses flavored caviars to enhance chilled oysters. Among the main courses, you can't go wrong with her hefty 16-ounce Kansas City sirloin, a fine cut of beef in an oxtail and red wine sauce, matched with a soufflé of goat cheese and horseradish, and barbecued onions. Nahabedian also offers a five-course degustation menu, as well as spa-style alternative cuisine. *$$$; AE, DC, DIS, JCB, MC, V; no checks;*

breakfast, lunch, dinner every day, brunch Sun; full bar; reservations accepted; www.fourseasons.com; between Burton Way and 3rd St. &

Ginza Sushi-Ko / ★★★

VIA RODEO, 218 RODEO DR, BEVERLY HILLS; 310/247-8939

Anxious to prove that mundane matters like cost do not affect their perceptions, critics tend to bury the fact that a meal at this starkly minimalist, rather intimidating sushi-and-sashimi bar can easily cost more than $300 per person. It should also be noted that there's no way to avoid the high cost, for the restaurant doesn't feature a menu—you're simply served tiny portions of seafood both perfect and rare until you say stop. (However, the chef asks customers whether they have any allergies or dislikes when planning the evening's menu, which does, in fact, begin at 300 bucks.) At that point, a check arrives covered with figures that look like phone numbers—the high cost of perfection. This is almost certainly the most expensive sushi bar in America, a bit of cognitive dissonance when you consider that it sits in a small room on the second floor of a Beverly Hills mall. Those with large-enough expense accounts claim it's the best sushi served this side of Tokyo. Expect to eat fish you've never heard of, shipped in specifically for the restaurant. We suspect the fish travel first class. *$$$; AE, MC, V; no checks; lunch, dinner Mon–Sat; sake and beer; reservations required; northeast corner of Wilshire Blvd and Rodeo Dr, upstairs from McCormick & Schmick's on the Via Rodeo shopping street.* &

Granita / ★★

23725 W MALIBU RD, MALIBU; 310/456-0488

After years of being forced to drive long distances to dine at a truly trendy restaurant, isolated denizens of Malibu now have their own high-profile Wolfgang Puck eatery: a restaurant that's been described as Spago-by-the-Sea, complete with a whimsical style of design that's reminiscent of both Captain Nemo's submarine and the Little Mermaid. As a reminder that this particular Spago cossets some of the top beachfront estaters in America, there's a stone near the entrance thanking Johnny Carson for his support—and, yes, Mr. Hey-Oh is a regular. In Puck style, the kitchen is open and bustling, and the food leans towards the well-loved Spago formula of designer pizzas and pastas. There's a wood-burning pizza oven, signature dishes such as the foie gras sandwich with Asian pears, and more seafood dishes than are found at the branches in town. They do wonderful things here with Santa Barbara spot prawns and monkfish. But Granita's most bountiful offering is its look and its vibe—this ain't your Malibu beach shack by any stretch of the imagination. *$$; AE, MC, V; no checks; dinner every day, brunch Sat–Sun; full bar; reservations recommended; in Malibu Colony Plaza shopping center on Malibu Rd west of Pacific Coast Highway.* &

The Grill on the Alley / ★★★

9560 DAYTON WAY, BEVERLY HILLS; 310/276-0615

Anyone who has had it up to his or her Oliver Peoples sunglasses with trendy California dining heads to the Grill, a classic American restaurant with hearty, straightforward fare. Awash in woods, brass, and leather, this old-boys'-club spot is the choice of power-dining businessmen who feast on huge plates of well-prepared steaks and chops and suck down martinis. (O. J. Simpson's dream team of lawyers dined here regularly during the "trial of the century.") Although the ambience is heavy on testosterone, the classic grill fare tempts both sexes with classic renditions of fresh oysters, plump crab cakes, a generous and classic caesar salad, and juicy porterhouse or New York steaks with such tasty side dishes as creamed spinach, fried onions, steamed vegetables, and shoestring potatoes. Sunday night is prime rib night, and the restaurant hosts year-round clambakes. But any night is right to sample the delicious homemade rice pudding or the hot fudge brownie sundae. If the surroundings seem familiar, it might be because this restaurant served as the inspiration for Southern California's Daily Grill chain. *$$$; AE, DC, MC, V; no checks; lunch Mon–Sat, dinner every day; full bar; reservations required; off Wilshire Blvd.* &

The Hump / ★★★

3221 DONALD DOUGLAS LOOP S, SANTA MONICA AIRPORT, SANTA MONICA; 310/313-0977

Despite its unappetizing name, the Hump, which sits atop the Typhoon Restaurant at the Santa Monica Airport, serves some of Los Angeles's best sushi in one of its most beautiful and unique dining rooms. With his love of history, owner Brian Vidor designed and named this restaurant to pay homage to the Himalayan wartime route the American pilots used to fly supplies from India to troops in China. The result is a sushi bar of remarkable quality, with a tarmac-front view and a spectacular setting designed by Steven Francis Jones (Spago Beverly Hills, Chinois Las Vegas, Barfly). The place is an elegant setting in which to consume great sushi prepared by Hiro Nishimura. Expect tuna, both big-eye and yellowfin, along with expensive (and worth it) toro. Luxuriate in the unabashed oiliness of Japanese sardines (*iwashi*), the slippery crunch of jumbo clam, the tidepool essence of sea urchin, the addictiveness of the rock shrimp tempura, or quick-sautéed abalone, and the collection of hot and cold sakes. Don't expect to find a Philadelphia roll or anything called "dynamite" on the menu. An eel roll with avocado is about as outlandish as things get here. Otherwise, this is sushi so pure, it's astonishing. *$$; AE, MC, V; no checks; lunch Mon–Fri, dinner every day; beer and wine; reservations recommended; south side of Santa Monica Airport, just off Bundy.* &

Il Cielo / ★★

9018 BURTON WAY, BEVERLY HILLS; 310/276-9990

Romance oozes through every room, patio, and garden at Il Cielo ("the sky"). Pasquale Vericella, scion of an Italian restaurant family that has long run the Albergo La Braida in Sorrento, took a red-brick house on a tree-shaded street and created *un ambiente d'amore* in each of the four sweetly shaded areas: there's a front patio facing Burton Way; a rear patio complete with arbors, bowers, and a fountain with water trickling from a lion's mouth; and two interior rooms each. Celebrities are especially fond of the place because they can slip in through the rear entrance just off the parking lot. (Frank Sinatra was a regular.) The food is Italian and pleasantly light; especially good are *bruschetta al pomodoro e basilico, risotto con porcini, petto di pollo alla Bolognese, branzino al forno* (whole baked sea bass, filleted tableside), and heart-shaped lobster ravioli. Service is properly obsequious. *$$; AE, MC, V; checks OK; lunch, dinner Mon–Sat; full bar; reservations recommended; south side of Burton Way just east of Doheny.* &

Indochine / ★★★

8225 BEVERLY BLVD, LOS ANGELES; 323/655-4777

Black-clad hipsters dine on elegant French-Vietnamese cuisine at this alluring West Coast branch of the celebrated New York dining establishment. Cozy into one of the restaurant's leather banquettes and order a selection of beautifully presented dishes that are perfect for sharing, such as fried spring rolls with shrimp and chicken wrapped in rice paper, steamed raviolis, spicy beef salad, striped bass steamed with ginger and asparagus, crispy salmon with lemongrass, and roast duck with Chinese broccoli. While most of the cuisine here is relatively healthy and comparatively low-calorie, desserts like the creamy coconut crème brûlée go a long way toward canceling out a health-conscious meal. Banana leaf murals, potted orchids, and bamboo accents give this sexy neighborhood favorite an exotic feel; however, the service and clientele can be pretentious. *$$$; AE, DC, MC, V; no checks; dinner every day; full bar; reservations recommended; between Fairfax Ave and La Cienega Blvd.* &

The Ivy / ★★★
The Ivy at the Shore / ★★★

113 N ROBERTSON BLVD, LOS ANGELES; 310/274-8303

1541 OCEAN AVE, SANTA MONICA; 310/393-3113

From big-shot Hollywood agents to A-list celebrities, this trendy restaurant is a long-time Hollywood hangout, where Julia Roberts has been known to drop by for the fantastic (though ridiculously priced) chopped salad and Tori Spelling is said to prefer the lime chicken. Aside from the fanfare and the constant parade of arriving Rolls-Royces and Mercedes sedans, the atmosphere is charming, especially along the front outdoor patio, where a white picket fence encloses comfy chintz seating and schmoozing power diners. The American fare is just as its clientele likes it: diverse and expensive, with such selections as sweet and spicy corn chowder, signature crab cakes, homey meatloaf, blackened shrimp, or Southern-style crisp fried chicken. The sitcom star at the table next to you may skip dessert, but if your goal isn't to share dress sizes with Calista Flockhart or Courteney Cox, try the pecan square (a pecan pie–like base topped with ice cream and butterscotch or fudge sauce), the warm and gooey fruit crumbles, or the homemade chocolate chip cookies. The restaurant's sister eatery, Ivy at the Shore, offers a similar country inn–like ambience, though chances are you'll have to settle for views of the Pacific instead of celebrity sightings. *$$$; AE, DC, MC, V; no checks; lunch, dinner every day, brunch Sun (The Ivy); lunch Mon–Fri, dinner every day, brunch Sat–Sun (The Ivy at the Shore); full bar; reservations recommended; south of Beverly Blvd (The Ivy); Ocean Ave at Colorado Ave (The Ivy at the Shore).* &

JiRaffe / ★★☆

502 SANTA MONICA BLVD, SANTA MONICA; 310/917-6671

JiRaffe became an instant hit under the partnership between chefs Josiah Citrin (the Ji) and Raphael Lunetta (the Raffe), the young culinary team who were named among the 10 "Best New Chefs" by *Food & Wine Magazine* in 1997. The pair separated in early 1999, with Citrin heading off to open his own more formally French place. Now the light, airy two-story dining room, decorated with 50 variations of the long-necked mammal (mostly gifts from satisfied customers) is overseen by Lunetta, who continues to serve excellent "rustic French/California" cuisine, explosively flavored yet not overly fussy. Signature dishes include a roasted rabbit appetizer; a crisp salad of roasted pears with mixed greens, hazelnuts, and *fourme d'Ambert* cheese; buttery salmon with parsnip puree, braised fennel, and balsamic *nage;* and zesty roasted chicken with Provençal stuffing, crushed Yukon gold potatoes, and a sauce of chanterelle mushrooms and fava beans. There's a nightly tasting menu, a vegetarian menu, and a Grand Chef's Menu, the last especially good on Wednesdays, after Lunetta has made his weekly trip to the local farmers' market. JiRaffe also offers a seasonal menu with or without paired wines. At this sophisticated yet unpretentious operation, you're perfectly safe putting yourself in the chefs' and sommelier's hands. Both the wine list and the menu are about quality rather than trendiness and flash. *$$$; AE, DIS, MC, V; no checks; lunch Tues–Fri, dinner Tues–Sun; beer and wine; reservations recommended; corner of 5th St.* &

Jitlada / ★★☆

5233½ SUNSET BLVD, HOLLYWOOD; 323/667-9809
For more than 20 years, Jitlada has been home to some of the best, most authentic, and spiciest Thai food to be found in the City of Angels. Though it's in a dicey section of Hollywood, it's the favorite of the local Thai community, who eschew many of the slicker places around town in favor of great food served in the two drab, incongruously furnished rooms within a mini-mall. This is spicy stuff, to be sure; the brave or foolish can even request extra chiles, while the saner might want a Thai beer (Amarit or Singha) to cool the fire. Sure, they've got excellent versions of *mee krob* and Thai toast, but try the Thai-style pomfret meunière, a whole fish, deep-fried and topped with garlic and chili sauce. *$; AE, DIS, MC, V; no checks; lunch, dinner Tues–Sun; beer and wine; reservations not necessary; between Western Ave and Normandie Ave.* &

Joe's / ★★★

1023 ABBOTT KINNEY BLVD, VENICE; 310/399-5811
Set in Hans Röckenwagner's former storefront eatery, this small, wildly popular restaurant combines the homestyle cooking of chef/owner Joe Miller with a stark modern ambience. Miller, who enjoys culinary exploration and utilizing the region's access to fresh seasonal ingredients, puts an innovative spin on virtually everything he does. An exotic example is his coconut-crusted soft-shell crab with a zesty green curry sauce, or his hazelnut-crusted goat chesse with roasted baby beets. Even the classics get a new spin, such as tender roast beef, which comes with creamy mashed potatoes, crispy artichokes, and balsamic vinegar; and homey port tenderloin, which also gets a dollop of mashed potatoes jazzed up with wild mushrooms and roasted garlic jus. Anyone up for an all-out culinary adventure should embark on one of the two four-course prix-fixe menus, which are offered nightly for $30 or $40 a person. Desserts like pistachio parfait with apricots, strawberries, and basil; or caramelized pineapple with mango sorbet go well with Joe's small but nice selection of port wines. Chocoholics shouldn't miss the warm chocolate soufflé cake that oozes with rich fudge. *$$; AE, MC, V; lunch and dinner Tues–Sun, Sat–Sun brunch; beer and wine; reservations recommended; between Main St and Westminster Ave.* &

Jozu / ★★★

8360 MELROSE AVE, LOS ANGELES; 323/655-5600
When executive chef Suzanne Tracht, formerly of Campanile, brought her unique California Pacific cuisine to quietly sumptuous Jozu, it was an instant success. The mostly seafood menu is served in a sleek, spacious, and dimly lit dining room. Eclectic and inventive options might include such blessings as tempura squash blossoms with shrimp and

wood-ear mushrooms in a spicy ponzu sauce or tender roasted Chilean sea bass with a fresh cabbage salad. To appeal to all taste buds, Tracht offers a few hearty meat dishes and great vegetarian entrees—such as scallion and black-rice crepes with braised leeks, mushrooms, and taro in a miso sauce—as well as a large nightly list of specials. Sake is a specialty of the house, with more than a dozen premium varieties at the bar, and owner Andy Nakano, a sake aficionado, wanders from table to table, pouring samples and describing his various offerings and how they pair with specific dishes. An added bonus is the tranquil atmosphere: this is one restaurant where you won't have to strain to hear the dinner conversation. *$$; AE, DC, DIS, MC, V; no checks; lunch Thurs–Fri, dinner every day; full bar; reservations recommended; www.jozu.com; between La Cienega Blvd and Kings Rd.* &

Kate Mantilini / ★★☆

9101 WILSHIRE BLVD, BEVERLY HILLS; 310/278-3699
Classic American cuisine is the focus at this eatery, where comfort foods like meat loaf, chicken pot pies, crab cakes, and garlic rotisserie chicken reign supreme in a rather sterile dining room marked with high ceilings, wooden booths, an open kitchen, and enormous black-and-white glamour photos. In addition to seafood, steaks, sandwiches, and salads, there's a large selection of healthy alternatives, from skinless chicken breasts to turkey burgers. Winning side orders, including broccoli with hollandaise sauce, fresh sautéed spinach with garlic and Parmesan cheese, and huge baked potatoes with all the fixings, are meals in themselves. Such daring choices as frogs' legs and calves' brains—which famed director Billy Wilder reportedly enjoys here on the average of twice a week—also grace the lengthy and diverse menu. For those in search of late-night dining after last call, the restaurant stays open until 2am on weekends. *$$; AE, DC, MC, V; no checks; breakfast, lunch, dinner every day, brunch Sun; full bar; reservations accepted for parties of 6 or more; at Doheny Dr.* &

Katsu / ★★☆

1972 HILLHURST AVE, LOS FELIZ; 323/664-1891
For a long time, this beautiful bento box of a restaurant, so spare in design that one entire room is dedicated to nothing but art on the walls, was perceived as the best sushi bar in Los Angeles. And to many, it still is, though the remarkable work at Matsuhisa and Sushi Nozawa (along with the awesomely expensive meals prepared at Ginza Sushi-Ko) now tend to eclipse the still-fine fish prepared nightly at this understated Los Feliz destination. After more than a decade, Katsu's rigidly austere black-and-white decor is still ahead of its time, and the sushi served here is utterly beyond reproach—perfect slices of richly flavored yellowtail (*hamachi*), silky sea bass (*shiromi*), blood-dark tuna (both *maguro* and the highly-prized, fat-marbled *toro*), exquisitely oily mackerel (*saba*),

jumbo clam (*mirugai*), and sea urchin (*uni*) that's like taking a bite out of the Mother Sea itself. *$$; AE, MC, V; no checks; lunch Mon–Fri, dinner every day; wine and beer; reservations recommended; east side of Hillhurst Ave, south of Los Feliz Blvd.* &

La Boheme / ★★

8400 SANTA MONICA BLVD, WEST HOLLYWOOD; 323/848-2360

An unlikely mix of Left Bank Paris and a Tuscan country villa, Boheme is the work of Kozo Hasegawa, one of Japan's flashiest restaurateurs. To make the otherwise cavernous room a bit more intimate, torches glow inside the enormous fireplace and tapestries and fabrics drape the walls. Tables, set well apart, fill the middle of the floor, and a row of curtained, wood-paneled leather booths lines the wall across from the fireplace. Upstairs, a narrow, catwalklike construction holds more tables, and a dumbwaiter at one end carries up drinks from the ground-floor bar. The menu sometimes leans toward bizarre combinations of ingredients, but if you stick to simple dishes, such as a zesty classic caesar salad, fresh oysters, crisp fried calamari, delicately seared tuna tataki, or filet mignon, both your palate and your dinner partner will be in the mood for love. *$$$; AE, DC, DIS, MC, V; no checks; dinner every day; full bar; reservations recommended; laboheme@netwood.net; www.calendarlive.com/cafelaboheme/; between La Cienega Blvd and Sweetzer Ave.* &

La Cachette / ★★★

10506 LITTLE SANTA MONICA BLVD, CENTURY CITY; 310/470-4992

Chef-owner Jean Francois Meteignier was already a local star by the time he opened La Cachette ("the hideaway"). During his 10-year stint at L'Orangerie he was recognized for four years running by the *Zagat Survey* for Best French Cuisine, and he was the opening chef at the original Cicada when the place was really jumping. But it's at formal and romantically lit La Cachette, which opened in late 1994, that Meteignier showcases his highly lauded lighter style of French cooking. The fare, which favors stocks and reductions over cream and butter, is served in two soft-white dining rooms whose simple splashes of color come from blue and beige banquettes and impressionist reproductions. While the decor is somewhat subdued, there's plenty of color to the food, which might include a salad of savory smoked whitefish over potatoes with capers, lemon, and olive oil; tangy double roast duck with honey orange zest; tender farm-raised New Zealand venison; grilled swordfish steak flavored with soy/wasabi/mustard sauce; and not-to-be-missed desserts such as dreamy chocolate soufflé with brandied cherries and a delightfully light apple tart with caramel sauce and vanilla ice cream. *$$$; AE, DC, DIS, MC, V; no checks; lunch Mon–Fri, dinner every day; full bar; reservations recommended; between Beverly Glen Blvd and Overland Ave.* &

La Serenata de Garibaldi / ★★

1842 E 1ST ST, BOYLE HEIGHTS (AND BRANCHES); 323/265-2887

A highly regarded family-run restaurant, La Serenata de Garibaldi serves some of the finest—and most authentic—regional Mexican cuisine in Los Angeles. The original Boyle Heights branch, which opened in 1983, closed for a while and then reopened in mid-1999. Like its sister restaurants, it uses family recipes, with menu highlights including two handmade moles—poblano (sweet and complex) and Oaxaca (black and spicy)—which are great with everything from enchiladas to chicken and fish or pork. Beef medallions arrive in *molcajete* sauce, which has plenty of spice from its mix of peppers, fresh-roasted tomatoes, onions, and chunks of avocado. For dessert, you can't go wrong with the simple, fresh strawberries or guavas in cream, or the house special *tres leches* cake, an unusually moist treat made with regular, condensed, and evaporated milks. The Rodriguez family recently opened a stylish new branch with hacienda-style decor in Santa Monica. That makes number three, after the casual store in the Westside Pavilion. *$$; AE, DC, MC, V; no checks; lunch, dinner every day, brunch Sat–Sun; full bar; reservations recommended; between Mission St and Soto St.* ♿

Lavande / ★★★

1700 OCEAN AVE, SANTA MONICA; 310/458-6700

Lavender is everywhere at Lavande, the relatively new French Provençal restaurant perched over the beach at Loews Santa Monica Beach Hotel. The aromatic, colorful herb is added to many of the main-course dishes, blended into ice cream and other desserts, and tucked into a little sachet that's presented with the check. The theme is well executed by Paris-born, Provence-raised chef Alain Giraud, who spent a decade at Citrus with star chef Michel Richard before opening this immediately revered spot. Giraud's cuisine is richly flavored, the result of fresh, first-rate ingredients and judicious use of herbs. House specialties include a thoroughly authentic fish soup with garlic croutons and rouille; a buttery *tartelette provençale* of Maine scallops; decadent sautéed foie gras with figs; and tender roasted Chilean sea bass with baby artichokes barigoule. "Alain's Tasting Menu," a five- or six-course meal, is based on the freshest available ingredients of the day. The wine list of nearly 200 selections is particularly strong in French bottles. *$$$; AE, DC, DIS, JCB, MC, V; no checks; breakfast every day; lunch, dinner Mon–Sat, brunch Sun; full bar; reservations recommended; www.calandarlive.com/lavande; between Pico and Santa Monica Blvds.* ♿

Lawry's The Prime Rib / ★★☆

100 N LA CIENEGA BLVD, BEVERLY HILLS; 310/652-2827
Lawry's is cooking from the very heart of America: a well-loved restaurant launched in 1938 and predicated on the simple pleasures of beef and cheerful service. It's also a restaurant straight out of Central Casting, with a serving staff that's corn-fed and raised on big glasses of milk—everybody's real friendly and nice. With only three items on the menu, there's no room for guessing what you'll have tonight: it's either prime rib (four selections), lobster, or the fresh fish special—all of which come with a pinwheel salad moistened with Lawry's dressing poured right out of the jar. Creamed spinach, creamed corn, and spuds both baked and mashed, slathered with creamery butter, arrive on the side. (Don't even think about cholesterol when dining at Lawry's.) The prices are right and the beef is good, though you've got to like prime rib. Your Aunt Matilda will love this place. Lawry's is family values incarnate, with lots of old-fashioned virtue in every swallow. *$$; AE, MC, V; no checks; dinner every day; full bar; reservations required; east side of La Cienega Blvd, north of Wilshire Blvd.* &

Le Colonial / ★★☆

8783 BEVERLY BLVD, WEST HOLLYWOOD; 310/289-0660
Clearly designed to evoke a prewar Saigon supper club, this elegant French-Vietnamese restaurant is downright sexy, with its ceiling fans, shuttered windows, and rattan and dark wood furnishings. The downstairs formal dining room and the front patio attract an eclectic assortment of patrons, from the suit-and-tie crowd to dressed-in-black hipsters, who come to graze on crisp spring rolls, shrimp–sugar cane sticks, and chicken-and-papaya salad with crunchy shrimp chips. Main courses such as whole sea bass wrapped in banana leaves—one of the best we've ever had—or filet mignon satay with spicy yams and long beans could easily become addictive. Upstairs, the restaurant's theme continues in the dimly lit lounge, which seduces the thin in-crowd with its comfy sofas, spacious seating areas, romantic nooks, and smokers-delight patio—prime turf for sipping Cosmopolitans and gossiping about industry happenings. *$$; AE, DC, MC, V; no checks; lunch Mon–Fri, dinner every day; full bar; reservations recommended; at Robertson Blvd.* &

Le Dome / ★★☆

8720 SUNSET BLVD, WEST HOLLYWOOD; 310/659-6919
Power lunch is such a way of life at this restaurant that magazines have actually published guides to which producers and which agents sit where on a regular basis. Le Dome functions as a French bistro, with a menu that's heavy with salads for the perennially diet-conscious regulars along with some very substantial bistro dishes for those who couldn't care less

if they fit into a designer dress come Oscar night. Despite the celeb-heavy crowd, the cooking is pleasantly egalitarian—cassoulet, tender leg of lamb, a healthy grilled chicken, fine french fries, hearty calf's liver, warm duck salad, a memorable tarte tatin. There's a view as well, of the city spread out before diners like a string of pearls against the neck of night. Or something like that. *$$; AE, MC, V; no checks; lunch Mon–Fri, dinner Mon–Sat; full bar; reservations required; south side of Sunset Blvd west of La Cienega Blvd.* &

Les Deux Cafe / ★★

1638 N LAS PALMAS AVE, HOLLYWOOD; 323/465-0509

Wander through Grant's parking lot in this seedy section of Hollywood and you'll find the unmarked front entrance to this ultra-hip French bistro, where proprietress Michele Lamy served up adequate French fare to Hollywood A-listers like Cameron Diaz, Cindy Crawford, and slews of others who rarely jaunt east of La Cienega. Guests dine on the charming garden patio, which embodies casual glamour and romance, or indoors in the woodsy bungalow-style dining room. While most of the clientele are here for the scene, the cuisine shouldn't be overlooked. Don't miss such starters as the lobster and tabbouleh salad with just a hint of mint, tender baked potatoes with osetra caviar, or the alluring fois gras terrine with fig compote. Entrees such as rich monkfish medallions with a lightly tarragon-scented vegetable salad, succulent rack of lamb with rosemary jus and eggplant caviar, and the obscenely decadent chicken breast with fois gras sauce make it easy to forget who's eating at the table next to you. For dessert, opt for the baked-to-order chocolate soufflé with pistachio ice cream, then stroll back to the bar/lounge where smoking is permitted and celebrities are known to join in with the evening's live entertainment. *$$$; AE, MC, V; no checks; lunch Mon–Fri, dinner Mon–Sat; full bar; reservations recommended; at Sunset Blvd.*

The Little Door / ★★

8164 W 3RD ST, LOS ANGELES; 323/951-1210

An L.A. hot spot that's so "in" it can't bother with a sign, this exclusive French-Mediterranean restaurant is nearly as dazzling as its twenty-something and wannabe twenty-something patrons. Ensconced behind heavy wooden doors—which are anything but little—the main dining area is actually a canopy-covered courtyard, lit mostly by candlelight. (A plus for smokers, who flout the no-smoking law in spades here.) From the sounds of the gurgling fountain to the heavenly aromas coming from the kitchen, the romantic ambience of this hip eatery makes you long to be in love just so you can bring a special someone here. Though the food is certainly secondary to the vibe, the Little Door specializes in decent organic fare, with such starters as a delicate tuna tartare and flavorful pistou soup paving the way for main courses like marinated swordfish, sautéed scallops, and fork-tender lamb. Wine buffs are wowed by the extensive selection of wines by the glass, but only Euro-transplants will appreciate the often-aloof service. *$$$; AE, MC, V; no checks; dinner every day; beer and wine; reservations required; east of La Cienega Blvd.* &

Locanda Veneta / ★★☆

8638 W 3RD ST, LOS ANGELES; 310/274-1893
Inside Locanda Veneta it's hard not to be struck by an overwhelming sense that you're in Venice. Not just because of the name, and not just because of the food, but because of the ineffable sense that you're in a place distanced from time and location. On a warm summer's evening you can feel the breeze flowing in through the windows, smell the green olive oil being poured over the carpaccio, hear the sizzle of roast lamb (served in a mustard and walnut sauce). Close your eyes (or, alternatively, drink enough pinot grigio) and you'll imagine hearing the songs of the gondoliers and the slap of the waves in the great lagoon. The menu is both simple and select, yet it's the sort of menu that bulges with dishes you must try. By all means, order the *trittico di mozzarelle*, which is nothing more than a wonderful trio of freshly made mozzarellas with tomatoes that actually taste like tomatoes, basil, and extra virgin olive oil. *$$; AE, MC, V; no checks; lunch Mon–Fri, dinner Mon–Sat; beer and wine; reservations required; west of San Vicente Blvd.* &

L'Orangerie / ★★★

903 N LA CIENEGA BLVD, WEST HOLLYWOOD; 310/652-9770
Housed in multimillion-dollar digs on La Cienega and lapped in the formality of truly upscale fine dining rooms, L'Orangerie is the most opulent classic French restaurant in Los Angeles—and the most expensive. Though the decor is relaxingly French-country-garden romantic, with a center atrium courtyard, sumptuous floral displays, and trellises, the place still requires your best duds and your special-occasion manners. Chef Ludovic Lefebvre's cuisine, described in the past as the finest French cuisine in America, is served by an appropriately professional staff, who might suggest that you begin your long and serious dining affair with fluffy scrambled eggs in a shell and topped with caviar, and proceed with whole rock lobster *fides* (vermicelli) seasoned with shellfish-and-cinnamon butter, or prime beef tenderloin masterfully roasted with six peppers, preserved shallot confit, baby carrots, and served with a light potato soufflé. The nightly prix-fixe menu is a six-course feast, and the wine list features 500 selections from France and the United States. *$$$; AE, MC, V; no checks; dinner Tues–Sun; full bar; reservations required; west side of La Cienega Blvd, south of Santa Monica Blvd.* &

47

Lucques / ★★★

8474 MELROSE AVE, WEST HOLLYWOOD; 323/655-6277

Take Caroline Styne, former manager of trendy Jones Hollywood, and Suzanne Goin, the executive chef from Campanile, mix them in a romantically minimalist space that used to be the carriage house for the Harold Lloyd estate, place them next door to celeb-heavy Ago, and the result is Lucques, the hot spot of the moment. In 1999 Goin was named one of the 10 Best New Chefs by *Food & Wine Magazine,* but her restaurant was packed long before she got major media recognition. The reason? The restaurant intentionally eschews Hollywood flash to focus on serving truly excellent food. Every meal at Lucques (say "Luke" with a French accent) begins with the dark, intense Provençal olives that give the place its name and almonds, which arrive soon after you sit down. The menu features the sort of casually satisfying French-Mediterranean food that matches the SoCal lifestyle to perfection—a heavenly soup of confit of tomatoes with crème fraîche, a flavorful salad of figs and prosciutto, light and delicate grilled bluefish with pancetta, an intense osso buco with haricots verts, and rabbit with escarole. Roasted beets, carrots, and potatoes are served on the side. There's even a cheese course, making this one of the few restaurants to risk such an offering in a town where cheese is usually found atop a hamburger. The scene crackles, from the large booths and tables indoors to the sleek patio seating, with diners who have had to make reservations close to a month in advance to enjoy the excellent fare and atmosphere of this West Hollywood gem. *$$; AE, MC, V; no checks; dinner Tues–Sun; full bar; reservations required; south side of Melrose Ave east of La Cienega Blvd.* &

Matsuhisa / ★★★☆

129 N LA CIENEGA BLVD, BEVERLY HILLS; 310/659-9639

Eating at Matsuhisa is an experience akin to having never eaten before— that is to say, never *really* having eaten before. Yes, we've all put chow in our gullets. But nothing like what chef Nobu Matsuhisa—who receives equal raves for his New York restaurant Nobu—creates here, which is a world of Japanese seafood dishes that's sure to make your taste buds seem as though they've been born again. The encyclopedic menu, complete with annotations, covers virtually every type of fish available through local Japanese markets, along with a fair number shipped in from Asia. Though the selection is overwhelming (reading the whole menu would take hours, time better spent indulging in the remarkable food), what catapults each and every morsel into the realm of otherworldly gastronomy are Matsuhisa's delicate and perfectly balanced sauces. Whatever accompaniment your fish comes swimming in or braised with, it's invariably a perfect marriage, allowing the subtle flavors of the sea to harmonize with creative combinations from the earth.

Try the shrimp in zingy pepper sauce, black cod in a miso sauce that redefines that trendy glaze, squid pasta, and the dish that may well exemplify Nobu's style—sea urchin wrapped in a shiso leaf and cooked tempura-style. We've seen tears trickle down the faces of committed foodies as they've nibbled, ever so delicately, on this remarkable creation. For its many fans, this understated, cramped—and surprisingly straightforward—space is home to the best restaurant in town. *$$$; AE, MC, V; no checks; lunch Mon–Fri, dinner every day; beer and wine; reservations required; west side of La Cienega Blvd north of Wilshire Blvd.* &

Michael's / ★★☆

1147 3RD ST, SANTA MONICA; 310/451-0843

Since the late '70s, Michael McCarty has done as much to define Cal-French cooking in Southern California as Alice Waters has at Chez Panisse in Northern California. Because this is Los Angeles, though, his methods are far more stylish and properly dressed. The food, though no longer as cutting-edge, is still a fine sampling of the cuisine that moved Los Angeles beyond surf 'n' turf, and nowadays it's executive chef Sang Yoon who's whipping it up. Despite the French overlay, Michael's is actually a very American restaurant—a sublime place to go for hearty crab cakes, whole lobster drizzled with basil butter, grilled pork tenderloin in star anise–pinot noir sauce, or grilled filet mignon wrapped in applewood-smoked bacon. When the seasonal meaty, but light, Baqueta bass in a Provençal purée of herbs with shaved fennel and mushroom-and-potato ragù is on the menu, it's one of the restaurant's best sellers. The setting remains wonderful and is home to one of the finest art galleries in town. There are few SoCal experiences more SoCal than a meal in the garden patio behind the restaurant, where the sound of falling water easily drowns out the parking lot beyond. Michael's also has a branch in New York City. *$$$; AE, DC, MC, V; no checks; lunch Tues–Fri, dinner Tues–Sat; full bar; reservations required; east side of 3rd St just north of Wilshire Blvd.* &

Mimosa / ★★☆
Cafe des Artistes / ★★☆

8009 BEVERLY BLVD, LOS ANGELES; 323/655-8895
1534 N MCCADDEN PL, HOLLYWOOD; 323/469-7300

While most restaurants claiming to be bistros are really bistro poseurs that serve lighter fare, Mimosa is the real thing—more or less. Here tables are cramped into a bright and cheery space where guests tend to focus on whom they're dining with instead of scanning to see who's sitting nearby. Sidewalk seating is especially appealing to true French expats who still can't get over California's anti-smoking laws. As the statement of purpose on the menu says: "No Truffles, No Caviar, No Bizarre Concoctions. Simply Our Interpretation of French Regional Cuisine." No proper meal can be consumed here without the tarte flambée Alsacienne as an opener, a wonderful thin-crusted "pizza" topped with the sweetest caramelized onions imaginable. The unabashedly caloric frisée salad with thick chunks of smoked bacon and a crowning poached egg is a dish to fall in love with. There's also an absolutely classic charcuterie platter, served with large pickle jars of house-made cornichons and black olives. The very best braised veal daube in town is found here. For dessert, there's floating island, an apple tart with vanilla ice cream, a pear clafouti, or a cheese plate that varies from day to day. Their sister restaurant, Cafe des Artistes, opened in 1999. *$$; AE, MC, V; no checks; lunch, dinner Mon–Sat; beer and wine; reservations required; north side of Beverly Blvd west of Fairfax Ave.* &

Morton's / ★★☆

8764 MELROSE AVE, WEST HOLLYWOOD; 310/276-5205

From hosting the *Vanity Fair* Oscars party to Madonna's post-MTV Music Video Awards bash, this restaurant is a Hollywood powerhouse, especially on Monday nights, when the show-biz crowd arrives in full force. Owned by Hard Rock Cafe co-creator Peter Morton and his twin sister, Pam (whose father is Arnie Morton, as in Arnie Morton's of Chicago steak houses), this stunning restaurant boasts high ceilings with skylights, big paintings, and lots of greenery—though chances are you'll be too busy watching the action to appreciate the decor. While moving and shaking is much of the experience here, the classic American grill food is also top-notch. Start with an impeccable caesar salad, or better yet the heavenly endive salad, or a spicy shrimp and black bean quesadilla, then move on to such entrees as the health-conscious free-range lime chicken with crisp shoestring potatoes, a well-prepared filet mignon, or tender sea bass on a bed of mashed potatoes. Chocolate fans swoon over a chocolate peanut butter cheesecake that's almost as rich as the clientele. *$$$; AE, DC, DIS, MC, V; no checks; lunch Mon–Fri, dinner Mon–Sat; full bar; reservations recommended; at Robertson Blvd.* &

Mr. Chow / ★★☆

344 N CAMDEN DR, BEVERLY HILLS; 310/278-9911

Perhaps the best-known low-profile restaurant in Beverly Hills, Mr. Chow is actually more famous for its celebrity clientele than for its upscale Chinese food. In fact, we've never been here when there wasn't an A-lister (L.L. Cool J, Goldie Hawn, Joe Pesci, Seal) dining beside us. Fortunately for everyone, mirrors are strategically placed along the walls so that rubbernecking is kept to a minimum. Considering the prices, it's fair to argue you're paying for more than great dim sum. Regardless, the quality is good, the style is rather '80s moderne, and the atmosphere is about as enjoyably insider-Hollywood as you can get. Bankable selections include delicious house-made garlic noodles—which on occasion the chef makes before diners' eyes—the absolutely sumptuous Gambler's Duck, and buttery black pepper lobster that's sure to inspire you to use the provided fingerbowls. Order for yourself instead of letting the waiter choose for the table (usually a more expensive gambit), and the combined food and scene make it well worth the price. *$$; AE, MC, V; no checks; lunch Mon–Fri, dinner every day; full bar; reservations required; east side of Camden Dr north of Wilshire Blvd.* &

Musso & Frank's Grill / ★ ★

6667 HOLLYWOOD BLVD, HOLLYWOOD; 323/467-7788
The story goes that everyone from F. Scott Fitzgerald to Frank Sinatra has drunk and dined at this classic Hollywood landmark restaurant. Dating back to 1919, Musso & Frank's is reminiscent of bygone glamorous dining with its enormous dining room of dark wood, red booths, and career waiters, many of whom've been around since the Kennedy era. Though the retro restaurant serves breakfast all day, if you come for its famous flannel cakes you must do so by 3pm. The novella-length menu features every old-fashioned dish imaginable, from shrimp cocktail, short ribs, chicken pot pie, and an open-face prime rib sandwich to steak with grilled liver and onions, creamed spinach, macaroni and cheese, and peas and carrots. Unfortunately, prices are at a premium for nostalgic dining; everything is served à la carte, including—oddly—salad dressing, which can run you an extra $3 for a smattering of blue cheese. But when all's said and done it's worth the expense. The food may not be the best in town, but the atmosphere—and some argue the martinis—are definitely contenders. *$$; AE, DC, MC, V; no checks; breakfast, lunch, dinner Tues.–Sat; full bar; reservations recommended; east of Highland Ave.* &

Nic's & The Martini Lounge / ★ ★ ☆

453 N CANON DR, BEVERLY HILLS; 310/550-5707
Larry Nicola (previously of Silver Lake's LA Nicola and downtown's Nicola's) is the brain/chef behind Nic's & The Martini Lounge in Beverly Hills—perhaps his best endeavor yet. The lovely, lively restaurant, with fresh flowers everywhere, dramatic fiberglass lamps, and striking contemporary art on the walls, is the backdrop for Nicola's seasonal contemporary American menu, which incorporates ethnic influences in such dishes as grilled prime rib of pork with tomatillos and Piedmont potatoes, or the now-classic Nic's oysters sautéed with walnuts and garlic. A strong chocolate theme runs throughout the exceptional desserts, such as Nic's chocolate martini, a creamy and intense bittersweet chocolate mousse with berry juice and squiggles of chocolate syrup, served, of course, in a martini glass. As the name suggests, the bar may be the best place in town for a classy, retro cocktail—especially when the nightly live music jazzes up the room. What else would you expect from a place

whose logo features a toothpick shooting through an olive for an apostrophe? *$$$; AE, DC, DIS, MC, V; no checks; lunch Tues–Fri, dinner Mon–Sat; full bar; reservations recommended; between Santa Monica Blvd and Brighton Way.* &

Nouveau Café Blanc / ★★★☆

9777 LITTLE SANTA MONICA BLVD, BEVERLY HILLS; 310/888-0108
Though chef/owner Tommy Harase is a top contender for the most talented chef in Los Angeles, his restaurant magically remains one of Beverly Hills's best kept secrets. After a stint in the kitchen at Chinois, Harase opened his first place, Café Blanc, in East Hollywood, and later relocated to this spare spot, where he continues to create his very personal version of French-Japanese cuisine. Nouveau Café Blanc is small (just 24 seats) and straightforward, with an all-white decor, a few pieces of art, and a sprinkling of fresh flowers. The only change over the years is the addition of a small but diverse wine list, with everything from Veuve Clicquot and Schramsberg to rieslings, gewürztraminers, and assorted California wines, all reasonably priced and selected to match Harase's cooking. His fragrant, intense soups and sorbets offer proof of his talents, and all of his food is light and clean, with pure yet delicate flavors. No one does better lobster or foie gras, both of which are often found on his seasonal, multicourse, prix-fixe menus. Harase's crème brûlée ranks easily among the best in town, with its perfectly creamy and thick texture and mica-like crust. If the coffee jello, a delicate, flavorful confection infinitely better than its name can convey, is on the menu, take our advice: order it. *$$$; AE, DIS, MC, V; no checks; lunch, dinner Tues–Sat; beer and wine; reservations recommended; between Wilshire Blvd and Linden Dr.* &

Off Vine / ★★

6263 LELAND WAY, HOLLYWOOD; 323/962-1900
Tucked into a side street and enclosed by a towering wooden fence, this Craftsman-style bungalow stands out as a beacon of country charm in the midst of gritty Hollywood street life. It's a favorite luncheon option for nearby Paramount Pictures employees, but the only clue to the oasis within is the valet out front and the parade of sunglasses-sporting movers and shakers on their way in and out of the restaurant. On a typical sunny California day, lunch or brunch on the bougainvillea-curtained porch or patio is L.A. at its most civilized. On the rare evening when it's cold enough to actually consider wearing socks, diners gather inside at tables dispersed within the little house that's accented by hardwood floors, cheerful art, and a blazing fireplace. The simple American menu features house-made soups, an Oriental chicken salad large enough to feed a small family, capellini pomodoro, grilled New York steak, and several fresh-fish options, doused with a whimsical fruit salsa or an Asian-influenced

sauce and served with sautéed vegetables and a creamy purée of carrots. *$$; AE, MC, V; no checks; lunch Mon–Fri, dinner every day, brunch Sun; beer and wine; just east of Vine St south of Sunset Blvd.* ⅃

One Pico / ★★☆

1 PICO BLVD, SANTA MONICA; 310/587-1717

Until Lavande opened at the nearby Loews, this dining room at Shutters on the Beach was almost certainly the best hotel restaurant on the beach. It may receive less fanfare these days, but it's still a respectable California style dining room with a large fireplace, a good ocean view, and a menu filled with what the restaurant calls New American cooking. Others might consider the food high-end Beach Cuisine, but that's not a bad thing—long before they were doing that sort of sandy comfort food at the terminally trendy Beach House, they were cooking it at One Pico. Here you'll find mussels steamed in chardonnay, a rich corn chowder dotted with smoked shrimp, big hunks of salmon smoked long and slow over applewood, and a seriously hearty rack of lamb. Show up in time to sip a cocktail while the sun sinks into Santa Monica Bay and the lights come alive on the Santa Monica Pier, and you'll find a civilized moment in the midst of a most uncivilized city. *$$; AE, MC, V; no checks; lunch, dinner every day, brunch Sun; full bar; reservations recommended; north side of Pico Blvd at the beach.* ⅃

Orso / ★★

8706 W 3RD ST, WEST HOLLYWOOD; 310/274-7144

Although it's overlooked by many, this noisy, affable, and very reasonably priced restaurant is popular with celebs who linger on the surprisingly intimate and romantic outdoor patio concealed behind a set of stucco walls and an almost overwhelming forest of ficus trees. The Northern Italian menu includes crisp-as-a-cracker pizzas, classic pastas (no one makes a better order of farfalle with smoked salmon), and pride-of-the-house seafood. An added bonus: Orso is very popular during the day with internists from Cedars hospital across the street. If you choke on a chicken bone, there'll be lots of physicians to give you a Heimlich and then send you a bill for it. *$; AE, MC, V; no checks; lunch, dinner every day; full bar; reservations required; south side of 3rd St 2 blocks east of Robertson Blvd.* ⅃

Pacific Dining Car / ★★★

1310 W 6TH ST, LOS ANGELES; 213/483-6000

2700 WILSHIRE BLVD, SANTA MONICA; 310/453-4000

A refuge for serious carnivores as well as lovers of big, tannic red wines, the Pacific Dining Car has been serving excellent steaks for nearly 80 years. The restaurant owes its name to the front room, a faux train car, while the other rooms have a more clubby style—both of which are ideal venues for the red-meat renaissance. All of the substantial beef entrees (more than a dozen) are USDA Prime Eastern corn-fed, dry-aged on the premises, cut by PDC's own butcher, then cooked as simply as possible over high-heat mesquite charcoal to sear in the juices. Add the requisite baked potato, french fries, mashed potatoes, or rice plus steamed spinach, creamed spinach, or broccoli hollandaise and you've got yourself a good old-fashioned dining experience. Alternatively, you can fake it with lime chicken or Maine lobster. The wine list, overseen by sommelier Ron Washam, has more than 400 beef-friendly choices. Best of all, the original downtown location is open 24 hours a day, 7 days a week, and even at breakfast there are some great steak options. Weekday happy hour in the cozy bar features great—and free—hors d'oeuvres like baby back pork ribs, broiled chicken wings, and shrimp. Their Santa Monica location is open for lunch and dinner daily but closes at 2am. *$$$; AE, DC, MC, V; no checks; breakfast, lunch, dinner every day (L.A. location); lunch, dinner every day (Santa Monica location); full bar; reservations recommended; www.moshix2.net/pdc; between Wilshire and 6th St on Witmer St (L.A. location); at Princeton and Wilshire (Santa Monica location).* &

The Palm / ★★

9001 SANTA MONICA BLVD, WEST HOLLYWOOD; 310/550-8811

For the movers and shakers of Hollywood, especially those exuding testosterone, this is the place to go for prime, aged, Eastern corn-fed steaks or for lobsters from the cold waters off Nova Scotia. There are also chops, chicken dishes, a number of salads, and pastas, although this might come as a big surprise to many who've been eating at the Palm for years without knowing it was an American continental restaurant. The scene continues to be absolutely frantic and lots of fun, due largely to the studiously rude waiters serving oversized portions of everything and to the ubiquitous general manager Gigi, after whom the signature salad (one of the best salads to be found in a salad-obsessed town) is named. Lobsters, served grilled, cost about as much as a new Volkswagen Beetle . . . and are often larger. *$$; AE, MC, V; no checks; lunch Mon–Fri, dinner every day; full bar; reservations recommended; north side of Santa Monica Blvd east of Doheny Dr.* &

Patina / ★★★★

5955 MELROSE AVE, HOLLYWOOD; 323/467-1108

 Patina's exterior is so understated you can easily drive by without seeing the restaurant, but it's no secret that most gourmands deem this the best fine dining experience in town. Chef/owner Joachim Splichal's flagship restaurant has a variety of "givens": it's given that the service is the most professional in town, that each eclectic dish will be artfully presented and prepared, and that even in this image-obsessed town the most important attraction here is the impeccable and creative cooking. The small, rather cramped contemporary dining room, filled with muted tones, soft light, and lots of little tables placed so close together you can listen in to many conversations at once, bears out the point: it's not the ambience, but the spectacular, ever-changing menu that has kept guests' attention since Patina's 1989 opening. Over the years the menu has demonstrated Splichal's whimsy with dishes such as a corn blini "sandwich" filled with marinated salmon, a soufflé of grits with Herkimer cheddar and an apple-smoked bacon sauce, New York duck liver with blueberry pancakes and blueberry sauce, and a red bell pepper soup with a tiny bacon, lettuce, and tomato sandwich on the side. Along with the playful additions, however, are a variety of classic Splichalian dishes such as the crisp-skinned delicate seared whitefish accompanied by "French fries not fried" (cubed poached potatoes that taste worlds better than they sound) or the scallops rolled in a sheet of potato and served with a brown-butter vinaigrette. For those who can't make up their minds there's a prix-fixe menu that changes regularly. Service, as befits the crème-de-la-crème clientele, is excellent without being intrusive. The wine list bubbles with creativity, listing enough standards to please regular folks and enough obscure vintages to keep oenophiles happy. For reasons that have long eluded us, lunch is served only on Tuesdays. The lunch menu is lighter—easier on the digestive system and the wallet—but it's still a meal that can take a couple of hours to go through. *$$$; AE, MC, V; no checks; lunch Tues only, dinner nightly; full bar; reservations required; north side of Melrose Ave. west of Vine St.* &

Peppone / ★☆

11628 BARRINGTON CT, BRENTWOOD; 310/476-7379
Gianni Paoletti, the original chef and partner at Santa Monica's Valentino, went off on his own and has run Peppone now for nearly 25 years. It's a classic Hollywood hangout, with a large following of celebrities who are lured by both the food and the dark, romantic setting. Paoletti's Italian cuisine, from fresh artichokes in olive oil, garlic, and broth to pork-loin scaloppine, calf's liver Venetian style, and homemade tiramisu, is a tribute to his flamboyant character and passionate love of wine and food. The wine list is nothing short of spectacular, and very reasonably priced, owing to the great volume and foresight of Paoletti's purchases, with great French, Italian, and California wines from major vineyards and vintages. Peppone is popular among Westside locals but not widely known beyond, which keeps the crowds under control. *$$$; AE, DC, MC, V; no checks; lunch Mon–Fri, dinner every day; full bar; reservations required; N69JPC@aol.com; south of Sunset Blvd.* &

Pinot Hollywood / ★★☆

1448 N GOWER ST, HOLLYWOOD; 323/461-8800
Pinot Hollywood, like Disneyland, consists of several discrete but shared worlds and an array of attractions to help you feel jolly. The restaurant, the natural evolution of Joachim Splichal's Patina in Hollywood and his Pinot Bistro in Studio City, is divided between the warm, bright dining room and the power-lunch patio. In the back, sprawling across several rooms, is the Martini Bar and lounge that's popular with the Johnny Depp/Jennifer Aniston–wannabe crowd. Though much of the menu is SoCal light and casual (delicately grilled ahi with baby artichokes, goat cheese terrine with grilled ratatouille, herb-crusted John Dory with pea

 pods), this is a true bistro, with all the solidity that that implies. You could pretend to be on the Left Bank in a snowstorm as you tuck into dense, cold-weather dishes such as French onion soup with a Gruyère topping as thick as a brick, braised veal shank, roasted leg of lamb with flageolets, roasted rabbit, and roasted venison. But since this is California, and since this is Splichal, you can simultaneously dine as though you were in Cannes on a warm summer's evening. For dessert, along with a serious chocolate mousse and a Cognac truffle cake, there're also a nice light trio of ice creams and sorbet and a sinfully memorable chocolate croissant pudding. *$$; AE, MC, V; no checks; lunch Mon–Fri, dinner Mon–Sat; full bar; reservations required; southeast corner of Sunset Blvd. and Gower St.* ⑤

Remi / ★

1451 3RD ST PROMENADE, SANTA MONICA; 310/393-6545
One of the few grown-up restaurants on the Third Street Promenade, this elegant Italian restaurant specializes in the good cooking of Venice, with nautical decor to match, and the largest collection of grappas in town. Indoors the environment is relaxing and brightly lit. The outdoor dining area facing the open-air mall can be hectic because of the nonstop show of the Promenade's oddities and entertainers. But it did come in handy during the restaurant's pre-smoking-ban cigar dinners, when Cohiba smokers sent up quite a cloud over mimes and domicile-challenged Santa Monica residents. As befits a Venetian restaurant, the menu features a good deal of fish, lots of fine pasta (such as linguine with scallops and broccoli rabe), and a remarkably tender Italianate steak. All told, this ambitious eatery, a branch of a well-respected New York trattoria, offers some of the best dinner theatre around. *$$; AE, MC, V; no checks; lunch, dinner every day; full bar; reservations recommended; east side of 3rd St Promenade just north of Broadway.* ⑤

The Restaurant at Hotel Bel-Air / ★★★

701 STONE CANYON RD, LOS ANGELES; 310/472-1211
There's no lovelier setting in Los Angeles than the rustic Hotel Bel-Air. Those seeking formality opt for the dining room; others prefer the rustic romance of the bougainvillea-draped garden terrace, with its heated stone floor. However, everyone appreciates executive chef Gary Clauson's excellent food and the superb wine list orchestrated by new sommelier Robert Cross. Clauson likes playful presentations; he often sends out appetizers on hefty rabbit statues—he calls it the Rabbit Surprise—and a dessert of petits fours might arrive on a miniature old-fashioned stove. But as whimsical as he is, British-born Clauson is a serious, albeit creative, chef. In his kitchen Dover sole is done Caribbean-style and is accompanied by banana chutney, sweet-potato purée and, most exotic, a vanilla-perfumed curry sauce with only the mildest hint of heat. Moroccan influences pervade the loin of lamb, sliced into tender little pieces, fanned out atop a disc of couscous and a layer of ratatouille and figs, all bound together with a rich lamb-reduction sauce. Best among the kitchen's many impressive dessert creations is a pear tart with ice cream, made of white chocolate and mascarpone, and drizzled with crème anglaise. Clauson's Cuisine Légère menu gives guests lighter, spa-style options such as a warm lentil salad or carrot-ginger soup. *$$$; AE, DC, DIS, JCB, MC, V; no checks; breakfast, lunch, dinner every day; full bar; reservations recommended; about 1 mile north of Sunset Blvd.* &

Rix / ★★½

1413 5TH ST, SANTA MONICA; 310/656-9688
After dazzling diners at Boxer, the always-creative Neal Fraser relocated to this '40s-style supper club and designed a very '90s California menu that fits perfectly with the restaurant's hip-meets-haute clientele. While he left the kitchen in 1999, the food remains intact under the direction of chef Gordon Naccarato, who hails from Michael's, Aspen's, Gordon's, and the infamous Monkey Bar. There's a '50s-style bar menu here divided into two sections—"Rix Classics" and "From the Tiki Bar"—while the kitchen straddles the lines between Old American and New American cooking. A good example of that stance is shrimp cocktail, available in two forms—traditionally prepared or cooked tempura-style with ponzu sauce. There's white radicchio salad with pine nut brittle on the one hand, and a caesar salad on the other; a pork chop with mashed potatoes from the old world, and a goat cheese–stuffed portobello mushroom from the new. Carnivores will exult in the venison and be befuddled by the kabocha squash flan. But regardless of your penchant, the kitchen delivers excellent renditions from both sides of the culinary coin. On a good night, the bar upstairs, often with live music, is the liveliest in town; culture shock becomes Los Angeles well. *$$; AE, MC, V; no checks;*

lunch Mon–Fri, dinner Mon–Sat; full bar; reservations required; east side of 5th St. just south of Santa Monica Blvd. ⅃

Röckenwagner / ★★☆

2435 MAIN ST, SANTA MONICA; 310/399-6504

After years in a funky storefront on Abbott Kinney in Venice, Hans Röckenwagner moved his California Eclectic cooking to an equally eclectic setting on Main Street, in the Frank Gehry–designed Edgemar Center. The wood-accented interior with vaulted exposed ceilings is spacious to the point of being cavernous, though they've made an effort to cozy the room with whimsical decoration and a deli area where fresh bread is sold on weekends. The same creative dishes—decadent crab soufflé; lamb; splendid smoked salmon and potato chips, prosciutto, and foie gras with grilled pears; air-dried duck; tender grilled scallops; every type of white asparagus dish imaginable (in season); and terrific European brunches of bread and cheese—all these are pleasures available nowhere else in town. Every Tuesday Hans offers a *Stammtisch,* or community-based dinner, served at a large table where locals congregate, discuss the evening's topic, and sample born-again versions of dishes from the chef's German childhood. *$$; AE, MC, V; no checks; lunch Thurs, dinner every day, brunch Sat–Sun; full bar; reservations recommended; east side of Main St south of Pico Blvd.* ⅃

Ruth's Chris Steak House / ★★★

224 S BEVERLY DR, BEVERLY HILLS; 310/859-8744

The constant crowds here are further proof (as if any is needed) that steak is back in a big way. A prime contender for the title of Best Steak House in Los Angeles, this Beverly Hills branch of a New Orleans beef eatery rose from the ashes of a fire a few years ago, returning as a larger, more elegant, even better restaurant. The beef here is prime, Midwestern, and perfectly selected—New York strip, porterhouse, T-bone, rib eye, filet mignon—all of which are perfectly cooked (served in butter unless you request otherwise) and accompanied by what many say are the best side dishes of any steak house in town, including terrific spinach, fries, and onion rings. For those who can still manage another bite, there's bread pudding for dessert. *$$; AE, MC, V; no checks; dinner every day; full bar; reservations required; east side of Beverly Dr south of Wilshire.* ⅃

Seoul Jung / ★★

930 WILSHIRE BLVD, LOS ANGELES; 213/688-7880

This restaurant in downtown's Wilshire Grand Hotel is an unusually lovely space, with several large dining areas and smaller, elegant private rooms, all geared toward the celebration of Korean barbecue. The tables are marble, with a grill built into the center of each to accommodate the grill-intensive cuisine of Korea. Among the various tabletop barbecue selections, *bul go gi* means blood-red raw strips of marinated beef rib eye, marbled with fat. Salad, rice, soup, and side dishes in many small bowls accompany the order, including several versions of *kim chee*, the fermented cabbage-based dish that defines Korean cuisine. Diners grill the meats themselves, and then roll them in lettuce leaves with assorted vegetables and condiments. Portions are substantial, but if room allows, begin with an appetizer of *pa jun*, a briny, pizza-sized pancake of seafood, including baby shrimp and calamari, mixed with scallions and strips of red and green bell pepper—a very satisfying dish with its latke-like texture. Korean Hite beer is a perfect match with any of the foods. *$$; AE, DC, DIS, JCB, MC, V; no checks; lunch, dinner every day; corner of Figueroa and 7th St.* &

72 Market Street / ★★☆

72 MARKET ST, VENICE; 310/392-8720

72 Market Street has long been known for its Modern American food with Asian and Latino influences; but since 1994 the sexy neighborhood restaurant and oyster bar has had a French chef, and that French chef, Roland Gibert, was doing French stuff until his 1999 departure when French chef Robert Roaquin stepped in to manage the menu. Consider it a sort of Franco-American cuisine, where the grilled filet that used to come with garlic butter and fries now arrives in a Roquefort and walnut sauce. These days, the menu also lists a fine torte of warm pears and Roquefort, a terrine of artichoke mousse and leek-wrapped asparagus, and a brightly colored terrine of eggplant, zucchini, and red and green peppers. Grilled salmon comes with a very French Dijon-Pommery mustard sauce. Dungeness crab arrives with a crisp noodle galette. The style has shifted, but the quality is still high, the service very fine, and the room comfortably relaxed, with interesting art on the walls that changes from time to time. The Oyster Bar was recently shucking a fine assortment of Malpeques, Eagle Creeks, Kumamotos, Fanny Bays, and Trail's Ends— all the right oysters for the right crowd. Wednesday is table d'hôte night, when a prix-fixe "peasant" meal of salad, a main course, and dessert is served family style at a long table. Sunday is "Wine Dregs" night, when wines coming off the menu sell at very low prices. *$$; AE, MC, V; no checks; lunch Mon–Fri, dinner every day; full bar; reservations required; west end at the beach.* &

Sonora Cafe / ★★☆

180 S LA BREA AVE, LOS ANGELES; 323/857-1800

Sonora Cafe was a favorite in downtown Los Angeles before owner Ron Salisbury (who also owns L.A.'s and Santa Monica's El Cholo restaurants) relocated it five years ago to a massive space on La Brea Avenue. As it did downtown, Sonora serves up some of the best New American Southwest cuisine around, with a rich variety of gourmet Mexican-influenced dishes. Duck is a specialty of the house, from the lunch-only duck tacos with duck confit in whole wheat tortillas with a honey-ancho sauce to the evening entree of Long Island duckling glazed with a tequila-pomegranate sauce. Banana leaf–wrapped sea bass is spectacularly moist, and the nachos teeming with goodies accompany the premium margaritas perfectly. The signature dessert is Sonora's Southwest Sundae: a gourmet banana split, laid out as artistically as a sand painting and topped with *cajeta* (a sauce made from burnt-sugar caramel and goat's milk). Sonora's dining room is comfortable, spacious, and a step above casual, while the splendid bar area is the prime spot for sampling one of the city's finest selections of tequila and mescal and a superb array of top-shelf margaritas. *$$$; AE, DC, MC, V; no checks; lunch Mon–Fri, dinner every day; full bar; reservations recommended; at 2nd St.* &

Spago Beverly Hills / ★★★★
Spago Hollywood / ★★☆

176 N CAÑON DR, BEVERLY HILLS; 310/385-0880
1114 HORN AVE, HOLLYWOOD; 310/652-4025

What La Cirque 2000 is to New York, Spago Beverly Hills is to Los Angeles. Ever since designer/wife Barbara Lazaroff and superstar chef/hubby Wolfgang Puck unveiled their Xanadu-like dining room in April 1997, it's been Los Angeles's defining restaurant and the hottest reservation around. Executive chef Lee Hefter, a veteran of Puck's Granita in Malibu, oversees the menu, which includes notably Asian influences in the rare grilled steak salad with crushed peanuts and chiliginger vinaigrette, deliciously understated marinated Japanese hamachi with seaweed salad, seared scallops with crisp noodles and ginger–lemongrass curry, and roasted Cantonese duck with ginger, kumquats, and Chinese greens. This is also the venue where Puck explores his Austrian roots with selections called "Wolfgang's Childhood Favorites." If you've never tried *Wienerschnitzel vom Kalb mit Kartoffeln und Vogersalat* (wiener schnitzel with warm potato and mâche) or *Rindgulasch mit Spätzle* (beef stew with spaetzle), this is the place to do it. Austrian memoirs continue through dessert menu, where *Kaiserschmarren* (soufflé pancakes) and *Apfelstrudel* (apple strudel) sit between strawberry-rhubarb soup and a glazed chocolate and orange ganache tarte. The original Spago Hollywood, which is a little more low-key than its Beverly Hills counterpart, still crackles with originality; the open kitchen is a sculpture in motion; and the food—from trademark pizzas to wood-grilled meat and fish—is sublime. *$$$; AE, DC, DIS, MC, V; no checks; lunch Mon–Sat (Beverly Hills), dinner every day (Beverly Hills); dinner Tues–Sun (Hollywood); full bar; reservations required (Beverly Hills); reservations recommended (Hollywood); east side of Cañon Dr at Wilshire Blvd (Beverly Hills); north of Wilshire Blvd (Hollywood).* &

Tahiti / ★★

7910 W 3RD ST, LOS ANGELES; 323/651-1213

The tropical decor of this stylish restaurant celebrates its namesake with fun island overtones—from a thatched-hut patio to a decidedly South Pacific restroom—that are just one step away from being over the top. Fortunately, the cuisine of chef/owner Tony Di Lembo (a former co-owner of Indigo) is far better than any found in the unimpressive restaurants of French Polynesia. His eclectic, exotic menu combines Italian, Asian, and Pacific Rim cuisines and features such lovely starters as pot stickers (which come with a spicy-minty dipping sauce), a refreshing shrimp and mango salad, and an unusual rendition of crab cakes, packed with tender crab meat and crisp angel hair pasta. Main courses tend to be less exciting than the starters, but include grilled chicken with pineapple rice, seafood pasta, spicy sea bass, and thin-crusted pizzas. Diners looking for a little romance should ask for a candlelit table on the patio—squint a little and you could almost imagine you're in Bora Bora. For dessert, don't miss the Valrhona chocolate pudding cake that oozes gooey warm chocolate. *$$; AE, MC, V; no checks; lunch Mon–Fri, dinner Mon–Sat; beer and wine; reservations recommended; west of Fairfax Ave.* ⅄

Valentino / ★★★★

3115 W PICO BLVD, SANTA MONICA; 310/829-4313

Deemed one of the primo Italian restaurants in the entire country, Sicilian-born chef/owner Piero Selvaggio's dining room has topped culinary charts since 1972 with sophisticated, swoon-inducing authentic contemporary Italian cuisine. But since 1984 the magic has been more of a team effort, with Bergamo-born chef Angelo Auriana heading up Selvaggio's kitchen. Though a dinner here can add up to a moderate mortgage payment, it's the price many pay for perfection. The kitchen uses only the best ingredients, from fresh fish—both local and imported from Italy—to generous shavings of white truffles. Deep-pocketed regulars know to let the chef select the evening's meal, which might include several small courses such as delicate cuttlefish capellini, pappardelle tossed with broccoli and ricotta, a risotto rich with white truffles (Selvaggio dubs this rice dish "the Lord's porridge"), perfectly grilled Chilean sea bass, and a sublimely seasoned rack of lamb. Valentino's wine cellar has repeatedly been honored each year since 1981 with the Grand Wine Award from *Wine Spectator,* with 13,000 bottles ranging from $30 to $10,000. From the understated elegance of the dining room to the attentive service to the wonderful food and wine, an evening at Valentino is one of those rare experiences that turns dining into a passionate love affair between your plate and your palate that will not soon be forgotten. *$$$; AE, DC, MC, V; no checks; lunch Fri, dinner Mon–Sat; full bar; reservations recommended; west of the 10 Fwy.* ⅄

Versailles / ★

10319 VENICE BLVD, CULVER CITY (AND BRANCHES); 310/558-3168
Garlic lovers gather at Versailles, where they often wait in line for a table to order the garlic chicken. Sure, there are other dishes available at this very casual, dark and dive-ish restaurant, some of them very good—especially seafood and pork—but the half bird long marinated in garlic is a must, especially on a first visit. Like many other dishes, it's served with rice, black beans, and chewy fried plantains. Portions are huge and prices are amazingly low. And the pungent scent of garlic fills the air, since virtually every table has at least one order of the chicken. There are other Cuban places in town, but this is the closest you can get to Havana and its food. Culver City was the original of this small chain that's now grown to four, with branches in Manhattan Beach, West Los Angeles, and Encino. *$; AE, MC, V; no checks; lunch, dinner every day; beer and wine; reservations not accepted; between Motor St. and Overland Ave.* ♿

Vincenti Ristorante / ★★★

11930 SAN VICENTE BLVD, BRENTWOOD; 310/207-0127
Since its opening in late 1997, the chance of scoring a weekend reservation at this loud and swanky Italian restaurant has often been as likely as winning the Lotto. Owners Maureen Vincenti (widow of Mauro Vincenti of Rex il Ristorante) and chef Gino Angelini are responsible for starting the stir with their trattoria, which serves alluring pastas, rotisserie meats, and fresh fish along with a hearty dose of haute attitude. The dining room borders on the cold side of modern, but polished servers and the overall vibe make a visit here more of an experience than a straightforward meal. Winning pastas include potato gnocchi with tomato-squab sauce and spaghetti loaded with lobster. Any of the rotisserie meats, cooked over a wood fire, are awesome, as are the freshly prepared evening specials—from beef or pork tenderloin to duck, rabbit, and exotic wild game—which are wheeled in on a cart and carved tableside. The exclusive restaurant boasts an avid Hollywood following, including Dustin Hoffman, Brooke Shields, and Cindy Crawford. Director Bruce Paltrow is a part owner, so look for daughter Gwyneth and her hunk of the moment cozying up in a corner. *$$$; AE, MC, V; no checks; lunch Fri, dinner Tues–Sun; full bar; reservations required; west of Montana Ave.* ♿

Yang Chow / ★★

819 N BROADWAY AVE, LOS ANGELES; 213/625-0811
It's not much to look at, but this straightforward Chinese restaurant is downright famous for its slippery shrimp. The rest of the extensive menu, though not as reputed, is well priced and of good quality. For a full review of Yang Chow, see the review of its Pasadena location in the Pasadena Restaurants section. *$$; AE, DC, MC, V; no checks; lunch, dinner every day; beer and wine; reservations recommended; between Alpine and College Sts.* ♿

Zankou Chicken / ★

5065 SUNSET BLVD, HOLLYWOOD (AND BRANCHES); 323/665-7845

If the old Armenian saying "Anyone can learn to cook, but you must be born knowing how to roast" is true, the Lebanese-Armenian family behind Zankou was gifted at birth. Zankou is truly the temple of roasted chicken—and you'll find dozens of birds slowly spinning on rotisseries, cooking to crisp-skinned perfection. Though fowl is king here, its palace is anything but regal. There's no option but to enjoy tender, fall-off-the-bone meat in the charmless dining room in a Hollywood mini-mall. The ramekin of garlic paste, which can be slathered on the juicy fowl or used as a dip, will surely spice things up. But be warned: You'll be sweating the stuff for days. Zankou also offers a smattering of typical Middle Eastern dishes such as hummus, tahini, and shawarma, all quite good and dirt cheap. Two newer branches offer the same wonderful food in Glendale and Van Nuys. *$; no credit cards; no checks; lunch, dinner every day; no alcohol; reservations not accepted; corner of Sunset Blvd and Normandie Ave.* &

LODGINGS

Argyle / ★★★

**8358 SUNSET BLVD, WEST HOLLYWOOD; 323/654-7100
OR 800/225-2637**

If you like Deco, you'll love the Argyle. The 15-story building originally opened in 1931 as the first all-electric apartments in California. The luxurious abodes were home to Bugsy Siegel, Charlie Chaplin, Marilyn Monroe, and Errol Flynn long before the building was listed on National Register of Historic Places. Today the stunning tower has been converted to a boutique hotel whose 64 guest rooms are smallish but extremely well furnished with period pieces and Italian reproductions that fit the architecture's Deco and Moderne lines. Especially chic are the oval scalloped beds, credenzas that electronically lift and lower the TV and VCR, ultra-cool ice buckets, and south-facing rooms with spectacular city views on the higher floors. Anyone desiring a truly glamorous stay should opt for one of the huge rooftop penthouse suites, whose balconies are a prime location for a cocktail party. There's a small but well-equipped gym, complete with sauna, cardiovascular machines, and free weights, and a small terrace swimming pool with fabulous plaster palm trees. Round-the-clock concierge service helps guests track down anything the hotel itself doesn't offer. The restaurant, fenix, is hot under chef Brandon Boudet, who previously worked with New Orleans's famed Emeril Lagasse and serves New American Cuisine with an emphasis on the Gulf Coast. The restaurant has recently become a hip cocktail spot with the young

Hollywood set. $$$$; AE, DC, DIS, MC, V; checks OK; www.argyle
hotel.com; between Sweetzer Ave and La Cienega Blvd. &

Avalon Hotel / ★★★

9400 W OLYMPIC BLVD, BEVERLY HILLS; 310/277-5221 OR 800/535-4715
Cashing in on the retro craze, this stylish new 88-room boutique hotel is
the latest incarnation of the historic Beverly Carlton Hotel, a former
haunt of such Golden Era celebs as Marilyn Monroe, Mae West, and
Lucy and Desi. The Avalon is situated in three distinct buildings: the original Landmark, the two-story '50s style motor inn (which offers some
rooms with kitchenettes), and the five-story Cityscape, with an alluring
top-floor penthouse ideal for parties and business meetings. Guest rooms
 in all three structures combine sophisticated period design elements such
as Heywood-Wakefield chairs, Eames cabinets, and George Nelson
bubble lamps with such modern-day conveniences as VCRs, CD players,
big-screen televisions, multiple phone lines with voice mail, fax machines,
and dataport connections. While the hotel's sleek, clean design and sunny
pool area with exclusive poolside cabanas attracts the terminally hip, reasonable rates starting at $165 per night make it possible for posers-in-
training to check in here as well. A small bar and restaurant in the
Landmark building serve hungry guests daily. $$$; AE, DC, MC, V; no
checks; east of Beverly Dr. &

The Beverly Hills Hotel and Bungalows / ★★★★

9641 SUNSET BLVD, BEVERLY HILLS; 310/276-2251 OR 800/283-8885
No hotel in town embodies Hollywood glamour like the Beverly Hills
Hotel. Built in 1912, this enormous legendary pink palace with its 12-
acre grounds (a preferred spot for fashion shoots) has hosted a slew of
famous guests, including Marilyn Monroe, Howard Hughes, Katharine
Hepburn, and Elizabeth Taylor, who spent six of her honeymoons here.
A massive $170-million renovation by the current owner, the Sultan of
Brunei, returned the glamorous retreat to its former glory, with picture-
 perfect surroundings: banana-leaf wallpaper, a vivid pink and green color
scheme, and lush gardens of banana-leaf palms and flowering plants. The
203 guest rooms and bungalows are large and lavishly adorned,with
plenty of gilded furnishings, stereos with CD players, VCRs, and bath-
rooms often large enough to live in. Bed and bath linens are designer, and
many rooms feature secluded private patios. Some rooms, and all 21
bungalows, have separate entrances for greater privacy. Bungalow #5 has
its own private pool, while #7, Marilyn Monroe's favorite, is decorated
to her taste. Sun worshipers and deal makers of several generations con-
tinue to congregate at the utterly glamorous Olympic-sized pool and its
in-demand cabanas, decked out with televisions, fax machines, direct dial
phones, and more, which rent for $150 per day. The property also boasts
a number of chic boutiques, a salon, spa, gym, and afternoon tea in the

lobby lounge. If more than a few of the famous Polo Lounge's regulars are now deceased, a new and younger crowd has adopted it as a favorite eating and drinking venue, especially for the classic steak tartare—made tableside—and the Sunday brunch, served inside or in the garden patio. *$$$$; AE, DC, MC, V; checks OK; sales@thebeverlyhillshotels.com; www.beverlyhillshotel.com; corner of Rodeo Dr.* &

Beverly Laurel Motor Hotel / ★

8018 BEVERLY BLVD, LOS ANGELES; 323/651-2441 OR 800/962-3824

"Retro-chic" would be a good way to describe this cool 52-room lodging just down the road from the Beverly Center. From the exterior, the Beverly Laurel resembles the '50s-style motel that it is: outdoor hallways overlook the ground floor's postage-stamp pool. But inside, spotless rooms have been stylishly redecorated with brilliant blue walls, Deco furnishings, and wooden headboards inlaid with black-and-white photos. Built-in dressers and other fun bygone design elements, mini-refrigerators, and microwaves give the place the convenience of home. Some rooms have kitchenettes, but guests not inclined to cook can head to Swingers diner for coffee-shop cuisine in an ultratrendy setting. Open till the wee hours, this diner-with-an-attitude attracts Hollywood hipsters, so people-watching is definitely on the menu, along with juicy burgers, tuna melts, fries, and creamy milk shakes. Discerning travelers would undoubtedly consider this gussied-up motel nothing more than a dive, but location and would-be stylishness don't come any cheaper than they do at the Beverly Laurel. *$; AE, DC, MC, V; no checks; west of Fairfax Ave.* &

Beverly Plaza Hotel / ★★★

8384 W 3RD ST, LOS ANGELES; 323/658-6600

Remodeled in 1996, this stylish boutique hotel is known for its 98 handsome oversized guest rooms and for the little extras often overlooked at many larger hotels. The well-appointed accommodations are decorated in chic Pottery-Barn-meets-Ethan-Allen fashion and include comfy beds, casual sitting areas, and smallish bathrooms. But where this hotel really goes to town is with amenities: such goodies as complimentary taxi service within a five-mile radius, a daily newspaper, natural soaps and shampoos, and Joseph Schmidt chocolates with the nightly turn-down service. There's also an in-house gym, an absolutely tiny outdoor pool, and a spa with services ranging from facials and massages to body waxing and personal training. The shoebox lobby is not large enough to linger in, but it is the place to rev up on complimentary gourmet coffees and fresh fruit each morning. Adjacent to the lobby, Cava Cafe & Tapas Bar is a festive spot frequented by loyal locals who sample sangria and tapas in the loud downstairs room or head upstairs for an elegant setting, a flavorful dinner of Spanish-influenced fare by chef/owner Toribio

Prado, and live entertainment. *$$$; AE, DC, DIS, MC, V; checks OK; east of La Cienega Blvd.* ♿

Casa Malibu Inn on the Beach / ★★

22752 PACIFIC COAST HWY, MALIBU; 310/456-2219 OR 800/831-0858

If you don't have a friend who lives on the beach, a stay at the revamped Casa Malibu Inn is the next best thing. Set on some of California's most coveted coastline, this two-story beachfront motel may not look like much from the street, but pass through the lobby to its charming, flower-filled brick courtyard, and you'll discover a peaceful 21-room hideaway with its own private stretch of sand and surf that even Frankie and Annette would envy. Guests chose from four types of immaculately kept accommodations: a beachfront suite with a private deck literally on the sand; oceanview rooms; garden-view rooms, which face the alluring *copa de oro*–draped courtyard; or one of two minisuites, which have four-star luxury bathrooms. A private seaside deck, fireplace, Jacuzzi bathtub, and kitchen make the Malibu Suite a slice of SoCal heaven. The Catalina Suite, which was Lana Turner's favorite room, overlooks the courtyard, ocean, and Catalina Island. Whichever room you chose, all are tastefully furnished and provide refrigerators, two-line phones with dataports, and coffeemakers stocked with Kona-blend coffee. Many also feature fireplaces or kitchens. Book your beach weekend well in advance, as this popular inn often fills up months ahead. *$$; AE, MC, V; no checks; casamalibu@earthlink.com; south of the Malibu Pier.* ♿

The Channel Road Inn / ★★☆

219 W CHANNEL RD, SANTA MONICA; 310/459-1920

This historic former home of Texas oil baron Thomas McCall was originally built in 1910 on Second Avenue and was moved to its current location—near Rustic Canyon and a few blocks from the beach—in 1977. The cheerful blue-shingle-clad Colonial Revival home was converted into a 14-room B&B in 1988, but the spirit of the McCall family lives on today, with family pictures decorating the walls and letters written by Thomas McCall to his youngest daughter, Grace, on display in the inn's well-stocked library. An elegant antique-filled living room with a grand fireplace decorated with Batchelder tiles serves as the inn's gathering spot, where guests enjoy complimentary afternoon tea or wine and cheese. Cozy guest rooms are reminiscent of a charming country inn, with a few featuring decks and fireplaces. Romance reigns in the one suite, where a white-canopied four-poster bed and a Jacuzzi tub for two make for a cozy love nest. Mornings begin with home-baked goods, egg dishes, and gourmet coffees served in a sunny breakfast room that overlooks a patio with bougainvillea and morning glories and the hillside beyond. *$$; AE, MC, V; no checks; channelinn@aol.com; east of Pacific Coast Hwy.* ♿

Chateau Marmont / ★★★

8221 SUNSET BLVD, HOLLYWOOD; 323/656-1010 OR 800/242-8328
This funky seven-story gray castle overlooking the Sunset Strip has wel comed Hollywood's royalty since it opened in 1935. Over the years it's been a temporary home to everyone from F. Scott Fitzgerald, Greta Garbo, and Errol Flynn to Kevin Bacon, Minnie Driver, and the unfortunate John Belushi, who met his demise here in a hotel bungalow. After decades of wear and tear, a recent renovation helped restore the grand chateau, but the cosmetic changes haven't altered the unpretentious, casual vibe that can be felt, from the antique-filled lobby and splendid garden to the rooms and the adorably cozy bungalows. Regardless of the type of room you choose, expect large apartmentlike accommodations with fashionably homey furnishings, tiled full kitchens and bathrooms, VCRs, cordless phones, and an entertainment center stocked with stereo equipment. There's the requisite pool and fitness center, and the Chateau Marmont offers additional perks such as complimentary cell phones, stereo systems, and a CD library. The small nameless restaurant serving casual California cuisine is one of the Strip's most intimate rooms, while around the corner trendy Bar Marmont is the spot to throw back a couple of cocktails and snack on Asian-inspired appetizers, grilled steaks, and seafood in the best of style. *$$$; AE, DC, MC, V; no checks; chateaula@aol.com, www.prima-hotels.com/US-holly.htm; west of Crescent Heights Blvd.*

Clarion Hollywood Roosevelt Hotel / ★★

7000 HOLLYWOOD BLVD, HOLLYWOOD; 323/466-7000
Once one of Hollywood's grandest hotels, today the Roosevelt caters largely to tourists who crave being in the heart of Hollywood—on Hollywood Boulevard across from Mann's Chinese Theatre. Unfortunately, what these out-of-town visitors don't realize is that "The Avenue of Dreams" isn't all that glamorous. However, the historic hotel offers plenty of Golden Era nostalgia. Opened in 1927, the Roosevelt was the site of the first Academy Awards ceremony and counted Marilyn Monroe as one of its famous residents for more than eight years. Today the Art Deco lobby and the abundance of Hollywood memorabilia are beautiful to behold. Unfortunately, even a 1985 renovation couldn't alter the fact that rooms are small, bathrooms are tiny, and walls are thin. The floral bedspreads and dark wood furnishings do help some, but not enough to be considered impressive. If ghosts count as celebrity sightings, the Roosevelt is a prime spot to be on the lookout. Rumor has it that the otherworldly spirits of several old Hollywood clients continue to frequent the hotel, including Montgomery Clift, who supposedly haunts room 928, and Marilyn Monroe, whose face has reportedly appeared in her old wardrobe mirror, which now hangs in the lower lobby. The hotel's

Olympic-size pool, with its bottom that was painted by David Hockney, is where living (and not-so-famous) guests now tend to commune—especially when the sun is shining and the Tropicana Bar serves up poolside libations. Steaks, seafood, and pastas are available in a casual setting at mediocre Theodore's; or you can order appetizers while watching live music or dancing at the historic Cinegrill. *$$; AE, DC, DIS, JCB, MC, V; checks OK; www.hollywoodroosevelt.com; east of La Brea Ave.* &

Figueroa Hotel / ★

939 S FIGUEROA ST, LOS ANGELES; 213/627-8971 OR 800/421-9092
Step into this 12-story Spanish-style hotel, which was built in 1925 as a YWCA, and you're immediately transported to a Mexican oasis, even though the downtown skyline and the nearby L.A. Convention Center make up the backdrop for the enchanting 285-room hostelry. It's not a luxury property by any stretch of the imagination, but the architecture, the hotel's efforts to gussy up the place, and the relatively inexpensive price tag make a stay here a bargain. The grand, intricately detailed lobby is a glorious sight to behold, with its towering hand-painted ceilings, Southwestern tiles, wrought-iron chandeliers, and exotic potted palm trees. The Spanish influence carries over into the terra-cotta–colored rooms, where a jumble of hand-painted Mexican furnishings, funky worn appointments, old TVs, ceiling fans, and limited amenities manage to magically work together to create cheap-chic style. Behind the hotel is the patio's small pool, which is surrounded by flowering vines and potted plants, and the festive poolside Verandah Bar, an ideal spot for afternoon margaritas. The hotel's lobby restaurant, Pasta Frenzy, serves American breakfasts every morning and Italian food every night. Free parking is an especially welcome bonus. *$; DC, JCB, MC, V; no checks; at Olympic Blvd.* &

Four Seasons Hotel at Beverly Hills / ★★★★

300 S DOHENY DR, LOS ANGELES; 310/273-2222 OR 800/332-3442
The Four Seasons at Beverly Hills is a refined and legendary Hollywood hot spot. As expected from a hotel catering to a distinctively demanding clientele, the 16-story Beverly Hills beauty is known for its amenities and impeccable service—so much so that it ranked number 9 in all of North America in the *Conde Nast Traveler* Readers' Awards. Public spaces are adorned with exquisite art, delicious sitting areas, and grand floral arrangements—all surrounded by small but masterfully manicured gardens. The 285 guest rooms were recently redecorated in a residential style with blond woods and pastels, but what remains are the chain's heavenly legendary mattresses, VCRs, ministereos with CDs, state-of-the-art telephone system with IPORT jacks for direct access to T1 lines, and superb bathrooms. The splendidly chichi fourth-floor terrace pool has lovely views of Beverly Hills and the Hollywood hills, although it's just as gratifying

to cast your sight on the clientele basking in their bronzed beauty—especially from one of the six cabanas, which, unlike at most other local hotels, are available at no charge. Adjoining the pool is the fabulous fitness center, housed in a chic tented space and stocked with various workout machines, most with individual televisions. The hotel's business center offers IBM and Macs with T1 connections. Gardens chef Carrie Nahabedian makes dining a worthy endeavor and power-breakfasting an L.A. tradition (see review), while the newly revamped Cafe offers lighter fare in a more casual setting. The hotel's bar is notable for its fabulous martinis and its savvy singles. Guests can request the hotel's limousine for a quick shopping excursion to nearby Rodeo Drive in Beverly Hills. *$$$$; AE, DC, DIS, JCB, MC, V; no checks; www.fourseasons.com; between Burton Way and 3rd St.* &

The Georgian Hotel / ★★

1415 OCEAN AVE, SANTA MONICA; 310/395-9945 OR 800/538-8147
A favorite hangout of Clark Gable and Carole Lombard, this 84-room Art Deco gem was restored to its original grandeur with a $5-million renovation in 1994. During its colorful history the building has functioned as one of L.A.'s first speakeasies during Prohibition, a favorite watering hole for Bugsy Siegel and Fatty Arbuckle, and, in the '60s, a senior citizens' hotel. Today, the yellow-and-light-blue beauty, with its stately period facade, looks like a South Beach Miami transplant overlooking Palisades Park and the beach. The graceful archways and ornate moldings in the 1930s lobby are truly reminiscent of a bygone era and is worthy of its recognition from the National Trust for Historic Preservation's Historic Hotels of America. Guest rooms are decorated in period style, with floral bedspreads, sleek chaise longues, and such modern conveniences as fax machines, dataport telephones, coffeemakers with Starbucks coffee, and video games. A complimentary breakfast is served each morning on the veranda (allegedly one of Arnold Schwarzenegger's favorite power-dining spots) or in your room. *$$$; AE, DC, JCB, MC, V; no checks; georgianhotel@georgianhotel.com; www.georgianhotel. com; between Santa Monica Blvd and Broadway.* &

Hotel Bel-Air / ★★★★

701 STONE CANYON RD, LOS ANGELES; 310/472-1211 OR 800/648-4097
Hotel Bel-Air is Los Angeles's most romantic luxury hotel. Its exclusive Bel-Air address, pastoral atmosphere, and superb accommodations, amenities, and service are the reason even locals are willing to pay a premium to retreat to one of its 92 guest rooms (including 40 suites) located on 11½ acres. The ultimate Bel-Air escape begins when guests enter the property via a short bridge over a creek inhabited by a trio of white swans. Charming pathways wind through lushly grown gardens of bougainvillea, azaleas, and camellias to stellar accommodations scattered

throughout the mostly pink Mission-style hotel. Every sweetly appointed guest room is unique—some have Jacuzzis, many have fireplaces and patios—but all share country French decor, high-tech amenities—including VCRs and ministereos with CD players—and Bulgari bathroom accessories. The secluded garden pool, once a riding ring, is a peaceful spot to unwind with a good book, but those in need of a more active pastime can head to the well-equipped gym, housed in a bungalow that was once Marilyn Monroe's favorite retreat. With dignitaries and high-profile celebrities invariably lounging in the romantic wood-paneled bar, formal restaurant, and bougainvillea-draped patio, it's no surprise cameras are not allowed. Under executive chef Gary Clauson, The Restaurant, with its year-round roaring fire and patio with heated floors, is one of L.A.'s favorites—especially for Sunday brunch (see review in the Restaurants section). *$$$$; AE, DC, DIS, JCB, MC, V; checks OK; 1 mile north of Sunset Blvd.* &

Hotel Del Capri / ★☆

10587 WILSHIRE BLVD, LOS ANGELES; 310/474-3511 OR 800/44HOTEL
Its exterior gives little indication that this homey hotel/motel is a tropical oasis, sandwiched between Westwood's chichi high-rise condos. But once you're inside the door there's no escaping the relaxing, kick-back vibe. Tropical fish tanks dot the property, and to get to your room in either building you'll have to pass a sunny courtyard where the pool, garden, and fountains are surrounded by blossoms and trumpet vines. With motel-room entrances facing the pool, the 79-room property does have a *Melrose Place* apartment complex feel, but that's generally fine with the clientele, since many are touring dance or other performance companies who enjoy the community atmosphere. Standard rooms are fairly large, but more than half of the units are one- and two-bedroom suites, with a separate bedroom, living room, pull-out sofa, and kitchenette. Hotel rooms are in an older building next door. Hotel Del Capri has been owned by the same family since it opened in 1954. It's especially known for its friendly staff, who gladly assist with travel plans or arrange for a free shuttle to nearby UCLA or Westwood Village. A complimentary breakfast (including a bagel with cream cheese or Danish, cereal, juice, and coffee) can be delivered to your room each morning or served poolside. While there's no restaurant, the hotel has worked out agreements with 35 local dining establishments to deliver lunches and dinners. *$; AE, DC, MC, V; no checks; www.hoteldelcapri.com; east of Westwood Blvd.* &

Hotel Nikko at Beverly Hills / ★★★

465 S LA CIENEGA BLVD, LOS ANGELES; 310/247-0400
This gem of a hotel doesn't always get the attention it deserves—overlooked, perhaps, because of its boxlike exterior. Inside, though, it's understated and elegant, designed with a strong—and well executed—

Japanese influence. The Nikko, conveniently located just south of the Beverly Center, has an inviting lobby filled with black granite, beautiful plants, and a Japanese rock garden with a constantly changing fountain. The 295 guest rooms (including 8 suites) are attractive yet spartan in the Nikko's blend of Eastern minimalism and high-tech elegance. In-room cordless phones work anywhere on the property. Translucent shoji screens block the glare of outside light during the day, and a second opaque screen slides over the windows at night to filter out the morning sun. Every item of furnishing is well chosen, from the single print that adorns the bedroom to the attractive armoire that contains a television, VCR, and compact disc player. Luxuries are of the functional kind, such as the deep Japanese soaking tubs in each modern bathroom—unless, of course, you check into a suite, which are contenders for the most stylish in town. A medium-sized pool is adjacent to the lobby, and the larger-than-average gym is well stocked with cardiovascular equipment, free weights, and television sets. The Hana Bar is a fine place to enjoy a cocktail, while Pangea serves "Asian-infused world cuisine," except during its Sunday brunch, when live smooth jazz accompanies classic American dishes from eggs Benedict to made-to-order omelets. *$$$$; AE, DC, DIS, JCB, MC, V; checks OK; between 6th and 3rd Sts.* &

Hotel Oceana / ★★☆

849 OCEAN AVE, SANTA MONICA; 310/393-0486
Colorful whimsy and 63 one-bedroom suites set this bright yellow three-story hotel apart from other options in the area. While its courtyard setting with a centerpiece swimming pool is meant to evoke the south of France, its atmosphere could be likened to a modern *Melrose Place*—minus the melodrama. But there is a sense of drama in the rooms, where the owners' playful taste is conveyed through vivid yellows, blues, and pinks and artsy furnishings combined with all the comforts of home. All guest accommodations come complete with marble bathrooms stocked with Neutrogena amenities and fully equipped gourmet kitchens. The bedroom's linens are Frette (100% Egyptian cotton), duvets are down, and the designer headboards are reminiscent of Matisse. Breakfast is delivered daily along with a newspaper, and, for those who don't want to cook or go out for the other meals, there's room service from the nearby Wolfgang Puck Cafe. Despite its small size, the hotel does its best to accommodate guests, with a concierge and a business center. But most visitors check in here to enjoy the beach (across the street) and the central location, near all of Santa Monica's action. *$$$$; AE, DC, DIS, MC, V; checks OK; beachsuite@aol.com; www.smweb.com/oceana; between Montana Ave and Wilshire Blvd.* &

Hotel Sofitel / ★★☆

8555 BEVERLY BLVD, LOS ANGELES; 310/278-5444

This 10-story French-owned hotel is a peaceful and sophisticated European oasis in the midst of the central Los Angeles action. You need only step into the impeccable lobby, and the soothing piped-in classical music erases all big-city angst. But should you choose to submerge yourself, the Beverly Center mall is across the street and Restaurant Row is a few blocks down. The grand staircase may be more for show than for use (since most guests take the elevator), but it is an attractive introduction to the 311 rooms, which are decorated in French-country splendor, with lush fabrics in vibrant shades of navy and terra-cotta, cushy sofas, and lovely floral wallpaper. Even the hotel's small 24-hour fitness center has French-country appointments. There's a good-sized pool and sun deck, but the echoing sounds of Beverly Boulevard and La Cienega traffic make relaxation a challenge. Regardless, it's the little extras—from a red rose, a bottle of Evian, and chocolates at nightly turn-down service to a fresh-baked baguette upon checkout—that keep foreign tourists and business people returning again and again. Gigi, the hotel's casual brasserie, serves traditional bistro fare such as quiche, steak frites, and chicken. *$$$; AE, DIS, JCB, MC, V; no checks; sofireserv@aol.com, www.sofitel.com; at La Cienega Blvd.* &

Inn at Playa del Rey / ★★☆

435 CULVER BLVD, PLAYA DEL REY; 310/574-1920

From its Cape Cod–style architecture to its location on the edge of the 350-acre Ballona Wetlands bird sanctuary, this 21-room B&B has a distinctly East Coast feel. Distressed wood furnishings and designer beds—four-posters or hand-painted antiques—give the artfully decorated rooms a country inn appeal, although bathrooms are notably modern, with shower tubs or Jacuzzis. Couples in search of romance should check into one of the intimate inn's spacious View Suites, overlooking the wetlands and nearby Marina del Rey. Their wrought-iron four-poster beds are seductive, but the romantic pièce de résistance is their two-sided fireplace, which warms the bedroom and casts a heavenly glow on the bathroom's Jacuzzi tub for two. Guests can also soak under the stars in the inn's garden hot tub out back. In the morning hours, the enticing aroma of gourmet coffees and homemade muffins and coffee cakes lures guests to a sunny nook with hardwood floors and a roaring fireplace, where baked goods, soufflés, made-to-order egg dishes, juices, and coffees await. The bright and airy living room—with its French doors opening out onto the wetlands—serves as the site for an afternoon toast at the inn's daily wine and cheese gathering. *$$; AE, DIS, MC, V; checks OK; playainn@aol.com; www.innaccess.com/pdr/; south of Jefferson Blvd.* &

Le Merigot / ★★★

1740 OCEAN AVE, SANTA MONICA; 310/395-9700 OR 800/926-9524

Santa Monica may be California casual, but this brand-new European-inspired hotel, which opened in late 1999, is bringing a bit of French Riviera sophistication to the quasi-cosmopolitan beach town. Situated next to Loews Santa Monica Beach Hotel and across the street from the beach, the elegant new property attracts tourists with its luxurious, contemporary decor and business travelers with its professional amenities, including executive desks and work areas, modem hookups, voice mail, and two phone lines in each of its 175 rooms. An extensive fitness center and spa boasts saunas, steam rooms, massage facilities, Pilates, kickboxing, and aerobic training. A member of Preferred Hotels and Resorts Worldwide, the hotel has two restaurants: the casual Café Promenade serves up light California cuisine, while the hotel's formal dining room, Cézanne, specializes in an interesting fusion of French, Asian, and Latin-American fare. *$$$$; AE, DC, JCB, MC, V; no checks; near 5th St and Colorado Ave.* &

L'Ermitage / ★★★★

9291 BURTON WAY, BEVERLY HILLS; 310/278-3344 OR 800/323-7500

The newest luxury property in Beverly Hills, L'Ermitage is sleek, sophisticated, and very contemporary, which is not surprising, since the 124-room hotel just underwent a $60 million renovation. Today it's a very design-conscious hotel, with a staff in Armani-esque uniforms and a rule that no brass or bronze fixtures are to appear anywhere. The chic-minimalist guest rooms, accented with quarter-paneled English sycamore, are unusually large—beginning at 675 square feet—and overflowing with amenities. An entertainment center opens to showcase a 40-inch Mitsubishi TV, complete with DVD player (and a library of CDs and DVDs for guests to borrow), and an in-room fax. Five telephones include a cell phone for guests to use around the city during their stay. A wet bar comes stocked with liquor, complimentary nonalcoholic drinks, and real crystal. And the enormous modern bathrooms have no shortage of Aveda products. Topping it off are fantastic frivolous goodies such as personalized cards and stationery with your private phone and fax numbers and a lovely Japanese-style box of chocolate and dried fruit presented upon check-in. As if that weren't enough, the high-tech hotel has in-room motion sensors that tell housekeeping whether guests are in or out. The rooftop pool, with its 360-degree views, is equally lovely by day or night, and the seasonal Pool Terrace offers light fare. The large and well-equipped gym greets guests with fresh-squeezed juice and Beverly Hills views. The small, very beautiful Restaurant, with its high domed ceiling, runs smoothly under chef Serge Falestich, who offers his "cuisine du soleil," a blend of Provence and Tuscany with Asian flair. Smokers can retreat to the Executive Center, with its private humidors and honor bar. *$$$$; AE, DC, DIS, JCB, MC, V; no checks; www.lermitagehotel.com; between Doheny Dr and Rexford Dr.* &

Loews Santa Monica Beach Hotel / ★★☆

1700 OCEAN AVE, SANTA MONICA; 310/458-6700 OR 800/235-6397
Perched above the beach, Loews' dramatic eight-story glass atrium manages to telegraph both sophistication and casual beach vibe, from its sunny and enormous lobby to the 343 rooms and suites. Guest rooms can be small, but are pleasantly decorated in beach resort style, with bleached rattan and wicker furniture and windows that open to the sound of crashing waves. While the hotel is only a minute's walk from a good stretch of Santa Monica beach, it also has its own recreation, from the new Pritikin Longevity Spa & Fitness Center with its spacious gym stocked with high-tech workout machines, to a half-covered pool area where deck chairs and chaise longues surround the water and spread out to the end of the deck overlooking the beach. The Ocean Lounge is a full bar with nightly live music, from solo piano to jazz trio and vocalist. But the most exciting news at Loews is the arrival of chef Alain Giraud, who spent a decade at Citrus with star chef Michel Richard. Now Giraud runs Lavande, the delightful Provençal restaurant at the hotel, where guests receive a sachet of the herb with their checks (see review). *$$$$; AE, DC, DIS, JCB, MC, V; checks OK; www.loewshotels.com; between Pico Blvd and Colorado Ave.* &

Luxe Summit Hotel Bel-Air / ★★☆

11461 SUNSET BLVD, LOS ANGELES; 310/476-6571 OR 800/468-3541
Situated in the backyard of the Getty Center Museum, this 162-room hotel attracts loads of art enthusiasts who opt to take the hotel's shuttle to and from the busy museum rather than wait months to score a parking reservation. Set on 7 acres, the former Radisson hotel offers enough tropical greenery to keep a slew of gardeners eternally busy. Though dated, the simply decorated rooms are well kept and fairly good sized, with many featuring patios and balconies that overlook the expansive grounds. A pool, tennis courts, and a small fitness center provide plenty of activity options. There's also an impressive menu of spa services, with excellent facialists who attract a local Bel-Air clientele. If you don't have a problem ordering rack of lamb or filet mignon from a laminated menu, you can dine in the hotel's Cafe Bel-Air. However, the restaurant's lunch menu of salads and sandwiches is a safer bet. Off the lobby, Oasis piano bar and patio is a nice place to relax and unwind. On weekends, this hotel is a popular wedding reception site, so be prepared for lots of lobby traffic. *$$$; AE, DC, DIS, JCB, MC, V; checks OK; west of the 405 Fwy.* &

Malibu Beach Inn / ★★☆

22878 PACIFIC COAST HWY, MALIBU; 310/456-6444 OR 800/4-MALIBU
Everyone can reside on beachfront property—at least for a couple of nights—at this Spanish-style inn, set on the sand near the Malibu Pier. The inn's Spanish theme travels from the lobby—with its gurgling terracotta fountains and paver tile floors—to guest rooms and bathrooms decorated with hand-painted tiles, and white stucco walls accented with pastels. Modern amenities—honor bar, coffeemaker, VCR, and in-room safe—are neatly integrated into the well-stocked rooms, and plush robes are provided. Each of the three-story pink palace's 47 rooms features dazzling Pacific views from private balconies, with all but six offering fireplaces (also adorned with hand-painted tiles) and many with two-person Soft Tub Jacuzzis on the balconies. Fire pits light the evening skies on the hotel's oceanfront patio—and when the sun rises and the fires have died out, this sunny terrace serves as the setting for a complimentary continental breakfast. Though there's no pool and no restaurant on the premises, steps lead to the pristine Pacific shore, and 24-hour room service is provided by nearby Marmalade Cafe. *$$$; AE, DC, JCB, MC, V; no checks; www.malibubeachinn.com; adjacent to the Malibu Pier.*

Malibu Country Inn / ★★

6506 WESTWARD BEACH RD, MALIBU; 310/457-9622 OR 800/FUN-N-SURF
Whether you're trying to finish that big screenplay or looking for a discreet locale to carry on an affair, this 16-room inn in northern Malibu is a great place to escape for a secluded getaway. The reclusive retreat sits high on a bluff overlooking the Pacific, surrounded by 3 acres of flowering rose bushes and tropical gardens. The inn itself is covered with bougainvillea and other flowering shrubs, which add to its private, pastoral ambience. Wicker furnishings and floral prints give the smallish rooms a country feel, while French doors lead out to sunny individual patios, many of which feature Jacuzzis. In-room refrigerators and coffeemakers make it possible to hole up in your room for days. But for those who want to enjoy the surroundings, there's a pool and plenty of spots to soak up the Malibu sun. The tiny, casual Hideaway Cafe serves a complimentary breakfast daily. Salads and sandwiches are offered for lunch, with dinner served on weekends only. *$$$; AE, MC, V; no checks; at Pacific Coast Hwy.* &

Miramar Sheraton Hotel / ★★

101 WILSHIRE BLVD, SANTA MONICA; 310/576-7777 OR 800/325-3535
The Miramar Sheraton, which recently underwent a $50 million renovation, is a casually elegant property that happens to be President Clinton's preferred L.A. hotel. Accommodations—302 of them in all—are divided among the 10-story tower, the 6-story Palisades building, and

bungalows, but all are situated atop the scenic bluffs overlooking Santa Monica beach and the Pacific Ocean. The seaside setting is key, but the interior ambience has its own merits, such as an impressive art collection and a striking lobby with rattan furnishings, Persian throw rugs, and stunning Jupirana marble floors trimmed with pink and white marble. Rooms in the tower feature ocean views, balconies, and contemporary furnishings. The Palisades building, built in 1924, has more traditional appointments and larger rooms. The 32 garden bungalows, some of which are bi-level suites, offer the most privacy and luxury and have hardwood floor entrances, CD players, and marble baths. Some bungalows have special equipment for the physically challenged. Every room has three phones and two lines, a coffeemaker and complimentary Starbucks coffee, and daily newspaper delivery. A 4,000-foot health center is open 24 hours and has sauna, steam room, Jacuzzi, and cardiovascular and weight training equipment. The salon, Club Sante, offers massage, hair care, and manicures. The Grille, which has a few tables overlooking the pool, serves contemporary California cuisine, with everything from seafood to lamb. More casual, the Cafe offers choices from meatloaf to sandwiches. The hotel also has a health spa and fitness center, as well as a pool and Jacuzzi. *$$$$; AE, DC, DIS, JCB, MC, V; checks OK; www.sheraton.com/miramar; between Ocean Ave and 2nd St.* ♿

Mondrian / ★★☆

8440 SUNSET BLVD, LOS ANGELES; 323/650-8999

Hotelier Ian Schrager, with the assistance of terminally trendy designer Philippe Starck, has converted the Mondrian into a shrine to all things hip. The 30-foot mahogany doors on Sunset dwarf the Range Rovers and Porsches waiting for valet parking. Modelesque doormen, in Armani-like beige uniforms, welcome guests to the lobby. Young black-clad hipsters loll at the lobby bar's one long table or in the small gift shop that sells only the coolest of knickknacks. White is the dominant color in all 238 of the guest accommodations, which are an intriguing blend of spartan and luxurious with their modern decor, single orchid, and faint messages painted on the walls. Unfortunately, the hotel's veneer of fabulousness is thinned by the often inattentive staff, who were clearly hired more for their looks than for their professionalism. Still, the eye candy is abundant, and there's also a gym, interesting art, and designer furniture sprinkled throughout the property. But the most talked about attraction is the perennially hip SkyBar, an open-air lounge run by Cindy Crawford's husband, Rande Gerber, who revitalized the town's velvet rope policies. By day the lounge, which is brilliantly designed with huge mattresses for lounging, enormous pots harboring small trees, and a pool overlooking the flatlands, is the prime spot to watch young Hollywood flaunt bikini bodies. At night, hotel guests are guaranteed admission, while the Sunset

Strip minions have to wait outside for the doorman's nod of approval. New York's Asia de Cuba recently took over the restaurant's dining room and terrace. *$$$$; AE, DC, DIS, MC, V; checks OK; www.mondrian hotel.com; between La Cienega Blvd and Olive St.* &

New Otani Hotel & Garden / ★★

120 S LOS ANGELES ST, LOS ANGELES; 213/629-1200 OR 800/273-2294
This very Japanese hotel is found, appropriately enough, in the Little Tokyo section of downtown Los Angeles. During the week, the 21 story, 434-room hotel draws a crowd of business people. But as the lawyers and others head home for the weekend, the New Otani lays out the weekend welcome mat for vacationers with a variety of special packages, including "The Japanese Experience," complete with massage, Japanese-style room with futon bed, deep soaking tub, and in-room tea-maker, which make it easy to enjoy the hotel's relaxing, slightly exotic atmosphere. (Western-style rooms are also available.) A Thousand Cranes, which serves classical Japanese cuisine, has a koto player and offers a lovely view of the hotel's elaborate garden. Diners sit either at standard Western tables, or on the floor, at traditional Japanese-style settings, and waitresses wear formal kimonos. The menu lists several sakes of varying degrees of dryness; all are served in beautiful, jewel-like, clear glass containers and cups. The Garden Grill offers *teppanyaki,* in which the food is prepared and cooked tableside, while Azalea serves American cuisine. A half-acre garden on a third-floor setback, created by landscape artist Sentaru Iwaki, employs the technique of *shakkei* ("borrowed scenery") to make use of distant landscapes—the skyline of downtown Los Angeles, in this case—to frame the garden. The *tsuro,* or path, through tiny ponds, miniature waterfalls, and distinctive stone lanterns in New Otani's garden is not just a walkway, but with each step becomes a separation from the gritty realities of modern city life. *$$$; AE, DC, DIS, JCB, MC, V; no checks; www.newotani.com; between 1st and 2nd Sts.* &

Peninsula Beverly Hills / ★★★★

**9882 S SANTA MONICA BLVD, BEVERLY HILLS; 310/551-2888
OR 800/462-7899**
The only AAA five-diamond and Mobil five-star hotel in Southern California, the Peninsula is also one of the most refined hotels. Formality begins with dapper white-clad doormen and continues through the lobby, the utterly distinguished Living Room, where high tea is one of the best in town, and into the mahogany bar, where CAA agents and clients share the men's-club atmosphere with players and aspirants. The 196 guest rooms offer a level of luxury rarely matched, with plush beds sporting Frette linens, bedside automated service panels (for lighting, temperature, and do-not-disturb button), fax, Italian marble bathrooms, and 24-hour personal room valets. Hotel amenities are equally impressive, with a 3,500-

square-foot gym and spa (recently refurbished to include a hydrotherapy bath and Vichy shower) and a to-die-for rooftop pool and grass-encircled hot tub, the latter a top contender for L.A.'s most romantic spot when the sun sets over the distant Pacific. Heaven forbid guests would have to hoof it to nearby Rodeo Drive; here a complimentary chauffeured escort in the hotel's Rolls-Royce is just a request away. The hotel's award-winning Belvedere restaurant, now under executive chef Bill Bracken, continues to draw locals and visitors with its lovely formal setting and colorful and creative California-Asian cuisine (see review). A lighter, spa-style menu is available at the Roof Garden cafe. $$$$; AE, DC, DIS, JCB, MC, V; checks OK; pbh@peninsula. com; between Wilshire Blvd and Lasky Dr. &

Regal Biltmore Hotel / ★★★

506 S GRAND AVE, LOS ANGELES; 213/624-1011 OR 800/245-8673

The 11-story Regal Biltmore is the oldest and grandest hotel in the downtown area. Since opening its doors in 1923, the Italian-Spanish Renaissance beauty has hosted everyone from the Beatles and Princess Margaret to Presidents Ford, Carter, and Reagan, as well as today's slew of tourists and conventioneers. Ongoing restoration and renovations have secured the hotel's reputation as a tribute to Old World luxury. It's impossible not to be impressed by the enormous and utterly refined lobby and galleria with hand-painted frescoes, bas-relief decor, and stunning florals; the pristine Gallery Bar and Cognac Room; and the original lobby on the Olive Street side, which is now used for afternoon tea. Its 683 rooms, including those on the more expensive Regal Club and Regal Class floors, are not as stunning as the public areas, but they are all to be completely renovated by the end of 1999, keeping the traditional decor but freshening the rooms with new paint, carpeting, and bedspreads. An additional visual treasure is the Art Deco Health Club, which originally opened in 1926, and now includes the latest Nautilus and Lifecycle-type equipment plus a Roman-style Pompeii replica pool ornamented with imported blue Italian tile, brass railings, and pillars with picture-story tiles. Of the three restaurants, Bernard's closed in 1999 to reopen as a steakhouse. Sai Sai offers superb Japanese cuisine, from sushi to elaborate multicourse *kaiseki* meals. For more casual dining, there's Smeraldi's, named for the Italian artisan who originally painted many of the public spaces, with California and Northern Italian cuisines. $$$$; AE, DC, DIS, JCB, MC, V; checks OK; www.regal-hotels.com/losangeles; corner of 5th St. &

Regent Beverly Wilshire / ★★★★

9500 WILSHIRE BLVD, BEVERLY HILLS; 310/275 5200 OR 800/427-4354

The Regent Beverly Wilshire may be forever known for its starring role in *Pretty Woman,* but this regal hotel been the celebrity and business constituency's second home since it opened in 1928. It seems everyone knows that grand-hotel ambience, superlative service, and a can-do attitude come with check-in at the Regent. Warren Beatty actually lived here during his playboy years. Larry King has moved in on more than one occasion after separating from the wife du jour. Middle Eastern royalty take over several floors at a time. The classy four-star property is remarkably fit for a septuagenarian building, and that's due to a combination of ongoing restoration and renovation. The lobby, with its raised ceiling and beautiful Aubusson tapestries, sparkles with its original grandeur. Each of the two wings—the original Wilshire and the Beverly, which was built in 1971—emphasizes its own style, from the Wilshire's traditional elegance to the Beverly's contemporary flair. Elegant guest rooms are generally spacious, with ovation-worthy bathrooms. When guests aren't lounging by the small pool, exercising in the gym, or pampering themselves in the salon and spa, they tend to mingle at the bar, which specializes in classic cocktails, or relax over a fine dinner in the Dining Room, where Beverly Hills native J. P. Amateau serves his California/Provençal–style cooking (see review). After dinner on the weekends, a jazz trio plays and tables are cleared to create a dance floor. *$$$; AE, DC, DIS, JCB, MC, V; no checks; www.rih.com; between Rodeo Dr and El Camino Rd.* &

Renaissance Beverly Hills Hotel / ★★☆

1224 S BEVERWIL DR, LOS ANGELES; 310/277-2800 OR 800/HOTELS-1
The bland high-rise may appear charmless from the outside, but until 1998 it was owned and operated by San Francisco's creative hoteliers the Kimpton Group, and their colorful and whimsical influence still pervades every nook and cranny. The sumptuous lobby—where complimentary morning coffee and afternoon wine are served daily—is awash in bold stripes and fanciful colors, original artworks, and topiaries, and features a blazing fireplace. Playful design extends to the rooms, where stripes, florals, oversized furnishings, hand-painted accoutrements, fax machines, VCRs, coffeemakers, and CD players mix to create a cozy but modern European atmosphere. Each room also has a tiny private balcony—which, unfortunately, overlooks either the parking lot and the hills to the north or the flats to the south. The small pool surrounded by trellised arbors is a wonderful place to relax after a busy day, while the limited fitness center allows guests to work off extra energy. Tiara at the Renaissance, with its warm woods, colorful glass fixtures, and lively bar, is an appealing spot for drinks or a leisurely meal. Open for breakfast, lunch, and dinner, the restaurant serves inspired California/continental cuisine, including salads, sandwiches, pastas, and such ubiquitous main courses as sea bass, grilled New York steak, and seared ahi. *$$$$; AE, DC, DIS, JCB, MC, V; checks OK; www.renaissancehotels.com; at Rodeo Dr and Pico Blvd.* &

Ritz-Carlton Marina Del Rey / ★★★

4375 ADMIRALTY WAY, MARINA DEL REY; 310/823-1700 OR 800/241-3333
Set on more than 5½ waterfront acres, this Ritz has a nautical theme in its decor and a more casual atmosphere than its California counterparts, although it's still notably formal by Southern California standards. The building was designed to accentuate the pleasant views of the calm Pacific and bobbing boats, which means that whether you're sitting in the luxuriously appointed and spacious lobby or the formal restaurant, you'll see firsthand why this area is known simply as "the Marina." Each of the 14-story property's 306 guest rooms has a terrace with French doors, a marble bathroom, tasteful traditional Ritz decor, and the kinds of amenities one expects from a first-class hotel. One natural amenity is especially enticing: even when Los Angeles is sweltering, Marina del Rey is almost always substantially cooler. But guests can plunge into the large pool when the mercury rises, or hit the Jacuzzi when it falls. There are also plenty of options for the sports-inclined, from a workout room to tennis courts and rental bicycles. For those who prefer stretching their legs, the Marina is great for walking and sightseeing. The Dining Room serves elegant, French-inspired cuisine in a lovely, formal room. A less dressy and expensive alternative is the Terrace Restaurant, with both indoor and outdoor dining overlooking the pool and marina. The hotel's concierge can help book reservations at popular spots like neighboring Cafe Del Rey (see review). *$$$$; AE, DC, DIS, JCB, MC, V; checks OK; www. ritzcarlton.com/marinadelrey; between Bali Way and Via Marina.* &

Shutters on the Beach / ★★★

1 PICO BLVD, SANTA MONICA; 310-458-0030 OR 800/334-9000
Cape Cod meets Santa Monica at this elegant, exquisite boutique hotel situated right on the beach. Though the views are definitely Southern California at their finest, everything else here feels East Coast. Artworks by Lichtenstein and Hockney hang in the lobby (where two fireplaces warm the seating areas), and guest rooms are plush yet not cluttered, with unusually comfortable beds and tasteful decor. Many feature whirlpool tubs which, when the shutters between bedroom and bathroom are open, look out toward the ocean. This thoughtful hotel even provides a candle for romantic baths à deux. About the only shortcoming at this property is a cramped driveway, but if that's the biggest complaint about a place, they're doing all right. In the restaurant, One Pico, relatively new chef Desi Szonntagh serves New American cuisine amidst blissful beach views, a gentle fire in the oversized limestone fireplace, and flickering candles on each table (see full review). Petals Cafe serves California continental cuisine in a more casual setting. *$$$$; AE, DC, DIS, JCB, MC, V; checks OK; sotb@earthlink.net; www.shuttersonthebeach.com; on the beach at Ocean Ave.* &

The Standard / ★★

8300 SUNSET BLVD, WEST HOLLYWOOD; 323/650-9090
This too-cool-for-words hotel is the Sunset Strip's latest entrant in the trendiness sweepstakes. The former retirement home is the latest endeavor for hotelier Andre Balazs of Chateau Marmont and New York's Hotel Mercer. To attract the young and perenially hip clientele, the building does its best to stand out, with its all-white exterior, frosted glass, and row of balconies, each lit by a single light bulb. The hotel's interior design definitely steals a trick or two from the neighboring Mondrian. However, the Standard puts a fresh, younger spin on things, with vibrantly colored carpeting and well-lit public spaces mixing with the subtle pastel walls and minimalist furnishings. Each evening the lobby comes to life with a DJ spinning groovin' tunes, so you can boogie down while you check in. "Classic-modern" guest rooms look as though they could have been decorated by Marcia Brady, with platform beds, beanbag chairs, and (a more contemporary touch) cordless phones. If you don't mind staying on the ground level in a room facing the noisy action on Sunset Boulevard, the eight Budget Sunset rooms go for $95 a night. A barbershop, a 24-hour diner serving "international comfort food," and several happening bars give this lively hotel a clublike feeling, making it a fun stop on the young-set-on-Sunset-Strip jaunt. *$$; AE, DC, DIS, MC, V; no checks; at Sweetzer Ave.* &

Summit Hotel Rodeo Drive / ★★

360 N RODEO DR, BEVERLY HILLS; 310/273-0300 OR 800/468-3541
When your trip to L.A. calls for shopping—and we mean big-time shopping—make a reservation at this 86-room boutique hotel, located on Rodeo Drive near such exclusive stores as Louis Vuitton, Tiffany & Co., Gucci, and Van Cleef & Arpels. While the its location on the famed boutique-lined thoroughfare is ideal for Gold Card–wielding shoppers, those who want to savor the California sun will have to take the hotel's complimentary shuttle to its property, Summit Hotel Bel-Air, in Bel-Air to swim, play tennis, or get pampered in the spa. (There is, however, a sun deck on the Summit's second floor, if you don't mind sun-worshipping without a pool.) Guest rooms, decorated with a European flair, feature small sitting areas; bathrooms are unimpressive. Fresh fruit and tea are sent to arriving guests in their room—a classy welcoming touch that reminds you of the advantages of smaller hotels. The ground-floor restaurant, Cafe Rodeo, serves continental breakfast to hotel guests, and cold sandwiches, salads, and drinks for lunch and dinner, with desserts and coffee in the evenings. *$$$; AE, DC, DIS, JCB, MC, V; checks OK; north of Wilshire Blvd.* &

Sunset Marquis Hotel & Villas / ★★★

1200 N ALTA LOMA RD, WEST HOLLYWOOD; 310/657-1333 OR 800/858-9758
It's easy to drive right past this quiet, secluded hotel, which is why the Sunset Marquis attracts a host of music and film celebrities looking for solitude during their stay in the heart of La-La Land. Once a part of the Lionel Barrymore estate, the expansive compound is nestled among 3 ½ acres of private gardens, with 102 stylishly decorated one- and two-bedroom suites, some with private patios and all with CD players and VCRs. The 12 Mediterranean-style villas—each with its own butler—are exclusive (and expensive) enough to attract the likes of Phil Collins, Julio Iglesias, Aerosmith's Steven Tyler, and members of the Rolling Stones, who, when feeling social, might choose to strut their celebrity stuff at the see-and-be-seen pool and the oh-so-hip Whiskey Bar or might prefer to lurk low profile at the second, more secluded pool. The hotel also boasts the ultimate rock-'n'-roller amenity: an on-site recording studio. On a sunny California day, dining is available poolside at the Patio Restaurant or inside in the elegant and petite dining area, The Room. Both serve California cuisine with Pacific Rim overtones, including such appetizers as blue cheese–stuffed prawns, spring rolls, vegetarian pizzas, and entrees like duck salad, grilled salmon, and beef short ribs. *$$$$; AE, DIS, MC, V; checks OK; www.srshotels.com/namerica/sunset.html; south of Sunset Blvd.* &

Venice Beach House / ★★

15 30TH AVE, VENICE; 310/823-1966
Built in 1911, this Craftsman-style B&B was once the summer home of the families of Venice Beach founder Abbott Kinney and *Daily News* founder Warren Wilson. Today, guests at the all-nonsmoking, antique-filled inn can look at historic photos of its former residents while enjoying the comfy surroundings of this peaceful retreat, which stands just a stone's throw from the sand and the wacky goings-on of Venice Beach. The cozy living room, with several sitting areas, a brick fireplace, and bookshelves crammed with classics, gives way to a staircase leading to the second-floor accommodations. The inn's nine rooms (four of which share bathrooms) boast beautiful period antiques, rustic wood detailing, and wool-upholstered walls. Surrounded by a wall of shrubs and trees, the slightly bohemian inn doesn't provide views of the Pacific, but the enticing gardens and veranda do beckon you to curl up with a good book and enjoy the fresh ocean air. Continental breakfasts include gourmet coffees and teas and homemade breads. *$$; AE, MC, V; checks OK; northwest of the Washington Blvd and Pacific Ave intersection.* &

W Los Angeles / ★★★

930 HILGARD AVE, WESTWOOD; 310/208-8765

At press time this hotel, which was known as the Westwood Marquis for many years, was undergoing a transformation and change of ownership. It is scheduled to reopen at the end of 1999 as W Los Angeles, part of a nationwide chain of similar properties owned by Starwood Hotels & Resorts. As the Westwood Marquis, the property has long been a fine Westside hotel, rating four stars and four diamonds, with 257 suites, a fine restaurant, well-landscaped grounds, and a pool. Under the new name, it remains an all-suite hotel aimed at business clientele. *$$$$; AE, DC, DIS, MC, V; checks OK; at Sunset Blvd.* &

Westin Bonaventure / ★

404 S FIGUEROA ST, LOS ANGELES; 213/624-1000

With its five cylindrical black-glass towers and dozens of feature-film appearances, the Westin Bonaventure is one of the city's most recognizable hotels. With 1,295 rooms, it's also one of the city's largest. In this virtual mini-city, crowds amble through the massive lobby, shops, and restaurants, or hitch a ride on the elevators, which glide up and down the hotel's exterior, to get to any of the 35 floors. Standard guest rooms are on the small side, owing in part to the limits imposed by the shape of the hotel, but have floor-to-ceiling windows and streamlined modern decor. Tower Suites, which are clustered in one tower, are twice the size of standard rooms and a far better way to go when staying here. Another must-do is the Bonaventure Club, an Asian-style spa with full massage and beauty services in a clubby setting. A recent renovation added, among other things, lively fountains and topiaries in the convention center of a lobby. There's a happy hour in the lobby-level Flower Street Bar, but the place to go for drinks is the Bonaventure's revolving Bonavista Lounge on the 34th floor, which makes one complete revolution per hour. One floor higher takes guests to Top of Five, the hotel's main restaurant, which has tremendous views to complement the continental cuisine. *$$$$; AE, DC, DIS, JCB, MC, V; no checks; labon@westin.com; www. westinbonaventurehotel.com; between 4th and 5th Sts.* &

Wyndham Bel Age / ★

1020 N SAN VICENTE BLVD, WEST HOLLYWOOD; 310/854-1111 OR 800/WYNDHAM

Once part of the empire of the Ashkenazy brothers, Los Angeles' art-collecting hoteliers, the Bel Age is now under Wyndham management. The legacy of the Ashkenazys is found in the art that fills the hotel, from the dramatic sculptures in the lobby to the prints and paintings that decorate the halls and guest rooms. (The latter are large and comfortable, though sometimes more reminiscent of apartments than of a luxury hotel.)

The location is ideal: just off the Sunset Strip in West Hollywood, central and convenient to most parts of town. Local music hot spots, from Johnny Depp's Viper Room to the Roxy and the Whiskey, are a short walk away. The Bel Age has two restaurants: the opulent, Old World Diaghilev, with its Franco-Russian cuisine, house-flavored vodkas, and live music; and the Brasserie, with a Californian-Tuscan menu, great live jazz several nights a week, and wide-open views of the city lights below. There's a fitness center and a rooftop pool with its own fabulous panoramic views as well. *$$$$; AE, DC, DIS, JCB, MC, V; checks OK; www.wyndham.com; between Sunset and Santa Monica Blvds.* &

Wyndham Checkers Hotel / ★★☆

535 S GRAND AVE, LOS ANGELES; 213/624-0000 OR 800/WYNDHAM
After a lengthy and award-winning restoration, Checkers was born in 1989 on the site of the 1926 Mayflower Hotel. Today, Checkers still feels like a lovely boutique hotel that's rarely noisy or crowded, though it is as conveniently located as its chain-hotel neighbors. And, perhaps due to its size, it's more intimate and personal than most downtown hotels, with a very high level of service. Its 188 rooms are decorated tastefully with a restrained palette of beige, taupe, and cream. All of the rooms (some of which are on the small side) share a sense of comfort and understated opulence. There's a small fitness center, and a truly lovely pool and Jacuzzi on the roof; at night, it's one of the loveliest places in all of downtown Los Angeles, with tremendous views of the surrounding skyscrapers. The elegant dining room no longer receives raves quite as glorious as those it garnered when renowned chef Thomas Keller put the hotel on the culinary map before departing to launch Napa Valley's French Laundry. But there have been a string of talented chefs since, including the latest, Tony Hodges. The adjacent bar, with its collection of cognacs, Scotches, and ports, is equally appealing, and it's a popular after-work spot for downtown business people. *$$$$; AE, DC, DIS, JCB, MC, V; checks OK; checkersla@aol.com; www.wyndham.com; between 5th and 6th Sts.* &

South Central Los Angeles

At the turn of the century, the area surrounding Exposition Park was filled with stately homes and high-profile residents. While the years haven't been particularly kind to this neighborhood, the **UNIVERSITY OF SOUTHERN CALIFORNIA**, one of California's premier and most expensive private colleges, and the Exposition Park museum complex continue to lure outsiders, for at least a brief stopover, to the otherwise questionable area.

Seven-acre **EXPOSITION PARK** seems a bit shabby and underused these days, but nonetheless, there is a lot to see in this 160-acre public space. The **ROSE GARDEN**, boasting over 200 varieties, is surrounded on three sides by museums. These include the recently renovated **CALIFORNIA SCIENCE CENTER** (700 State Drive; 213/SCIENCE), which is filled with interactive exhibits incorporating computers, virtual reality, and a space docking simulator; the **IMAX THEATER** (213/744-2014), where you can witness an elephant stampede or a Mount Everest expedition on a seven-story screen; the **NATURAL HISTORY MUSEUM** (900 Exposition Boulevard; 213/743-4861); and the **CALIFORNIA AFRICAN-AMERICAN MUSEUM** (600 State Drive; 213/744-2060), which explores the history, art, and cultural legacy of black people in the United States. The **AEROSPACE HALL** is closed for renovation and isn't slated to reopen until 2001.

RESTAURANTS

Harold & Belle's / ★★

2920 W JEFFERSON BLVD, LOS ANGELES; 323/735-9023 OR 323/735-9918
A class act in a seedy neighborhood, Harold & Belle's has been serving down-home Southern cooking in an atmosphere of understated elegance to the affluent black community for 30 years. The original Harold has passed away, but Harold Jr. and his wife, Denise, continue the tradition, welcoming their guests into the dimly lit dining areas, which are separated into several intimate and cozy rooms with fresh flowers gracing every table. Ambience is certainly part of the draw, but the food—well, let's just say it offers more comfort than your favorite easy chair, and there's plenty of it. We're talking good old hold-on-to-your-heart, down-home Southern cooking: fried chicken coated in peppery, snappingly crisp batter and filé gumbo, a tasty mix of shrimp, crab, sausage, chicken, and ham in a spicy Creole sauce. There are also traditional Creole standbys such as crawfish and shrimp étouffées, jambalaya with red beans and hot sausage, and enormous po-boy sandwiches. Considering the neighborhood, some folks feel more comfortable coming for lunch, but there's comfort in knowing there's valet parking at night. *$$; AE, DC, MC, V; no checks; lunch, dinner every day; full bar; reservations recommended; between Western and Crenshaw Aves.* &

Inn at 657 / ★

657 W 23RD ST, LOS ANGELES; 213/741-2200 OR 800/347-7512
Owner Patsy Carter has turned a 1940s apartment building sweetened with fountains and a flowering garden into a homey B&B haven for travelers who want to be close to downtown, the University of Southern California, and the Exposition Park museum complex. Each of the five spacious units in an individual apartment handsomely furnished with

elegant upholstered couches and wing chairs, Oriental carpets, polished wooden armoires, and crystal chandeliers. Besides a kitchen stocked with coffee, tea, and soft drinks, a hearty homemade breakfast is included in the price. Breakfast typically starts with seasonal fresh fruit, followed by a hot entree such as an avocado-and-cheese omelet with home fries and a toasted English muffin, and, if you're lucky, homemade tapioca with fresh whipped cream. While plenty of people are put off by the neighborhood, those who transcend the surroundings consider the Inn at 657 a tastefully appointed and well priced hotel alternative with all the comforts of home. *$$; no credit cards; checks OK; www.patsysinn657.com; just west of Figueroa St.* &

Huntington Park

RESTAURANTS

Avila's El Ranchito / ★

6703 SANTA FE AVE, HUNTINGTON PARK (AND BRANCHES); 213/585-5055
When you see the vibrant mural on the side of the corner building and the line waiting to get inside, you'll know you're at Huntington Park's favorite Mexican restaurant. Inside the spacious dining room, Mexican-style festivities begin with comfortable booths, wrought-ron accents, and plenty of south-of-the-border knickknacks, which make you feel more like you're dining in Ensenada or Mazatlan than in SoCal suburbia. The homemade fare includes regulation tacos, enchiladas, and chiles rellenos, but it's worth being adventurous and trying one of the house specialties, such as the baby pork ribs or the ranchero beef tongue, served with tomatillo sauce. The chicken breast with salsa ortega and the tamales are also top-notch. The restaurant is very popular with locals, and the employees make any meal here seem like a festive occasion. *$; AE, DC, MC, V; no checks; breakfast, lunch, dinner every day; full bar; reservations not necessary; corner of Zoe, between Gage and Florence.* &

Whittier

Whittier was founded as a Quaker community in 1887, and though its name in a sense does reflect its heritage, the town wasn't named after its founding family, the Baileys, but after the Quaker poet John Greenleaf Whittier of Pennsylvania—who never even saw California, much less the town of Whittier.

Whittier also has the dubious distinction of being the town that raised Richard M. Nixon. Nowadays more emphasis is put on former first wife Pat Nixon's Whittier connections than on Tricky Dick's.

Nonetheless, the only U. S. President ever to resign from office graduated from a local school and set up his first law practice here.

Nowadays, Whittier is simply another of Southern California's bedroom communities, although a charming one. One of the nicest things about the town is tree-shaded Greenleaf Avenue, with its meterless parking and historic buildings. Known as **HISTORIC UPTOWN**, this old-time downtown area manages to hold its own against strip malls and shopping centers. There are some vacant storefronts, but most of the buildings are occupied by restaurants, specialty and antique shops, or pubs.

On Friday mornings a **FARMERS MARKET**, from 8:30am to 1pm on the corner of Bailey Street and Greenleaf Avenue, adds to the daily hustle and bustle. For information on special events in the Uptown area, call 562/696-2662.

Just a couple of blocks west of Greenleaf Avenue is the well-organized and unassuming **WHITTIER MUSEUM** (6755 Newlin Avenue; 562/945-3871). Housed in a 1940s Pacific Telephone toll switching office, it offers a small-town personal look at Whittier's history. Replicas of a Quaker meeting house and a Victorian home share space with early day town memorabilia and old photographs, and the museum archives include copies of local newspapers as far back as the 1890s. The **PAGEANT OF ROSES** garden at **ROSE HILLS MEMORIAL PARK** (yes, a cemetery, located at 3900 S Workman Mill Road; 562/699-0921) is a must-see—and smell, for that matter. Packed into a mere 3.5 acres are 7,000 rose bushes in more than 600 varieties, including some that date from the 1600s.

RESTAURANTS

Dattilo Restaurant / ★

6746 S GREENLEAF AVE, WHITTIER; 562/693-3051
Francisca and Achilles Dattilo have been serving fresh, high-quality Italian food in a sweet Italian courtyard-like setting since 1981. Though the walls in the main dining room could use a touch-up, the room's skylights, Romanesque statues, and glass-topped wrought-iron tables make the ambience cozy enough. A smaller dining room, where the bar is located, is a more formal and dapper, as well as more intimate, environment in which to savor hearty salads, wood-fired pizzas, pasta, fresh fish specials, and an ever-popular seafood ravioli, to the sound of the Three Tenors playing over the sound system. Francisca makes all the sauces herself, and the bread is baked daily on the premises. It ain't Florence, but it's about as close as you're going to find this far off the beaten track. *$; AE, DC, DIS, MC, V; no checks; lunch, dinner Mon–Sat; full bar; reservations not necessary; in Historic Uptown.* &

Downey

Downey, an unassuming suburb of Los Angeles, may lack spectacular attractions, but it does have one monumental memento that no other destination can boast. On the corner of Lakewood Boulevard and Florence Avenue is a landmark of the purely American kind: the third-oldest, and only remaining, **ORIGINAL MCDONALD'S.**

You gotta love the bygone Mickey D's sign featuring a funny little '50s cartoon character, "Speedee"—the original company logo, who symbolizes his fast-food clientele because he's literally on the run. The '50s throwback building with its understated golden arches opened on August 18, 1953, under a McDonald Bros. license and still serves standard McDonald's fare. The only McDonald's that didn't affiliate with the McDonald's Corporation after Ray Kroc bought out the brothers in the mid-1950s, it did finally become part of the McDonald's system in 1990, although today it still stands out from the rest of the chain. The tiles, walls, and signage remain virtually original, the crew and managers wear white Speedee uniforms like those worn by workers in the 1950s, all the paper products are custom-made to resemble those in the early days, milk shakes are made using mixers, and buns are toasted on a flat grill using custom bunboards as they were before automation became the norm. Adjoining the restaurant is a small museum where you can buy McDonald's souvenirs.

RESTAURANTS

Sambi / ★

8649 FIRESTONE BLVD, DOWNEY; 562/869-1171

A vast Japanese restaurant with soaring ceilings, dark walls, huge prints, and black lacquer furniture, Sambi looks as if it belongs in San Francisco rather than in humble downtown Downey. But this combination teppan, sushi bar, cocktail lounge, and restaurant has been serving its inland community for 25 years. Despite the burly sumo wrestlers hurling each other about in almost-life-sized panels hanging high above the diners, the overall atmosphere is quite gentle. The cocktail lounge has cozy tables with comfy chairs facing a big-screen TV, and a piano player tickles the ivories somewhere in the further reaches of the restaurant. Though the menu isn't particularly unique, it covers fresh and flavorful renditions of Japanese favorites: teriyaki, tempura, yakitori, and kushiyaki. The $10.95 Sunday champagne brunch brings in budget-minded bingers for regulation salads, egg dishes, and breakfast meats, along with Asian dishes, sushi, and made-to-order dessert crepes. *$; AE, DC, MC, V; no checks; lunch Mon–Fri, dinner every day, brunch Sun; full bar; reservations not necessary; between Lakewood and Paramount Blvds.* &

Szechwan / ★

11010 PARAMOUNT BLVD, DOWNEY; 562/923-3277 OR 562/923-3278
A meal at Szechwan probably isn't worth a special trip to Downey, but if you're in the neighborhood and have a yen for Chinese, you won't be disappointed at this Art Deco/minimalist dining room with a few Asian touches. The staff is friendly, the clientele loyal and local; and while the menu isn't particularly innovative, it's been a traditional fresh and tasty Chinese food standby for the past 15 years. For lovers of fiery Szechwan cooking, there are two-star "extra hot and spicy" specialties such as the hot and spicy chicken in orange flavor and braised whole fish. Milder palates are satisfied with familiar dishes such as sweet and sour pork and almond chicken. Sunday champagne brunch offers about 30 items, including lemon chicken, barbecued pork, and an assorted seafood buffet. *$; AE, DIS, MC, V; no checks; lunch, dinner every day, brunch Sun; full bar; reservations not necessary; 1 block northeast of Firestone Blvd.* &

South Gate

RESTAURANTS

La Barca Jalisco / ★

3501 FIRESTONE BLVD, SOUTH GATE; 323/564-5141
From the outside, La Barca Jalisco may look like nothing more than a pink house surrounded by car lots, but inside is a Mexican dining experience as authentic as any south of the border. The cheerful dining room is usually jam-packed as bilingual waiters and waitresses serve freshly made corn and flour tortillas, fresh fish, and such house specialties as *birria* (stewed goat) to a mostly Latino clientele. A concoction of freshly squeezed orange and carrot juices is the restaurant's specialty nonalcoholic drink, but it's hard to pass up a beer or a margarita; they are as essential to a great Mexican dining experience as salsa is to tortilla chips. On weekends *menudo*, a spicy soup of hominy and tripe, and *pozole*, another hearty hominy dish, are served, along with enormous omelets for the less-adventurous palate. *$; AE, DC, MC, V; no checks; breakfast, lunch, dinner every day; full bar; reservations accepted Sat and Sun only; corner of California Ave.* &

Gardena

At face value, Gardena isn't much more than a town of uninspired strip malls and industrial parks. It does, however, have two unique characteristics: it's home to one of the largest Japanese populations in the United

States, and it has a city ordinance that allows certain kinds of gambling—which means you can purchase excessive amounts of *nigiri* from local restaurants with your card-table winnings.

The **NORMANDIE CASINO** (1045 W Rosecrans Avenue; 800/540-8006), which sits at the far end of an optimistically huge parking lot, has been around since the late 1940s and now acts as a round-the-clock card players' haven with ongoing exotic games such as Texas Hold-'em and Pai-Gow Poker.

RESTAURANTS

Tsukiji / ★★

1745 W REDONDO BEACH BLVD, GARDENA; 310/323-4077
You won't hear much English spoken in this tiny sushi restaurant, tucked into a mundane shopping mall. This is a Japanese dining experience aficionados consider the real thing. Besides the sushi bar and a couple of Western-style tables, there are a few Japanese-style sit-on-the-floor tables. Most people shed their shoes on entering, as Japanese tradition dictates, and there are slippers for those who didn't bring their own. The two sushi chefs prepare unerringly fresh seafood delicacies with specials including sea urchin, tuna, eel, salmon, shad roe, and squid. Be prepared to wait in the stream of transplanted Japanese who come here to get sushi like they had in Japan. *$; AE, DC, MC, V; no checks; lunch Mon–Fri, dinner Mon–Sat; full bar; reservations not accepted; corner of Western Ave.* &

Bellflower

RESTAURANTS

Café Camellia / ★★★

16916 BELLFLOWER BLVD, BELLFLOWER; 562/866-2824
Can you believe an award-winning French restaurant in a town best known for its automobile dealerships? Café Camellia has won all sorts of distinguished dining and wine awards, and its faithful clientele isn't limited to the locals. People who have dined here once will often drive impressive distances to have another meal. The decor is very chic 1950s, with a hand-painted ceiling that sports abstract shapes in blue, red, yellow, and green. Café Camellia is particularly good at creating luscious sauces. A particular favorite, confit of duck breast, is poached in a cabernet/pear/banana/rum sauce. Another intriguing entree is prosciutto-wrapped free-range chicken breast, stuffed with spinach and red bell pepper, topped with a delectable goat cheese cream sauce. *$$; MC, V; no checks; lunch Mon–Fri, dinner Mon–Sun; full bar; reservations recommended; 4 blocks north of 91 Fwy.* &

Johnny Rebs' / ★

16639 BELLFLOWER BLVD, BELLFLOWER; 562/866-6455

Johnny Rebs' is a fun and friendly place where you can get good ol' Southern barbecue served with a dash of good ol' Southern hospitality. Considering the cholesterol-heightening properties of most of the entrees, it's ironic that the place is right next to a health food store. But the hostess was fast to point out that "Most of our meats are smoked, so the fats are drained out." That may be, but this place still isn't going to be a contender for a heart-smart dining experience. What it does have is succulent barbecued chicken, ribs, beef, sausage, and pork. It also features other Southern specialties such as catfish, collard greens, black-eyed peas, Cajun rice, and home-baked biscuits. The walls are unfinished wood and red brick, decorated with license plates and other folksy memorabilia, and college pennants hang from the ceiling. There are bowls of unshelled peanuts on each table, and southern beers, such as Dixie Jazz Light and Mississippi Mud Black & Tan, are featured. *$; MC, V; no checks; breakfast, lunch, dinner every day; beer and wine; reservations accepted for parties of 6 or more only; 3 lights north of 91 Fwy at Flower St.* &

Marino's / ★★

17126 BELLFLOWER BLVD, BELLFLOWER; 562/866-9260 OR 562/867-4225

Forget your trendy Northern Italian cuisine: Marino's is proud to announce that it's strictly an old-time Sicilian-red-sauce restaurant. For more than 20 years this Bellflower institution has served regulation Italian, and all the old favorites are on the menu: chicken cacciatore, cioppino, eggplant parmigiana, veal scaloppine. The food is always fresh, and the red sauce just peppery and spicy enough. The interior is more reminiscent of a country cafe in the Midwest than of Italy, with its chintz and lace cafe curtains and grainy wood, but the photographs on the walls are strictly Old World Italian. These fascinating pictures, which date back as far as the turn of the century, chronicle the lives of Italian immigrants both at work and at play. The atmosphere is warm and homey, the food is familiar, and it doesn't take much imagination to feel as though you're having dinner in an Italian family's home, with mama doing the cooking. *$; MC, V; no checks; lunch Mon–Fri, dinner every day; beer and wine; reservations accepted for large parties only; 1 block north of 91 Fwy.* &

San Fernando Valley

When most people think of the San Fernando Valley—known simply as "the Valley"—two things come to mind: the Northridge earthquake, and Frank and Moon Unit Zappa's satiric homage to Valley Girls. Thankfully, this northwestern region of Los Angeles County, which spreads from the Ventura County border to Glendale, has surmounted both of those claims to fame. What was once considered a bedroom community for neighboring Los Angeles is now a thriving business and entertainment-industry region, as well as a nice and relatively affordable place to live away from the hustle and bustle of the metropolis—if you can deal with the daily commute on gridlocked freeways. Though the Valley is often maligned as the lesser part of the Los Angeles basin, it could actually be considered the workaday heart of the entertainment industry, with **WALT DISNEY STUDIOS, WARNER BROS., UNIVERSAL STUDIOS, NBC, CBS STUDIO CENTER,** and **DREAMWORKS SKG ANIMATION** all within its boundaries. With show-biz roots growing into a concrete jungle of opportunity, the Valley's creative community is growing rapidly, as are new malls and office buildings, which are popping up with regularity. However, most visitors come here to attend various television tapings or visit the Universal Studios Hollywood working studio/theme park.

ACCESS AND INFORMATION

The Valley is just a short drive "over the hill" from Los Angeles. Cruising north on the 101 Freeway will take you through the southern part of the Valley starting at Universal City and on to the western boundaries of the Valley near Woodland Hills. Or take the 101 north to the 170 Freeway to traverse the mid-Valley region, traveling through such communities as North Hollywood and Van Nuys. The 5 Freeway skirts the eastern boundaries of the Valley starting near Burbank and traveling up to Santa Clarita and beyond. The 5 Freeway merges with the 170 Freeway in the northeast Valley near Pacoima. The 405 Freeway is a direct route up the middle of the Valley.

The **BURBANK-GLENDALE-PASADENA AIRPORT** (2627 N Hollywood Way, Burbank; 818/840-8847), served by Southwest Airlines, Alaska Airlines, American Airlines, Skywest Airlines, America West, and United Airlines, is the Valley's most convenient airport and is often preferred by Los Angeles residents for commuter flights. Nearby **LOS ANGELES INTERNATIONAL AIRPORT** (1 World Way, at the intersection of Century and Sepulveda Boulevards, Los Angeles; 310/646-5252) is a short drive from the Valley and can be easily reached with service on the Fly-A-Way bus based in Van Nuys; call 818/994-5554. **RENTAL CAR COMPANIES** are available at locations throughout the Valley. Most major rental car agencies have offices at the Burbank-Glendale-Pasadena Airport. **METROLINK** (800/371-5465) trains connect sections of the North Valley, including Chatsworth, Sylmar, and San Fernando, with the southeast Valley cities of Burbank and Glendale, as well as downtown Los Angeles. The Valley is also serviced by **GREYHOUND** buses (800/231-2222),

MTA buses (888/266-6883), and AMTRAK (800/872-7245), which offer stops at Glendale, the Burbank Airport, Van Nuys, and Chatsworth.

For more information, contact the SAN FERNANDO VALLEY CONFERENCE AND VISITORS BUREAU (15205 Burbank Boulevard, 2nd Floor, Van Nuys, CA 91411, 818/782-7282), or visit their Web site at www.sfvalley.org/sfvcvb.

As Beverly Hills has Rodeo Drive, Paris the Champs-Elysées, and Rome the Via Veneto, the Valley is known for its famous—although notably less glamorous—thoroughfare, VENTURA BOULEVARD. Lined with shops, cafes, boutiques, and fine restaurants, this major east–west artery stretches across the southern Valley from Universal City to Calabasas. (In most Valley circles, living "south of the Boulevard," or closer to the hills leading to Los Angeles, is a status symbol.) Though 20 years ago this shopping mecca may have been frequented by big-hair babes exclaiming the likes of "That shirt is totally bitchin'," today the area is a tad more sophisticated. Though you still have to trek over the hill to Los Angeles for Barneys or Saks, there is a new Bloomingdale's in Sherman Oaks, which in these parts means that the Valley has arrived.

Calabasas

RESTAURANTS

Saddle Peak Lodge / ★★★

419 COLD CANYON DR, CALABASAS; 818/222-3888

A century-old hunting lodge that's a true destination high in the mountains of Malibu houses one of the grandest American restaurants in Southern California. Not far from where $M*A*S*H$ was shot, this very manly hunting lodge is decorated with heads and horns and with fireplaces that blaze all year long. The Modern American menu, which leaves few alternatives for vegetarians, features in-season game—ostrich, boar, venison, elk, and their ilk. Those who'd rather not eat Bambi and Thumper can choose from fine renditions of chicken, tuna, and salmon. An unforgettable journey into the hills for red-flannel hash and eggs, caviar-topped poached eggs on crab cakes, and other dishes makes Sunday brunch worth the trip. This, at its best, is a breathtaking destination and a restaurant worth getting to an hour before your reservation so you can sit on the patio and watch the sun set over the Coast Range. *$$; AE, MC, V; no checks; dinner Wed–Sun, brunch Sun; full bar; reservations required; Cold Canyon Dr east of Malibu Canyon Rd.* &

Topanga Canyon

RESTAURANTS

Inn of the Seventh Ray / ★★

128 OLD TOPANGA CANYON RD, TOPANGA CANYON; 310/455-1311

Just because much of the cuisine offered at this fantastically romantic, ethereal canyon hideaway is organic and macrobiotic doesn't mean it doesn't taste good. Organic meats, grains, and eggs, fresh herbs, home-made breads of unbleached flour, and raw butter and cream are used to prepare such health-conscious (and tasty) selections as the hearty porto-bello mushroom sandwich, a satisfying *seitan* veggie burger, and fresh steamed vegetables with brown rice. Sure, there's an abundance of tofu, brown rice, and vegan selections, but you'll also find the unexpected— like a juicy steak sandwich or mango-papaya duck. The atmosphere of this rustic mountain eatery, however, is what makes dining here special. Designed around an old church, Inn of the Seventh Ray is set high in the canyon, with towering oaks, flowering shrubs, and a babbling creek running through the outdoor patio seating area, creating a magical setting unparalleled by almost any in the Los Angeles area. On the seventh day, try the Inn's Sunday brunch. With more than 20 salads (two-thirds of which are vegan or macrobiotic), a bagel bar with spreads ranging from salmon to flavored cream cheeses, quiche, organic cereals, and chicken, fish, and vegetarian dishes, this feast is a great way to celebrate the weekend. *$$; AE, MC, V; no checks; lunch Mon–Sat, dinner every day, brunch Sun; beer and wine; reservations recommended; just off Topanga Canyon Blvd about 4 miles north of Pacific Coast Hwy.* ら

Tarzana

RESTAURANTS

Kushiyu / ★★☆

18713 VENTURA BLVD, TARZANA; 818/609-9050

What sets this modest Japanese eatery apart from other neighborhood sushi haunts is its *kushiyaki*—tender skewers of chicken, beef, tuna, swordfish, scallops, quail eggs, mushrooms and onions, pork-wrapped asparagus, and more, which are grilled to perfection on the restaurant's imported kushiyaki grill. Though the swordfish skewers are a melt-in-your-mouth starter, they only inspire further exploration of the traditional Japanese fare, including *nabe* (pot-boiled dishes such as a seafood soup with huge portions of salmon), tempura, and inventive sushi such as the Tarzana roll, a delicate combination of white albacore sashimi, vegetables, and smelt eggs. Be sure to try the specials of the day; with fish delivered three times a week, the seafood is always fresh. *$$; AE, MC, V; no checks; lunch Tues–Fri, dinner Tues–Sun; beer, wine, and sake; reservations recommended; near Reseda Blvd in a mini-mall.* &

Encino

One of the Valley's most exclusive neighborhoods, Encino is known for its high-priced hillside houses south of Ventura Boulevard, which such celebs as the Jackson family, Dick Van Dyke, Teri Hatcher, Cybill Shepherd, and Cher have called home at one time or another. Encino is also the site of the Valley's largest and most popular park, **BALBOA PARK** (set along Burbank Boulevard and Woodley Avenue; 818/756-9642). Part of the 2,000-acre Sepulveda Dam Recreation Center, Balboa Park offers much more than swing sets and picnic tables; there are three 18-hole golf courses, tennis courts, running and biking trails, an archery range, bird-watching, fishing in Balboa Lake, and a bicycle velodrome. The city's other well-known park, **LOS ENCINOS STATE HISTORIC PARK** (16756 Moorpark Street, 818/784-4849), is more about history than recreation. The 5-acre property was once part of the 4,460-acre **LOS ENCINOS RANCHO OF FRANCISCO REYES,** and today visitors can tour the rancho's original stone buildings, which document the life of this early Valley settler.

RESTAURANTS

Delmonico's Seafood Grille / ★★☆

16358 VENTURA BLVD, ENCINO; 818/986-0777
9320 W PICO BLVD, WEST LOS ANGELES; 310/550-7737

Reserve one of the high-backed wooden booths at this upscale San Francisco–style seafood eatery and you'll enjoy a little privacy along with strategic views of the seafood restaurant's coming and goings. The restaurant's primary attraction is its wide selection of fresh, cooked-to-order fish. Most of the slightly older, well-heeled crowd that frequents Delmonico's prefer their fish grilled or sautéed and a bit on the plain side or drowned in an accompanying sauce, but you can order yours the way you want it. The Boston clam chowder appeals to anyone with a preference for thick and creamy, as does the spicy *zuppa alla pescatore,* whose fresh shellfish is served in a broth with respectable zing. Grilled swordfish is a generous portion of the tender fish with a light rum glaze, accompanied by crisp crab pancakes. Anti-seafoodites appreciate the alternative selections of pasta, steak, veal, and chicken, the last three of which come with a side of addictive garlic mashed potatoes. Delmonico's original location in West Los Angeles is also still going strong. *$$$; AE,*

MC, V; no checks; lunch, dinner every day; full bar; reservations recommended; east of Havenhurst St (Encino); between Beverly Dr and Doheny (West Los Angeles). &

Sherman Oaks

RESTAURANTS

Café Bizou / ★★★

14016 VENTURA BLVD, SHERMAN OAKS; 818/788-3536

This perennially packed restaurant run by chef/co-owner Neil Rogers and partner Philippe Gris attracts throngs of foodies with its hearty portions of reasonably priced delicious French-California fare. How reasonably priced? Order the delicate roasted monkfish with saffron risotto, a rich lobster sauce, and deep-fried carrots; textural sesame seed–encrusted salmon perched on potato pancake triangles and set in a red wine sauce; steak *au poivre* with peppered veal jus; roasted chicken breast in a tangy balsamic vinegar sauce; or any other main course, and you'll find the bill still hovers at remarkably reasonable (and you can tack on a house salad or homemade soup, such as the velvety lobster bisque, for just $1). Café Bizou offers a small wine list, but if you bring your own, the corkage fee is a measly $2. Tables are packed tightly together in the unassuming and rather noisy dining areas and garden room, so forget about intimate conversation, but chances are you'll be so busy savoring your menu selections that it won't matter. What's the secret to getting a table on Friday night at 8pm at this bustling French restaurant? Call at least a month in advance. *$$; AE, DC, MC, V; no checks; lunch Mon–Fri, dinner every day, brunch Sat–Sun; full bar; reservations recommended; at Hazeltine Ave.* &

Joe Joe's / ★★★

13355 VENTURA BLVD, SHERMAN OAKS; 818/990-8280

This American-style bistro, formerly owned and operated by Los Angeles restaurateur Joe Miller, is one of the Valley's best, for the same reason that its sister eatery, Joe's in Venice Beach, is so popular: sophisticated California cuisine at reasonable prices. Miller sold his share of the successful restaurant to founding chef and partner Tom Munoz and manager James Dresser, but the small storefront restaurant continues to crank out classic American bistro fare at great prices. An artfully presented tuna tartare with cucumbers, preserved lemons, and tomatoes, or the roasted beet, goat cheese, and arugula salad are winning ways to start a meal. Then move on to such alluring main courses as baked salmon with a savory lemongrass-crusted couscous and braised fennel; grilled shrimp perched high on a flavorful saffron risotto; or pork tenderloin served with creamy mashed potatoes and vegetables. Two seasonal prix-fixe menus help indecisive diners select their meals, with each including two starters, a main course, and a dessert for either $26 or $32. Forget about counting calories and try the buttery tarte tatin or the warm chocolate soufflé cake with a gooey fudge center for dessert. The softly lit dining room, decorated with contemporary art, may be crammed with tables, but it gives guests a good excuse to mingle with other diners, who range from well-dressed thirty-somethings to older business executives. *$$; AE, MC, V; no checks; lunch Tues–Fri, dinner every day, brunch Sat–Sun; beer and wine; reservations recommended; between Coldwater Canyon Blvd and Woodman Ave.* &

Mistral Brasserie / ★★☆

13422 VENTURA BLVD, SHERMAN OAKS; 818/981-6650

Crystal chandeliers, wood-paneled walls, black-and-white tile flooring, and crisp linen tablecloths give this charming French bistro a warm and authentically Parisian feel. Surprisingly, owner Henri Abergel is Moroccan, and he's a long-standing Valley restaurateur who once served as manager at the Valley's bygone La Serre. His cozy dining room attracts everyone from romancing couples to large birthday parties as well as a slew of regulars who apparently can't go long without a fix of French chef Gilles Dirat's steak-frites, served *au poivre* with garlic, parsley, and butter and accompanied by a salad. Onion soup gratinée, homemade rabbit pâté, stewed chicken, and grilled entrecôte round out the traditional bistro menu, with chocolate soufflé the perfect selection to finish your night off right. *$$$; AE, DC, MC, V; no checks; lunch Mon–Fri, dinner Mon–Sat; full bar; reservations recommended; between Coldwater Canyon Blvd and Woodman Ave.* &

Paul's Cafe / ★★☆

13456 VENTURA BLVD, SHERMAN OAKS; 818/789-3575

Working as a restaurant manager at bustling Café Bizou, Paul Lloyd learned what excites Valley diners, and today he's putting that knowledge to use at his own dining establishment. Paul's Cafe serves well-priced, sophisticated French/California cuisine, with soup or a salad just a dollar with entrees and a mere two-dollar corkage fee when you BYOB. The small, simply decorated storefront restaurant may still be perfecting its winning formula, but diners are flocking to the happening eatery to savor the cuisine of chef/co-owner Darin Eckermann, who previously worked as a sous chef at Joe's in Venice Beach. Appetizers such as the lobster and wild mushroom cannelloni, served with a rich chive beurre blanc, and grilled scallops with grilled asparagus, marinated artichokes, and a light lemon vinaigrette, start the meal off right. Fish entrees dominate main-course selections, with pepper-crusted salmon with artichoke, potato, and wild mushroom hash, and roasted whitefish with mashed potatoes both winning a big thumbs up. Garlic-rubbed rack of lamb and phyllo-crusted shrimp with seafood ravioli also score big. For dessert, try the restaurant's classic take on crème brûlée. *$$; AE, DC, MC, V; no checks; lunch Mon–Fri, dinner every day; beer and wine; reservations recommended; east of Woodman Ave.* &

Posto / ★★★

14928 VENTURA BLVD, SHERMAN OAKS; 818/784-4400

When renowned restaurateur Piero Selvaggio, owner of Los Angeles's Valentino and Primi, entrusted the kitchen duties of his Valley restaurant to chef Luciano Pellegrini, he made a smart move. This inventive chef delivers some of the most innovative Italian cuisine in the valley. The menu is seasonal, changing every couple of months to highlight local fresh ingredients. The menu might feature crisp Parmesan cheese chips, buttery polenta, shrimp and lobster cakes, creamy risotto with porcini mushrooms, and grilled rabbit fillet with an exotic pomegranate sauce. But whatever the time of year, it's sure to include delectable pastas, such as conchiglione stuffed with rich lobster and ricotta cheese, or delicate agnolotti with fresh artichokes served with a rich spinach-flavored cream sauce; Pellegrini makes both dishes from scratch. Uncork a bottle of wine from the restaurant's impressive wine list, and sit back and enjoy the

THAT'S THE TICKET

Attending the taping of a television show may seem like a touristy thing to do, but it can actually be a lot of fun. The best way to obtain a ticket to your favorite show is to write to an official ticket outlet (see below), requesting the show and date you would like and enclosing a self-addressed stamped envelope. Once you have the tickets in hand, show up at the studio at least an hour early so you'll be sure to get a seat.

Keep in mind that most television production seasons run only from August through March. Folks line up each morning to attend tapings of *Third Rock from the Sun, Just Shoot Me,* and *Caroline in the City,* which are filmed at **CBS Studio Center** (424 Radford Avenue, Studio City; 818/655-5000; for tickets call 818/506-0043). **NBC**'s taping of *The Tonight Show with Jay Leno* (3000 W Alameda Boulevard, Burbank; 818/840-3537) is, however, taped year-round. If you don't get tickets in advance, you can go down to the studio the day of the taping and stand in line for available seats. For more information, contact the following ticket request handlers: **Audiences Unlimited** (100 Universal City Plaza, Bldg. 153, Universal City, CA 91608; 818/753-3483; www.tvtickets. com.), **NBC Studios** (3000 West Alameda Avenue, Burbank, CA 91523; 818/840-3537), or **Hollywood Group Services** (1918 West Magnolia Boulevard #203, Burbank, CA 91506; 818/556-1516).

beautiful dining room and first-rate service, because when the bill comes you'll find out you're paying for the whole experience. *$$$; AE, DC, MC, V; no checks; lunch Mon–Fri, dinner Mon–Sat; full bar; reservations recommended; at Kester Ave.* &

Studio City

Back in the 1920s when Keystone Cops creator Mack Sennett outgrew his Silver Lake studio, he built a new facility near Ventura Boulevard and Laurel Canyon Boulevard. When he started calling the community "Studio City," the moniker stuck. With its location close to the surrounding studios and the L.A. side of the hill, today this area is widely considered the hippest neighborhood in the Valley—with some of the highest-priced real estate, especially south of Ventura Boulevard.

A wide selection of respectable **RESTAURANTS AND SHOPS** line Ventura Boulevard. Television show tapings, such as *The Price is Right*, welcome studio audiences at **CBS STUDIO CENTER** (see "That's the Ticket," above, for more information).

RESTAURANTS

The Bistro Garden at Coldwater / ★★½

12950 VENTURA BLVD, STUDIO CITY; 818/501-0202

The Beverly Hills outposts of this elegant eatery have closed their doors, but their Valley sibling serving continental cuisine is still very much alive. Set in a formal winter garden with skylights, latticework, and ficus trees strung with little white lights, the Bistro Garden's dining room oozes romance. Co-executive chefs Harry Klibingat and Karl Rohner stick to the expected classics, such as French onion soup au gratin, roast rack of lamb with rosemary jus, and filet mignon with three-peppercorn sauce; but they also exercise their agility with more modern entrees such as sesame-crusted salmon with soy and wasabi or chicken curry with mango chutney, chopped bananas, almonds, and shredded coconut. The menu changes with the seasons, but one thing remains a Bistro Garden standard: the decadent chocolate soufflé, baked to order and served with mounds of freshly whipped cream. On most nights, the mahogany bar area teems with the business crowd who relax over martinis after a long day at the office or sip wine spritzers as they entertain clients. Perhaps no one verbalizes it, but we're convinced the bar's baby grand piano player should keep his day job. Just next door, BG To Go has several tables and an outdoor patio, where you can eat more casual fare like salads, rotisserie chicken, pasta, and chicken burgers—and even their famous chocolate soufflé, or grab it to go. Call 818/FOOD-2-GO. *$$$; AE, DC, MC,*

V; no checks; lunch Mon–Fri; dinner every day; full bar; reservations recommended; west of Coldwater Canyon Blvd. &

Pinot Bistro / ★★★

12969 VENTURA BLVD, STUDIO CITY; 818/990-0500

With high-beamed ceilings, a roaring fire, crisp white linen tablecloths, and kitchen hutches displaying fine French china, this charming bistro possesses the comfortable, homey feel of a French inn. But don't let the neighborhood-cool vibe fool you. Thanks to restaurateur Joachim Splichal and executive chef/partner Octavio Becerra's award-winning food, 7,000-bottle wine cellar, and courteous service, this is one of the valley's top restaurants. A memorable dinner might begin with onion soup with perfectly caramelized onions in a beefy stock and topped with bubbling, golden brown Swiss cheese; a rich caramelized-onion and salmon tart; or fresh oysters, followed by such impressive entrees as oxtail ragout, whitefish with roasted garlic sauce, or linguine with shellfish. With 20 wines by the glass and 260 selections by the bottle, you'll be hard pressed not to find the ideal pairing. Whatever you do, save room for the chocolate croissant bread pudding, a sinfully spectacular dessert that, along with practically everything on the menu, exemplifies why this dining room consistently ranks at the top of dining critics' lists. Pinot Bistro is also a great people-watching spot, with celebrity sightings likely most nights. *$$$; AE, DC, DIS, JCB, MC, V; no checks; lunch Mon–Fri, dinner every day; full bar; reservations recommended; west of Coldwater Canyon Blvd.* &

Sushi Nozawa / ★★☆

11288 VENTURA BLVD, STUDIO CITY; 818/508-7017

Located in a nondescript mini-mall, this tiny sushi restaurant with 10 sushi-bar seats and five tables has a word-of-mouth following that keeps it full at all times. The loyal patrons come for fresh, innovative sushi made by sushi master Kazunori Nozawa, whose sashimi, hand rolls, and nigiri combinations depend on what fish is freshest that day. If you have a craving for tuna or yellowtail and it wasn't really fresh when chef Nozawa was selecting his fish, you may be out of luck. But you can revel in the much-anticipated specials, including a scallop roll, a creamy deviled-scallop concoction tightly wrapped with rice and toasted seaweed; jumbo crab hand rolls chock-full of sweet crab and sticky rice; tender soy-glazed octopus sprinkled with sesame seeds; thin slices of salmon layered with seaweed noodles; and ultrafresh hamachi, which is luxuriously soft—like butter. If you sit at one of the tables, you get a menu; but adventurers should opt for the sushi bar, where Nozawa generally doesn't tell you what he's bringing you (if you ask, he ignores you) but will tell you how to eat it, like "Eat this first" and "No soy sauce." Chef Nozawa prefers that you trust him to order for you, and he doesn't believe in making such ubiquitous fare as California rolls. But if you are game to try anything, this is one of the best places to go. *$$; MC, V; no checks; lunch, dinner Mon–Fri; beer and sake; reservations not accepted; west of Vineland Ave.* &

LODGINGS

The Sportsmen's Lodge / ★★

12825 VENTURA BLVD, STUDIO CITY; 818/769-4700 OR 800/821-8511
A Valley landmark for more than 50 years, this 200-room hotel is a sort of upgraded California-style motel, with exterior hallways and Astroturf lining the deck of its Olympic-sized pool area. Though there's a definite retro-kitsch value here, the hotel's lush grounds, with waterfalls, wooden bridges, and a swan-filled lagoon, really set the hotel apart from prospective competitors. Spacious rooms are decorated in mauves and blues, and studio suites with private patios provide extra space for families or those staying a while. Tourists benefit from the complimentary shuttle to Universal Studios and the Burbank Airport. There's a coffee shop in the hotel, but just across the parking lot is the Sportsmen's Lodge Restaurants & Special Events Center (12833 Ventura Blvd; 818/755-5000). The center, a popular site for weddings and business events, offers two restaurants: Caribou, a rustic lodge setting that specializes in such wild game dishes as buffalo, venison, and boar, and the Muddy Moose Saloon, a more casual eatery offering pizzas, sandwiches, and salads. *$$; AE, DC, DIS, JCB, MC, V; checks OK; www.SLHOTEL.com; at Coldwater Canyon Blvd.* &

Universal City

Movie mogul Carl Laemmle built **UNIVERSAL STUDIOS** back in 1915 on the site of a former chicken ranch and began giving behind-the-scenes studio tours himself, charging guests a quarter for a glimpse of the moviemaking process. Over the following years, Laemmle's early vision evolved into a massive hilltop attraction, featuring not only the largest working film and television studio in the world, but a bustling promenade, **UNIVERSAL CITYWALK**, whose shops, restaurants, and movie theaters are frequented more by tourists and loitering teenagers than by locals. Though a small upscale community has sprung up in the vicinity, Universal City is basically Universal Studios (see below), and it's the only real reason to visit the area aside from fall's annual **AMERICAN FOOD & WINE FESTIVAL** (310/652-3706), which is held on Universal Studios' back lot.

Part behind-the-scenes studio tour and part theme park, **UNIVERSAL STUDIOS HOLLYWOOD** (1000 Universal Center Drive; 818/508-9600) is the number-one visitor attraction in Los Angeles County, according to the Los Angeles Visitors and Convention Bureau. Its highlights include a tram tour where visitors learn a thing or two about movie-making as they traverse the back lots and sound stages and meet the main star of *Jaws,* experience the sensation of an 8.3 earthquake, and get up close and personal with King Kong. Well-polished tour guides (most of them aspiring actors) spout interesting facts and stories about the studio. Other attractions include the "Back to the Future," "E.T.," and "Jurassic Park" rides, the new interactive Totally Nickelodeon, and live-action shows based on such Universal Pictures films as *Waterworld* and *Beetlejuice.* A new virtual-reality attraction, "Terminator 2 3-D," created by the self-proclaimed King of the World James Cameron, opened in May 1999.

Within **UNIVERSAL CITYWALK**'s (818/622-4455) minivillage of tourist attractions, some of the most popular venues are **WIZARDS MAGIC CLUB AND DINNER THEATER** (818/506-0066), which serves up dinner and a magic show; **GLADSTONE'S UNIVERSAL** (818/622-3474), the Valley outpost of the popular Malibu fish eatery; **COUNTRY STAR** (818/762-3939), which looks like a giant jukebox from the outside, serves barbecue, and plays country music videos; and **MARVEL MANIA RESTAURANT** (818/762-7835), a kid-friendly theme restaurant inspired by Marvel comic book characters. **ALL-STAR COLLECTIBLES** (818/622-2222) is filled with sports memorabilia, and **JAMS WORLD** (818/761-6340) is a retail store for Jams surfer/Hawaiian-style clothing.

LODGINGS

Sheraton Universal / ★★

333 UNIVERSAL TERRACE PKWY, UNIVERSAL CITY; 818/980-1212
OR 800/325-3535

Situated at Universal Studios' back door, this 442-room hotel caters to both tourists and business travelers. Its elegant beige and gray lobby attempts a setting of sophistication with rich Oriental overtones, including Chinese lion statues, Buddha sculptures, and potted plants. Rooms, which are rather standard and corporate, with a desk, in-room coffee, minibar, and iron and ironing board, are located in the 24-story tower that overlooks the surrounding Hollywood Hills and the Valley, and in a 3-story wing with small balconies that surrounds the pool. Club Level bonuses include a complimentary continental breakfast, evening hors d'oeuvres, and cocktails in the Club Lounge, as well as upgraded bathroom amenities. The hotel's 22 state-of-the-art meeting rooms, complete with automated screens with overhead projectors, keep the business crowd happy. And while the hotel's tropical garden pool area definitely caters to kids, mom and dad can kick back with cocktails served at the Baja Bar. However, the real family attraction here is easy access to fun—a free shuttle outside the lobby whisks hotel guests across the street to the gates of Universal Studios. The hotel's coffee shop–style Californias Restaurant offers a breakfast and lunch buffet, as well as sandwiches, salads, and pastas for dinner. Auditions lobby bar offers libations with live piano entertainment nightly. *$$$$; AE, DC, DIS, JCB, MC, V; checks OK; www.sheraton.com; Lankershim Blvd exit off the 101 Fwy.* &

Universal City Hilton & Towers / ★★

555 UNIVERSAL TERRACE PKWY, UNIVERSAL CITY; 818/506-2500 OR 800/HILTONS

With its hilltop location just across the street from Universal Studios and an extensive amount of conference and ballroom spaces, this 24-story glass high-rise is literally crammed with tourist groups and convention-eers. If you didn't come to join the masses, know in advance there's no chance of beating them and you'll be better prepared to appreciate the hotel's attributes. Free shuttles leave the hotel regularly for Universal Studios, and after a day of crowded tourist attractions, the oversized guest rooms, decorated in warm tones of burgundy and green and affording great views of the surrounding Hollywood Hills, are a welcome retreat. There's no real reason to hang in the bustling lobby, though its all-about-glass construction allows views of garden-filled courtyards with trickling fountains from virtually every angle. The hotel's pool and whirlpool are idyllic for lounging, while the limited fitness center is the spot for sculpting the Southern California–style bod. The hotel's Tower Floors, accessed only by special elevator keys, offer concierge service and a lounge with complimentary food throughout the day. On the lobby level, you can sip cappuccinos or order something a little stiffer in the Lobby Lounge. Nautical-themed Cafe Sierra offers a breakfast, lunch, and dinner buffet and features enough of an international food selection to satisfy the United Nations—although none of it is exactly memorable. *$$$$; AE, DC, DIS, JCB, MC, V; local checks only; www.hilton.com; Lankershim Blvd exit off the 101 Fwy.* &

North Hollywood

Located just north of Universal City, North Hollywood is best known for its trendy arts district, NoHo, which runs along Lankershim Boulevard between Chandler and Otsego. Lined with equity-waiver theaters like the **RAVEN PLAYHOUSE** (5233 Lankershim Boulevard; 818/509-9519) and the **AMERICAN RENEGADE THEATER** (11136 Magnolia Boulevard; 818/763-4430), artist studios, coffeehouses, eclectic boutiques and restaurants, this recently revitalized section of town is also the home of the **ACADEMY OF TELEVISION ARTS AND SCIENCES COMPLEX** (5220 Lankershim Boulevard; 818/754-2800), where TV fans can wander through the outdoor Hall of Fame Plaza to admire statues of their favorite television legends, including Bob Hope and Lucille Ball.

Each June, NoHo celebrates the arts with its annual **NOHO ARTS FESTIVAL**, a street fair that includes musical performances, dancing, an arts and crafts show, and free performances at many area theaters. For more information, call the North Hollywood/Universal City Chamber of Commerce at 818/508-5155.

RESTAURANTS

Barsac Brasserie / ★

4212 LANKERSHIM BLVD, NORTH HOLLYWOOD; 818/760-7081
With its close vicinity to the studios, this dining establishment is an industry hangout often filled with studio suits doing business deals over above-average French-Italian fare. To take advantage of seasonal ingredients, the menu here changes every three months. Start with the wild mushroom and anchovy tart or the grilled eggplant rolls stuffed with goat cheese, sun-dried tomatoes, and pine nuts, and then move on to the tortelloni with wild duck, served with a slightly heavy shiitake and oyster mushroom cream sauce, or the spaghetti and rabbit in a Burgundy ragout with peas, onions, and garlic. Roasted game hen with fresh tarragon and rack of lamb served with a puree of pumpkin and yams are other menu highlights. The open-air kitchen facing the busy dining room makes it impossible to savor a quiet meal, but the studio crowd makes people-watching almost as much fun as eating. *$$$; AE, DC, MC, V; lunch Mon–Fri, dinner Mon–Sat; full bar; reservations recommended; just north of Universal Studios.* &

Ca' del Sole / ★★☆

4100 CAHUENGA BLVD, NORTH HOLLYWOOD; 818/985-4669
This rustic Italian eatery transports diners to the Mediterranean with its trellised vine terrace and countryside-inn atmosphere, fireplace, and antique wood hutches. The mouth-watering aroma of garlic and herbs wafting through the busy dining room only helps the illusion. Waiters, many of whom are Italian, will encourage you to *mangia* by sharing such starters as baked Roma tomatoes, lobster- and crabcakes sautéed with cannellini beans and green lentils, and rich broccoli and cauliflower soufflé served with roasted plum tomato sauce. Pasta lovers enjoy the hearty bowls of freshly made pastas, including *bigoli alla Ca' del Sole,* a fragrant seafood pasta overflowing with lobster, clams, shrimp, and crab; and pumpkin raviolis accented with sage. The marinated corn-fed chicken

with lemon zest and herbs and the free-range wine-braised veal shank with vegetables and potato gnocchetti sautéed in sage butter are also good choices. Forget about fat grams and sample the restaurant's homemade gelati for dessert. Adding to the relaxed atmosphere, Ca' del Sole (which means "House of the Sun") also offers dinner in the casual-but-cramped jazz room, where live jazz is performed nightly. But if you are planning to have dinner, stick to the dining room. *$$$; AE, DC, MC, V; no checks; lunch Mon–Fri, dinner every day, brunch Sun; full bar; reservations recommended; between Lankershim Blvd and Moorpark St.* &

LODGINGS

Beverly Garland's Holiday Inn / ★★

4222 VINELAND AVE, NORTH HOLLYWOOD; 818/980-8000
OR 800/BEVERLY

This 258-room hotel's moniker refers to the actress who played Fred MacMurray's wife on *My Three Sons*. While you can look at movie stills from her other roles in the Mission-style lobby, chances are you'll be more interested in checking out the property's meticulously landscaped seven acres, which include a pool and two lighted tennis courts, or the historical pictures of the area from the early 1900s. The good-sized rooms, located in two seven-story buildings, are quaint, and their distressed pine furniture provides a distinctly California feel. With Universal Studios just down the street and the 101 and 134 Freeways right out the front door, the hotel's location can't be beat. Unfortunately, immediate freeway access also means there's the constant buzz of traffic, so be sure to ask for a room facing Vineland Avenue. Additional perks include a free shuttle to Universal Studios and the Burbank Airport. The hotel's Paradise Cafe & Bar serves breakfast, lunch, and dinner, including everything from cheesy omelets to sandwiches and seafood. *$$$; AE, DC, DIS, JCB, MC, V; checks OK; exit 101 Fwy at Vineland Ave.* &

Van Nuys

RESTAURANTS

Dr. Hogly Wogly's Tyler Texas BBQ / ★

8136 SEPULVEDA BLVD, VAN NUYS; 818/782-2480

This authentic barbecue joint may lack ambience and may be located in a not-so-desirable part of town, but all is forgiven the minute diners catch a glimpse of the juicy, mega-sized portions of barbecued and smoked meats served here. Dr. Hogly Wogly's Tyler Texas BBQ was named by its original owner, Johnny Greene, who as a chubby little kid back in the

105

early 1930s used to deliver groceries for a Piggly Wiggly market in Texas. But around these parts he's better known for launching this ultra-casual place offering a barbecued half chicken that easily serves two, especially considering the enormous drumsticks look like something straight out of the *Flintstones*. Barbecued beef ribs are also reminiscent of a Fred and Barney 'cue sizewize, although Dr. Hogly Wogly's is probably tenderer—it practically falls off the bone. Texas hot links offer a spicy kick, and side orders include home-baked bread, barbecued beans, and fresh coleslaw. Career waitresses who greet you as "Honey" or "Doll" fit just fine into the kitschy atmosphere of vinyl booths and Formica tables. Though it's tempting to overeat, save room for the pecan and sweet potato pie, and ask for your leftovers to go; the staff will gladly dump your remaining food into a giant plastic bag and seal it with a knot. *$; AE, DC, DIS, MC, V; no checks; lunch, dinner every day; beer and wine; reservations not necessary; south of Roscoe Blvd.* &

LODGINGS

Radisson Valley Center Hotel Los Angeles / ★★

15433 VENTURA BLVD, VAN NUYS; 818/981-5400 OR 800/333-3333
Located at the junction of the 405 and 101 Freeways, this contemporary chain hotel redefines the term "freeway-accessible." Because of its convenient location, it has become Tourist Central, with Gray Line Tour buses departing from outside the lobby daily for such sights as Disneyland, the San Diego Zoo, and Sea World. However, freeway-savvy visitors can opt to rent a car from the Avis location in the lobby and visit the sights on their own. Conventioneers also make up a good portion of the hotel's clientele, utilizing the executive suites. After the Northridge earthquake, this hotel underwent an extensive renovation, including everything from retrofitting to decor, and today boasts pastel interiors with whitewashed wood furnishings. A state-of-the-art fitness center occupies the top floor, and there's a heated outdoor pool and spa. Windows Bar & Grill serves traditional American cuisine, including salads, steaks, shrimp, and chicken. *$$$; AE, DC, DIS, JCB, MC, V; checks OK; www.radisson.com; at the junction of the 405 and 101 Fwys.* &

Burbank

Although Johnny Carson may have had reason to mock Burbank during his years on *The Tonight Show*, today "beautiful downtown Burbank," as he dubbed it, is actually pretty neat—thanks to a renovation that transformed its main street, San Fernando Road, into a hip promenade lined with restaurants, bookstores, cafes, and movie theaters.

In addition to its newly revitalized downtown, Burbank seems to have a movie or television studio on every corner, with Disney, Warner Bros., and NBC all calling this busy city home. For a two hour behind-the-scenes tour where such shows as *E.R.* and *Friends* are produced, make a reservation for the **WARNER BROS. STUDIOS VIP TOUR** (4000 Warner Boulevard; 818/972-TOUR; www.studio-tour.com). The Peacock Network also offers a tour; call **NBC STUDIOS** (3000 W Alameda Avenue; 818/840-3537) for more information.

RESTAURANTS

Cafe N'Awlins / ★★

122 N SAN FERNANDO RD, BURBANK; 818/563-3569

This tiny storefront Cajun-Creole eatery might not be much to look at, but the food makes up for the lack of ambience. Owner/chef Mark Antoine Foster learned to cook authentic New Orleans cuisine in all the right places, working under Cajun master chef Paul Prudhomme and at the stoves of such famed New Orleans establishments as Court of Two Sisters and Commander's Palace. There he mastered such Cajun/Creole traditions as shrimp Creole, jambalaya, redfish étouffée, and hearty seafood gumbo, all of which he now serves at his downtown Burbank restaurant. Hearty portions of Foster's spicy fare come with red beans and rice, vegetables, and homey potato salad. No alcohol is served, but you can bring your own beer or wine. Be sure to save room for the sweet potato/pecan pie, served with freshly whipped cream. *$; no credit cards; checks OK; lunch Tues–Fri, dinner Tues–Sun; reservations not accepted; 4 blocks from Burbank Media Center Mall.* &

LODGINGS

Safari Inn / ★

1911 W OLIVE AVE, BURBANK; 818/845-8586

Used as the exterior location for Christian Slater and Patricia Arquette's hideaway in *True Romance,* this cool retro motel recently underwent a complete renovation, though its Deco neon sign welcoming visitors remains intact. From the outside, the two-story lodging may look like your basic motor lodge, but thanks to its recent gutting, everything inside the 55-room motel is brand-spanking new—from paint and bathroom fixtures to mattresses and the contemporary furnishings. Guest rooms are fairly small, but wrought iron and upholstered headboards with a David Hockneyesque red, green, and blue design and colorful framed prints of the same pattern create a lively, IKEA-like atmosphere. Several of the rooms have a small kitchenette and wet bar. Guests can take a dip in the tiny pool that sits in the middle of the motel's parking lot, or soak up the Southern California sunshine on a rooftop sundeck above the front office. There's no restaurant, but breakfast, lunch, and dinner are available via room service from the Olive Bistro, located next door at the Safari Inn's sister property, the Anabelle Hotel (2011 W Olive Avenue; 818/845-7800). The small eatery's classic bistro fare runs the gamut from sandwiches and salads to roasted chicken and steaks. $$; AE, DC, DIS, MC, V; no checks; between Buena Vista and Victory Blvds. &

Glendale

Like Burbank, Glendale has been revitalizing its downtown area over the last several years, and today its Brand Boulevard is lined with shops, cafes, restaurants, movie theaters, bookstores, and neighborhood pubs. Its historic Art Deco ALEX THEATER (216 N Brand Boulevard; 818/243-2539) was recently restored and today hosts concerts, musicals, and vintage movie screenings. Shoppers can hit the GLENDALE GALLERIA (north of Colorado Boulevard, between Central Avenue and Brand Boulevard; 818/240-9481), which snakes its way across several blocks of town. In addition to hundreds of boutiques, the massive indoor mall features Nordstrom, Macy's, Mervyn's, and Robinsons-May.

Nearby at the eastern tip of GRIFFITH PARK, western fans can pay tribute to the Old West at the AUTRY MUSEUM OF WESTERN HERITAGE (4700 Western Heritage Way, Griffith Park, Los Angeles; 323/667-2000) and visit animals from around the world at the Los Angeles Zoo (5333 Zoo Drive, Griffith Park, Los Angeles; 323/644-6400; www.lazoo.org).

RESTAURANTS

Cinnabar / ★★☆

933 S BRAND BLVD, GLENDALE; 818/551-1155

The neon sign outside casts a strange reddish hue over Cinnabar's eclectic dining room, and the faux-leopardskin chairs and white parasols hanging from the ceiling complete the uniquely exotic ambience. However, that just sets the mood for this out-of-the-ordinary dining establishment. Housed in an old moving-company warehouse, Cinnabar combines a casual atmosphere with elegant French/Pacific Rim fare. Owner Alvin Simon, former co-owner at Pasadena's now-defunct Cafe Jacoulet, has a winner with chef Damon Bruner, whose menu emphasizes creative seafood, with such specialties as spicy lemongrass bouillabaisse chockfull of salmon, clams, lobster, rock shrimp, scallops, and rice noodles; swordfish with pea purée; and a deep-fried red snapper served whole. Start with crisp spring rolls, tangy tomato bisque, or a light mixed green salad with homemade vinaigrette. Save room for the homemade desserts, such as a delicious banana–chocolate mousse tart. And be sure to pay homage to the ornate bar, which was imported from Yee Mee Loo in Chinatown; try the intoxicatingly refreshing Moscow Mule, a bubbly combination of vodka, ginger beer, and lime juice served in a festive tin cup. A major bonus: Many of the restaurant's entrees are available as half orders, which are still more than ample in size. *$$; DC, DIS, MC, V; no checks; lunch Mon–Fri, dinner Tues–Sun; full bar; reservations recommended; 1 block north of Chevy Chase Dr.* &

Fresco Ristorante / ★★

514 S BRAND BLVD, GLENDALE; 818/247-5541
Set amid Glendale's strip of car dealerships, this Italian restaurant has made a name for itself by serving inventive, reasonably priced Northern Italian fare with an emphasis on fresh ingredients. Owner/chef Antonio Orlando makes his breads, pastas, gelati, sorbetti, and pastries on the premises. Entrees include such delicious creations as gnocchi with wild mushrooms, smoked chicken and asparagus ravioli, and creamy saffron risotto. You can't go wrong with the garlicky caesar salad, prepared for two tableside by tuxedo-clad waiters. Orlando also does a well-seasoned take on duck, pheasant, and a delightful thinly pounded and breaded veal chop with capers, garlic, and lemon in a light white wine sauce. The romantically lit dining room, bordered by Roman columns and archways and a glass-encased wine cellar, gives Fresco a feeling of elegance at affordable prices. *$$; AE, DC, DIS, MC, V; no checks; lunch Mon–Fri, dinner Mon–Sat; full bar; reservations recommended; between Chestnut St and Colorado Ave.* &

Mission Hills

Named after its resident **MISSION SAN FERNANDO REY DE ESPAÑA**, this northeast Valley community is home to several historical landmarks. Founded in 1797, the city's namesake mission (15151 San Fernando Mission Boulevard; 818/361-0186) suffered extensive damage in the Northridge earthquake but has recently been restored to its former grandeur. Today, busloads of schoolchildren wander the historic site with their teachers, and daily religious services attract devoted worshipers. While this is a holy place, the surrounding neighborhood is a bit sketchy, so think twice before wandering far from the grounds.

Just down the street from the mission, history buffs might want to stop at the **PICO ADOBE** (10940 Sepulveda Boulevard; 818/365-7810), the second-oldest building in Los Angeles and today home of the San Fernando Valley Historical Society.

Valencia

Sure, everything kind of looks the same in this master-planned community where housing, parks, walkways, and streets were all a part of a unified design. But affordable homes and safe public schools give parents reason to deal with the lengthy commute to work in the city. There's lots of open land for horse ranches and for the ever-expanding 100-acre **SIX FLAGS MAGIC MOUNTAIN** (26101 Mountain Parkway; 805/255-4111), which attracts tourists as well as packs of teenagers who seem more interested in flirting with members of the opposite sex than enjoying the rides. You'll find some of the best rock-'em-sock-'em thrill rides in the West here, among them Riddler's Revenge—which claims to be the world's tallest stand-up roller coaster, Psyclone (think Coney Island's Cyclone)— and Superman: The Escape—your heart will be in your mouth during the moment of zero gravity and the subsequent 41-story plunge. For kids not old enough (or tall enough) to enjoy the park's thrill rides, Bugs Bunny World is dedicated to kiddie rides. Youngsters can also enjoy Six Flags' shows such as the Batman and Robin Live Action Show.

Adjacent to Six Flags Magic Mountain is their **HURRICANE HARBOR WATER PARK** (26101 Magic Mountain Parkway; 661/255-4527), which is open May through September and features top-ten-best-in-the-world water fantasy rides, including the stirring Black Snake Summit and the Bamboo Racer, a six-lane racing water slide.

San Gabriel Valley

Set in the foothills of the San Gabriel Mountains, the San Gabriel Valley, with its suburban landscape and laid-back Southern California lifestyle, is in stark contrast to the hustle and bustle of city living. What was once a rural area of orange, lemon, and walnut groves and ranches is today a largely residential region with a growing Asian and Hispanic population—an addition that has brought cultural diversity to the area. From the charming town of Pasadena, the San Gabriel Valley spans eastward, including such neighboring communities as San Marino, Arcadia, and Monrovia, with Pomona and Claremont defining the region's eastern borders. Though you'll find turn-of-the-century estates nestled on tree-lined streets and sprawling horse ranches with plenty of rugged terrain, much of the San Gabriel Valley is populated with boxy stucco homes and historic downtown sections that are hard to differentiate from city to city. New housing developments and up-and-coming businesses are forcing the region to expand haphazardly, but despite its commercial growth the valley still boasts vast expanses of picturesque countryside—from the

TEATIME IN THE VALLEY

Forget a quick stop at Starbucks. When in the San Gabriel Valley, do as the locals do and take a break for a leisurely afternoon tea. Although most people assume that little old ladies wearing hats still dominate this age-old pastime, in these parts the tradition has become quite hip. Besides, what's not to like about relaxing in a beautiful setting, sipping tea, and nibbling on scones, finger sandwiches, and pastries? Perhaps the San Gabriel Valley's most formal afternoon tea is to be found in the Lobby Lounge at the **Ritz-Carlton Huntington Hotel** (1401 S Oak Knoll Street, Pasadena; 626/568-3900), where guests choose from a selection of teas such as lapsang souchong and gunpowder green, poured through elegant little silver strainers into fine china. Freshly baked scones with Devonshire cream, finger sandwiches, and perfect petit fours are served as musical strains from a baby grand piano fill the air. Opt for the hotel's Royal Tea, and an elegant afternoon ends with champagne kir and strawberries marinated in Grand Marnier or Chambord and served with whipped cream. For a more British experience, head to the **Rose Tree Cottage** (828 E California Boulevard, at Lake Street, Pasadena; 626/793-3337; www.rosetreecottage.com), which serves tea in an English-style cottage and includes a very civilized spread of traditional tea sandwiches, fresh fruit, and scones with Devonshire cream and jam. The ideal way to end a meander through the grounds of the **Huntington Library, Art Collections, and Botanical Gardens** is over tea in the **Huntington's Rose Garden Room** (1151 Oxford Road, San Marino; 626/683-8131). The elegant surroundings overlooking the Huntington Rose Garden set the mood for a sophisticated English tea service, with the requisite edibles. Reservations are recommended at all afternoon tea locales.

hiking paths of Angeles Crest National Forest to equestrian trails in the neighboring foothills.

There are those who complain that the San Gabriel Valley is too hot during summer, has too much smog, and is too far from downtown L.A. Though these accusations are true, on a balmy winter day when the foothills rise proudly against a clear sky and traffic is at a minimum, even a cynic would have to agree that this valley is a lovely place to call home.

ACCESS

The 210 Freeway traverses the northern cities of the San Gabriel Valley, while the 10 Freeway travels through the southern boundaries. The 605 Freeway travels south from the northeastern San Gabriel Valley to where it crosses the 10 Freeway near El Monte. To the east, the 57 Freeway links the 210 Freeway to the 10 Freeway.

BURBANK-GLENDALE-PASADENA AIRPORT (2627 N Hollywood Way, Burbank; 818/840-8847), located to the west of the San Gabriel Valley in Burbank, and **ONTARIO INTERNATIONAL AIRPORT** (at the intersection of Airport and Archibald Aves, Ontario; 909/937-2700), 12 miles to the east of the San Gabriel Valley, are the region's two major airports, though **LOS ANGELES INTERNATIONAL AIRPORT** is a short drive away. Ontario is served by 26 carriers, including Delta, Northwest, TWA, and United.

METROLINK'S RIVERSIDE LINE (800/371-5465) links Pomona, City of Industry, and Montebello with downtown Los Angeles. The San Bernardino Line stops in Claremont, Pomona, Covina, Baldwin Park, and El Monte on its way to downtown Los Angeles. **FOOTHILL TRANSIT** (800/RIDE-INFO) provides 30 fixed-route local, express, and rail-feeder bus lines. The **MTA** (800/266-6883) also services the San Gabriel Valley.

Pasadena

The crown jewel of the San Gabriel Valley, Pasadena is an oasis of style and culture. In the early 1900s, this one-time stretch of orange groves beneath the picturesque San Gabriel Mountains attracted wealthy East Coasters looking to escape harsh winters. But once the sun-seeking aristocrats arrived, many decided to stay. Elaborate Victorian mansions, Craftsman-style bungalows, and other lavish edifices soon sprang up around the rural community, and a sophisticated society with theater, museums, and elegant gardens quickly followed.

Today, this refined city possesses an air of old money, with its restored historic district and vast cultural offerings; and in contrast to neighboring Los Angeles's flashy community, it attracts more of a pearls-and-loafers crowd, who reside in lavish bungalows and drive Volvos.

Pasadena is perhaps best known for its January 1 **TOURNAMENT OF ROSES PARADE AND ROSE BOWL** football game (626/449-7673), where the annual Big 10 versus Pac 10 football rivalry is played out. For the rest of the year the city's most popular draw is **OLD TOWN** (bordered by Arroyo Parkway on the east, Pasadena Avenue on the west, Walnut Street on the north, and Del Mar on the south), a 20-block stretch of shops, restaurants, cafes, art galleries, and movie theaters. This bustling district, awash with restored buildings from the late 1800s, has in recent years attracted a whole new crowd to Pasadena, who come for the newly chic historic atmosphere, shopping, and restaurants and only later discover the historic city's museums and cultural attractions.

At the western end of Old Town, the **NORTON SIMON MUSEUM** (411 W Colorado Boulevard; 626/449-6840) offers an impressive collection of Impressionist works by the likes of van Gogh, Renoir, Degas, and Monet. Farther east, the **PACIFIC ASIA MUSEUM** (46 N Los Robles Avenue; 626/449-2742), complete with Chinese-style garden and koi pond, celebrates Asian-inspired art from the Far East. For a close-up look at Pasadena's early architecture, the **GAMBLE HOUSE** (4 Westmoreland Place; 626/793-3334) is the area's finest example of Craftsman style and is open for public viewing. Built in 1908 by famed architects Greene & Greene, the bungalow features amazing hand-crafted teak woodwork, Tiffany glass, and many of the home's original furnishings.

The Rose Bowl may be best known for its annual namesake New Year's Day football game and as the home of UCLA football, but the stadium also hosts an amazing **FLEA MARKET** (RG Canning Flea Market at the Rose Bowl; 213/560-7469) on the second Sunday of every month, when the stadium parking lot is overflowing with collectibles, albums, antiques, furniture, carpets, and virtually everything else you can imagine.

For more information on the Pasadena area, call the **PASADENA CONVENTION & VISITORS BUREAU** (171 S Los Robles Avenue; 626/795-9311; www.PasadenaCal.com).

RESTAURANTS

Arirang / ★★☆

114 W UNION ST, OLD TOWN PASADENA; 626/577-8885
In a rambling warehouselike space just north of Colorado Boulevard in Old Town, Airang is a Korean barbecue culinary adventure raised to the level of, if not haute cuisine, at least highly sophisticated cooking. Most diners go for the various barbecue selections—marinated rib-eye steak, short ribs, pork, beef tongue, chicken, prawns, scallops, and the like, all of which arrive with the usual entourage of soup, rice, lettuce, raw garlic, sliced peppers, and sundry kimchees. But those who have been there and done that expand their horizons to include the remarkable pan-fried dumplings, the equal of anything found in the better Chinese restaurants in San Gabriel, along with the spring onion pancake, the kimchee and pork pancake, the dazzling tartare steak, and the various hotpots of braised tripe and vegetables or sliced pork with salted cabbage. To wash it all down, there's OB Beer from Korea, as good as if not better than the fine beers of Japan. *$; AE, MC, V; checks OK; lunch Mon–Fri, dinner every day; full bar; reservations not necessary; south side of Union St west of Fair Oaks Ave.* &

Arroyo Chop House / ★★★

536 S ARROYO PKWY, PASADENA; 626/57-PRIME

At the Arroyo Chop House, in a setting heavy with wood, glass, and brass, the pure-classic menu items start with salads: there's a salad of mixed greens, a caesar, a plate of sliced beefsteak tomatoes with sliced red onions (in the style of New York's Peter Luger's), a salad of spinach and hearts of palm, and the pride of the house—a chilled heart of iceberg lettuce (yes!) drenched in blue cheese dressing. The steaks, equally classic, are USDA prime, every one of them—from the filet mignon (rarely found graded prime because of the heavy, even marbling that defines prime; fat is not common in filet mignon), through the rib-eye, the porterhouse, the New York strip, and the Delmonico cut. The porterhouse is a fine piece of meat, cooked to perfection in a high-temperature broiler (akin to the one pioneered at the Ruth's Chris chain) that seals in the juices, giving the meat a well-cooked crust on the outside and lots of well-blooded goodness on the inside. *$$; AE, MC, V; checks OK, dinner every day; full bar; reservations required; northeast corner of Arroyo Pkwy and California Blvd.*

Bistro 45 / ★★★

45 MENTOR AVE, PASADENA; 626/795-2478

At the highly respected Bistro 45 (named one of the best restaurants in Los Angeles by *Wine Spectator* and by the readers of *Gourmet* magazine), owner Robert Simon (formerly of Pasadena's Cafe Jacoulet) took one of the fussiest spots in town and gave it an Art-Deco-at-the-end-of-the-decade look—very angular, very medium-cool, very edge-of-decadence. (He's also put in some terrifically comfortable seats; this is art that feels good to sit in, which is not often the case.) The cuisine here is basically California Bistro, and it changes often. On any given evening, the menu might include such pleasures as the salmon and tuna tartares, flavored with cilantro; rock shrimp risotto with saffron; pan-roasted monkfish with garlic polenta; roasted veal loin filled with Roquefort; Fanny Bay oyster salad; and Nebraska pork with figs. The wine dinners here, generally built around a particular winery and often attended by the winemaker, are almost certainly the most popular in town. The waiters define the California style of affable and knowledgeable at the same time—the only attitude here is a good one. *$$; AE, MC, V; lunch Tues–Fri, dinner Tues–Sun; full bar; reservations required; www.bistro45.com; west side of Mentor Ave south of Colorado Blvd.* &

Buca di Beppo / ★★

80 W GREEN ST, OLD TOWN PASADENA (AND BRANCHES); 626/792-7272

Buca di Beppo is often compared to Carmine's in New York, for both are notable for red-sauce chow served in giant portions. But where the food at Carmine's is simply okay, Buca serves good stuff—as long as you don't mind blowing your diet for the whole rest of the year on one meal. The folks responsible for the national Buca di Beppo chain describe their creation as "a Southern Italian immigrant restaurant" and a recreation of the "Italian supperclubs of the '40s and '50s." Actually, it's closer to a Smithsonian of Italiana, with hundreds of photographs on the walls of gangsters, priests, pretty girls, grouchy mamas, and musicians. Buca is to Italians what Sammy's Roumanian in New York is to Jews—a place where you can revel in your roots and chuckle at them at the same time. The trick to eating here is to go with a lot of people. (There's even a Pope's Table that can accommodate probably 20 hungry souls.) All the portions are for groups of four, which makes the prices—in the high teens—a terrific deal. And this is chow that sticks to your ribs (and various other internal organs)—garlic bread, roasted peppers with garlic and anchovies, good pizzas as big as breadboards (try the one topped with Gorgonzola, provolone, mozzarella, and Romano), rigatoni tossed with white beans and sausage, chicken cacciatore served over garlic mashed potatoes, and linguine topped with an ocean of seafood. There's a commitment here to piling as many calories on the plate as possible, so don't expect to undereat. Additional locations are in Encino (17500 Ventura Blvd; 818/995-3288) and Redondo Beach (1670 S Pacific Coast Highway; 310/540-3246). *$; AE, MC, V; checks OK; dinner every day; full bar; reservations recommended; southeast corner of DeLacey and W Green Sts.* &

Cafe Santorini / ★

64 W UNION ST, OLD TOWN PASADENA; 626/564-4200

Cafe Santorini sits around the corner from the AMC Multiplex in Old Town, down an alleyway, with a single neon sign overhead. While the large upstairs room with bare brick walls and polished wood floors has a number of pleasant tables, they aren't nearly as popular as the tables outside. The patio is clearly the place to sit at Cafe Santorini, overlooking the crowds coming and going at the theater complex below. The thing to do here is to start with the mezze platter, a bounty of stuffed grape leaves, spanakopita and tiropita, fried kibbeh, tabbouleh, and feta cheese that's enough for a light meal for two. From there, things wander a bit—from a caesar salad with salmon, a cheeseburger made with kasseri cheese, Armenian sausage pizza, and an oxtail pizza made with shiitake mushrooms, through the realm of pasta, finally refocusing on souvlaki, lule (ground meat) kebab, a terrific oven-baked chicken with ratatouille and kalamata olives, and a casual bouillabaisse of prawns and scallops in a swell tomato broth. Prices are right. And sitting on the patio, you won't feel like you're in Pasadena anymore. You can almost smell the Mediterranean in the air. *$; AE, MC, V; no checks; lunch, dinner every day; full bar; reservations recommended; north side of Colorado Blvd west of Fair Oaks Ave.*

Celestino / ★★

141 S LAKE AVE, PASADENA; 626/795-4006

Celestino is the creation of chef Celestino Drago, formerly of Il Giardino, Chianti Cucina, and currently behind Santa Monica's stylish Drago, and Beverly Hills' Il Pastaio. Here Chef Drago (along with his brother Giacomino) has created his own version of Il Fornaio, with a dominant motif of light, casual, surprisingly inexpensive cooking. This is a great spot for serendipitous dining; you show up, look at the menu, and find something you want, even though you didn't know you wanted it. It's unlikely you'll find a better bruschetta this side of the Po River—wonderfully crisp bread, topped with just the right balance of garlic, tomato, and arugula. The less-traditional *arancine di riso* (literally, "little rice oranges") look like inverted ice cream cones filled with a dollop of beef stew, peas, and provolone. Pastas come in two forms—egg or durum wheat. Drago is a master of risottos—flavored with such combinations as beets and goat cheese, porcini and mascarpone, lobster and peppers, or squid and scallops. Think of Celestino as a casual Italian cafe where you can feast (lightly) on dishes that always satisfy, no matter what you're in the mood for. *$$; AE, MC, V; no checks; lunch Mon–Fri, dinner Mon–Sat; full bar; reservations recommended; west side of S Lake Ave south of Green St.* &

Clearwater Seafood / ★★

168 W COLORADO BLVD, OLD TOWN PASADENA; 626/356-0959

At Clearwater Seafood (formerly Clearwater Cafe) you'll find New Wave seafood in a comfortably modernistic setting. Call it seafood for the '90s: the freshest of fish cooked in a wide variety of ways, a good deal of heart-healthy Mediterranean ingredients thrown in for good measure, a fair number of vegetarian dishes, served in a setting complete with a dramatic outdoor patio. Oysters are whatever happens to be fresh and available— perhaps nothing more complex than Blue Points from Long Island and Dungeness Bays from up north. Though the menu changes regularly expect a fine cioppino (award-winning, since they're using a similar recipe as at their sister restaurant, Ocean Avenue Seafood in Santa Monica), roasted halibut on greens with sweet potatoes and mushrooms, crisp striped bass on teriyaki noodles, mahi mahi with basil-flavored mashed spuds, and the like. Prince Edward Island mussels and Hog Island Manila clams are steamed. Soups and salads abound. This is easily some of the best seafood in Pasadena. *$; AE, MC, V; no checks; lunch, dinner every*

day; full bar; reservations recommended, southeast corner of Colorado Blvd and Pasadena Ave. &

Crocodile Cafe / ★

140 S LAKE AVE, PASADENA (AND BRANCHES); 626/449-9900

The Crocodile Cafe (a creation by those behind the upscale Parkway Grill) is the sort of restaurant where you can drop by for a casual burger or where a sizable group can go for a jolly and festive birthday celebration. It's a dandy place, with smart young waitpersons and a sense of being on the cutting edge, at prices that are more than reasonable. What they do, they do very well—the black bean and sirloin chili is one of the best in town. The quesadilla is packed to overflowing with jack and ranchero cheeses and topped with salsa and guacamole. There are potstickers filled with shrimp and veggies in a lime-ginger-soy dip. They make a classic hamburger here, oak-wood grilled, served with fries, and with or without grilled onions. The pizzas and calzones are fine, variations on the Spago/California Pizza Kitchen style, with the barbecue chicken pizza a real standout; smoked gouda is a swell pizza cheese. Of the large plates, the Cuban chicken breast is quite a feed, a big plate of cinnamon-and-raisin sweetened chicken, with bananas and rice on the side. It's easy to get stuffed here for very little and have a heck of a good time in the process. Other locations include Old Town Pasadena (88 W Colorado Boulevard; 626/568-9310); Burbank (201 N San Fernando Boulevard; 818/843-7999); Glendale (626 N Central Avenue; 818/241-1114); and Santa Monica (101 Santa Monica Boulevard; 310/394-4783). *$; AE, MC, V; no checks; lunch, dinner every day; full bar; reservations not necessary; east side of S Lake Ave near Green St.* &

DeLacey's Club 41 / ★

41 S DELACEY ST, OLD TOWN PASADENA; 626/795-4141

DeLacey's is one of the most comfortable steak houses around. It's a manly establishment, heavy with wood, glass, and brass, with a fine bar at which a thirsty cove can pause for a beverage, and spacious booths where an affectionate couple can lose themselves, gazing deep into each other's eyes over a nice shrimp and crab Louis, or perhaps some lovely crab cakes, properly crisped, sufficiently padded with crab. Though DeLacey's is just a decade old, it smacks of early times. Service is the style you'd expect at Musso & Frank's in Hollywood, or the Dal Rae in Pico Rivera—efficient without being abrupt. The menu is classic—there's a whole section of dipped sandwiches (roast beef, roast pork, roast lamb), along with "hot plate specialties" of the same roast threesome, plus roast turkey, meat loaf, London broil, and calf's liver. Spinach salad is served with a proper hot dressing; filet mignon is wrapped in bacon; there's veal chop bordelaise, chicken piccata, chicken Marsala, even fettuccine alfredo. But mostly, there's meat. They make a very nice 10-ounce pepper

117

steak at DeLacey's—not a big piece, but a very satisfying one, crusted with peppercorns, dripping juice, just terrific accompanied by some garlic mashed potatoes, home-fried potatoes, or French fries. *$; AE, MC, V; no checks; lunch Sun–Fri, dinner every day; full bar; reservations recommended; west side of DeLacey St south of Colorado Blvd.* &

Derek's / ★★☆

181-185 E GLENARM ST, PASADENA; 626/799-5252

What used to be Dickenson West has been transmuted into Derek's (half of the same ownership, new chef, spiffed-up decor), a casually elegant Cal-American restaurant where the simplest way to approach dinner is to head straight for the Chef's Menu. It changes weekly, shifting with the seasons and with the whimsy of the moment. A typical menu (at $39 a person) went from seared foie gras with caramelized mango (so indulgent it was almost embarrassing) and a plate of happily plump grilled Santa Barbara shrimp atop mashed spuds flavored with truffle oil to roast duck with a perfect risotto flavored with sweet sautéed onions. After the cheese course, dessert might seem a bit extraneous. But desserts here are awfully hard to pass on—especially the tart lemon tart with a sauce of wild huckleberries, the fig-and-raspberry tarte tatin, or the lemon verbena crème brûlée. Those who opt against the Chef's Menu might consider the absurdly addictive tower of ahi and salmon tartare, the blue plate special of lamb curry, the impressively moist pork tenderloin, or the perfect rack of lamb with peppered gnocchi. Derek's needs looking for; even those driving down Glenarm might not notice it. But as an exercise in serendipity, it's worth sleuthing out. *$$; AE, MC, V; no checks; lunch Tues–Fri, dinner Tues–Sat; full bar; reservations recommended; north side of Glenarm St east of Arroyo Pkwy.* &

The Grill at the Ritz-Carlton Huntington Hotel & Spa / ★★★

1401 S OAK KNOLL AVE, PASADENA; 626/577-2867

Dining is more of an event than a meal in this elegant hotel restaurant. Wood-paneled walls, crystal sconces, seascape paintings, and a collection of antique carved ships create a sophisticated clubby atmosphere that perfectly accentuates the menu of continental classics. Although executive chef Denis Depoitre, who has been with the hotel since 1993, oversees the hotel's restaurants, chef Fabrice Huet, who hopscotched from Ritz-Carltons in Shanghai and Seoul to his current post, presides over the kitchen in the hotel's most formal dining room. Appetizers here, as refined as the setting, might include salmon gravlax with a marinated vegetable salad, lamb confit in crépinettes, and roasted squab with Moroccan couscous, baby artichokes and yellow curry vinaigrette—all served by tuxedoed waiters whose professionalism is quintessential Ritz-Carlton. A respectable selection of grilled prime-aged meats includes tender double lamb chops and succulent chateaubriand à deux, each served with a rich béarnaise, merlot, or peppercorn sauce. Norwegian salmon, Atlantic grouper, and Lake Superior whitefish are among the fresh seafood entrees, grilled, poached, or sautéed. A classic rendition of herb-crusted rack of lamb for two is beautifully presented, as is the roasted wild sturgeon with an accompanying crab soufflé. An impressive wine list of more than 350 vintages ensures you'll find the perfect bottle to complement your meal. *$$$; AE, DC, DIS, JCB, MC, V; no checks; lunch Sun, dinner every day; full bar; reservations required; www.ritz carlton.com; exit 210 Fwy at Lake Ave and go south until it becomes Oak Knoll St.*

Houston's / ★★

320 S ARROYO PKWY, PASADENA; 626/577-6001

Houston's is a burgeoning chain now numbering some two dozen, with restaurants in Southern cities like Atlanta, Dallas, and, yes, Houston. It's an interesting concept in terms of large-market dining—a good-looking, steakhouse-like setting with an open kitchen and a menu that mixes burgers with barbecue. A sizable number of menu items run under $10, a surprise for a relatively upscale eatery. Though the beef choices, like the filet mignon, the New York strip, and the prime rib, hover in the high teens, they're also large enough to feed two persons with ease. The thing to chomp on while you wait for your meal at Houston's is the Chicago-style spinach and artichoke dip, a ridiculously caloric bowl of creamed spinach and artichoke hearts topped with melted cheese, accompanied by sour cream and salsa, and tortilla chips. Main courses are straightforward and to the point—good, solid, culinary Americana. There's a fine hickory burger, and an intriguing firehouse chili–topped Texas burger that's served only on Saturdays. And there's everybody's favorite dish of choice, the barbecued ribs. The menu says "Our Knife and Fork Version," but that isn't really true: pick up the tender ribs with your fingers, and the meat absolutely drops off the bone. *$; AE, MC, V; no checks; lunch, dinner every day; full bar; reservations recommended; east side of Arroyo Pkwy south of Colorado Blvd.* &

Il Fornaio / ★★

1 COLORADO BLVD, OLD TOWN PASADENA (AND BRANCHES); 626/683-9797

This outpost of the Il Fornaio chain is noisy in the way that restaurants filled with people having a very good time tend to be noisy. It's a happy noise, with lots of waving of arms at old friends, and air kisses flying. It's very much like being in Italy, with food to match: soft polenta (not fried and rubbery) with mushrooms and Parmesan, an outstanding and a perfect eggplant dish with goat cheese, sun-dried tomatoes, onions, capers, and balsamic vinegar. They make a heck of a fine Tuscan bean and barley soup and a tomato soup with Tuscan bread that's good enough to raise the dead. The pizza is crispy-crunchy, thin-crusted, topped with the sort of stuff you might find in the Piazza Navona in Rome—mozzarella, provolone, grilled eggplant, ricotta, red onions, garlic, and so forth. It works perfectly as an appetizer for two or as a main course for one. Their pizza permutation of focaccia bread stuffed with gorgonzola, pine nuts, basil, and onions is what sandwiches dream of someday becoming. Additional Southern California locations include Beverly Hills (301 N Beverly Drive; 310/550-8330) and Santa Monica (1551 Ocean Avenue; 310/451-7800). *$; AE, MC, V; no checks; breakfast, lunch, dinner every day; full bar; reservations recommended; north side of Colorado Blvd west of Fair Oaks Ave.*

Kingston Cafe / ★

333 S FAIR OAKS AVE, PASADENA; 626/405-8080

The Kingston Cafe looks as if it was someone's home in the not-too-distant past—a nice frame house several blocks south of the manic energy of Old Town's Colorado Boulevard. It's divided into four separate rooms, in which you can enjoy a distinctive amount of privacy and friendly service along with your good Jamaican meal. The menu here offers a fine cross-section of that cuisine that hits all the right notes—many of them, though not all, at the spicy end of the spectrum. The option is yours, but know that if you ask for a dish to be prepared hot, it will indeed be very much that. The ubiquitous specialty of Jamaican restaurants is jerk chicken, which here is titled Hot Flashes and is so tender it falls right off the bone. Curried chicken is named Yellow Glow, curried goat is Kingston Glow, and their chicken rich with the taste of molasses is known as Air Condition. Their Matrimony bread pudding is sweeter than most marriages, and holds together far better. *$; DIS, MC, V; no checks; lunch, dinner Tues–Sun; beer and wine only; reservations not necessary; west side of Fair Oaks Ave south of Colorado Blvd.*

Kuala Lumpur / ★

69 W GREEN ST, OLD TOWN PASADENA; 626/577-5175

At Kuala Lumpur (named for the capital of Malaysia), dishes are both familiar and unfamiliar. The satay is as good as any in town—skewered beef, chicken, pork, or shrimp with a peanut-chili sauce so good it could be served for dessert. The *puteri* roll is a good-sized Malaysian egg roll, very crisp, filled with what seems to be just about everything in the kitchen. Kung pau mango shrimp involves tiger shrimp stir-fried with mango, mango juice, chile sambal, garlic, and onions. The deep-fried pulau shrimp's flavor is tempered with a sauce of lemongrass, garlic, and shallots, which allows you to encounter a new flavor every time you take a bite: a remarkable experience. Fish comes cooked in a tamarind sauce over noodles, a dish with a flavor that's hard to identify and harder to forget. Chicken is grilled in a *ketjap* sauce, the granddaddy of our far more mundane ketchup. For dessert, among others, there's durian ice cream, which neither smells as bad as its press implies nor tastes nearly as sweet. *$; AE, MC, V; no checks; lunch, dinner Tues–Sun; beer and wine only; reservations recommended; north side of Green St at DeLacey St.*

Market City Caffe / ★

33 S FAIR OAKS AVE, OLD TOWN PASADENA; 626/568-0203
164 E PALM AVE, BURBANK; 818/840-7036
There are few pleasures more satisfying than finding a nice table on the outdoor patio at the Market City Caffe and spending a long evening sipping a glass or two of pinot grigio while nibbling on dish after dish from the antipasto buffet (one of the best around, with a rich assortment of recipes handed down from the owner's grandmothers). This is a trattoria in the best meaning of the word—a casual, family-oriented sort of place where eating and drinking can be done at ease in comfort, and the cost doesn't cause any indigestion afterwards. They make quite a pizza, and the great bar at the other end of the patio—martinis on one side, antipasti on the other—certainly makes for one of the clearer definitions of heaven on earth. *$; AE, MC, V; no checks; lunch, dinner every day; full bar; reservations recommended; west side of Fair Oaks Ave south of Colorado Blvd.* &

Marston's / ★★

151 E WALNUT ST, PASADENA; 626/796-2459
Marston's is not an old restaurant, but within a decade it has become a Pasadena tradition. It's not a big place, so come lunch time, there's always a wait. Breakfast is a gala affair, a meal for those who like their first meal of the day big and sumptuous and couldn't give a fig about cholesterol. The menu includes arguably the best French toast in town—two fat slabs of sourdough soaked in egg batter, rolled in cornflakes, griddled to marvelous brownness, and served with hot syrup and soft butter. There are also fine macadamia nut–blueberry pancakes with enough blueberries to keep the usual "what berries?" grumbles to a minimum. For lunch, the best of the best is the Pasadena Salad, an incredible mixture of spinach, avocado, candied pecans, chicken, scallions, and bacon in the slightly sweet house dressing served with a basket of crunchy cheese popovers. You might also consider the superb Cobb salad, grilled chicken caesar, grilled chicken breast club sandwich with black bean mayonnaise, white lightnin' chili with chicken, or a grilled chicken and Gorgonzola melt. *$; MC, V; no checks; breakfast, lunch Tues–Sat; no alcohol; reservations not accepted; north side of Walnut St east of Raymond Ave.* &

McCormick & Schmick's / ★★

111 N LOS ROBLES AVE, PASADENA (AND BRANCHES); 626/405-0064
This is seafood, done both traditionally and California-style, in a setting right out of downtown San Francisco. Those with a piscatorial bent can usually be found crowding the bar, feasting on an impressive selection of oysters on the half shell—Dungeness Bays, Olympias, Samish Bays, Quilcenes, Eagle Creeks, and Snow Creek Belons, all from Washington State and all so fresh as to be transcendent in terms of oysterness. And they're just the start of an encyclopedic seafood menu that runs from steamed Manila clams in garlic and white wine broth, Penn Cove or Emerald mussels steamed with garlic and herbs, and traditional oyster stew, to fine popcorn rock shrimp, very good Dungeness crab cakes, one of the best salades niçoises around, and a particularly rich clam chowder. There's much more, some of it on the line between creative and utterly wild-eyed—Chilean white sea bass grilled with mango aioli and red potatoes, ling cod with pesto and sun-dried tomatoes, and white Alaskan king salmon pan-fried with Moroccan black barbecue sauce. Additional locations include one in Beverly Hills (2 Rodeo Drive; 310/859-0434), another in downtown Los Angeles (633 W 5th Street, in Library Towers; 213/629-1929), and one in El Segundo (2101 Rosencrans Avenue; 310/416-1123). *$$; AE, MC, V; no checks; lunch, dinner every day; full bar; reservations required; west side of Los Robles Ave north of Colorado Blvd.* &

Mi Piace / ★★

25 E COLORADO BLVD, OLD TOWN PASADENA; 626/795-3131
801 N SAN FERNANDO BLVD, BURBANK; 818/843-1111
Mi Piace is a phenomenon—a restaurant that's never without customers. Even on nights when the streets of Old Town Pasadena are empty and most local restaurants are sending their excess staff home, you can bet your bottom dollar Mi Piace will be full. The formula is simple—lots of good Italian comfort food freshened up with California touches, served in a cheerful setting, at very reasonable prices. The room is warmly high-tech, with massive mirrors hanging from the back walls, an open kitchen, and a busy bar that separates the restaurant from the adjacent bakery. You can easily mix and match a meal of classic pasta, chicken and veal dishes with cutting-edge carpaccios, risotti, and seafood, all made with state-of-the-art olive oils and balsamic vinegars. The pizzas are wonderful, too, with a good crunchy crust and enough toppings to satisfy even the most persnickety pizza lover. *$; AE, MC, V; no checks; lunch, dinner every day; full bar; reservations accepted for groups of 4 or more; north side of Colorado Blvd between Fair Oaks and Raymond Aves.* &

Parkway Grill / ★★★

510 S ARROYO PARKWAY, PASADENA; 626/795-1001
Commonly regarded as the Spago of Pasadena and certainly one of the best restaurants in town, the Parkway Grill offers utterly and totally revisionist American fare. When you enter, you're overlooking the open kitchen, in which a bevy of chefs are making pizzas and composing salads. The room itself is warm and welcoming, wonderfully open, and filled with a small forest's worth of plants and trees. All told, it's a nearly perfect piece of design. The design of the menu is fairly perfect as well. Consider appetizers like delicate corn cakes with warm oysters, small sausages, and a vaguely spicy tomatillo sauce; black bean soup with smoked pork and a lime cream; or roasted chiles filled with smoked chicken, corn, cilantro, and cheese. Think of marvelous pizzas topped with lamb sausage, grilled eggplant, clams, and scallops; smoked chicken and cilantro; and even black beans and smoked pork, or roasted Chinese air duck with apricot-ginger glaze, long beans, and Napa cabbage; and whole catfish fried crispy with ginger lime soy sauce and caraway rice. They sound silly, but they sure do taste good. *$$; AE, MC, V; checks OK; lunch Mon–Fri, dinner every day; full bar; reservations required; east side of Arroyo Pkwy north of California Blvd.*

Pinot Restaurant & Martini Bar / ★★★

897 GRANITE DR, PASADENA; 626/792-1179
What began as Pinot at the Chronicle is now the Pinot Restaurant & Martini Bar, superchef Joachim Splichal's hometown operation (he lives in nearby San Marino). It's an excellent, elegant, yet easygoing place to go for an encyclopedic assortment of martinis along with an equally extensive selection of classic and modern bistro dishes—including everything from grilled chicken with garlic-flavored French fries, crisp duck leg confit with red lentils, braised veal short ribs with horseradish mashed potatoes, and potato and goat cheese terrine to crisp sweetbreads, endive and Roquefort salad, oven-baked onion soup, grilled lamb sirloin, and an awesome smoked salmon club sandwich. There's a spa menu for those who worry about such things, but in the face of food this good, we recommend just buying a larger size of clothing. *$$; AE, MC, V; no checks; lunch Mon–Fri, dinner Mon–Sat; full bar; reservations required; on tiny Granite Dr, northeast of the intersection of Lake Ave and California Blvd.* &

The Raymond / ★★

1250 S FAIR OAKS AVE, PASADENA; 626/441-3136

The Raymond is, in its own understated way, one of the most traditionally romantic spots in Southern California—a place that doesn't scream romance but subtly lets it get beneath your skin. It's actually the sort of romantic restaurant makes guys feel rather comfortable—all that nice wood in a lovingly restored California bungalow (formerly the caretaker's cottage at the Raymond Hotel), the kind of place that Tim Allen might like. The food is also special without being overly fussy—Long Island roast duckling with fresh pomegranate and cranberry sauce, softshell crabs with sliced oranges and toasted almonds, rack of lamb chops with fresh rosemary and garlic, and medallions of beef with Stilton cheese and port wine cream sauce. Nothing precious here, but there is music, wonderful service, and soft lighting. She'll love it; he won't mind it. *$$; AE, MC, V; checks OK; lunch, dinner Tues–Sun; full bar; reservations recommended; east side of Fair Oaks Ave north of Pasadena Fwy.*

Shiro / ★★★

1505 MISSION ST, SOUTH PASADENA; 626/799-4774

Shiro is named for its chef, who first leaped to prominence with his fine cooking at Pasadena's long-departed Cafe Jacoulet. In the tradition of many of L.A.'s Cal-Asian restaurants, the room is high-ceilinged and noisy. The virtually all-seafood menu, printed daily, is as stripped down as the setting: it might consist of no more than six appetizers and six entrees plus a couple of specials. The Asian influence is manifest in dishes such as the superb Chinese ravioli filled with the most delicate shrimp-salmon mousse and nestled in a mild fennel sauce; smoked salmon with masago roe on potato pancakes (Jewish-Japanese cooking?); California king salmon napped in a ginger-lime sauce; and Shiro's signature dish, a whole sizzling catfish (you can order either medium or large) served with sweet ponzu sauce. This last is arguably the best catfish this side of N'Awlins, and may be even better than anything down there. Shiro is, genuinely, one of the restaurants that makes life in Southern California so very . . . livable. *$$; AE, MC, V; dinner Tues–Sun; beer and wine; reservations required; south side of Mission St west of Fair Oaks Ave.* &

Twin Palms / ★★

101 W GREEN ST, OLD TOWN PASADENA; 626/577-2567

When it comes to re-creating the feeling of a bistro-cafe by the Mediterranean, there are few settings more dramatic or successful than Twin Palms. This is a Disneyland version of a cafe in Nice or Cannes, with a billowing tent wrapped around the central patio like Christmas wrapping. The cooking has evolved over the years from the California-French cuisine of Michael Roberts to the California Coastal cooking of Tony

Zidar, who's given the menu a fresh approach that works especially well on warm January days following the Rose Parade. Main courses include roast chicken and bacon Bric crostada, and herb-crusted filet mignon with potato leek gratin in a port wine sauce. There are 450 seats here that are almost always full—and are definitely packed come Sundays, when Twin Palms erupts with the joy of a wonderful gospel-music buffet brunch. Praise the Lord and pass the eggs Benedict. *$$; AE, MC, V; no checks; lunch, dinner every day; full bar; reservations required; northwest corner of DeLacey and Green Sts.* ໄ

Xiomara and Oye! / ★★

69 N RAYMOND AVE, OLD TOWN PASADENA; 626/796-2520
Xiomara and Oye! are two restaurants under one roof, a brilliant concept engineered by wildly energetic restaurateur Xiomara Ardolina, with Xiomara in the front and Oye! in the back. Xiomara is home to New World cuisine, the sort of dishes found down in Miami at hot spots like Mark's Place and Chef Allen's. Oye! is where Xiomara serves a sort of Cuban-Asian amalgam that's not so odd when you consider that Cuba has long had a sizable Asian population. Oye! translates as "Listen!" So listen: It's well worth trying. Go here for Peruvian *jalea* (marinated, breaded, deep-fried seafood), *churrasco anticucho* (pesto-flavored skewered skirt steak) with sweet-potato fries, Ecuadorian ceviche (rock shrimp, scallops, and avocado), traditional Galician appetizers (cured Spanish ham, wonderfully dry manchego cheese, cantimpalo sausage), pork-filled wonton taquitos with a snappy chipotle dip, and warm duck salad with what has to be the world's only Key lime–hoisin dressing. There's nothing quite like the place. *$$; AE, MC, V; no checks; lunch Mon–Fri, dinner every day; full bar; reservations recommended; west side of Raymond Ave north of Colorado Blvd.* ໄ

Yang Chow / ★★

3777 E COLORADO BLVD, PASADENA (AND BRANCHES); 626/432-6868
Yang Chow has long been the place to go for well-nigh perfect versions of the Top 100 Chinese dishes. Although the menu does offer sea cucumber (served with either brown sauce or shrimp eggs), generally you won't find the sort of dishes that only restaurant critics trying to prove how cool they are order. This is the sort of place to go for a Platonically perfect experience. No meal should be embarked upon without orders of spicy Szechwan wontons, which are soft and hot-sweet in a broth the color of a fire engine; cold noodles tossed with shredded chicken and warm-cool sesame sauce; steamed pork dumplings; hot and sour soup; or the dish that most people think of when Yang Chow comes up in conversation—the slippery shrimp. It's a wonderful dish—plump shrimp in a crisp batter under a sweet-sour-hot sauce. One bite and you're hooked. The restaurant's two other locations (819 N Broadway Avenue, Los

Angeles; 213/625-0811 and 6443 Topanga Canyon Boulevard, Woodland Hills; 818/347-2610) offer the same menu. *$; AE, MC, V; no checks; lunch, dinner every day; beer and wine; reservations recommended; north side of Colorado Blvd east of Rosemead Blvd.*

Yujean Kang's / ★★★

67 N RAYMOND AVE, OLD TOWN PASADENA; 626/585-0855
8826 ROBERTSON BLVD, WEST HOLLYWOOD; 310/288-0806

There's a subtlety to Yujean Kang's cooking that one needs to be prepared for. It's quintessentially understated—so much so that it's hard to say whether the food is Chinese or Kangian. His menu changes with clockwork regularity, for there is a restless imagination at work here. Typical of his twists are his Chinese dumplings with hot chili oil, tiny, perhaps a quarter the size of the normal model—a bit like gnocchi filled with minced pork and garlic chives. Kang is fond of sweetness, a trait found in appetizers like the catfish with kumquats and passion fruit. Tender and moist, elegantly swimming in a stream of kumquats, silver sprouts, red and green bell peppers, and chiles, it's a catfish dish for people who never knew they liked catfish. The soup called Pictures in the Snow is a brown stock with julienne of chicken, ham, and mushrooms, and a floating island depicting a scene created out of vegetable bits. Additional offerings might include beef with oyster mushrooms, chicken with glazed cashew nuts, Santa Barbara prawns in a green herb sauce, salmon sautéed with garlic chives, and tea-smoked duck. Whatever is on the menu, this is very impressive, very personal cooking, and like nothing we've had before. *$$; AE, MC, V; no checks; lunch, dinner every day; beer and wine; reservations required; west side of Raymond Ave north of Colorado Blvd.* &

LODGINGS

Artists' Inn and Cottage Bed and Breakfast / ★★★

1038 MAGNOLIA ST, SOUTH PASADENA; 626/799-5668 OR 888/799-5668

Interior designer Janet Marangi acquired this 1895 Victorian farmhouse, originally owned by C. R. Johnson, in 1989, and she has restored it in a style that would make Old Man Johnson proud. A flourishing rose garden and white picket fence surround what is clearly the most handsome home on the quiet residential street. The public rooms are adorned with choice antiques, original art, rich fabrics, and luxurious Oriental rugs. The nine guest rooms, each with its own bathroom and air conditioner, were inspired by different artists or art periods: Van Gogh, Expressionist, Italian Suite, Gauguin, Degas, Impressionist, 18th-Century English, Georgia O'Keefe, and Grandma Moses. The comfy, artsy rooms may be inviting, but that doesn't dissuade guests from heading to the dining room each morning for a fabulous breakfast spread, including fresh fruits, homemade muffins, waffles, pancakes, eggs Benedict, and cappuccinos. On a sunny Southern California day, breakfast or tea on the inn's old-fashioned porch overlooking the blooming rose garden will make you feel right out of the pages of *Martha Stewart Living*. *$$; MC, V; no checks; artistsinn@artistsinn.com; www.artistsinn.com; west of Fair Oaks Ave and north of Mission St.*

The Bissell House Bed & Breakfast / ★★★

201 ORANGE GROVE AVE, SOUTH PASADENA; 626/441-3535
It's not a far stretch to fantasize you're visiting your millionaire socialite friend at this Victorian mansion on Pasadena's Millionaire's Row. The former home of Anna Bissell McCay (as in Bissell vacuums), this B&B is set on a half-acre lot surrounded by 40-foot hedges designed to keep the noise from busy Orange Grove Avenue to a minimum. Owners Russell and Leonore Butcher and their dog, Domino, actually reside at this 1887 Historical Landmark and are on hand to help prepare homemade breakfasts on the weekend and an extended continental breakfast on weekdays. The property's trellised grounds and sweeping porch are alluring, but it is the Bissell House's elegant interior, with mahogany flooring and lushly appointed antique-filled rooms, that makes the quaint inn seem straight out of a different era. Each of the five guest rooms is individually decorated with an English flair and has its own bathroom and individual heating and air-conditioning. The Garden Room is utterly romantic, with an antique hand-carved queen-size bed, floral chintz decor, and a Jacuzzi for two. The Morning Glory, decorated in china blue and white, and The Prince Albert Room, with its double corner leaded glass window, have bathrooms that beckon for a bubble bath in their claw-footed tubs. Gable ceilings and tall windows that look out onto the exclusive neighborhood make the Rose Room an ideal spot for snuggling up with a good book. Afternoon tea and evening refreshments are served each day in the inn's parlor. A small unheated pool and spa just behind the house welcome guests to take a dip. *$$; AE, MC, V; no checks; southeast corner of Orange Grove Ave and Columbia St.*

Pasadena Hilton / ★★

150 S LOS ROBLES AVE, PASADENA; 626/577-1000 OR 800/HILTONS
This Pasadena hostelry may be a Hilton, but its upscale interior design is more reminiscent of an Ethan Allen showroom than a standardized mega-chain hotel. From the stylish lobby with its glistening marble floors, slipcovered couches, and antique hutch, to the well-appointed rooms—decorated in soft blues and greens—with minibars, coffeemakers, and dataports, it does its best to be anything but generic. Located in an office-tower complex across from the Pasadena Convention Center, and close to the Rose Bowl, the 14-story, 291-room lodging often

doubles as home-away-from-home for both business travelers and traveling sports teams. If you're not lucky enough to score a ticket to the big game, the hotel's woodsy Sports Edition pub is a prime spot to watch sporting events and swill a beer or two. Trevos Restaurant, a combination hotel coffee shop/Mediterranean-style eatery, offers a breakfast and lunch buffet, as well as salads, pastas, sandwiches, and pizzas. *$$; AE, DC, DIS, JCB, MC, V; checks OK; www.hilton.com; south of Colorado Blvd.*

The Pasadena Hotel Bed & Breakfast / ★★

76 N FAIR OAKS AVE, PASADENA; 626/793-9313 OR 800/OLD-8886
Set in the heart of Old Town, this historic bed-and-breakfast inn is only about a hundred steps from such shops and restaurants as J. Crew, Pottery Barn, the Cheesecake Factory, and Mi Piace, but it's so enticing that most guests prefer to hang out and enjoy the antique-filled surroundings. One of the oldest hotels in Pasadena, it was restored in 1994. Though skylights were added to its 12 Edwardian-inspired rooms, great care was taken to preserve the alluring architectural features that make the historic property—well, historic. Such modern-day amenities as central air-conditioning and color TVs bring it up-to-date, but not entirely—some guest rooms still share bathrooms, with five spacious period-style options that lack tubs but are well equipped with showers. Still, queen-size beds, antique furnishings, and turn-of-the-century decor create a comfortable setting, especially in the accommodations that overlook a European-style courtyard with an Italianate fountain. On occasion, traffic clamor and merriment from the nearby Old Town bars and restaurants can disrupt the hotel's tranquillity. A complimentary continental breakfast of fresh fruit and baked goods is offered each morning. *$$; AE, DIS, MC, V; no checks; pasadena@travelbase.com; www.travelbase.com/pasadenahotel; north of Colorado Blvd.*

The Ritz-Carlton Huntington Hotel & Spa / ★★★★

1401 S OAK KNOLL ST, PASADENA; 626/568-3900
Originally built in 1906, this Pasadena landmark is the most stunning and understated grand dame in the entire region, the kind of place where once you check in there's no reason to leave. But it hasn't always been such an alluring retreat. After a disastrous first season, the failing resort was purchased by railroad tycoon and art collector Henry Huntington, who turned the majestic property into an exclusive winter resort for elite East Coasters. During World War II, the gracious hotel was rented to the U.S. Army. In 1954 it became a Sheraton, but it was forced to close in 1985 because its aging fabrication didn't meet earthquake codes. Enter Ritz-Carlton Hotels, who purchased the run-down gem and spent two and a half years lovingly restoring the historic relic to its former glory. Reopened in 1991, the grand hotel sits on 23 acres and boasts 392 guest rooms, 26 suites, and 7 cottages. Although the renovation brought the

swanky resort into the '90s—adding such luxury hotel touches as spacious guest rooms with classical decor, elegant marble bathrooms, tennis courts, and a restored Olympic-size pool and spa—much attention was paid to preserving the property's original attributes. The hotel's rare covered picture bridge, with 40 paintings depicting California's most beautiful spots, has been restored; the alluring Horseshoe Garden and Japanese Garden have been replanted and landscaped to appear as they did during the resort's early years; and exquisite stained-glass windows that were once blacked out during the war have been refinished in the grand ballrooms. In 1997, the Huntington added a world-class spa, complete with 17 treatment rooms, a state-of-the-art fitness center featuring a virtual-reality Stairmaster and Lifecycle, a beauty and nail salon, and a spa boutique. The Ritz-Carlton Club offers guests private concierge levels on the 7th and 8th floors, with complimentary snacks and libations throughout the day and an attentive staff to fawn over their every need. The elegant Grill restaurant serves food as refined as its setting. The Terrace, overlooking the pool area, serves casual California cuisine, including a champagne buffet brunch on Sundays, and the Lobby Lounge offers afternoon tea Wednesday through Sunday. $$$$; AE, DC, DIS, JCB, MC, V; no checks; www.ritzcarlton.com; exit 210 Fwy at Lake Ave and proceed south until it turns to Oak Knoll St.

La Cañada/ Flintridge

Set on the northwestern edge of the San Gabriel Valley, this suburban neighborhood of rolling hills and rugged countryside is where avid equestrians reside on pastoral ranches and gardeners come to swoon over the utterly romantic and pastoral DESCANSO GARDENS (1418 Descanso Drive; 818/952-4400). The stately 165-acre property features a California live oak forest—with an abundance of camellias and azaleas—that's straight out of A Midsummer Night's Dream, plus elaborate rose gardens, an iris garden, lilac garden, Japanese tea garden, art gallery, gift shop, cafe, and picnic area.

San Marino

Founded in the early 1900s by railroad tycoon and art collector Henry Huntington, this exclusive neighborhood is the land of debutantes and bluebloods, with enough palatial estates to fill the pages of Architectural Digest well into the new millennium. You could easily spend the day just driving around looking at fabulous homes, but make a point of stopping at THE HUNTINGTON LIBRARY, ART COLLECTION, AND BOTANICAL GARDENS (1151 Oxford Rd; 626/405-2100). Its more than 130 acres of beautifully landscaped grounds on the former estate of the city's founder are considered one of Los Angeles County's finest outdoor treasures. The library also boasts an impressive collection of rare books and artworks, including a Gutenberg Bible and Gainsborough's *Blue Boy*.

RESTAURANTS

Julienne / ★★☆

2649 MISSION ST, SAN MARINO; 626/441-2299

Julienne is where affluent San Marino goes to eat out casually, for this is a major destination for that wondrous breed known as the ladies who lunch. It's a fine place—warm and cozy with really terrific food. And you can sit outdoors and watch (to quote T. S. Eliot), "The women come and go/Talking of Michelangelo." There are actually two parts to Julienne: the cafe, with its cool, calm interior and its exceedingly pleasant sidewalk dining area, and the cuisine-to-go shop. As you might expect at a major watering hole for the lunching ladies, *les salades* abound—baby greens topped with warmed cornmeal-encrusted chèvre and herbed croutons, salade niçoise with seared ahi, caesar Julienne tossed with rosemary-spiked croutons and grilled chicken breast, garden greens with sautéed crab cakes and a marjoram–red pepper marmalade, and an array of other upscale combinations. There are also combos of soup and salad, quiche and salad, or half sandwich and salad, as well as a renegade sandwich of tarragon chicken salad on rosemary raisin bread. Unfortunately, Julienne is open only for breakfast and lunch, which is a pity, for this would be a nifty spot to go for dinner on a warm summer's evening. *$; AE, MC, V; checks OK; breakfast and lunch Mon–Sat; no alcohol; reservations required; north side of Mission St near El Molino.* &

San Gabriel

One of the San Gabriel Valley's oldest cities, this largely Hispanic neighborhood is the home of the **MISSION SAN GABRIEL ARCHANGEL** (428 S Mission Drive; 626/457-3035). Founded in 1771 on a spot intersected by three heavily trafficked trails leading new settlers into California, the mission was once one of the state's wealthiest, featuring a copper baptismal font that was a gift from the King of Spain. Though it has suffered extensive earthquake damage over the years and even had to close for a time because its structure was deemed unsafe, restorations have allowed it to reopen to the public for self-guided tours, guided tours by appointment, and mass twice daily on Sunday.

RESTAURANTS

El Emperador Maya / ★★

1823 S SAN GABRIEL BLVD, SAN GABRIEL; 626/288-7265

That the cooking of Mexico can be hot is a given. But that the cooking of the Yucatan may produce the most complex hot dishes in an already overheated cuisine is a difficult matter to debate; there are simply too few Yucatecan restaurants around for proper research. El Emperador Maya is the best of our few Yucatecan eateries, a shrine to one of the finest indigenous cuisines to be found in the Americas, and a hotbed of hot. The chef contends that his *biftek con patas* is his hottest dish, flavored with a rich sauté of chiles, garlic, tomatoes, onions, cloves, cumin, and epazote (a pungent wild herb). But we like the sizzle in the *cochinito pibil,* an

ancient Mayan dish of pork steamed in banana leaves (originally the leaves were placed in a *pib,* the Mayan word for "pit"), flavored with onions, garlic, many chiles, achiote, tomatoes, and more. If you want to reach something akin to a nirvana of hot, ask for a side order of chile habanero, which is bound to fry your poor palate to cinders. In this case, the drink of choice is *horchata,* a beverage that tastes amazingly like liquid rice pudding and stands as the perfect antidote to too much capsaicin. For dessert, there are two of the best flans in town, one plain, the other banana-flavored, each a further soothing emollient for the agonies of the tummy. *$; AE, MC, V; lunch Tues–Fri, dinner Tues–Sun; beer only; reservations recommended; west side of San Gabriel Blvd, north of 210 Fwy.*

Tung Lai Shun Islamic Restaurant / ★★

140 W VALLEY BLVD, SAN GABRIEL; 626/288-6588

Tung Lai Shun is a large, handsome restaurant on the ground floor of sprawling San Gabriel Square Shopping Center (a.k.a. the Great Mall of China) that serves the kind of cooking you'd find in the Islamic Chinese restaurants of Hong Kong and Taipei. That cuisine is marked by a love of breads, dumplings, lamb, mutton, and spices, so it's not surprising to

find wonderful boiled lamb dumplings on the menu here, along with lamb pancakes, hot pots of lamb and pickled cabbage, soup of lamb and cabbage and mutton haslet (read: innards), more cold and hot lamb dishes, and Beijing-style ox tongue. (Because it's an Islamic restaurant, you'll notice there's no pork on the menu.) Otherwise, the five-spice eggplant is spiced enough to raise a bit of a sweat on your upper lip and the noodle dishes are more than sufficient for a main course. One item everyone orders is the sesame bread, served plain or, better yet, stuffed with scallions. This massive plate of soft bread that's steamed, then baked, and topped with lots of sesame seeds can suffice as a meal in itself. You can, however, order a half portion, which is enough for four. *$; AE,*

MC, V; no checks; lunch, dinner every day; no alcohol; reservations not necessary; southwest corner of Del Mar and Valley Blvd.

Monterey Park

RESTAURANTS

Harbor Village / ★★

111 N ATLANTIC BLVD, MONTEREY PARK; 626/300-8833

Conventional wisdom has it that you may find better Cantonese seafood next door at Ocean Star, but that the dim sum is better at Harbor Village. Harbor Village is the Southern California branch of a hugely successful Hong Kong restaurant. And when it comes to dim sum, this is among the best dim sum–eries in town. Service here is done in the Hong Kong fashion: if you want something, you have to flag down one of the many dim sum ladies—and then fend her off as she tries to turn your request for one or two items into a dozen. (Are the dim sum ladies working on commission?) As you order, the bill on your table is stamped (the tradition of counting dishes has begun to vanish), with a mark placed next to each item ordered, ranging from $1.50 a plate up to $3 a plate. The sweet roast pork filling in the steamed *cha siu bao* is rich with flavor, sweet yet quite subtle. The shrimp *har gow* and *shui mai* (little pastry flowers stuffed with a variety of meats) are well-nigh perfect, presented hot in their little steamers. If you feel up to venturing off the well-beaten dumpling path, try the marinated octopus or the intensely crispy ribs—dim sum, and then some. *$; AE, MC, V; no checks; lunch, dinner every day; full bar; reservations recommended; northwest corner of Atlantic Blvd and Garvey Ave.* &

Lake Spring / ★★☆

219 E GARVEY AVE, MONTEREY PARK; 626/280-3571

Lake Spring is one of the few Shanghai-style restaurants this side of Hong Kong. The heavy, rich cooking of Shanghai stands in direct contrast to the lighter, simpler style found at most Cantonese eateries. One of the great delights of Shanghai cuisine is the hairy crabs that show up on the menu every autumn, filled with roe and served steamed, with ginger tea and vinegar sauce—a true delicacy. Shanghai cooking involves a lot of sauces—both a pungent red sauce, and an intense brown one, as well as soy sauce and sesame oil. The meat of choice here, visible on virtually every table, is pork, served as a large rump roast cooked long and slow in a sauce of soy and rock sugar. It's a wonderful creation, but one that tends to completely obliterate your ability to eat anything else on the menu as it could easily feed four. Much of the rest of the menu is pork-based as well: shrimp and shredded pork with bean curd soup; salted pork with bamboo shoot casserole; shredded dry bean cake and pork; pepper-seasoned pork chops; sweet-and-sour pork chops; and more. *$; AE, MC, V; no checks; lunch, dinner every day; beer only; reservations recommended; north side of Garvey Ave east of Atlantic Blvd.*

Ocean Star / ★★★

145 N ATLANTIC BLVD, MONTEREY PARK; 626/308-2128
The dominant Hong Kong–style seafood palace in the San Gabriel Valley rambles through a series of large rooms, which can be reconfigured to hold parties of various sizes. On a good evening the main dining room is full, offering the opportunity to watch dozens of family groups convene for a fine feed of fresh-from-the-tanks lobster, crab, shrimp, abalone, oysters, clams, and a wide assortment of still-twitching fish. If there's a special on the lobster, by all means order it—"special" usually means half price. The deal often extends to shrimp as well, and there's hardly anything better than a platter of flamingo pink shrimp fresh from the wok, lightly flavored with garlic. Pan-fried oysters with spicy salt are also remarkable; their crisp salty crust crackles when you bite into it. But don't just stick to the menu. Check out what others are eating and you might see unlisted dishes like stir-fried pea vines, one of the great vegetables of the world. If you're lucky enough to be here when a wedding is going on, you'll be entertained by guests who, after downing a bottle of Chivas Regal that they've brought in, head for the mike to serenade the bride and groom with Cantonese love songs. *$$; AE, MC, V; no checks; lunch, dinner every day; beer and wine only; reservations required; northwest corner of Atlantic and Garvey.* &

Pico Rivera

RESTAURANTS

Dal Rae Steak House / ★★

9023 E WASHINGTON BLVD, PICO RIVERA; 562/949-2444
At this grand old steak house from the early '50s in the wilds of Pico Rivera, they still make dishes that have long vanished most everywhere else—spinach salad tossed at your table, lobster Thermidor, even chicken under glass. Here you'll find a virtual Smithsonian of cuisine, a taste of how it was and how it is again. The Dal Rae has been around since Dwight Eisenhower was in the White House, and it's one of the last bastions of real American cuisine. The pride of the house is their awesome pepper steak. Perhaps the best anywhere, it can easily feed two, with enough left over for lunch the next day. It's a huge chunk of seared cow, covered with peppercorns cut so roughly they're little more than chopped in half. At the start of the meal, there's a relish tray, and at the end there

are desserts made tableside (yes, including cherries jubilee). *$$; AE, MC, V; checks OK; lunch Mon–Fri, dinner every day; full bar; reservations recommended; north side of Washington Blvd at Rosemead.* &

Arcadia

Established around the turn of the century as the personal utopia of millionaire "Lucky" Baldwin, Arcadia is today publicized by the local chamber of commerce as "the community of homes." But this quiet residential neighborhood offers more than just tree-lined streets rife with sprawling ranch-style homes.

RESTAURANTS

The Derby / ★★

233 E HUNTINGTON DR, ARCADIA; 626/447-8173
545 W ALOSTA AVE, GLENDORA; 626/914-2977
This legendary steak and chop joint has been feeding racing aficionados for close to three quarters of a century—no small accomplishment in a land where after ten years a restaurant is considered a venerable institution. But then, as a booklet available near the entrance says, "The Derby is not one of the best because we are the oldest, we are the oldest because we are the best." A restaurant that resolutely and enthusiastically embraces the past, it's a place where you can order a Gibson or a Negroni without getting a funny look from your waiter, and where men and women drink spirits and eat meat with no need to apologize for either. The dish of choice here is the "Odds-On Favorite . . . The Derby's Famed . . . Bacon Wrapped Filet Mignon." And for good reason—it's a lovely hunk o' meat, tender as a filet should be, girdled with a belt of thick bacon that keeps the beef from drying out while giving it a rather rakish flavor. It can, and should, be preceded by the thickly cheesed onion soup, and garlic bread that adds a touch of heady exotica to the whole evening. An additional location is in Glendora. *$$; AE, MC, V; no checks; lunch, Mon–Sat, dinner every day; full bar; reservations recommended; across from Santa Anita Racetrack.* &

LODGINGS

The Santa Anita Inn / ★★

130 W HUNTINGTON DR, ARCADIA; 626/446-5211 OR 888/584-7068

The 5½-acre grounds surrounding this rambling two-story inn are lush and wonderfully pastoral—enough so that it's easy to forget that Santa Anita Racetrack is across the street. Rose gardens, Italian fountains, waterfalls cascading into rocky grottoes, stately trees that change colors with the seasons, and perfectly manicured lawns also make it easy to forget that the peaceful inn is situated right off busy Huntington Drive. The large and elegant rooms, most of which face away from the street traffic noise, are casually decorated with European furnishings such as sturdy armoires and brass beds, fireplaces, and fabric-covered valances. Curiously, racetrack photos in some rooms go a long way toward canceling the overall charm. However, judging from the number of horse trailers in the hotel parking lot, this inn does attract an equestrian crowd. Guests have free run of the grounds, including an outdoor heated pool and a Jacuzzi, which are surrounded by giant rocks with cascading waters. Friendly staffers at the front desk are happy to direct you to nearby eateries. The inn's Finish Line Restaurant opens only for banquets and weddings. *$; AE, DC, DIS, MC, V; no checks; across from the main entrance to Santa Anita Racetrack.*

Monrovia

RESTAURANTS

Devon / ★★★

109 E LEMON AVE, MONROVIA; 626/305-0013

Devon is what local critics like to call "a Westside restaurant," working under the false assumption that only the residents of Brentwood and Beverly Hills can be counted on to eat ostrich carpaccio for dinner. But Devon is powerful proof that chèvre is no longer haute. The restaurant, a pair of storefronts with a few tables on the sidewalk and a glassed-in wine cellar off to one side of the single dining room, sits on quiet Lemon Avenue in the heart of historic downtown Monrovia. The menu changes with the seasons, but the casual California vibe is always the same. Since eating light is one of the hallmarks of California cuisine, it's easy to eat much and feel largely guilt-free here—from the sweet acidity of a marvelously intense tomato cappuccino soup (tomato and basil topped with foamed milk) or the happy crunch of the shrimp-and-shiitake-filled spring rolls or the goat cheese–layered wontons to some delicious sea scallops and shrimp in a tempura batter so light it couldn't possibly be fattening. The sweet orange cake finishes things off just right. There's rarely an empty seat at Devon—Monrovia has a healthy respect for this place. *$$; AE, MC, V; checks OK; lunch Tues–Fri, dinner Tues–Sat; beer and wine; reservations required; north side of Lemon Ave just east of Myrtle Ave.*

La Parisienne / ★★

1101 E HUNTINGTON DR, MONROVIA; 626/357-3359
A friendly, homey place, La Parisienne is a genuine institution. Once you leave the traffic and mini-malls of Huntington Drive and enter the fine old wood-lined room, with flowers and French fabrics, it's not hard to believe after a glass or two of wine that you're in Lyon, eating at a pleasant little brasserie. Fare is both French classic and new at the same time. The right dishes are all here—*escargots, moules marinières, terrine de canard au foie gras, soupe a l'oignon gratinée, canard a l'orange, bouillabaisse.* But in most cases, they've been reexamined, rethought, and neatly freshened up. Snails are simply a treat, richly flavored with garlic, parsley, and herb butter; mussels are perfectly cooked with shallots, parsley, white wine, and cream; salmon Alexandra (stuffed with minced seafood and topped with an infinitely delicate shallot-butter sauce) is a signature dish, the sort of creation that tastes fresh and new every time you order it. *$$; AE, MC, V; checks OK; lunch Mon–Fri, dinner Mon–Sat; full bar; reservations required; north side of Huntington Dr at Mountain Ave.*

LODGINGS

Aztec Hotel / ★

311 W FOOTHILL BLVD, MONROVIA; 626/358-3231
Built in the early 1900s, this funky Historic Landmark hotel is hard to miss with its stucco facade adorned with Aztec relief designs. Inside, the lobby is equally eclectic, with Aztec-inspired murals and a smattering of vintage collectibles, including an antique gas pump, an archaic Coke machine, a tobacco-store Indian who greets guests at the reception desk, and old-fashioned barbershop chairs. The hotel's 38 rooms vary in size and are sparsely decorated with musty vintage furnishings, which aren't impressive but complement the overall ambience in a Route 66–kitschy-charming kind of way. For those who get attached to this earthy lodging, eight apartments in back are rentable for long-term stays. Just off the lobby, the Brass Elephant restaurant is more like a dimly lit roadhouse (after all, Foothill Boulevard used to be Route 66), where locals drink long-neck beers and shoot pool. In addition to cocktails, the Brass Elephant grills burgers, steaks, and chicken. *$; no credit cards; no checks; at Magnolia Ave.*

Duarte

LODGINGS

White Horse Estate Bed and Breakfast Inn / ★★☆

330 LAS LOMAS ROAD, DUARTE; 626/358-0798 OR 800/653-8886
Ranch-style gates emblazoned with white horses lead the way to this Queen Anne–style inn set amidst an acre of gardens on a quiet residential street in the Duarte foothills. Once the home of the Maddock ranching family, the turn-of-the-century house was restored and converted into a five-room bed and breakfast in 1994. Today, fancifully filled with Victorian antiques and period furnishings, it offers a quiet, easily accessible country getaway. Accommodations include the Bridal Room, with a fireplace, a cozy sitting room, and an antique vanity that's perfect for primping brides on their way to take the plunge; the Honeymoon Suite, located in an octagonal tower and featuring a claw-footed bathtub for a little post-nuptial soaking; the Rose Room, decorated with floral designs and offering views of the garden; the Garden Room, with hand-painted floors, a personal library (including an impressive Victor Hugo collection), and a balcony overlooking the inn's vast grounds; and the Celestial Room, an almost-spiritual retreat decorated with cherubs. Central air-conditioning and a private bathroom in each room make a stay here that much more soothing. Mornings begin with a hearty complimentary breakfast, which includes home-baked goods, fruit, and egg dishes, served in the formal dining room or on the sunny glass-enclosed veranda. Afternoons are passed with a leisurely complimentary tea service. *$$; AE, DIS, MC, V; no checks; pasadena@travelbase.com; www.citycent.com/whitehorse; just north of Huntington Dr near the junction of the 605 and 210 Fwys.*

Covina

RESTAURANTS

Hayakawa / ★★★

750 TERRADO PLAZA, COVINA; 626/332-8288
Hayakawa sits in the Terrado Plaza mini-mall, just a short distance north of the San Bernardino Freeway. It has that generic sushi-bar look—which is to say it's neat as a pin, with tables for those who want to sit at tables and a sushi bar for those who like their food participatory. But behind the bar chef Kazu Hayakawa does his masterful work, creating sushi at a slow, steady pace, the way the best sushi chefs always do. At first glance, this may appear to be a fairly standard issue Japanese restaurant, with

beef and chicken teriyaki and vegetable and shrimp tempura for those who think raw fish is a curious and potentially deadly aberration. But a quick glance at both the à la carte menu and the daily special menu gives the sense that something else is going on here. Along with old favorites like tuna, yellowtail, salmon, and whitefish are more rarefied sushi dishes like *kohada*, red clam, *toro*, and *kampachi*. Then there are simple pleasures of deep-fried soft-shell crab in a spicy garlic sauce, snow crab in a spicy cream sauce, broiled black cod with miso, and monkfish pâté topped with freshwater caviar. You might want to simply order the *omakase*, the chef's choice, which begins at $45 and works its way up from there. At Hayakawa, it's sure to be good. *$$; AE, MC, V; no checks; lunch Tues–Fri, dinner Tues–Sun; beer and wine; reservations required; east side of Citrus Ave north of the 10 Fwy.*

San Dimas

Some movie buffs might remember San Dimas as the hometown of the two goofy stars of *Bill and Ted's Excellent Adventure* but most outsiders think of this suburban community as the home of **RAGING WATERS** (111 Raging Waters Drive; 909/802-2200), a 50-acre aquatic park complete with water slides, activities pools, and artificial beaches. With one of the country's longest man-made rivers and one of the tallest vertical-drop water slides among its features, this busy attraction draws busloads of teenagers looking for a diversion from the malls and the beach. Raging Waters has seasonal hours, so call before you head to this fun waterworld.

Pomona

Pomona is best known as the home of the Los Angeles County Fairgrounds (1101 W McKinley Avenue; 909/623-3111), which hosts the **LA COUNTY FAIR** every September as well as computer shows, auto races, and business expos throughout the year. Downtown Pomona has been undergoing an extensive renovation and, though the neighborhood remains lacking, its **ANTIQUE ROW** (south of the 10 Freeway approximately 2 miles from the Garey Avenue exit) is lined with vintage shops and surplus stores full of undiscovered treasures.

LODGINGS

Sheraton Suites Fairplex / ★★☆

601 W MCKINLEY AVE, POMONA; 909/622-2220 OR 800/325-3535
From families planning to spend the day at the Los Angeles County Fair
to businesspeople participating in trade shows at the Fairplex Exposition
Complex, this 247-suite hotel was created for those attending events at
the Fairgrounds. Actually located within the 487-acre fairgrounds site,
the eight-story hotel includes many of the amenities of home in each of
its spacious guest rooms, including a separate living room, refrigerator,
microwave, coffeemaker, and iron with full-size ironing board. Traveling
businesspeople appreciate modem hookups and voice-mail messaging.
The lobby is generically decorated in varying shades of mauve. Massive
conference and banquet space is available just about everywhere you
turn. A heated outdoor pool gives kids a place to splash around and
mellow out after the excitement of a day at the fair, while parents and
business travelers can unwind in the poolside Jacuzzi, the sauna, or the
small fitness center. The hotel's Brass Ring restaurant is more of an
upscale coffee shop, serving sandwiches and salads. Guests can enjoy a
drink and munch on such bar food as nachos and chicken wings while
they watch the game on overhead televisions in Banners Pub, located just
off the lobby. *$$; AE, DC, DIS, MC, V; checks OK; www.sheraton.com;
exit 10 Fwy at Fairplex Dr and go north to McKinley Ave.*

Claremont

Set against the dramatic backdrop of the San Gabriel Mountains, this
quaint little town possesses an East Coast charm. Students at the six pres-
tigious **CLAREMONT COLLEGES** (Pomona College, Claremont Graduate
School, Scripps College, Claremont McKenna College, Harvey Mudd
College, and Pitzer College) make up a good percentage of the town's
population, but generations of families also call this tight-knit commu-
nity of Victorian homes and peaceful wide streets home. Claremont's old-
fashioned downtown, dubbed **THE VILLAGE** (between First and Fourth
Streets and Yale and Harvard Avenues), is a fun place to window shop,
with clothing boutiques, art galleries, and antique stores. While yuppies
with strollers wander past The Village's sidewalk cafes, neighborhood
coffeehouses are filled with caffeinated students working on laptops.
Gardening enthusiasts will enjoy a day at the **RANCHO SANTA ANA
BOTANIC GARDENS** (1500 N College Avenue; 909/625-8767), which is
dedicated to native California plants and flowers. Amidst its 82 acres,
gardens are broken down into three areas: Indian Hill Mesa, a flat-topped
hill featuring wild lilacs, desert manzanitas, and California cultivars; East

Alluvial Gardens, featuring plants native to California deserts, the garden's largest oak tree, a fan palm oasis, and plants indigenous to the Channel Islands; and Plant Communities, filled with plant life from Baja and the Mojave Desert, Joshua trees, oak woodlands, and chaparral. Visit from February through June when the gardens are in bloom.

RESTAURANTS

Aruffo's Italian Cuisine / ★★

126 YALE AVE, CLAREMONT; 909/949-8426

Vintage posters, wine displays, an exposed brick wall adorned with delicately painted cherubs, and fresh flower arrangements create an elegant atmosphere at this charming trattoria featuring owner/chef Tom Aruffo's traditional Italian fare. Homey classics such as creamy fettuccine alfredo, house-made spinach-and-egg tortellini stuffed with veal and Parmigiano cheese, and buttery scampi are as authentic as they come. The hearty eggplant lasagne—generously layered with rich ricotta, mozzarella, thinly sliced breaded eggplant, noodles, and homemade marinara sauce topped with steamed asparagus and squash—is a fresh spin on the traditional Italian favorite. A tender breast of fragrant rosemary chicken and a charbroiled New York sirloin steak with mushrooms, Marsala, prosciutto, and melted mozzarella are also pleasingly straightforward and well prepared. Pastas and entrees come with either soup or salad and homemade garlic bread, which arrives piping hot and topped with a dollop of fresh tomato sauce. Save room for the creamy tiramisu; it's worth every calorie. *$$; AE, MC, V; no checks; lunch, dinner every day; full bar; reservations recommended; north of 1st St.* &

Harvard Square Cafe / ★★

206 W BONITA AVE, CLAREMONT; 909/626-7763

Housed in the former home of Claremont's historic Village Theatre, this casual bistro-style eatery attracts everyone from college professors and students to the ladies who stop in for lunch after browsing the nearby antique and collectibles boutiques. Lace curtains and dark woods add a relaxed charm to the interior of this cozy eatery, but the spacious outdoor patio is a popular spot to linger and people-watch on a sunny Southern California day or indulge in Sunday brunch. Though the restaurant's lunch menu sticks to basic California cuisine such as salads, sandwiches, pasta, and pizza, dinner selections have a decidedly French (and more caloric) overtone. The way to go here is to start with the garlicky escargots bourguignon or the rich lobster crepes topped with a creamy hollandaise sauce and nestled in a bed of flavorful lobster sauce, and then follow up with grilled lamb cutlets with Provençal herbs and roasted garlic sauce or filet au poivre, a tender piece of beef sautéed with cracked black pepper, flambéed with brandy, and laced with cream. The newly expanded wine cellar seems a little overpriced, but it does contain more than 40 vintages ranging from Australia, German, and French wines to those from Central and Northern California. *$$$; AE, MC, V; no checks; lunch Mon–Sat, dinner every day, brunch Sun; full bar; reservations recommended; at Harvard Ave.*

Heroes Bar and Grill / ★

131 YALE AVE, CLAREMONT; 909/621-6712

Like "Cheers," this friendly neighborhood pub is the kind of place where everybody knows your name. Or at least they will by the time you're seated for dinner, since the wait for a table at this charming little eatery on weekend nights has been known to last an hour. Once you've put your name on the list, the order of business is to belly up to the bar and sample one of 46 beers on tap, which include Portland Honey Ale and Belgium Double Bach. Some choose to sample bar food—such as zesty chicken wings and nachos with all the fixings, but it's recommended that you save room for Heroes' generous-sized entrees, which arrive on enormous plates that dominate every dinner table. Beef stroganoff perched on a creamy bed of mashed potatoes is comfort food at its most comfortable, and the whiskey chicken with apple-walnut stuffing, rice pilaf, and fresh vegetables is a carbo-loader's dream. Steak lovers will appreciate the tender New York steak served with a baked potato stuffed with sour cream and chives. For those with less-hearty appetites, juicy burgers served with baskets full of crisp curly fries and a tender chicken sandwich with jalapeño cheese and avocados are about as light as it gets here. *$$; AE, MC, V; no checks; lunch, dinner every day; full bar; reservations not accepted; north of 1st St.* &

LODGINGS

The Claremont Inn

555 W FOOTHILL BLVD, CLAREMONT; 909/626-2411

This nondescript inn looks rather like a 1970 condo complex, where several brown three-story wings linked by cement walkways all lead to a clover-shaped swimming pool and tiny spa in the center of the grounds. However, what the Claremont Inn lacks in character it makes up for with location, as it's within easy walking distance of the ivy-covered Claremont Colleges and The Village. Though they're dated, the simply decorated guest rooms are immaculately kept, and most offer a patio or a veranda. In keeping with the inn's trapped-in-a-different-era vibe, it's affiliated with the adjacent Candlelight Pavilion Dinner Theater, perhaps one of the few dinner-and-a-Broadway-show venues left west of Branson, Missouri. The Bakery Café, located just across the front parking lot, serves a daily breakfast buffet, sandwiches, and average coffee-shop fare. The Bar & Grill opens for dinner and drinks, serving chicken, steaks, and sandwiches. Complimentary shuttle service is provided from the Ontario Airport. *$$; AE, DC, DIS, MC, V; checks OK; exit 10 Fwy at Indian Hill Blvd, go north to Foothill Blvd and turn left.*

The South Beaches

Strung along Los Angeles county's southern shores, in the figurative shadow of the "Big City," several disparate communities provide a haven for urban escapees who eschew L.A. proper. Each community has developed a distinct personality, especially the three beach towns collectively known as the South Bay (Manhattan Beach, Hermosa Beach, and Redondo Beach). Daily life revolves around the ocean, pleasant weather, and sparse parking, which has led to a laid-back walking-bicycling tradition. As Santa Monica Bay curves into its southern crescent, the Palos Verdes peninsula looms tall over the ocean. Once literally an island, "P.V." is now only figuratively one—a hard-to-reach enclave of affluent neighborhoods and breathtaking coastline. Past the peninsula, sandwiched around the enormous Port of Los Angeles, you'll find blue-collar, industrial San Pedro, and adjacent Long Beach, where harborside attractions and an almost Midwestern sensibility contrast sharply with cosmopolitan Los Angeles. Then there's Santa Catalina Island, an idyllic and cozy offshore retreat often compared to Mediterranean jewels like Capri and Malta.

Playa del Rey

Tucked away on the far side of Marina del Rey, the tiny bedroom community of Playa del Rey might have surprised the unfortunate speculators who attempted at the end of the 19th century to turn the tiny lagoon into a full-blown tourist attraction. Between 1887 and 1917, an Asian-style entertainment pavilion, the 50-room Del Rey Hotel, an elegant boathouse, and grandstand seating for boat-race audiences all fell victim to wicked tides and furious storms that conspired to return the lagoon to marshland. Today's beachy cottages and ocean-view condos are built only on solid land, and the murky Ballona wetlands that isolate Playa del Rey from the ultra-developed Marina del Rey to the north are now a protected **BIRD SANCTUARY**. The neighborhood is funky and unspoiled, despite the inevitable higher rents that ocean-front real estate brings. There's not much to attract outsiders, but enough to ensure that PDR locals don't have to venture far from their "village" unless they want to.

RESTAURANTS

Caffe Pinguini / ★★☆

6935 PACIFIC AVE, PLAYA DEL REY; 310/306-0117

This small, nearly invisible trattoria might be the least obvious of Playa del Rey's assortment of taverns and comfort food joints, but throngs of devotees fill the casually elegant dining room every night. There's a pleasant European feel to the place, from the brick and wood patio enclosed with enormous palm fronds to simply-set tables whose crisp linens are accented only by golden cruets of herb-infused olive oil in which to dip Pinguini's chewy, addictive bread. The strains of vintage jazz and classic crooners waft gently throughout the restaurant, which is nearly the last building before the sea and thus immune from traffic noise. The menu is simple, but you can count on a subtlety of preparation many overzealous trattorias miss. A crisp arugula and radicchio salad is dressed with just enough—but not too much—balsamic vinegar; perfectly thin pizzas aren't weighed down with too many ingredients; pasta is prepared *al dente* with unfussy and economically applied sauces; and even the delicately flavored grilled chicken or fish shines in its simplicity. You don't have to hear the owner's unmistakable Italian accent to know this is the genuine article. *$–$$; AE, MC, V; no checks; lunch Tues–Fri, dinner Tues–Sun; beer and wine; reservations recommended; at Culver Blvd.* &

LODGINGS

Inn at Playa del Rey / ★★☆

435 CULVER BLVD, PLAYA DEL REY; 310/574-1920

From its Cape Cod–style architecture to its location on the edge of the 350-acre Ballona Wetlands bird sanctuary, this 21-room B&B has a distinctly East Coast feel. Distressed wood furnishings and designer beds—four-posters or hand-painted antiques—give the artfully decorated rooms a country inn appeal, although bathrooms are notably modern, with shower tubs or Jacuzzis, and amenities such as voice mail and data-ports attest to the inn's popularity among savvy business travelers. Couples in search of romance should check into one of the intimate inn's spacious View Suites, overlooking the wetlands and nearby Marina del Rey. Their wrought-iron four-poster beds are seductive, but the romantic pièce de résistance is their two-sided fireplace, which warms the bedroom and casts a heavenly glow on the bathroom's Jacuzzi tub for two. Guests can also soak under the stars in the inn's garden hot tub out back. In the morning hours, the enticing aroma of gourmet coffees and homemade muffins and coffee cakes lures guests to a sunny nook with hardwood floors and a roaring fireplace, where baked goods, soufflés, made-to-order egg dishes, juices, and coffees await. The bright and airy living room—with its French doors opening out onto the wetlands—serves as the site for an afternoon toast at the inn's daily wine and cheese gathering. *$$–$$$$; AE, DIS, MC, V; checks OK; playainn@aol.com; www.innaccess.com/pdr/; south of Jefferson Blvd.* &

Manhattan Beach

In the early 1950s surfing's popularity crested with a group of local kids called the Beach Boys, who spent their days catching waves at Manhattan Beach and their nights recording what would become classic "surf music." Today the casual summer shacks that old-time surfers remember have been replaced with stellar ocean-view homes, and real estate prices edge steadily higher as the beach town takes on an upscale tone. **MANHATTAN STATE BEACH** is as popular as ever, a wide white swath bordered by the Strand, a broad paved path crowded with walkers and skaters, and a steep hillside of homes boasting breathtaking views. The surfing is some of the best in the county, and volleyball nets stretch as far as the eye can see. For more information, contact the **MANHATTAN BEACH CHAMBER OF COMMERCE** (425 15th Street; 310/545-5313) or log onto www.beach-web.com.

RESTAURANTS

Anacapa Restaurant / ★★☆

304 12TH ST, MANHATTAN BEACH; 310/546-4777
Named for one of the offshore Channel Islands, Anacapa, which launched in 1998, is the most refreshing and sophisticated restaurant to open here in a long time and reflects restaurateur Greg McNally's time spent honing his craft in San Francisco's competitive food scene. Sporting a low-key but chic decor of sisal flooring, sandy celadon walls, and warm, subdued lighting, the interior strives for a Key West ambience accented by weathered trunks, starfish, and faded nautical maps. Comfy wicker chairs fill a dining room enclosed by greenhouse windows that afford sunset views, and the menu features both New American dishes and compositions influenced by chef Jason Segal's island experience with Hawaiian Regional cuisine. Look for fresh fish specials—flown in daily from Hawaii—like *ono* (wahoo) prepared Pacific Rim–style with Thai sticky rice, black bean sauce, and fresh ginger. Ahi tuna gets two treatments, either blackened with pickled Napa cabbage and black bean–sesame vinaigrette, or barely seared and glazed with tangy soy mustard. High-quality filet mignon comes with fragrant thyme-cabernet sauce and creamy Gorgonzola potatoes, and the crab cake appetizer is

also a winner. Anacapa also earns kudos for its user-friendly wine list, organized by price and featuring expertly chosen bottles from California's underrated Central Coast. *$$; AE, DC, MC, V; no checks; dinner Tues–Sun, brunch Sun; full bar; reservations recommended; ½ block east of Highland Ave.* ♿

Cafe Pierre / ★☆

317 MANHATTAN BEACH BLVD, MANHATTAN BEACH; 310/545-5252

For years this small bistro has been considered one of the South Bay's premier dining spots, and crowds of locals reluctant to drive to L.A.'s Westside still fill the place every night of the week. Though no longer cutting-edge, the restaurant continues to hold its own within the context of this laid-back beach community, offering a smidgen of pretension along with its self-coined "Cali-Franco" cuisine. The decor is bright and brassy, with gold and copper tones and black lacquer tempered by a collection of Art Deco lithographs. Picture windows open onto the sidewalk scene along busy Manhattan Beach Boulevard, making the cafe less romantic than you might expect. Once seated, you can begin nibbling on marinated kalamata olives or a selection of fresh crusty bread with gourmet dipping oils. Cafe Pierre serves excellent martinis, especially those made with fruit-infused vodkas (watermelon, pineapple, or mango) from decorative jars adorning the bar. The restaurant also boasts a superior wine list. The menu, which combines straightforward bistro favorites with dishes given an eclectic fusion twist, makes for mouthwatering reading, but those in the know stick with reliable standards like roasted salmon atop fennel mashed potatoes crowned with a crispy potato bird's nest; or peppered filet mignon with either cognac or Roquefort sauce and accompanied by a mound of *pommes frites*. Linguine and risotto are both prepared with a medley of fresh seafood (baby octopus, rock shrimp, scallops, mussels, clams), and ahi tuna tartare joins a list of more traditional starters like escargots and French onion soup gratinée. *$$–$$$; AE, MC, V; no checks; lunch Mon–Fri, dinner every day; full bar; reservations recommended; ½ block east of Highland Ave.* ♿

Fonz's Restaurant / ★★

1017 MANHATTAN AVE, MANHATTAN BEACH; 310/376-1536

Opened in 1997 by renowned surfer and local hero Mike Dodd, this casual gourmet-tinged bistro is named in tribute to Dodd's dad, nicknamed "Fonz" for his retro 1950s hairstyle. Amidst a decor that blends richly sponge-painted walls and bright watercolors with tables dressed down by brown paper laid over white linen tablecloths, Dodd and his wife proudly but discreetly display family photos and mementos of athletic victories. Fonz, who passed away in 1994, was beloved for making the family home a welcome place for the kids and their friends, and the Dodds bring the same spirit to their restaurant, where even new customers are treated like expected friends. Long before any tables are filled, crowds have already gathered at the long bar that's separated from the dining room by a simple partition. The menu is strong on steaks and seafood, featuring the kind of hearty dinners you might get at your best friend's house—if their mom or dad had been perusing the latest foodie magazines. Seared Australian rack of lamb is soaked with rosemary garlic sauce, blackened swordfish is dressed with a delicious tropical fruit salsa, filet mignon arrives atop seared spinach and surrounded by Marsala-shallot sauce, and even that old stand-by meat loaf is gussied up with whole-grain mustard sauce. Fish selections vary with the day's haul, but can include grilled escolar, fresh ahi tuna, or rock shrimp in a variety of preparations. Potatoes are a common side dish—rich, creamy, and flavored with roasted garlic, tomato-basil, or wasabi. *$$; AE, MC, V; no checks; dinner every day, brunch Sun; full bar; reservations recommended; between 10th and 11th Sts.* よ

Good Stuff / ★☆

1300 HIGHLAND AVE, MANHATTAN BEACH (AND BRANCHES); 310/545-4775

A mainstay of local casual dining, this popular crowd-pleaser suits beachgoers, lunch-breakers, and families alike because there's something for everyone. Inside the gray clapboard corner restaurant you'll find brightly painted marine-themed murals and lifeguard memorabilia; picture windows let in the sunshine. On nice days the outdoor patio fills first, built with glass railings to ensure a good vantage on bustling downtown M.B.'s human parade. Cheerful servers positively bounce through the restaurant, clad in casual sport togs and ferrying generous platters of food that's fresh, carefully prepared, and very affordable. The mile-long menu runs the gamut, featuring standouts like Santa Fe chicken omelet, cinnamon swirl French toast, a superb homemade veggie burger, turkey or tuna wrapped in gourmet tortillas, burritos and Mexican favorites, enormous main course salads, steaming hot pastas, and a selection of dinner-only entrees. Nightly bargain "get stuffed" dinners are sized for satisfaction (but priced under $10)—the seafood stew, for example, is guaranteed to be filling or your second bowl's on the house. You can't beat an offer like that, and you can't top Good Stuff. Other locations include one on the Strand near the Hermosa Beach pier (1286 The Strand; 310/374-2334) and in Redondo Beach (1617 Pacific Coast Highway; 310/316-0262). *$; AE, DC, DIS, MC, V; no checks; breakfast, lunch, dinner every day; beer and wine; reservations not accepted; www.eatgoodstuff.com; at the corner of 13th St.* よ

LODGINGS

Barnabey's Hotel / ★★

**3501 SEPULVEDA BLVD, MANHATTAN BEACH; 310/545-8466
OR 800/552-5285**

Step from laid-back Southern California into Merry Olde England at this high-concept hostelry that surprises with dedicated attention to personal comfort and service. Located just a mile from the beach but a world removed, the hotel is shielded from busy six-lane Sepulveda Boulevard by privacy walls, abundant foliage, and a clever design that focuses attention on Barnabey's relaxing interior courtyard. It's easy to play along with the Victorian manor house theme when you're surrounded by dark wood paneling, ornate red gas lamps, quintessentially British oil paintings in wide gilded frames, and plenty of polished brass and frilly floral decor. Guest rooms have the rich masculine aura of a turn-of-the-century library, complete with filled bookshelves. They're also exceedingly comfortable, featuring fluffy comforters (the copper bed warmer hanging outside is for looks only!), coffeemakers, and small bathrooms outfitted with towel-warming racks, extra sundries for the forgetful, and pretty tile work. Deluxe rooms sport a mantel-topped faux hearths and private balconies overlooking the wisteria-draped patio. Refrigerators are available for any room. Despite its size (120 rooms) and its popularity with business travelers, the hotel successfully gives guests the sense of a boutique inn. There's a canopied heated pool outdoors, and free shuttles to the airport, beach, and local shopping malls.

The hotel's restaurant, Auberge, is an ornate Edwardian parlor with correspondingly formal service. Once a bastion of heavy British favorites, the kitchen now prepares a lighter, California-Mediterranean cuisine. They also offer traditional afternoon tea, and a lavish Sunday Champagne brunch complete with carving station, design-your-own omelets, and mounds of fresh seafood on ice. $$–$$$; AE, DC, DIS, MC, V; no checks; at Rosecrans Ave. &

Hermosa Beach

In Spanish, *hermosa* means "beautiful," and this tiny seaside community is named for the pristine beach that is its central feature. HERMOSA CITY BEACH is 2 miles of wide, pearly sand dotted with endless volleyball nets and lined by the STRAND, a pedestrian and bicycle/skate path that stretches the entire length of the city. If you want to join in, bike and in-line skate rentals are available at HERMOSA CYCLERY (20 13th Street; 310/374-7816), a block from the Strand near the pier. In the early 20th century, Hermosa Beach was a summer vacation spot for folks from Los

Angeles, who built many opulent cottages and bungalows along the Strand—then a wooden boardwalk. In the 1920s, concrete replaced the wood, and today the homes on this prime real estate are small, expensive, and intimately close together. Many celebrities have lived here, including comedian Charlie Chaplin, filmmaker Warren Miller, and Ozzie and Harriet Nelson. If David and Ricky were boys today, they'd undoubtedly have skateboards and hang out around the **HERMOSA PIER,** which is popular with anglers topside, and brave surfers—who thread their way between the pilings—underneath. **PIER PLAZA** is a pedestrian-only block of Pier Avenue, lined with bars and restaurants known for raucous happy hours and party-all-night crowds. If you're looking for more information, contact the **HERMOSA BEACH CHAMBER OF COMMERCE,** at 1007 Hermosa Ave; 310/376-0951; www.hbchamber.net.

RESTAURANTS

The Bottle Inn / ★★☆

26 22ND ST, HERMOSA BEACH; 310/376-9595
A local favorite, the Bottle Inn consistently garners awards for Best Italian Food, Most Romantic, and especially Best Wine List, and owner Silvio Petoletti has been honored with *Wine Spectator* commendations for several years running. The restaurant is refreshingly cozy and quiet, located several blocks from the loud, bright, center of town. Inside, its vaguely European decor has remained unchanged since the Bottle Inn opened in 1974, and everything here evokes fancy restaurants from that decade. Surprisingly, it still works—much thanks to the expert kitchen and exceptional wine list, a fat notebook of 250 selections ranging from affordable bottles from the best California vintners to a full page of "Opus One" vintages and a library of the finest Italian Chiantis. True wine aficionados call ahead to reserve the single table in the 65-degree wine cellar, then dine in solitude surrounded by great wines. The servers are knowledgeable, accommodating, and well versed in a classic menu that stars veal piccata, chicken cacciatore, osso buco, fettuccine Bolognese, rich minestrone soup, and seafood risotto. Practiced to the point of near perfection, the food here is wonderful, with attention paid to making even the accompanying vegetables so delicious there's rarely a morsel left. For dessert, the housemade cannoli is a rare treat: impeccably flavored thick mascarpone freshly piped into a crisp shell and garnished with chocolate chips and chocolate shavings. Despite being fancy by South Bay standards (no beach flip-flops, no cut-off jeans), the Bottle Inn is comfy and casual. *$$; AE, MC, V; no checks; lunch Mon–Fri, dinner every day; beer and wine; reservations recommended; between Hermosa Ave and the Strand.*

Club Sushi / ★★

1200 HERMOSA AVE, HERMOSA BEACH; 310/372-5939
This place is to sushi what rock 'n' roll is to the symphony—there's not a kimono in sight, and the sushi chefs are more likely to give you a high-five than a deferential bow. Situated at the ground-zero intersection of the raucous Hermosa scene, Club Sushi is high-tech, youth-oriented, loud, and beachy—it even has a half-price sushi happy hour daily (5 to 7pm). Crowds pack into an industrial-style space filled with small tables, shoulder-to-shoulder sushi bar-stools, and a dozen TV screens showing sportscasts muffled by the sounds of jazz, rock, and calypso music (live five nights a week). But Club Sushi is more than a hangout. It boasts a line of sushi chefs whose flashing hands churn out a mind-boggling amount of great sushi, from the standard varieties to special house creations with names like volcano roll, shrimp dynamite, garlic yellowtail sashimi, and a terrific spicy tuna/asparagus tempura roll. An added draw is the regular menu, which runs a surprising gamut from teriyaki chicken and traditional Japanese dishes to pizzas, pastas, burgers, and American favorites like steak Diane. Thanks to the creativity of "Chef Bruno," whose experience includes stints as personal chef for Dan Ackroyd and David Geffen, the restaurant holds its own among local foodies. Just don't be surprised to see bikini-clad diners at the next table. *$–$$; AE, DC, DIS, MC, V; no checks; lunch, dinner every day; reservations not accepted for fewer than 6; at the corner of Pier Ave.*

LODGINGS

Beach House at Hermosa Beach / ★★★

1300 THE STRAND, HERMOSA BEACH; 310/374-3001 OR 888/895-4559
Your every need is addressed at this chic and luxurious new hotel, which is more akin to the historic Surf & Sand beach club that once stood on this spot than to the motels further down the Strand. Sporting a Cape Cod style with white wood accents and stylish beige furnishings, the

Beach House frequently draws comparisons to L.A.'s Shutters on the Beach—but it's only about half the price. Most rooms have at least a par-

tial ocean view; the very best are just inches away from the Strand, with an unobstructed view of the pier, Palos Verdes, and the entire Santa

Monica Bay. Completed in 1998, the hotel is a breath of fresh air, from the stylish furnishings evoking a classic California beach cottage to the gracious staff, whose respectful but casual attitude make it as suited for beach-loving families as Fortune 500 CEOs. Each of the 96 rooms is equipped with a queen sleeper-sofa, complete micro-kitchen (plus dishes and flatware for four), elevated king-bed sleeping niche, plush down comforters and flannel robes, and mood-enhancing stereo/CD player.

You're always within arm's length of one of the four phones, and business travelers will find an ergonomic computer space with good lighting, dataport, and handy outlets. The bathroom is a study in relaxation, with clean white tile and chrome lines, extra deep soaking tub, and pampering Aveda products. In the morning, a generous continental breakfast is laid out downstairs, with to-go trays if you prefer yours on the beach or your private balcony. Room service is available from Strand fixture Good Stuff, and beach toys and towels are provided. Despite the summertime carnival atmosphere of the Strand, the Beach House keeps serene with double-paned windows and "quiet" walls; packages are available with spa or romance themes. $$$$; AE, DC, DIS, JCB, MC, V; checks OK; www.beach-house.com; at 14th St. &

Torrance

RESTAURANTS

Depot / ★★☆

1250 CABRILLO AVE, TORRANCE; 310/787-7501

Set in a restored train station, this eclectic eatery is a spin-off of Redondo Beach's Chez Melange, with chef-owner Michael Shafer serving an imaginative assortment of ethnic cuisines. Start your meal off with a creative cocktail, like the Red Berry Rising, a refreshing blend of Stoli vodka, homemade berry sauce, and a lime twist; or a zesty Tex-Mex, made with vodka, sweet and sour mix, and a jalapeño. Garlicky rock shrimp sausage with chile–goat cheese wontons, delicate Thai dumplings steamed in ale, or a rich ahi tuna and wasabi caviar tartate are all great ways to start your meal. While daily specials like killer meatloaf with creamy mashers and pepper stew or Thai-barbecued New York steak with cashew rice make up a big portion of the menu, pasta dishes such as rock shrimp linguine and bow-tie pasta with house-smoked chicken, roasted corn, and chile cream sauce always hit the spot. The chef's spicy "Thai-dyed" chicken has become somewhat of a house specialty. For special occasions, gather of group of 8 to 12 friends and order the Chinese slow-roasted suckling pig, cooked with 100 cloves of garlic and served with such tasty side dishes as mu shu pancakes, cashew rice, and spicy vegetable bowls. Aspiring gourmets can sign up for Shafer's monthly cooking classes.

Redondo Beach

RESTAURANTS

Chez Melange / ★★

1716 PACIFIC COAST HWY, REDONDO BEACH; 310/540-1222
Located inside the modest Palos Verdes Inn, this well-regarded brasserie has been presenting artful California cuisine so long it's become a Redondo Beach institution. The menu may no longer be cutting-edge, but it does seem to get more and more eclectic, moving seamlessly from Japanese to Cajun, Italian to Chinese, and keeping up to date with premium vodkas and a mouth-watering oyster-and-seafood bar. The decor has a dated, late 1980s feel, but the conservative, moneyed crowd here doesn't seem to mind a bit. During the day, a wide wall of picture windows makes the restaurant light and airy; at night, it feels decidedly more formal. Each meal begins with a basket of irresistible breads before you move on to a dizzyingly international entree such as shrimp and chicken in orange vindaloo curry over basmati rice with sweet, chunky chutney; rosemary-laced pork tenderloin and shallot-sherry cream sauce; Parmesan-crusted albacore with Greek feta salad and tabbouleh; or spicy blackened halibut sauced with horseradish and served with seafood gumbo. Spa cuisine selections are available at every meal. *$$; AE, DC, MC, V; no checks; breakfast, lunch, dinner every day; full bar; reservations recommended; www.chezmelange.com; between Palos Verdes Blvd and Prospect Ave.* &

Kincaid's Bay House / ★★☆

500 FISHERMAN'S WHARF, REDONDO BEACH; 310/318-6080
Opened in 1999, this branch of the venerable San Francisco/Hawaii surf 'n' turf specialists is the classiest joint on the reborn Redondo Beach pier. Sporting a Craftsman-inspired chunky architecture and sleek, clubby decor, the restaurant boasts panoramic ocean views, a relaxed bar with outdoor seating, and an open kitchen starring a huge hardwood spit-roaster redolent with the aroma of sweet, smoky Nebraska-bred beef. A grand entryway of marble flooring gives way to rich burgundy carpeting and the warm glow of Deco-inspired wall sconces. Composed by Kincaid's Hawaiian executive chef James Nalu Miller, the menu offers island-influenced dishes like char-sui pork skewers that are grilled over applewood to caramelize the sweet-tart honey/soy/hoisin marinade. Fresh fish from the Pacific Northwest and Hawaii are featured each day; other seafood specialties include wood-smoked prawns flavored with chipotle-ancho rub and Kincaid's signature barbecue hollandaise, plus crab-and-shrimp hash served with sherry-cream sauce. Meat lovers can

catch a whiff of the spit-roasted prime rib on the way in . . . if that doesn't entice you, consider seasoned and buttered sirloin, or pan-seared venison flavored with blackberry and sage. For dessert there's Key lime pie—the pale yellow color lets you know it's authentic—or pear bread pudding baked in individual ramekins and served with bourbon-custard sauce. *$$–$$$; AE, DC, DIS, MC, V; checks OK; lunch Mon–Sat, dinner every day; full bar; reservations recommended; www.kincaids.com; at the south end of Harbor Dr.* &

LODGINGS

The Portofino Hotel and Yacht Club / ★★★

260 PORTOFINO WAY, REDONDO BEACH; 310/379-8481 OR 800/468-4292
Built on a promontory jutting into the main King Harbor channel, this contemporary resort has a relaxed elegance that perfectly fits its yacht club personality. The main level features an exquisite light-filled atrium lounge with cheerfully upholstered armchairs that invite you to sit before the marble fireplace and gaze oceanward through tall windows. Guest rooms are on three floors; views improve (and rates rise) as you ascend, and every room has a private balcony. Rooms on the ocean-facing side have a panoramic view past the breakwater, while those on the marina side spy on private yachts docked in the Portofino Marina—and the massive Wyland whale mural adorning the concrete power plant on Harbor Drive. All are well outfitted with clean and bright French country furnishings that team broad plaids with richly colored florals and pale wood furniture. Though the rooms are modestly sized, they provide every comfort from coffee service to ironing boards and irons—the same goes for the bathrooms, stocked with plush towels and luxury toiletries. The morning newspaper is complimentary, and all of King Harbor is within walking distance. *$$$–$$$$; AE, DC, DIS, MC, V; checks OK; www. noblehousehotels.com; west of Harbor Dr.* &

Palos Verdes Peninsula

Home to some of the most insulated and affluent residential neighborhoods in L.A. County, the Palos Verdes peninsula has been discovered by geologists to have once been one of the Channel Islands chain, which accounts for its unusual height at the coastline and its abrupt drop to sea level around inland San Pedro. Years ago "P.V.," as it's locally known, was home to the aquatic theme park Marineland, which was popular for a time but ultimately succumbed to the disadvantage of its isolated location. Since then, there's been little to draw visitors here—and it's a shame, considering the drive around the peninsula shoreline is spectacularly enjoyable. Begin at the southern end of Redondo Beach by turning onto Palos Verdes Drive. After you pass Malaga Cove Plaza, home to the grandiose Neptune Fountain, continue along the blufftop road to **POINT VICENTE LIGHTHOUSE AND INTERPRETIVE CENTER** (31501 Palos Verdes Dr W; 562/377-5370). The Center features a small marine museum and is positioned to observe the annual migration of the California gray whale—the view from their second-floor gallery is impressive on any clear day but is most rewarding between December and March, when the graceful mammals pass surprisingly close to the point on their way to and from warm-water Baja breeding grounds. Built in 1926, the nearby **LIGHTHOUSE** still protects boaters from Palos Verdes' treacherous rocks, though the lamp has been automated since 1939.

San Pedro

South of magnificent Palos Verdes, the city of San Pedro is an often gritty, blue-collar port town; most of its residents work in the harbor, which has grown through the years to literally and figuratively dwarf any other interests in the city. The **SAN PEDRO PENINSULA CHAMBER OF COMMERCE** (390 W 7th Street; 310/832-7272; www.sanpedrochamber.com) publishes visitor brochures and maintains an informative web site. Learn about maritime history at the **LOS ANGELES MARITIME MUSEUM** (Berth 84, at the foot of 6th Street; 310/548-7618), housed in a beautifully restored 1941 WPA Streamline Moderne building on the waterfront. In addition to exhibits on Native American navigation, ship figureheads, the whaling industry, and other topics, the museum offers classes in topics such as celestial navigation, scrimshaw, and model ship building. A different kind of glimpse into maritime history is waiting at the **SS** *Lane Victory* (Berth 94, adjacent to the World Cruise Center; 562/519-9545; www.lanevictoryship.com), a 10,000-ton World War II cargo ship restored and operated by the Merchant Marine. This national historic landmark saw service through the Vietnam War and now operates as a working museum that offers guided ship tours, displays of memorabilia, and occasional all-day voyages. A particularly impressive harbor site is the soaring **VINCENT THOMAS BRIDGE**, San Pedro's answer to the Golden Gate. It crosses from San Pedro to **TERMINAL ISLAND**, an uninviting industrial jungle of canneries, loading cranes, and a federal penitentiary. But it wasn't always this way—as you drive across, try to imagine the island circa 1899, as an appealing resort with its own pleasure pier and beach pavilions. The island was also home to a close-knit community of Japanese-American fishermen and their families, most of whom were removed for internment during World War II and never returned.

RESTAURANTS

Papadakis Taverna / ★★

301 W 6TH ST, SAN PEDRO; 310/548-1186

Papadakis has been here as long as anyone can remember and still draws crowds nightly with traditional Greek recipes from genial host John Papadakis' family. Every evening runs like a successful Vegas-style production. Arriving ladies get a kiss on the hand from one of the Papadakis brothers, and then diners are shown to a table in this bright banquet room decorated with equal parts Aegean murals and football art (in deference to John Papadakis' glory days as a USC football legend). Start with a bottle of wine from a list that combines good California vintages with traditional (but sometimes inferior) Greek wines, and consider some *mezes* (small plates) to share such as *spanakopita* (spinach-filled phyllo pastries) or thick, satisfying *tsatziki* (garlic-laced cucumber and yogurt spread) with pita bread. Before long the lights dim, and any empty-handed waiter gets called upon to sing and dance through the aisles to traditional Greek music. As the evening wears on, these interludes grow more raucous, as enthusiastic diners get into the act and the classic ritual of breaking plates begins (a special tray of throwaways is wheeled out for that purpose). It's easy to make a complete meal of varied appetizer plates, or you can opt for grilled lamb, pork, citrus-laced fish, or other Mediterranean specialties. Plan on a relaxed pace—since your waiter might be otherwise engaged during the meal—and a festive, party atmosphere more suited to groups and families than to romantic couples. *$$; DC, MC, V; checks OK; dinner every day; beer and wine; reservations recommended; at Centre St.*

Long Beach

Formerly ranchland dating back to early Spanish land grants, the modern city of **LONG BEACH** was named during the real estate boom of the 1880s and conceived as a seaside resort community. But industry and commerce quickly took over, with the discovery of oil and the development of Long Beach Harbor (along with adjacent San Pedro) as the primary Port of Los Angeles. Despite a devastating 1933 earthquake, downtown Long Beach enjoyed a steady prosperity throughout the first half of the 20th century, acquiring the nickname of "Iowa by the Sea" due to the many Midwest transplants who made their home here—and whose conservative, pragmatic culture still pervades the area. An aggressive downtown redevelopment plan that began in the 1970s has helped draw visitors back with new tourist attractions, an expensive waterfront Convention Center, and the small-town flavor of remarkably well-preserved residential neighborhoods. Visitor information and maps are available from the **LONG BEACH AREA CONVENTION & VISITORS BUREAU** (One World Trade Center, Suite 300; 562/436-3645 or 800/4LB-STAY; www.golongbeach. org). Each April the star-studded **LONG BEACH GRAND PRIX** races through the streets around the Convention Center and harbor, attracting the likes of Jason Priestley and Paul Newman to burn some serious off-screen rubber; get schedule and ticket information through 562/981-2600 or www.longbeachgp.com.

Mention Long Beach to many people, and they're apt to associate the name with this city's biggest tourist attraction, and one that virtually saved it from bankrupt obscurity in the 1970s. Once the world's largest and most luxurious Atlantic ocean liner, the regal **QUEEN MARY** (located at the end of I-710; 562/435-3511; www.queenmary.com) sits permanently docked in Long Beach harbor, open to visitors, diners, and overnight guests. Easy to dismiss as a tourist trap, the ship is really a living museum, the only surviving example of a particular kind of 20th-century elegance and excess that's hard to imagine until you actually stroll the gangways and grand salons of this splendid vessel. Vast teakwood decks, priceless interiors, and lavish staterooms once occupied by notables like Winston Churchill, the Duke of Windsor, and Greta Garbo all tell the story of a vanished era. Kiosk displays of historic photographs and memorabilia are everywhere, and guided tours take you from poop deck to pump room, passing through perfectly preserved crew quarters along the way. The ship is a must-see for nautical history buffs. Across the waterway is Long Beach's newest attraction, the **AQUARIUM OF THE PACIFIC** (100 Aquarium Way; 562/590-3100; www.aquariumofpacific. org), which opened in 1998. City planners gave their all to the project, hoping that what worked in Baltimore and Monterey would re-energize the waterfront. Re-creating three separate regions of the Pacific, the Aquarium features animals native to tropical lagoons, coral reefs, the chilly Bering Sea, and temperate Baja waters. Kids and adults alike can learn little-known facts about sea creatures from sharks and sea lions to delicate sea horses and moon jellies—three-story-high tanks let you get nose-to-nose with these denizens of the oceans. Across the way is the aging **SHORELINE VILLAGE**, a shopping/dining/marina complex disguised as a 19th-century fishing village. Savvy crowds seem no longer enchanted by its kitschy theme, but it still makes a pleasant stroll if you're in the area, and it's also home to a 1906 Charles Looff carousel. Nearby Rainbow Harbor is where the tall ship **CALIFORNIAN**, flagship of the Nautical Heritage Society, is docked during the winter months. A day sail aboard this two-masted, 145-foot wooden cutter offers passengers a chance to help raise and lower the eight sails, take a turn at the helm, and experience the "romance of the high seas"; call the **NATIONAL HERITAGE SOCIETY** (800/432-2201), for reservations and schedule.

The **LONG BEACH MUSEUM OF ART** (2300 E Ocean Blvd; 562/439-2119; www.lbma.com) is situated on a prime waterfront knoll along Ocean Boulevard, in one of the several grand old mansions that still line this picturesque stretch. Built in 1912 as the summer home of New York philanthropist Elizabeth Milbank Anderson, the house was designed by the firm that built Los Angeles's landmark Chinese and Egyptian theaters, and it functioned as a private social club and WWII officers' club before becoming the museum's home in 1957. In 1999 a yearlong expansion project began to restore the home to its original state and build a complementary gallery annex on the property. In addition to its interest as an historic site, the museum is notable for its collection of 20th-century European modernists, post–World War II art from California, and the largest video art archive in the nation.

If you travel east of downtown Long Beach, you'll quickly find yourself in the neighborhood communities of **BELMONT SHORE** and **NAPLES,** whose quaint village feel and prewar bungalow-lined streets are in sharp contrast to the harbor district's industrial energy. East Second Street and East Broadway bisect Belmont Shore—known locally as "the Shore"—and provide hours' worth of strolling amongst **ANTIQUE AND COLLECTIBLE SHOPS, CAFES, BOUTIQUES,** and an increasing number of high-profile retailers like The Gap, Banana Republic, and Jamba Juice, happily co-existing alongside old-style hardware stores, barbershops, and delicatessens. The Belmont pleasure pier offers a romantic bayfront stroll; a bait-and-tackle shop, snack bar, and ice cream stand operate at the pier's end in summer. Naples is a manmade island community of picturesque canals, boardwalks lined with million-dollar homes, tiny sandy lagoons, and the romantic **GONDOLA GETAWAY** (562/433-9595; www.clever.net/gondolas). Since 1982 these authentic Venetian gondolas have been snaking through the canals, camping it up with experienced gondoliers ready to belt out an Italian aria at the drop of a straw hat. Passengers are encouraged to bring a beverage—the fee includes a nice basket of bread, cheese, and salami, plus wineglasses and a full ice bucket.

RESTAURANTS

Belmont Brewing Company / ★★☆

25 39TH PL, LONG BEACH; 562/433-3891
The best of the local brewpubs, this spot at the base of Belmont Pier features an outdoor patio with a million-dollar harbor view that takes in the *Queen Mary,* fiery sunsets, and the unusual multicolored street lamps that illuminate the pier after dark. The five respectable house brews include Top Sail (amber) and Long Beach Crude (porter). Inside, the

restaurant has an undersea theme, with a giant aquarium and murals featuring tropical fish against a turquoise background. But nearly everyone opts for the relaxing wind shielded patio, with umbrellas for the midday sun and heat lamps to warm chilly evenings. Seated here, you can listen to the water lapping at the sand, envy the lucky folks whose condos line the waterfront promenade, and enjoy food that goes a step beyond the usual tavern fare. There are plenty of appetizers, of course—favorites like crab cakes, fried calamari, and bruschetta as well as fresh ceviche and steamed artichokes. Pizzas, pastas, main-course salads, and sandwiches round out a menu that also features lots of seafood and delectable baby back ribs. This casual eatery is ideal for whiling away a pretty afternoon or a low-key evening. *$; AE, DC, MC, V; no checks; lunch, dinner every day, brunch Sat–Sun; beer and wine; reservations not accepted; www.belmontbrewing.com; west of Ocean Blvd.* &

Delius / ★★☆

3550 LONG BEACH BLVD, LONG BEACH; 562/426-0694

You might not expect an ambitiously conceived concept restaurant located in a mini-mall close to the freeway to last three months, but Louise and Dave Solzman's Delius has been going strong since 1996. Serving just one seating each evening, Delius offers a prix-fixe dinner according to a menu that changes weekly and reflects British-born chef Louise's excellent culinary sense. Despite its out-of-the-way location a 10-minute drive from downtown Long Beach, Delius creates an intimate romantic ambience insulated from the world outside. Once you enter the richly furnished, Victorian-flavored lounge and dining room, heavy velvet draperies enclose you in a 45-person salon whose tables are set with a full complement of flatware for each course and stemware for every carefully chosen wine. Cocktails are at 6:30, and dinner begins at 7:15. The seven-course extravaganza includes hors d'oeuvres, soup, appetizer, first course, entree, fruit and cheese, and dessert; a five-wine sampler complements each selection and is just $15 per person. Recent menus have featured crab-and-shrimp-stuffed zucchini flowers, sautéed halibut on penne pasta with porcini sauce, rosemary-and-feta-stuffed filet mignon, grilled chicken with Indian mango chutney, and chipotle crab cakes with ginger-cilantro butter. A harpist entertains on Fridays, and the restaurant really pulls out the stops for frequent winemaker and holiday dinners. *$$$; DC, DIS, MC, V; checks OK; dinner Tues–Sat; beer and wine; reservations required; between Wardlow Rd and 36th St.* &

Lasher's / ★★☆

3441 E BROADWAY, LONG BEACH; 562/433-0153

Part of the newly hip Broadway corridor through a mainly residential neighborhood, this comfy eatery occupies a masterfully restored historic house, offering dining in a number of rooms or on a quiet brick patio.

157

Billing itself as "an American Restaurant," Lasher's boasts that every menu ingredient is U.S. grown except the imported English Stilton (because "there's just no substitute for real Stilton"). The regional American menu features standout dishes like slow-roasted turkey served Thanksgiving-style year-round, with rich herb-sausage stuffing and pan gravy; Maryland crab cakes available as an appetizer or a main course; and home-style meat loaf baked with sweet-tangy cranberry glaze and surrounded by rich gravy. Meal presentation is meticulous, with delicate herb sprigs adorning carefully composed plates, and servers are professional and knowledgeable. You'll regret not ordering dessert, especially the genuine Key lime pie or the decadent white chocolate bread pudding accompanied by two-chocolate sauce. Weekend champagne brunch is meant to evoke a Southern plantation feast, with fancy French Quarter egg dishes, spicy catfish etouffée, and Cajun-spiced fried green tomatoes. *$$; AE, DC, DIS, MC, V; no checks; lunch Thurs–Fri, dinner Tues–Sun, brunch Sat–Sun; beer and wine; reservations recommended; corner of Newport Ave.* &

The Madison Restaurant & Bar / ★★★

102 PINE AVE, LONG BEACH; 562/628-8866

Set in one of Pine Avenue's most stunning historic buildings, this elegant 1920s-style supper club offers the grand experience of fine dining in a majestic setting reminiscent of opulent ocean liner dining salons of the day. Coffered mahogany walls, gilded ceiling beams, sparkling oversize crystal chandeliers, and enormous two-story windows framed with rich brocade draperies provide the backdrop for service that's deferential without being stuffy, and a menu that delivers on its promise of fine quality and reliable steaks and seafood. Originally a bank and more recently a private club, the 1890s building has been beautifully restored and features a lavish bar where a library ladder lets the staff reach the highest shelves. Next to the bar, a quiet combo entertains with dinner music from the 1940s, while diners ensconced in padded crescent booths and high-backed chairs unfurl napkins folded to resemble tuxedo jackets. The Madison serves exceptional dry-aged beef broiled and accompanied by à la carte sides like buttery garlic potatoes, tender asparagus hollandaise, and perfectly seasoned creamed spinach. The menu includes seafood dishes like grilled salmon atop mussels and clams with a creamy ginger-citrus sauce, or oyster-stuffed sole breaded and drizzled with beurre blanc and fragrant fresh dill. The house caesar salad is a winner— crisp romaine wedges with the traditional dressing but with the surprise of capers to provide the salty tang usually expected of anchovies. Desserts are artistic renditions of reliable favorites like sugary apple crumble, or a s'mores sundae with roasted-marshmallow "antennae." *$$$; AE, MC,*

V; no checks; lunch Mon–Fri, dinner every day; full bar; reservations recommended; www.madisonsteakhouse.com; at 1st St. &

Shenandoah Cafe / ★★

4722 E 2ND ST, LONG BEACH; 562/434-3469
In an era when "New American" is the culinary buzzword, here's a place where "American" food means only one thing—big, filling portions of regional home-style cuisines. Located in trendy upscale Belmont Shore, the restaurant was part of the first wave of new businesses to open on Second Street and has been a popular mainstay since 1987. The high-ceilinged parlor is decorated with hanging quilts, floral wallpaper, and ornate columns; regulars agree it's equal parts New Orleans mansion and Grandma's house. Dinner here is definitely not for vegetarians or light eaters; even fresh fish specialties are given rich and heavy Southern treatments, and meats take up most of the menu. Start by nibbling on the irresistible apple fritters and yeasty dinner rolls brought fresh from the oven by strolling servers, and loosen your belt a notch in anticipation of an enormous meal that also includes soup or salad and starchy side dishes. Recommended specialties include Texas-sized chicken-fried steak with country gravy, Santa Fe–style baby back ribs glazed with smoky chipotle, Cajun-blackened fresh catch of the day, and Granny's deep-fried chicken. Even after stuffing yourself, don't be surprised if you're tempted by rich desserts like bananas Foster or Shenandoah's special double fudge brownie with ice cream and two chocolate sauces (one order is enough for the whole table). *$$; AE, DIS, MC, V; no checks; dinner every day, brunch Sun; beer and wine; reservations recommended; at Park Ave.*

LODGINGS

Hotel Queen Mary / ★★

1126 QUEEN'S HWY, LONG BEACH; 562/432-6964 OR 800/437-2934
If you're too young to have made an Atlantic crossing on one of the grand old luxury liners, staying here might be the closest you'll come to reliving the romance of those historic voyages. A grand stateroom once occupied by royalty or the wealthy elite can be yours for a night—or longer—on the *Queen Mary*, permanently docked in Long Beach (see the Long Beach introduction for information about tours). You'll need a sense of adventure and some imagination, though, because these once-lavish quarters aren't that exceptional when compared to contemporary hotels, and few modern amenities have been added lest they destroy the historic authenticity of the ship. Some notable exceptions are private phones and TVs, but the idea is to enjoy the novelty and charm of features like the original porcelain bathroom fixtures, priceless walls paneled in now-extinct tropical hardwoods with intricate Art Deco designs, and the aura of history that pervades each hallway, stateroom, and well-walked deck. Just

as in the ship's 1930s heyday, quarters vary widely; try to splurge on an ocean-view first-class or deluxe stateroom. Because it's a bona fide tourist attraction, the *Queen Mary* features a full complement of restaurants and bars. Sir Winston's is the ship's very formal dining room, a pricey continental affair best suited for special occasions and expense accounts. The Chelsea is a slightly less fancy seafood grill, and the Promenade Cafe is open all day for casual dining. We recommend Sunday's Champagne Brunch, an overwhelming orgy for gourmands that includes unlimited champagne, ice sculptures, and a harpist. It's served in the ship's Grand Salon, the original ballroom that's so lovely it's worth the price of admission. Don't miss the Observation Bar, a chic Art Deco cocktail lounge with panoramic skyline view and an interior that's been featured in countless films and TV shows. *$–$$$; AE, DIS, MC, V; checks OK; www.queenmary.com; from the end of I-710, follow signs to ship.*

Lord Mayor's Inn / ★★☆

435 CEDAR AVE, LONG BEACH; 562/436-0324
Situated in a formerly elite residential neighborhood downtown, this elegant Edwardian home was built in 1904 and belonged to Long Beach's first mayor, Charles H. Windham. He earned his unofficial title of "Lord Mayor" from a group of British beauty contestants visiting the seaside resort, and the nickname stuck. In 1988, after a sensitive restoration that earned a National Trust for Historic Preservation award, innkeepers Laura and Reuben Brasser opened the area's best bed and breakfast. The main house offers five guest rooms, each furnished with impeccably chosen antiques, luxurious high-quality linens, and heirloom bedspreads and accessories. Though only one bathroom is original to the house, all rooms now boast private baths so cleverly recreated with vintage fixtures and painstakingly matched materials that it's impossible to tell the new from the old. All the rooms are upstairs, and utterly charming; three open onto a wooden deck overlooking the back garden, including the cozy Hawaiian Room, which re-creates the feel of the Victorian Era with an ornately carved wedding bed and other island memorabilia. A white-wicker sun porch overlooks the street, and the entire house radiates the warmth of original wood floors and walls, a Vermont granite hearth, and vintage clocks whose gentle chiming enhances the historic ambience of the inn. Seven more rooms—four with private baths—are available in two less-formal adjacent cottages, also dating from the early 20th century; they offer a private option for families or those seeking seclusion. Guests gather at their leisure in the main-house dining room for Laura's lavish breakfasts, which include specialties like Old World pancakes with fried apples, delicate asparagus eggs, and hearty stuffed French toast. *$–$$; AE, DIS, MC, V; checks OK; www.lordmayors.com; between 4th and 5th Sts.*

SASQUATCH BOOKS

BUSINESS REPLY MAIL
FIRST-CLASS MAIL   PERMIT NO. 998   SEATTLE WA

POSTAGE WILL BE PAID BY ADDRESSEE

SASQUATCH BOOKS
615 2ND AVE STE 260
SEATTLE   WA   98104-9841

BEST PLACES®

You don't have to stop with just one Best Places® guidebook.
We offer a complete line of guides to Alaska, the Northwest, and California,
as well as regional favorites in cooking, gardening, and literature.

Call toll-free 1-800-775-0817
or visit us on the web at www.SasquatchBooks.com

Yes, please send me a FREE copy of the Sasquatch Books catalog.

Name _____

Address _____

City _____ State _____ Zip _____

Phone _____ I've purchased Best Places® guides for _____ years.

Yes, please send me the FREE Sasquatch Books enewsletter.

Email address _____

Catalina Island

Often compared to Mediterranean jewels like Malta or Capri, this local island—easternmost in the Channel Island chain—offers sun-filled skies, clean sea air, and shimmering azure waters just 22 miles off the California coast. **AVALON**, named after the Arthurian paradise as described in Tennyson's *Idylls of the King*, is the island's only town, occupying barely a square mile; 86 percent of the island is wilderness under the protection of the Catalina Island Conservancy. The Avalon you see today owes its popularity to chewing-gum magnate and baseball fan William Wrigley Jr., who purchased the island around 1918, constructed a Wrigley Field replica here so his Chicago Cubs could come for spring training (1929 to 1959), and channeled his considerable resources into making his beloved island a stylish offshore playground. Today Catalina is a mecca for outdoor enthusiasts, who come to kayak, fish, dive, hike, bike, camp, and much more. It also draws day trippers eager to stroll the streets of charming bayfront Avalon, live out *Gilligan's Island* fantasies, and absorb the infectious, laid-back island vibe.

The usual way to reach Catalina Island is via **CATALINA EXPRESS** (310/519-1212 or 800/464-4228), which operates up to 22 daily departures from San Pedro and Long Beach. The trip to Avalon takes about an hour on their high-speed catamarans. **CATALINA CRUISES** (800/CATALINA) also ferries passengers from Long Beach to Avalon, and offers lower fares by running monstrous 700-passenger boats that take almost twice as long to make the crossing. If money is more of a concern to you than time, they're your best bet; call for schedules.

You can't get lost in Avalon. Aptly named Crescent Avenue follows the bay's horseshoe curve from end to end, and nearly everything is on this main street or one of the half-dozen side streets radiating outward from it. At the center is the 1909 **GREEN PLEASURE PIER**, which is still a hub of activity even though visitors now arrive at a high-volume terminal across the bay. The **CATALINA ISLAND CHAMBER OF COMMERCE & VISITORS BUREAU** (310/510-1520; www.catalina.com) operates at the base of the pier, answering questions and distributing tons of helpful brochures and guides. The town is easily explored on foot, and rental cars are nonexistent (most residents motor around in golf carts, and many homes have only cart-sized driveways). Other options include renting a bicycle from **BROWN'S BIKES** (107 Pebbly Beach Road, near the passenger terminal; 310/510-0986). Gas-powered golf carts are available for rent on an hourly basis from **CARTOPIA** (on Crescent Ave at Pebbly Beach Rd; 310/510-2493).

Avalon's most distinctive landmark is the elegant **CASINO**, an Art Deco masterpiece housing a theater and a ballroom, and featuring spectacular murals, revolutionary engineering, and impeccable design. You can see the theater any night for the price of a movie ticket—the Casino screens first-run films—but the tenth-floor ballroom is accessible only by guided tour (see below) or during one of the many special dance events throughout the year. These include June's SWING CAMP CATALINA (call 626/799-5689 for information), CATALINA JAZZ TRAX FESTIVAL in October (contact them at 800/866-TRAX), and the gala NEW YEAR'S EVE CELEBRATION (the Visitors Bureau has complete details). In the ground floor of the Casino is the CATALINA ISLAND MUSEUM (310/510-2414), featuring exhibits on island history and archeology, plus a con-tour relief map of Catalina that's helpful to hikers. Other landmarks visible from the bay include Wrigley's stately mansion, built on the hill-side and now the exclusive INN ON MOUNT ADA (see Lodgings, below). Nearby is the distinctive HOLLY HILL HOUSE, easily recognized by its Queen Anne frills and prominent striped cupola. Built in 1888–1890 by Peter Gano, who used his blind horse Mercury to haul most of the mate-rials uphill, the house was meant, according to legend, as a wedding present for Gano's intended—who then refused to move to the isolated island and ultimately married another. Gano lived alone in Holly Hill House, never marrying, and posting "No Women Allowed" signs at the threshold. The home, listed on the National Register of Historic Places, is privately owned and superbly restored with period antiques. Once-monthly tour days are conducted during the summer; call the Catalina Island Museum Society (310/510-2414) for tour dates and reservations.

Much of the most interesting stuff on Catalina Island—rugged back roads, dramatic shoreline palisades, pristine isolated coves, the Art Deco Casino Ballroom, Arabian horses at the Wrigley family's El Rancho Escondido—is either restricted or too remote for the casual visitor. Luckily, there are numerous options for guided excursions, ranging in length from a couple of hours to three-quarters of the day. Santa Catalina Island Company's DISCOVERY TOURS (310/510-TOUR or 800/626-7489) offers the greatest variety: In addition to day and night scenic tram tours of Avalon, glass-bottomed boat cruises, and bus trips into the island's interior, it conducts some unusual outings none of the other oper-ators offer. These include the UNDERSEA TOUR of Lovers' Cove Marine Preserve in a semi-submerged boat, nighttime boat trips to see Catalina's famed FLYING FISH, and an exclusive tour of the landmark CASINO THE-ATER AND BALLROOM. Call for prices, schedules, and tickets.

Around the point marked by the Avalon Casino lies the DESCANSO BEACH CLUB, (310/510-1226), nestled in its own small cove and looking like a mini–Club Med. Facilities include showers, changing rooms, a restaurant and bar, volleyball nets, and thatched beach umbrellas. Year-round rentals of KAYAKS, SNORKEL GEAR, RAFTS, AND WETSUITS are available. If you're interested in a SPORTFISHING or DIVING excursion, they depart from the Green Pleasure Pier in the bay; call the Visitors Bureau for details. If you venture into the island's interior, be sure to look out for wild buffalo—descendants of a long ago herd brought over for a movie shoot, then abandoned—who meander the hillsides (and sometimes block auto traffic).

RESTAURANTS

The Channel House / ★★

205 CRESCENT AVE, AVALON; 310/510-1617
With a secluded outdoor patio that's generally agreed to be the most romantic dining spot in Avalon, this very traditional continental restaurant manages to attract jeans-clad vacationers as well as dressed-to-the-nines islanders. The patio is the way to go (put in a request when making your reservation), festooned with twinkling lights and surrounded by vine-covered trellises that obscure the sidewalk traffic along busy Crescent Avenue. Indoor seating is refreshingly quiet, aided by plush carpeting and a pitched, open-beam ceiling; the Channel House projects an aura of elegance without pretension. Dinner always begins with an enormous platter of crisp, fresh crudités and creamy dip, whose bounty unfortunately dispels any thought of a first course, even the bread-bowl clam chowder or the tableside-prepared caesar salad. The menu here is enticing, with local seafood offerings like mako shark, fresh Catalina lobster, or grilled island sand dabs. Meat and poultry are invariably served sauced; you'll see plenty of rich touches like goose liver, béarnaise, and butter galore. Surprisingly, the restaurant offers just a couple of perfunctory desserts, hardly the lavish selection of mousses and rich cakes you might expect. *$$; AE, DIS, MC, V; local checks only; lunch every day (July–Oct only), dinner every day (subject to Mon–Tues closure in winter); full bar; reservations recommended; at Sumner Ave.* &

Clubhouse Bar & Grille / ★★

1 COUNTRY CLUB DR, AVALON; 310/510-7404
The most elegant meals in this typically casual town can be found here, at the historic Catalina Country Club. A 1997 renovation upgraded the stunning golf course and tastefully restored this Spanish-Mediterranean clubhouse, built by William Wrigley Jr. during the 1920s and designed by the same team responsible for the stylish casino. It's now got a chic and historic atmosphere, favored by well-heeled golfers with a taste for its California/Pacific Rim cuisine. The menu is peppered with historic anecdotes and photos of the many celebrities who've frequented the club throughout the years. Seating is either outdoors, in an elegant tiled courtyard complete with splashing fountain and Mediterranean earthenware, or in an intimate, clubby dining room filled with dark woods and pol-

ished brass fixtures. Much of the menu is served all day, including gourmet pizzas (such as smoked prime rib with sweet peppers, pesto, and caramelized onions), appetizer samplers (seared jerk ahi, Southwest satay, seafood pot-stickers, and more), and soups (fisherman's bisque, or French onion with apple, shallots, and Gruyère—try either in a sourdough bowl), plus thick, satisfying sandwiches. Dinner offerings follow a similar fusion-style pattern, such as tender New Zealand lamb sirloin accented with a piquant mango-mint chutney; cioppino with Gulf shrimp, scallops, clams, Alaskan king crab and mahi-mahi; and pad thai. Sunday brunch is a genteel treat, especially in nice weather on the sun-splashed courtyard. The club is a few blocks uphill, so shuttle service is available from Island Plaza (on Sumner Avenue) on weekends. *$$; AE, DIS, MC, V; local checks only; lunch, dinner every day, brunch Sun; full bar; reservations recommended; from the bay, take Sumner Ave to Country Club Dr.* &

El Galleon / ★★☆

411 CRESCENT AVE, AVALON; 310/510-1188

Here at Catalina's answer to Disney's *Pirates of the Caribbean,* diners step from the busy bayside promenade into a fantastic collage of brass portholes, ship's rigging, ample red-leather booths, and wrought-iron conquistador decor. Owner Jack Tucey consciously preserves El Galleon as a tribute to the restaurants of Avalon's vacation heyday (circa 1959)—places with names such as Tally-Ho, Waikiki, Chi-Chi Club, and the Flying Yachtsman. This setting feels just right for the hearty menu of steaks and seafood, featuring enormous cuts of aged Midwest beef (petite filets and smaller cuts are available) and fresh local and regional fish (Catalina swordfish, Hawaiian mahi-mahi, Alaskan halibut). The traditional special-occasion splurges are all here; prime rib complete with all the fixings, and Maine or local lobster with ramekins of drawn butter. You can also make a respectable meal—think of it as "grazing"—from the many appetizer selections, each large enough to be a main course. Choose from zesty barbecue pork ribs with a mesquite tang, Cajun crab cakes with Creole remoulade sauce, or a whole steamed artichoke with Thai peanut or roasted-pepper sauce. The house specialty "sourdough ensemble" is highly recommended—a basket of chewy bread accompanied by warm spinach-artichoke dip, roasted-garlic olive oil, and crumbly Romano cheese. The bar does a brisk business all day long. *$$; AE, DIS, MC, V; no checks; lunch, dinner every day; full bar; reservations recommended; on the bay between Catalina and Claressa Aves.*

LODGINGS

Hotel Metropole / ★★☆

205 CRESCENT AVE, AVALON; 310/510-1884 OR 800/300-8528

When Avalon was in its infancy, around 1887, a large, elegant hotel was constructed on the crescent-shaped bay. The old Metropole was a destination hotel in the Victorian style, and its distinctive green paint and imposing facade dominated early picture postcards. Today's Metropole, built on the spot formerly occupied by this historic grande dame, is the cornerstone of a shopping plaza that looks like Disneyland's New Orleans Square. Much smaller than its namesake, this modern replacement has 48 rooms and the ambience of a boutique inn. Built in the early 1990s, the hotel is sleek and well appointed, affording nice views from almost every room on its three floors. There's a wind-shielded rooftop deck and whirlpool overlooking the harbor, and rooms have luxurious touches like bathrobes, snack bars, air-conditioning, and in-room phones; some have fireplaces, whirlpool bathtubs, and balconies. Furnishings throughout public areas and guest rooms alike are contemporary with a tropical air, reminiscent of a Florida plantation. Rates include a continental breakfast, and just outside the front door is all of Avalon Bay's activity, starting with the theme-y Metropole Market Place in the ground-floor courtyard. It may look touristy from the outside, but the Metropole shapes up as a classy, comfortable retreat that's equally suitable for romantic interludes or family getaways. $$–$$$; AE, MC, V; metropolcatalinas.net; www.catalina.com/metropole; on Crescent Ave between Metropole and Whitley Aves. ♿

The Inn on Mount Ada / ★★★

398 WRIGLEY RD, AVALON; 310/510-2030 OR 800/608-7669

William Wrigley Jr. purchased Catalina Island in 1918, and by 1921 he built this ornate Georgian Colonial mansion on the best hillside property in Avalon, which he promptly named for his wife, Ada. Home to the Wrigley family for 37 years, the house is now an intimate and luxurious bed and breakfast that's consistently rated one of the finest small hotels in California. The ground-floor salons include a clubroom with warm hearth, a plush-seated formal library, and a wicker-filled sun room where tea, cookies, and fruit are always available. The wraparound main porch still offers the same spectacular vista of Avalon Bay that inspired Wrigley to build on this spot. Each of the six guest rooms and suites upstairs has breathtaking ocean views and a private bath; the best is the Grand Suite, which boasts a fireplace and a large private patio. The innkeepers' meticulous attention to detail will make you feel like the special guest at the summer home of wealthy friends, especially since you need never leave this hilltop Eden. Rates are always American plan, with hearty full

breakfast, light deli-style lunch, and beautiful multicourse dinner (complemented by a limited wine selection) included. For those who aren't content to merely bask in this pampering solitude, your stay also includes a
private golf cart for exploring Avalon. And don't fret about lugging your
bags uphill—the inn will arrange to have a car meet you when you arrive
on the island. The price of such luxury *can* be rather steep; if you've got
champagne taste on a beer budget, try staying midweek between November
and May, when rates plummet by $100 or more. *$$$$; MC, V; checks
OK; www.catalina.com/mtada; from the harbor, take Claressa Ave to
Beacon St, turn right to Wrigley Rd, then left uphill.*

Snug Harbor Inn / ★★★

108 SUMNER AVE, AVALON; 310/510-8400

Avalon's newest luxury hotel has been getting lots of attention since
opening in mid-1997, and this aptly named small spot is an ideal place
to drop anchor. The owners (who already operate the more affordable
European-flavored Vista del Mar around the corner) spared no expense
in renovating a dark rooming house (circa 1895) into a skylit, intimate
retreat in the heart of the action. Located above shops on a prime
bayfront street corner, these six upstairs rooms are light, airy, and impec-
cably decorated in a relaxing Nantucket theme, with hardwood floors,
thick hooked rugs, and the maximum amount of pampering comfort per
square inch. Solid new doors and double-paned windows keep street
noise out of your boudoir, leaving you to enjoy your goose-down com-
forter, cozy gas fireplace, TV, VCR, CD player, Jacuzzi bathtub, plush
terry robe (and slippers!), and the convenience of an in-room phone. The
tasteful seashore/nautical decor is worthy of *House Beautiful*—water-
color lighthouses, wooden model sailboats, striped beach umbrellas, and
well-chosen colors work together to create a truly soothing environment.
The inn provides coffee, tea, juice, and muffins set up on a hallway buffet
each morning, along with complimentary wine and cheese in the late
afternoon. The rooms are all modestly sized—with the exception of the
Santa Catalina room, sporting two bay windows and a panoramic ocean
view—and offer either partial or full bay views. If cost is a consideration,
opt for a partial view and try to visit between November and April, when
off-season and midweek rates offer a substantial discount. *$$$–$$$$;
AE, DIS, MC, V; snug@catalinas.net; www.catalina.com/snug_harbor_
inn; on the bay at Crescent and Sumner Aves.*

Zane Grey Pueblo Hotel / ★★

199 CHIMES TOWER RD, AVALON; 310/510-0966 OR 800/3-PUEBLO

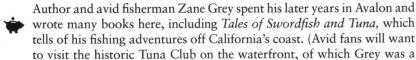

Author and avid fisherman Zane Grey spent his later years in Avalon and
wrote many books here, including *Tales of Swordfish and Tuna*, which
tells of his fishing adventures off California's coast. (Avid fans will want
to visit the historic Tuna Club on the waterfront, of which Grey was a

member). His home, named The Pueblo, is built on a hilltop with superb bay views and reflects Grey's love of the Arizona desert as well as his frequent South Seas fishing expeditions. Now a hotel, the house is built from teak beams imported from Tahiti, and sports Hopi touches like rough-hewn exposed beams and a mosaic-tile arrowhead set into the pool bottom (the Pueblo is one of only two hotels in Avalon with its own swimming pool). It's a welcoming, unfancy house, with a fireplace, grand piano, and TV in the intact original living room. The 17 simply furnished guest rooms have been updated with private baths and ceiling fans, gaze upon either the bay or the hills, and are named for Grey's various novels. Complimentary coffee, tea, and morning toast is served, and a shower room is conveniently available after checkout. The hotel also offers complimentary shuttle service to and from town for those hesitant to make the aerobic uphill climb. $-$$; AE, MC, V; checks OK; www.virtualcities. com; north of Hill St.

CENTRAL
CALIFORNIA COAST

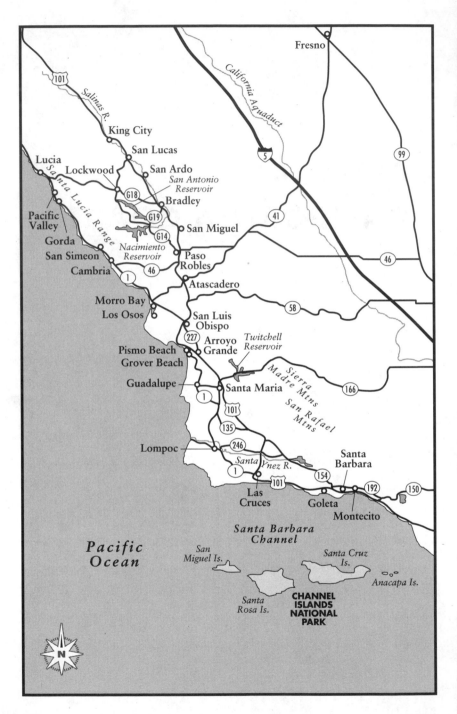

CENTRAL CALIFORNIA COAST

The dramatic scenery of California's Central Coast unfolds like an accordion of picture postcards: pristine beaches, windswept cliffs, cow-studded pastures, historic mission towns, tree-shaded country roads. The area's diversity is part of its continued appeal. You can bask in sunshine at ocean's edge, bicycle through lush vineyards, ride horses along rural backroads, and shop a boulevard of chic boutiques—all in one day.

Glorious vacation destinations are sprinkled throughout the beachfront towns. The coastline itself has a distinct personality: sunny white-sand beaches segue into rocky, cliff-lined shores, then give way to calm, picturesque bays. Quintessential Californian beach towns reflect the influence of the Native American tribes who first lived here, and residents of upscale suburbs retain something of the frontier flair of pioneer ranchers.

Though the name "Central California Coast" refers primarily to the coastline between Cambria on the north and Ventura County on the south (and though the region is best known for attractions such as the opulent tourist mecca Hearst Castle and the wealthy beach city of Santa Barbara), some equally intriguing destinations are tucked into the inland mountains and valleys, where citrus orchards and vineyards beckon to the discerning traveler. Agriculture is the economic mainstay of both Santa Barbara and San Luis Obispo Counties. Everywhere you drive you'll see roadside stands peddling fresh-from-the-fields strawberries, apples, oranges, avocados, corn, tomatoes, cucumbers, and more. The weekly farmers market is a Central Coast tradition in San Luis Obispo and many neighboring towns.

Central Coast residents are as diverse as the region itself. Well-heeled urban escapees coexist with lifelong farmers who still work the land; bohemian artists inspired by their surroundings are juxtaposed with college students whose presence brings up-to-date trends. Yet all share an appreciation of this laid-back collection of old-fashioned communities, close to, yet a world apart from, the bustling metropolis of Los Angeles.

ACCESS AND INFORMATION

The Central Coast stretches from San Luis Obispo County in the north down to Ventura County, almost nudging the Los Angeles city limits. US HIGHWAY 101, a major four-lane freeway, nicely bisects the region, complemented by scenic HIGHWAY 1 (PACIFIC COAST HIGHWAY, or PCH). (In spots, notably from San Luis Obispo to Grover Beach and from Gaviota to Oxnard, the two highways share the same roadbed.) Smaller scenic highways, such as Highways 33, 46, 150, 154, and 246, provide access to inland destinations. CAR RENTALS and major travelers' services are available primarily in Santa Barbara and San Luis Obispo. Airports in

Santa Barbara and San Luis Obispo are served by Skywest Airlines and American Eagle; Santa Barbara is also served by United Express and USAirways Express; flights are frequent from Los Angeles, less frequent from San Francisco.

San Simeon

Though it started out as a Portuguese whaling port, today the town of San Simeon is synonymous with HEARST CASTLE (750 Hearst Castle Road; 800/444-4445 for information on tour schedules, prices, and advance ticket purchases (recommended); 805/927-2020 reaches the information center; www.hearstcastle.org) and the stretch of highway-side motels catering to the one-million-plus tourists who flock here annually. The lavish palace that publishing magnate William Randolph Hearst always referred to as "the ranch" sits high above the coastline. It's opulently and almost haphazardly furnished with museum-quality treasures purchased by Hearst, a collector with indiscriminate taste and inexhaustible funds who spent years traveling to Europe buying up complete interiors and art from ancestral collections. Touring the house you'll see carved ceilings from Italian monasteries, fragments of Roman temples, lavish doors from royal castles, and a breathtaking collection of Greek pottery carelessly displayed amongst equally priceless volumes in the library. The estate boasts two swimming pools—one indoor, one outdoor—whose grandiose opulence must be seen to be believed. Besides viewing the palatial grounds and interiors, visitors learn about Hearst's Hollywood connection and the countless celebrities who were weekend guests. Now operated as a State Historic Monument by the Department of Parks & Recreation, the landmark Hearst Castle can be seen only by guided tour; four separate itineraries cover different areas of the estate.

If you've got a few minutes left over and want to see the other side of San Simeon's history, cross Highway 1 to the sheltering bay where W. R. Hearst's father in the 1880s built a wharf, pier, and Mission-style warehouses for the operation of what was then a massive cattle ranch. His son would later use the port to bring in the voluminous building materials and furnishings for the castle, including crates of exotic animals for his private zoo (the zebras you see grazing with cattle alongside the highway are remnants of that short-lived endeavor). Near the end of San Simeon Point, stop into SEBASTIAN'S GENERAL STORE (442 San Luis Obispo–San Simeon Road; 805/927-4217; www.sebastians.com); the rustic country store, which has been in operation since 1852, dispenses basic groceries and souvenirs and operates a small snack bar.

CENTRAL CALIFORNIA COAST THREE-DAY TOUR

DAY ONE. Get an early start at San Simeon's **Hearst Castle** to avoid midday crowds. After touring this landmark, enjoy lunch on the dramatic cliffs at **Ragged Point Inn,** followed by a leisurely afternoon strolling the antique stores and boutiques of **Cambria's Main Street.** Have dinner by the welcoming fireplace at the **Sow's Ear Cafe,** then bed down in one of Cambria's charming B&Bs, such as the **Olallieberry Inn.**

DAY TWO. After breakfast, head down scenic Highway I toward **San Luis Obispo,** where you can explore the historic mission and see the downtown sights. Take a lunch break at the eclectic and colorful **Big Sky Cafe** in the heart of town. When you're ready, continue to funky **Pismo Beach** and check into an oceanfront room at luxurious **SeaVenture Resort.** If the weather's nice, take a pre-dinner stroll on the pier, perhaps stopping for a bowl of clam chowder. Or proceed directly to dinner at popular **Giuseppe's Cucina Italiana.**

DAY THREE. Leave the beach behind for a day of wine touring in the idyllic **Santa Ynez Valley.** Stop first in tiny **Los Olivos** for lunch provisions, then ramble leisurely from winery to winery. When you get hungry, buy a bottle of wine and enjoy the **picnic grounds at a vineyard** such as Gainey, Sunstone, or Zaca Mesa. Later on (perhaps after an afternoon nap), make your way to the Danish storybook town of **Solvang** for a relaxed dinner at intimate **Brothers Restaurant.** Spend the night at the cozy **Ballard Inn** before heading to Santa Barbara for a few days (see Santa Barbara Three-Day Tour, page 223, for complete details).

One of the most spectacular natural attractions along this stretch of rugged coast is its abundance of marine mammals. Seals and sea lions are often spotted along Cambria's Moonstone Beach, but the area most popular with ELEPHANT SEALS is the rocky shoreline below PIEDRAS BLANCAS LIGHTHOUSE, about 12 miles north of Cambria. These enormous creatures are practically year-round residents, allowing visitors the opportunity to eavesdrop on their always intriguing—and frequently noisy—society. The most active time is mating season in December, when females who have just given birth to the pups conceived the previous year almost immediately conceive again. Mothers and pups hang out on shore for several months. Meanwhile, other seals return for molting, and younger seals are nearly always present, as they need to reach maturity before they're able to spend long periods out at sea.

RESTAURANTS

Ragged Point Inn / ★★

19019 HIGHWAY 1, SAN SIMEON; 805/927-5708

Ragged Point shares with its adjacent motel a million-dollar view and a dramatic clifftop location. The dining room is classic California-redwood architecture with plenty of view-enhancing windows, and there's a partially enclosed patio for alfresco dining when the weather allows. The menu is California cuisine, with hearty American favorites and gourmet European touches. Recommended choices include herb cheese-stuffed mushrooms, baby back ribs in ginger-barbecue sauce, and home- made ravioli in orange-sage sauce. At lunchtime there's a variety of gourmet sandwiches. You'll want to be here during daylight to enjoy the scenery, so plan on lunch or a reasonably early dinner (the dining room serves lunch until 4pm, with dinner starting at 5pm) and make a point of strolling the well-landscaped, Japanese-inspired gardens. Ragged Point also serves up a hearty and satisfying breakfast. *$$; AE, DIS, MC, V; checks OK; breakfast, lunch, dinner every day; full bar; reservations recommended; 15 miles north of Hearst Castle.* ᕲ

LODGINGS

Best Western Cavalier Oceanfront Resort / ★

9415 HEARST DR, SAN SIMEON; 805/927-4688 OR 800/826-8168

Of the dozen or more budget and midrange hotels and motels clustered along Highway 1 just south of Hearst Castle, this surprisingly nice Best Western is the only one that's actually an oceanfront property. Composed of a handful of buildings sprawled across a gentle slope, the hotel offers a wide range of accommodations. Every room—whether you choose a basic double or opt for extras such as a fireplace, ocean view, wet bar, or oceanfront terrace—features a stocked minibar, hair dryer, computer jack, and cable TV with VCR (rentals are next door). Two outdoor pools are shielded from the wind—but not from the exceptional view—thanks to glass walls, and guests are invited to huddle around cliffside bonfires each evening. There are several casual dining options within walking distance, plus an exercise room, coin laundry, and telescopes set up for whale- or porpoise-watching. Though travelers focusing on Hearst Castle are probably the only ones who'll choose to stay along this motel-heavy stretch, the Cavalier is top-notch in its class. *$$; AE, DC, DIS, MC, V; checks OK; on Hwy 1, 3 miles south of Hearst Castle.* ᕲ

California Seacoast Lodge

9215 HEARST DR, SAN SIMEON; 805/927-3878

If you're looking for a bed-and-breakfast ambience super-close to Hearst Castle, this innlike property really stands out from its motel neighbors.

Although most of the rooms have no ocean view, and although the small swimming pool is good for a quick dip but not pretty enough to lounge by, the Seacoast Lodge's loyal followers are drawn by the plush comfort of homey country French rooms featuring canopy beds and plenty of flowered prints and flounces. You'll never awaken thinking you're in an impersonal chain hotel here. Some rooms have fireplaces or whirlpool tubs to add a romantic mood, and a complimentary continental breakfast is served each morning in the sunny parlor. If the mediocre dining options nearby don't interest you, Cambria is a mere 10-minute drive away. Between September and May, low-season rates offer substantial bargains. *$$; AE, DIS, MC, V; no checks; on Hwy 1, 3 miles south of Hearst Castle.* &

Ragged Point Inn & Resort

19019 HIGHWAY 1, SAN SIMEON; 805/927-4502

The number one reason to stay here—make that the *only* reason—is the breathtakingly dramatic setting. Perched on a grassy cliff high above the ocean, this little 20-room motel offers views as spectacular as any further north in pricey Big Sur. Part of an upscale rest stop complex that includes a gas station, minimart, gift shop, snack bar, and the Ragged Point Inn restaurant (see review in Restaurants, above), the motel itself is folksy and basic—and reminds many of Alan Alda's and Ellen Burstyn's secluded oceanside tryst in *Same Time, Next Year*. Each spacious room features an oceanfront balcony or patio, along with separate heating controls for getting cozy on blustery nights. The furnishings, though well maintained, are mismatched and far from stylish; bathrooms are small but serviceable; and the motel is set back a ways from the other roadside facilities; so you can count on silence and seclusion. Foxes and raccoons are often spotted scurrying around the grounds. San Simeon and Cambria are a 25-minute drive south, but the restaurant is good enough to eat all your meals here if you want. Ask for an upstairs room to get the best view—and the most privacy. *$$; AE, DIS, MC, V; checks OK; 15 miles north of Hearst Castle.* &

Cambria

Many vacationers discover Cambria only when they visit Hearst Castle for the first time, but after that they're hooked on the sophisticated little village that combines the best elements of both northern and southern California. The town's name reportedly compares the natural beauty of the area to the lush, rolling countryside of Wales, whose ancient name was Cambria. This place truly has a split personality. The main part of town is known as the **VILLAGE**, a charming enclave of restored Victorians, art galleries, antique stores, boutiques, and exceptional restaurants nestled among pine-blanketed hills. Across the highway, however, **MOON-STONE BEACH** (named for the translucent stones that wash ashore) is lined with inns offering an opportunity to sleep alongside the breaking surf and stroll windswept beaches populated by seals and sea lions. For an introduction to the area, stop by the **CAMBRIA CHAMBER OF COMMERCE** (767 Main Street; 805/927-3624; www.cambria-online.com).

Shopping is a major pastime in the village; boutique owners are hyper-savvy about keeping their merchandise current—and priced just a hair lower than in L.A. or San Francisco. This close-knit community has always attracted artists and artisans of the highest quality, so listen when you hear phrases like "important piece" and "museum quality" bandied about. The finest hand-crafted glass artworks, from affordable jewelry to investment-scale sculpture, can be found at **SEEKERS COLLECTION & GALLERY** (4090 Burton Drive; 805/927-4352; www.seekersglass.com). Nearby, at **MOONSTONES GALLERY** (4070 Burton Drive; 805/927-3447), you'll find a selection of works ranging from woven crafts to jewelry and an exceptional selection of woodcarvings and other crafts.

About 10 minutes east of town, on a rambling country road, sits **LINN'S FRUIT BINN** (east of town on Santa Rosa Creek Road; 805/927-8134), a family farm known statewide for freshly baked pies and other goodies. The Linns' cash crop is the olallieberry, a tart blackberry hybrid used in pies, preserves, salsas, teas, mustards, candies, and anything else they dream up. Their most popular pies are apple-olallieberry and rhubarb, which are even sold frozen for easy transport home. Their goods are also available in town at **LINN'S MAIN BINN** (2277 Main Street; 805/927-0371; see review, below).

RESTAURANTS

The Brambles Dinner House / ★

4005 BURTON DR, CAMBRIA; 805/927-4716

Looking at the exterior of this Old English cottage–style lodge, it's easy to predict the menu: prime rib, of course, and Continental/American specialties reminiscent of the 1950s, when the Brambles first opened. But the Greek influence of owner Nick Kaperonis is everywhere, as *dolmades* and *saganaki* share billing with oysters Rockefeller, chicken cordon bleu, and rack of lamb. Since the dining room's romantic retro atmosphere alone isn't enough to compete with the culinary excellence elsewhere in town, Brambles stays on the top with the freshest fish and beef, expert preparation, and fair prices; they've also augmented the menu with some lighter Mediterranean fare. To do it right, however, forget the diet for a night and order sour cream for your baked potato, extra butter for your lobster, and one of the restaurant's tempting chocolaty desserts. Locals grouse that the place is too popular with busloads of tourists, whose package deals often include the restaurant's early-bird dinner, so it's wise to dine later. *$$; AE, DIS, MC, V; checks OK; dinner every day, brunch Sun; full bar; reservations suggested; 2 blocks south of Main St.* ♿

Linn's Main Binn / ★★

2277 MAIN ST, CAMBRIA; 805/927-0371
The in-town outlet for popular Linn's Fruit Binn (see the Cambria introduction, above), this casual all-day restaurant also carries decorative housewares, gifts, and a selection of Linn's food products. You can't go wrong with a steaming hot chicken or beef pot pie, which seems natural, since Linn's most famous products are their superlative berry pies. Other winners are homemade daily soups, hearty sandwiches, and fresh-from-the-farm salads; at breakfast, sweet treats like berry-covered waffles and pancakes prevail. Every town should have a place like this, where a reliably good meal doesn't have to be an event and where you'll feel equally welcome stopping in for just a slice of warm pie and a glass of ice-cold milk. *$; DIS, MC, V; checks OK; breakfast, lunch, dinner every day; beer and wine; reservations not accepted; 1 block east of Burton Dr.* ♿

Robin's / ★★

4095 BURTON DR, CAMBRIA; 805/927-5007
"Home Cooking from Around the World" is the slogan at this adventuresome and eclectic cafe that's been a local favorite for many years. Located on the east side of Cambria's still-expanding village, Robin's has a cozy, casual, almost hippie ambience, and a menu that runs the gamut from exotic Mexican-, Thai-, or Indian-tinged recipes to simple vegetarian salads, pastas, and sandwiches. The robust flavors of extremely fresh ingredients shine through every dish, and the food manages to taste well composed yet distinctly homemade. Best bets include the soup of the day; the "black bean surprise," a tortilla dip appetizer of beans, cheese, guacamole, salsa, and sour cream; salmon fettuccine in cream sauce with fresh dill sprigs; and *roghan josh,* a North Indian lamb dish in a richly spiced nutty yogurt sauce accompanied by sweet-tangy chutneys. Much of the menu is somewhat health oriented, giving many diners the justification to indulge in one of Robin's to-die-for desserts, like vanilla custard bread pudding in Grand Marnier sauce. *$$; MC, V; local checks only; lunch, dinner every day; beer and wine; reservations recommended; www.robinsrestaurant.com; 1 block south of Main St.* ♿

Sea Chest Oyster Bar & Seafood Restaurant / ★★

6216 MOONSTONE BEACH DR, CAMBRIA; 805/927-4514
No nautical items were spared in decorating this gray clapboard cottage festooned with brass portholes, anchors, fishing nets, buoys, and virtually anything else to accentuate the seaside atmosphere. Warm and welcoming, the Sea Chest even has a game-filled lounge complete with cribbage,

checkers, and chess to keep you amused while waiting for your table. Once you're seated—either gazing out at the waves rolling ashore or next to a cozy pot-bellied stove—choose from an extensive menu of very fresh seafood from local and worldwide waters. Oysters are the main attraction: oysters on the half shell, oyster stew, oysters Casino, oysters Rockefeller, or devils on horseback (oysters sautéed in wine and garlic, then topped with bacon and served on toast). The menu also features steamed New Zealand green-lipped mussels, steamed clams and other clam preparations, halibut, salmon, lobster, and scampi, plus whatever looked good from off the boats that morning. There's a respectable list of microbrews and imported beers, along with a selection of Central Coast wines. *$$; no credit cards; checks OK; dinner Wed–Mon; beer and wine; reservations not accepted; west of Hwy 1 at Windsor.* &

The Sow's Ear Cafe / ★★☆

2248 MAIN ST, CAMBRIA; 805/927-4865

If it were in Los Angeles or San Francisco, the Sow's Ear would cost twice as much and you'd never get a reservation—it's that good. One of Cambria's tiny old cottages has been transformed into a warm, romantic hideaway right on Main Street, where the best tables are in the fireside front room, lit just enough to highlight its rustic wood-and-brick decor. Pigs appear in oil paintings, small ceramic or cast-iron models adorning the shelves, and the Americana woodcut sow logo. Though the menu features plenty of contemporary California cuisine, the most popular dishes are American country favorites given a contemporary lift; these include a warmly satisfying chicken-fried steak with outstanding gravy, chicken and dumplings any grandmother would be proud of, and zesty baby pork ribs. Other standouts are salmon prepared in parchment and grilled pork loin glazed with chunky olallieberry chutney. Although dinners come complete with soup or salad, do share one of the outstanding appetizers—the calamari is melt-in-your-mouth, and marinated goat cheese perfectly accompanies the restaurant's signature marbled bread baked in terra-cotta flowerpots. The wine list is among the area's best, featuring outstanding Central Coast vintages with a large number available by the glass. If you have only one nice dinner in town, make this the place. *$$; AE, DIS, MC, V; local checks only; dinner every day; beer and wine; reservations recommended; ½ block east of Burton Dr.* &

LODGINGS

Beach House Bed & Breakfast / ★☆

6360 MOONSTONE BEACH DR, CAMBRIA; 805/927-3136

If you've ever been jealous of friends with vacation homes and wished for your own casual, comfy cabin or beachfront cottage, this is the place for you. Reconfigured as a B&B, this three-story, A-frame wood house still has the vibe of a 1950s vacation retreat, happily sporting unchic decorative touches and a communal kitchen and living room. Guests gather around the main fireplace or on the seaside deck for wine and appetizers each afternoon and take full advantage of the telescopes and binoculars provided for bird-, dolphin-, seal-, and whale watching. All six quirkily individual rooms have either a full or a partial ocean view, private bath, and cable TV. Consider splurging on one of the best ocean-view rooms (worth every penny), which have private fireplaces to chase the evening chill away. Hosts Penny and Tom Hitch also own the Moonstone Beach Bar & Grill a few doors down, where full breakfast is provided each morning. The restaurant is also a great place to end a sunset stroll or enjoy a nightcap. *$$–$$$; MC, V; no checks; west of Hwy 1 at Windsor.* &

Cambria Pines Lodge

2905 BURTON DR, CAMBRIA; 805/927-4200 OR 800/445-6868

Nestled as it is in 25 acres of wild Monterey pine woods, it's hard to believe this old-style enclave is just minutes from the crashing surf and only a few blocks from the center of town. Equal parts vacation lodge and summer camp, the lodge is composed of 31 different buildings, from rustic, secluded cabins to two-bedroom hotel-style units. At the heart is the main lodge, built in the early 1990s around the great stone hearth of the original 1927 building (which was destroyed by fire). It all has a welcoming, communal feel. Nearly all the rooms have fireplaces; a 1999 upgrade replaced worn furnishings with contemporary (though plain) pieces and added amenities like coffee-makers and cable TV. The only swimming pool on the village side of town is on these grounds, a gorgeous indoor Olympic-sized one heated for year-round use. At press time, the circa-1950s pool complex, which includes a separate whirlpool, sauna, and massage room, was slated for a complete refurbishing. Inside the main lodge, there's a moderately priced restaurant and large fireside lounge with occasional live music. A full breakfast buffet is included in the rate. *$–$$; AE, DIS, MC, V; checks OK; www.moonstonemgmt. com; take Burton Dr uphill from the center of town.* &

FogCatcher Inn / ★

6400 MOONSTONE BEACH DR, CAMBRIA; 805/927-1400 OR 800/425-4121
This contemporary hotel's faux English style—featuring thatched-look roofing and rough-hewn stone exteriors—fits right into the architectural mishmash along funky Moonstone Beach, even though the hotel is one of the newest properties here. Its 60 rooms are contained in a U-shaped building situated so that many have unencumbered views of the crashing surf across the street, while some gaze oceanward over a sea of parked cars, and others are hopelessly landlocked. Rates vary wildly according to the quality of view, but all rooms have identical amenities. Inside you'll find a surprising attention to comfort, especially considering the Fog-Catcher's prices, which can drop dramatically midweek and off-season. Rooms are immaculately maintained and furnished in a comfy cottage style with oversize pine furniture, floral accents, and stylish fixtures. Each is made cozier by a gas fireplace and also boasts a microwave oven, coffeemaker, and stocked refrigerator; the rate also includes a continental breakfast buffet. Unlike many comparably priced Moonstone Beach lodgings, the FogCatcher also has a heated swimming pool and whirlpool. *$$; AE, DIS, MC, V; checks OK; www.moonstonemgmt. com; west of Hwy 1 at Windsor.* &

J. Patrick House / ★★

2990 BURTON DR, CAMBRIA; 805/927-3812 OR 800/341-5258
Hidden in a pine-filled residential neighborhood overlooking Cambria's East Village, this picture-perfect B&B is cozy, elegant, and welcoming. The main house is an authentic two-story log cabin, where each afternoon innkeepers Barbara and Mel Schwimmer host wine and hors d'oeuvres next to the living room fireplace, and each morning serve breakfast by windows overlooking a garden filled with hummingbirds, Chinese magnolias, fuchsias, white and pink Japanese anemones, flowering Jerusalem sage, primrose, and bromeliads. The eight guest rooms, most of which are in the adjacent carriage house, are named for Irish counties. Each features a private bath, wood-burning fireplace, feather duvets, bedtime milk and cookies, and country elements like knotty wood, bent-twig furniture, calico prints, and hand-stitched quilts—all of which combine for ultra-charming accommodations that may teeter on the side of too-cute for some. Still, every guest is made to feel special with the personal attention and consideration that Cambria's B&Bs are known for. *$$; AE, DIS, MC, V; checks OK; jph@jpatrickhouse.com; www. jpatrickhouse.com; take Burton Dr uphill from the center of town.* &

Olallieberry Inn / ★★☆

2476 MAIN ST, CAMBRIA; 805/927-3222 OR 888/927-3222

Cambria's bed and breakfasts are standard-setters for aspiring innkeepers, and this charming nine-room B&B is one of the best in town. Innkeepers Carol Ann and Peter Irsfeld have spent years honing their craft—and it shows in the way they meticulously attend to every detail while staying graciously relaxed. Besides lovingly maintaining this 1873 Greek Revival house—a convenient two-block stroll from the heart of Cambria's east end of the village—they show their skills in the lush but perfectly manicured gardens (including an herb garden once featured in *Sunset* magazine) and in the treats that come from chef Peter's kitchen. Guests are served afternoon wine and delectable hors d'oeuvres (baked Brie, and a trio of homemade gourmet salsas). Breakfast is an impressive spread that includes house specialties such as creamy, nutty stuffed French toast or cheddar-topped eggs in a crust of hash brown potatoes. Tangy olallieberry jelly is always alongside. Like the home's parlor and breakfast room, guest quarters are teeming with antiques, floral wallpaper, and Victorian lace. Six are in the main house; though all have private baths, three of the baths are across the hall rather than en suite. The nicely renovated carriage house has three spacious rooms overlooking a creek; one is a suite for up to four people. Six rooms have fireplaces. The most charming room is Room at the Top, a sunny nook where you can relax fireside in a white wicker chaise or soak in the antique claw-footed tub. *$$; AE, MC, V; checks OK; from Hwy 1, turn east on Main St.* &

Harmony

Along Highway 1 just a few minutes south of Cambria lies a town whose big reputation belies its tiny size. The sign says "Harmony, California, Population 18," and this hamlet is truly not much larger than a postage stamp. Highway 1 used to pass right through the center of town along what's now known as Old Creamery Road. It's named for the once-vital dairy operation that provided milk, cream, and butter throughout the county; William Randolph Hearst even used to stop in to stock the weekend larder on his way up to San Simeon. The **OLD CREAMERY BUILDING** now houses a few gift shops and a U.S. postal station.

Far from languishing as a 19th-century ghost town, Harmony has an enduring appeal among folks from all over. You can take home a souvenir Harmony snowdome, or even get married in the town's tiny wedding chapel. Like its neighbor Cambria, Harmony also has an **ARTS AND CRAFTS** movement, and most visitors stop off here to shop at one of three serious galleries, all on the same street. Inside the barnlike **PHOENIX STUDIOS** (10 Main Street; 805/927-0724) you can watch the resident glassblowers create superbly designed vases, lamps, and bowls. Their organic patterns are smooth, iridescent colors have a sophisticated Art Nouveau style. Next door is **BACKROADS** (2180 Old Creamery Road; 805/927-2919), a gallery displaying mainly small items like jewelry, glassware, and handmade paper goods by regional artists. Across the street, the cavernous **HARMONY POTTERY STUDIO/GALLERY** (Old Creamery Road; 805/927-4293) displays ceramic artwork ranging from inexpensive painted bathroom accessories to elegant glazed platters and vases, with hundreds of pieces in between.

Paso Robles

Although its Spanish name means "pass of oak trees," Paso Robles is today better known for the grapevines that blanket the rolling hills of this inland region. Part of the up-and-coming Central Coast Wine Country, Paso Robles currently boasts almost 40 wineries (see Wineries, below). The town is also proud of its faintly checkered past: it was established in 1870 by Drury James, uncle of outlaw Jesse James (who reportedly hid out in these parts). In 1913, pianist Ignace Paderewski came to live in Paso Robles, where he planted zinfandel vines on his ranch and often played in the Paso Robles Inn (which today maintains a small exhibit in his honor).

Paso Robles is blessed with a well-preserved turn-of-the-century downtown that could have leapt from the play *The Music Man*. At the center of town is **CITY PARK** (at Spring and 12th Streets), a green gathering place—complete with festival bandstand—anchored by the 1907 **CARNEGIE HISTORICAL LIBRARY** (805/238-4996), a Classical Revival brick masterpiece that today houses an exhibit of area maps, early photographs, and historical documents. Several downtown side streets are lined with splendid historic Victorian, Craftsman, and Queen Anne homes all shaded by grand trees. Drive along Vine Street between 10th and 19th Streets for a superb peek into the past, including the **CALL-BOOTH HOUSE** (1315 Vine Street; 805/238-5473), a carefully restored Victorian on the National Register of Historic Places, which is now an art gallery featuring local painters and artisans. The **PASO ROBLES PIONEER MUSEUM** (2010 Riverside Avenue, near 21st Street across the railroad tracks; 805/239-4556) is worth a visit for insight into the heritage of a working frontier town. The small museum is filled with donated artifacts presented as a series of life-size dioramas illustrating the town's history, ranging from Native American settlements and vintage ranching equipment to a primitive turn-of-the-century medical-surgical office.

Antique hounds have been flocking to Paso Robles since long before the wine-country explosion, and downtown still proves fertile hunting ground for treasure-seekers. The best are the giant mall-style stores representing dozens of dealers each; you can easily spend hours in just one building. Two reliable choices are **ANTIQUE EMPORIUM MALL**(1307 Park St; 805/238-1078) and **GREAT AMERICAN ANTIQUES MALL** (1305 Spring St; 805/239-1203). For more information, contact the **PASO ROBLES CHAMBER OF COMMERCE** (1225 Park St; 805/238-0506 or 800/406-4040; www.pasorobleschamber.com).

RESTAURANTS

Bistro Laurent / ★★

1202 PINE ST, PASO ROBLES; 805/226-8191
Although it was inevitable that fine dining would follow on the heels of fine wine, chef Laurent Grangien nevertheless created quite a stir when he opened this cozy yet sophisticated bistro in a town unaccustomed to innovations like a chef's tasting menu. With his extensive French cooking background and his Los Angeles restaurant experience, Grangien offers a California-tinged style of French cuisine while maintaining an unpretentious atmosphere that locals have come to love. Banquette-lined walls make virtually every table in the historic brick building a cozy private booth, and there's alfresco dining on a romantic patio. While you peruse Bistro Laurent's impressive list of Central Coast wines, you'll enjoy a complimentary hors d'oeuvre (goat cheese toasts, perhaps). Menu highlights include traditional bistro fare such as roasted rosemary garlic chicken, pork loin bathed in peppercorn sauce, or ahi tuna in red-wine reduction. If you're daring, choose the four-course tasting menu, which changes nightly to reflect the chef's current favorite ingredients or preparations. On busy nights, the kitchen can be uneven, but Bistro Laurent is still the best place in town. *$$; MC, V; no checks; dinner Mon–Sat; beer and wine; reservations recommended; at the corner of 12th St.* &

Busi's on the Park / ★

1122 PINE ST, PASO ROBLES; 805/238-1390
Busi's is indeed across from downtown's City Park, but don't expect this friendly local fave to be snooty and scenic. It's a comfortable tavernlike joint whose capable kitchen always works with the freshest local ingredients. A short, seasonally changing menu offers eclectic fare: Southwestern chicken salad with refreshing cilantro-lime *crema;* Chinese stir-fry beef tinged with orange and sesame; a supreme cannelloni rolled in freshly made basil-egg pasta, ladled with roasted tomato sauce, and accompanied by sautéed spinach. Everything comes with garden-fresh soup or the colorful dinner salad, and mouth-watering desserts tantalize from a nearby tray. Busi's on the Park is a perfect lunch or weekend brunch choice and is a fine option for an affordable dinner as well. *$; AE, MC, V; checks OK; lunch, dinner Tues–Sun, brunch Sat–Sun; full bar; reservations recommended; between 11th and 12th Sts.* &

PASO ROBLES WINERIES

Although vines have been tended in Paso Robles's fertile foothills for 200 years, the area has until recently been overlooked by wine aficionados—even though it was granted its own appellation in 1983. But sometime around 1992 wine grapes surpassed lettuce as San Luis Obispo County's primary cash crop, and now the whole character of the area has shifted into Wine Country mode—albeit without the pretension and stifling crowds of California's more established Napa Valley wine region. Wine touring in Paso Robles is reminiscent of another, unhurried time; here it's all about enjoying a relaxed rural atmosphere and driving leisurely along country roads from winery to winery. The region's friendly ambience and small crowds make it easy to learn all about the winemaking process as you go along—often from the winemakers themselves. The **Paso Robles Wine Festival** each May started out in 1983 as a small, neighborly gathering but has grown into the largest outdoor wine tasting in California. Nearly a dozen events make up the three-day weekend, including winemaker dinners with guest chefs, a golf tourney, a 5K run, a 10K bike ride, concerts, winery open houses and tastings, plus the carnival-like festival itself in City Park. For more information on seasonal events and area wineries, contact the **Paso Robles Vintners & Growers** (805/239-8463 or 800/549-WINE; www.pasowine.com). Meanwhile, any time of year is fine for dropping by the following wineries.

Eberle Winery: Winemaker Gary Eberle is sometimes called the "grandfather of Paso Robles's wine country" by the local vintners who honed their craft under his tutelage. A visit to Eberle includes a look at its underground caves, where hundreds of aging barrels share space with the Wild Boar Room, site of Eberle's monthly winemaker dinners. Located on Highway 46 E (3.5 miles east of US 101); 805/238-9607.

EOS Estate Winery at Arciero Vineyards: Follow the checkered flag to the 800 acres of wine grapes owned by former race-car driver Frank Arciero, who specializes in Italian varietals like Nebbiolo and Sangiovese. The facility includes a self-guided tour, race-car collection, spectacular rose garden, and a picnic area. Located on Highway 46 East (6 miles east of US 101); 805/239-2562 or 800/249-WINE; www.eosvintage.com.

Justin Vineyards & Winery: At the end of a scenic country road lies the boutique winery of ex-Angelenos Justin and Deborah Baldwin, whose best wine is Isosceles, a sophisticated Bordeaux-style blend with splendid aging potential. Since 1987 the Baldwins have commissioned a different artist each year to interpret their gorgeous Tuscan-style property for the label, and the results are on display throughout the complex. Located at 11680 Chimney Rock Road (15 miles west of US 101), 805/237-4150; www.justinwine.com.

Meridian Vineyards: Meridian is the largest local producer, the Central Coast's best known label, and where you'll get the most polished, Napa-like tasting experience. The grounds are beautiful, featuring a man-made lake surrounding by rolling hills. Located on Highway 46 E (7 miles east of US 101); 805/237-6000; www.meridianvineyards.com.

Tobin James Cellars: With a Wild West theme based on the unpredictable personality of colorful winemaker "Toby" James (who claims a dubious lineage from the James Gang), this winery is fun and unpretentious. Don't think he's not serious about his craft, though—Tobin James's zinfandel and late-harvest zinfandel are both award winners. Located at 8950 Union Road (at Highway 46 E 8 miles east of US 101); 805/239-2204.

York Mountain Winery: The first winery to be established in Paso Robles, York Mountain stands on land originally deeded by Ulysses S. Grant. Inside the 100-year-old stone tasting room, look for a dry chardonnay with complex spice overtones, and Reserve cabernets made from hand-selected grapes. Located at 7505 York Mountain Road (off Highway 46 W 7 miles west of US 101); 805/238-3925.

LODGINGS

Adelaide Inn / ★

1215 YSABEL AVE, PASO ROBLES; 805/238-2770 OR 800/549-PASO

Though its neighbors are gas stations and coffee shops, this freeway-friendly motel is nicely isolated from its bustling surroundings. Lush, manicured gardens are screened from the street by foliage, a relaxing outdoor hot tub is secluded inside a redwood gazebo, and there's even a miniature golf course/putting green. The result is a surprisingly quiet, comfortable property tended with a loving care that's rare among lower-priced accommodations—and this place is truly a bargain. The rooms are clean and comfortable, with an extra warmth that's a cut above standard motels; unexpected amenities include refrigerators, coffeemakers, hair dryers, and complimentary newspaper, plus work desks and dataports designed specifically for the business traveler. An outdoor heated pool is in the center of the complex, and morning fruit and muffins are provided in the lobby. *$; AE, DC, DIS, MC, V; www.adelaideinn.com; at 24th St just west of US 101.* &

The Arbor Inn / ★★

2130 ARBOR RD, PASO ROBLES; 805/227-4673

Across from Treana Winery about a five-minute drive from the center of town, this elegant bed and breakfast is a favorite with honeymooners because of its splendid setting and luxurious hospitality. Though the main building—a white clapboard cross between Queen Anne and

Southern plantation style—looks old, it was actually built in 1994. This means that guest rooms are extra-spacious and bathrooms ultra-modern, though the entire inn is furnished with formal English country antique reproductions. Treana's vine-planted acres are just steps from the inn's back patio and visible from every room's private balcony. Each of the nine rooms is named for a wine (Syrah, Bordeaux, Chardonnay, etc.) and has a gas fireplace, color TV, telephone, terry bathrobes, and bedside bottled water. Luxury is achieved through small, thoughtful touches; you'll find fresh flowers accompanying everything from the chocolate on your pillow with turn-down service to the morning coffee tray left discreetly outside your door. The room rate includes full breakfast, afternoon wine and hors d'oeuvres, and late-night cookies. If you're looking for a romantic splurge, the Moscato Allegro room features an in-room whirlpool-for-two, and the top-floor Cabernet Suite is as rich and decadent as an aged wine, with sumptuous furnishings, a seven-headed shower, and an ultra-private patio with a view. *$$$; MC, V; checks OK; at Hwy 46 W, 1 mile west of US 101.* &

Gillie Archer Inn / ★★

1433 OAK ST, PASO ROBLES; 805/238-0879

Architecture buffs love poking around this small bed-and-breakfast inn, just a couple of blocks from the heart of town on a quiet residential street lined with fabulously restored historic homes. Although the exterior of the 1917 transitional Craftsman home has an unfortunate layer of stucco, it can't obscure its classic structure. No luxury was spared when this house was built for a prominent Paso Robles attorney—at extraordinary expense for the time—and subsequent owners have worked hard at maintaining its historical integrity. Expect to find original built-in shelves and storage in nearly every room, original electrical fixtures (along with well-designed reproductions), and light, airy sun porches. Named for an ancestor of genial innkeeper Kathleen Stratton-Haas, the inn has five warmly decorated and unfussy rooms. Two have private bathrooms, one has a fireplace, and all have cable TV and VCR. The morning breakfast buffet includes treats such as apple strudel or fruit crepes along with a large spread of fresh fruit from the local farmers' market; the sunny breakfast room overlooks a delightful garden whose gazebo is often used for small gatherings and events. *$$; AE, DIS, MC, V; gillie@tcsn.net; www.virtualcities.com; 1 block west of Spring St between 14th and 15th Sts.* &

Paso Robles Inn / ★

1103 SPRING ST, PASO ROBLES; 805/238-2660

If you're attracted to the retro 1940s look of this sprawling downtown inn, you'll enjoy learning about the *first* El Paso de Robles Hotel, a grand landmark favorably compared to the finest hotels in San Francisco.

Designed by famed architect Stanford White and built in 1891, the "absolutely fireproof" structure burned to the ground in 1940, leaving only the ballroom wing that sits, boarded up and off limits, behind the hotel. Many photographs and relics of the old hotel are on display in the lobby, whose Spanish-style architecture and tile reflect the passion for Mission Revival that was in full swing when this replacement was built. A stroll through tranquil and lovely grounds leads guests to a footbridge over the creek meandering through this oak-shaded property and to 68 bungalow-style motel rooms with convenient carports. Well shielded from street noise, these units are simple and plain, lacking in modern amenities and appointments, but many guests consider them charming and nostalgic. (Avoid room numbers beginning with 1 or 2, however—they're in a less desirable building near the street.) A large heated pool near the creek makes for great afternoon dips, and the dining room (with cocktail lounge) serves three diner-style meals daily. *$; AE, DC, DIS, MC, V; between 10th and 12th Sts.* &

San Miguel

Eight miles up the road from Paso Robles lies San Miguel, site of **MISSION SAN MIGUEL ARCHANGEL** (on old US Highway 101; 805/467-3256), founded in 1797 and still run by the Franciscan order. It's not uncommon to see brown-robed friars going about their daily business on the grounds. Less extensively restored than many others in the state, San Miguel's modest exterior hides a breathtakingly elaborate and well-preserved church, which was painted and decorated by area Native Americans under the supervision of Spanish designer Estevan Munras. The walls and woodwork glow with luminous colors untouched since their application in 1820. Behind the altar, with its statue of San Miguel (St. Michael), is splendid tile work featuring a radiant Eye of God.

Templeton

Located just a few minutes south of Paso Robles, Templeton sports an almost cartoonlike Old West flavor, with wooden boardwalks and antique-style signage. But this agrarian frontier town is the genuine article, continuing to flourish ever since its founding during the Civil War era. The grain elevator of Templeton Feed & Grain is still the centerpiece of downtown business; across the street, period storefronts house modern establishments.

RESTAURANTS

Mcphee's Grill / ★★☆

416 MAIN ST, TEMPLETON; 805/434-3204

Inside what used to be Templeton's general mercantile store (circa 1860), chef/restaurateur Ian McPhee has created an eatery that manages to perfectly balance the town's rural Americana with the big-city culinary eclecticism he honed so successfully at Cambria's much-missed Ian's. An old-fashioned pressed-tin ceiling complements sponge-painted walls adorned with English livestock prints and stenciled barnyard animals. Through the open kitchen chefs can be seen busily garnishing McPhee's most popular plates: chewy ancho chile strips adorn the Mexican tortilla soup, and baby orange wedges frame the rustic bread salad—country bread draped with warm Duberki cheese and topped with vinaigrette-tossed mesclun. Main courses range from lighter fare, like shiitake-mushroom ravioli in macadamia-nut butter dotted with sun-dried tomatoes, to hearty peppered filet mignon in cabernet-olive reduction over tangy blue cheese potatoes. Fresh fish specials always reflect McPhee's innovative style, and wife June presents delectable desserts. An impressive list of Central Coast wines, many available by the glass, ensures a perfect match for your meal. *$$; MC, V; checks OK; lunch Mon–Sat, dinner every day, brunch Sun; beer and wine; reservations recommended; between 4th and 5th Sts.* &

Morro Bay

Vast and filled with birds and sea mammals, scenic Morro Bay is named for the peculiarly shaped **MORRO ROCK** anchoring the mouth of the waterway. This ancient towering landmark, whose name comes from the Spanish word for a Moorish turban, is a volcanic remnant inhabited by the endangered peregrine falcon and other migratory birds. Across from the rock, a monstrous oceanfront electrical plant mars the visual appeal of the otherwise pristine bay.

Morro Bay Boulevard is the main route into town from the freeway; it will drop you at the harborfront Embarcadero, site of a **GIANT CHESS-BOARD**, inspired by open-air boards in Germany, with 3-foot-tall redwood pieces. Further down the Embarcadero is the **MORRO BAY AQUARIUM** (595 Embarcadero; 805/772-7647). This modest operation with its tanks displayed in a dank and grim basementlike room won't be putting SeaWorld out of business any time soon, but it is officially sanctioned to rehabilitate injured and abandoned sea otters, seals, and sea lions. During their stay, all the animals learn to perform tricks for a morsel of fishy food (50 cents a bag). If you're new to town, stop in at the **MORRO BAY CHAMBER OF COMMERCE** (880 Main St; 805/772-4467 or 800/231-0592; www.morrobay.com) for helpful information. Water recreation is a mainstay in the bustling marina, and you can venture out on a kayak tour from **KAYAKS OF MORRO BAY** (on the Embarcadero at Pacific Street; 805/772-1119). If you've always yearned for sailing lessons, call ahead to the **SAILING CENTER OF MORRO BAY** (551 Embarcadero; 805/772-6446). They're next to the Morro Bay Yacht Club and offer everything from one-day intro classes to week-long series and scheduled sunset sails. Just south of Morro Bay is the 8,400-acre **MONTANA DE ORO STATE PARK** (805/528-0513), encompassing sand dunes, jagged cliffs, coves, caves, and reefs. Named "mountain of gold" by the Spanish for the golden poppies that carpet the hillsides each spring, the park contains trails for hiking, biking, and horseback riding as well as restrooms and picnic facilities.

RESTAURANTS

Hoppe's at Marina Square / ★★☆

699 EMBARCADERO, MORRO BAY; 805/772-0677
If you're looking for a special meal in Morro Bay, you'll find it at this respected restaurant overlooking the waterfront and distinctive Morro Rock. An airy, high-ceilinged, multilevel space that takes full advantage of bay views, the bistro has Tuscan golden-ochre walls nicely complemented by dark wood accents. But chef Matthew Yakabowski's cuisine—a California/French/pan-Asian hybrid incorporating local fresh seafood and produce—is the main attraction, and it's presented with a welcome level of sophistication. On any given evening, the menu might boast seared sea bass on spinach with lemon and olive oil, or roasted rack of lamb with white beans and curried sausage. Dessert is a must here, with tempting choices like dense chocolate-pistachio terrine surrounded by fresh raspberry coulis or lemon crème brûlée with a sugar cookie crust. The wine list is composed of the choicest Central Coast vintages and selected French wines. All in all, Hoppe's is one class act. *$$; AE, DC, DIS, MC, V; local checks only; dinner every day, brunch Sun; full bar; reservations recommended; at the end of Pacific St.* &

Hoppe's Hip Pocket Bistro / ★☆

901 EMBARCADERO, MORRO BAY; 805/772-9012
After leaving stylish Hoppe's at Marina Square in capable hands, chef/owner Bill Hoppe now devotes his attention to this more casual bistro. A wide-open space with wood floors and an outdoor deck for fair-weather dining, the Hip Pocket offers a simple but expertly executed seasonal menu of country French dishes with a fusion twist. Sautéed sole is fairly traditional, with brown garlic butter and a sprinkling of fresh

herbs, but the grilled portobello mushroom surprises with a stuffing of black beans and Thai-spiced tempeh. Roasted duck comes accompanied by artichokes and lentils, and a perfectly seasoned steak au poivre is paired with creamy potatoes gratinée. Among the best appetizers are warm goat cheese salad in a citrusy vinaigrette and seared foie gras with a rich duck reduction and fresh mango compote. *$$; AE, DC, DIS, MC, V; local checks only; lunch, dinner every day (closed Mon–Tues in winter); full bar; reservations recommended; at the end of Harbor St.* &

LODGINGS

The Inn at Morro Bay / ★★

60 STATE PARK RD, MORRO BAY; 805/772-5651 OR 800/321-9566
Though its sleek brochure hints at a snooty, ultra-glamorous resort, you'll be pleasantly surprised by this exceedingly comfortable and affordable place that's smart enough to let its splendid natural surroundings be the focus of attention. Two-story Nantucket-style buildings have contemporary interiors tempered by blond-wood cabinetry, polished brass beds, and reproduction 19th-century European furnishings. Rates vary wildly according to the view; the best rooms enjoy unobstructed views of Morro Rock plus convenient access to a bayfront sun deck, while those in back face the swimming pool, gardens, and eucalyptus-forested golf course at Morro Bay State Park. Guests receive a discount on pampering treatments at the on-site Therapeutic Massage Center, and the hotel has a romantic bayside lounge and dining room, which serves California/ Mediterranean cuisine and three meals daily. *$$–$$$$; AE, DC, DIS, MC, V; checks OK; www.innatmorrobay.com; take Main St south past park entrance.* &

Baywood Park

LODGINGS

Baywood Inn Bed & Breakfast / ★★☆

1370 2ND ST, BAYWOOD PARK; 805/528-8888
 Nestled in one of the southernmost inlets of vast Morro Bay, the tranquil little community of Baywood Park is popular with folks who like to explore nearby Montana de Oro State Park or quietly launch their kayaks from the small wooden landing right across the street from this romantic bed-and-breakfast. At first glance, the two-story gray inn facing out onto Morro's "back" bay looks like a garden-style office building. Though indeed the building was constructed in the 1970s for business tenants, its spacious interiors lent themselves perfectly to a remodel into

B&B suites, each furnished in a distinctive theme. From the knickknacks and ruffles of Granny's Attic to the pale pastels of California Beach or the rough cedar beams and stone fireplace of Appalachian, there's a room for every taste and preference. Our favorite is Quimper, a country French room with a tiled hearth and vaulted ceiling illuminated by a clerestory window. Every room has a separate entrance, fireplace, microwave oven, coffeemaker, and refrigerator stocked with complimentary snacks and nonalcoholic beverages; many have bay views. Included in your stay is full breakfast each morning and a late-afternoon wine and cheese reception highlighted by a tour of many of the rooms. If you're looking for solitude, the Baywood Inn fits the bill; and there are a couple of decent restaurants on the block, so you never really have to wander far. *$$; MC, V; checks OK; innkeeper@baywoodinn.com; www.baywoodinn.com; 2 blocks south of Santa Ysabel Ave.* &

San Luis Obispo

Pretty San Luis Obispo can't be seen from the 101 Freeway and, as a result, many motorists think the garish pink, roadside Madonna Inn (see review in Lodgings, below) is all there is to the place. But nothing could be further from the truth—just ask some of the big-city transplants flocking to live in this relaxed yet vital college town. With its beautiful surrounding countryside, charming neighborhoods of historic cottages, and developing wine region nearby, SLO—as the locals call it—has been growing by leaps and bounds. Recently, the town's population topped 42,670, a magic number for corporate marketing gurus, which explains why big-name businesses like the Gap, Barnes & Noble, Victoria's Secret, and Starbucks have been popping up all over the place. But even with the influx of new residents and commerce, SLO's downtown is wonderfully compact and perfect for exploring on foot, while the sparkling coastline is only minutes away.

Like several other charming Central Coast towns, this one began life as a Spanish mission outpost. Founding friar Junípero Serra chose this valley in 1772, based on reports of friendly natives and bountiful food, and established **MISSION SAN LUIS OBISPO DE TOLOSA** (782 Monterey Street; 805/543-6850). The hospitality of the local Chumash Indians had been greatly exaggerated, though—the mission became the first to use the now-traditional red-tile roof after its original thatched roofs repeatedly fell to burning arrows. The well-restored mission church, padres' quarters, and colonnade are in the heart of town, fronted by the pedestrian-friendly **MISSION PLAZA**, a pretty park that serves as SLO's town square for festivals and other events. Around the corner the **SAN LUIS OBISPO CHAMBER OF COMMERCE** (1039 Chorro Street; 805/781-2777;

www.VisitSLO.com) offers a colorful, comprehensive *Visitors Guide* and the self-guided *Mission Plaza Walking Tour.* On Thursday nights everyone comes out for the **FARMERS' MARKET** (Higuera St, between Osos and Nipomo Streets), a beloved local tradition. Emptied of auto traffic, Higuera Street fills with a colorful and festive assemblage of vendors and entertainers. Shoppers stroll through, clutching bags of luscious fruits and vegetables, fresh flowers, locally made arts and crafts, and warm baked goods. The sounds of Peruvian street musicians, old-fashioned brass bands, or lively dance troupes fill the air as the tantalizing aroma of oak barbecue wafts from sidewalk grills. Come hungry and graze your way through a classic SLO evening. Thursdays, 6:30 to 9pm (rain or shine).

Another favorite attraction for kids and parents is the **SAN LUIS OBISPO CHILDREN'S MUSEUM** (1010 Nipomo Street; 805/544-KIDS), which helps youngsters learn about the past with an authentic reproduction Chumash cave dwelling, and inspires their imaginations in a music room, computer corner, pint-sized bank and post office, and more. This area is also a terrific region for **BICYCLING**, with scenic terrain for riders of all levels. Pick up the *San Luis Obispo County Bike Map,* a color-coded guide that includes mileage, terrain descriptions, and a list of local bike shops, which is available at the Chamber of Commerce (see above for address and phone). **ALAMO BICYCLE TOURING COMPANY** (805/781-3830 or 800/540-BIKE) offers bicycle rentals and to-your-door delivery, as well as guided specialty bike tours that range from 3 hours to 3 days.

RESTAURANTS

Big Sky Cafe / ★★

1121 BROAD ST, SAN LUIS OBISPO; 805/545-5401

Anyone who's familiar with L.A.'s Farmers' Market knows funky Kokomo Cafe and its cousin, the Gumbo Pot, and will recognize some signature recipes on the menu of this eclectic, imaginative restaurant opened by a former Kokomo chef. At breakfast they serve the same red-flannel turkey hash and a beet-fortified ragout topped with basil-Parmesan glazed eggs, and the Cajun-Creole influence spices up the menu at almost every turn. In fact, Big Sky might be the only place on the Central Coast to find decent jambalaya, gumbo, or authentically airy beignets. The menu is self-classified "modern food," a category that here means a dizzying international selection including Caribbean shrimp tacos with chipotle-lime yogurt, Thai curry pasta tossed with sautéed tiger shrimp, Moroccan pasta with spicy tomato-cumin-peanut sauce, and Mediterranean broiled chicken infused with garlic, rosemary, and olive oil. The setting is comfy casual; creative paint treatments and weathered furniture create a vaguely Southwestern ambience accented by local art and a blue, star-studded ceiling. Big plush booths and small wooden tables coexist happily and complement the long counter/bar. Big Sky is well known and well liked, as evidenced by the benches thoughtfully placed outside for customers who encounter a wait. *$; AE, MC, V; local checks OK; breakfast, lunch, dinner every day; beer and wine; reservations not accepted; between Higuera and Marsh Sts.* ⅃

Buona Tavola / ★★★

1037 MONTEREY ST, SAN LUIS OBISPO; 805/545-8000

Situated next to the Art Deco masterpiece Fremont Theater, this upscale dining room and its charming outdoor patio offer well-prepared Northern Italian cuisine in a setting that's fancy enough for special occasions but welcoming enough for the casually dressed. Checkerboard floors and original artwork adorn the warm, intimate interior, while lush magnolias, ficuses, and grapevines lend a garden atmosphere to terrace seating out back. Begin by choosing one of the traditional cold salads on the *antipasti* list, then proceed to a main course menu that highlights delicious homemade pastas. Favorites include *agnolotti di scampi allo zafferano*, half-moon purses pinched around a scampi filling then smothered in saffron-cream sauce, and *spaghettini scoglio d'oro*, a rich pasta dish overflowing with lobster, sea scallops, clams, mussels, shrimp, diced tomatoes, and saffron sauce. The balance of the menu can be equally tongue-twisting, filled with rich, intense sauces and satisfying meat dishes. The wine list is a winner, with traditional Italian offerings complemented by stellar choices from the surrounding wine region. *$$; AE, DIS, MC, V; local checks only; lunch Mon–Fri, dinner every day; beer and wine; reservations recommended; between Osos and Santa Rosa Sts.* ⅃

SLO Brewing Company

1119 GARDEN ST, SAN LUIS OBISPO; 805/543-1843

Hang out with the area's collegiate population at this local-brewpub-makes-good success story. Their homemade beers—Pale Ale, Amber Ale, and Porter—have created such a buzz (no pun intended) that they're now nationally distributed. Located downtown in an historic 100-year-old brick commercial building, the Company offers a bar (all beer, all the time) downstairs and a cavernous dining room upstairs. Illuminated by industrial skylights and filled with hardy wooden tables and chairs, the restaurant is comfortable, although it can get loud. The menu—burgers, deep-fried appetizers, and other pub basics—is far from gourmet, but quite satisfying with a tall, cold one. All in all, this is a great place to meet friends, celebrate a sports victory, or grab a pre-movie bargain bite. *$; AE, DIS, MC, V; local checks only; lunch, dinner every day; beer and wine; reservations not accepted; www.slobrew.com; between Higuera and Marsh Sts.* ⅃

LODGINGS

Apple Farm Inn / ★★

2015 MONTEREY ST, SAN LUIS OBISPO; 805/544-2040 OR 800/255-2040
Even though it's adjacent to busy US 101, this ultra-popular frilly get-away is remarkably quiet and always booked well in advance. The entire complex—which includes a restaurant, gift shop, and working cider mill—exhibits an over-the-top Victorian-style cuteness, with floral wall-paper, fresh flowers, and sugar-sweet touches. No two guest rooms are alike, although each has a gas fireplace, large bathroom with plush terry robes, canopy or brass bed, and lavish country decor. Some bedrooms open onto cozy turreted sitting areas with romantic window seats, while others have wide bay windows overlooking the creek that rambles through the property. Morning coffee and tea are delivered to your room, or you can opt for breakfast in bed at an additional cost. Rooms in the motel-style Trellis Court building have virtually the same amenities as those in the main inn (including fireplaces and cozy decor), but cost less and include a discount voucher for breakfast at the restaurant. The hotel's also got a heated outdoor swimming pool and Jacuzzi, and there's unlimited hot apple cider on hand in the lobby. *$$$ (Main Inn); $$ (Trellis Court); AE, DIS, MC, V; checks OK; www.applefarm.com; just south of US 101.* &

Garden Street Inn / ★★

1212 GARDEN ST, SAN LUIS OBISPO; 805/545-9802
The prettiest accommodations in town are to be found in this gracious Italianate/Queen Anne bed and breakfast near downtown. Built in 1887 and fully restored in 1990, the house is a monument to Victorian gen-tility and to the good taste of owners Dan and Kathy Smith. Each bedroom and suite is decorated with well-chosen antique armoires, opulent fabric or paper wall coverings, and vintage memorabilia. Choose one with a claw-footed tub, fireplace, Jacuzzi bath, or private deck—whatever suits your fancy. Breakfast is served in the morning room as the sun filters through original stained-glass windows, and each evening wine and cheese are laid out for guests. The well-stocked library is always available to guests. *$$; AE, MC, V; checks OK; innkeeper@gardenstreetinn.com; www.gardenstreetinn.com; between Marsh and Pacific Sts.* &

Madonna Inn / ★

100 MADONNA RD, SAN LUIS OBISPO; 805/543-3000 OR 800/543-9666
Conjured from the fertile imaginations of owners Alex and Phyllis Madonna, this eccentric hotel is a wild fantasy world where faux-rock waterfalls, velvet-flecked wallpaper, marbled mirrors, and deep shag car-

peting are just the beginning. The only consistent element of the decor is Phyllis Madonna's favorite color, a ubiquitous pink that pops up even on the specially printed bottles of Neutrogena bath products. The 109 rooms are individually decorated in themes so unusual the Madonna Inn sells 109 different postcards—just in case your friends can't believe you slept in digs reminiscent of *The Flintstones*. Everybody's favorites include the all-rock Caveman rooms, featuring waterfall showers and giant animal-print rugs. Other over-the-top options include Swiss Chalet and English Manor, which look like they sound. Many guests of this Disneyland for adults request their favorite rooms annually, celebrating anniversaries or New Year's Eve, and the Madonnas host hundreds of honeymooners each year. Although it's best known for its outlandish features, the Inn pays attention to guests' comfort—after all, it takes more than kitsch to keep 'em coming back. The rooms are spacious and very comfortable; if the loud decor doesn't keep you up, there's a very good night's sleep to be had. A surprisingly good coffee shop adjoins a delectable European bakery. Don't miss the formal Gold Rush dining room, an eyeful beyond description that's flaming with fuchsia carpet, pink leather booths, and gold cherub chandeliers. Even those checking out early are treated to coffee and tea in the registration office. *$$–$$$; AE, MC, V; checks OK; www.madonnainn.com; Madonna Rd exit off US 101.* &

Avila Beach

Half the fun of Avila Beach might be getting here; from San Luis Obispo, scenic San Luis Bay Road leads toward the ocean. During the late summer and fall harvest seasons, take a detour into woodsy, sun-dappled **SEE CANYON**, where makeshift roadside fruit stands and U-Pick signs mark this apple-producing region. Continuing on, you'll come to **SYCAMORE MINERAL SPRINGS RESORT**, a 100-year-old therapeutic hot springs that's also popular as a day spa. **SAN LUIS OBISPO BAY** is as lovely as ever, with its azure, crescent-shaped natural harbor filled with bobbing sailboats. Follow its natural curve to the **OLD SAN LUIS PIER** for a day's sport fishing or a hearty fresh-caught meal. At press time, the town of Avila Beach itself was in terrible shape: years of seepage from underground crude oil extraction were finally being addressed, which unfortunately meant leveling the several commercial blocks along the waterfront, and the excavation was scheduled to be completed in 2001.

RESTAURANTS

Olde Port Inn / ★☆

PORT SAN LUIS, AVILA BEACH; 805/595-2515

You can drive all the way out onto the pier, but if the handful of parking spaces are filled you'll have to park on shore and stroll out past sportfishing outfitters and snack stands to reach this unique seafood restaurant. In the mornings, the wooden platform bustles with commercial fishermen unloading their daily catch of rock cod, halibut, crab, and the like, while pelicans and seagulls vie with sea lions for undersize fish. You can count on the family-run Olde Port Inn to serve the absolute freshest seafood, from their hearty fresh-catch cioppino (a house specialty) to the morning's fresh scallops and shrimp tossed in pasta. (There are also filet

mignon and chicken piccata for any landlubbers tagging along.) They make clam chowder, of course, and also offer fish and chips, scallops and chips, and shrimp and chips. Dinners, sized for hungry dock workers, include soup or salad, potatoes, vegetables, and plenty of warm sourdough bread. Though the upstairs dining room has a nice bay view through picture windows, request one of the glass-topped tables downstairs if you want a straight-down view of the churning waters below through a mirror-lined cut-out. Gooey, decadent desserts include a homemade peach cobbler that's well worth the extra calories. *$$; AE, MC, V; no checks; lunch, dinner every day; full bar; reservations recommended; 4 miles west of US 101 via Avila Beach Dr.* &

LODGINGS

Sycamore Mineral Springs Resort / ★★

1215 AVILA BEACH DR, SAN LUIS OBISPO; 805/595-7302 OR 800/234-5831

First discovered in 1886 by prospectors drilling for oil, these natural bubbling mineral springs provide relaxation and rejuvenation in an idyllic natural setting. Until the mid-1970s, the spa facility was a therapeutic center staffed by doctors and nurses. Today no one feels obliged to plead medical necessity in order to enjoy the sensuousness of Sycamore Springs.

There are close to 75 private mineral baths on the property—one on each room's private deck or balcony, with two dozen more tucked away on the wooded hillside above the spa. Hot-tub rentals for nonguests are available 24 hours a day, and a half-hour soak is included with massage and facial services. The spacious guest rooms, many of which have fireplaces, are in contemporary condo-style two-story buildings. During the monarch butterfly nesting season (October to March) you can spot hundreds of the splendid orange-and-black insects around the property's dense sycamore trees.

The resort's Gardens of Avila restaurant isn't much to look at, but its outdoor setting shines and its casually elegant, if slightly expensive, California eclectic menu is often hailed as one of the Central Coast's finest. Seafood is prepared especially well, so you can't go wrong with one of the fresh-catch specials. Other offerings include red curry–coconut chicken potstickers, tiger shrimp in a Mediterranean ragout, and an excellent prime rib. All overnight guests receive a breakfast credit for the restaurant. *$$$ $$$$; AE, DIS, MC, V; local checks only; info@smsr. com; www.sycamoresprings.com; 1 mile from US 101.* &

Pismo Beach/Shell Beach

The native Chumash, who lived here as far back as 9,000 years ago, named Pismo Beach for the abundance of *pismu,* or tar, found in the sand. In the 1900s, with saloons, brothels, and a dance hall established, the town had become a tourist getaway for wild times, and that reputation was furthered during the Depression when Pismo Beach became a well-known source for illicit booze. Currently, it's merely a time-warp shrine to days when California beach towns were unpretentious places meant for just goofing off. Surfers roam the sands year-round, drawn by the timeless song of that siren, the perfect wave—and upscale weekenders come to let it all hang out (even though the new beachfront resorts are the height of luxury).

Here is where you'll find the acclaimed Pismo clam, which reached near-extinction in the mid-1980s due to overzealous harvesting. If you'd like to get your feet wet digging for bivalves, you'll need to obtain a license and follow strict guidelines. Or come for the annual **CLAM FESTIVAL.** Held at the pier each October since 1946, the weekend celebration features a chowder cook-off, sand-sculpture contest, Miss Pismo Beach pageant, and competitive clam dig. For more information on this and other local attractions and events, visit the **PISMO BEACH CHAMBER OF COMMERCE** (581 Dolliver St; 805/773-4382 or 800/443-7778; www. classiccalifornia.com or www.pismochamber.com). If you're around between October and March, don't miss the **MONARCH BUTTERFLY** preserve on Pacific Coast Highway in nearby Grover Beach. The brilliantly colored monarchs nest in a grove of eucalyptus and Monterey pine, where an information board tells you about their unique habits. During cold weather (below 40°F), they remain densely clustered on tree branches, but on warm days you'll see their stately orange-and-black wings fluttering throughout the area as they search for flower nectar.

Near Pismo Beach—and claimed by Oceano, Grover Beach, and even inland Nipomo—lies a stretch of extraordinary **SAND DUNES.** Walk along the shifting sands at Pismo State Beach, or, alternatively, visit the livery stable in Oceano; they'll outfit you with a horse to match your riding ability and send you (alone or with a guide) along their private trail to the dunes, where you can gallop along the surf's edge or just mosey around. The Pismo dunes are also the only place in California where it's legal to drive on the beach—in the specially designated OCEANO DUNES STATE VEHICULAR RECREATION AREA (805/473-7230), accessed via a ramp from Pier Avenue in Oceano. A 5½-mile "sand highway" at the ocean's edge parallels the mountainous dunes; you can take the family car onto the sand, but the dunes are off-limits to all but 4WDs and ATVs.

RESTAURANTS

F. McLintocks Saloon & Dining House / ★

750 MATTIE RD, SHELL BEACH; 805/773-1892

If you've got a hankerin' for stick-to-your-ribs ranch-style meals in a corny Old West setting, then mosey up to the table at McLintocks. Set in a 100-year-old former farmhouse (later the local speakeasy), this headquarters of the McLintocks chain offers ocean views and abundant meals. Best known for oak pit–barbecued steaks and ribs, they also feature fresh local shellfish and a few oddball selections like chicken cordon bleu and liver and onions. Stick with the basics, though, and you won't be disappointed by either the quality of beef or the gargantuan portions. Every dinner starts with onion rings and salsa, then salad, and includes sides of barbeque beans, garlic bread, and fried potatoes, plus ice cream or an after-dinner liqueur. Parents are relieved to know there *is* a kids' menu. The staff is spirited and helpful—all part of that "genuine Western hospitality," we reckon, which means you can't help but roll up your sleeves and enjoy yourself—unless, that is, you had a romantic evening in mind. *$$; DIS, MC, V; local checks only; breakfast, lunch Sun, dinner every day; full bar; reservations accepted Sun–Thurs only; www. mclintocks.com; at Hwy 101 (Shell Beach exit).* &

Giuseppe's Cucina Italiana / ★★

891 PRICE ST, PISMO BEACH; 805/773-2870

The enticing aroma wafting from this always-crowded standout on Pismo Beach's Italian restaurant row is enough to lure you inside. Known countywide for consistently good home-style food, generous portions, and a friendly, casual ambience, Giuseppe's can get a little boisterous, but it retains a classy touch just a notch above the usual a family-style pizza joint. Even Paso Robles vintner Gary Eberle even chose to have one of his famed Winemaker Dinners in Giuseppe's private rear cottage— a 40-minute drive from the winery itself. White linen rather than red-checked tablecloths set the stage for a menu that offers both traditional southern Italian-style fare (pizza, lasagne, veal parmigiana), and trattoria-influenced California cuisine such as peppercorn-seared ahi tuna, grilled portobello mushrooms in an arugula-tomato salad, and individual gourmet pizzas. Dinners come with soup or salad; try the highly recommended "alternate" salad, butter lettuce with creamy Gorgonzola. Appropriately, given its seaside location, Giuseppe's menu includes plenty of ocean fare—favorites include an appetizer of clams stuffed with shrimp, scallops, and lox, baked in the wood-fired oven and served with aioli. *$$; AF, DIS, MC, V; local checks only; lunch Mon–Fri, dinner every day; full bar; reservations not accepted; at Pismo Ave.* ⅚

Splash Cafe / ★

197 POMEROY AVE, PISMO BEACH; 805/773-4653
You might expect Pismo Beach restaurants to sell a lot of clam chowder, and you'd be right—although the bivalves are actually imported, since Pismo's famous clams aren't sold commercially. But that doesn't stop Splash from serving up a darn good bowl of the stuff. Although Splash is a beachy burger stand with a short menu and just a few tables, locals agree its creamy, New England–style chowder is the best in town, which explains why the place makes 10,000 gallons annually. If you like, you can order it in a sourdough bread bowl. If that's not enough of a meal, the menu also includes fish and chips, hamburgers, hot dogs, and other sandwiches. *$; no credit cards; no checks; lunch, dinner every day; beer and wine; reservations not accepted; www.splashcafe.com; between Dolliver St and the pier.* ⅚

LODGINGS

The Cliffs at Shell Beach / ★★

2757 SHELL BEACH RD, SHELL BEACH; 805/773-5000 OR 800/826-7827
What it lacks in personality, this efficiently luxurious clifftop resort hotel makes up for in comfort. Guest rooms are light and airy, stylishly furnished with antique reproductions, and outfitted with extras like hair dryers, irons, and private balconies. Poolside beverages and snack service give more reason to recline by the heated swimming pool and whirlpool, which are shielded from the wind and situated to capitalize on the bay views. The Cliffs has its own spa, so a massage or facial is a convenient reward after a workout at the on-site fitness center. However, a more leisurely treat is accessible via the private staircase, which zigzags down to a prime, albeit small, strip of sandy beach. (However, be forewarned that high tide comes nearly to the base of the cliffs.)

The adjacent Sea Cliffs Restaurant features an eclectic menu of grilled meats and fish accented by international flavors (a little Caribbean here, a little Pacific Rim there) and is more formal than it ought to be considering the area. However, it does have a terrific wine list featuring Central Coast labels reasonably priced and available by the glass. The only Sunday brunch more extensive and formal than the one served here is down the coast at Santa Barbara's Four Seasons. *$$$–$$$$; AE, DC, DIS, MC, V; local checks only; www.ihc-hotels.com; north of Spyglass Dr.* &

Kon Tiki Inn / ★★☆

1621 PRICE ST, PISMO BEACH; 805/773-4833 OR 888/KON-TIKI

The over-the-top Polynesian architecture of this three-story gem is easy to spot from the freeway—and once you're inside it fulfills that kitschy promise, with decor reminiscent of Waikiki hotels of the 1960s. Rooms are modest, small, and simply furnished with faux bamboo and island prints, yet each has an oceanfront balcony or patio, refrigerator, TV with free HBO, convenient in-room vanity separate from the bathroom sink, and groovy retro-style stationery on the bureau. If the weather turns raw once the sun sets, individual heaters quickly and quietly toast your room. Outside, vast lawns slope gently toward the cliffs, broken only by the wind-shielded, kidney-shaped heated swimming pool flanked by twin whirlpools. This humble hotel—which is privately owned and does no advertising—has several advantages over most along these Pismo cliffs, including a sandy beach with stairway access, lack of highway noise, and ground cover that discourages gatherings of pesky seagulls. At press time, the restaurant attached to the Kon Tiki was undergoing renovation and was scheduled to reopen as an oyster bar/seafood grill run by F. McLintocks's management. *$; AE, DIS, MC, V; checks OK; info@kontikiinn. com; www.kontikiinn.com; 8 blocks north of the pier.* &

SeaVenture Resort / ★★★☆

100 OCEAN VIEW AVE, PISMO BEACH; 805/773-4994 OR 800/662-5545

Guests are pleasantly surprised to find that this heavenly beachfront resort offers exceptional pampering without a trace of pretentiousness. Each room is decorated in a soothing blend of deep greens, with thick carpeting, white plantation-style furnishings, and a gas-burning fireplace. With the beach directly below, private balconies or decks are welcoming enough, but in addition almost all rooms have irresistible private hot tubs with soft leatherette rims. Whether the night is foggy or clear, slide into the spa tub, and the invigorating yet ethereal experience is worth the entire cost of the room. It's almost as enticing to release your cares without leaving your feather bed as you loll in a terrycloth robe, splurge on refreshments from the excellently stocked wet bar, or slip into mindlessness with a rental movie from the hotel's video library. Morning wake-up is both melodic and flavorful, thanks to the CD alarm clock and the continental breakfast basket delivered to your door. If you're still having problems relaxing, SeaVenture has an on-site therapeutic massage center, and their restaurant offers dinner room service and a lovely brunch.

$$–$$$$; AE, DC, DIS, MC, V; checks OK; seaventure@fix.net; www. seaventure.com; from Price or Dolliver Sts, follow Ocean View to the beach. &

Arroyo Grande

Although Arroyo Grande is now more or less a suburb of San Luis Obispo, residents work hard to maintain the small-town atmosphere and Old West heritage of their "village." The main interest of visitors seems to be shopping the many **ANTIQUE STORES** that line Branch Street, the village's main drag, but an ice-cream stop at **BURNARDO'Z** (114 W Branch St; 805/481-4021), an antique ice cream parlor with plank floors, marble-topped tables, and vintage soda-fountain equipment, is practically mandatory. The annual gathering that began in 1983 as a small-town ice-cream social has grown into Memorial Day weekend's **STRAWBERRY FESTIVAL**, which draws a quarter of a million people to locations around town for game and craft booths, music, and entertainment, plus every strawberry treat imaginable. For more information on this and other happenings around town, contact the **ARROYO GRANDE VILLAGE IMPROVEMENT ASSOCIATION** (805/473-2250; www.arroyogrande.com), which also offers a self-guided walking tour of historic sites that includes the **SWINGING BRIDGE** across Arroyo Grande Creek and the 1895 Victorian **HERITAGE HOUSE AND MUSEUM** (126 S Mason Street), which displays photographs and artifacts from Arroyo Grande's history as farmland, railroad route, and occasional outlaw hideout.

RESTAURANTS

The Hunt Club Restaurant / ★★☆

789 VALLEY RD, ARROYO GRANDE; 805/481-1854 OR 800/ROSE-INN
Housed in a modern addition behind the Victorian-era Crystal Rose Inn (see review in Lodgings, below), this quiet, romantic restaurant opens onto the Inn's manicured gardens and enjoys a reputation for creative and meticulously prepared California/Mediterranean cuisine. The dining room is dominated by an enormous floor-to-ceiling brick hearth, whose muted crackle produces a warm, relaxed mood that's enhanced by soft French ballads playing in the background. Chef Bonnie Royster's unique menu reflects a variety of ethnic influences with a nod to California trends. She also offers an equally creative vegetarian menu. Among the best appetizers are Andalusian pork rolls with fresh mozzarella wrapped in prosciutto with a honey-Dijon sauce; warm spinach salad with red potatoes and bacon dressing; and poached pear salad with locally farmed greens and apple-walnut dressing. Main courses are available either à la

ARROYO GRANDE WINERIES

Often overshadowed by the Central Coast wine regions in Paso Robles and the Santa Ynez Valley, the wineries around Arroyo Grande are slowly but surely coming into their own. Growing conditions have long been ideal, as ancient volcanoes created soil rich in granite and tufa, which, combined with cooling ocean breezes, make for a long, fruitful growing season. The **Edna Valley/Arroyo Grande Valley Vintners Association** (11545 Los Osos Valley Road #2; 805/541-5868; www.thegrid.net/vintners), which used to be headquartered at Corbett Canyon Vintners, has since moved into San Luis Obispo proper, and is an excellent source for wine country information. A helpful map of the wine region is available from their office or at many participating wineries. (**Corbett Canyon Vintners,** the best-known area winery, is sadly not open to the public.)

Claiborne & Churchill Winery: Specializing in the dry Alsatian riesling and gewürztraminer varietals, Clay Thompson's boutique winery might be best known for its unusual hay-bale construction. Though the foot-thick walls have been stuccoed over for looks, you can peek through a "truth window" and see the naturally insulating walls beneath. Located at 2649 Carpenter Canyon Road (Highway 227), San Luis Obispo; 805/544-4066.

Edna Valley Vineyard: Edna Valley's beautiful tasting room also has an impressive selection of Provençal pottery and wine-country gifts; stand at the wine bar to get the best panoramic view of the valley below. Outside is our favorite feature—demonstration vines that illustrate the art of grape growing. Located at 2585 Biddle Ranch Road, San Luis Obispo; 805/544-5855; www.EdnaValley.com.

Laetitia Vineyard & Winery: The former Maison Deutz still boasts superior sparkling wines, along with a selection of Burgundy-style whites. Stylish gourmet oils and specialty foods bear the Laetitia label as well. Located at 453 Deutz Drive, Arroyo Grande; 805/481-1772.

Talley Vineyards: An 1860 two-story adobe house stands atop a quiet, peaceful hill amidst the grapevines of this out-of-the-way winery—it's one of the area's more unusual tasting rooms. Talley's pinot noir grapes are hand-tended and aged only in French oak, resulting in a locally respected wine whose small production always sells out quickly. Located at 3031 Lopez Drive, Arroyo Grande; 805/489-0446.

carte or as a three-course meal (for about $10 more), with choices ranging from seared salmon with spinach and champagne *beurre blanc,* to mustard-crusted rack of lamb to local halibut with cilantro–green chile sauce. The quality of the food here, always creative and meticulously prepared, is fully matched by the quality of service, and the wine list features moderately priced Central Coast vintages. *$$; AE, DIS, MC, V; checks OK; dinner Tues–Sun; full bar; reservations recommended; www.crystal roseinn.com; between Fair Oaks Ave and Hwy 1.* &

LODGINGS

Crystal Rose Inn / ★★☆

789 VALLEY RD, ARROYO GRANDE; 805/481-1854 OR 800/ROSE-INN
When it was built in 1885 as an opulent farmhouse, this distinctive four-story Victorian gingerbread house stood alone amidst crop acreage. Today, sporting a colorful pink paint job, it's still surrounded by fields but is only a few blocks away from the modern city that has encroached upon it. Talented innkeepers Dona Noland and Bonnie Royster clearly cherish this landmark, maintaining its excellent condition. They have carefully furnished each of the eight guest rooms (all with private baths) with period antiques and suitably Victorian lace and frills. Dozens of carefully tended rosebushes surround the rose-hued Crystal Rose Inn, and you'll find the floral/color theme repeated in everything from wallpaper to outdoor lighting. The only nonpink guest room is the lacy white Honor Suite, which boasts a claw-footed soaking tub. The Queen Elizabeth Tower Suite features a hidden staircase to its own private tower sitting room, with awesome views and a table perfect for an intimate breakfast. Rates include a lavish full breakfast and afternoon high tea, and the on-site Hunt Club Restaurant is available for dinner (see review in Restaurants, above). Considering the property's decidedly feminine ambience, it's not surprising this spot is popular for weddings, anniversaries, and other romantic trysts. Kids are welcome but may be daunted by the abundance of breakable ornaments in every room. *$$$; AE, DIS, MC, V; checks OK; stay@crystalroseinn.com; www.crystalroseinn.com; between Fair Oaks Ave and Hwy 1.* &

Santa Maria

The largest city in the region, Santa Maria is a bustling community of aerospace and farm employees, drawn by both nearby **VANDENBERG AIR FORCE BASE** and the wealth of profitable agriculture throughout the Central Coast valleys. Although tourism has never been a great draw, one local gastronomic tradition has taken on such legendary proportions that word of it has traveled far beyond the city limits. We're talking about **SANTA MARIA STYLE BARBECUE**, the featured grub at all festive occasions, both public and private. In the early days of huge ranchos, the *rancheros*, the *vaqueros* (cowboys), and their families and friends would gather midday under the towering oaks to enjoy Spanish barbecues. The recipe is deceptively simple: sirloin tri-tip steak is seasoned with salt, pepper, and garlic (and sometimes parsley, depending on whom you ask) and then cooked over the hot coals of a red-oak fire. The red oak is important; unlike Southern-style barbeque, which hides underneath tangy glazes, the Santa Maria variety is all about simple seasoning and the freshness of the meat, which must be served immediately after cooking. Customary accompaniments are sweet-and-spicy barbeque *piquinto* beans, garlic toast, salsa, and green salad. On weekends throughout Santa Maria, the tangy aroma of barbecue floats on the air from streetside vendors and local restaurants (although the Far Western Tavern in neighbor Guadalupe usually wins the Santa Maria Style Barbecue Cook-Off—see the review in the Guadalupe section, below).

LODGINGS

Santa Maria Inn

801 S BROADWAY, SANTA MARIA; 805/928-7777 OR 800/462-4276
The best hotel in Santa Maria is happily the one with the most character, even if it does have a split personality. Originally opened in 1917, the Santa Maria Inn does indeed have a charming historic side. One entire wing of rooms occupies the original building, as does the hotel's Garden Room restaurant, a reasonably good place completely upstaged by its vintage decor. What was formerly an outdoor promenade is now a relaxing enclosed porch, and there's also a cozy taproom. To the other side is a newer six-story tower whose oversized guest rooms sport bay window seats and decorative crown molding, tasteful decor uncommon in this price range, and modern conveniences including refrigerators, VCRs, hair dryers, and coffeemakers. The original wing offers very small rooms (with large closets), and unfortunately all the original bathroom tile here was demolished in a careless renovation. Perhaps retaining more original detail would've been enough to make up for small space and no air-conditioning, but most guests do prefer the tower. A secluded stone patio with trickling fountain is a nice place for strolling or relaxation, and beyond the garden lies a swimming pool and heated spa. *$$; AE, DC, DIS, MC, V; checks OK; north of Stowell Rd.* &

Guadalupe

RESTAURANTS

Far Western Tavern

899 GUADALUPE ST, GUADALUPE; 805/343-2211

A frequent winner of the Santa Maria Style Barbecue Cook-Off, this hearty eatery is a real hoot. Operating in a reclaimed Old West theater (whose entire lobby is now a raucous barroom), the restaurant packs 'em in for every variety of steak and chop, each given the traditional barbecue treatment and each presented in a cowboy-size portion. They've got it down to a science, seasoning sirloin tri-tip, rib-eye, or New York with a dry rub of salt, pepper, garlic, and parsley, then throwing the meat on a sizzling oak fire until it's perfectly done. The menu also includes Alaskan king crab, scampi, lobster, pasta primavera for the faint of heart, and a "Little Wrangler" menu for the kids. Appetizers run the gamut from nachos to crisp mountain oysters. Breakfast here invariably involves meat, served with the classic Santa Maria sides—barbecue beans, salsa, and potatoes. The dining room is a decorator's nightmare, a 19th-century Western saloon ambience celebrated with red velvet wallpaper, fuzzy cowhide draperies, enormous mounted steer heads, and plenty of cowboy hats—oh, wait, those are on the patrons. If you've got a hankering to sample the legendary Santa Maria style barbecue, this is the only place to come. *$$; AE, DIS, MC, V; local checks only; lunch Mon–Sat, dinner every day, brunch Sun; full bar; reservations recommended; on Hwy 1 at 9th St.* &

Los Alamos

Founded in 1876, Los Alamos became a Wells Fargo stagecoach stop in 1880 with the inauguration of the old Union Hotel. Though the original structure burned to the ground and was rebuilt in 1915, Los Alamos continued to be a traveler's stop and local gathering place well after the demise of the stagecoach route. When the streamlined US Highway 101 was completed in the 1960s, though, it circumvented little Los Alamos, and now you can't even see the town from the freeway. Not content to slide quietly into ghost-town status, the hamlet reinvented itself as an authentic Old West attraction, complete with wooden boardwalks, an historic hotel and bed and breakfast (the restored **UNION HOTEL & VICTORIAN MANSION**), and the Old Days festival and barbecue each September. The growth of the surrounding wine country has also helped, since many **VINEYARDS** are within easy driving distance of town. Several **ANTIQUE STORES** have sprung up along the main drag, including the enormous Los Alamos Depot Mall (in the old Pacific Coast railroad station at the south end of town; 805/344-3315), a 17,000-square-foot warehouse with a surprisingly good selection of antiques and collectibles, especially furniture. Don't be surprised to find yourself asking that all-important question, "Will it fit in the trunk?"

LODGINGS

Union Hotel & Victorian Mansion / ★

362 BELL ST, LOS ALAMOS; 805/344-2744 OR 800/230-2744

This lodging duo, a fantastic time-travel fantasy set in a sleepy historic town, must be seen to be believed. Like the original 1880 building, the Union Hotel, once a stagecoach stop, has boardinghouse-style rooms upstairs and a dining room and saloon below. In 1972 the late Dick Langdon began painstakingly restoring the hotel to 19th-century authenticity, using old photographs to ensure an exact re-creation. Walk through the front door and it's like entering the *Wild Wild West* TV series' sound stage. Overstuffed velvet wing chairs adorn the front parlor, gilded wrought-iron grating frames the bell desk, and swinging saloon doors lead into the adjacent barroom. Upstairs, where fading carpet runners and creaky hardware reinforce the illusion, most of the rooms share a common bath (although they're equipped with in-room sinks). A single shower room is the hotel's only concession to modernity; the few rooms with private bath have only a tub—claw-footed, of course. Even though

the double beds overwhelm the simple, tiny bedrooms, the charm of this place is truly infectious. Breakfast—a generous family-style feast—is included, and diversions like billiards, shuffleboard, and card tables provide entertainment. The hotel's dining room also serves dinner on weekends, offering steaks, seafood, and a nightly family special.

As if the Union Hotel weren't enough, next door stands the Victorian Mansion, an ornate Queen Anne built around 1890 in nearby Nipomo. Langdon moved it here, then spent nine years creating over-the-top B&B theme rooms. Each has a fireplace, a hot tub, a chilled bottle of champagne upon arrival, and a secret door through which breakfast appears each morning. Sleep in the '50s Room and you'll bed down in a vintage Cadillac at a drive-in movie, watching *Rebel Without a Cause*. The Pirate Room is a schooner's stateroom where lanterns sway gently and the sound of seagulls provides the backdrop for the 1938 film *Buccaneer*. The Egyptian Room, a tapestry-laden sheik's tent, boasts a hieroglyphic-papered bathroom entered through a mummy's sarcophagus while *Cleopatra* plays onscreen—you get the idea. *$$ (Union Hotel); $$$$ (Victorian Mansion); AE, DIS, MC, V; no checks; Hwy 166 at Centennial St.* &

Lompoc

Nicknamed "Valley of the Flowers," the fertile, flat Lompoc Valley is probably best known for its vast **FLOWER FIELDS**, which supply more than half the world's seeds. Since the early 1900s, flower farmers—beginning with W. Atlee Burpee, whose name would eventually grace seed packets in potting sheds throughout the world—have been cultivating flowers for seed here, and today nearly 2,000 acres of the valley floor are planted with more than 30 different kinds of blossoming plants. In peak blooming season, between May and September, colorful and fragrant sweet peas, larkspur, petunias, asters, marigolds, zinnias, and others create a splendid rainbow as majestic as New England's fall foliage display. The **LOMPOC CHAMBER OF COMMERCE** (111 South I Street; 805/736-4567 or 800/240-0999; www.lompoc.com) publishes a map to guide you along country roads to the various fields and to a designated Observation Point in town that offers a panoramic look at the patchwork valley floor. In June the annual **LOMPOC VALLEY FLOWER FESTIVAL** (805/735-8511) begins with a colorful downtown parade and continues with many bus tours through acres of brilliant blooms. (You can also follow a self-guided tour.) Festivities continue with a carnival, flower show, arts and crafts fair, and more.

While you're in Lompoc it's worth admiring the results of the **LOMPOC MURALS PROJECT,** an ongoing effort in which enormous murals depicting Lompoc's heritage and natural history are being executed on building extensions scattered through downtown. Often painted by nationally renowned muralists, these public works of art currently number around 40. For a map and guide to each mural's subject matter, contact the Chamber of Commerce (see above).

Anyone who grew up in California learned all about the Spanish mission chain in grade school, and Lompoc's **MISSION LA PURISIMA** (2295 Purisima Road; 805/733-3713) is widely accepted as the best preserved and most educational surviving example of these 18th-century colonial outposts. Founded in 1787 along El Camino Real, the original Spanish road from Mexico, La Purisima has been completely reconstructed in its still-rural setting, and its intricate water-supply system of elaborately tiled aqueducts and fountains is still relatively intact. As a California State Historic Park, La Purisima is constantly visited by busloads of schoolchildren taking their turn to learn this chapter in early California history, especially during **MISSION LIFE DAYS**, once a month from spring through autumn, when costumed docents provide a living history lesson in tortilla-baking, candle-dipping, soap-making, and other once-essential chores.

Buellton

RESTAURANTS

Pea Soup Andersen's

376 AVENUE OF THE FLAGS, BUELLTON; 805/688-5581

Nearly everyone puzzles over the unconventional syntax of the name of this highway mainstay whose familiar billboards—and far-flung franchises—dot Southern California. Shouldn't it be "Andersen's Pea Soup"? Opened in 1924 by Anton and Juliette Andersen as a little roadside cafe, the original restaurant was called Andersen's Electrical Cafe in honor of its newfangled electric range, but it was soon renamed for Juliette's specialty, which was gaining statewide popularity. And what about those trademark pea-splitters? The cartoon pair of workmen wielding hammer and chisel were originally drawn for a magazine feature depicting "little-known occupations," but were licensed to Andersen's in 1946, who then held a contest to name them. The winning names: Hap-Pea and Pea-Wee. You can pose outside the chain's original restaurant with your face filling a cutout of one of the two (kids love this). Except for what could be in the running for the world's largest restaurant gift-shop, Andersen's itself is simply a familiar coffee-shop kind of place where split-pea soup is always on the menu. Because surrounding Buellton offers little else, Andersen's makes a welcome highway stop; Solvang and the Los Olivos wine country are a 5-minute drive away. *$; AE, MC, V; no checks; breakfast, lunch, dinner every day; full bar; reservations not necessary; splitpea@silcom.com; www.silcom.com/~splitpea; at Hwy 246.* &

Solvang

One of the state's most popular tourist stops, nestled in the Santa Ynez Valley, the town of Solvang would look out-of-place cutesy if everyone weren't so accustomed to it by now. Here everything that *can* be Danish *is* Danish: You've never seen so many windmills, cobblestone streets, and wooden shoes and so much gingerbread trim—even the sidewalk trash cans look like little Danish farmhouses with pitched-roof lids. At night, though, the village truly does radiate a storybook charm, as twinkling lights in the trees illuminate sidewalks free of the midday throngs. Solvang (whose name means "sunny field") gets a lot of flak for being a Disneyfied version of its founders' vision, but it does possess a genuine Old World lineage, which you can learn about with a quick visit to the small **ELVERHØJ MUSEUM** (1624 Elverhoy Way; 805/686-1211). Set in a traditional hand-crafted Scandinavian-style home, the museum consists of fully furnished typical Danish rooms and artifacts from Solvang's early days. Most intriguing are promotional pamphlets distributed in Nebraska and Iowa nearly 100 years ago to lure more Danes to sunny California. Solvang can be easily explored on foot, but you might like to pedal your way around town in a fringe-top surrey from **SURREY CYCLES** (at Mission Drive and First Street, on the park; 805/688-0091), which also offers 18-speed bikes suitable for exploring the surrounding hills and wine country. In the center of town, upstairs from the Book Loft and Kaffe Hus, you'll find the **HANS CHRISTIAN ANDERSEN MUSEUM** (1680 Mission Drive; 805/688-2052), which is more interesting than it sounds. The gallery is filled with memorabilia pertaining to Andersen, father of the modern fairy tale and Danish national hero. In addition to rare and first editions of his works, displays include manuscripts, letters, photographs, and a replica Gutenberg printing press. But most folks come to Solvang to enjoy groaning Danish **SMORGASBORDS**; sample delectable Old World pastries, such as those found at the best storefront, **BIRK-HOLM'S BAKERY** (1555 Mission Drive; 805/688-3872); and shop in town for gifts and souvenirs—or for bargains at **SOLVANG DESIGNER OUTLETS**. You can get more information by picking up a glossy *Destination Guide* at the **SOLVANG VISITOR BUREAU** (1511 Mission Drive; 805/688-6144 or 800/GO-SOLVANG; www.solvangca.com). The Bureau also has details about **DANISH DAYS**, a three-day festival of Old World customs and pageantry held during September. There's a parade, demonstrations of traditional Danish arts, dancing by the Solvang Dancers, and a raffle to win a trip to Denmark. Of course, plenty of *aebleskiver* (Danish apple fritters) are served up along with the fun. February's **FLYING LEAP STORYTELLING FESTIVAL** (805/688-9533) grows in popularity each year, with events ranging from nationally renowned storytellers to local folks swapping impromptu tales in the park or ghost stories in the school barn.

On the edge of town is an historic building *without* windmills, roof storks, or other Scandinavian foofaraw—the Spanish **MISSION SANTA INES** (1760 Mission Drive; 805/688-4815; www.oldmission@santaincs. org), built of adobe by Native Americans in 1804, destroyed by the earthquake of 1812, partially rebuilt, and then burned in 1824 in a violent Native American revolt. Santa Ines never regained its initial prosperity or its harmonious existence. Today little of the original mission remains, but the structures you see painstakingly replicate the originals. The chapel, still in use for daily services, features the ornate painting and tile work typical of Spanish missions. The grounds also include the well-restored and well-maintained monks' garden.

RESTAURANTS

Bit O' Denmark

473 ALISAL RD, SOLVANG; 805/688-5426

It's nearly impossible to visit Solvang without sampling the Danish fare that traditionally fills the groaning smorgasbord table, and Bit O' Denmark has the freshest and highest-quality offering around. It's not only the oldest restaurant in town, it's also housed in Solvang's oldest building. Constructed in 1911, the two-story wood-frame structure served first as a college and later as a church before it welcomed its first diners in 1929. Inside, pleasant farmhouse tables are scattered throughout, and collections of blue-and-white china adorn every wall. The traditional all-you-can-eat smorgasbord (offered at both lunch and dinner) consists of a variety of hot and cold dishes, many pickled according to Scandinavian custom, and includes sauerbraten, roast pork, mashed potatoes, Danish salami, gravlax, marinated herring, pumpernickel, deviled eggs, salads, Jell-O molds, and more. The regular menu includes Scandinavian fare such as roast beef with red cabbage and applesauce and *frikadeller* (Danish meatballs), sautéed golden and drenched in brown gravy. At breakfast you'll enjoy Solvang's famous *aebleskiver,* deep-fried apple dumplings served with powdered sugar and raspberry jam. Casual and convenient, Bit O' Denmark is sometimes *too* popular—in other words, expect crowds when tour buses are parked outside the front door. *$$; AE, DIS, MC, V; no checks; breakfast, lunch, dinner every day; full bar; reservations recommended; between Copenhagen and Mission Drs.* &

Brothers Restaurant / ★★☆

409 FIRST ST, SOLVANG; 805/688-9934

Brothers Jeff and Matt Nichols are two intrepid chefs who came to Solvang in 1996 (by way of L.A.'s revered Spago and Ocean Avenue Seafood) and quickly won the hearts of smorgasbord-weary Solvangites. Together they bring over 30 years' combined experience to this intimate restaurant in the front room of the Storybook Inn. Even the setting is refreshing, with its simply furnished and romantically lit parlor, a mere nine tables, windows framing a tree-shaded side street, and a carefully chosen, moderately priced selection of Central Coast wines displayed on a grand antique buffet. The California/international menu changes seasonally and according to Matt and Jeff's whims, but you can count on dishes that emphasize the bounty of the fertile surrounding valley. There are always numerous selections from the grill, such as swordfish on vegetable rice, splashed with Thai curry sauce and accented with mango salsa. A tender rack of lamb is fanned over mashed potatoes studded with tangy black olives on a rich rosemary sauce. Dessert selections, often as numerous as entree choices, might include a fudge brownie with

homemade roasted-banana ice cream and passion fruit cheesecake. *$$;
MC, V; no checks; dinner Wed–Sun; beer and wine; reservations rec-
ommended; between Oak and Copenhagen Sts.* &

Paula's Pancake House / ★

1531 MISSION DR, SOLVANG; 805/688-2867

There's something for everyone on Paula's menu, which begins with three
full pages of *just breakfast.* Wafer-thin Danish pancakes are served plain
and simple, sweet and fruity, or with sausage and eggs. Buttermilk and
whole wheat–honey pancakes can be topped with fresh fruit or chopped
pecans. Paula's French toast is made with dense sourdough bread. There's
every omelet you can imagine, plus egg dishes served with country or
Danish sausage. Farmhouse breakfasts like pork chops and eggs share
menu space with more timid Egg Beaters and granola. Paula's, friendly
and casual, is right on Solvang's busiest street, so you can eat on the patio
and watch the world go by as the seasoned staff makes sure your coffee
is always hot. Breakfast is served all day, and there's also a lunch menu
with burgers, sandwiches, homemade soups, and Santa Maria–style chili
with ham, all of which go down smoothly with an ice-cold beer. Cham-
pagne is also available to turn any breakfast into a mind-tingling mimosa
morning. *$; AE, DIS, MC, V; local checks only; breakfast every day,
lunch Mon–Sat; beer and wine; reservations not accepted; at Fourth Pl.* &

LODGINGS

Alisal Guest Ranch & Resort / ★★

1054 ALISAL RD, SOLVANG; 805/688-6411 OR 800/4-ALISAL

Part of a working cattle ranch, this rustic yet quietly posh retreat is ideal
for anyone who wants an Old West vacation. But you certainly won't be
asked to pitch hay or groom horses—it might interfere with your golf
game, guided horseback ride, or poolside lounging. *Alisal* is Spanish for
"alder grove," and the ranch is nestled in a vast, tree-shaded canyon,
offering 73 guest cottages equipped with wood-burning fireplaces, refrig-
erators, and covered brick porches ideal for sitting and soaking up the
scenery. There aren't any TVs or phones to spoil the serenity, but restless
visitors will never tire of the resort activities, which include hiking trails,
tennis, croquet, bicycling, and fishing in the Alisal's private lake, where
sailboats, pedal boats, and canoes sit ready for guests. Wildlife abounds
on the ranch's 10,000 acres, so don't be surprised to see eagles, hawks,
deer, coyotes, and mountain lions. Golf here is top-notch, with two cham-
pionship 18-hole courses, both of which offer impeccably maintained fair-
ways accented by mature oak, sycamore, and eucalyptus trees. The River
Course, which is also open to the public, winds along the Santa Ynez River
and offers spectacular mountain vistas. Resident PGA and LPGA pros are

on hand for instruction. As if a visit here weren't sybaritic enough, breakfast and dinner, featuring fresh local ingredients and a wide range of choices, are included, and during the day a poolside snack bar and a golf-course grill make it entirely possible to never leave this peaceful getaway. In the evening the upscale ranch-style Oak Room lounge features live entertainment in a comfortable setting. *$$$$; AE, MC, V; checks OK; info@alisal.com; www.alisal.com; 3 miles south of Mission Dr.* ⅋

Inn at Petersen Village / ★

1576 MISSION DR, SOLVANG; 805/688-3121 OR 800/321-8985

Anchoring a small plaza of shops, cafes, and cobblestone paths, this boutique inn eschews ubiquitous Danish kitsch in favor of a more elegant Old World style. Mahogany lines the lobby and hallways, rich carpeting muffles the passing of tour groups, and strategically placed antiques lend a touch of class. Each of the 39 rooms is different, but all are decorated in a subdued country motif with print wallpaper, canopy beds, and high-quality antique reproductions. Some overlook the bustling courtyard, while others face the scenic hills. The smaller rooms have private balconies, and the more spacious ones have noisier outlooks. But it's the impressive little touches that set this hotel apart: dimmable bathroom lights, lighted magnifying mirrors, and free coffee/tea service in your room. Complimentary wine and hors d'oeuvres each evening in the piano lounge and desserts served while a pianist tickles the ivories are included in the cost of laying your head. The reasonable rates here even include a generous breakfast buffet with sit-down coffee and juice service, and two decent cafes are right outside in the plaza. *$$; AE, MC, V; no checks; www.peterseninn.com; just east of 4th Pl.* ⅋

Royal Scandinavian Inn

400 ALISAL RD, SOLVANG; 805/688-8000 OR 800/624-5572

Solvang's largest hostelry is this full-service hotel neatly tucked away from the town's congested main drag. Attractive and comfortable, the Royal Scandinavian is also popular with convention and tour groups (and, as a result, it can be fully booked at unexpected times). Guest rooms are furnished in vaguely Danish country decor, and the hotel does a good job with maintenance by replacing soft goods before they show wear, and keeping bathrooms sparklingly up to date. Most rooms look out onto the lovely Santa Ynez Valley; some have private balconies overlooking the courtyard, where a heated swimming pool and whirlpool provide welcome refreshment in the summertime. There's an all-day restaurant and a cocktail lounge. The hotel is within easy walking distance of village attractions, and it offers some terrific golf and breakfast packages featuring play at the nearby pristine Alisal River Course. *$$; AE, DC, DIS, JCB, MC, V; checks OK; sroyal@silcom.com; www.solvangrsi.com; between Mission Dr and Oak St.* ⅋

Ballard

Occupying just a few square blocks, Ballard is the Santa Ynez Valley's smallest community, but it still lays claim to a popular gourmet restaurant and to the Valley's most charming bed and breakfast. Situated midway between Los Olivos and Solvang, Ballard is surrounded by **APPLE ORCHARDS** and **HORSE FARMS** kept with as much care as any Kentucky breeding farm. **SHETLAND PONIES** abound along Alamo Pintado Road near town—drive through slowly (especially if you're with children) to see these darlings frolicking in their pastures. In Ballard itself, stroll past the **BALLARD SCHOOL** (School Street, between Cottonwood and Lewis Streets), an archetypal "little red schoolhouse" with a wooden steeple accented by white gingerbread trim. Built in 1883, it's been in continuous use as an elementary school; Ballard youngsters spill out the front door, *Little House on the Prairie*–style, at morning recess.

RESTAURANTS

The Ballard Store / ★★

2449 BASELINE AVE, BALLARD; 805/688-5319

The façade may look like a country general store, but this is hardly the place to come for a sack of flour. Built in 1939, the former market/gas station was purchased in 1971 by the Elliott family who began serving French/continental cuisine to a farming community unaccustomed to such gentility. These days it seems more at home, a natural complement to the many local wineries and the upscale Ballard Inn across the street, and folks from throughout the region come here for the Elliotts' unique blend of haute cuisine and down-home hospitality. Each meal starts with a basket of warm homemade bread, and the long list of appetizers includes oysters offered five ways, mussels, escargots, baked artichoke hearts, and veal sweetbreads. Dinners, hearty affairs here, begin with soup or salad and include traditional French bouillabaisse, lobster and scallop Thermidor, veal Oskar with shrimp, German *rouladen*, New Zealand rack of lamb, and other rich culinary classics. Anyone with room left to indulge in dessert will revel in the chocolate mousse or bananas flambé. Gourmet picnic boxes, complete with plastic wine glasses, are available with a day's advance notice. *$$; AE, DC, DIS, MC, V; local checks only; dinner Wed–Sun, brunch Sun; full bar; reservations recommended; just east of Alamo Pintado Rd.* &

213

LODGINGS

The Ballard Inn / ★★★

2436 BASELINE AVE, BALLARD; 805/688-7770 OR 800/638-2466

Built to look as though it had been standing proud for 100 years, this two-story gray-and-white inn is actually of modern construction, offering contemporary comforts to gentleman farmers and city-weary celebs alike. Charming country details abound, from the wicker rocking chairs that decorate the inn's wraparound porch, to the white picket fence and the carefully tended rosebushes. Step inside, and the first thing you'll notice is a fire warming the giant hearth that serves both the lobby and the inn's restaurant. The downstairs public rooms, including an enormous, sunny parlor, are tastefully furnished with a comfortable mix of antiques and reproductions, hand-hooked rugs, bent-twig furniture, and vintage accessories. Upstairs, each guest room is decorated according to a theme from the Valley's history or geography. Some have fireplaces and/or private balconies. All have well-stocked bathrooms, and many feature an antique washbasin in the room as well. Though a few have overly feminine decor of lace and florals, more than half are tastefully unfrilly. The best (and most expensive) is the Mountain Room, a mini-suite decorated in rich forest green, with a fireplace and a private balcony. Other favorites are the hardwood-floored Vineyard Room, with a grapevine motif and a large bay window, and Davy Brown's Room, whose tall stone fireplace, wood paneling, and hand-stitched quilt lend a log-cabin appeal. Included in the rate are a gracious wine-and-hors-d'oeuvres reception each afternoon, evening coffee and tea, and a delicious full breakfast each morning; be forewarned, however, that a 10 percent service charge for the staff is added to your bill. Here in the heart of wine country, the staff can provide advice on wine touring or even arrange a full-day wine-tasting excursion.

Cafe Chardonnay is the inn's own restaurant, tucked into a cozy room downstairs by a crackling fire. The short, often inspired (though occasionally uneven) menu can include grilled meats, seafood pastas, and catch-of-the-day specials. Dinner might start with baked goat cheese salad garnished with kalamata olives, move on to roasted and grilled prime rib of pork with a glaze of caramelized shallots and port wine sauce, and end with an orange-infused crème brûlée. Inn guests and nonguests alike need to reserve in advance, since Cafe Chardonnay's few tables are always in demand. *$$$–$$$$; AE, MC, V; checks OK; innkeeper@ballardinn.com; www.ballardinn.com; just east of Alamo Pintado Rd.* &

Los Olivos

Looking exactly like the movie set for a small town, this former stage-coach stop has a giant flagpole instead of a traffic light to mark its main intersection. Along the town's three-block business district, a wooden boardwalk contributes to the Wild West atmosphere. But although this tiny dot on the map has starred as a backwards Southern hamlet in such TV shows as *Return to Mayberry*, Los Olivos sits squarely at the heart of the Wine Country—and it boasts all the upscale sophistication you'd expect from a place that attracts big-city transplants and cosmopolitan tourists. Next to wine touring and dining, the favorite pastime here is shopping, and Los Olivos has more than its share of art galleries and antique shops. **GALLERY LOS OLIVOS** (2920 Grand Avenue; 805/688-7517) is for serious collectors of regional artists; **JUDITH HALE GALLERY** (2890 Grand Avenue; 805/688-1222) showcases paintings and Navajo-crafted silver jewelry; and **PERSNICKITY** (2900 Grand Avenue; 805/686-8955) is a darling niche filled with antique linens and laces.

RESTAURANTS

Los Olivos Cafe / ★

2879 GRAND AVE, LOS OLIVOS; 805/688-7265
This local favorite is always filled with folks waving to friends from tables on the trellis-shaded wooden porch and enjoying uncomplicated but thoughtfully prepared Mediterranean meals. Inside, the simple cafe resembles an Italian country kitchen. Lunch consists mainly of sandwiches prepared in the gourmet deli (also a great place for buying a picnic lunch), including the favored smoked turkey on a baguette with oven-dried tomatoes, radicchio, and creamy aioli and a roasted-vegetable sandwich with a smoky undertone that calls out for a glass of wine. At dinner the short menu consists of chicken (Marsala, piccata, cacciatore, or parmigiana), several light and savory pastas, and specialty pizzas. You can't go wrong by starting with the roasted-vegetable appetizer served with smoked mozzarella and olive tapenade. Always packed at lunch, Los Olivos Cafe is also a pleasantly casual dinner alternative to the ritzy Vintage Room across the street. *$; DIS, MC, V; local checks only; lunch, dinner every day; beer and wine; reservations recommended; south of Alamo Pintado Ave.* &

Mattei's Tavern / ★

HIGHWAY 154, LOS OLIVOS; 805/688-4820

Italian-Swiss immigrant Felix Mattei built this roadside tavern in 1886 to accommodate stagecoach travelers preparing for the mountainous journey to Santa Barbara, and today the rambling white Victorian, sub-

SANTA BARBARA COUNTY WINERIES

You might think of Santa Barbara County as a "new" wine region, but winemaking here is a 200-year-old tradition, first practiced by Franciscan friars at the area's missions. In the past 20 to 30 years, area vintners have been gaining recognition, and today wine grapes are one of the top crops in the country. To understand their success, you need only look at geography. Like most renowned wine regions, the Santa Ynez and Santa Maria Valleys are bounded by transverse (west-to-east) mountain ranges, which allow ocean breezes to flow in and keep the climate temperate. Variations in temperature and humidity within the valleys create numerous microclimates, in which vintners have learned how to cultivate nearly all the classic grapes. White grapes flourish here, so everyone makes a chardonnay, but several reds are also well regarded, including cabernet sauvignon, syrah, and viognier, a Rhône varietal that's gaining in popularity. A good way to familiarize yourself with the local wine country is by contacting the **Santa Barbara County Vintners' Association** (3669 Sagunto Street, Unit 101, Santa Ynez; 805/688-0881 or 800/218-0881; www.sbcountywines.com). Be sure to pick up a copy of their *Winery Touring Map*, which is also available at hotels and the wineries themselves. If you'd like to sample wines without driving around, head to **Los Olivos Tasting Room & Wine Shop** (2905 Grand Avenue; 805/688-7406), located in the heart of town, or **Los Olivos Wine & Spirits Emporium** (2531 Grand Avenue; 805/688-4409; www.sbwines.com), a friendly barn in a field half a mile away. Both offer a wide selection, including wines from vintners—like Au Bon Climat and Qupé—who don't have their own tasting rooms.

Fess Parker Winery & Vineyard: Part of a Santa Barbara dynasty that also includes an oceanside resort, cattle ranches, and a chic B&B, this grandiose operation turns out some critically acclaimed syrahs and chardonnays. Lest you think Parker has forgotten his Hollywood past (he played Davy Crockett and Daniel Boone), the winery's gift shop even peddles coonskin caps. Located at 6200 Foxen Canyon Road, Los Olivos; 805/688-1545; www.FessParker.com.

Firestone Vineyard: Started by Brooks Firestone of tire-manufacturing fame, this winery is one of the county's largest producers and now includes two "second" labels, one of which specializes in Chilean-grown grapes. The tasting room and gift shop are a three-ring circus of merchandise, but Firestone offers a quick, worthwhile tour. Located at 5017 Zaca Station Road, Los Olivos; 805/688-3940; www.firestonevineyard.com.

The Gainey Vineyard: This visitor-oriented winery has a large terra-cotta–tiled tasting room, plenty of logo merchandise, and a deli case for impromptu lunches at their garden tables. Gainey draws huge crowds thanks to a prime location on Highway 246 and the in-depth tours it offers seven days a week. Located at 3950 East Highway 246, Santa Ynez; 805/688-0558.

Sunstone Vineyards & Winery: This classy winery's wisteria-wrapped stone tasting room and lavender-fringed picnic courtyard lie nestled in an oak grove overlooking the river. Don't be misled by the rambling dirt entrance road—Sunstone boasts a superior merlot (their flagship varietal) and features a sophisticated gift shop with gourmet foods, cigars, and souvenirs. Located at 125 N Refugio Road, Santa Ynez; 805/688-WINE or 800/313-WINE.

Zaca Mesa Winery: Situated on a serene plateau, Zaca Mesa offers the usual syrahs and chardonnays plus Rhône varietals such as grenache, roussanne, and viognier. Located at 6905 Foxen Canyon Road, Los Olivos; 805/688-9339 or 800/350-7972.

merged in wisteria, has successfully retained its historic charm. Although the tavern stopped accepting overnight guests in the 1960s, Mattei's is well known throughout the county for fun and good food. You might find yourself seated in one of several downstairs dining rooms: in the Mattei family's formal dining room, on the white-wicker enclosed sun porch, or inside the former water tower, looking up through the skylight at nesting owls atop the structure. Rumors abound of high-stakes poker games in Mattei's back room, where many an early rancher literally lost the farm. As befits a family-run joint with such a colorful history, Mattei's has a light-hearted ambience and good-neighborly attitude. The fare is heartily American, including fine steaks and steak-seafood combos; chicken piccata, Marsala, or teriyaki; lobster tail; rainbow trout; burgers; prime-rib chili; and the house soup, a dill-tinged tomato bisque. Dinners, all of which are generous, include soup or salad and sides. *$$; MC, V; local checks only; lunch Fri–Sun in summer, Sat–Sun the rest of the year, dinner every day; full bar; reservations recommended; west of Grand Ave.* ⅙

Panino / ★★

2900 GRAND AVE, LOS OLIVOS; 805/688-9304

For the best gourmet sandwiches in the wine country, head to this charming little cafe just a stone's throw from the flagpole that marks the center of Los Olivos. You can dine at simple bistro tables on their garden patio (cooled by a fine mist during the hotter months) or pack an upscale picnic lunch for a day of wine touring, bicycling, or boating. Choose from 31 sandwiches—all served on fresh-baked Italian-style breads—including grilled chicken with sun-dried tomatoes, fresh basil, and provolone; Genoa salami with kalamata-olive tapenade, basil, and roasted red peppers; smoked salmon with Caprino goat cheese, capers, and olive oil; or English Stilton with Asian pear on fresh walnut bread. Several Mediterranean salads are also available, and the shop is great at arranging easy-to-carry box lunches complete with all the necessary utensils. *$; no credit cards; checks OK; lunch every day; beer and wine; reservations not accepted; at Alamo Pintado Ave.* &

LODGINGS

Fess Parker's Wine Country Inn & Spa / ★★

2860 GRAND AVE (PO BOX 849), LOS OLIVOS; 805/688-7788 OR 800/446-2455

With an elegance (and a price) that comes dangerously close to being out of place in this unpretentious town, the newest holding in the wine-country dynasty of Fess Parker prides itself on state-of-the-art pampering. The first thing Parker did after taking over the former Los Olivos Grand Hotel was to inaugurate a deluxe spa featuring French Sea Spa treatments that use ocean products such as seaweed, algae, and mud in a variety of exfoliating and soothing therapies. Each of the spacious guest rooms is luxuriously appointed, with a fireplace, oversize bathroom (some have Jacuzzi tubs), wet bar, and cozy down comforter. A turn-down fairy leaves Godiva chocolates on your pillow. The inn's decor conjures up the tasteful French country home of a Parisian dignitary. Staying in the main building makes you feel more like a country-house guest, but the annex across the street has easier access to the heated outdoor swimming pool and whirlpool. A warm lobby/sitting room woos guests with its fire roaring in the main hearth; there's also a quiet cocktail lounge and a pretty back garden often used for weddings or small luncheons.

Parker brought in some culinary heavy hitters for the inn's restaurant, The Vintage Room, a polished spot that wouldn't be out of place in one of L.A.'s or San Francisco's choicer hotels. Breakfast and lunch are both a notch above average, but chef Calvin Francis—formerly with the Ojai Valley Inn—pulls out the stops with dinner entrees like pan-seared venison medallions atop a couscous flan accented with Asian pear–molasses chutney, or herb-crusted halibut alongside Dungeness crab dumplings bathed in tamari-ginger jus. Starters can be even more intriguing, with choices like pan-seared scallops glazed with pinot noir served atop potatoes whipped purple with beets; grilled quail with spinach–goat cheese stuffing drizzled with aged balsamic; or venison carpaccio layered with fennel and arugula and topped with dried-cherry aioli. *$$$$; AE, DC, DIS, MC, V; checks OK; www.FessParker.com; south of Alamo Pintado Ave.* &

Santa Ynez

The center of cattle ranching in this valley since the 1880s, Santa Ynez remains a farm town whose centerpiece is the historic Santa Ynez Feed & Mill, which still supplies hay, grain, and tack to valley ranchers and cowboys. Spanning just two blocks, downtown Santa Ynez sports false-front Old West facades and down-home hospitality—notably illustrated by the local service station, which cheerfully offers full service at the self serve price. For a look at conveyances of yesteryear, stop into the **PARKS-JANEWAY CARRIAGE HOUSE** (corner of Sagunto and Faraday Streets; 805/688-7889), operated by the Santa Ynez Valley Historical Society. This small but exceptional museum comprises the largest collection of horse-drawn vehicles west of the Mississippi, featuring rare examples of stagecoaches, covered wagons, a horse-drawn hearse, personal surreys, and more. Tour-bus groups are common in the valley, drawn to nearby Solvang and to Santa Ynez's **CHUMASH CASINO** (on Highway 246 in Santa Ynez; 805/686-0855 or 800/728-9997), where high-stakes bingo, Las Vegas–style video gaming, and spirited card games entertain 24 hours a day (on certain days) while adhering to state guidelines that permit gaming on Native American lands.

Follow Highway 154 south from here and you'll soon see pictur-esque **CACHUMA LAKE** (805/686-5054). The reservoir, created in 1953 by damming the Santa Ynez River, is the primary water source for Santa Barbara County and the centerpiece of a 6,600-acre county park with a flourishing wildlife population and well-developed recreational facilities. Migratory birds—including **BALD EAGLES**, rarely sighted in these parts—abound during the winter months, and full-time residents include blue herons, osprey, red-tailed hawks, golden eagles, deer, bobcats, and moun-tain lions. The best way to appreciate all this bounty is by taking a nat-uralist-led **EAGLE CRUISE** or **WILDLIFE CRUISE**, offered year-round on the lake; call 805/686-5050 for reservations. Camping, boating, and fishing are all popular activities centered around a small marina.

Nearby is the new 18-hole **RANCHO SAN MARCOS GOLF COURSE** (on Highway 154 south of the lake; 805/683-6334), designed by Robert Trent Jones Jr. to wind scenically along the Santa Ynez River next to the Los Padres National Forest.

RESTAURANTS

The Vineyard House

3631 SAGUNTO ST, SANTA YNEZ; 805/688-2886
Until the 1980s, this lavish Victorian on Santa Ynez's main drag was a private residence. Now it serves as a welcome addition to the valley's interesting, but limited, dining scene. Though the food served here—a

pleasant mix of American standards and lighter California-style dishes—isn't always competitive with some other gourmet hot spots, the Vineyard House's utterly charming setting is a winner. Diners who choose a table on the wide front deck enjoy a bucolic view that has changed little since the house was built over a century ago. Diners inside are treated to the same picturesque vista through a giant picture window. Standout dishes include a souplike venison chili verde made with tomatillos and served with avocado salsa, a main-course salad topped with beer-battered fried chicken and creamy Gorgonzola cheese, and some inventive pastas. Other choices include rack of lamb, filet mignon, and salmon in an aromatic fennel sauce with spinach. The menu is complemented by a reasonably priced list of fine Central Coast wines and a worthy dessert list. *$$; AE, MC, V; local checks only; lunch, dinner Wed–Mon, brunch Sun; beer and wine; reservations recommended; 3 blocks from Hwy 246 via Edison St.* &

San Marcos Pass

California Highway 154 is a beautiful drive, and one we highly recommend as a scenic alternative to US 101 as it traverses the Santa Ynez Mountains on its way to Santa Barbara. After passing Cachuma Lake, the San Marcos Pass climbs to around 2,200 feet amidst thick chaparral-covered hillsides, brightened each spring with blooming wildflowers. Whatever the time of year, a stellar ocean view comes into sight just as you reach the summit. This mountain pass has been used by people for centuries, including Colonel John Frémont, who sneaked through to surprise a band of Mexican soldiers during the American conquest of California in 1846. Stagecoach Road traces the original pathway through the pass, and until a bridge was built in 1963 this winding and rugged road served as the only way across 400-foot-deep Cold Spring Canyon near the top of the pass. Unfortunately, most drivers never appreciate the marvelous **COLD SPRING ARCH BRIDGE,** since its graceful, swooping arc (supporting the roadway in a single 700-foot span) cannot be seen as you cross it. For a glorious view of the bridge, turn off the main highway at Stagecoach Road.

The earliest evidence of inhabitants in the pass can be seen at **CHUMASH PAINTED CAVE HISTORIC PARK,** a worthwhile 10-minute detour from Hightway 154. Turn off onto Painted Cave Road; after two miles, look for the small sign and parking turnout. On foot, follow the rocky path a few yards to the cave. It's dark inside, but not too dark to distinguish the vivid drawings, probably made by Chumash shamans, which include geometric and swirling designs, horned animals, human figures, and a sun drawing believed to represent a 17th-century eclipse.

Santa Barbara

For a relatively small town, Santa Barbara has a tremendous amount to offer. Self-proclaimed as "the American Riviera," the city of 87,000 residents is indeed breathtaking, from its picturesque hills to its wide sandy beaches and dolphin-filled Pacific waters. Adding to the area's natural beauty is the town itself, whose rich Spanish/Mexican history is evident in today's culture and architecture. And did we mention the near-perfect weather year-round (70 degrees average), and the obscure fact that more species of trees grow here than in any in other city?

ACCESS AND INFORMATION

Santa Barbara is 92 miles from Los Angeles and 332 miles from San Francisco, on Highway 101. Highway 154, through the San Marcos Pass, joins 101 from the Santa Ynez Valley to the north. United Airlines offers the most flights daily, but American also flies from L.A. into the **SANTA BARBARA MUNICIPAL AIRPORT**, which is located in Goleta (15 minutes north of downtown Santa Barbara; 805/967-7111). Most major **CAR RENTAL COMPANIES** are conveniently located at the airport, and the Superride (805/683-9636) **SHUTTLE SERVICE** provides passengers with advance-reservation rides to and from the airport. The **AIRBUS COACH** (800/733-6354) arrives daily from Los Angeles. **AMTRAK** (209 State Street; 800/872-7245 or 805/963-1015) makes several stops daily at State and Yanonaly Streets. Local **TROLLEYS AND BUSES** are easy to use and stop at most hotels and places of interest. The Santa Barbara Trolley Co. (805/965-0353) offers all-day fares for only $5 ($3 for children). The MTD Shuttle Bus operates every 10 minutes between downtown and Stearns Wharf and every 30 minutes between the harbor and the zoo (in the Santa Barbara Zoological Gardens), at a one-way cost of a quarter. For more information contact the **SANTA BARBARA VISITORS BUREAU** (1 Santa Barbara Street, Santa Barbara, CA 93101; 800/927-4688 or 805/966-9222; www.santabarbaraca.com).

MAJOR ATTRACTIONS

At the **SANTA BARBARA BOTANICAL GARDENS** (1212 Mission Canyon Road; 805/682-4726; www.sbbg.org.) flora, fauna, and weather come together perfectly—particularly in the spring and summer months, when most of the 1,300 indigenous and rare plants are in bloom. But the lovely trails are worth a rambling walk any time of year. In the same area you can find the much-admired **SANTA BARBARA MISSION** (2001 Laguna at Los Olivos; 805/682 4713), one of 21 Catholic missions built on former Spanish territory. Services are still held regularly in the majestic adobe church with its double bell tower and rose garden. Nearby is the oldest bridge in the county.

The paintings, photographs, furniture, clothing, and artifacts at the **SANTA BARBARA HISTORY MUSEUM** (136 E de la Guerra Street; 805/966-1601) portray town life from the 1780s to the 1920s, with scenarios depicting the lives of the Spanish, Mexican, Chumash, Chinese, and American pioneers. The diverse collection of objects includes a magnificent Chinese altar, an original Pony Express saddle, an unusual Victorian hair wreath, and the beautiful 17th-century oil *Coronation of the Virgin* by Miguel Cabrera. Across the courtyard is the Gledhill Library, a researcher's paradise where newspapers and periodicals dating back over a hundred years are bound in huge leather volumes and available for your perusal. For more information, or group tours, contact the **SANTA BARBARA HISTORICAL SOCIETY** (805/966-1601) or the **ARCHITECTURAL FOUNDATION OF SANTA BARBARA** (805/965-6307), which offers informative walking tours of the city.

Santa Barbara boasts its own **SANTA BARBARA MUSEUM OF ART** (1130 State Street; 805/963-4364) with an impressive collection of 18th-, 19th-, and 20th-century American and European paintings and sculpture, as well as decorative arts from Asia. For a more child-friendly environment, the **SANTA BARBARA MUSEUM OF NATURAL HISTORY** (2559 Puesta del Sol Road; 805/682-4711) has a planetarium, lizard lounge, insect arena, and exhibits of everything from a 72-foot whale skeleton to a space lab and outstanding Native American artifacts. The **SEA CENTER** (211 Stearns Wharf; 805/962-0885) is run in cooperation with the museum, and in addition to a touch tank for children has well-stocked aquariums and shipwreck artifacts. The **SANTA BARBARA ZOOLOGICAL GARDENS** (500 Ninos Drive; 805/962-5339) consists of a quaint zoo on 30 acres of well-landscaped gardens, with a small but well-rounded collection of animals, many of which are endangered species. The zoo can be toured in a bright-red miniature train.

ARCHITECTURE

The streets of Santa Barbara may not be paved with gold, but many of its sidewalks are adorned with terra-cotta, and surrounding walls and fountains are decorated with beautiful Spanish tile circa 1920. Though the town is steeped in Spanish heritage, the picture-perfect downtown landscape is actually a result of a massive earthquake that leveled much of State Street in 1925. As bizarre as it seems, the architectural commission of Santa Barbara saw the earthquake as a godsend of sorts, as they had been drawing up plans to rebuild the town in keeping with its Spanish heritage. They had, in fact, already begun implementing the design concept a couple of years before with **EL PASEO** (15 E de la Guerra Street), which is now a complex of shops and restaurants. The complex was restructured from a section of the **CASA DE LA GUERRA**, built in 1819 for the fifth commandante of the Presidio. One block over is the

SANTA BARBARA THREE-DAY TOUR

DAY ONE. Start your day with a frothy cappuccino and a breakfast pastry at **Aficionado** in the old-town section of Santa Barbara. Walk past **Casa de la Guerra** to the **History Museum** and acquaint yourself with the town's past. Walk up Anacapa Street to the **County Courthouse,** whose magnificent 360-degree view gives you a good visual sense of your surroundings. Then hop on the shuttle bus and head over to **Stearns Wharf** at the harbor for a seafood lunch at **Brophy Bros. Clam Bar & Restaurant.** Spend part of the afternoon enjoying the beach and views of the Channel Islands, and then take the shuttle bus as far as the **Zoological Gardens**. Or, if you are feeling energetic, rent a bike and follow the coastal path from Stearns Wharf to **Montecito**. Have afternoon tea at the **Four Seasons Biltmore,** or stroll on clothing-optional **Butterfly Beach**. Cycle back, ending the day back on State Street to browse some shops and dine at the **Wine Cask**.

DAY TWO. Take scenic **Cliff Drive**, starting at Cabrillo Drive near the harbor and following the signs all the way to the **Brown Pelican** in the Arroyo Burro County Beach Park for a beachfront breakfast. Continue on the scenic drive past Hope Ranch. Drive up Las Palmas Drive back onto State Street to the **Santa Barbara Mission**, situated off Los Olivos. Walk through the nearby **Botanical Gardens** before heading into the hills for an amazing view and lunch on the terrace of **El Encanto**, high up in the wealthy Riviera section of town. After lunch, drive along Alameda Padre Serra through the scenic area and continue on Alston Road to Montecito. Visit **Lotusland** (by appointment only) or shop on **Coast Village Road** in the charming village. Dine at **Pane e Vino** or the Stonehouse restaurant, both in Montecito, and tuck into bed at the pastoral **San Ysidro Ranch**.

DAY THREE. Depending on the day and time of year, go **whale watching**, **sailing**, or just spend the morning kicking back at any of the area's pristine beaches. In the afternoon look for antiques on State Street or Brinkerhoff Avenue, then drive through Los Padros National Forest over the San Marcos Pass for a hearty lunch at **Cold Springs Tavern**. Head back to Santa Barbara to the **Santa Barbara Museum of Art** or the **Santa Barbara Museum of Natural History**, then browse the out-of-print titles at the **Book Den**. Dine at the charming **Meritage** or the harborside **Emilio's**.

remains of **EL PRESIDIO** (129 E Cañon Perdido Street; 805/966-9719), now a state park that commemorates the site where Santa Barbara was originally settled in 1782. The original fortress was one of four built in California by the Spanish as a seat of government and military headquarters (the other three are in San Diego, San Francisco, and Monterey).

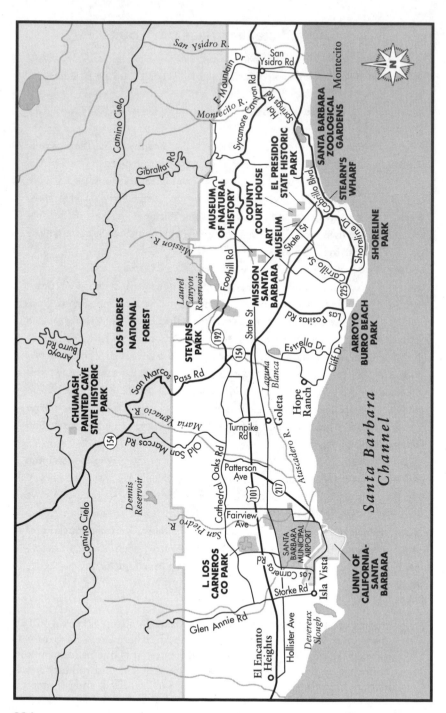

The Santa Barbara Trust (805/966-9719), which is painstakingly restoring all the buildings, offers **GUIDED TOURS**. The **SANTA BARBARA COUNTY COURTHOUSE** (1100 Anacapa Street; 805/962-6464) is a distinctive piece of Spanish colonial revival architecture, resplendent with its stunning painted ceilings and tiled walls and easy to find by its four-story clock tower.

ACTIVE EXCURSIONS

For activity of a more participatory kind, **HIKING** and **BIKING TRAIL MAPS** are available at the Visitor Center main office (on the corner of State Street and Cabrillo Boulevard at the Ocean; 805/965-3021) or in downtown Santa Barbara at 504 State Street; 805/568-1811 or the Chamber of Commerce Visitor Center (1 Garden Street; 805/965-3021 www.sbchamber.org). **BIKES** and **IN-LINE SKATES** are available for rent at Beach Rentals (22 State Street; 805/966-6733). If you'd rather travel by four-legged friend, call the people at **CIRCLE B STABLES** (1800 Refugio Road; 805/968-3901), who arrange all kinds of rides, including sunset and sunrise, English- or Western-style excursions. You can rent a **SAILBOAT, JET SKI**, or **SPEEDBOAT** from the Sailing Center of Santa Barbara (at the breakwater, enter from Shoreline Drive; 800/350-9090), or let someone else steer your craft with Sunset Kidd Sailing Charters (at the breakwater; 805/962-8222), which offers **DAY TOURS, SEASONAL WHALE WATCHES**, and **SUNSET CRUISES** on a 41-foot Morgan. The *Condor* (board at SeaLanding at the harbor, 888/77-WHALE or 805/882-0088), operated through the Natural History Museum, is an 88-foot boat that offers educational trips with knowledgeable volunteers (during the months of February, March, and April only). For the more adventurous, Truth Aquatics (Sea Landing at the harbor; 805/962-1127) offers **CHANNEL ISLANDS TRIPS** including kayaking, snorkeling, scubadiving, and hiking.

SHOPPING

Santa Barbara's shopping is excellent. There are specialty stores and boutiques in historic **EL PASEO** (State Street, above de la Guerra Street) and **LA ARCADA** (State Street, above Figueroa Street) and the beautiful modern mall **PASEO NUEVO** (State Street at de la Guerra Street). While State Street is the **MAIN SHOPPING AREA** and the prime destination for antiques and vintage clothing, some of the best shops are on side streets. For bibliophiles, The **BOOK DEN** (11 E Anapamu Street; 805/962-3321) has been the place to go for used books since 1979; **SULLIVAN GOSS** (7 E Anapamu Street; 805/730-1460) stocks old and new prints, photographs, and paintings such as those of revered local wine-label painter James Paul Brown. For really serious antique hunters, Brinkerhoff Avenue between Cota Street and Haley Street is a row of landmark preservation houses overflowing with expensive knickknacks, turn-of-the-century antiques, and vintage oil paintings capturing local vistas.

BEACHES

The broad stretch of beach hugging the ocean from **STEARNS WHARF** to Montecito is **EAST BEACH**, which is the most popular along with the more intimate (and clothing-optional) **BUTTERFLY BEACH**, further east near the Biltmore Hotel. Restrooms, showers, a playground, and volleyball courts are scattered in the area, and the Cabrillo Pavilion Bathhouse (1118 Cabrillo Boulevard; 805/965-0509) provides lockers and use of their weight room for a minimal fee. At **SHORELINE PARK** (Shoreline Drive, north of the harbor), take the steps down to the secluded white sand beach to escape the crowds, or for an even more remote spot head to **MESA LANE BEACH** (north, at Mesa Lane, off Cliff Drive), a very private strip of sand hidden by bluffs, which is also a good surf spot. Also off Cliff Drive is the beach locals refer to as **HENDRY'S BEACH**, with good picnic areas, snack bars (such as the **BROWN PELICAN**), and excellent swimming, fishing, and surfing. (Its official name is **ARROYO BURRO NATURE RESERVE**; 2981 Cliff Drive; 805/687-3714.)

NIGHTLIFE

Most of the nightlife scene is centered in **OLD TOWN SANTA BARBARA**, particularly on State Street. **Q'S** (409 State Street; 805/966-9177) and **ZELO** (630 State Street; 805/966-5792) are great for dancing to the latest sounds. The sound at SoHo (1221 State Street; 805/962-7776) changes nightly, from jazz, blues, dance, funk, and reggae to Eastern European traditional folk. Also on State, in the Paseo Nuevo is the popular **ROCKS** (801 State Street; 805/884-1190), where lemon-drop martinis and cigars are practically mandatory. A more sophisticated crowd is drawn to the bar scene and upstairs lounge at **BLUE AGAVE** (20 E Cota Street; 805/899-4694). During warmer months **THE SANTA BARBARA BOWL** (805/962-7411), an outdoor arena set into the Santa Ynez foothills, attracts all the major concert tours.

RESTAURANTS

Aficionado European Bakery / ★★☆

10 E CARRILLO ST, SANTA BARBARA; 805/963-8404
If you doubt for a moment that this bakery is anything other than what its name implies (by extension, "dedicated"), just stroll by on a Sunday and peer through the closed storefront to the busy kitchen beyond that's churning out rack upon rack of freshly baked breads and pastries. Most of the bounty is headed to many of Santa Barbara's finer tables (Simpson House, the Four Seasons Biltmore, bouchon, and Wine Cask are a few). But, happily, there's plenty left over for all the folks who come here the

rest of the week. Regional bread specials are featured and include herbed *fougasse, levain boules* (sourdough), onion focaccia, sweetly perfumed olive rolls, simple flatbreads, and Tuscan breadsticks. At lunchtime the breads become sandwiches: tuna with sesame-ginger mayonnaise, rosemary-marinated chicken, or roasted vegetable with crumbly feta. Start the day on a sweet note with a fruit-filled pastry or a lemon blueberry muffin and a foamy cappuccino, and savor it outside on a cafe table or perched on a stool inside. *$$; AE, DC, MC, V; checks OK; breakfast, lunch Mon–Sat; on Carrillo St, just east of State St.* &

AJA / ★★

1812 CLIFF DR, SANTA BARBARA; 805/962-0337

A newer restaurant, AJA (pronounced "Asia") is situated in a strip mall in the little-known residential neighborhood known as "the Mesa." What this small and casual cafe lacks in stylish decor, it certainly makes up for in flavor. "Pacific Rim" describes most of the menu accurately, from the exotic Indonesian corn fritters or tender Kahlua pork with polenta to the rich coconut shrimp with pilaf. Some of the fried items tend toward greasy, so you may want to stay with lighter fare such as the lollipop scallops (grilled scallops in a spicy brown sauce) or the well-seasoned paper-wrapped roasted chicken. Thin-crust pizzas with the topping of the day are also light and delicious. *$; MC, V; local checks only; lunch Tues–Fri, dinner Tues–Sun; beer and wine; reservations not necessary; take Cabrillo Blvd west until it becomes Shoreline, left on Cliff Dr.*

bouchon / ★★★☆

9 W VICTORIA ST, SANTA BARBARA; 805/730-1160

Although the name means "wine cork" in French, almost all of the corks are coming out of local bottles at this newcomer serving Wine Country cuisine. Owner Mitchell Sjerven and chef Charles Fredericks worked at many of the town's finer eating establishments before teaming up in 1998. The list of local wines by the glass is impressive, as is the wine list in general, including such selections as an excellent sangiovese from the Cambria region and a viognier from Santa Ynez. The well-informed staff love to help with menu selections; seasonal dishes they might recommend might include the velvety potato-leek soup or saffron-roasted monkfish. Local escargots and pepper-seared ostrich loin are two more exotic offerings, but you can also count on well-prepared standards such as grilled veal chop, Angus steak, or rack of lamb. The simple dining room is adorned with paintings by Paul Brown (a respected local painter of wine labels), the kitchen is in view beyond beautiful etched glass panels, and the garden patio is heated. An adjoining wine bar is open on weekends. *$$$; AE, MC, V; checks OK; dinner every day; beer and wine; reservations recommended; between State and Chapala Sts.* &

The Brown Pelican / ★★

2981½ CLIFF DR, SANTA BARBARA; 805/687-4550

The Brown Pelican, a lone building tucked perfectly into a sunny cove on a beach in the Arroyo Burro Nature Reserve, is unparalleled for pure scenic beauty. It's possible that on a clear day a patio seat overlooking the vast expanse of ocean and surrounding cliffs makes the food taste better than it actually is. However, the food is actually quite good if you stick to the fresh fish specials: good old fish and chips in an ale batter, light but hearty seafood linguine, crab cakes, or steamed local mussels. The ahi tuna on focaccia and the grilled chicken sandwich are simple and tasty, and there's a children's menu with the usual requests—grilled cheese, pasta, burger and fries. Breakfast is especially satisfying, with delectable offerings such as fluffy French toast, buttermilk pancakes, and ocean hash (poached eggs, crab cake, and a potato sauté). An even sweeter temptation is the heavenly chocolate chip pancakes. Don't worry: Afterwards you can just step down onto the picture-perfect 2-mile stretch of beach to walk it off, along with a multitude of dogs walking their owners on what is known locally as "dog beach." *$; AE, MC, V; no checks; breakfast, lunch, dinner every day; full bar; reservations accepted Mon–Thurs only; Cabrillo Blvd W, right on Loma Alta, left on Cliff Rd about 3 miles.*

Brophy Bros. Clam Bar & Restaurant / ★★★

119 HARBOR WAY, SANTA BARBARA; 805/966-4418

Unrivaled harbor views and famous clam chowder are the main draws at this cheerful, lively restaurant. However, there're plenty more treasures from the sea served amidst the ocean breezes: cioppino; the cold combo platter of shrimp, crab, oysters, clams, and ceviche; or its hot counterpart with steamed clams, oysters Rockefeller, and beer-boiled shrimp. The fresh fish menu changes daily; you may find local yellowtail lovingly grilled with lemon, rosemary, and shallots; traditional lobster; fresh mahi-mahi; or succulent swordfish steak grilled and topped with tarragon-and-crab cream sauce. Meat eaters, however, needn't be disappointed; the burgers here aren't bad either. Lunch outside on the balcony and absorb the sights and sounds (and sometimes smells) of the fisherman's world around you, or in the evening join regulars at the inside bar as they trade tales of the sea over draught beer and steamers. *$$; AE, MC, V; no checks; lunch, dinner every day; full bar; reservations recommended; enter the harbor off Cabrillo Blvd.*

Cold Springs Tavern / ★★★

5995 STAGECOACH RD, SANTA BARBARA; 805/967-0066

This charming moss-covered shingle cabin with gingham-draped windows and cozy fireplace nooks, nestled among the trees next to a babbling brook, is truly a testament to old-fashioned carnivorous dining. After 100-plus years, the former stagecoach stop is still a popular watering hole. The simple, hearty lunch menu features burgers of buffalo or beef, plus sandwiches, salads, and Cold Springs' renowned chili. Dinner is more elegant than you might expect, with excellent-quality cuts of meat and fresh vegetables, stuffed chicken with sherry–sour cream sauce, barbecued baby back ribs, or rack of lamb with champagne-mint glaze. Venison sausage–stuffed mushrooms in garlic butter are the house appetizer, a tasty but rich artery-clogger best shared. Not surprisingly, trophy heads and photographs line the walls; a plaque reads "God go with you, we haven't got time." Weekends and nights, especially during summer, the saloon-style bar next door is packed with revelers singing along to Wurlitzer classics or dancing to local bands. In addition to visiting the rustic restaurant and bar, you can roam around the remaining outbuildings and the namesake artesian springs. Don't miss the resident 19 cats, all named George. It'll take you 20 minutes to drive here from downtown, but the incredible coastline views along the way make the trip worthwhile. $$; AE, MC, V; no checks; breakfast Sat–Sun, lunch, dinner every day; full bar; reservations recommended; cst@silcom.com; from Hwy 154, turn west on Stagecoach Rd.

Downey's / ★★★

1305 STATE ST, SANTA BARBARA; 805/966-5006

A Santa Barbara classic, Downey's has become synonymous with great California food during its lengthy tenure on State Street, although its unassuming appearance inside and out offers no hint of its reputation. Chef John Downey, who honed his talents on that most royal of cruise liners, the QE2, has perfected the art of taste-bud awakening with his simply prepared but unerringly conceived creations. Melt-in-your-mouth smoked pheasant with ginger-infused pear, Sonoma foie gras with buttery potato and Madeira-soaked raisins, and tenderloin of lamb floating in a veal stock reduction with roasted eggplant are only a few of his magical offerings. The menu changes daily, so it's hard to predict what will be featured, but everything is guaranteed to be fresh and delicious. Indulge in the special house dessert—a rhapsody of white chocolate cream and raspberries sandwiched between two layers of buttery sweet flaky pastry. $$$; AE, DIS, MC, V; local checks OK; lunch, dinner Tues–Sun, brunch Sat–Sun; full bar; reservations recommended; between Sola and Victoria Sts.

El Encanto / ★★☆

1900 LAUSEN RD, SANTA BARBARA; 805/687-5000

It's set in an area of Santa Barbara known locally as "the Riviera," and the mountain-to-ocean views from this restaurant's rambling perch are second to none. Whether you're enjoying lunch on a sunny afternoon or dinner under the stars, the food just makes the view seem even grander. As of mid-'97, Chef Phillipe Berger has overseen the California cuisine menu with seafood specialties such as smoked salmon on a leek pancake; risotto of lobster, scallops, and rock shrimp; and a perfectly seasoned paella brimming with mussels, clams, chicken, scallops, and spicy sausage. The menu changes with the seasons (and indeed with the days) but always features chicken (perhaps poached with black truffles), veal (perhaps roasted with foie gras sauce), great pastas, and superb desserts—which are served as the stars compete with the harbor lights. *$$$; AE, DC, MC, V; checks OK; lunch, dinner every day, brunch Sun; full bar; reservations recommended; www.placestostay.com; past the Mission to Laguna, right onto Los Olivos, right onto Alameda Padre Serra, to Lausen.*

Emilio's Ristorante and Bar / ★★☆

324 W CABRILLO BLVD, SANTA BARBARA; 805/966-4426

At this romantic Italian restaurant, arched windows open to Pacific breezes on warm nights and candles provide the only light as evening sets in. As if that weren't enchanting enough, add whitewashed walls, exposed wood beams, soft jazz, and clinking wineglasses and you've got yourself one amorous dining room. Soulful dishes include a rich osso buco, oak-grilled salmon, and a traditional paella overflowing with mussels, clams, and spicy sausage. As you feast, enjoy the ever-changing display of works by local artists. The prix-fixe dinner is highly recommended (it always includes a vegetarian option), offered for the entire table and served family-style Sunday through Thursday. Chef Pete Clements, having once been a vegetarian himself, knows how to create some of the tastiest nonmeat fare we've ever sampled. You may want to become a temporary vegetarian just to experience the excellent truffle-laced wild mushroom spring roll served over a dollop of creamy mashed potatoes, endive salad with toasted pistachios, and butternut squash tortellini bathed in sage butter and walnuts. Whatever your choice, arrive with a good appetite; the beautiful painted Italian plates bear hefty portions. *$$; AE, MC, V; no checks, dinner every day; full bar; reservations recommended; 2chefs@msn.com; www.emilios.com; near Castillo St; city parking across the street.*

La Super-Rica / ★☆

622 N MILPAS ST, SANTA BARBARA; 805/963-4940

The dichotomy of Santa Barbara's ultra-wealthy, yet kick-back-casual lifestyle is well exemplified in this little roadside Mexican place. For many years it's been celebrated as the area's most famous restaurant, thanks to the praise of such renowned critics as part-time Santa Barbara resident Julia Child. The turquoise-trimmed white shack with its blackboard menu is not the place you would expect to find some of the most consistently superlative, authentic, and entirely unfussy Mexican food this side of the border; but as you bite into your first soft taco filled with steak, pork, or chile and cheese—all with soft buttery onions—you know it will not be your last. Try the *sopes* (corn tortillas filled with spicy chicken, avocado, and cheese), or the *chilaquiles* (eggs, cheese, and tortilla strips with a spicy tomato sauce), the quesadillas, or the special corn tamales (served only on Friday and Saturday)—and don't forget to check the daily specials board. And if somehow you still have room, try the hot *atole* (a delicious milk drink laced with vanilla and cinnamon). Though most menu items cost less than $5, you're likely to end up spending more than you anticipated because the selections are too delicious to pass up and because they generally come in rather small portions. *$; cash only; lunch, dinner Mon–Sat; beer only; reservations not accepted; between Cota and Ortega Sts.* &

Meritage / ★★☆

920 DE LA VINA ST, SANTA BARBARA; 805/882-1200

Walking into Meritage for the first time is like arriving at the home of an old friend. The carefully restored 1920s cottage is warm and inviting, and the congenial staff welcome you into one of three adjoining rooms—the main room with its two fireplaces, a semiprivate room for larger groups, or the cozy and relaxed bar, perfect for solo dining. Each space has retained its exquisite original detailing, from leaded windows to etched light fixtures. The American classic cuisine is as lively and charming as its creator, Lydia Gaitin, whose travels to other states for inspiration are evident in dishes such as fried chicken salad in a creamy dressing on a bed of greens or the incredible award-winning seafood cioppino. Inventive soups such as carrot-fennel, perfect french fries with aioli dipping sauce, and old favorites such as rack of lamb or New York steak are sure winners, as is the dreamy apple napoleon drizzled with warm caramel. *$$–$$$; AE, MC, V; no checks; lunch Mon–Fri, dinner every day; beer and wine; reservations recommended; between Carrillo and Cañon Perdido Sts.*

The Palace Cafe / ★★☆

8 E COTA ST, SANTA BARBARA; 805/966-3133

Fun is a complimentary side order at this lively Cajun-style eatery where spicy temptation starts with the cocktails (lemon-drop or Cajun martinis are limited to one per customer, and not because of the spices). Warm jalapeno-cheddar and molasses-date muffins start you in the right direction. Then it's a matter of grilled or blackened steak; chicken, salmon, or redfish; sweet coconut shrimp or spicy Creole shrimp or savory crab cakes. However, the food is only half the reason lines form out the door here. The award-winning staff also deserves credit, along with the festive atmosphere and the great music (sometimes live, and often a group effort when the entire restaurant takes part in a rendition of Louis Armstrong's "What a Wonderful World"). There are lots of good places to eat in Santa Barbara, but for pure fun, this place is number one. Incidentally, the bread pudding soufflé with warm—and potent—whiskey cream sauce should also be limited to one per person. *$$–$$$; AE, MC, V; no checks; lunch, dinner every day; reservations required; full bar; Cota St, just off State St.*

Paradise Cafe / ★★

702 ANACAPA ST, SANTA BARBARA; 805/962-4416

The Paradise's secluded patio, shaded with market umbrellas and palm fronds, has been a local alfresco lunch favorite for over 15 years. Equally appealing is the vintage diner-style interior, with its chrome bar stools and wide array of exotic tequilas. A small but creative wine list pairs well with the menu, which ranges from tasty local mussels, oak-grilled swordfish, and New York steak to the delectable teriyaki burger, Greek salad, and an interesting penne with peppery sausage and onions. *$$; AE, MC, V; no checks; lunch, dinner every day, brunch Sun; full bar; reservations accepted for large groups only; on the corner of Anacapa and Ortega Sts.*

Stella Mare's / ★★★

50 LOS PATOS WAY, SANTA BARBARA; 805/969-6705

The house now known as Stella Mare's was built by a sea captain in 1872 and moved a hundred years later from its original site in town to a charming and tranquil spot overlooking a pond that's a haven for birds. The friendly personalities of owners Eva Ein and Philipe and Kym Rousseau pervade this inviting country farmhouse with its painted pine chairs, distressed fireplace mantels, and hand-painted Italian plates on the walls. A private dining room is great for small parties, but the crowning glory, a restored greenhouse with a bar and cozy fire-front sitting area, where every Wednesday night a jazz trio performs, makes departing a serious challenge. All entrees from the wood-fired grill (swordfish, steak, jumbo shrimp) are excellent, as are the meaty crab cakes and Kym's meat loaf with garlic mashed potatoes. Lunch favorites include croque monsieur (French-style grilled ham and cheese sandwich) and a steak sandwich topped with caramelized onions. For dessert, try the crème brûlée of the day. *$$; AE, MC, V; no checks; lunch, dinner every day, brunch Sat–Sun; full bar; reservations recommended; off Channel Rd.*

Wine Cask / ★★★☆

813 ANACAPA ST, SANTA BARBARA; 805/966-9463

Informal elegance in the tradition of great European restaurants has been captured within these stucco walls, which are accented by a stunning hand-stenciled ceiling and a grand stone fireplace. Owner Doug Margerum, who began his restaurant career with a love of wine and a small adjoining wine shop, now presides over a vast cellar of over 2,000 labels. Chef David Cecchini (recognized by the prestigious James Beard Foundation for his culinary masterpieces) has expertly matched them with dream-worthy dishes such as a delicate shrimp tamale, tangy duck spring rolls, porcini-crusted salmon, Belgian endive baby romaine and apple salad with toasted pecans, goat cheese, and lemon mustard vinaigrette, and filet mignon on a bed of truffle-laced potatoes. We recommend reserving a table for the Sunday or Monday prix-fixe tasting, which has become a popular event among local food and wine connoisseurs. If enamored of a particular vintage, you can pop next door for an excellently priced bottle or two in the adjoining retail wine shop. An outdoor patio offers a charming alternative to the main room, especially on warmer nights. *$$$; AE, D, MC, V; no checks; lunch, dinner every day, brunch Sat–Sun; reservations recommended.*

Your Place / ★★

22 MILPAS ST, SANTA BARBARA; 805/965-9397

Simple rattan furniture and bamboo paneling, traditional music, and wall hangings leave no question that this is a Thai restaurant. And framed awards on the walls testify to the accolades it has won for over a decade. You might want to start with a classic soup such as *tom kah gai,* laden with chunks of chicken and delicately flavored with lemongrass, or the grilled beef salad with spicy lime dressing, which is guaranteed to jump-start your taste buds. Choosing from the huge menu is the hardest thing you'll do here; go with a bunch of friends so you can order as many dishes as possible. Try the divine *massamun,* a beef curry with onions and peanuts in coconut milk. Eggplant tofu is an excellent vegetarian alternative. The deep-fried garlic/pepper spareribs are divine, as is the *pra luck* chicken, diced with spinach and served in a peanut sauce. Along with the requisite satay (barbecued pork or beef on skewers with a peanut dipping sauce), honey duck, and pad thai, you can also find some more unusual items, including squid, abalone, and frogs' legs stir-fried with bamboo shoots and basil. *$; AE, MC, V; local checks only; lunch, dinner Tues–Sun; beer and wine; reservations not necessary; Milpas exit, just north of 101 Fwy.*

LODGINGS

The Bath Street Inn / ★★☆

1720 BATH ST, SANTA BARBARA; 805/682-9680 OR 800/549-2284 (WITHIN CA) OR 800/341-2284 (OUTSIDE CA)

If homey charm is what you're looking for, you'll find it at this friendly and comfortable bed and breakfast, set back from a quiet street in a well-kept, quaint area of old Santa Barbara. The house is large enough to afford privacy, and the sitting area with comfy chairs and Victorian antiques is very cozy with its fireplace and library. On warmer days, breakfast and afternoon tea, wine, and cheese are served on the lovely trellised patio under a canopy of wisteria and in the dining nook off the main room. The Country Suite, the largest accommodation, boasts a canopy bed, fireplace, Jacuzzi tub, fully equipped kitchen, and mountain views. A more secluded guest house in the garden has a sweetly romantic bedroom with a private balcony. All the rooms are clean and comfortable, with their own unique features: a claw-footed tub in the Partridge Room, a window seat with ocean view in the Wedgewood Room, and our personal favorite, the Tiffany, where you can luxuriate in a bubble bath with mountain views. *$$–$$$; AE, MC, V; checks OK; between Valerio and Arrellaga Sts.* &

El Encanto Hotel and Garden Villas / ★★★

1900 LAUSEN RD, SANTA BARBARA; 805/687-5000 OR 800/346-7039

This romantic retreat's 84 cottages are perched high above the town on 10 lushly landscaped acres. Some were built as early as 1912 in the popular Craftsman style, and others have a Spanish colonial sensibility, but all are set among tropical foliage, waterfalls, arbors, a Japanese garden, and lawns rolling down to views of the ocean beyond. In 1999 the hotel underwent a much-needed $10 million renovation, which only added to its charm. Many of the cottages have fireplaces, porches, and French doors; some are ideal for families, with two separate rooms. The plantation-like main building houses a lounge and bar area, with high-back wicker chairs, shutters, and colorful florals, and the award-winning El Encanto restaurant (see the review in the Restaurants section, above), which offers delicious food along with outstanding views. The history of the hotel dates back to the days when railway lines brought families from the East Coast, and continues today with extended families booking adjoining cottages and taking pleasure in all the hotel has to offer, including the Olympic-size pool and clay tennis courts. *$$$; AE, DC, MC, V; checks OK; www.placestogo.com; from Mission, left on Laguna, right on Los Olivos, right on Alameda Padre Serra, left on Lausen.*

Simpson House Inn / ★★★☆

121 E ARRELLAGA ST, SANTA BARBARA; 805/963-7067

The superlative B&B experience begins the moment your car comes to a stop at the end of the driveway leading to this imposing Victorian gem. A staff member will greet you, show you around the estate, and offer you a refreshment before settling you into your amazingly well stocked room. If you have chosen accommodations in the main house, you won't be disappointed; period detailing on the painted ceilings is color-coordinated with the Oriental rugs and plush upholstery, and complemented with brass beds and elegant antiques. In back, beyond the stone patio and lawn (the domain of Bella, the most petted black Lab in town), guests are afforded more privacy in old barn suites and two-story cottages with private courtyards and stone fountains, tucked between tall oaks and magnolias. Each is stylishly modern country-cottage in decor, with open-beam ceiling, river-stone fireplace, Jacuzzi tub, and wet bar. A complete gourmet breakfast—with china and silver—is delivered to your room or secluded patio. A facial or a massage can be arranged, and a game of croquet on the lawn is most civilized entertainment. Wine and a lavish array of hors d'oeuvres are served nightly in the sitting area or can be enjoyed on the main house's wisteria-draped porch. Bicycles and beach equipment are also offered, along with an extensive collection of videos. $$$; AE, DIS, MC, V; checks OK; simpsonhouse@compserve. com; www.simpsonhouseinn.com; between Anacapa and Santa Barbara Sts. &

The Upham / ★★

1404 DE LA VINA ST, SANTA BARBARA; 805/962-0058 OR 800/727-0876

Unlike many local bed and breakfasts, this one didn't begin life as a private home. It was built in 1871 as a hotel, and retains the distinction of being the oldest continually operating hotel in Southern California. Furnishings echo the period architecture, which works particularly well in Rose Cottages 28 and 31, with their four-poster beds and mahogany desks overlooking the main garden area. The Lotus and Iris rooms are equally charming, and each has a sitting area in front of a gas log fire. The Jacaranda junior suite has a separate sitting area with chess table and comfy down sofa, and from its king-size bed you look out onto a private, vine-covered patio. The ultimate in luxury here, however, is the secluded Sycamore master suite, which has a large enclosed patio with a cafe table and chairs and a hammock, plus a double Jacuzzi tub in the bathroom. A walkway with trellised arches and a gazebo weaves its way around the pretty garden and into the main building, where continental breakfast, afternoon cheese and wine, and evening milk and cookies are served. The Upham also boasts its own highly regarded bistro-style eatery, Louie's, which serves lunch and dinner daily. It fills up with more than just hotel guests, so be sure to make a reservation. *$$$; AE, DIS, MC, V; checks OK; on the corner of Sola St, 2 blocks west of State St.*

Villa Rosa / ★★☆

15 CHAPALA ST, SANTA BARBARA; 805/966-0851
In the boutique-hotel tradition of London and Paris, the Villa Rosa is sparsely but tastefully decorated: soft desert and ocean hues, simple carved furniture that gives a nod to Santa Barbara's Spanish and Mexican heritage. The beautiful building with its red tiled roof and scrolled iron detail wraps around a secluded pool and spa. Some of the rooms overlook the pool, while others have ocean, harbor, or mountain views. Some have tiled adobe fireplaces and sitting areas, and all have beamed ceilings and louvered doors and windows. The location, near the harbor, is convenient yet quiet. In-room continental breakfast and a newspaper are included in the price, as are afternoon and evening aperitifs. The affable staff have good knowledge of the local scene. Day membership at the nearby athletic club and massage, available on request, adds to the appeal of this small inn with big value. *$$$; AE, MC, V; checks OK; Cabrillo Blvd to Chapala St.*

Montecito

The home of two of California's top-notch accommodations (San Ysidro Ranch and the Four Seasons Biltmore), this exclusive pastoral community of country lanes and gated multimillion-dollar haciendas is an idyllic retreat for the moneyed few who can afford to live in relative privacy among the shady oaks and smell the jasmine-scented air. Visitors (and residents) who venture beyond their glamorous digs meander to the town's charming **MAIN STREET** (Coast Village Road), the central village area and gathering spot. If you continue west from here on E Valley Road to where it meets Hot Springs Road, you will stumble onto the beautiful adobe **MOUNT CARMEL CHURCH,** with its primitive painted interior complete with Mexican silver chandeliers, set in a cactus garden typical of the area. Continue west and follow Sycamore Canyon Road to Cold Springs Road and you will behold **LOTUSLAND** (by appointment only; 695 Ashley Road; 805/969-9990), the best-kept secret in town. Unless you are staying at one of the local hotels, call well ahead for reservations to experience the beauty of this 37-acre property. Its spectacular exotic gardens, ponds, and waterfalls are the loving creations of Ganna Walska, whose husband was a pioneer nurseryman and horticulturist.

RESTAURANTS

Little Alex's / ★★☆

1024A COAST VILLAGE RD, MONTECITO; 805/969-2297

In a busy local shopping center that also houses everything from a barber to a gas station, you'll find a very busy Mexican eatery that makes up for in taste what it lacks in charm. Whatever your choice from the variety of enchiladas, burritos, tacos, or chimichangas, know that the portions are huge (even the ones that claim to be small)—so come here with an appetite. From the popular primo burrito, chile verde, and chile relleno to the house-special *arroz con pollo* (chicken breast simmered in ranchera sauce), you won't be disappointed. Phone ahead for to-go orders to take to the beach. *$; checks OK; breakfast, lunch, dinner every day; beer and wine; reservations not accepted; at the junction of Coast Village Rd and Hot Springs Rd in the Vons Shopping Center.*

Pane e Vino / ★★★

1482 E VALLEY RD, MONTECITO; 805/969-9274

It takes more than luck to keep a restaurant open for over 12 years, especially one tucked into the corner of a quiet shopping center. However, at this popular Italian trattoria it's the patrons who are truly lucky. The authentic country fare attracts well-heeled locals and many local restaurateurs, who rave about the fresh pasta (Thursday-night gnocchi is legendary), risotto, simple grilled fish, *bistecca alla fiorentina*, and juicy veal chops. Daily specials—which sometimes outnumber regular menu items—include seasonal items such as local mussels in garlic sauce or spaghetti with rock shrimp and radicchio. The wine list is largely Italian; desserts include classically good tiramisu, crème caramel, and an assortment of gelati. The outdoor patio, which is especially appealing on balmy summer nights, provides the largest seating area, but the more intimate interior, which evokes Old World charm and comfort, is equally coveted and replete with its shelf of assorted plates, bowls and children's soccer trophies. *$$–$$$; AE, MC, V; no checks; lunch Mon–Sat, dinner every day; beer and wine; reservations recommended; San Ysidro Rd to Montecito Village.* &

Pierre Lafond Deli / ★★☆

516 SAN YSIDRO RD, MONTECITO; 805/565-1502

Early risers need only to follow the aroma of freshly brewed coffee to this gourmet deli, which offers a large selection of delicious pastries and bagels to be savored on a vine-covered patio. Long after the deli's crack-of-dawn opening hour, they begin filling breakfast burritos with eggs and cheese. When lunchtime rolls around it's a treat to sample their rolls filled with crab cake or duck sausage, caesar chicken wrap, black-bean burger, individual quiche, or salad bar. You might want to pair a cappuccino or chai tea with one of their famous farmcakes—a dense and decadent chocolate muffin swirled with cream cheese and chocolate chips. *$–$$; AE, MC, V; local checks only; breakfast, lunch, dinner every day; no alcohol; reservations not accepted; in Plaza del Sol Center, north in downtown Santa Barbara, at 5116 State St between Cota and Gutierrez, and in the Paseo Nuevo Shopping Center.*

LODGINGS

Four Seasons Biltmore / ★★★★

1260 CHANNEL DR, MONTECITO; 805/969-2261 OR 800/332-3442

This elegant 236-room property, loaded with the luxury associated with the Four Seasons chain, is one of the state's most beautiful Old World hotels. The regal main Spanish revival building, which was built in 1927, stands amidst towering palm trees overlooking the Pacific. Magnificent wrought iron gates lead into a pale-hued lobby with hand-decorated archways, bowls of orchids, and polished antiques resting on waxed terra-cotta tiles. Rooms are tastefully furnished in soft tones with beds of the utmost comfort, plantation shutters, botanical prints, and marble bathrooms with big fluffy towels and robes. Heat lamps, hair dryers, book lights, and bowls of candy are some of the extra amenities, and at the touch of a button, earplugs, hot water bottles, non-allergenic soap, and even that toothbrush you forgot will magically appear. We especially love the green trimmed California bungalows, many of which have fireplaces and patios with wrought iron lounge chairs. In addition to the pool and tennis courts, the expansive lawn area behind the main building is home to croquet, shuffleboard, and an 18-hole putting green. The gym is fully equipped and bikes are at the ready along with a map of local bike paths. Complimentary day passes to the exclusive Coral Casino Beach and Cabana Club across the street are available for guests who want to swim in an Olympic-size pool or try some surfing. The Patio restaurant, with its retractable glass roof offers casual fare and also hosts a famous Sunday brunch where chefs man a multitude of food stations serving everything from roast beef to custom omelets. La Marina is an elegant, timber-beamed dining room that serves an array of continental and American cuisine such as truffled Brie and cauliflower soup, lobster, salmon, and beef tenderloin. (Try to reserve the table by the arched ocean-view window.) La Sala, afternoon tea, served cozily by the fire, gives way to live jazz nightly, with dancing on Friday and Saturday. *$$$$; AE, DIS, MC, V; www.fshr.com; Olive Mill Rd exit from 101 Fwy to Channel Dr.* &

Montecito Inn / ★★

1295 COAST VILLAGE RD, MONTECITO; 805/969-7854

Although this Mediterranean-style red-tiled stucco hotel is now identified with Charlie Chaplin (whose image is everywhere, from the etched glass doors to the vintage movie posters lining the hallways), it only seems fair to note that fellow actor Fatty Arbuckle was Chaplin's business partner in the hotel (although his name is never mentioned). It also seems fair to note that the 101 Freeway runs directly alongside, where once only Coast Village Road offered access, and that guests can hear the train as it passes on the nearby tracks. However, this doesn't seem to deter most people; the hotel is as popular now as when it opened in 1928 and

hosted Hollywood royalty from Norma Shearer to Marion Davies. Its popularity is due in part to its prime location in Montecito Village, which is within walking distance of a beautiful beach shared with the nearby

Biltmore. The 60 rooms with their Victorian decor tend toward the feminine, with small but pretty tiled bathrooms, while the suites are more neutrally furnished in creams, golds, and olives. Luxury suites have Jacuzzi tubs set in marble, fireplaces, and arched windows, some with incredible views. The much-sought-after Tower Suite has two-story ocean and mountain vistas. California cuisine is served daily in the casual cafe. A central sitting area leads to a large pool—which, unfortunately, is not immune to the noise from the 101 below. The attached gym fares better. A video library that includes all of Chaplin's work is also available to guests. $$$; AE, DC, DIS, JCB, MC, V; checks OK; info@montecitoinn.com; www.montecitoinn.com; Olive Mill Rd exit from 101 Fwy. &

San Ysidro Ranch / ★★★★

900 SAN YSIDRO LANE, MONTECITO; 805/969-5046 OR 800/368-6788

If you want to know how it feels to live in a country cottage, get married in style (like Vivien Leigh and Laurence Olivier did), or luxuriate on a dream honeymoon (like Jackie and J. F. Kennedy did), then this is the place for you. On the other hand, if all you want is the best of comfort and style that money can buy (some of the cottage suites do run into quadruple digits), you will not be disappointed at this 540-acre hedonistic slice of heaven secluded in the foothills of the Santa Ynez mountains. From the moment you find which white cottage has your name by the door (and your dog's name on the bowl, presuming your pet also travels in style), luxury awaits you in the form of carefully selected antiques, Frette bed linens, goosedown-filled comforters on beds high enough that some offer a stepping stool, toiletries worth taking home, and robes you can buy. You are also guaranteed a view of beautiful landscaped terraced gardens, mountains, canyons, or ocean from your private porch or outdoor hot tub. The pool, gym, and tennis courts are grouped at the top of the property. A minihike away is the casual Plow & Angel, which serves tasty pub grub, and the renowned Stonehouse restaurant. Under the guidance of wonderfully talented chef David Adjey, Stonehouse offers one of the most exciting culinary experiences in the area. Adjey's cuisine echoes worldly influences, but he never fuses them. Instead, each dish, whether Jamaican-, French-, or Asian-influenced, maintains the integrity of its origins. Combine that with peaceful, country-formal surroundings, a fine wine list, and professional service, and Stonehouse guarantees a night to remember. With all the luxurious pampering San Ysidro Ranch has to offer, and such fine dining so near, the only problem with a stay here is that you will never want to leave— except perhaps to move next door to another cottage. $$$; AE, MC, V; checks OK; jansyr@west.net; www.sanysidroranch.com; take the San Ysidro exit from the 101 Fwy, drive North to San Ysidro Lane, turn right. &

Summerland

This tiny coastal suburb of Santa Barbara has an intriguingly colorful past and a countrified present, though the boundaries it shares with upscale Montecito are growing fuzzier by the moment. Founded in 1883 by an eccentric rancher and spiritualist named Henry L. Williams, Summerland was originally conceived as a secluded community where mediums would congregate each summer to swim, sunbathe, and conduct séances. But when a few intrepid settlers digging water wells struck oil, it triggered a full-scale oil boom instead. Williams built an ornate Victorian home for himself (now the **BIG YELLOW HOUSE** restaurant).

After the wells went dry in the 1950s, bikers, surfers, and hippies moved in and erected shanties that earned Summerland the epithet of "Where the Debris Meets the Sea." As land values soared in the 1980s, yuppies took over, building quaint hillside cottages and restoring decrepit Victorian houses. Today the town is a great place for strolling around antique shops and boutiques along Lillie Avenue, having a seaside lunch, and even spending a night or two. Summerland's tiny beach is secluded **LOOKOUT COUNTY PARK** (take Evans Street under the freeway to the small parking lot), where you have the option of hanging out on the wooded bluffs or playing on the white sand below.

RESTAURANTS

Stacky's Seaside / ★★

2315 LILLIE AVE, SUMMERLAND; 805/969-9908

Looking as though it had stepped from the Technicolor frames of a classic beach-party flick, this ivy-covered shack is filled with fishnets, surfboards, and local memorabilia. The menu of sandwiches is enormous, just like most of the pita pockets, hoagies, and club sandwiches that emerge from a deceptively small kitchen. A sign proudly proclaims "Half of Any Sandwich, Half Price, No Problem"—and Stacky's has made plenty of friends with that policy. Eat inside or out on the shaded wooden deck, or join the legions of beachgoers, picnickers, and road-trippers picking up lunch to go. Sandwiches include the Santa Barbaran (roasted tri-tip and melted Jack cheese on sourdough with lettuce, salsa, and mayonnaise); the Rincon pita (Jack and cheddar, green chiles, onions, lettuce, tomato, and ranch dressing); and the hot pastrami hoagie (Swiss, mustard, and onions). The menu also lists burgers, fish 'n' chips, and hearty soups, and there's Dreyer's ice cream for dessert. Stacky's serves fantastic breakfast items: most have a south-of-the-border flair, such as the fat breakfast burritos with your choice of bacon, sausage, chili, or roast beef, but the classic scrambled-egg sandwich is all-American goodness that goes perfectly with thick-cut French fries. *$; no credit cards; no checks; breakfast, lunch, dinner every day; beer and wine; reservations not necessary; Summerland exit from US 101.* &

Summerland Beach Cafe / ★

2294 LILLIE AVE, SUMMERLAND; 805/969-1019

Set in a gray Victorian beach cottage in the heart of town, this funky and casual cafe is the trendiest eatery in the vicinity, yet it's still a place where comfortable workout clothes or beach thongs are appropriate. Most seating is on the wraparound porch to take advantage of sea breezes and sunshine, though tables inside get pressed into use during inclement weather. Serving only breakfast and lunch, the Summerland specializes in omelets (from plain-Jane to everything-but-the-kitchen-sink), waffles, French toast, and egg dishes such as huevos rancheros or eggs Benedict. All items have cutesy names like Belgian Wonder Wa-Fulls, Singin' the Bleus, and Indian Summerland, but the food is fresh, hearty, and always satisfying. If you opt for a burger or sandwich (Cobb salad pita, tuna-filled croissant, grilled veggie, or club), get a side of the thick, beer-battered onion rings—you'll be glad you did. *$; AE, DIS, MC, V; no checks; breakfast, lunch every day; beer and wine; reservations not accepted; Summerland exit from US 101.* &

JUNÍPERO SERRA AND
THE BIRTH OF THE CALIFORNIA MISSIONS

Throughout California you'll find highways, canyons, schools, and monuments bearing the name of Junípero Serra (pronounced who-NEE-per-oh SARE-uh). Who was this Spaniard and why is he held in such high esteem?

Junípero Serra, born on Mallorca in 1713, was a Franciscan friar who was sent to the New World to administer the church's missions in Baja ("lower") California (in present-day Mexico). He was later sent north to found missions in the ports of San Diego and Monterey in the little-explored Alta ("upper") California, a Spanish territory populated with "heathen" natives and threatened by Russian imperialism. Though small of stature and quiet of nature, Father Serra led his expedition on a six-week march north to San Diego in May 1769. Discouraged by the failure of previous expeditions and facing dwindling supplies and escalating illness, the group survived on the strength of the determined friar's faith and will. They finally staggered into San Diego in July, raised a wooden cross, and conducted Mass before a crowd of curious Native Americans.

On reaching Monterey Bay, Serra and his men found that a cross erected by an earlier expedition had been surrounded by offerings—arrows and feathers stuck in the ground, a string of sardines, pieces of meat and fish—placed there by wary natives to appease the unfamiliar gods. A few days later Father Serra conducted, with great pageantry, the services that finally symbolized the definitive presence of the Spanish in Alta California.

Constantly challenged by insufficient supplies, resistant natives, and Spanish bureaucratic red tape, Serra ultimately went on to found a total of 9 thriving missions before his death in 1784. The mission chain eventually totaled 21, situated a day's travel apart (on horseback) along El Camino Real ("the royal road"), which stretched up through present-day California from Mexico. U.S. Highway 101 runs along this historic route for most of its concrete path, and intact portions of the original road can be seen at several mission sites. Recognized for the role he played in spreading the Christian faith and establishing a strong Spanish legacy in California, Father Junípero Serra was beatified by the Vatican in 1988.

LODGINGS

Inn on Summer Hill / ★★

2520 LILLIE AVE, SUMMERLAND; 805/969-9998 OR 800/845-5566
This beige Craftsman-style inn may look as vintage as the town of Summerland, but inside it's brand-spanking new, with all the modern amenities. If you simply can't live without a fireplace, VCR, and whirlpool bathtub, this luxury bed and breakfast is for you. Each of the 16 guest rooms also has a balcony or patio. Decor is heavy-handed English country (think layers and layers of fabric prints and frills, romantic canopy beds, fluffy down comforters). If you'd like an ocean-view room, ask when you book, but remember that you'll have to look across the 101 Freeway, which zooms the length of Summerland like an inescapable concrete-and-steel river. Inside the inn, however, pampering is taken to the highest level: rooms have instant hot water taps for coffee or tea, small refrigerators, and even bathroom phone extensions. A video library is available for those who want to cocoon in their room. Rates include a lavish gourmet breakfast each morning, as well as hors d'oeuvres and wine in the afternoon. Before bedtime, the dining room is sweetened with complimentary desserts. A variety of celebration packages, custom gift baskets, and a breakfast-in-bed option make this B&B a popular anniversary getaway. *$$$$; AE, DIS, MC, V; no checks; innkeeper@ innonsummerhill.com; www.innonsummerhill.com; Summerland exit from US 101.* &

Ojai

Ojai sits in a secluded crescent-shaped valley, a spot whose natural beauty has inspired Hollywood filmmakers, artists, and free spirits for decades. Still blanketed with citrus groves stretching toward wild, rocky foothills, the Ojai Valley can trace its popularity back to the 1870s, when journalist Charles Nordhoff praised its ideal climate, natural mineral baths, and spectacular setting. The farmers who began settling the area named the new town in Nordhoff's honor, but anti-German sentiment during World War I led to its being renamed in 1917. *Ojai* is a Chumash word that can mean either "nest" or "moon." Bohemian artisans, well-heeled equestrians, camera-shy celebs, and New Age gurus have all embraced idyllic Ojai and left their mark on the valley. This area still radiates the magic that captivated movie producer-director Frank Capra who, when scouting locations for *Lost Horizon* in 1936, selected sleepy little Ojai to stand in for legendary utopia SHANGRI-LA. To see the spectacular vista admired by Ronald Colman in the movie, drive east on Ojai Avenue, continuing uphill until you reach the gravel turnout near the top; a stone bench provides the perfect spot for contemplation. Another mystical phenomenon praised by residents and visitors alike is the "pink moment," when the brilliant sunset over the nearby Pacific is reflected onto the Topa-Topa mountains, creating an eerie and beautiful pink glow. Although you can catch a glimpse from town, the effect is amplified when you ride uphill with PINK MOMENT JEEP TOURS (805/653-1321), whose four-wheel-drive excursions position you at the valley's perfect vantage point just in time for sunset.

Ojai's downtown is both charmingly rustic and pleasantly sophisticated, thanks to the influence of urban émigrés from Los Angeles and Santa Barbara. Shops, galleries, and cafes are concentrated in the ARCADE, whose Mission-revival arches shade pedestrians from the midday sun. Across the street is LIBBEY PARK, centerpiece of the community and home to open-air LIBBEY BOWL, where musical notes enhance many summer evenings. Classical music fans throughout the state look forward to June's OJAI MUSIC FESTIVAL (for schedule information and tickets, call 805/646-2094), which has been drawing world-class performers since 1947. Past appearances by Igor Stravinsky, Aaron Copland, the Juilliard String Quartet, and others of their caliber ensure sold-out crowds—and sold-out lodgings—each year. While strolling downtown, pick up a free *Visitors Guide* at the OJAI VALLEY CHAMBER OF COMMERCE (150 West Ojai Avenue; 805/646-8126; www.the-ojai.org).

There's no understating the powerful influence of the visual arts on Ojai. The town is home to more than 35 well-regarded artists working in a variety of mediums. Most have home studios and are represented in one of Ojai's many galleries. Every October visitors get a chance to enter the private studios of many area painters, sculptors, potters, and wood-carvers during the two-day OJAI STUDIO ARTISTS TOUR. This unique event includes an evening reception and benefit art auction, and it's also a great way to bring home an original piece without paying the gallery markup; for tickets and information, call the CHAMBER OF COMMERCE (805/646-8126).

You can't visit Ojai without hearing about local legend BEATRICE WOOD, an internationally acclaimed ceramic artist responsible for putting Ojai on the art world's map. Wood, who was declared a California Living Treasure, worked up until her death in 1998 at 104 years of age. Her luminous lustreware pottery and whimsical sculpture are occasionally displayed in local galleries but are more commonly found at museums such as New York's Whitney or San Francisco's Craft & Folk Art. Numerous galleries represent other Ojai artists, including HUMA-NARTS (310 East Ojai Avenue; 805/646-1525); MILAGRO'S NEST (307 East Ojai Avenue #104; 805/640-1453); and PRIMAVERA (214 East Ojai Avenue; 805/646-7133).

Any bibliophile who's been to Ojai knows about used-book purveyor **BART'S BOOKS** (302 West Matilija Street; 805/646-3755), a quirky local institution whose books are displayed in every nook and cranny of a converted cottage, including the patio, garden shed, and even along the sidewalk outside the entrance gate. After hours these sidewalk racks are on the honor system, and patrons drop money into a little payment box. If browsing bookshelves isn't active enough for your tastes, rent a bicycle from **BICYCLES OF OJAI** (108 Canada Street; 805/646 7736) or a horse (the Ojai Valley Inn offers guided horseback rides; 805/646-5511) and hit the **OJAI VALLEY BIKE & EQUESTRIAN TRAIL**, which winds scenically for 8.8 miles, most of it parallel to Ojai Avenue. Even more recreational activities are available at sparkling **LAKE CASITAS** (follow Highway 150 northwest from Ojai until signs direct you to Lake Casitas; 805/649-2233), hidden just minutes uphill from the valley floor. Site of the 1984 Olympic rowing events, the lake boasts a shoreline full of coves and inlets. Swimming is not allowed because the lake serves as a domestic water supply, but you can rent rowboats and small motorboats from the boathouse (805/649-2043).

RESTAURANTS

Boccali's / ★★

3277 SANTA PAULA–OJAI RD, OJAI; 805/646-6116

You'll find this small wood-frame restaurant set among citrus groves, in a nostalgic pastoral setting that hasn't changed for decades. Sit outdoors at one of the picnic tables shaded by umbrellas and twisted oak trees, or inside where the tables are covered with red-and-white-checked oilcloth. Like an old-style roadhouse, Boccali's has a complete lack of pretension, coupled with excellent homestyle Sicilian grub, including a lasagne that could win a statewide taste test hands down. An equally delicious meatless version is available, with spinach filling and marinara sauce. Their pizzas run a close second, even though they can be topped with suspiciously trendy ingredients like crab, whole garlic cloves, shrimp, and chicken. Fresh lemonade, squeezed from fruit plucked off local trees, is the usual drink of choice. Come hungry, and plan on sharing. *$; no credit cards; local checks only; lunch Wed–Sun, dinner every day; beer and wine; reservations recommended; on Highway 150 at Reeves Rd.* &

L'Auberge / ★★

314 EL PASEO, OJAI; 805/646-2288

Often touted as the most romantic restaurant in Ojai, L'Auberge is a swank holdover from the days when classic French cuisine was the epitome of fancy dining. Housed in a 1910 mansion with fireplace and ornate chandeliers, a short, pleasant walk from downtown, the restaurant has a charming terrace with a marvelous view of Ojai's "pink moment" at sunset. The French-Belgian menu is unswervingly traditional, and L'Auberge is known for its exceptional escargots and sweetbreads. Among the other selections are scampi, frogs' legs, poached sole, tournedos of beef, and duckling à l'orange. The weekend brunch menu offers a selection of perfectly prepared crêpes. This kind of place has gone seriously out of style, so if you love classic French you'd do well to take advantage of this still-excellent grande dame. *$$; AE, MC, V; no checks; dinner every day, brunch Sat–Sun; full bar; reservations recommended; corner of Rincon St.* &

The Ranch House / ★★★

SOUTH LOMITA AVE, OJAI; 805/646-2360

If you're going to have only one meal in Ojai, have it here. The name may suggest, steaks 'n' spuds, but the reality of this Ojai Valley gem couldn't be more different. Originally conceived in 1949 by Alan and Helen Hooker—two Krishnamurti followers drawn to Ojai's natural beauty— the restaurant began life as a vegetarian boarding house. The Hookers were hippies before hippie was hip, and it wasn't long before they turned their "ranch house" into a full-fledged restaurant, adding meat dishes and exceptional wines to a menu that continues to emphasize the freshest vegetables, fruits, and herbs in what is now ubiquitously known as California cuisine. Freshly snipped sprigs from the lush herb garden will aromatically transform your simple meat, fish, or game dish into a work of art, and diners are encouraged to stroll through this splendid kitchen garden during their visit. From an appetizer of Cognac-laced liver pâté served with its own chewy rye bread to leave-room-for desserts like fresh raspberries with sweet Chambord cream, the ingredients always shine through. With guests driving in from as far as Los Angeles just for a Ranch House meal, everything has to be perfect, and this peaceful and friendly retreat never disappoints. Equally impressive are the polished yet friendly service and magical setting, with alfresco dining year-round on a wooden porch facing the scenic valley, as well as in the romantic garden amid twinkling lights and stone fountains. *$$; AE, DC, DIS, MC, V; checks OK; dinner Wed–Sun, brunch Sun; beer and wine; reservations recommended; www.TheRanchHouse.com; south of El Roblar Dr off Hwy 33.* &

Suzanne's Cuisine / ★★☆

502 WEST OJAI AVE, OJAI; 805/640-1961

Ojai's roster of exceptional restaurants includes this understated charmer a few blocks from the center of town where every little detail bespeaks a preoccupation with quality. Each ingredient is as fresh and natural as it can be, and these recipes—a blending of California cuisine with Italian recipes from chef-owner Suzanne Roll's family—show them off to advantage. Every meal begins with a basket of homebaked rolls served with butter squares, each accented by a single pressed cilantro leaf. Vegetables are al dente, and even the occasional cream sauce tastes light and healthy. A highlight of the lunch menu is the Southwest salad: wild, brown, and jasmine rice tossed with smoked turkey, feta cheese, veggies, and green chiles. At dinner, pepper-and-sesame-crusted ahi is served either sautéed or seared (your choice). Suzanne's covered outdoor patio should be your first seating choice. Its marble bistro tables are shaded in summer by lush greenery and warmed in winter by a fireplace and strategically placed heat lamps. When it rains, a plastic cover unfurls to keep water out while maintaining an airy garden feel. This is the kind of restaurant that makes you long for three-hour lunches and decadently unhurried dinners; so sit back, enjoy, and—by all means—don't skip dessert! *$$; DC, DIS, MC, V; local checks only; lunch, dinner Wed–Mon; full bar; reservations recommended; east of Bristol Rd.* &

LODGINGS

The Moon's Nest Inn / ★★

210 E MATILIJA ST, OJAI; 805/646-6635
Ojai's oldest building is now its newest lodging. The former schoolhouse (circa 1872) has been reborn as a bed and breakfast that stays charmingly historic while offering every modern comfort. This old-fashioned clapboard building, located within easy walking distance of downtown shopping, dining, and attractions, was fully renovated in 1998 by innkeepers Rich and Joan Assenberg, who carefully preserved, replaced, or complemented the inn's historic details. Five of the seven guest rooms now boast private bathrooms, and several also enjoy private balconies. In addition to being greeted by an afternoon wine reception, you'll find bottled water and chocolates in each room. Throughout the house, from the cozy fireplace parlor to the sunny breakfast room, architectural features like crown molding are highlighted by dramatically painted walls, and the entire inn is furnished with a mix of carefully chosen antiques and quality contemporary pieces. A once-neglected side lawn has been transformed into a restful tree-shaded garden retreat, complete with a rock-lined pond and a large trellised veranda where breakfast is served on pleasant days. A cottage on the grounds houses a friendly beauty-and-massage salon (in-room massage is available), and guests enjoy full day-use privileges at the Ojai Valley Athletic Club for a nominal fee. *$$; AE, MC, V; checks OK; info@moonsnestinn.com; www.moonsnestinn.com; 1 block north of Ojai Ave between Signal and Montgomery Sts.* &

The Oaks at Ojai Health Spa / ★★☆

122 E OJAI AVE, OJAI; 805/646-5573 OR 800/753-6257

Physical fitness guru Sheila Cluff opened this low-key, affordable spa in the heart of downtown in 1977, and it remains one of Ojai's most enduring draws. Leave your designer sweatsuits at home; the Oaks capitalizes on its spectacular natural setting and Ojai's laid-back personality to encourage people—mostly women, but men aren't uncommon—to focus on personal renewal and stress reduction. Rates here are full board and include a 1,000-calorie-a-day diet consisting of three meals plus snacks. The spa cuisine is surprisingly good, incorporating a variety of flavorful accents and ethnic influences to help compensate for the lack of fat and salt. (Guests are free to go snacking off the grounds, but don't tell them we said so.) The spa specializes in providing a custom-tailored experience: you can plan a day of fitness classes and activities (morning hikes, step aerobics, yoga, body sculpting, and so on), or simply float from one pampering spa treatment to another (choose from massage, facial, body wraps, reflexology, salon treatments, and more). There's a swimming pool that's often filled with aquarobicizers, plus saunas and whirlpools—and all of Ojai is outside the front door. Rates are per person, per day, and vary depending on your accommodation choice. The spa offers private or shared rooms in detached cottages or the main lodge; all are comfortably appointed but otherwise unremarkable. The Oaks also offers day-spa packages that include lunch and use of the entire facility. *$$; DIS, MC, V; checks OK; www.oaksspa.com; at Signal St.* &

Ojai Valley Inn & Spa / ★★★

905 COUNTRY CLUB RD, OJAI; 805/646-5511 OR 800/422-OJAI

Chic travelers have been sojourning at this genteel resort since 1923, when Hollywood architect Wallace Neff designed the clubhouse that's now the focal point of the quintessentially Californian, Spanish colonial–style complex. Guest accommodations on the sprawling ranch can be individual cottages, low-rise buildings, or modern condos. Many of the unusually spacious rooms have fireplaces; most have sofas, writing desks, and secluded terraces or balconies that open onto picturesque views of the valley and mountains. A beautiful oak-studded Senior PGA Tour golf course ambles throughout the property, offering moderately challenging play in a stunning setting. Gracious elegance pervades the property, along with a "something for everyone" philosophy. "Camp Ojai" offers kids' programs during peak holiday periods; a pampering "Pet Package" includes a sleeping mat, food bowl, and poo-poo-pick-up kit; tennis courts, complimentary bicycles, horseback riding, and two swimming pools provide active recreation.

Next to the golf course, the jewel of the resort is pampering Spa Ojai, where stylish spa treatments—many modeled on Native American traditions—are administered inside a beautifully designed and exquisitely tiled Spanish-Moorish complex. Mind/body fitness classes, art classes, nifty workout machines, and a sparkling outdoor pool complete the relaxation choices; it's easy to spend an entire splendid day at this rejuvenating spot.

The inn's formal dining room is Maravilla, whose excellent and intriguing Mediterranean/California menu can derail even the most frugal intentions. Yes, it's *very* expensive, but if you're looking for a supremely gourmet splurge, this is the place. Choose from an à la carte menu featuring seasonal creations like bacon-wrapped quail resting on tangy red onion and raisin salad, seared blue prawns atop asparagus-barley risotto with a citrus accent, or a superb tenderloin in port wine–mustard-Roquefort reduction accompanied by a leek cake. Also offered each evening are an equally inspired (but less rich) four-course spa menu and a six-course "menu gastronomique," with each dish matched to a different wine. Mere mortals might opt for the more affordable Oak Cafe & Terrace, whose scenic golf-course views are a nice backdrop for a menu that's also in the Mediterranean family and uses plenty of fresh local ingredients. Recommended choices are caesar salad (which they do exceptionally well), any of the fish dishes, venison chili with black beans and goat cheese, and any of several light pastas always included in the offerings. *$$$$; AE, DC, DIS, MC, V; checks OK; www.ojairesort.com; turn off Ojai Ave at the west end of town.* ఈ

Theodore Woolsey House / ★★☆

1484 E OJAI AVE, OJAI; 805/646-9779
Built in 1887 by Theodore S. Woolsey, attorney and Yale University dean, this grand American colonial stone and clapboard home was converted into a bed and breakfast exactly 100 years later by innkeeper Ana Cross. Don't expect a perfectly restored "museum" of a house, though. The Woolsey-Cross home displays many idiosyncrasies, ranging from an incongruous (but refreshing) 1950s kidney-shaped swimming pool to a curious mix of antique furniture and modern tchotchkes throughout. A virtual backyard playground also includes a fish pond, putting green, horseshoe pit, volleyball court, and croquet lawn, all scattered amongst seven acres of countryside near Ojai's citrus orchards. The six guest rooms are decorated in an old-fashioned lace-and-floral fashion, each with equally frilly private bath (although some baths aren't en suite). Be sure to get all the specifics when booking, since there are rooms offering fireplace, claw-footed tub, or other extras. A one-bedroom country cottage with kitchenette is available as well. What the inn lacks in polish, it makes up for in character, with a virtually unchanged living room and plenty of corners for some discreet snooping. *$$; no credit cards; checks OK; www.theodorewoolseyhouse.com; on Hwy 150 east of Gridley Rd.* ఈ

Mussel Shoals

LODGINGS

The Cliff House Inn / ★★

6602 W PACIFIC COAST HWY, MUSSEL SHOALS; 805/652-1381 OR 800/892-5433

This small hotel perched cliffside is often booked solid by intrepid guests seeking a dramatic vantage point for watching winter storms—though it has plenty of appeal during the calm warmer months as well. Located between Ventura and Santa Barbara where US 101 snakes right alongside the rocky beach, the Cliff House punctuates an isolated strip of beach houses overlooking an artificial reef. The inn makes the most of its dramatic surroundings; every room has a spectacular ocean view, as does the impressive swimming pool, which is surrounded by deck lounges and graced by an enormous Chilean wine palm whose fronds rustle seductively. Guest rooms are just large enough to hold a few basic pieces of white wicker furniture with cheerful floral upholstery, and bathrooms are equally utilitarian. The location, though untouristy, is a good one: decent beaches and surfing are close by, as are Santa Barbara's restaurants and attractions, and even Ojai is only a short jaunt inland.

The hotel's own Shoals restaurant boasts the same stunning ocean view—they even serve poolside in pleasant weather. The dining room is simple and sparsely adorned, but the restaurant does a good job of creating a mood with subdued lighting and polished service. Not surprisingly, seafood figures prominently on a seasonally composed menu that highlights fresh local ingredients and familiar California cuisine. Standout dishes include the appetizer of herb-crusted seared ahi lightly bathed in sesame-ginger sauce, or creamy goat cheese baked in phyllo and topped with roasted pears (served over greens, this large starter is perfect for sharing). For a main course, look for the Shoals cioppino—a glorious jumble of scallops, prawns, clams, mussels, and potatoes in a pungent stew of tomato, saffron, and garlic; pan-roasted sea bass in tangy caper-citrus sauce; or rich braised lamb shank with shallot confit. A very nice lunch menu features lighter adaptations of dinner entrees. Fill up if you want, because desserts unfortunately fall short of a dedicated sweets-lover's expectations. *$$; DC, DIS, MC, V; local checks only; info@cliffhouseinn.com; www.cliffhouseinn.com; Mussel Shoals exit from US 101.* &

Ventura

Nestled between gently rolling foothills and the sparkling blue Pacific, Ventura is endowed with the picturesque setting and clean sea breezes typical of the California coast. Since most of the city's development has taken place inland and to the south, there's a charming small town character to the historic district, known nostalgically by its Spanish mission name, San Buenaventura. To learn more, make the **VENTURA VISITORS AND CONVENTION BUREAU** (89-C South California Street; 805/648-2075 or 800/333-2989; www.ventura-usa.com) your first stop, since their office is in the heart of old downtown. The town grew up around **MISSION SAN BUENAVENTURA** (225 East Main Street; 805/643-4318), which was founded in 1782 as one of the California mission chain. Still in use for daily services, the current buildings date from 1815 and have been restored to depict the everyday mission life of the 19th century. Touring the interior garden, you'll see the antique water pump and olive press once essential to survival, and get a look at the whitewash-and-red-tile architecture whose influence can be seen throughout town. Across the street is the **VENTURA COUNTY MUSEUM OF HISTORY AND ART** (100 E Main Street; 805/653-0323), worth a visit for its rich Native American Room, filled with Chumash treasures, and its enormous archive of historical photos depicting Ventura County from its origin to the present time. Don't miss the majestic **SAN BUENAVENTURA CITY HALL** (501 Poli Street; 805/658-4726), which presides over town from a hillside at the end of California Street. Built in 1912 to serve as the county courthouse, this neoclassical landmark is filled with architectural detail, inside and out—look for the carved heads of Franciscan friars whimsically adorning the facade. In the summertime, City Hall can be fully explored by escorted tour.

Antique hounds have been flocking here for many years, and even casual browsers can spend the better part of a day shopping for collectible treasures along Main Street. Start with one of the mall-style places, where dozens of different sellers present a mind-boggling selection that ranges from Hawaiian aloha shirts to antique armoires, from fine china to Art Deco lithographs, or even *Star Wars* lunch boxes and Nancy Drew first editions. Our favorites are **HEIRLOOMS ANTIQUES** (327 E Main Street; 805/648-4833); **TIMES REMEMBERED** (467 E Main Street; 805/643-3137); **NICHOLBY ANTIQUES** (404 E Main Street; 805/653-1195); and **SEVOY ANTIQUES** (494 E Main Street; 805/641-1890),an antique furniture warehouse.

If the weather's nice—and it usually is—take a stroll along the **VENTURA PROMENADE**, a paved oceanside pathway wide enough to accommodate bicyclists and in-line skaters. On the weekends, **BICYCLES** and

CANOPIED SURREYS are available for rent in front of the Holiday Inn (450 E Harbor Boulevard, at California St; 805/648-7731) at the boardwalk.

A short drive south of old San Buenaventura lies picturesque **VENTURA HARBOR**, headquarters of Channel Islands National Park (see Channel Islands, later in this chapter). Nearby is **VENTURA HARBOR VILLAGE** (on Spinnaker Drive off Harbor Boulevard; 805/644-0169), a vaguely Mediterranean shopping/entertainment complex spread along the length of the marina. In addition to waterfront restaurants, gift shops, and paddle boat rentals, there's a small carousel for kids and a fresh fish market. Sport fishing and dive charters operate nearby, and a narrated **HARBOR CRUISE** departs from the village aboard the *Bay Queen* (805/642-7753). If you're here during the annual gray whale migration season—from late December through March—consider taking a **WHALE-WATCHING CRUISE** to observe the graceful leviathans up close. **ISLAND PACKERS** (1867 Spinnaker Drive; 805/642-1393) offers half- and full-day excursions. Inland from the harbor lies the historic **OLIVAS ADOBE** (4200 Olivas Park Drive; 805/644-4346). Built in 1847 as the showplace of prosperous Rancho Miguel, the restored two-story house is filled with antiques and surrounded by tranquil, century-old gardens; one grape arbor dates to the 1840s. The grounds are open daily, but the adobe is open only on weekends.

RESTAURANTS

Eric Ericsson's on the Pier / ★

668 HARBOR BLVD, VENTURA; 805/643-4783
When the coveted restaurant space on Ventura's pleasure pier became vacant, this local crowd-pleaser wasted no time moving from its landlocked former spot. Perched atop the beach, an airy, multistoried building echoes the simple wood construction of the pier itself, with huge windows lining the walls to exploit a terrific view (and let in ocean breezes). The crowd here is varied: scruffy beachgoers mingle with suited business folk at lunch, sports fans and twenty-somethings scarf down shellfish and deep-fried appetizers at cocktail hour, families come early for generously sized dinners, and dating couples linger at window tables past sunset. The staggering array of seafood includes clams, oysters, mussels, shrimp, scallops, cod, halibut, lobster, and calamari. Add specialties like Mexican cioppino or traditional clambake, plus a handful of non-fish entrees, and it's hard to imagine anyone being stumped by this menu. No one expects subtlety from the kitchen, just gobs and gobs of food. The service is equally unpolished, but that doesn't stop Eric Ericsson's from packing 'em in. *$; AE, MC, V; no checks; lunch, dinner every day; full bar; reservations recommended; where the pier meets Harbor Blvd, south of California St.* &

Rosarito Beach Cafe / ★☆

692 E MAIN ST, VENTURA; 805/653-7343

Got a hankering for traditional Baja-style and regional Mexican cooking, spiked with tangy elements borrowed from the West Indies? Here's where you'll find a culinary sophistication that's rare in modest Ventura. The staid appearance of this 1938 Aztec Revival Moderne building (the historical marker out front reveals that it was originally a bank) is deceiving. Inside, bright Pacific colors and intoxicating aromas pervade the dining room and wide outdoor patio. If you're lucky, the resident tortilla maker will be in plain view, patiently patting disks of flour and corn masa for the cafe's trademark fresh tortillas. Resist the temptation to fill up on these warm treats, though, to save room for truly superb specialties like pork *adobado* (rubbed with ancho chiles and mesquite-grilled), chicken in savory dark *mole* sauce, crab and white cheddar chile relleno, or lobster-spinach lasagne made with chile-spiked pasta. In true Baja style, seafood is the main attraction here: a daily selection of fresh fish or shrimp can be prepared in one of five regional ways ("Veracruz" is poached with capers, olives, onions, and tomatoes; "Yucatan" is marinated with achiote and citrus, then mesquite-grilled), and you can always fall back on a platter of fish tacos served with *crema*, cabbage, and lime. *$$; AE, DIS, MC, V; no checks; lunch (summer only) Tues–Sat, dinner Tues–Sun; full bar; reservations recommended; corner of Fir St.* ♿

71 Palm Restaurant / ★

71 N PALM ST, VENTURA; 805/653-7222

Recently opened in a charmingly restored 1910 Craftsman home just a block off Main Street, this ambitious restaurant is still working out some details. Quality of service can be uneven, and the well-composed country French menu sometimes promises better than the kitchen can deliver. Still, the delightful setting helps make 71 Palm a pleasant change of pace in a town of few dining options. The two-story house was once a showplace home, and you can still see the ocean from the airy upstairs dining room. Downstairs, simple bistro tables are arranged around the original tile fireplace, which crackles pleasantly during nearly every meal. The decor features the warm woods and rich muted colors associated with the Arts and Crafts period, and the home's original moldings and built-in features have been expertly preserved. As a rule, dinner is more thoughtfully prepared than lunch, and you won't go wrong sticking with bistro basics like steak *au poivre* with crispy *pommes frites,* Provençal lamb stew, or roasted Chilean sea bass with horseradish-Dijon crust. Authentic French appetizers shine at both lunch and dinner; coarse country pâté is served with crusty bread and tangy *cornichons,* the charcuterie sampler is sized for two, and the onion soup *gratinée* is rich and cheesy—just the way it should be. Be sure to visit the antique-filled original restrooms upstairs. *$$; AE, DC, DIS, MC, V; no checks; lunch Mon–Fri, dinner Mon–Sat; full bar; reservations recommended; between Main and Poli Sts.* &

LODGINGS

Bella Maggiore Inn / ★★

67 S CALIFORNIA ST, VENTURA; 805/652-0277 OR 800/523-8479

 Looking as though it had just jumped out of a European art film into Ventura's historic downtown, this intimate Italian-style hotel scores points for affordability, character, location, and hospitality. From the sidewalk, step through Bella Maggiore's Romanesque entrance into a lobby filled with classic antiques, sparkling chandeliers, a cozy fireplace, and a grand piano. Up a shapely marble staircase are 24 simply furnished rooms, each overlooking either the romantic courtyard or the roof garden. Each Mediterranean-casual room is unique; some have extras like fireplace, balcony, bay-window seat, air-conditioning, or kitchenette, and all have shutters, ceiling fans, and fresh flowers. A full breakfast is included in the room rate, as well as complimentary beverages and appetizers each afternoon. A central courtyard is the inn's focal point, with fountains and flowering trees. Adding to its European-plaza ambience is Nona's Courtyard Cafe, the hotel's charming restaurant—a favorite with locals, who stop in to dine in the small dining room or on the pleasant canopied patio. The menu offers bistro basics with a Mediterranean flair. *$; AE, DC, DIS, MC, V; no checks; between Main and Santa Clara Sts.*

La Mer European Bed & Breakfast / ★★

411 POLI ST, VENTURA; 805/643-3600

 Visit La Mer and you'll soon discover why this quirky little inn bills itself as "European." Most obvious are the colorful foreign flags flying outside this 1890 Cape Cod–style house, whose perch near Ventura's imposing neoclassical City Hall is within convenient walking distance of San Buenaventura's historic district and the beach. The distinctive mark of German proprietor Gisela Baida is evident everywhere, from the charmingly askew colloquialisms of her brochure to the Old World furnishings of the five guest rooms, each enthusiastically decorated (with very fine antiques) to evoke the style of a different country. Whether you choose the Madame Pompadour chamber with its wood-burning stove, the Vienna Woods hideaway with its sunken bathtub, the Norwegian Captain Coje with its nautical theme, or one of the others, you'll enjoy a private entrance, a private bath, and complimentary wine in your room. There's a spectacular coastal view from two of the five guest rooms as well as the parlor. The rest of the cottage is small and cluttered with antiques (definitely not a place for kids), including a cozy parlor where breakfast is served. Gisela's Bavarian-style breakfast features traditional foods like muesli and Black Forest ham in addition to cakes, breads, cheeses, fresh fruits, and plenty of strong coffee. Generous packages for couples can include gourmet candlelight dinners, cruises to Anacapa Island, country carriage rides, therapeutic massage/mineral bath . . . or all of the above. *$$; MC, V; no checks; www.vcol.net/LaMer; at Oak St.* &

Pierpont Inn / ★

550 SANJON RD, VENTURA; 805/643-6144 OR 800/285-4667
One of those places you see from the freeway but never learn about, the Pierpont is a landmark property well worth further investigation. Inside the main building—a 1908 California Craftsman—the Arts and Crafts style reigns, and photos from the inn's rich and colorful past adorn the warm wood-paneled walls. When it was built, the hotel enjoyed unobstructed views of and access to the beach, but the 101 Freeway rudely intruded in 1962. Today clever landscaping manages to obscure the highway without hiding the Pacific, but some automobile noise is inevitable. Though the property is no longer luxurious, it doesn't take long to appreciate the sense of history, style, and dedication to hospitality that pervade here. The guest rooms are spacious but otherwise unremarkable. Many have terrific (freeway notwithstanding) ocean views, and the best also have fireplaces to cozy up the evenings. Two utterly darling cottages—displaced from their original spot on the old beach path—are available as well; they're a short stroll from the main hotel but are happily insulated from the freeway. There's a classic kidney-shaped swimming pool, and massage and spa services on the premises.

Room rates include a full breakfast in the Pierpont's dining room, the ocean-view Mattie's restaurant. Open to the public for lunch and dinner, this relaxing spot is best appreciated by sitting at a window table so you can gaze over the large, sunny lawn dotted with Adirondack chairs to the sea beyond. Informal but dignified, Mattie's offers the same reasonably priced menu throughout the day, featuring an amalgam of California cuisine, European specialties, and American classics. Recommended dishes are soup (gazpacho, clam chowder, and French onion are always on the menu), fresh and crisp main-course salads, seafood "shepherd's pie," and traditional bouillabaisse. *$$; AE, DC, DIS, MC, V; checks OK; info@www.pierpontinn.com; www.pierpontinn.com; near Harbor Blvd.* &

Oxnard

LODGINGS

Embassy Suites Mandalay Beach Resort / ★★☆

2101 MANDALAY BEACH RD, OXNARD; 805/984-2500 OR 800/EMBASSY
Oxnard is a rather unlikely home for such an impressive getaway, which is run by the equally unlikely Embassy Suites chain. Feeling more like a privately owned retreat, the hotel would be as at home on Hawaiian shores as it is on these pristine sands (which are enjoyed mainly by residents of chic surrounding condos). In sharp contrast to nearby marshes where the Chumash once hunted, the posh Spanish-colonial complex sports a red-tile roof, tall palm trees and lush tropical plants, a sparkling blue swimming pool, and a variety of luxurious one- and two-bedroom suites with garden or ocean views. Guest rooms are tastefully decorated with neutral furniture, Mexican tile, marble flooring, and two of everything: telephones, TVs, even two full bathrooms. Room rates include full sit-down breakfast plus afternoon snacks and free well drinks. A recreation shack rents bikes and skates on weekends—bicycles are complimentary for midweek guests.

The restaurant, Capistrano's, serves three meals daily as well as a Sunday brunch and features decent California-Mediterranean fare in a pleasant indoor/outdoor patio setting. There's a tropical-themed indoor cocktail lounge and a poolside bar. If the beach, pool, or tennis courts lose their appeal, Channel Islands Harbor is a short drive or a healthy walk away. Much smaller and less commercial than Ventura Harbor up the coast, it's a pretty enclave of marina homes with private docks and a small shopping and restaurant complex, and it's a jumping-off point for harbor cruises, whale-watching excursions, and fishing charters. *$$$–$$$$; AE, DC, DIS, MC, V; checks OK; www.embassysuites.com; at Costa de Oro, west of Harbor Blvd.* ♿

The Channel Islands

CHANNEL ISLANDS NATIONAL PARK consists of five unspoiled islands a mere 25 to 40 miles offshore from Ventura and Santa Barbara. Remote and wild, the islands are said to closely resemble what Southern California's landscape looked like hundreds of years ago when Native Americans were the only inhabitants—here *and* on the mainland. Facilities are few—just primitive campgrounds and ranger stations—so visitors are usually hikers, divers, kayakers, and wildlife watchers. Relative isolation has led to the development of distinct species like the island fox. The rocky shorelines are home to sea lions and seals, and provide nesting areas for dozens of species of seabirds. The many coves make for colorful scuba diving and snorkeling. During the annual gray-whale migration in winter and early spring, pods of the graceful mammals pass close to the islands with their newly born young in tow. The unpredictable climate on the islands adds to the wildness; though breezy, clear days with strong, hot sun are the norm, thick fog banks or howling windstorms can often descend suddenly.

Each island has a distinct personality. **ANACAPA** is the most commonly visited, being the closest to shore. Ninety minutes is all it takes to reach this tiny (1.1 square miles) isle, whose principal appeal is a network of easy hiking trails that lead to scenic overlooks. **SANTA CRUZ** is the largest in the chain—nearly 100 square miles—and the most diverse, with huge canyons, beaches, cliffs, Chumash village sites, and a copious variety of flora and fauna. Nine-tenths of the island is protected by the Nature Conservancy. The remaining tenth was, for many decades, a privately held sheep ranch; when the National Park Service took over that property in 1997, it eliminated the Channel Islands' only noncamping accommodations, lodges that are being converted to interpretive centers. Windy **SANTA ROSA** also has a strong ranching past, one that ended in 1998 in a storm of controversy that pitted the Park Service against both environmental groups and the 97-year-old Vail & Vickers cattle ranch. The cows are all gone now, taking with them a slice of history and leaving uncertainty that nature's balance can ever be restored on Santa Rosa. Ranger-led tours explore the island's canyons, beaches, and unique endangered plant species. **SAN MIGUEL**, the farthest west in the chain, is also the wildest, a collection of contradictory images: picture-postcard lagoons belie dangerous waters, and constant howling winds can't drown out the barking from crowded seal and sea lion breeding grounds. Explorer Juan Cabrillo is rumored to be buried here; a simple memorial cross stands in his honor. Grass-blanketed **SANTA BARBARA** sits alone to the southeast, an isolated isle out of visual range of the other islands, and often of the mainland as well. Other than the landing cove, the island has no boat access, since it is rimmed with rocky cliffs inhabited by elephant seals, sea lions, and abundant seabirds.

Visiting the Channel Islands requires some advance planning. Your first step should be to contact the **CHANNEL ISLANDS NATIONAL PARK VISITORS CENTER** (1901 Spinnaker Drive; 805/658-5700; www.nps.gov/chis) in Ventura Harbor, where you can get maps, weather reports, and individual guidance. The park's official concessionaire for boat transportation is **ISLAND PACKERS** (1867 Spinnaker Drive; 805/642-7688; www.islandpackers.com), next door to the Visitors Center. Regularly scheduled boat excursions range from 3½-hour nonlanding tours to full-day naturalist-led trips. The Visitors Center has information on scuba, kayak, and whale-watching tours.

ORANGE COUNTY

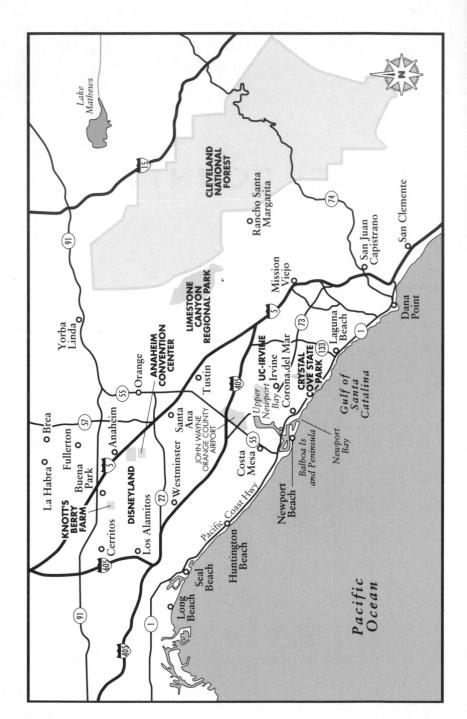

ORANGE COUNTY

For centuries, this 800-square-mile region has been populated by wave after wave of settlers who saw what they liked and stayed. The inrush began with Native Americans who fished the waters and farmed the hills. Sixteenth-century Spanish explorers and 17th-century missionaries arrived next, followed by the land barons of the 18th-century rancho era, the oil magnates of the 19th century, and the World War II GIs who trained here and returned in droves after the war. In recent years Los Angeles yuppie émigrés have been responsible for the latest Orange County influx, chasing, if not a saner existence, then a cleaner one—not to mention one with less-inflated real estate prices (which, much thanks to them, is no longer the case).

The county's motto has always been "If you can dream it, you can find it in the County of Orange." It does have something of a boomtown atmosphere, and it is a region of contrasts: exceedingly wealthy communities next to extremely poor ones, characterless non-communities next to communities that are loaded with identity, housing developments in the middle of cow pastures. And while the county seat may be the salt-of-the-earth community of Santa Ana, paradoxically, the county's most renowned attraction is Disneyland.

Orange County also holds the deed to more than 40 miles of California's premier shoreline. The ravishing light and superbly benevolent climate of this lovely stretch, often referred to as the Gold Coast, are the basis of frequent comparisons to the French Riviera. From indolent and funky Seal and Sunset Beaches at the county's northern tip to San Clemente at the southern county line, each beach, and the community that has grown around it, has its own singular attributes and idiosyncrasies rather than simply being an alias for "Pacific Coast Highway." The disdain many Angelenos feel for Orange County—they sneer at its white-breadness, strip malls, lack of sophistication, and conservatism—is equivalent to a San Franciscan's condescending view of San Jose. However, on a hot summer afternoon when surfers wait to catch that dream wave off Bolsa Chica State Beach, amateur marine enthusiasts explore the ankle-deep cool water of a Laguna Beach tidal pool, and children of all ages miraculously rejoice amidst the heat and crowds at Disneyland, the Orange County moment is the only part of the area's zeitgeist that has relevance.

ACCESS AND INFORMATION

Orange County stretches from Fullerton at the north to the beach community of San Clemente down south, from the Pacific Ocean on the west to a part of the Cleveland National Forest to the east. From West Hollywood, Hollywood, the Hollywood Hills, parts of the San Fernando

Valley, and downtown Los Angeles, Orange County is most easily reached by taking the 101 (Hollywood) Freeway to the 5 (Santa Ana) Freeway to the 405 (San Diego/Santa Ana) Freeway. From Hollywood take the 10 (Santa Monica) Freeway, then transfer to the 405 Freeway south. From San Diego, take the 5 (San Diego/Santa Ana) Freeway north.

The recently expanded **JOHN WAYNE/ORANGE COUNTY AIRPORT** (949/252-5200) often far more convenient than LAX if your destination is in Orange County, is located in the community of Irvine on MacArthur Boulevard near the 405 Freeway. It's served by many of the major carriers, and most who don't fly into Orange County have arrangements with air shuttle services. There are major car rental agencies available at the airport, and each community is served by **SUPERSHUTTLE** (714/517-6600). Orange County is also served by **METROLINK** (call Orange County Transit, 714/636-7433). **AMTRAK** (800/872-7245, www.amtrak california.com) stops in Fullerton, Anaheim, Santa Ana, Irvine, San Juan Capistrano, and San Clemente.

Seal Beach

RESTAURANTS

Walt's Wharf / ★★

201 MAIN ST, SEAL BEACH; 562/598-4433
Justly revered for fresh seafood expertly grilled over oak embers, this village fixture is a casual favorite with both locals and visitors. Once the wood fire leaves its oaky accent behind, the kitchen adds layers of flavors with creative sauces that complement (not overwhelm) the varied fresh catches. Although the line-up changes daily, good examples include Alaskan halibut with roasted yellow bell pepper cream sauce and orange roughy with papaya/red chile salsa. Entrees include al dente vegetables and a choice of five side dishes (including garlic mashed potatoes, a nutty wild rice, or pasta marinara). But not everything gets a grilling. Traditionalists can enjoy the fresh fish and chips (with shoestring fries), the beer-batter jumbo shrimp, or a cream-laden clam chowder. Fresh oysters, crispy pizzas, choice beef, and lively pastas also have their place—the menu seems to stretch on forever. Even the wine list is ample, featuring well-chosen bottles at fair prices. *$$; AE, DC, MC, V; no checks; lunch, dinner every day; full bar; reservations recommended; at Central Ave.* &

ORANGE COUNTY THREE-DAY TOUR

DAY ONE. In **San Juan Capistrano,** begin with fresh-roasted java and a delicious muffin at **Diedrich Coffee,** then spend the morning meandering through the historic **Mission San Juan Capistrano.** Have lunch at **Ramos House Café,** take the Historic Walking Tour of old San Juan Capistrano, wander along Antique Row, and stop and visit the old **Capistrano Depot.** Drive south on Camino Capistrano to Pacific Coast Highway and the beach, then head northwest to **Dana Point** to check into the incomparable **Ritz-Carlton, Laguna Niguel.** Have drinks on the terrace and watch the sunset. Dine in the Ritz-Carlton **Dining Room,** have a nightcap in the Lobby Bar, and sleep in a room fit for royalty.

DAY TWO. In the morning, enjoy breakfast in the Ritz-Carlton's **Terrace Restaurant.** Arrange to play tennis on the hotel's courts, or ask the concierge to set up a round of golf at the **Links at Monarch Beach Club** next door. Drive north on PCH to **Laguna Beach.** Stop at **Taco Loco** for lunch, then spend the afternoon lying on beautiful **1000 Steps Beach.** Check into the **Hotel Laguna,** have dinner at **Five Feet,** then catch one of the stellar performances at the **Laguna Playhouse.**

DAY THREE. After breakfast at the hotel, spend time perusing the galleries and shops in the village of Laguna Beach before continuing up the coast to **Newport Beach.** Have lunch at **JackShrimp,** then take the ferry to **Balboa Island** and window-shop along Marine Avenue. Drive to Balboa Peninsula and check into the **Doryman's Inn Bed & Breakfast.** Sip a glass of wine with some savory tidbits while enjoying the breathtaking ocean view, and then make the brief drive south along PCH to scenic **Corona del Mar** for dinner at **Five Crowns.** Finish off the evening with drinks and dancing at **Bob Burns** club at **Fashion Island.**

LODGINGS

The Seal Beach Inn & Gardens / ★★☆

212 5TH ST, SEAL BEACH; 562/493-2416 OR 800/HIDEAWAY

This B&B with bright blue awnings, shuttered windows, wrought-iron grillwork, hanging baskets of geraniums, and old-fashioned lamp posts looks as though it belongs in New Orleans' Garden District, although it's only a block from the beach. The check-in desk in the main building shares space with an elaborate gift shop selling reproduction Tiffany-style lamps and expensive toiletries; beyond are a bright, sunny coffee bar, wicker and wingback chairs, and three oak bookcases crammed with reading material. French doors lead out to the kidney-shaped pool surrounded by greenery, lounge chairs, and a fountain, all of which make a prime setting for the full breakfast on warm mornings and tea, wine, and cheese in the evenings. When a chill sets, in the Tea Room's mammoth gas-burning fireplace is the place to cozy. The inn's 24 rooms, which include 13 suites, are decorated in highly distinctive style. The Primrose Room has a gas-burning fireplace, raspberry flower wallpaper, a coffered ceiling with a deep purple inset, and a bathroom with a Jacuzzi tub for two. The Azalea King Suite is larger, with a bright pink floral theme, a canopy bed covered in white flouncy gauze, a kitchen, and a Roman soak tub in the bathroom. Most, but not all, of the rooms and suites have kitchenettes, fireplaces, and Jacuzzi tubs. If you're a light sleeper, avoid the first-level rooms at the front next to the parking lot. *$$$; AE, DC, DIS, MC, V; checks OK if reservation is made a month ahead; hideaway@ sealbeachinn.com; www.sealbeachinn.com; 4 blocks west of PCH.* &

Huntington Beach

We're not sure the "two girls for every boy" ratio has any basis in fact here in Surf City, USA. A mile east of Pacific Coast Highway, the community of Huntington Beach could pass for a middle-class suburb in Anywhere, USA, with hundreds of square miles of scarily indistinguishable rabbit-warren housing developments and an excess of strip malls. However, as the community's sobriquet implies, the coastal area offers visitors and residents alike the chance to experience quintessential Beach Boys and Jan & Dean beach life.

In summer, parking in Huntington Beach's coastal communities is a nightmare, restaurants are packed, and accommodations are scarce and expensive. **BOLSA CHICA STATE BEACH** (714/846-3460), however, which parallels PCH from the town's northern tip to its most southern edge, and the oft-perfect waves that pound it, are all about California dreamin'. The southern end of Bolsa Chica is also the location of the **BOLSA CHICA ECOLOGICAL RESERVE** (714/846-1114), where many species of marine life are protected. Anyone interested in the history of surfing will surely find gratification in the exhibits at the **HUNTINGTON BEACH INTERNATIONAL SURFING MUSEUM** (411 Olive Avenue, between Main and Fifth Streets; 714/960-3483), where the history of the sexy sport is illustrated. Pictures and biographies of surfing hall-of-famers are displayed in the museum, and not far away, at PCH and Main Street, they're immortalized (à la the Hollywood Walk of Fame) in polished granite stars on the **SURFING WALK OF FAME**. Huntington Beach's visitor's bureau is located in the **CHAMBER OF COMMERCE** (2100 Main Street #200, at Yorktown Avenue; 714/536-8888).

After a long day of shooting the curl, hanging ten, and soaking up rays, big kahunas and their wahines want to party. **AMATO'S THE BAR** (18862 Beach Boulevard, between Garfield and Ellis Avenues;

714/963-8341) has pool, darts, and a terrific jukebox. At the **MAJESTIC** (18582 Beach Boulevard, at Ellis Avenue; 714/963-1089), there's ballroom and freestyle dancing during the week, and renowned Vietnamese performers appear regularly. At **GECKOS** (7887 Center Avenue, near the 405 Freeway; 714/892-2227) an offhand, all-age crowd bops to Top-40 hits in an unpretentious atmosphere Thursday through Sunday.

SURFING AND THE CALIFORNIA DREAM

Whether the world's first surfers were Hawaiian kings riding wooden boards or (as some anthropologists have recently suggested) Peruvian Indians on reed rafts, no one disputes that the heart and soul—and booming industry—of global surfing is Southern California.

The sport of surfing was first imported in 1910 to L.A.'s Manhattan Beach by Oahu's legendary surfer Duke Kahanomoku. As it gained popularity among SoCal beach boys, wave-riding not only carved itself an identity as a sport and a lifestyle, but also evolved into a two-billion-dollar global industry, shaping the world's perception of surfing, surfers, and California culture through the sale of clothing, music, and accessories.

Surfers now number 750,000 in California, compared to half that number in Hawaii and four times that in surfing's other heartland, Australia. But beyond its devout enthusiasm and sunny climate, the reason Southern California is the true heart of global surf culture is because it's fortunate enough to possess surfing's most essential element: good waves. Along Orange County's coast there are more than 50 prime surf spots, not to mention nearby headquarters of industry giants such as Quicksilver, OP, Gotcha, Rip Curl, and the sport's twin bibles, *Surfing* and *Surfer* magazines.

For the visitor, the best place to watch surfers ripping into Pacific waves is off the legendary pier at Huntington Beach, also known as Surf City, U.S.A. As the longtime host to professional surfing contests such as the Katin Challenge and the OP Pro (both held annually in August), the old pier tends to build up sand around its pilings, which results in consistent and well-shaped waves. The pier is a safe, dry vantage point from which spectators can hear the yells of surfers continually attempting to outmaneuver each other for the best waves, see the spray as riders hit the lip and carve tight cutbacks, and feel the mist and salt as the waves smash against the pilings below. From the pier it's only a few steps across the asphalt of Pacific Coast Highway to Main Street's Surfing Walk of Fame. Bronze plaques embedded in the sidewalk recognize surfers influential to the sport, from *Endless Summer* filmmaker Bruce Brown, to six-time world surfing champion Kelly Slater. And there's a bust of the man who started it all, Duke Kahanomoku.

LODGINGS

Hilton Waterfront Beach Resort / ★★★

21100 PACIFIC COAST HWY, HUNTINGTON BEACH; 714/960-7873 OR
800/HILTONS

One of the prettiest in the Hilton chain, this large establishment has a special ambience that makes it seem much smaller than its 290 guest rooms and 12 stories would suggest. The reason is obvious: It's directly across from the ocean, and it's at the quieter south end of Huntington Beach. Awash with sunlight reflecting on the water, the hotel's exterior wears a perpetual rosy gold glow. The marble lobby is light, airy, and impressive, with its coffered ceiling and skylight. It's peaceful to rest a while in the cushy padded wicker armchairs and the overstuffed sofas in conversation-group arrangements. The staff are helpful, and the bellhops   seem to whoosh your luggage to your room in record time. All the rooms have privates lanais and ocean views, but the corner suites are the best because they have wraparound terraces that seem to turn the Pacific Ocean into a roommate. There is a beautiful simplicity to these suites, with their soft beige and warm peach décor and fabric-covered headboards that match the satin brocade coverlets. The bathrooms are polished travertine, extraordinarily clean and spacious, and the suites have both wet bars and fully stocked minibars. Added perks include an outdoor pool, fitness center, spa, and restaurants The Palm Court, which serves Mediterranean influenced cuisine; the West Coast Club, a more formal library-like dining room; and Surf Hero, which serves coffee drinks, fresh sandwiches, and pizza. The Surf Hero will also sell you firewood, hot dogs, and all the fixings for s'mores so you can make a fire in one of the rings on the beach just across from PCH. On the concierge level, continental breakfast, soft drinks, and afternoon tidbits are gratis. *$$$$; AE, DC, DIS, MC, V; checks OK; www.hilton.com; between Golden West St and Beach Blvd.* &

Newport Beach

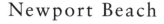

With its glittering harbors, seven islands, expensive waterfront homes, thousands of seagoing vessels, miles of gorgeous beach, tanned natives in elegant shabby-chic garb, and most especially its atmosphere of wealth and ease, Newport Beach could easily pass for Newport, Rhode Island. Newport West has one advantage, however: The season here doesn't end with the Labor Day regatta. Plainly put, the lovely seaside jewel is among the best destinations Orange County has to offer and is easily accessible via PCH or the 405 Freeway south to the 55 Freeway, which becomes Newport Boulevard and crosses over the PCH overpass. The NEWPORT

BEACH CHAMBER OF COMMERCE AND VISITORS BUREAU (3300 West Coast Highway; 949/722-1611) offers a **24-HOUR INFORMATION CENTER** (949/729-4400).

Of the abundant picturesque attractions, a good starting point is **BALBOA PENINSULA**, an historic area lined with homes and shops featuring vintage clothing, antiques, curios, and eateries surrounding Newport Boulevard. The waterfront village on **LIDO ISLE** (at Balboa Boulevard) and the cobblestoned and leafy **VIA OPORTO** are perfect places to enjoy a latte at one of the outdoor cafes and shop in the charming boutiques and galleries. Southeast on Newport Boulevard is the quaint and historic **CANNERY VILLAGE**, home to a commercial fishing fleet, shops, and galleries. Nearby **NEWPORT PIER** boasts the **DORY FISHING FLEET**, an energetic and resourceful cooperative established in 1889 where you can shop the open-air market for the catch of the day, and a beach that's an extremely popular surfing spot, with a horseshoe-shaped strand lined with fun and funky food concessions and beachwear shops. The roller-skate, blade, and bicycle rental concerns usually do a land-office business because there are miles of smooth boardwalk and bicycle paths. At **BALBOA PIER**, where the harbor meets the jetty, is a body-surfers' and boogie-boarders' heaven called **THE WEDGE**. The waves are powerful—and so is the undertow. **THE BALBOA PAVILION** (end of Main Street, at the intersection of Edgewater Street; 949/673-4633) is a wooden, gabled, cupola-topped confection more reminiscent of the other Newport. Constructed in 1905, it's the city's most famous landmark. The pavilion is the departure point for **WHALE-WATCHING** (in-season from December through March) and **SPORTFISHING**, both of which are available through Davie's Locker (949/673-1434), as well as **HARBOR CRUISES** and **CATALINA ISLAND JAUNTS** via Catalina Passenger Service (949/673-5245). The kiosk at the pavilion's entrance is full of brochures about all the tours and other available activities. The **BALBOA FUN ZONE** (beyond the intersection at Washington Street and Edgewater; 949/673-0408), another Newport institution, boasts a Ferris wheel, carousel, bumper cars, and arcade games.

Across the harbor is **BALBOA ISLAND**, an excellent excursion via the **BALBOA ISLAND FERRY** (ferry landing off Main Street; 949/673-1070). The charming, spic-and-span auto/pedestrian shuttle has been in operation since 1919 and accommodates three vehicles per trip. Drivers are free to leave their vehicles at the craft's gunwales and admire the harbor's blue sparkle. Balboa Island is a tiny community with an East Coast fishing village ambience, its narrow streets lined with a jumble of cottages and garage-top apartments. The island's main drag, Marine Avenue, leads to the tiny village's Shangri-La of unique boutiques and diminutive restaurants.

On the other side of PCH a few turns in the car lead to one of the entrances to **BACK BAY**, the name residents have given to **UPPER NEW-PORT BAY ECOLOGICAL RESERVE AND REGIONAL PARK** (600 Shellmaker Island; 949/640-1751). The 752-acre saltwater marsh is a protected sanctuary for 200 species of birds and encompasses six different habitats. Rowing and kayaking are excellent ways to explore the area. Contact the **NEWPORT AQUATIC CENTER** (One Whitecliffs Drive, located below the reserve and PCH; 949/646-7725) for information on kayak and canoe rental.

The **ORANGE COUNTY MUSEUM OF ART** (OCMA) (850 San Clemente Drive; 949/759-1122; www.ocarts.org/ocma/), formerly the Newport Harbor Art Museum, may seem unprepossessing, but the collection of works inside by California artists is spectacular, from dreamy impressionist-style paintings from the turn of the century to edgier postmodern installations. More attainable visuals are abundant at **FASHION ISLAND** (401 Newport Center, between MacArthur and Jamboree; 949/721-2000 or 800/495-4753), Newport Beach's premier outdoor shopping oasis complete with koi pond and a dog-friendly attitude. Newport nightlife is best at **BOB BURNS** (37 Fashion Island; 949/644-2030), where there's dancing and live music nightly for sophisticates.

RESTAURANTS

Aubergine / ★★★☆

508 29TH ST, NEWPORT BEACH; 949/723-4150

The celebrated team of Tim and Liza Goodell began their rise to culinary fame in 1994 when they transformed a tiny florist shop into Aubergine, a dainty California-French charmer. Instant success soon led to broader horizons, and the duo shuttered tiny Aubergine for renovation while they opened Troquet, their wildly triumphant French bistro. Almost 18 months later, Aubergine reopened with an ambitious, all-prix-fixe tasting menu of three, five, or nine courses that's bound to impress the savviest palates. Typical examples: Maine lobster strudel with fresh tarragon and julienned leeks; roasted chestnut soup with crumbled pancetta, crème fraîche and fresh truffles; confit of veal heart with potatoes, haricots verts, and organic baby greens; and squab breast with roasted sweetbreads and melted savoy cabbage. Tim is also acclaimed for his desserts, which include a peerless warm Valrhona chocolate soufflé cake and a daring roasted pineapple–cornmeal cake with vanilla bean ice cream and pink peppercorn infusion. A creative, sometimes quirky wine selection with plenty of boutique choices is enhanced by adept service and proper stemware. The remodeled cottage now includes a roomier dining room and new front and rear patios. Stone floors, antique furnishings, and an embossed zinc-topped bar add to the space's charm. Limoges china,

Christofle flatware, and Spigelau crystal add notes of undeniable elegance to what is clearly one of Orange County's most refined dining experiences. $$$; AE, MC, V; no checks; dinner Tues–Sat; full bar; reservations recommended; off Lido Park Dr. ᕗ

Bistro 201 / ★★☆
3333 W PACIFIC COAST HWY, NEWPORT BEACH; 949/631-1551
Although Orange County boasts plenty of waterfront real estate, precious few of its restaurants manage to combine a great view with commendable cuisine. In fact, locals often lament the common pairing of a killer view with deplorable fare. Bistro 201 defies that tradition by offering likable, reliable contemporary bistro fare with a sparkling view of prosperous Newport Harbor. The handsome split-level room affords a view from almost any table, but spacious booths on the lowest deck are preferred for both comfort and unimpeded vistas. The menu here offers something for everyone. Signature dishes include excellent seared crab cakes with a crisp-flavored red pepper sauce and buttery sea bass with whole-grain mustard sauce, supplemented by specials that reflect more seasonal flavors. Live music on weekends adds zest to this already spirited spot. $$$; AE, DC, MC, V; no checks; lunch Mon–Fri, dinner every day, brunch Sun; full bar; reservations recommended; at the Newport Marina. ᕗ

Issay / ★★☆
485 N NEWPORT BLVD, NEWPORT BEACH; 949/722-2992
This sleeper of a dinner spot isn't widely known, isn't easy to find, and doesn't have a good view, a full bar, or entertainment, yet it stays very busy. Why? Because the food is fabulous. The name sounds Japanese, but the menu is Northern Italian all the way, with a big emphasis on fresh, meticulously prepared seafood and beautifully dressed pastas. A converted beach cottage on a quirky back street, Issay is a petite place with only 15 or so tables surrounding an open kitchen. Flowers on the wood porch, creaky wood floors, and lace curtains fluttering in the ocean breeze supply lots of relaxed charm. Regulars rarely consult the appealing menu of pastas, seafood, and other standard fare. Instead, they wisely order from chef Paolo Pestarino's 10 or so daily specials—we've never had one that wasn't outstanding. Sure bets include a roasted Chilean sea bass, salmon filet with a balsamic vinegar reduction, and lobster ravioli topped with grilled shrimp and a rich "pink" sauce. The cioppino is hugely popular and perhaps the best buy on the menu. There's an imaginative wine list appropriate to the food, but prices include an ample markup. Service is quite professional, though not stuffy, and the waitstaff knows the menu well. $$$; AE, DC, MC, V; local checks only; dinner every day; beer and wine; reservations recommended; near Industrial Blvd. ᕗ

JackShrimp / ★★☆

**2400 W PACIFIC COAST HWY, NEWPORT BEACH (AND BRANCHES);
949/650-5577**

Spicy, addictive, and dripping with butter, Louisiana-style peel-and-eat crustaceans are the key draw at this laid-back restaurant chain where locals get top-drawer eats at back-door prices. Working from a carefully protected recipe of Cajun spices, owner Jack Jasper cheerfully supplies a taste of the South from a compact menu of classics including pastas (for the timid), a mean jambalaya (for the ravenous), and the aforementioned shrimp (with loads of fresh bread to dunk in the sauce). At all three locations, the settings tend to be more basic than fancy, the better to focus on the food. The original Newport Beach site stays pretty busy; the Irvine location (3041 Michelson Drive; 949/252-1023) does a brisk office lunch trade; and the downtown Laguna Beach spot (361 Forest Avenue; 949/376-8982) has a cigar patio and live music on weekends. *$; AE, MC, V; no checks; lunch Fri, dinner every day; beer and wine; reservations not accepted; between Tustin and Riverside Aves.* ⅃

Pascal / ★★★

1000 N BRISTOL ST, NEWPORT BEACH; 949/752-0107

Long before Provence was popular, French chef-owner Pascal Olhats began wooing an upscale clientele with the authentic, earthy flavors of the South of France at this homespun bistro opened in 1988. Success was almost immediate and today this cozy, rose-filled dining room is widely considered one of Orange County's premier culinary destinations. The menu is characterized by rustic dishes prepared with meticulous care from premium ingredients. (Pascal's kitchen has schooled some of the area's most acclaimed young chefs, including Tim Goodell of Troquet and Florent Marneau of Pinot Provence.) Signature dishes like the aromatic and delectable thyme-roasted sea bass and the duck confit salad share billing with rotating items such as sautéed sea scallops, with the unusual pairing of lentils, and roasted duck breast with another unique sidekick, green olives—all ably supported by a discerning selection of French wines from Languedoc, Provence, and the Rhone Valley. Olhats's wife Mimi runs the homey room with gracious efficiency, ensuring that the well-dressed crowd is served with a polish that belies the strip-mall location. The adjacent Epicerie is a gourmet jewel box stocked with beautiful cheeses, breads, wines, and other edibles. *$$$; AE, DC, MC, V; no checks; lunch Mon–Fri, dinner Tues–Sat; full bar; reservations recommended; www. pascalnewportbeach.com; between Spruce Ave and Dore St.* ⅃

Pavilion / ★★★

FOUR SEASONS HOTEL, 690 NEWPORT CENTER DR, NEWPORT BEACH; 949/760-4920

Commendable for its excellent service and top-notch treatment of Cal-continental cuisine, this lovely low-key dining room, which exudes elegance while remaining tastefully understated, is something of a sleeping beauty, often overshadowed by glitzier competitors in the neighborhood. But those who prefer substance over sizzle will appreciate the splendid room's quiet magic, colossal pillars and oversized floral arrangements. Civilized service is just what you'd expect from a Four Seasons operation, and the food matches that mood. Much of the menu borrows from the Mediterranean, but seasonal changes and daily specials add many California touches. Representative appetizers include a sculptural ahi tartare with won ton spirals and sweet corn soup with smoked shrimp, while entrees might include Canadian salmon en croute with roasted shallots, grilled veal chop with sweet corn polenta in truffle jus, pepper-crusted lamb with port wine reduction, or roasted vegetable ravioli with root-vegetable ribbons and Madeira sauce. Housemade desserts are fabulous and first class. *$$$; AE, DC, DIS, MC, V; no checks; breakfast, lunch, dinner every day; full bar; reservations recommended; near Fashion Island center at Fashion Center Dr.* &

Restaurant Abe / ★★

2900 NEWPORT BLVD, NEWPORT BEACH; 949/675-1739

Few Orange County sushi bars stand out enough to be worthy of a drive across the county, but this spot qualifies. Chef-owner Takashi Abe's enticing (if pricey) line-up of hot and cold "platters" is a gourmet effort that will appeal most to seafood connoisseurs. The menu's spare descriptions scarcely do justice to creative offerings that taste (and look) more lovely than expected. Rock shrimp tempura drizzled with truffle oil is a good place to start. Decadent bets from the hot side of the menu include broiled sea bass and foie gras with shiitake mushrooms, crisp soft-shell crab *kara-age* with ponzu and a spicy tomato sauce, or the mixed *kinoko tobanyaki* (three varieties of deftly sautéed mushrooms). Cold-side winners include toro tartare with caviar or salmon *kinuta*, a cylinder of delicate vegetables surrounding the freshest of salmon. Ambience is spare here, the lighting too harsh, and the chefs not overly chatty. The real art is on the plate, not the walls. But for sushi zealots, it's worth the trip. *$$; AE, DC, MC, V; no checks; lunch Mon–Fri, dinner Mon–Sat; beer and wine; reservations not accepted; at 28th St.* &

The Ritz / ★★★☆

NEWPORT FASHION ISLAND, 880 NEWPORT CENTER DR, NEWPORT
BEACH; 949/720-1800

Dining at the Ritz (no relation to the hotel empire) is a time-honored
Orange County treat. The classic continental fare is nearly perfect, and
the luxurious, clublike setting is easy to savor. Impeccable service makes
everyone feel like royalty—it's no surprise the Ritz consistently gets top
ratings for both food and service from critics and publications. Cordial
owner Hans Prager and his expert team deftly deliver memorable meals
served with panache. Popular dishes include American rack of lamb
rotisseried with rosemary and thyme, chateaubriand adorned with diced
truffles, and their legendary Harlequin Soufflé, made with Belgian chocolate and Grand Marnier. In addition to the handsome dining room
(briefly notorious for its collection of tasteful nude paintings), guests now
have the option of dining in the beautiful new garden room. All this glorious elegance only gets better after dark, when one of two accomplished
piano vocalists performs on Fridays and Saturdays. Cole Porter, George
Gershwin, and Nat King Cole add a nostalgic note just right for the ele-
gant bar. *$$$; AE, DIS, MC, V; no checks; lunch Mon–Fri, dinner every
day; full bar; reservations recommended; Newport Fashion Island at
Santa Barbara.* ᕓ

Sid's / ★

445 OLD NEWPORT BLVD, NEWPORT BEACH; 949/650-7437

This eccentric tavern/steak joint bends all the rules when it comes to
prices, service, and location. Don't look for a sign because there isn't
one—just a blank space where a sign used to be. Don't expect classy
service because there isn't any—just a couple of friendly, overloaded
waitresses who do the best they can with a very slow kitchen. Don't count
on a big tab because it can't be—not when a steak dinner costs under
$10. The small menu is for beef lovers, with a few exceptions for chicken
fans (brochettes or simply sautéed breast meat). The bacon-wrapped filet
mignon is as tasty as most at any price. Not fancy, just tasty. Entrees are
served with a hearty green salad, a wild rice blend, and "Sid's carrots,"
a sugary concoction of carrots and onions. Spend the extra buck for the
super garlicky bread. The massive bar packs premium labels, poured at
low prices, and the surprisingly large wine list boasts a good number of
bottles for $18 or less. The small, casual quarters are usually jammed
with a cross-generational, antistyle beach crowd. *$$; AE, MC, V; no
checks; lunch, dinner every day; full bar; reservations recommended;
turn onto Hospital Rd from Newport Blvd.* ᕓ

LODGINGS

Doryman's Inn Bed & Breakfast / ★★☆

2102 W OCEANFRONT, NEWPORT BEACH; 949/675-7300

This splendid little place with only 10 rooms is in sharp contrast to the fun funk of the beachwear and surf shops just up the block. Guests who enter the elegantly etched glass front doors and step into the old elevator to the second-floor wood-paneled lobby are likely to feel as though they are in one of the posh smaller hotels in the Mayfair district of London. Each lovely room is decorated in plush, comfortable (and genuine) Victoriana and luxuriously appointed with marble window seat, sunken marble tub, deep-pile carpeting, and gas-log fireplace. Some rooms have ocean views. Although each room is special in its own way, the master suite, fabled Room 8, with its brocade canopy bed and deep-blue-tiled bathroom, is guaranteed to add a little vacation zing to any relationship. Breakfast, served in the parlor, consists of cereal, fruit, yogurt, pastries, and hard-boiled eggs. In summer the rooftop view overlooking the Newport Pier and surrounding beach is fantastic. The 21 Oceanfront restaurant, just below, provides room service. $$$; AE, MC, V; cashier's checks only; on Balboa Peninsula off Newport Blvd.

Four Seasons Hotel Newport Beach / ★★★

690 NEWPORT CENTER DR, NEWPORT BEACH; 949/759-0808
OR 800/268-6282

A stay at a Four Seasons hotel in any part of the world is always a treat, and this one is no exception. Perhaps it's the thick, soft carpet underfoot, or maybe it's the bowl of gleaming red crunchy apples placed within easy reach on the check-in desk. Whatever the case, guests are soothed the moment they enter the magnificent lobby, with its coffered ceiling and gorgeous floral arrangements. Within the 19 stories are 285 rooms, including 96 suites. All have terraces with views of the surrounding area and/or the Pacific in the distance. Spacious guest rooms are furnished with cushy modern pieces in neutral tones and have minibars. Large bathrooms sparkle and are well stocked with hair dryer, terrycloth robe, and top-of-the-line toiletries. Additional services include 24-hour room service, twice-daily maid service, complimentary shoe-shine, one-hour pressing, and overnight dry cleaning. As if that isn't enough, the property also boasts an excellent landscaped pool, a state-of-the-art fitness center, and a full spa where facialists and massage therapists are ready to smooth away any tension not already erased by a night spent in this haven. Dining options include the world-class Pavilion and the more casual Gardens Lounge and Café. $$$$; AE, DC, MC, V; checks OK; www.fourseasons.com; near Fashion Island. &

Portofino Beach Hotel / ★★

**2306 W OCEANFRONT BLVD, NEWPORT BEACH; 949/673-7030
OR 800/571-8749**
You can't miss this two-story oceanfront hotel; it's painted a cheery and pleasing vermilion. The cushy interior, done up in a style something between Old World elegance and New World glitz, is full of pleasant surprises and charming idiosyncrasies. There are half a dozen charming areas to sit and socialize or have a quiet moment, including an inviting corner with a large gas-burning fireplace. The 15 guest rooms are upstairs along a long carpeted corridor, which is pleasantly spooky (as the best old buildings are), and are flouncily furnished with a blend of genuine antiques—Edwardian and Victorian, predominantly—and attractive older, but not quite antique, pieces. All have cable TV. Only premier rooms have ocean views, although a few others have ocean "peeks" through side windows; five options have spa tubs and some have gas-log fireplaces. Complimentary continental breakfast, which is served each morning in the Portofino's Bar La Gritta lounge, consists of coffee, tea, fresh fruit, cereal, juice, muffins, and croissants. Wine, tea, and treats are served each afternoon. Patrons may also order room service (for dinner only) from Renato, the Italian restaurant downstairs. A bonus for families; the hotel also rents one- and two-bedroom furnished apartments, which come with full kitchens and daily maid service (for an additional fee). $$$; AE, DC, DIS, MC, V; checks OK; portofino@newportbeach. com; www.portofinobeachhotel.com; on Balboa Peninsula in Old Newport, near the Newport Pier.

The Sutton Place Hotel / ★★☆

4500 MACARTHUR BLVD, NEWPORT BEACH; 949/476-2001 OR 800/243-4141
From the subdued but cushy lobby with its tinkling fountain to the staff that absolutely heaps attention on guests, this 10-story establishment in the Newport Beach business center perfectly captures the cool California ease of the breezy, booming '80s. A small anteroom before the grand, main lobby lets you adjust your eyes to the light change by resting them on a beautiful flower arrangement. The interior corridor leading to Accents restaurant and the lobby bar is a veritable art gallery displaying stunning glass sculptures. Capacious, comfortable rooms are decorated in comfy modern style in tones of deep rose, peach, and gold, and offer amenities such as room service, cable TV with movies and games, robes, hair dryers, Gilchrist & Soames toiletries, and dataports—plus a cheery welcome of limited-edition Sutton teddy bears, tea, and fresh cookies. Each has a view of the surrounding—partially developed—countryside. Added amenities, such as a complimentary continental breakfast, large glass-enclosed pool, excellent fitness center, nail salon, concierge-arranged massages, and a shuttle service to shopping areas contribute to

the overall sumptuous atmosphere. Along with casual and comfortable Accents restaurant, Sutton Place also boasts a piano bar and another that also offers live music. Business travelers will appreciate the hotel's proximity to John Wayne Airport as well as the Panache Floor with its business center and private concierge. *$$$$; AE, DC, DIS, MC, V; checks OK; info@npb.suttonplace.com; www.suttonplace.com; near John Wayne Airport.* ♿

Corona del Mar

The topography of Orange County beaches begins its dramatic change in Corona del Mar, transitioning from smooth and broad shoreline to the north to sculpted and rocky, surrounded by steep bluffs. **LITTLE CORONA BEACH** (below Pacific Coast Highway and Ocean Avenue at Poppy Avenue) is a pretty cove with some of the best scuba diving and tide pools going. To rent scuba gear, try Newport Aquatic Center (see Newport Beach, above). **BIG CORONA BEACH** (off Marguerite Avenue below Ocean Avenue) is famous for its snorkeling. Surfboards and boogie boards can be rented at **HOBIE SPORTS LTD** (2831 E Coast Highway; 949/675-9700). Volleyball courts are available, too, along with picnic tables, fire rings, restrooms, showers, and a snack bar. Along PCH, Corona del Mar also offers several blocks of galleries, restaurants, and shops where handcrafted jewelry, Southwestern furniture, and antiques are available.

On the land side of the beach, exquisite homes cling to the terraced hillsides above PCH. The streets of the tiny community are named after plants, trees, and flowers, and appropriately so, since the **SHERMAN LIBRARY AND GARDENS** (2647 E Pacific Coast Highway, 2 blocks east of MacArthur Boulevard; 949/673-2261) is one of Corona del Mar's main attractions. Modestly begun in 1966, it now boasts more than 2,000 plant species in its carefully cultivated two acres. Stroll through the green and cool setting, past fountains, sculptures, and precisely maintained shrubbery, and view the bountiful botanical collection, which includes everything from rare cacti to tropical vegetation. The library includes an historical research center focusing on the Pacific Southwest, a prime lunch spot—**CAFÉ JARDIN** (949/673-0033), which serves Monday through Friday and requires reservations—and a gift shop absolutely crammed with cute garden and kitchen items.

Duffers will truly appreciate the Tom Fazio–designed courses at the **PELICAN HILL GOLF CLUB** (22651 Pelican Hill Road S; 949/759-5190), just past Corona del Mar. **CRYSTAL COVE STATE PARK/EL MORO CANYON** (south of the Corona del Mar city limits and approximately 2 miles north, within the boundaries of Laguna Beach at 8741 Pacific Coast Highway; 714/771-6731) offers 2,200 acres of back country with campgrounds, hiking trails, biking paths, horse trails, and 3.5 miles of unbelievably beautiful beaches. Exact change of two dollars is required for parking, and all vehicles are strictly prohibited beyond the parking area. There are restrooms off the parking lot, but hikers, bikers, and campers must carry in their own water. Fires are prohibited except for backpackers' camp stoves. Across PCH, about a quarter of a mile down, just beyond the entrance to Crystal Cove State Beach, the **CRYSTAL COVE SHAKE SHACK** (7408 Pacific Coast Highway; 949/497-9666), a Southern California institution, perches on the bluffs overlooking the beach. There's a weathered patio with tables and chairs next to the shack, and it's the perfect spot to enjoy a cool, creamy, surprisingly delicious date shake after a hike in the canyons or a jog along the beach. The **CORONA DEL MAR CHAMBER OF COMMERCE AND VISITORS BUREAU** (2843 E Coast Highway; 949/673-4050; www.cdmchamber.com) is a helpful source for further information.

RESTAURANTS

Five Crowns / ★★☆

3801 E PACIFIC COAST HWY, CORONA DEL MAR; 949/760-0331
Merrie Olde England lives again at this long-revered haven for beef lovers and special-occasion celebrants. Roaring fireplaces, low ceilings, dark wood beams, and ivy-draped walls set the stage for costumed servers plying guests with near-perfect platters of prime rib and Yorkshire pudding. But don't think it's just a kitschy theme joint—this Lawry's-owned operation consistently meets high standards for food and service. Though top-notch beef and other hearty continental fare are king, salads, seafood, and chicken choices abound. Of course with all that red meat on the menu, it only makes sense to offer equally mighty wine bottles, and the list here has garnered awards for decades. *$$$; AE, DC, MC, V; no checks; dinner every day, brunch Sun; full bar; reservations recommended; at Poppy Ave.* &

Laguna Beach

For many years visitors zooming along Pacific Coast Highway into Laguna Beach did a double-take when they spotted the cheery old gent standing at the side of the road waving them in. His name was Eiler Larsen, and he was the community's beloved greeter. Mr. Larsen is gone now, but in his place, in front of the Pottery Shack just inside the city limits, there's a statue commemorating him. There's another one at the opposite end of town, too, in front of Greeters Corner Restaurant. With or without an official greeter, visitors have been flocking to this friendly community for more than a century. By the late 1800s, they were camping on the beaches and exploring the tide pools. The early Hollywood community adored Laguna Beach: filmmakers appreciated the area's varied topography, and in the 1920s, 1930s, and 1940s stars such as Bette Davis, Victor Mature, and Judy Garland had vacation homes here.

Attracted by the spectacular ocean vistas, the hillsides covered with brightly colored wildflowers, and the intense Mediterranean light, artists flocked here, too, and they were in the vanguard of the California impressionist movement. By 1917 Laguna Beach was a recognized artists' colony, and it remains one to this day. In 1932, the artists formed a cooperative and presented the first **FESTIVAL OF ARTS/PAGEANT OF THE MASTERS** (949/494-1145), which became the annual event that has put Laguna Beach on the map. The Festival of Arts is a juried exhibit of original works from more than 150 local artists, displayed on a 6-acre patch of park land just off of Laguna Canyon Road, near PCH, on the property surrounding the Irvine Bowl. On festival evenings the Pageant of the Masters is presented inside the Bowl. Visitors are treated to *tableaux vivants*—live, staged re-creations of classical paintings, accompanied by orchestral music and narration. These evenings draw art lovers from all over the country, and tickets must be purchased months in advance (650 Laguna Canyon Road, just off PCH; 949/497-6582 or 800/494-1145). The annual **SAWDUST FESTIVAL** (949/494-3030), held concurrently with the Festival of Arts/Pageant of the Masters and directly across Laguna Canyon Road, is another popular Laguna Beach event. This festival provides a venue for local artisans to display and sell their pottery, jewelry, and much more, amidst food booths, entertainment, and hands-on demonstrations. Also concurrent is the annual **ART-A-FAIR** (949/494-4514), on the same grounds as the Sawdust Festival, where fine arts—predominantly paintings and sculpture created by artists from all over the world—are displayed and offered for sale.

In 1960 the stretch of North Coast Highway (in upper Laguna Beach numbered from 300 to 500) was dubbed **GALLERY ROW** because of the great number of galleries located there. Today more than a dozen display works of art to suit all tastes. The **FIRST THURSDAYS** program (949/497-0722), held on the first Thursday of each month, is an art walk sponsored by the city. Art lovers are shuttled around town to visit 35 different galleries and enjoy the artworks as well as wine and refreshments. The shuttle may be boarded outside the Laguna Museum at 6:35pm. Reservations are not necessary. The **LAGUNA MUSEUM** (307 Cliff Drive, near the intersection of North Coast Highway, just north of Laguna Canyon Road; 949/494-8971) focuses on California art and artists, and on Laguna Beach as an art colony. On First Thursday evenings its hours are extended and admission is free.

The village of Laguna Beach is best enjoyed on foot. There is ample metered parking on its three main streets, which are one-way east to west. The self-guided **HERITAGE WALK AND TOUR OF LAGUNA** is an excellent way to visit the numerous charming and unusual boutiques and galleries while glimpsing Laguna's historic past. Points of interest along the way include the Bette Davis home, Cope House (built in 1887, it's the oldest structure in downtown Laguna), and the Murphy-Smith Historical Bungalow, which was constructed in 1923 and now displays local photos and artifacts. To pick up a map for this interesting tour, drop by the **LAGUNA BEACH VISITORS CENTER** (in the Transit Center, 252 Broadway, just east of Beach Street; 949/497-9229). The **LAGUNA PLAYHOUSE** (606 Laguna Canyon Road, next to the Irvine Bowl; 949/494-8021), which opened its doors in 1920, is one of Orange County's most reputable professional theaters. The five-play main season runs from September to June.

Laguna Beach's main claim to fame may be its artist-colony status, but beach life along its craggy coast thrives too. Each gorgeous beach—and they're all gorgeous—from **CAMEO COVE** to the north to **THREE ARCH BAY** to the south—offers a unique experience, and surfing, tanning, volleyball, people-watching, and tide pool exploration as well. **1000 STEPS BEACH**, adored by locals for its rocky beach and surrounding steep bluffs, is in the South Laguna area below Ninth Avenue. For more information on the area's beaches, contact the Visitors Center (949/497-9229).

RESTAURANTS

Café Zinc / ★★☆

350 OCEAN AVE, LAGUNA BEACH; 949/494-6302
All the elements of Laguna Beach village life merge at this bustling Euro-style sidewalk cafe with zinc-topped tables. Its central location is only a minor reason for long lines at the counter; exceedingly tasty and creative morning and midday eats are the major draws (transcending service that is often coldly brusque). Superior baked goods, home-blended granolas, robust frittatas, and inventive sandwiches all share makings of the highest quality—even the coffee drinks meet sublime standards. The few inside tables fill up only when all of the patio spots are taken. Expect to witness a colorful display of locals at leisure—artists and writers noshing beside cyclists and CEO's, with plenty of dogs leashed to chair legs. The adjacent market is a good source for beach-picnic fixings. *$; no credit cards; checks OK; breakfast, lunch every day; beer and wine; reservations not accepted; between Ocean and Forest Aves.* ♿

Café Zoolu / ★★

860 GLENNEYRE ST, LAGUNA BEACH; 949/494-6825

Artsy, funky, crowded, noisy—this is dining in true Lagunatic style. The work of local artists provides much of the ambience here, and the varied crowd provides the rest. Villagers and inlanders alike flock to this pint-size eatery to dine on Cal-Eclectic dishes prepared in the open kitchen only a few steps from the front door. Hearty soups (often encircling a mound of their famous mashed potatoes), grilled meats, vegetarian fare, and plenty of daily specials make up a small but creative menu that also includes what many consider the best (and biggest) serving of swordfish on the coast. In keeping with the lack of square footage, the wine list is also small, but it's well chosen. Even with reservations, prepare to wait (sans drinks) on the sidewalk as tables turn over slowly. A speedier alternative can be a seat at the counter overlooking the kitchen action, an eye-opening entertainment for anyone who is starry-eyed about the restaurant biz. *$$$; AE, DC, MC, V; no checks; dinner only Wed–Sun; beer and wine; reservations recommended; between St. Ann's Dr and Thalia St.* &

Dexter's / ★★

2892 S PACIFIC COAST HWY, LAGUNA BEACH; 949/497-8912

Talk about an identity crisis. What would you call continental-meets-Pacific-Rim-meets-California-meets-farmer's-market? Imaginative chef-owner Scott Savoy labels it "Global Fusion," and his customers deem it irresistible. Well south of town and right on noisy PCH, this bantam bistro squeezes maximum style out of minimal space, enticing diners with techno-luxe decor and the likes of duck confit, shiitake mushroom and fresh spinach salad with Thai tahini dressing, sweet-and-spicy Jamaican jerk chicken with guava honey chili glaze, or pepper-crusted salmon with champagne sauce. Patrons are a buoyant mix, service is cheerful yet skilled, and the prevailing mood is affably hedonistic. Avoid sitting outdoors (unless you enjoy shouting over traffic); for a peek at chef Scott in action, request a seat at the exhibition kitchen's counter. *$$$; AE, DC, MC, V; no checks; dinner Tues–Sun; beer and wine; reservations recommended; at Nyes Pl.* &

Five Feet / ★★☆

328 GLENNEYRE ST, LAGUNA BEACH; 949/497-4955

What do we call this food? "Contemporary Chinese?" "Asian Eclectic?" "Nouvelle Pacific Rim?" Whatever it's called, chef-owner Michael Kang certainly pioneered it in Orange County, and it has remained popular for over a decade, long outliving the trendy stage. Seafood lovers are very happy here, and few can leave without ordering the signature whole catfish, first marinated in wine, then flash-fried and served with a tomato/peanut/citrus sauce. "Wild Vision" is a typical entree—fresh Hawaiian opakapaka grilled with a soy-balsamic reduction plus tempura soft-shell crab topped with mango-papaya relish and champagne ginger sauce. Prices can edge up here, but portions are hefty and even the wonderful appetizers can make a fantastic feast. The wine list is cleverly chosen. The feel of this place is pure Laguna Beach—small, unusual, and crowded. The joint bustles on weekends, so too much noise is inevitable. It's a rather petite space, boldly decorated with arty industrial flair (Kang, who studied architecture, designed the room). A word of warning: On busy nights, the too-small foyer makes waiting and checking in quite problematic, and parking is tough too. *$$$; AE, DC, DIS, MC, V; no checks; dinner every day; beer and wine; reservations recommended; between Forest Ave and Mermaid St.* &

Picayo / ★★☆

1155 N PACIFIC COAST HWY, LAGUNA BEACH; 949/497-5051

This enchanting cafe reflects the European character of Laguna Beach, offering delicious rewards for those who venture beyond downtown. Partners David Rubin and chef Laurent Brazier combine the flavors of the Mediterranean with the spirit of Southern France to create careful, pretty meals served with finesse. The attractive space with stone floors and Provençal fabrics handles only 20 at a time (dinner is split into two seatings on weekends), but the effect is totally engaging. Seafood often dominates the short dinner menu of select starters and entrees. Don't miss the silky lobster bisque accented with fragrant ribbons of orange zest. A typical entree might be sautéed sea scallops with braised fennel and curried zucchini in lemon chardonnay beurre blanc. Other dishes include pistachio-crusted halibut over mushrooms or charbroiled lamb chops in a beaujolais thyme sauce. The predominantly domestic wine list includes a few gems and a few European imports. Service is courteous and subdued, making this one of Laguna's finest hidden treasures. *$$$; AE, DC, MC, V; no checks; dinner Tues–Sat; beer and wine; reservations recommended; one mile north of Laguna Beach.* &

Taco Loco / ★

640 S COAST HWY, LAGUNA BEACH; 949/497-1635

For over 12 years, this quirky joint has attracted a steady stream of daring diners eager to feast on an offbeat menu of cheap, tasty Mexican munchies. A roster of nearly 20 tacos is the core of the menu here. You can order the standard beef, chicken, or carnitas versions, but that's almost missing the point. Instead, go for an uncommon taco interpretation such as blackened mushroom (tofu optional, but surprisingly good), blackened salmon, or mahi-mahi. The blackened lobster taco is the priciest choice, but worth it. Slapped together in the tiniest kitchen imaginable, tacos are drizzled with your choice of hot, hotter, or hottest sauce and are accompanied by a chunky relish of fresh avocados. The warm tortillas are super-fresh and may be made of corn, blue corn, or whole wheat, depending on what item you've chosen. After placing your order at the cramped counter, grab a wobbly patio table overlooking busy PCH. Add some sunshine, a cold microbrew, and amusing people-watching, and you have the quintessential Laguna Beach feast. $; AE, DC, DIS, MC, V; *no checks; lunch, dinner every day; beer and wine; reservations not accepted; vedamantra@msn.com; between Clio and Legion Sts.* ＆

LODGINGS

Aliso Creek Inn / ★★

31106 S COAST HWY, LAGUNA BEACH; 949/499-2271 OR 800/223-3309
This wonderful resort is a duffer's heaven. It offers a challenging 9-hole, par-32 golf course (part of it in rugged yet serene Laguna Canyon), driving range, excellent pro shop, and lessons from a golf pro. The folks at the inn, which was at one time an apartment building, like to say that they "never rent rooms." What they do rent are comfortable, tastefully appointed studio, one-, and two-bedroom *townhouses* with kitchens and private landscaped patios. One-bedrooms are neatly arranged on a single level, while two-bedrooms are two-story; all accommodations have a lodgelike feel, with comfortable furnishings accentuating the rustic theme. Canyon Lodge American Grill (formerly Ben Brown's), which has a terrace overlooking the golf course and a commanding canyon view, is a Laguna Beach tradition, and the cozy Ben Brown Lounge is the preferred spot for après putting. There's live entertainment and dancing in the lounge on weekends. Completing the sporty package are the large and very clean swimming pool, children's wading pool, and Jacuzzi, all of which are surrounded by thick trees. The business conference facility is excellent. Popular Aliso State Beach is just across PCH, 365 yards from the resort's front entrance. $$$; AE, DC, DIS, MC, V; checks OK; *sales@alisocreekinn.com, www.alisocreekinn.com; north of Dana Point, between Wesley Rd and Crown Valley Pkwy.* ＆

The Carriage House / ★

1322 CATALINA ST, LAGUNA BEACH; 949/494-8945
This disarming two-story seaside country inn is a designated landmark built in the early 1920s in French-Mediterranean style. Located in a pleasant villagelike neighborhood in Laguna's less bustling lower reaches, it's only a mile from the interesting shops, galleries, and eateries of Laguna proper, and the beach is right across Pacific Coast Highway (PCH), only two blocks away. Guests are welcomed with complimentary California wine, fresh fruit, and other goodies. Six suites—some of them with two bedrooms and/or kitchenettes—are built around an open, well-

manicured brick courtyard. Each has a sitting room, private bath, and TV, though no phone. Mandalay has a king bed, an ocean view, and an Asian tropical theme. In Primrose Lane, which has a queen bed, the theme is English country cottage and includes a pretty breakfast nook. Home Sweet Home, with its king bed, is a riot of calico and not unlike sleeping in granny's bedroom. Mockingbird Hill is a two-bedroom with country-French gray and rose decor, handsome fish pictures in the kitchen, and the feel of a wonderful old apartment. A generous breakfast, which is served family-style in the homey dining room or may be enjoyed in the courtyard, includes fresh homemade muesli and granola, a delicious egg dish, fresh baked goods, and more. For $10 extra per night pets are welcome, although leaving them in the room unattended is against the rules. One of the best features of the inn is the hosts'—Andy and Lesley Kettley—attention to detail and pride they take in every aspect of their establishment. *$$; AE, MC, V; checks OK; www.carriagehouse. com; from PCH (near the Pottery Shack), east onto Cress St, past Glenneyre St, south on Catalina St.*

Casa Laguna / ★

2510 S COAST HWY, LAGUNA BEACH; 949/494-2996 OR 949/233-0449
Entering the grounds of Casa Laguna is like stepping back in time to the days when Laguna Beach first gained status as an artists' colony. The establishment is an appealing series of miniature Mission-style structures, comprising 20 rooms and suites, the Mission House, and a cottage, all of which are terraced into the hillside. All are connected by a series of lush and green pathways, stone stairways, gardens, and a courtyard. The entire landscape burgeons with azaleas, hibiscus, bougainvillea, and impatiens. One- and two-bedroom accommodations are immaculate but basic, with cable TV, refrigerators, and furniture that has been around since the '20s and '30s, when the place was built. Courtyard rooms are secluded and open onto the garden. Balcony rooms are airy, open onto an upper terrace, and have a 180-degree view of the Pacific. But the most popular accommodation is the Cottage, which has a living room, dining room, stained-glass windows, a shower for two, and an ocean-view private deck. The Mission House, the owners' former residence, comes replete with its own cross and a bell tower with an observation deck where most guests repair at sundown for wine and tea. Breakfast is part of the deal here, and it's a decent one—nothing fancy, but including fresh fruit and baked goods, cereal, juice, tea, and coffee. Tea and wine, cookies, and hors d'oeuvres are laid out each afternoon. The swimming pool, surrounded by avocado and banana trees, is heated to 82 degrees year round. *$$$; AE, DIS, MC, V; no checks; between Laguna Canyon Rd and Crown Valley Pkwy.*

Eiler's Inn / ★

741 S COAST HWY, LAGUNA BEACH; 949/ 494-3004

Built around a lovely overgrown courtyard with a brick floor, comfy chairs, and a tinkling fountain, this French-Mediterranean–style establishment is located on a section of Coast Highway shaded by magnolia trees. Guests enter the charming brick foyer and get hints of the sweet appointments beyond: a phone booth reminiscent of the old London boxes, a cozy little parlor where one can enjoy a cup of tea or a glass of wine each evening, and a more formal but completely homey parlor with a gas-burning fireplace. Rooms are decorated in individual floral motifs with complementing bedspreads, throw pillows, and curtains. The eclectic mix of furnishings—wicker chairs, predominantly mahogany or cherry dressers, headboards, and side tables—aren't old enough to be classified as rare antiques, but they do give the impression that someone discovered a treasure trove of turn-of-the-century odds and ends in their granny's attic. Some of the ground-floor rooms aren't large, but all are cozy. We recommend snaring an upstairs room for more privacy. One such gem is the Larsen Suite, which has a large, comfortable sitting room with a gas-burning fireplace, full kitchen, bedroom with a king bed, the only TV and VCR in any room, a tremendous ocean view, and easy access to the rooftop patio, which welcomes guests with umbrella tables, chairs, and chaises. It's worth noting that the inn has no bathtubs or phones, but does offer a fine breakfast of fresh fruit, cereal, baked goods, boiled eggs, juice, coffee, and tea. Live music is often presented on weekends. *$$; AE, DIS, MC, V; no checks; near Cleo St.* &

Hotel Laguna / ★★

425 S COAST HWY, LAGUNA BEACH; 949/494-1151 OR 800/524-2927

Easily recognizable by its landmark bell tower, this lustrous old Spanish-style pearl is right on the water at the south end of Main Beach, where it has been weathering storms and earthquakes since 1888. The cream-colored lobby, with a Saltillo-tile floor and a comfortable sitting area, isn't much to look at, but it leads to a charming rose garden that displays many varieties of fragrant roses and brilliant hibiscus, which are in bloom almost year round. It's a favored spot for weddings, with its handsome white gingerbread gazebo near the back wall. Just past the garden are the restaurants: Claes Seafood, Etc., the more casual open-air Terrace Café, and Le Bar. Patronizing any of them is like having a picnic right on the beach, with the sun streaming down and waves crashing onto the sand only yards away. Because this little gem harbors the most popular terrace in the city, count on crowds—usually including a high percentage of Europeans—during fair weather. The 65 pastel-decorated rooms are not nearly as impressive; they're on the small side, and the furnishings, although comfortable, are a bit motelish. Bathrooms are tiny with showers, but only a few have tubs. On the bright side, all the rooms have cable TV and are very clean, and your reservation ensures access to the hotel's private beach club. Even considering the downsides, staying here is a quintessential Southern California experience, best enjoyed by securing an ocean room, where the roar of the waves can actually be heard through a closed window. *$$$; AE, DC, DIS, MC, V; no checks; hotellaguna@ msn.com; www.hotellaguna.com; just south of Main Beach.* &

Surf and Sand Hotel / ★★☆

1555 S PACIFIC COAST HWY, LAGUNA BEACH; 949/497-4477 OR 800/524-8621

Beach lovers think they've died and gone to oceanfront heaven in this place. It's a great environment for kicking back and being lazy. Nothing, except the elevator in the center of this building of 164 rooms and suites, obscures the view of the shimmering Pacific. Upon entering, guests' eyes are immediately drawn past the handsome wooden plantation shutters on the sliding glass doors to the terrace and the sensational view beyond. The new decor throughout is peaches-and-cream, with cushy beds, luxurious modern furnishings, in-room movies, velour robes, hair dryers, a minibar, a spacious marble bath, two-line phones, and a dressing area. VCRs are available through the concierge. Suites have hydro-spa baths and wood-burning fireplaces. But whichever room you choose, at sundown, with the tangerine rays of light beaming through the glass, all the guest rooms and everything in them positively glows. The restaurant, Splashes, has ocean views of the hotel's 500-foot stretch of beach, and there's a lovely, glass-enclosed sea-view pool with a surfside bar. *$$$$; AE, DC, DIS, MC, V; checks OK; www.jcresorts.com; near Bluebird Canyon Rd.* &

Dana Point

Cape Cod architecture and evocatively named streets are only part of the charm this tiny community holds for residents and visitors. It was named in homage to Richard Henry Dana, who immortalized the area in his much-adored *Two Years Before the Mast*, which he penned after a sail around Cape Horn in 1835 aboard the *Pilgrim*. The author wrote admiringly about the region's windswept headlands, sweeping ocean vistas, steep bluffs, and the violent smash of the sea against them. In the early 19th century, the coves along the beach were a haven for pirates raiding the nearby Catholic mission, San Juan Capistrano. Today you can gaze down from any of the dizzying blufftop vantage points at the replica of the tall ship *Pilgrim* anchored in the harbor below, and imagine those bygone days. Under the auspices of the **ORANGE COUNTY MARINE INSTITUTE** (24200 Dana Point Harbor Drive; 949/496-2274), there are activities aboard the *Pilgrim*. The Institute also sponsors marine-mammal-watching expeditions and educational cruises aboard the research vessel *Sea Explorer*. **DANA COVE PARK**, a popular picnicking spot, is on the left abutting the institute. To the south is the entrance to **DOHENY STATE BEACH** (949/496-3627). Managed by the Department of Parks and Recreation, the beach park is a 62-acre site with tide pools, a mile of sandy beach, some of the best surfing in the county, camping, and picnicking. North of Doheny State Beach at the north end of Dana Point is **STRANDS BEACH**, perhaps Orange County's most beautiful beach. Here, the steep and rocky headlands gently smooth out. Further south, **CAPISTRANO STATE BEACH**, followed by **PRIMA DESHECHA CANADA BEACH**, are both broad, sandy, and exquisite, with plenty of parking along the way. The **DANA POINT/CAPISTRANO BEACH CHAMBER OF COMMERCE AND TOURIST BUREAU** (24681 La Plaza; 949-496-1555) has a hotline with tourist information.

RESTAURANTS

Ritz-Carlton Dining Room / ★★★☆
Ritz-Carlton Club Grill & Bar / ★★★

I RITZ-CARLTON DR, DANA POINT; 949/240-5008
One of the county's choicest venues for a formal, opulent evening, the Dining Room at the Ritz-Carlton Laguna Niguel is favored by traditionalists for its serene setting and first-class approach to service and cuisine. As is the Ritz-Carlton custom, menu choices are many, but all make use of the finest ingredients available. Much of chef Yvon Goetz's seasonal menu borrows from Southern France and the Mediterranean with a welcome touch of his native Alsace added. Entrees include wild mushrooms and foie gras–crusted fillet of turbot with champagne and watercress cream, or Colorado lamb medallions with cannellini beans, roasted eggplant, thyme flowers, and red pepper essence. The prix-fixe menu pairing five courses with wines is always noteworthy—and a (relative) value. The hotel's Club Grill & Bar is less ceremonious, slightly more affordable, and somewhat more approachable. Here, guests enjoy more traditional but still outstanding fare like whole roast baby chicken with garlic potatoes and chardonnay jus or ale-marinated rib eye with crisp zucchini and potato herb hash. *$$$–$$; AE, DIS; MC, V; no checks; lunch, dinner every day; full bar; reservations recommended; www. ritzcarlton.com/location/NorthAmerica/LagunaNiguel/dining.htm; off Pacific Coast Hwy, north of Dana Point.* &

LODGINGS

Blue Lantern Inn / ★★

34343 STREET OF THE BLUE LANTERN, DANA POINT; 949/661-1304 OR 949/950-1236

Located on a bluff above lovely Dana Point Harbor, the Blue Lantern Inn may be part of a chain (Four Sisters Inns), but it doesn't feel like it. There are so many niceties that despite its 29 rooms, the atmosphere is more like that of an intimate bed and breakfast than a small hotel. Almost every window in the Cape Cod–style structure offers a panoramic ocean view. The complimentary full breakfast, including a hot egg dish, cereal, fresh fruit, and baked goods, with the morning sunlight streaming in, couldn't be more pleasant as the deft and courteous waitstaff moves quietly about refilling cups of coffee. Each of the rooms, decorated in luxurious-seaside-shanty style, has a queen or king bed, a large bathroom with a spa tub, a sitting area, and a gas-log fireplace. The Tower and Pacific Edge rooms have private decks that offer especially spectacular views of the bluff and of Dana Point Harbor. There's also a meeting room, a fitness center, and bicycles available for exploring the coast and pretty Dana Point. Each afternoon, hors d'oeuvres and wine await guests in the cozy library. *$$$; AE, MC, V; no checks; turn west from PCH/Pacifica Del Prado.* &

The Ritz-Carlton, Laguna Niguel / ★★★☆

I RITZ-CARLTON DRIVE, DANA POINT; 949/240-2000 OR 949/241-3333

Nestled within a tranquil blufftop grove overlooking the sea, this swank Mediterranean-style palace reminds us what gracious living is all about. "Choice" is the adjective that describes everything here, from the manicured grounds and the two mammoth swimming pools—especially the glittering aquamarine Dana Pool surrounded by towering palms—to the magnificent lobby with its plush carpets, gleaming woodwork, and lavish floral arrangements. The guest rooms—393 of them, including suites and Club Suites—are spacious, yet cozy and hushed. Every possible concession to comfort has been made including plush terry robes, marble tubs, hair dryers, toiletries, twice-daily maid service, laundry service, 24-hour room service, and a well stocked minibar. Not all the rooms have ocean views, and it's worth it to pay extra to get one, but each one has French doors that open onto a terrace furnished with a white wrought-iron table and chairs. The ultra-chic and exclusive Ritz-Carlton Club Floor has a private concierge, open bar, all-day light meals, and a secluded after-dinner lounge. Reservations may be made through the concierge for golf at the challenging 18-hole Links at Monarch Beach, adjoining the property. There are four tennis courts on the hotel property along with a top-of-the-line gym. The gleaming spa offers aromatherapy, Swedish and shiatsu massage, steam and sauna rooms, and a full-service salon—everything, in short, to encourage the sense of being pampered that surrounds guests the moment they enter the lobby. In the Ritz-Carlton's elegant Dining Room, the French-Mediterranean menu changes daily. More casual dining is available in the Supper Club Grill. For casual, outdoor, ocean-view dining all day (weather permitting) there's the Ocean Terrace Restaurant, and California cuisine is served all day in the Terrace Restaurant, which also has a commanding view of the Pacific. Drinks are available in the Lobby Bar, and tea is served every day in the snug and comfortable Library. The use of beach equipment—chairs, towels, umbrellas, and boogie boards— is included in the price of the room, and arrangements can be made for baby-sitting. One of the most marvelous aspects of this place, for all its poshness, is that guests pad through the lobby, and back and forth along the beach path, in their bathrobes. At sunset, the best place to be is relaxing, drink in hand, in a cushy lounge chair on one of the terraces, just sitting back and watching the show. It's *all* good. *$$$$; AE, DC, DIS, MC, V; checks OK; off Pacific Coast Hwy, north of Dana Point.* &

San Clemente

This relaxed and uncomplicated little beach town is something of a wel-come respite after the frenetic activity in Huntington, Newport, and Laguna Beaches. The village, which runs along Avenida del Mar below N El Camino Real, is comfortably down-at-heel and crammed with antique shops and resale clothing shops a bit more downscale than those in Corona del Mar and Newport Beach. The **HERITAGE OF SAN CLEMENTE MUSEUM** (415 N El Camino Real (PCH), between Avenida Palizada and Avenida del Mar; 949/369-1299) strives to maintain the uniquely sleepy charming character of the community, modeled on turn-of-the-century developer Ole Hansen's idea of a Spanish village. The museum has several interesting permanent exhibits including "Remem-brances of San Clemente—Photos of the 1920s and 1930s," "Legends of Surfing," and "The Western White House—President Nixon's Years in San Clemente." On palm-fringed **SAN CLEMENTE STATE BEACH** (949/492-3156), near the historic **SAN CLEMENTE PIER**, volleyball playing and watching are favored activities. The pretty 1-mile stretch of beach, abut-ting headlands with landscaped blufftops, also offers opportunities for scuba and abalone diving (seasonal), swimming, and board and body surfing. For beach equipment rentals, try **ROCKY'S SURF CITY** (100 S El Camino Real, at the corner of Avenida Del Mar; 949/361-2946). The **CALAFIA PARK** beach area is just south of the state beach. It's wilder and more secluded and has great surfing. The staff of the **SAN CLEMENTE CHAMBER OF COMMERCE/TOURIST INFORMATION CENTER** (1100 Camino Real; 949/492-1131) is extremely helpful and friendly.

LODGINGS

Beachcomber Motel / ★★

533 AVENIDA VICTORIA, SAN CLEMENTE; 949/492-5457 OR 888/492-5457
There's nothing even remotely fancy about this 50-year-old place. Don't expect any frills, any extra services, or even a lot of privacy. But this is one of the few Orange County hostelries that fulfill your primary reason for visiting the region in the first place: it's virtually on the beach. The glistening Pacific is just beyond a green grassy bluff fronting each of the motel's 12 vaguely Spanish-style cottages. Rooms are studios or one bedrooms, each with cable TV and a kitchenette. The decor is strictly motel (though it's shabby in a friendly way rather than a depressing one), and there's not much in the way of added amenities; but the place is exceedingly clean and tidy inside and out. Each cottage has its own porch with a set of comfortable chairs. Barbecue facilities and picnic tables are scattered over the lawn. It's also right next to the San Clemente Pier, and an easy walk to San Clemente shops and restaurants. Relaxing in a chair on the porch of a Beachcomber cottage and gazing out over the sea, you'll really appreciate San Clemente's city motto: "Where the good life comes in on waves." *$$; AE, DIS, MC, V; no checks; near San Clemente Pier.*

San Juan Capistrano

Father Junípero Serra and his brown-robed group of Franciscan missionaries were drawn to San Juan Capistrano in the 18th century by the area's abundance of fresh water, its fertile land, and its extensive population of Native American prospective converts. Construction on the **MISSION SAN JUAN CAPISTRANO** (at the intersection of Ortega Highway and Camino Capistrano; 949/248-2040), the seventh in the Spanish mission system in California, began in 1776. It was periodically expanded to accommodate the increasing number of "neophytes" enslaved to work the hundreds of acres of surrounding farmland, herd the livestock, and man the weaving, soap- and candle-making, tanning, and iron-smelting operations the mission's economy depended on, and by 1796 its population had swelled to almost 2,000. The crown jewel of California's mission chain, which has undergone constant restoration, still stands on the original 10-acre plot. The historical site's attractions include the ruins of the original stone church, the cool white Serra Chapel (one of the oldest Spanish structures in California), the museum where the mission's founding documents are on display, the friars' quarters, soldiers' barracks, the ancient olive mill, the cemetery full of broken headstones, and the well-tended gardens that lead to the lovely central courtyard.

For a larger taste of the area's history, try the city-sponsored, do-it-yourself **SAN JUAN CAPISTRANO WALKING TOUR**. The tour includes

Rios Adobe house, constructed in 1794, the Los Rios area (California's first residential neighborhood, circa 1870), Garcia Adobe house (circa 1880), and Egan House. Maps may be obtained from the helpful folks at the **CHAMBER OF COMMERCE** (2nd Floor, El Adobe Plaza, on Camino Capistrano between Forster and Del Obispo Streets; 949/493-4700).

Apart from its historical importance, the city itself is as attractive for visitors as it is for the **SWALLOWS** who instinctively return each March and stay through October. The birds may be indifferent to the community's wide array of gift and clothing boutiques, cafes, and numerous antique shops along **ANTIQUE ROW** (at Camino Capistrano between Acjachema and Del Obispo Streets; 949/493-4700), but they're wild about the mission, the power lines, and the eaves of many other town structures. The red-brick **CAPISTRANO DEPOT** (26762 Verdugo Street, below Camino Capistrano; 800/USA-RAIL) is noteworthy for its dome as well as historical significance. Constructed in 1894 by the Santa Fe railroad, the miniature station (still an Amtrak stop) now houses a restaurant and shops too. The **VINTAGE BRICK JAIL**, out of use since the mid-1800s but great for photo ops, is just across the tracks. Both are adjacent to the beautifully landscaped red-brick **CAPISTRANO PLAZA**, one of the most pleasant and pretty spots in the entire community. For nightlife, try the popular **COACH HOUSE** (33157 Camino Capistrano, just north of Stonehill Drive; 949/496-8927).

RESTAURANTS

Ramos House Café / ★★

31752 LOS RIOS ST, SAN JUAN CAPISTRANO; 949/443-1342

Talented and inventive chef-owner John Humphries plays seasonal changes on a small but ever-changing menu of New and Regional American daytime meals. But equally beguiling is the Old California character of this tiny, virtually hidden historic structure (circa 1881) whose dining room is simply a lush brick patio shaded by mature trees and colorful vines. A hearty spinach, bacon, and caramelized-onion scramble is typical morning fare, joined by sautéed potatoes, spiced applesauce, and one perfect biscuit. Lunch might be an ample crock of garden-inspired soup with cheesy bread twists, a robust warm salad, or a smoked turkey and wild mushroom sandwich. Humphries is a gifted baker as well, so it pays to order any dish involving his oven skills (try warm berry and banana shortcake for dessert). Partner Lisa Waterman oversees the front of the house, ably leading a breezy crew of young locals sporting denim overalls and warm smiles. The city's historic Rios District offers lots of charm, and live entertainment is provided by the rumbling and whistle of the train you can almost touch from your table. *$; AE, DC, DIS, MC, V; no checks; breakfast, lunch Tues–Sun; beer and wine; reservations accepted for large parties only; at Del Obispo St.* &

Irvine

The original Irvine Ranch, acquired by James Irvine and his partners in 1864, was composed of acreage included in Spanish and Mexican land grants dating back to the 16th and 17th centuries. In 1894 James Irvine II incorporated the land and formed the Irvine Company. The 200 square miles of the original ranch represented a full quarter of Orange County's land area. Although the Irvine Company has sold off more than half its holdings for development, it still retains more than 54,000 acres. Today's community of Irvine, incorporated 25 years ago, is a meticulously planned, frighteningly homogeneous group of single-family-dwelling developments, more than 50 apartment communities, and a number of towering glass and steel business mega-complexes. Surrounding the cookie-cutter communities are 20,000 acres of open pasture where cattle still roam and 8,000 cultivated acres producing citrus, avocados, and various other food crops plus flowers, trees, and shrubs for Southern California commercial nurseries. In an emphatic nod to ecological concerns, the Irvine Company has apportioned more than 21,000 acres as a reserve for endangered species of plants and animals, which will become the center of a 36,000-acre Orange County Nature Reserve.

The community of Irvine sprang up around the **UNIVERSITY OF SOUTHERN CALIFORNIA'S IRVINE CAMPUS (UCI)** (bounded by University Drive to the north, Culver Drive to the west, Bonita Canyon Drive to the south, and Newport Coast Drive to the east; 949/824-5011; www.uci.edu), constructed on land donated by the Irvine Company. The focus at the cool, quiet, and spartan **IRVINE MUSEUM** (12th floor, 18881 Von Karman Avenue, near Campus Drive; 949/476-2565; www.irvine-museum.org) is California impressionism between 1890 and 1930, a regional offshoot of the American impressionism movement. Though its permanent collection once consisted almost exclusively of the works of Joan Irvine Smith (now exhibited at UCI), in recent years the museum has built a wider collection, and in addition presents a variety of shows that change quarterly.

Built into a hillside, **IRVINE MEADOWS AMPHITHEATER** (8808 Irvine Center Drive; 949/855-8096) is Irvine's answer to the Hollywood Bowl—sort of. It *is* possible to picnic there on delicacies from your own basket, but only before performances of the Pacific Orchestra. For other large-venue musical events, unimpressive food and drink must be purchased inside the grounds. Still, with 10,000 reserved seats and 4,500 lawn seats, it's one of Irvine's main draws.

For a change of pace, try Irvine's **OLD TOWNE**. It was established in 1887 by James Irvine II as the shipping center for produce from the Irvine Ranch. There are shops and restaurants, and among the historic buildings you may tour are the blacksmith shop, the old garage, a tenant farm-house, the general store, and La Quinta Inn (see Lodgings, below). The **IRVINE CHAMBER OF COMMERCE** (17755 Sky Park E, Suite 101; 949/660-9112, www.irvinechamber.com; icc@irvinechamber.com) is a useful source of tourist information.

RESTAURANTS

Bistango / ★★★

19100 VON KARMAN AVE, IRVINE; 949/752-5222
A happening scene ever since it opened in 1987, stylish Bistango continues to attract the movers and shakers of corporate Irvine. A sprawling art gallery, lively jazz club, and dashing restaurant fused together under one atrium, Bistango hums with energy from lunch to happy hour to dinner to late-night dancing. Austrian-born Chef Paul Gstrein offers a modern take on continental cuisine, featuring such entrees as melt-in-your-mouth tuna grilled rare on Asian vegetables with subtle sesame vinaigrette and green horseradish, and juicy rack of lamb with mashed potatoes and a rich port wine sauce. Daily specials always include one of the county's best-value prix-fixe dinners. There's a long list of wood-oven pizzas, deservedly favored by many. Weekly wine and champagne tastings are well run and a great value for discriminating palates. *$$$; AE, DC, MC, V; no checks; lunch Mon–Fri, dinner every day; full bar; reservations recommended; Bistango@net999.com; www.Bistango.com; ground floor of Atrium office complex.* &

Prego / ★★☆

18420 VON KARMAN AVE, IRVINE; 949/553-1333
Given its mundane location in the maze of corporate Irvine, it's rather amazing that Prego oozes so much undiluted Italian style and spirit. Sleek and chic (think Milan, not Florence), the inflection here is utterly Italian, from the pop songs and magazines in the bar to the dapper waiters to the basket of grissini that begins every meal. All pastas are homemade and of the highest quality; some of the best are spinach gnocchi with gorgonzola, pumpkin tortelloni with mascarpone sauce, and lobster-filled agnolotti with lemon sauce. Rotisserie meats (duck, rabbit, chicken) are also handled well, and grilled items like veal chops, rack of lamb, and flank steak round out the diverse menu. Crisp white linens, gleaming wood floors, and low-slung banquette seating give the room an air of sophistication. The executive crowd adds its own panache. *$$$; AE, DC, MC, V; no checks, lunch Mon–Fri, dinner every day; full bar; reservations recommended; between Main St and Michelson Dr, entrance faces Michelson Dr.* &

Ruth's Chris Steak House / ★★☆

2961 MICHELSON DR, IRVINE; 949/252-8848

The richly marbled USDA Prime and other premium cuts of steak here are the best that money can buy. Midwest-bred and aged to exacting standards are Ruth's Chris's claims to steak fame. They insist the reason portions are so large—12 to 22 ounces—is because larger cuts retain more natural juices during broiling. Cooked to your taste and delivered sizzling in butter, the beef here is exceptionally tender and flavorful. A variety of fresh vegetables, including seven styles of potato, salads with made-fresh dressings, and homemade desserts complete the feast. More relaxed than its chief competitor, Morton's of Chicago (you can leave your suit jacket in the car), Ruth's Chris still retains a trace of its easygoing New Orleans origins. Since the kitchen is out of sight and out of earshot, the wood-paneled room with its roomy leather booths is spared the accompanying frenzy. Service is gracious and personalized. An extensive wine list offers suitable bottles at nearly every price. Another location of this national chain is on Beverly Drive in Beverly Hills (see the L.A. Restaurants section). *$$$; AE, DC, DIS, MC, V; no checks; dinner every day; full bar; reservations recommended; www.ruthschris.com; in Park Place center, off Michelson Dr at Jamboree Rd.* &

Trilogy / ★★☆

18201 VON KARMAN AVE, IRVINE; 949/955-0757

Tucked into Irvine's hyper-corporate zone, Trilogy succeeds by supplying a warm, handsome gathering place that's short on attitude and long on comfort. Muted acoustics allow easy conversation, even when a jazz combo performs (generally Wednesday through Saturday). The owners label the cuisine Creative American, though it also qualifies as New Continental. Whatever the designation, it could also be dubbed scrumptious. The menu offers a balanced mix of the fantastic and the familiar. Commendable starters include spicy Maryland crab cakes with parsnip slaw and saffron aioli or the rich corn chowder with rock shrimp and the mellow zing of chiles. Entree choices are enticing: Pacific halibut in a golden crust of potato slices with a side of "melted" leeks, crisp Muscovy duck breast with tart cherries in a zinfandel reduction, or seared ahi enhanced with smoked-trout hash and braised baby artichokes. The seasonally changing menu is reinforced by a fitting wine list with some excellent by-the-glass options. Service is adept without being overly mannered. When weather permits, consider the green, serene, bamboo-walled patio—one of the area's better outdoor rooms. *$$$; AE, DC, DIS, MC, V; no checks; lunch Mon–Fri, dinner Mon–Sat; full bar; reservations recommended; between Main St and Michelson Dr on ground floor of TransAmerica Bldg.* &

LODGINGS

La Quinta Inn / ★

14972 SAND CANYON AVE, IRVINE; 949/551-0909 OR 949/687-6667
A large portion of this establishment, which is listed on the National Registry of Historic Places and is located at the edge of Irvine's Old Towne, once functioned as an Irvine Ranch granary for the storage of several hundred tons of lima beans. The hexagonal granary's 98 honeycomb silos have been converted to comfortable, pleasant, and atmospheric guest rooms, decorated in a sophisticated country style. The newer part of the inn features 50 more straightforward rooms, which have big-screen TVs, cable, in-room movies, video games, and dataports. The inn is very clean, and the staff is accommodating. The continental breakfast is complimentary, and there's a free shuttle to the airport. One of the pluses of staying here is its proximity to the Irvine Spectrum business complex and the Irvine Spectrum Center entertainment complex. *$$; AE, DC, DIS, MC, V; no checks; www.laquinta.com; off the 5 Fwy's Sand Canyon Ave exit.* &

Costa Mesa

Costa Mesa is one of the fastest growing cultural, retail, and business centers in the U.S. It's also the location of **TOWN CENTER**, universally accepted as Orange County's cultural core. At first glance, the Town Center complex resembles just another concrete-and-glass corridor of professional office buildings, a place one passes through on the way to somewhere else. Take a closer look and you'll see that the façade of one of the buildings—Segerstrom Hall—is graced with Richard Lippold's stunning steel-and-aluminum *Fire Bird*. Segerstrom Hall and its companion tower, the more intimate Founders Hall, compose the **ORANGE COUNTY PERFORMING ARTS CENTER (OCPAC)** (600 Town Center Drive; 714/556-ARTS; www.ocpac.org). Segerstrom Hall, with its 3,000-seat capacity, fantastic acoustics, and excellent sightlines, hosts **OPERA PACIFIC**, the **PACIFIC SYMPHONY ORCHESTRA**, **PACIFIC POPS**, and the **PACIFIC CHORALE**, along with engagements by such world-renowned performers as the **AMERICAN BALLET THEATER** and Sir Neville Marriner's **ACADEMY OF ST. MARTIN-IN-THE-FIELDS** Orchestra. Founders Hall hosts the **CHAMBER MUSIC SERIES "A LITTLE LUNCH MUSIC"** as well as a wide variety of concerts offering jazz, blues, and other forms of popular music. Tours of both halls are available Monday, Wednesday, and Saturday. Adjacent to OCPAC is the outdoor **NOGUCHI SCULPTURE GARDEN**. It parallels Anton Boulevard (the intersection just east of Town Center Drive) and features Noguchi's visually startling *California*

Scenario, which simultaneously captures the essence of the area's Southwestern soul and the terror of the yawning San Andreas fault, all in the tranquil setting of a Japanese rock garden. There are notable works by **HENRY MOORE, JOAN MIRÓ,** and others as well.

Costa Mesa's ascension to the throne as the county's cultural crowned head began more than 35 years ago, when **SOUTH COAST REPERTORY** (655 Town Center Drive; 714/708-5500) opened its doors. Like Los Angeles's Mark Taper Forum, SCR mounts consistently fine productions of wide appeal, often featuring big-name L.A. talent. And, like the Taper's, several of SCR's productions have gone on to the Great White Way and have earned Tony awards there.

Blessed with lovely tinkling fountains, elegant courts, and an ornate and lovely children's carousel, **SOUTH COAST PLAZA** (Bristol Street between Anton Boulevard and Sunflower Avenue, directly across from OCPAC) and its adjacent partners—**CRYSTAL COURT, SOUTH COAST VILLAGE,** and **METRO SQUARE**—compose one of the largest shopping megalopolises in the world, where the best major department stores and designer boutiques are only steps apart. Another nice stop to make in this area is the **ROBERT MONDAVI WINE & FOOD CENTER** (1570 Scenic Avenue, off S Harbor Boulevard; 714/979-4510) where, in a building set in a rose garden and a sculpture garden, the Mondavi chefs share their secrets, wine experts offer lectures, and there are various other wine and food events.

In amusing contrast to the ultra-modern, ultra-high-hat Town Center and South Coast Plaza, Costa Mesa is also the location of the **ORANGE COUNTY FAIR AND EXPOSITION CENTER** (88 Fair Drive; 714/708-3247). The County Fair runs annually in July, but almost every weekend of the year there's a **SWAP MEET**—the best in the county—and admission is only a dollar. In addition, there's a **FARMERS MARKET** each Thursday morning in the parking lot, with incredibly fresh and delicious produce. In spring, summer, and fall, enjoy hair-raising motorcycle racing at the **SPEEDWAY,** and tour **CENTENNIAL FARM,** a genuine working farm, any time of the year.

Information on the above attractions is available by calling the fairgrounds (714/708-3247). The **COSTA MESA CHAMBER OF COMMERCE** (1700 Adams Avenue; 714/885-9090) offers further information on the town's attractions.

RESTAURANTS

Diva / ★★☆

600 ANTON BLVD, COSTA MESA; 714/754-0600

As any producer will tell you, divas are gorgeous, theatrical, enchanting, and capricious, and this one is no exception. Just a short, pleasant walk from the Orange County Performing Arts Center and the South Coast Repertory, upscale Diva is a natural for pre- or post-theater dining with a dramatic flourish. Seductively lit with a soaring ceiling and lavishly adorned with jewel tones and an imposing gilded mirror, this is clearly a Big Night Out destination. Featuring contemporary creations by Orange County chef-entrepreneur John Sharpe (also of Bistro 201 and Topaz Café), Diva's menu is organized into "small" and "large" plates, such as the house seafood sampler and grilled hearts of romaine with Stilton/port swirl (both small plates) and grilled prawns on spaghetti squash or roast rack of lamb on wilted spinach with crisp fingerling potatoes (large plates). Appearances reign supreme here, from the sky-high food presentations to the spiffily dressed waitstaff to the designer-clad diners. Kitchen performance is solid (if slightly uninspired), but service is frustratingly uneven, bouncing from adroit to amateurish. Live jazz on weekends makes the lounge a stylish choice for nightcaps or dessert. *$$$; AE, MC, DC, V; no checks; lunch Mon–Fri, dinner Mon–Sat; full bar; Divascp@ aol.com; lobby level of Plaza Tower building.* &

The Golden Truffle / ★★

1767 NEWPORT BLVD, COSTA MESA; 949/645-9858
Maverick chef/owner Alan Greeley uncharacteristically understates his position when he says "It's never boring here; we cook on the edge." Indeed, Greeley continues to excite chefs, foodies, and other daring souls with his broadly eclectic cuisine. With a menu that bounces between "utility foods" such as macaroni and cheese with black truffles and weekly specials on regional, ethnic, or ingredient themes, diners should expect the unexpected (duck tacos, veal dumplings). A decidedly unchic location in a quirky strip mall hardly deters fans of this low-key bistro. Insiders call ahead to be sure Greeley is in the kitchen. Also noteworthy is Greeley's adventurous approach to his wine selections, featuring unsung varietals from far-flung locales. *$$$; AE, MC, V; no checks; lunch, dinner Tues–Sat; beer and wine; reservations recommended; www. thegoldentruffle.com; between 17th St and Industrial Wy.* &

Memphis / ★★

2920 BRISTOL ST, COSTA MESA; 714/432-7685
Housed in a former tavern of dubious repute, Memphis preserves a bit of the previous tenant's funkiness while adding a spin all its own. It's pretty much Aunt Lizzie's kitchen meets *Melrose Place* and takes her act to Orange County. The backbone of the compact menu here is Southern cooking, updated with contemporary ingredients and the quirky vision of chef-partner Diego Velasco. Diners here get a lot of talent on their plate for little cash. A grilled center-cut pork chop is accompanied by grits and a balsamic-cherry sauce. Creole shrimp gets its fire from chipotle chile vinaigrette. Roasted chicken breast with mustard greens and grilled corn

295

is set off with a lemon-thyme sauce. The feisty gumbo is also a winner. The scene is pretty basic—a simple room of spare tables, good tunes, and retro touches. The mixed crowd stays jovial even when service fluctuates from positively gracious to perfunctory. *$$; AE, DC, MC, V; no checks; lunch Mon–Fri, dinner every day, brunch Sat and Sun; beer and wine; reservations recommended; between Randolph and Baker Aves.* &

Pinot Provence / ★★★

686 ANTON BLVD, COSTA MESA; 714/444-5900

Orange County foodies were positively giddy in 1998 when celebrity chef Joachim Splichal, longtime darling of the L.A. gourmet scene, opened this addition to his empire. Gastronomes familiar with Splichal's other efforts (Patina in Hollywood, Pinto Bistro in Sherman Oaks, Pinot Hollywood) will note that this bistro has its own distinct personality—that of a Provençal château complete with village antiques, a mammoth fireplace, and a limestone archway. French-born Florent Marneau (formerly of Aubergine and Pascal) is executive chef here, executing a novel menu divided between Provençal dishes and those from other regions of France. Marneau, who shops local farmers markets for the freshest ingredients, presents somewhat lighter French fare than the bistro menus at other Splichalian haunts. If you're lucky, it will include appetizers such as a melange of marinated haricots verts, baked tomatoes, sautéed fennel, quail egg–topped brioche, and a pungent olive tapenade; or perhaps a sampling of seasoned olives; chilly raw oysters; or fritters of *brandade*, a tasty salt-cod purée. Noteworthy entrees include heaven-scented lavender lamb chops, tender rack of pork with cherries, and plats du jour such as a hearty *daube* of stewed lamb shanks with couscous. Yellow-striped banquettes with pillows provide tasteful seating indoors, and two cozy garden rooms make for lovely patio interludes. At press time the waitstaff had not yet hit its professional stride, but management is earnest, and the wine service supporting an inviting list can be quite expert. *$$$; AE, DC, DIS, MC, V; no checks; breakfast, lunch, dinner every day; full bar; reservations recommended; in South Coast Plaza, facing Bristol St.* &

Sidestreet Café / ★

1799 NEWPORT BLVD, COSTA MESA; 714/650-1986

Wedged into an offbeat shopping strip, Sidestreet Café is a tiny operation with a big heart. One glance at the handwritten menu in this homey, cheerful spot and it's clear breakfast is a passion here. Pages of appetizing scrambles, egg sandwiches, omelets, burritos, and "griddle goodies" make decisions difficult, and everything tastes even yummier than it sounds. Typical items include roasted corn cakes, spicy chorizo and eggs (including the essential beans, rice, and tortillas), and diced ham scramble loaded with cheese plus taters and toast. Rightfully billed as "huge and delicious," the cinnamon roll proved too big for two—but what a way to indulge. Hearty eaters will appreciate "Soul Food" platters of robust stuff like sirloin tidbits and eggs covered with mushroom-wine sauce. A loyal following creates long waits for only 40 or so seats. To avoid delays, come weekdays, or early (before 8am) or late (after 2pm) on weekends. *$; no credit cards; checks OK; breakfast, lunch every day; no alcohol; reservations not accepted; between 17th St and Industrial Wy.* &

Troquet / ★★★⯪

333 BRISTOL ST, COSTA MESA; 714/708-6865

Troquet is a bistro in the finest sense. Neither hectic nor noisy, it's a poised, seductive room where time slows and astute patrons savor the area's best French cuisine. Unlike some of Orange County's French restaurants, there is no worn-out reverence for all things Gallic; but chef-owner Tim Goodell's considerable talent is evident on every plate. He and wife Liza (also a chef, and the designer of the sensuous setting) have rapidly vaulted to the top of the culinary scene with their newest try. Originally the creators behind Aubergine (the tiny Newport Beach bistro with a big reputation), the duo closed their first effort to open this larger spot, awash in amber lighting, vintage French liquor posters, and fine crystal. One can easily build an impressive repast just from the many appetizer offerings, such as a tart of plump escargots and wild mushrooms with a pungent herb salad, or prawns wrapped in prosciutto atop fragrant curried couscous. As for entrees, options are dazzling. From potato-wrapped salmon with baby artichokes to crisp veal sweetbreads with sautéed leeks to an impeccably roasted chicken with perfect pommes frites, each plate is an indulgence. True foodies will fancy Troquet's tasting menu, several small courses that showcase the kitchen's many fortes. This is one of Orange County's few such menus—a special event with great value (you can drive to L.A. and pay more for less). Desserts are mostly divine, and the cheese platter positively seduces. *$$$; AE, DC, MC, V; no checks; lunch, dinner Mon–Sat; full bar; reservations recommended; third floor on the north side of South Coast Plaza near Nordstrom, near Sunflower Ave.* &

Tustin

RESTAURANTS

Caffé Piemonte / ★★⯪

498 E IST ST, TUSTIN; 714/544-8072

Even though Orange County has a surplus of notable Italian restaurants, this unassuming shopping-center trattoria stands out. Hard-working siblings Giovanni and Luigi Ravetto and Luigi's wife, Amy, have garnered both awards and a devout clientele by presenting a polished range of

Northern Italian dishes that stress quality over quantity. (Purists might note that the menu doesn't truly concentrate on the earthy flavors of Italy's Piemonte region, but no matter.) Every menu item is deftly prepared, with top ingredients and perfect balance. The divine lobster ravioli is perhaps the most popular offering, but regulars who order nothing else are missing out on other superb pastas and meats, such as the classic creamy polenta with fontina or the crisp veal schnitzel. The simple quarters are just a tad above basic (opt for a booth if you can), with glass-topped tables and white plantation shutters that add intimacy and shield diners from a mundane view of the parking lot. Service is polite (if brusque). The wine list needs more depth, though such quibbles don't deter loyalists. *$$$; AE, MC, V; no checks; lunch Tues–Fri, dinner Tues–Sun; beer and wine; between Prospect Ave and Centennial St.* &

Zov's Bistro / ★★☆
Zov's Bakery / ★★☆

17440 E 17TH ST, TUSTIN; 714/838-8855

What began as a first-timer's attempt at unpretentious bistro cooking has steadily evolved into a thriving culinary enterprise, carefully nurtured by quality-obsessed Zov Karamardian and her family. The contemporary bistro grows more stylish with each facelift and currently sports curved pillars, oversized floral arrangements, and dramatic gold and purple lighting. It still serves a pleasing (and ever-changing) selection of contemporary continental fare, often with authentic Mediterranean overtones. The main room is a bustling scene at both lunch and dinner, so many diners opt for the tented patio, where they enjoy favorites like rack of lamb, fresh seafood, and inventive pastas in relative calm. Zov's Bakery (around in back) offers slightly more casual all-day dining from an ample menu of salads, sandwiches, and entrees that includes a revered rotisserie chicken. Although the patio is inviting, many of the dishes travel well and make for great picnic fixings. The bakery side also does a brisk business in sublime artisan breads and scrumptious, sinful desserts. *$$; AE, DC, MC, V; no checks; Bistro: lunch Mon–Sat, dinner Tues–Sat; Bakery: breakfast, lunch Mon–Sat, dinner Tues–Sat; beer and wine; reservations recommended for the Bistro; www.zovs.com; at the east end of Enderle Center.* &

Orange

RESTAURANTS

Citrus City Grille / ★★

122 N GLASSELL ST, ORANGE; 714/639-9600

This 1996 addition to Old Towne, the charming historic heart of Orange, was heartily embraced by locals hungry for contemporary cuisine close to home. Almost hip for Old Towne (but in an easygoing way), the stylishly renovated space boasts lofty ceilings, daring colors, and giant reproductions of bright, vintage orange-crate labels. The strong selection of starters includes dishes like roasted tomato and mushroom napoleon with saffron essence, coconut shrimp tempura with a spicy apricot sauce, and potato and charred leek soup. On the entree side, pastas, fish, and meat dishes dominate. Solid bets include the sea bass in an oyster and lemongrass sauce with couscous and the grilled pork loin chop with fig-balsamic demi-glace, caramelized onions, and garlic mashed potatoes. The lunch menu features pizzas, sandwiches, and lighter entrees like blackened fish tacos with tomatillo salsa and black bean–corn hash. Service can be iffy, and the wine list needs depth, but that doesn't deter a diverse clientele that creates a din during peak hours. *$$; AE, DC, MC, V; no checks; lunch Mon–Sat, dinner Tues–Sun; full bar; reservations recommended; at Chapman Ave.* &

Santa Ana

RESTAURANTS

Antonello / ★★★

1611 SUNFLOWER AVE, SANTA ANA; 714/751-7153
This longtime darling of the power dining set maintains its lofty perch by consistently supplying premium service and refined Italian cuisine amid lavish surroundings. Gracious owner Antonio Cagnolo adds warmth and style to the proceedings, personally overseeing a highly skilled kitchen that turns out what Cagnolo calls *cucina nostalgica* (though we deem it mostly Northern Italian), handling special requests with aplomb. The broad menu touches on classics old and new such as delicate miniature veal ravioli with bolognese sauce (his mother's recipe) or creamy risotto blessed with shrimp and champagne—hardly the same old take on the dish. A notable wine list is well supported by a wine-savvy waitstaff. The meandering layout and faux-palazzo design of the dining room includes many nooks and crannies for privacy or romance. Utterly upscale yet perfectly, endearingly gracious, this top-notch enterprise offers some of Orange County's foremost Italian cuisine in a setting suited to any special occasion. *$$$; AE, DC, MC, V; no checks; lunch Mon–Fri, dinner Mon–Sat; full bar; reservations recommended; www.antonello.com; in South Coast Plaza Village.* &

Gustaf Anders / ★★★
Back Pocket / ★★★

3851 BEAR ST, SANTA ANA; 714/668-1737

Chef Gustaf Anders has a stellar reputation as a purveyor of superlative Swedish and continental cuisine. Virtually impossible to find by chance, this hidden treasure succeeds with its keen balance of style, civility, and culinary distinction. Partners Wilhelm Gustaf Magnuson and chef Ulf Anders Strandberg turn out meals that are memorable by virtue of both exceptional cooking and a serene setting that is sleek and spare, with muted hues accented with an occasional shock of bold color. Typical dishes include sugar-and-salt-cured salmon with creamed dill potatoes, filet of beef in Stilton/red wine sauce with creamed morels, and Arctic char roasted on savory vegetables with light tomato and extra virgin olive oil sauce. Also legendary are many signature breads and a host of herring preparations, all made on the premises. The partners recently fired up a wood-burning oven and rotisserie to anchor their adjacent Back Pocket cafe. In Sweden, *bakficka* ("back pocket") refers to a satellite eatery attached to a fine dining establishment. Here they offer similar fine food at popular prices with more casual surroundings. Though a few items are lifted directly from the main room's menu, there are plenty of comfort food dishes like sea bass with tomato broth, honey-glazed pork loin, and a baked gravlax sandwich dressed with Parmesan, fresh dill, and tomato *concassée. $$$; AE, DC, MC, V; no checks; lunch Tues–Sat, dinner Tues–Sun; full bar; reservations recommended; mailgustaf@aol. com; www.imenu.com; in rear of South Coast Village.* &

Morton's of Chicago / ★★★

1661 SUNFLOWER AVE, SANTA ANA; 714/444-4834

Owned by Hard Rock Cafe co-creator Peter Morton and his sister, Pam (their father is Arnie Morton, of Arnie Morton's of Chicago steak house fame), Morton's serves up classic American grill fare in a striking setting. For a full description of Morton's, see the review of its West Hollywood location in the L.A. Restaurants section. *$$$; AE, DC, MC, V; no checks; dinner every day; full bar; reservations recommended; south end of South Coast Plaza Village.* &

Topaz Café / ★★

BOWERS MUSEUM, 2002 N MAIN ST, SANTA ANA; 714/835-2002

Certainly one of the best finds in this part of town, Topaz Café is a visually appealing spot that makes creative use of its location within the highly regarded Bowers Museum. Added as part of an excellent renovation of this historic site, the cafe offers a laid-back early California charm thanks to a prime corner in the lovely Spanish-style courtyard graced by tiled arcades, towering palms, and historical mural. Inside, the Flintstones

Nouveau decor might be too cavelike if it weren't for the many doors and windows that open onto the big patio. The menu features World Cuisine items like Tunisian salad with grilled peppers, artichokes, eggplant, and endive in tahini dressing or grilled salmon wrapped in corn husks with cilantro pesto, served with a sweet-corn tamale and black beans. Less daring diners will be happy with soups (black bean and sweet corn), salads (grilled romaine wedge with creamy Maytag blue cheese dressing and caramelized pecans), and crisp roasted tarragon chicken with whole-grain mustard sauce and lumpy mashed potatoes. Daily specials are often inspired by current museum exhibits (Austrian dishes like onion tarts, venison stew, and assorted kuchen honored a recent Beethoven show). The pedestrian wine list won't excite, but they have recently added a commendable high tea nicely suited to warm afternoons on the shaded veranda. *$$; AE, DC, MC, V; no checks; lunch Mon–Sat, high tea every day, dinner Thurs–Sat, brunch Sun; full bar; reservations recommended; topazcafe@aol.com; www.westcoastproductions.com; in the courtyard of the Bowers Museum.* ಈ

Anaheim and Disneyland

German settlers initially bought the region they named Anaheim (derived from the German word for "home" plus the name of the local river) to establish vineyards—and did so for about $2 an acre. The vineyards thrived, and the region was for many years considered the wine-producing capital of the state. In the late 1880s, the vineyards were decimated by a blight, and the wine industry collapsed. Within a few years, however, the citrus industry developed, and by World War II Anaheim was considered a prosperous agricultural community.

But it was in 1955, when Walt Disney opened the doors to **DISNEY-LAND** (1313 Harbor Boulevard; 714/781-4565; www.disneyland.com), that Anaheim put itself on the global map. And today Disney Imagineers are hard at work to keep it that way. Within the land of the mouse are eight themed lands with more than 60 amusements. Perennial favorites like Pirates of the Caribbean, the Haunted Mansion, Country Bear Jamboree, and the musical comedy review *Animazement* continue to delight old and young alike. Newer ventures like Mickey's Toontown, the Indiana Jones Adventure, the fantastic Fantasmic laser and special effects show, and the completely rejuvenated Tomorrowland became favorites the instant they opened. Tomorrowland, ridiculously *de trop* before the renovation, now includes exciting new features like the comic, sensorially appealing and highly amusing Honey, I Shrunk the Audience ride; Rocket Rods, where test drivers with a need for speed have their need met; and the Astro Orbiter, where visitors burn through the cosmos in

THE DISNEYLAND STORY

As the "Happiest Place On Earth" rockets toward its 50th anniversary in 2005, the landmark theme park bears less and less resemblance to the original vision of its illustrious founder, but still inspires wonder in children and long-since-grown fans.

Animation king Walt Disney had been dreaming since the 1930s of an "amusement park" (he himself invented the phrase) where parents and children could enjoy good, clean entertainment together. In 1955, he blended the noble goal of embodying America's diverse past (in features like the replica 1800s Main Street, rugged Frontierland, and jazzy New Orleans Square), the ambitious vision of a World of Tomorrow (soon renamed Tomorrowland), fantasy settings from his features *Snow White* and *Sleeping Beauty*, and the astounding creativity and technological feats performed by his "Imagineering" department. Throw in a little typical Walt-style optimism in the form of employee "hosts" and "hostesses" who treat every tourist as a "guest" (and refer to each ride as an "adventure")—and the world's greatest family park was born.

Over the years, crowds have been delighted by the sight of celebrities and world dignitaries carousing inside Disneyland right alongside other visitors: Senator Robert Kennedy and astronaut John Glenn riding "Flight to the Moon" together, Japan's Emperor Hirohito inside "It's A Small World," President Dwight D. Eisenhower piloting a "Jungle Cruise," and President Harry Truman, who refused to ride Dumbo because of the Republican symbolism! Even reclusive pop star Michael Jackson—whose home is called "Never Never Land"—made little effort to disguise himself on frequent visits.

Disneyland hasn't escaped its share of controversy along the way, however. Opening-day debacles included ladies' high heels sinking into not-quite-cured asphalt, and too few drinking fountains due to an ill-timed plumbers' strike during construction. In 1970, a Vietnam war protest group seized Tom Sawyer Island. Public relations nightmares continue with the recent spate of guest injuries inside the park. Keeping up with the times has also proved difficult in the personnel realm (the original "host" hygiene code forbade facial hair on men) as well as the technological, such as the behind-the-scenes scurrying to update the once-speculative "Rocket to the Moon" attraction (even the replacement "Mission to Mars" ultimately became anachronistic).

As Disneyland enters the new millennium, it embarks on the loftiest undertaking ever: a massive expansion that will introduce an adjacent sister theme park ("California Adventure") and transform Disneyland into a self-contained resort with themed destination hotels, shopping, theaters, and restaurants. The city is chipping in, too, transforming the surrounding streets into manicured, tree-lined boulevards and building a dedicated Disneyland offramp from the Golden State Freeway. It might have dazzled even Walt Disney's monumental imagination!

their own private starships. Perhaps the most fascinating and fun new feature of Tomorrowland today is Innoventions, where visitors try out the latest techno whizbangs and gizmos invented to make life easier. The brand new tri-part California Adventure, scheduled to open in 2001, will include Golden State, Hollywood, and Paradise Pier. Those who have visited the park before will be happy to know it's as well manicured and maintained and as squeaky-clean as ever, and that neatly dressed, courteous park employees still whisk litter away before it hits the ground.

You can avoid some of the pitfalls of a trip to the land of Mouse-Mania by careful planning. The two cardinal rules are: Don't go if the day's predicted high will be above 85; and Always plan to arrive a bit before the park is scheduled to open. Early arrival will let you try out at least one of the attractions without the usual hour's wait in line. And remember, rain keeps the hordes away. A trip to Disneyland on a gray and drizzling day can be an extremely pleasant experience.

The reason behind the extensive construction is that Disneyland is busily turning what seems like the entire community into the Disneyland Resort, with the object of attracting *more* than the annual 38 million tourists who already visit Anaheim. When the construction, general reconfiguration, and traffic reconfiguration (the 5 Freeway is going to be widened to provide direct access to the resort) are concluded sometime after the year 2000, traffic—theoretically—will flow more easily. With the proposed pedestrian walkways, accompanying verdant landscaping, and uniform signage for all the streets, avenues, and boulevards, the apparent idea is to transform the area into a garden district. For answers to questions about the Disneyland Resort project, call 714/491-4660.

The **ANAHEIM CONVENTION & VISITOR CENTER** (800 W Katella Avenue; 714/999-8950) can offer helpful information on the area and its attractions.

The state-of-the-art **ARROWHEAD POND OF ANAHEIM** (2695 E Katella Avenue, between the 57 Freeway and Main Street; 714/704-2500) is the home of the NHL **MIGHTY DUCKS** of Anaheim. The **LOS ANGELES CLIPPERS** play a number of games here, but are relocating to the new Staples Arena near the Los Angeles Convention Center in late 1999. The Pond is also host to other high-profile sporting and musical events.

RESTAURANTS

Foxfire / ★★½

5717 E SANTA ANA CANYON RD, ANAHEIM HILLS; 714/974-5400

 What used to be a rather ho-hum restaurant is now a strong player in the north county's fine dining scene, thanks to a completely retooled menu and the talents of chef Eric Nguyen. The current menu is a spirited, distinctly up-to-date take on continental cuisine. Beef, lamb, duck, pork, game, shellfish, and seafood all receive tempting treatments and are well supported by side items that add interest and dimension. Tea-smoked duck is sided with grilled pears and wild rice pancakes stacked with creamed turnips and dressed with a cherry-port sauce, and pan-roasted *lotte* (a.k.a. monkfish) medallions are matched by crab-corn-risotto cakes topped with fresh spinach. Foxfire's setting has changed less than its menu: it remains a rambling series of smaller rooms that feel more intimate than the total square footage would suggest. Service varies considerably from server to server. Another warning: Dinner is Foxfire's forte, and lunch often falls short. The lively adjoining lounge attracts mostly baby-boomer singles. *$$$; AE, DC, MC, V; no checks; lunch Mon–Fri, dinner every day, brunch Sun; full bar; reservations recommended; www.foxfire.com; at Imperial Hwy.* &

Mr. Stox / ★★★

1105 E KATELLA AVE, ANAHEIM; 714/634-2994

Open since 1967, Mr. Stox could well be labeled an Old Reliable, but that would understate this restaurant's obvious enthusiasm for change and ever-higher levels of excellence. The current menu illustrates how well Mr. Stox blends the fresh with the familiar. Chef Scott Raczek has a gift for taking a basic like certified Angus beef culotte steak and gussying it up with red wine, caramelized onions, and a rosemary potato roll, or for siding mesquite-grilled swordfish with pesto risotto, grilled vegetables, and roasted red chili oil. Also on the menu are lamb, duck, rabbit, and several seafood selections. If you're fond of authentic crab cakes, order them here; the owners, former Marylanders Ron and Debbie Marshall, are justifiably proud of their lump-meat crab cakes, served on a light Dijon sauce with a medley of garden vegetables and peppered potatoes. Entrees are supported by incredible site-baked breads and an exquisite, widely praised wine cellar. Add polished service and tranquil, sumptuous surroundings, and you have an experience worth repeating for another three decades. *$$$; AE, DC, DIS, MC, V; no checks; lunch Mon–Fri, dinner every day; full bar; reservations recommended; between State College Blvd and Levis St.* &

Thee White House / ★★★

887 S ANAHEIM BLVD, ANAHEIM; 714/772-1381

Old World elegance applied to service, setting, and cuisine is the specialty at this restored 1909 Colonial-style home once surrounded by orange groves. Since 1987 Paris-born Bruno Serato has earned a loyal following by gracefully serving a Northern Italian menu (with a few French items tucked in) to those in search of a fine meal near Disneyland. Diners enjoy a choice of candlelit rooms with Victorian decor, though service seems most attentive downstairs (tables near the fireplace are highly coveted). Steak, veal, lamb, and pasta choices include all the standards we've seen before, but a capable kitchen does justice to every dish. Examples include filet mignon with baked polenta, caramelized shallots and thyme-scented veal reduction, or Italian potato dumplings in a silky Gorgonzola sauce. The widely praised wine list features over 200 California and European vintages, offering top choices befitting the many special occasions celebrated here. *$$$; AE, MC, V; no checks; lunch Mon–Fri, dinner every day; full bar; reservations recommended; www.imenu.com/theewhite house; between Ball Rd and Lincoln Ave.* &

LODGINGS

Anaheim Hilton and Towers / ★★☆

777 W CONVENTION WY, ANAHEIM; 714/750-4321 OR 949/222-9923
Perhaps because Disneyland is nearby, this branch of the Hilton chain is more garish than the others. As you enter the lobby, you wish they'd turn down the volume of the fountain because the rush of the water is so loud it's hard to hear yourself think. However, in customary Hilton style, management makes everything easy at this city within a city. Arrangements for outings to Disneyland and the region's other attractions are made with a wave of the concierge's hand. The 1,600 rooms and suites—some of them in a pretty, landscaped garden area—are uniformly cozy, designed for maximum efficiency and with plenty of amenities, including a free continental breakfast. They are spacious, decorated in modern style, in shades of mauve, pink, and green, with pale wood furniture. The excellent fitness center includes weight-training, aerobics and spinning (stationary bike) classes, and a basketball court. Guests also enjoy the spa, full-service salon, and gargantuan pool, replete with a pool bar and Jacuzzi, the rooftop gardens, and the sun decks. The hotel also offers lobby shops, a foreign currency exchange, a post office, and airline and car-rental offices. Dining options include Hastings Grill, Pavia for Italian specialties, and Café Express for quick bites. The Lobby Bar, oozing California cool, is a terrific spot for a drink. The Anaheim Convention Center is next door. *$$$$; AE, DC, DIS, MC, V; checks OK; www.hilton.com; 2 blocks from Disneyland.* &

Candy Cane Inn / ★★☆

1747 S HARBOR BLVD, ANAHEIM; 714/774-5284 OR 949/345-7057
A block south of Disneyland, this motel-style establishment has been newly redecorated and is now quite spiffy, sporting a handsome porte cochère over the entrance and a three-tiered fountain out front. The two- story U-shaped inn masterfully maintains its 172 spacious rooms and studio suites, which are decorated in deep pink with matching floral bedspreads. A large pool tucked into a neatly landscaped garden courtyard is preferred by après-Disneygoers, while the children's wading pool is almost always splashing with young bathers. Complimentary continental

breakfast is served in the courtyard or the dining room. Extra amenities such as valet services, self-serve laundry facilities, a helpful staff, and kid-friendly antics make this spot a family favorite. *$–$$; AE, DC, DIS, MC, V; no checks; near Katella Ave.* ⅋

The Disneyland Hotel / ★★

1150 W CERRITOS AVE, ANAHEIM; 714/778-6600

For the complete Disneyland Resort experience, this three-tower, 1,136-rooms-and-suites complex is the place to be. Just inside the lobby of the main building you'll be greeted by three-foot bronze statues of Mickey and Minnie. (Otherwise, the polished-granite, high-ceilinged lobby is surprisingly understated.) The hotel offers a variety of room choices, all of which are spacious, comfortable, and tastefully done in pastel pinks and blues. Suites have separate sitting areas with dark-wood furniture. Although most guests beeline it via tram or foot each morning to the Disneyland gates, there is reason to hang around. The large swimming pool is a blessing on sweltering summer days; the Team Mickey fitness center works out the adults; and a fun kids' arcade with miniature remote-control stock-car racing keeps the kids preoccupied. The hotel's dining options include Grenville's Steakhouse, Hook's Point, and Montreal Cafe, but the family favorite is Goofy's Kitchen, where children dine with Disney characters. Afternoon tea at the hotel's Practically Perfect Tea is another popular pastime. Another bonus: early entrance to Disneyland. *$$$; AE, DC, DIS, JCB, MC, V; checks OK; www.disneyland.com; next to Disneyland.* ⅋

Disneyland Pacific Hotel / ★★

1717 S WEST ST, ANAHEIM; 714/999-0990

Formerly the Pan Pacific Hotel, this 4.6-acre property—15 stories, 502 rooms—has been completely refurbished and appropriated by Disney to become part and parcel of the Disneyland Resort. Entering the lobby, small guests will be charmed by the playful Goofy, Mickey, and Daffy figurines on their bright yellow pedestals that dominate the area. The rooms are spacious and clean, decorated in pastel shades of pink and blue, and have such amenities as Disney-themed bathroom toiletries, individual temperature controls, refrigerators upon request, irons, ironing boards, hair dryers, and voice-message machines. There's also a fitness center, a gigantic pool, baby-sitting services, a foreign currency exchange, and interpreters available upon request. The staff is very helpful and extremely patient—crucial attributes when working within such a bustling establishment. Mary Poppins tea is served each afternoon, while for breakfast with Minnie and a magic show there's Goofy's Kitchen at the adjoining Disneyland Hotel. The Coffee House is open late, but the best dining room in either of the two hotels is Yamabuki, where Japanese food reigns. The more casual option is the PCH Grill, where burgers, pizza, and other standard American fare are served. The best thing about the place, of course, is its location; it's just a short walk to the Anaheim Convention Center and right next to Disneyland, and guests are entitled to extra park privileges such as early entrance. *$$$; AE, DC, DIS, JCB, MC, V; checks OK; www.disneyland.com; next to Disneyland between Katella Ave and West St.* ⅙

Buena Park

The sole attraction that lures tourists to Buena Park is **KNOTT'S BERRY FARM** (8039 Beach Boulevard; 714/220-5200; www.knotts.com), 10 miles northwest of Disneyland. At one time the property was indeed a boysenberry farm, belonging to the Knott family of jam fame. But ultimately the family re-created the ghost town that had once occupied the area and began allowing people to tour it, as well as inviting them to stay for hearty chicken suppers prepared in the old farmhouse kitchen. Today the spot is a sprawling amusement park that's no longer owned by the family, but the infusion of cash from new owners has underwritten several new attractions and other improvements. The Supreme Scream—the tallest structure in Orange County—propels thrill-seekers 30 stories up, then drops them straight down again. GhostRider, the new wooden coaster reminiscent of Coney Island's Cyclone, is wonderfully terrifying. Old favorites such as Montazooma's Revenge and Boomerang still pack a wallop, too. The "farm" is also a major venue for popular musical groups. Visitors may still pan for gold, and free tours of an exact replica of Independence Hall are interesting. Guest conveniences include lockers, ATMs, a foreign currency exchange, accessibility for disabled visitors, and free 45-minute passes for those who simply want to venture through the gates to shop. Best of all, they're still serving up the famous chicken dinners. Additional Buena Park information is available at the **CHAMBER OF COMMERCE AND VISITORS CENTER** (6280 Manchester Boulevard, off the 5 Freeway between Stanton Avenue and Beach Boulevard; 714/521-0261).

Yorba Linda

Whether you love or loathe the 37th President of the United States, the **RICHARD NIXON LIBRARY & BIRTHPLACE MUSEUM** (18001 Yorba Linda Boulevard; 714/993-3393 or 800/USA-8865; www.nixonfoundation.org) is absolutely extraordinary. The tiny farmhouse, built by Nixon's father in 1912 in the center of a citrus grove, is now a historic landmark. The library/museum itself is composed of 22 rooms offering permanent exhibits that chronicle Nixon's life and his years in office. There are many other exhibits, too, both permanent and traveling, on a variety of topics including China, Southeast Asia, Russia, and the Berlin Wall (see a three-ton hunk of it), as well as a painfully honest accounting of one of the biggest scandals of the century, Watergate. In the gallery space, every gift Mr. and Mrs. Nixon received while they occupied the White House is on display. The gallery also plays host to many traveling fine art shows. The structure is surrounded by beautifully maintained gardens.

Fullerton

The City of Fullerton, 22 miles from downtown L.A. and on the edge of the California coastal plain, is the home of **CAL STATE FULLERTON** (bordered by Yorba Linda Boulevard, the 57 Freeway, Nutwood Avenue, and State College Boulevard; 714/278-2011; www.fullerton.edu). The **FULLERTON ARBORETUM** occupies the northeast corner of the campus, where guided nature tours of the lush and green, 26-acre grounds and the lovely **HERITAGE HOUSE MUSEUM** (1900 Associated Road; 714/278-3404; www.arboretum.fullerton.edu/general/htm) are available October through July (by appointment only, a month in advance). The handsome **PLUMMER AUDITORIUM** (at the corner of Lemon Street and Chapman Avenue) is home to the popular **FULLERTON CIVIC LIGHT OPERA**, one of the largest professional musical groups in the state, and the recipient of numerous Drama-Logue and Robbie Awards (for tickets, call 714/879-1732). The **MUCKENTHALER CULTURAL CENTER** (1201 W Malvern Avenue; 714/738-6595; www.ci.fullerton.ca.us/muckenthaler/arts.shm), located in the former residence of an Orange County pioneer, presents a unique and imaginative schedule of exhibitions and performing arts events.

For nightlife, **STEAMERS CAFÉ** (135 W Commonwealth, west of Arbor; 714/871-8800) is one of the county's best jazz venues, presenting live music every night. The **CHAMBER OF COMMERCE** (219 E Commonwealth Avenue; 714/871-3100) provides useful information on the area and its attractions.

RESTAURANTS

The Cellar / ★★★

305 N HARBOR BLVD, FULLERTON; 714/525-5682

Long the top choice for fine dining in Fullerton, the Cellar has weathered over 30 years of culinary whims and trends to become a north county institution. It all began in 1969, when Disneyland craftsmen fashioned a romantic cavern in the cellar of the 1922 California Hotel (now the intimate Villa Del Sol complex). Today chef David Kesler oversees a classically French menu heavy with time-honored favorites like Dover sole meunière, sautéed calf's liver in Madeira butter sauce, chateaubriand with béarnaise sauce, and venison medallions in cranberry-port sauce. Many a longtime county resident savors the memory of a special-occasion dinner topped off with the Cellar's superb chocolate or Grand Marnier soufflé. Also of note is the extensive wine selection of over 1,300 bottles, which has rightfully earned a Grand Award from *Wine Spectator*. Though some modernists find the subterranean setting overly themed and a bit dated, many more are easily beguiled by the candlelit space and insist on booking tables near the fireplace months in advance. Top-notch, European-style service adds to the air of romance and elegance here. *$$$; AE, DIS, DC, MC, V; no checks; dinner Tues–Sat; full bar; reservations recommended.* &

Mulberry Street Ristorante / ★★

114 W WILSHIRE AVE, FULLERTON; 714/525-1056
Mulberry Street certainly doesn't feel like Orange County. This lively neighborhood bar and restaurant offers a tempting (if basic) Italian menu and something of a New York personality—almost a trip back East for the price of a meal. It's been open only since 1986, but Mulberry Street feels like it's been there forever, thanks to dark wood, brick, and a notable shortage of windows. Old friends, sociable warmth, good food, and white tablecloths pretty much compose the scene here. The menu is a classic Italian lineup emphasizing shellfish—clams, oysters, mussels, shrimp—plus fresh fish specials each day. We like the cherrystone clams, either raw on ice or with wine and garlic over linguine. But best bets aren't limited to seafood: other commendable choices include rich eggplant parmigiana, veal piccata, and a solid fettuccine carbonara. The food here is consistently solid even if it's rarely inspired. The compact wine roster is well chosen, and there are some nice vintages by the glass. Service can be exceptional or disastrous. Since the room appears to have no captain, request "your best waiter" when you make reservations. *$$; AE, MC, V; no checks; lunch Mon–Sat, dinner every day; full bar; reservations recommended.* &

La Habra

RESTAURANTS

Cat & the Custard Cup / ★★★

800 E WHITTIER BLVD, LA HABRA; 562/992-6496 OR 310/694-3812
A steadfast player on the north Orange County dining scene for decades, Cat & the Custard Cup excels in an admittedly restaurant-lean territory. Though the place looks and feels like the cozy British country tavern that its name evokes, the bill of fare here is strictly modern Cal-continental. But despite its curious choice of name, the setting is relaxed, the service

is able, and the cuisine is generally quite good. Starters and salads, such as the baby greens with red onions, sweet peppers, pecans, and goat cheese crouton, are appropriately tempting. Fish, meat, and poultry entrees are simply prepared, then dressed with jazzy sauces and partnered with creative side dishes. Broiled scallops rest on a crisp potato nest with pecans, red peppers, chives, and a drizzle of limed brown butter. Crisp roast duckling has a brandy–port wine–red currant sauce; grilled culotte steak is accented by port, blue cheese, and four kinds of peppercorns. Pan-roasted duck breast with a plum-pomegranate sauce is sided with wasabi-spiked mashed potatoes. An unusually canny selection of wines by the glass adds appeal. Rustic wood flooring, high brick walls, and a fireplace lounge create an inviting atmosphere. *$$; AE, MC, V; no checks; dinner every day; full bar; reservations recommended; south of the Whittier off Hwy 57; between N Harbor Blvd and N Euclid St.* &

Brea

RESTAURANTS

La Vie en Rose / ★★

240 S STATE COLLEGE BLVD, BREA; 714/528-8333

At first, it looks incongruous: a big French farmhouse wedged between a freeway and a major shopping mall. But once you're inside La Vie en Rose, it's easy to forget the suburban sprawl outside. Although it hardly counts as a trip to France, owner Louis Laulhere has successfully created a first-rate French restaurant, one with its culinary roots in the farms and seaside villages of Gascony. Typical starters include fresh mussels steamed in cider and sautéed veal sweetbreads with an Amaretto veal reduction. Entrees include veal medallions with Calvados demi-glace and caramelized apples, sautéed duck breast and leg confit with a dark cherry sauce, and grilled sea scallops wrapped in leeks with green peppercorn sauce. The wine list does a reasonable job of complementing the cuisine. On par with the rich cuisine are the solicitous service and the fanciful surroundings. A collection of rooms and private nooks, charmingly trimmed in floral prints and antique furnishings, creates warmth and privacy— and a welcome retreat from the hectic world beyond. *$$$; AE, MC, V; no checks; lunch Mon–Fri, dinner Mon–Sat; full bar; reservations recommended; www.lavnrose.com; southeast of Whittier and north of Fullerton off Hwy 57; near E Birch St.* &

Cerritos

The architecturally splendiferous **CERRITOS CENTER FOR THE PER-FORMING ARTS** (12700 Center Court Drive; 800/300-4345; www.cerritoscenter.com), designed by Barton Myers, is actually just over the line in Los Angeles County. Since its inaugural performances by Frank Sinatra in 1993, the center—possessing a 6,000-square-foot auditorium, which can be configured six different ways—has been hailed as one of the preeminent performance venues in the world, with a varied and exciting performance schedule. To reach the center, a 30-minute drive from downtown L.A., take the 5 Freeway to the 605 Freeway to the 91 Freeway east. Exit at Shoemaker Avenue, turn right at the first intersection. The center is the building on the right, topped with three flags.

SAN DIEGO COUNTY

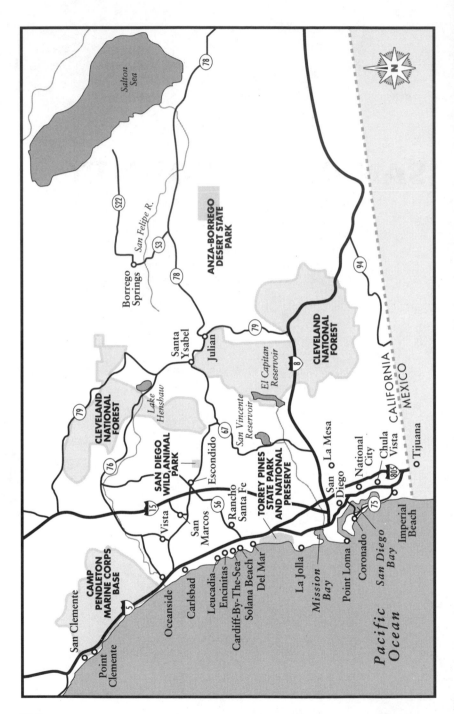

SAN DIEGO COUNTY

Perhaps the most shocking thing about San Diego County is that almost every single thing publicized about it is true. The climate is divine, the beaches are heavenly, and the healthy (some might say health-nut) inhabitants are laid back, good-looking, perpetually bronzed, and smiley-face friendly. They spend infinite amounts of time "getting in touch with their feelings," as well as everyone else's, and visitors are often taken aback—even repelled—to find themselves being bear-hugged by complete strangers.

San Diegans love to play outdoors, and there's plenty of opportunity, with more than 70 miles of beaches and bays, a plethora of world-class golf courses and tennis courts, some real show-off city parks, and semiisolated forests, mountains, and desert.

When it's time to get down to business, many San Diegans can be found ensconced in one of the ever-expanding number of high-tech firms or medical research facilities that have set up shop here; others devote their energies to hawking New Age wares, services, and religion in markets, offices, and pulpits throughout the county. This business boom, combined with an influx of those who couldn't live through one more icy winter or hellish summer in their own home states, may be economically rewarding, but it has unfortunately transformed many parts of the county into a snarl of condos, strip malls, and traffic jams. Nonetheless, this is the only place in the United States where within the span of one day you can jump ocean waves, frolic on a snowy mountain, hike a forest trail, off-road in the desert, attend a big-city event, and stroll across an international border.

ACCESS AND INFORMATION

Two major north-south routes traverse San Diego County. From Los Angeles, **INTERSTATE 5** (which originates at the Canadian border) more or less follows the coast, passing Camp Pendleton, the beach communities, the University of California at San Diego campus, and the turn-off to La Jolla, Mission Bay Park, Old Town, and San Diego proper, before ending at the Mexican border. **INTERSTATE 15**, from Las Vegas, is the inland route—skirting wine country, the city of Escondido, high-tech campuses, and Marine Corps Air Station Miramar (previously Miramar Naval Air Station), ending just south of San Diego, where it meets up with Interstate 5. From Arizona, **INTERSTATE 8** follows the Mexican border, moving slightly northwest as it enters San Diego County and connects with the interchanges. From the coast, **HIGHWAYS 76 AND 78** offer varied options for reaching Indian reservations, Mount Palomar, the Cleveland National Forest, the mining and tourist town of Julian (also reached via Highway 79, from Interstate 8), and the vast Anza-Borrego Desert State Park.

Major domestic and some international carriers serve **SAN DIEGO INTERNATIONAL AIRPORT–LINDBERGH FIELD** (3707 N Harbor Dr, near downtown; 619/231-2100), and **RENTAL CARS** are readily available through all the big-name chains. **TAXIS** are generally readily available, or you can grab a **SHUTTLE** from Cloud Nine (800/974-8885) or San Diego Xpress Airport (619/220-8454), or catch a San Diego Transit Bus (619/233-3004) for the short ride into the city. **MCCLELLAN PALOMAR AIRPORT** (2198 Palomar Airport Road; 619/431-4646), in Carlsbad (about 35 miles from San Diego), is served by American Eagle and United Express for flights in and out of Los Angeles. **AMTRAK** (800/872-7245) provides daily train service between Los Angeles and San Diego's Santa Fe depot (at Kettner Boulevard and Broadway), with additional stops in Oceanside and Solana Beach. **GREYHOUND** (120 West Broadway; 800/231-2222) runs buses from all major cities to its San Diego station.

The usually perfect-temperate **WEATHER** of San Diego is legendary. Even the dreaded "El Niño" in the winter of '98–'99 hit San Diego with only a few big storms. Daytime temperatures rarely dip below 55°F in winter or rise above 85°F in summer. Desert areas, however, sizzle well above the 100-degree mark most of the summer. Both deserts and mountains can turn bitterly cold during winter, with occasional frost and snow at higher elevations. June is traditionally foggy in the beach areas.

For more information, contact the **SAN DIEGO INTERNATIONAL VISITORS INFORMATION CENTER** (11 Horton Plaza, on the corner of First and F Streets; 619/236-1212), or visit its Web site at www.sandiego.org.

San Diego

California's second-largest city—tagged "America's Finest City" by its Convention and Visitors Bureau—is, if not the finest, certainly one of the prettiest and most low key big cities in the country, despite the fact that it still has a huge naval presence. Though it lacks the slick sophistication of San Francisco and the lovable gaudiness of Los Angeles, San Diego reigns as both year-round playground and thriving metropolis—all set against a backdrop of shimmering sea, open parklands, rugged cliffs, verdant valleys, and a blend of contemporary and Spanish architecture. One big-city component that visitors will probably not find, though, is attitude. Hyperactive egos are a distinct minority here—anyone getting pushy or aggressive is more apt to be confronted by healing crystals and aromatherapy potions than by angry words or weapons.

Considered the birthplace of California after Juan Rodriguez Cabrillo landed at the tip of Point Loma in 1542, San Diego wasn't actu-

SAN DIEGO COUNTY THREE-DAY TOUR

DAY 1. Begin the day in San Diego's **GASLAMP QUARTER.** Pick up a walking map at William Heath Davis House, and wander the **HISTORIC DISTRICT** with its renovated buildings and intriguing shops. Stop for a leisurely lunch at one of the sidewalk trattorias along Fifth Avenue (**BELLA LUNA** is always a good bet), then dive into downtown San Diego's **HORTON PLAZA** for an inside view at the whimsical architecture, picking up theater tickets at the **TIMES ARTS TIX** booth on the way out. Drive to **OLD TOWN STATE HISTORIC PARK** for a peek into San Diego's beginnings. After a Mexican dinner, catch a **PERFORMANCE** at Theatre in Old Town or one of the other local theaters, then spend the night at the US Grant Hotel or the Horton Grand Hotel.

DAY 2. Go directly to **BALBOA PARK.** Spend the morning oohing and aahing at the critters at the marvelous **SAN DIEGO ZOO.** Meander through the **SPANISH VILLAGE ART CENTER** toward **EL PRADO.** Grab something for lunch from one of the fast-food vendors and linger on the lawn in front of the **BOTANICAL GARDENS** or along El Prado to watch the street performers. Pick up a money-saving museum pass at the Visitor Center, then spend the rest of the day swept away by art, photography, history, or science at one or all of the city's incredible **MUSEUMS.** Anyone not in a museum mood will most likely be tail over fins for **SEA WORLD.** The Embarcadero area sets the scene for a seafood dinner and a sunset view—the **FISH MARKET RESTAURANT** is a perennial favorite. Then it's back to the Gaslamp Quarter and some hot jazz or cool blues at one of the music clubs, such as **PATRICK'S II** or **CROCE'S JAZZ BAR.**

DAY 3. Either grab the **SAN DIEGO WATER TAXI** or drive across the Coronado Bay Bridge, heading straight for the palatial **HOTEL DEL CORONADO.** Have a leisurely breakfast or brunch and daydream over the historic past of "The Dell." Spend the rest of the morning visiting **CABRILLO NATIONAL MONUMENT** and then head for the chic seaside communities of **LA JOLLA** and **DEL MAR.** Lunch at one of Del Mar Plaza's trendy eateries (such as **PACIFICA**). After lunch, wind back to La Jolla and visit the **STEPHEN BIRCH AQUARIUM** or the **MUSEUM OF CONTEMPORARY ART.** Dinner is a splurge at **GEORGE'S AT THE COVE.** Spend the night at luscious **LA VALENCIA** after a nightcap at the hotel's swank **WHALING BAR.** More active types will eschew the coastal route on Day 3 and point eastward toward the San Diego **WILD ANIMAL PARK** near Escondido. With afternoon light to spare, continue to the mining town of **JULIAN,** to feast on apple pie from one of the shops or stands and explore the old mine, cemetery, and rustic streets.

ally "put on the map" until 1769, when Franciscan padre Junípero Serra dedicated the Presidio and San Diego de Alcalá—first in the string of California's 21 missions. Nearly 100 years later, San Francisco merchant Alonzo E. Horton moved in and relocated the center of the city from Old Town (now preserved as a historical park) to its current site near the all-important harbor. Horton's "New Town" took on a sleazy ambiance during World War I and the Depression, when the area—then known as "the Stingaree"—was packed with brawling sailors, bawdy women, and a variety of sins and vice. That very same district—now called the GASLAMP QUARTER—has been restored and revitalized and is rife with swank hotels, chic cafes, funky shops, trendy boutiques, contemporary galleries, and performing arts venues, with the convention center and the Embarcadero nearby. Though the city sprawls for miles in three directions, most of the business and entertainment action is centered in or near the downtown core, giving San Diego yet another rub-their-nose-in-it-edge over its urban competitors: an upmarket and relatively crime-free downtown that attracts rather than repels visitors and residents.

More changes are blowing in the (barely discernible) breeze for this city. A new baseball stadium is in the works (scheduled opening: circa 2002); it will be located in the warehouse district, an area very close to the Gaslamp Quarter, presently filled with a conglomeration of converted lofts, artists' studios, manufacturing concerns, antique markets, and down-and-out dwellings. This quasi-community was once the dregs of the city but is now haughtily referred to as the "East Village."

ACCESS AND INFORMATION

San Diego is easily accessed by air via SAN DIEGO INTERNATIONAL AIRPORT–LINDBERGH FIELD (3707 N Harbor Drive, near downtown; 619/231-2100). Taxis and door-to-door shuttles are plentiful at San Diego International Airport, and a ride downtown is less than $10. For further information, see San Diego County "Access and Information" above.

Because of the influx of tourists and residents, DRIVING is becoming more and more of an L.A.–like pain. Visitors can expect freeway congestion throughout the day. Plentiful public PARKING is available at Horton Plaza (bounded by Broadway, G Street, and First and Fourth Avenues; 619/238-1596), and just about any shop or food outlet validates parking for up to three hours. Street parking is metered in downtown areas and in some uptown locations.

SAN DIEGO METROPOLITAN TRANSIT SYSTEM runs buses on more than 20 downtown routes, and DAYTRIPPER PASSES allow a full day of unlimited rides. Tickets can be purchased onboard, and exact change is required. For passes, maps, and information, contact the Transit Store (102 Broadway, at First Avenue; 619/234-1060). The bright red SAN

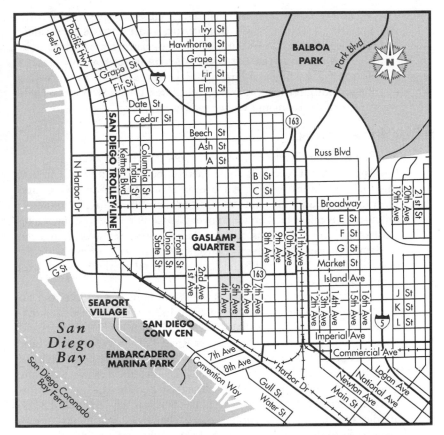

DIEGO TROLLEY (619/685-4900) whisks visitors south to the Mexican border, north to Old Town, and east to Mission Valley. Purchase tickets at self-service machines at station stops. **THE COASTER** (800/COASTER) commuter rail line operates between Oceanside and San Diego, with several stops en route (hooking up with the trolley at Old Town and downtown). **AMTRAK** (800/USA-RAIL) trains stop in Solana Beach and Oceanside as they chug up the coast toward Los Angeles.

Like many large cities, San Diego is composed of a downtown hub and neighborhood spokes—though here half those spokes dip into the bay or ocean. The **GASLAMP QUARTER** is the designated city center. This is where businesses, retail enterprises, commerce, tourism, transportation depots, and the convention center buzz—with Balboa Park and the San Diego Zoo on the periphery. The major neighborhoods include **HILLCREST,** the predominantly gay area (also referred to as "Uptown"); **KENSINGTON,** an older section with Spanish architecture and an "antique row"; and **OLD TOWN,** the city's historic heart. **MISSION BAY, PACIFIC**

BEACH, POINT LOMA, and **OCEAN BEACH** cluster between Old Town and San Diego's watery edges. **CORONADO** and **LA JOLLA** are distinct communities—notable for wealth, trendy shops, and historic dwellings.

The **SAN DIEGO INTERNATIONAL VISITOR INFORMATION CENTER** (11 Horton Plaza, corner of First and F Streets; 619/236-1212), with a multilingual staff, provides maps and brochures. Useful Web sites include www.infosandiego.com and www.sandiego.org.

MAJOR ATTRACTIONS

It's not a walking city like San Francisco, nor does it sprawl endlessly like Los Angeles. San Diego falls somewhere in between, and you can best enjoy its attractions by taking a combination of inner-city walks and short drives. In addition, **OLD TOWN TROLLEY TOURS** (619/298-8687) provides convenient bus service to over 100 points of interest, including most of the top attractions such as Balboa Park, Sea World, and the Gaslamp Quarter—allowing passengers to get on and off at leisure for one fee. Trolley buses make the loop (which takes about two hours) almost every day of the year.

One of the city's top draws is the world-famous **SAN DIEGO ZOO** (2920 Zoo Drive, Balboa Park; 619/234-3153), where more than 4,000 animals thrive in conditions that simulate their natural environments and about 6,500 plant species enrich Tiger River, Gorilla Tropics, Sun Bear Forest, Hippo Beach, and Polar Bear Plunge. The reptile house is home to scaly creatures including two-headed Thelma and Louise, while the Children's Zoo lets kids (and kids at heart) pet and snuggle newborn animals. **SEA WORLD** (500 Sea World Drive, Mission Bay; 619/226-3815), another famous local attraction, is one of the largest marine-life amusement parks in the world. Shamu, the kissing whale, has gained the most notoriety, while other exhibits include the Forbidden Reef, Wild Encounter, Penguin Encounter, and California Tide Pool. San Diego's other famous zoo, the **WILD ANIMAL PARK,** is located to the northeast in Escondido (see Escondido section).

Wander around the **GASLAMP QUARTER,** the 16-block national historic district bounded by Broadway and Market Streets and Fourth and Fifth Avenues, encompassing Victorian architecture, cool shops, hot restaurants, and the Disneyland-esque **HORTON PLAZA** retail complex (bounded by Broadway, G Street, First Avenue, and Fourth Avenue; 619/238-1596). Pick up walking maps or take a Saturday tour at **WILLIAM HEATH DAVIS HOUSE** (410 Island Avenue, at Fourth Avenue; 619/233-4692), one of the city's first residences, which was built in 1850 and is now the area's information center. The **CHILDREN'S MUSEUM OF SAN DIEGO** (200 West Island Avenue; 619/233-8792) mesmerizes kids with interactive exhibits, art studios, and improvisational theater, as well as a plethora of art supplies, dress-up costumes, and educational displays. **SEAPORT VILLAGE** (close to the Gaslamp, on the Embarcadero; 619/235-4014) is a New England–like, touristy waterfront retail development, but the Broadway Flying Horses Carousel is fabulous. The **MARITIME MUSEUM** (1306 North Harbor Drive, on the Embarcadero; 619/234-9153) provides a close-up exploration of three restored ships: the 1898 ferryboat *Berkeley,* the 1863 windjammer *Star of India,* and the 1904 steam yacht *Medea.* Hop a ferry over to Coronado, via scheduled **SAN DIEGO WATER TAXI** ferry service (Broadway and Harbor Drive; 619/235-8294) for a terrific view of the city and the Coronado Bridge. Explore Coronado's **FERRY LANDING MARKETPLACE** and the town's spectacular gingerbread icon, the 1888 **HOTEL DEL CORONADO** (1500 Orange Avenue, Coronado; 935/435-6611)—film site of *Some Like It Hot* and a longtime hangout for politicians and dignitaries. It's one of the city's (and the country's) most superb pieces of architecture, and still a top-notch people-watching spot.

OLD TOWN STATE HISTORIC PARK (4002 Wallace Street; 619/220-5422), north of downtown, affords a glimpse into San Diego's beginnings, though **PRESIDIO HILL,** which overlooks the park, is the site of the first mission and fort and is where the city actually began. **OLD TOWN'**s six square blocks encompass 20 historic buildings—most surrounding the Old Town Plaza (bounded by San Diego Avenue and Wallace, Calhoun, and Mason Streets), along with assorted restaurants, galleries, and come-hither tourist shops. Free daily **GUIDED WALKING TOURS** depart from Park Headquarters (in the Robinson-Rose Building, 4002 Wallace Street; 619/220-5422). California's first mission, **SAN DIEGO DE ALCALÁ** (10818 San Diego Mission Road, Mission Valley; 619/281-8449), is still an active parish, but was moved and later rebuilt near what is now condo-mania. Back at the coast and a slight jog south, **CABRILLO NATIONAL MONUMENT** (1800 Cabrillo Memorial Drive, Point Loma; 619/557-5450) commemorates Juan Rodriguez Cabrillo's 1542 exploration of California. The visitor center features films and lectures relating to the Portuguese explorer's landing, and both the promontory and the restored lighthouse provide dizzying views of the surrounding area, from the San Bernardino Mountains to the Mexican hills.

The coastal enclave of **LA JOLLA,** with its gorgeous coves and beaches (La Jolla Cove, Windansea Beach, La Jolla Shores), hillside mansions, and resort ambience, is San Diego's Beverly Hills—a tourist attraction in itself. The zip code called home by wealthy professionals and retirees lures locals, visitors, and visiting celebrities with ritzy shops, galleries, and restaurants along Prospect Street and Girard Avenue, and further tempts them with the wonderful **MUSEUM OF CONTEMPORARY ART** (700 Prospect Street; 858/454-3541) and the impressive **STEPHEN BIRCH**

AQUARIUM (2300 Expedition Way; 858/534-3474) at the Scripps Institution of Oceanography. For more information, contact **LA JOLLA TOWN COUNCIL** (7734 Herschel Ave, Suite F; 858/454-1444).

PARKS

San Diego's **BALBOA PARK** (2125 Park Boulevard; 619/239-0512) is a glorious 1,200-acre showpiece—and one of the largest and loveliest city parks in the country. The park houses the world-famous San Diego Zoo, most of the city's museums, the **SIMON EDISON CENTRE FOR THE PERFORMING ARTS** (which includes the Old Globe Theatre, 1363 Old Globe Way; 619/239-2255), the **REUBEN H. FLEET SPACE THEATER AND SCIENCE CENTER** (with hands-on science exhibits, plus an IMAX theater, 1875 El Prado; 619/238-1233), the awe-inspiring 4,445-pipe Spreckels organ (see Music, below), and a kid-in-a-candy-store slurp of other attractions. The park was the site of the Panama-Pacific Exposition in 1915, and many of the exuberant Moorish and Spanish Renaissance buildings built for that event remain along **EL PRADO,** the main boulevard, coexisting beautifully with the **BOTANICAL BUILDING'S** 500 species of tropical and subtropical plants (1550 El Prado; 619/235-1114), the contemplative-style **JAPANESE FRIENDSHIP GARDEN** (2215 Pan American Road E; 619/232-2780), and the regal **ALCAZAR GARDEN,** patterned after the gardens of Spain's Alcazar Castle (off El Prado, across from the Museum of Man). The cultural and educational cornucopia includes the **MUSEUM OF SAN DIEGO HISTORY** (1649 El Prado; 619/232-6203), **MUSEUM OF MAN** (1350 El Prado; 619/239-2001), **NATURAL HISTORY MUSEUM** (1788 El Prado; 619/232-3821), **HALL OF CHAMPIONS SPORTS MUSEUM** (2131 Pan American Road; 619/234-2544), **MODEL RAILROAD MUSEUM** (1649 El Prado; 619/696-0199), and **AEROSPACE MUSEUM** (2001 Pan American Plaza; 619/234-8291). (For art museums in Balboa Park, see Art Museums, below.) Not surprisingly, the park is jammed with locals as well as visitors (especially in summer and on weekends), and magicians, mimes, musicians, jugglers, palm readers, and performing monkeys all vie for the attention—and pocket money—of passers-by. Interspersed with all this activity are ice-cream vendors and hot-dog wagons, and the whole shebang is overseen by the 200-foot **CALIFORNIA TOWER,** whose 100-bell carillon signals approval every 15 minutes. For information, maps, and schedules for the free trams through the park, stop by the **BALBOA PARK VISITOR CENTER** (in the House of Hospitality, 1549 El Prado; 619/239-0512).

    MISSION BAY PARK, north of downtown and Old Town, is the sports-and-water equivalent of Balboa Park. This 4,600-acre aquatic park—once an unsightly marsh and swampland—was miraculously transformed into one humongous playground, encompassing 17 miles of ocean frontage, 27 miles of bayfront beaches, an artificial island, almost one hundred acres of parklands, and countless coves, bays, and hideaways, as well as plenty of parking spots and boat slips. Sailing, water skiing, jet skiing, windsurfing, swimming, golf, rollerblading, jogging, softball, and kite flying are just some of the hits. Boat, bike, and sports-equipment rentals are readily available at **MISSION BAY SPORTS CENTER** (1010 Santa Clara Place; 619/488-1004). Maps and guides are available at **MISSION BAY PARK HEADQUARTERS** (Quivera Basin, at the western edge of the park; 619/221-8900) and at the **VISITOR INFORMATION CENTER** (at the East Mission Bay Drive exit, off Interstate 5; 619/276-8200).

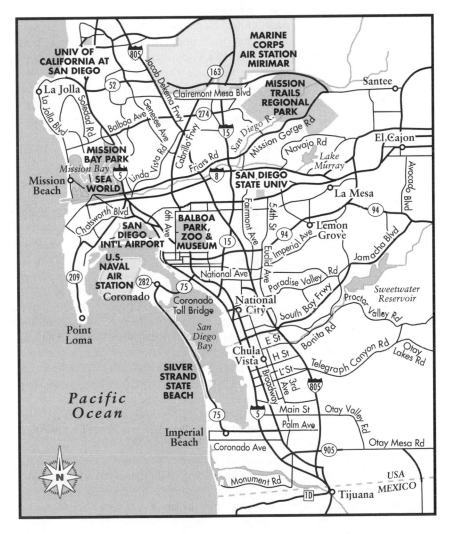

BEACHES

With 70 miles of Pacific coast, it would be difficult to not find a pleasing beach. Top bets are wide, sparkly, happy-to-be-alive **CORONADO BEACH,** fronting Ocean Boulevard and the Hotel del Coronado; funky, old hippie, dog-friendly **OCEAN BEACH,** north of Coronado and south of La Jolla, where experienced surfers challenge the riptides and gather around the pier; and **MISSION BEACH,** farther north on the ocean side of Mission Bay Park, good for surfing and *Baywatch* fantasies, with an L.A./Venice Beach ambience. Farther up the coast is Pacific Beach's **TOURMALINE SURFING PARK** (no swimming, only surfing), off La Jolla Boulevard at the end of Tourmaline Street. North of Pacific Beach, La Jolla is home to **WINDANSEA** (off La Jolla Boulevard, at the end of Nautilus Street), the famous surfing beach popularized in Tom Wolfe's *Pump House Gang.* **LA JOLLA COVE** (off Coast Boulevard) is a clear, calm, heaven-sent stretch for swimming, snorkeling, scuba diving, beginner surfers, and family dips; **LA JOLLA SHORES BEACH** offers a wide, flat expanse where families and beginning board- and bodysurfers gather. **BLACK'S BEACH** (off North Torrey Pines Road), a steep, dangerous climb from the Glider Port, is the officially illegal unofficial nude beach, where the shrubbery is often inhabited by an active gay crowd. For beach reports, call 619/289-1212.

ART MUSEUMS

SAN DIEGO MUSEUM OF ART (1450 El Prado, Balboa Park; 619/232-7931), with its striking replica Spanish Renaissance façade, exhibits everything from Renaissance and contemporary European and American paintings to Indian miniatures and Southeast Asian collections, along with six major traveling shows each year. The courtyard sculpture garden is a great place to linger with a journal or a sketchbook. For lovers of Russian icons, **TIMKEN MUSEUM OF ART** (1500 El Prado, Balboa Park; 619/239-5548), next door, offers a superb collection, as well as Old Master paintings. The **MUSEUM OF PHOTOGRAPHIC ARTS** (1649 El Prado, Balboa Park; 619/238-7559), across the way, is a world-class museum devoted to photography. At press time it was under renovation, scheduled to reopen in February 2000. Expect to see thought-provoking, sometimes-controversial works by world-class photographers (Mary Ellen Mark, Edward Weston, and others) as well as la crème of newcomers. The two-story **MINGEI INTERNATIONAL MUSEUM OF WORLD FOLK ART** (1439 El Prado, Balboa Park; 619/239-0033) presents permanent and changing exhibits of crafts, textiles, and wearable art from around the globe. Also in Balboa Park is the **SPANISH VILLAGE ART CENTER** (1770 Village Place, Balboa Park; 619/232-3522), with 35 studio galleries where working artisans show off their techniques in ceramics, woodcarving, glassblowing, jewelry making, and other artsy-craftsy pursuits. Though small, the downtown annex of the **MUSEUM OF CONTEMPORARY ART** (the main museum is in La Jolla; 1001 Kettner Boulevard, across from the Santa Fe Depot; 858/234-1001) features changing exhibitions by renowned contemporary artists. **ART WALK** (619/232-3101), a weekend event each April, is a self-guided bonanza of gallery receptions and artists' open houses.

SHOPS AND BOOKSTORES

Bright, colorful, multilevel **HORTON PLAZA** (bounded by Broadway, G Street, and First and Fourth Avenues; 619/238-1596) is the Gaslamp Quarter's centerpiece attraction. Architect Jon Jerde's tour de force is a sort of Alice in Wonderland retail paradise, containing 140 specialty shops, chic boutiques, fast-food stands, fine restaurants, book and record stores, high-tech and computer outlets, a multi-screen cinema, and three department stores including Nordstrom. Nearby, on the Embarcadero, New Englandesque **SEAPORT VILLAGE** (849 West Harbor Drive; 619/235-4014) is touristy but has some interesting finds. **FERRY LANDING MARKETPLACE** (1201 First Street, Coronado; 935/435-8895), across the bay

---

TIDE POOL TANGO

The small animals that inhabit coastal tide pools are some of the most adaptive and tenacious on the planet. Living in an environment that undergoes tidal changes four times a day, these little creatures are the commandants of compromise. At low tide their watery sanctuary disappears, exposing them to the broiling sun, increased salinity, and hungry predators. To survive, mussels collect seawater inside their bodies, then slowly release it to cool by evaporation. Sea anemones fold inward, trapping tiny drops of water to sustain themselves until the flow of water returns. At high tide, they are once again flooded, with rough swirls of seawater threatening to evict them from their homes. Barnacles hold on to rocks for dear life or risk being hurled up on the beach or out to sea. Sea urchins stay put by burrowing their spines deep into the rocks on which they live. There is a constant threat of being eaten by a neighbor. Clams, scallops, and oysters are the favored dinner of the carnivorous sea star, which in turn makes a fitting snack for a gull or a crow. If this wet, miniature-scale drama sounds interesting, San Diego has several prime spots for front-row viewing. Put on your rubber-soled tennis shoes and head for **Bird Rock** or the **Cove** in La Jolla, or the tide pools of **Point Loma**, located on the western side, near Cabrillo Monument. **Birch Aquarium at Scripps** offers classes on tide-pooling and can provide information on the best times for viewing. Call 858/534-7336 for more information.

in Coronado, features some unique gift, jewelry, and craft shops, as well as clothing stores and restaurants. Mall rats usually head for **MISSION VALLEY CENTER** (1640 Camino Del Rio North; 619/296-6375) and **FASHION VALLEY** (452 Fashion Valley Drive; 619/297-3381) in Mission Valley, where hundreds of shops and retail outlets await, including a branch of Neiman Marcus.

Antique-hunters should scout out one of the **ANTIQUE WAREHOUSES** that keep popping up in and around the Gaslamp Quarter. A couple of perennial favorites are the Olde Cracker Factory (448 West Market Street; 619/233-1669) and the Unicorn Company (704 J Street; 619/232-1696). Diehard antique hounds go snooping along Newport Avenue, in Ocean Beach, or Adams Avenue in the Normal Heights/Kensington section of town (between Park Boulevard and 40th Street). Bazaar del Mundo is the best place to go for Mexican arts, crafts, clothing, and textiles without making a trip across the border (2754 Calhoun Street, Old Town; 619/296-3161). The most extensive selection of travel guides, maps, and travel-related paraphernalia is at Le Travel Store (743 Fourth Avenue, across from Horton Plaza; 619/544-0005). San Diego Hardware is the premier "old-time" hardware store (840 Fifth Avenue; 619/232-7123).

Prowl the streets of the Gaslamp Quarter for hip and **TRENDY SHOPS**, Pacific Beach's Garnet Avenue for **RETRO AND RESALE** (and piercing and tattoos), Mission Boulevard and the beach towns for **BIKINIS AND SWIMWEAR**. La Jolla is the place to cruise for **UPSCALE SHOPPING**.

Alas, as with many cities, some **INDEPENDENT BOOKSELLERS** have been buried by the superstores. Good shops that still remain are the Blue Door (3823 Fifth Avenue, Hillcrest; 619/298-8610), which is particularly heavy on gay and lesbian titles as well as Beat and offbeat fiction; Libros Bookstore (2754 Calhoun Avenue, Old Town; 619/299-1139), which emphasizes California and Latin American fiction, arts, and history; and Upstart Crow and Company (835 West Harbor Drive, Seaport Village; 619/232-4855), a bookstore/café with reading gallery. Bookstar (3150 Rosecrans Place, Point Loma; 619/225-0465), housed in the refurbished 1945 Loma Theater where bestsellers are heralded on the tail-fin marquee, is one of the more interesting chain establishments.

PERFORMING ARTS

TIMES ARTS TIX (in Horton Plaza at Broadway and Broadway Circle, just steps from the San Diego Repertory Theater; 619/ 497-5000) sells day-of-performance half-price tickets to many theater, dance, and music events, as well as discounted admissions to various attractions and tours. Payment is cash only. Tickets for Sunday performances (when the office is closed) can be purchased on Saturday. Call the above number for recorded information, including which tickets are available. **TICKET-**

MASTER (619/220/8497) sells tickets by phone to most performing arts events, with an added service charge and handling fee. Call for information on TicketMaster locations throughout the county.

MUSIC

The SAN DIEGO OPERA (at the Civic Theatre, 202 C Street; 619/232-7636), still thriving under the 15-year leadership of artistic director Ian Campbell (whose contract doesn't end until 2011), presents five operas per season, January through May, performed and conducted by a trove of international superstars. Recent offerings have included *Falstaff*, *Of Mice and Men*, and *Hansel and Gretel*. The SAN DIEGO SYMPHONY (750 B Street; 619/235-0804) has made a happy, albeit shaky, recovery from bankruptcy—and is back at home in its own Symphony Hall, performing a variety of series from blue-jean casual to formal black-tie, October through May, plus a Summer Pops Festival July through September. Other classical groups include the SAN DIEGO CHAMBER ORCHESTRA (which plays at various locations; 760/753-6402 or 888/848-7326), LA JOLLA CHAMBER MUSIC SOCIETY (also various locations, 858/459-3724), LA JOLLA SYMPHONY AND CHORUS (various locations; 858/534-4637), and SAN DIEGO EARLY MUSIC SOCIETY (various locations; 619/291-8246).

In summer, Spreckels Organ Pavilion presents FREE SUNDAY AFTER-NOON CONCERTS at 2pm on the enormous 4,445-pipe outdoor organ in Balboa Park (2211 Pan American Road East; 619/702-8138). ANNUAL MUSIC FESTIVALS include the Mainly Mozart series (various locations, 619/239-0100); February's Bob Marley Day Festival (619/230-1190) at the San Diego Sports Arena (3500 Sports Arena Boulevard; 619/230-1190); and Street Scene (tickets available through TicketMaster; 619/220-8497), September's three-day music extravaganza in the streets of the Gaslamp Quarter, which draws more than 60 bands—including many big-name international entertainers—to ten stages.

DANCE

The class-act CALIFORNIA BALLET COMPANY (8276 Ronson Road; 619/560-6741), more than three decades old and under the artistic direction of Maxine Mahon, performs four or five traditional and contemporary productions a year at various venues throughout the county. The company's flagship *Nutcracker* runs from Thanksgiving through Christmas at downtown's Civic Theater. For MODERN AND CONTEMPO-RARY WORKS, seek out Malashock Dance & Company (PO Box 2171, San Diego 92112; 619/235-2266), San Diego Dance Theater (619/484-7791), or McCaleb Dance (619/551-5599). The San Diego Repertory Theater (79 Horton Plaza; 619/235-8025) is the scene for the annual

Nations of San Diego International Dance Festival (619/544-1000), featuring more than 150 dancers and musicians in a multitude of ethnic styles.

THEATER

The **OLD GLOBE THEATRE** (1363 Old Globe Way, Balboa Park; 619/239-2255) is California's oldest professional theater and San Diego's grande dame, staging 12 productions from January to October (often with guest actors such as Jon Voight, Marsha Mason, and John Goodman), which include classics, contemporary dramas, musicals, experimental works, and the famed summer **SHAKESPEARE FESTIVAL**. The Old Globe is part of the Simon Edison Centre for the Performing Arts, which is also home to the Cassius Carter Centre Stage (same address and phone number as above). The **LA JOLLA PLAYHOUSE**, winner of a Tony Award for best regional theater, not only draws professional touring groups and big-name talent such as Holly Hunter and Linda Hunt, but also previewed Broadway shows such as *Tommy, Big River,* and *How to Succeed in Business Without Really Trying* before the shows ever took a bite out of the Big Apple. Six productions are mounted, May through November, in the Mandell Weiss Center for the Performing Arts on the UCSD campus (2910 La Jolla Village Drive, at Torrey Pines Road, La Jolla; 858/550-1010). **SAN DIEGO REPERTORY THEATRE**—the city's first resident acting company—performs a broad range of classic and contemporary dramas, along with musicals and comedies, at the Lyceum Theater (79 Horton Plaza; 619/235-8025). Its two-week run of *A Christmas Carol*—with a new version each year—is a local favorite. Musicals are performed by the **SAN DIEGO COMIC OPERA COMPANY** (Casa del Prado, Balboa Park; 619/239-8836) October through June, and in Balboa Park's outdoor amphitheater by the **STARLIGHT MUSICAL THEATRE** (Starlight Bowl, Balboa Park; 619/544-7827) mid-June through mid-September.

The roster of small local theatres is burgeoning. **HORTON GRAND THEATRE** (444 Fourth Avenue; 619/234-9583) focuses on contemporary works; **THEATRE IN OLD TOWN** (4040 Twiggs Street; 619/688-2494) is a popular stage for revues; **SAN DIEGO JUNIOR THEATRE** (Casa del Prado, Balboa Park; 619/239-8355) is a hit with youngsters and young-actors-to-be; and **LAMB'S PLAYERS THEATRE** (1142 Orange Avenue, Coronado; 935/437-0600) offers first-rate productions in an intimate setting. For avant-garde, cutting edge works, it's **SLEDGEHAMMER THEATRE** (1620 Sixth Avenue; 619/544-1484) or the **FRITZ THEATER** (420 Third Avenue; 619/233-7505), a cool location for provocative and experimental offerings. **DIVERSIONARY THEATRE** (4545 Park Boulevard; 619/220-0097) presents gay- and lesbian-friendly works; and **MYSTERY CAFÉ** (505 Kalmia Street, at the Imperial House Restaurant; 619/544-1600) is a mecca for those who like to combine dinner with murder. **SUSHI PERFORMANCE AND VISUAL ART** (320 Eleventh Avenue; 619/235-8466), not recommended for prudes, showcases often-controversial performance artists, including top talents from New York, Los Angeles, and San Francisco.

FILM

Though San Diego movie theaters (and the films shown therein) tend to be of the multiplex variety, **FOREIGN AND ART FILMS** are shown regularly at the Ken Cinema (4061 Adams Avenue, Kensington; 619/283-5909); Hillcrest Cinemas (3965 Fifth Avenue, Hillcrest; 619/299-2100); and The Cove (7730 Girard Avenue, La Jolla; 619-459-5404). UCSD hosts the **SAN DIEGO INTERNATIONAL FILM FESTIVAL** (Mandeville Auditorium, UCSD; 619/534-8497) from February through May, screening premieres of more than 18 international films, as well as short subjects. Animated-film aficionados beeline to the annual **FESTIVAL OF ANIMATION**, held April through May at Museum of Contemporary Art (700 Prospect Street, La Jolla; 858/234-1001). For several days each September, the **UNDERWATER FILM FESTIVAL** allows celluloid glimpses into watery realms at the Civic Theatre (San Diego Concourse; 619/615-4100).

During summer months, **REVIVAL FILMS** can be enjoyed alfresco at Garden Cabaret (4040 Goldfinch Street, Mission Hills; 619/295-4221), while in August everything from mainstream to classic films are projected onto **SCREENS ON BARGES** that float between San Diego and the Mexican border, while movie buffs gawk from the beach. For movies and barge locations, call the Cinema Society (619/280-1600). Other venues combining water with water-theme films are Dive-In Movies at The Plunge (3115 Ocean Front Walk, Mission Beach; 619/488-3110), where viewers nonchalantly watch *Jaws* and other flicks as they float atop rafts in a bathtub-warm indoor swimming pool; and Movies Before the Mast (1306 North Harbor Drive; 619/234-9153), which projects the films onto a "screensail" from April to October aboard the 1863 windjammer *Star of India*. The **IMAX** screen at the Reuben H. Fleet Space Theater and Science Center (1875 El Prado, Balboa Park; 619/238-1233) affords practically-in-the-picture views of everything from Alaska and Mount Everest to outer space and race-car driving.

NIGHTLIFE

BARS: A longtime favorite with San Diego politicians and sophisticates is **DOBSON'S** (956 Broadway Circle, near Broadway, across from Horton Plaza; 619/696-0398). Equally trendy **FIO'S** (801 Fifth Avenue, at F Street; 619/234-3467) has a corner location for extra see-and-be-seenability. More casual **CAFÉ LULU** (419 F Street, near Fourth Avenue;

619/238-0114) is open late for beer and wine. Sports-bar powerhouses include **SEAU'S** (1640 Camino del Rio North, in Mission Valley Center; 619/291-7328), which is owned by San Diego Charger Junior Seau, and **FUNDIDO'S** (1775 East Mission Bay Drive, at the San Diego Hilton Resort; 619/276-4010). Folks in search of a quiet drink try the **PALACE BAR** (311 Island Avenue, in the Horton Grand Hotel; 619/544-1886), while the pints-and-darts crowd hit **THE PRINCESS PUB AND GRILLE** (1675 India Street, at Date Street; 619/702-3021). College-type ragers favor raunchy **DICK'S LAST RESORT**, which is so disgustingly rowdy and rude it's almost lovable (345 Fourth Avenue; 619/231-9100). **KARL STRAUS BREWERY & GRILL** (1157 Columbia Street; 619/234-2739) continues to win multiple awards for best microbrewery.

CLUBS: CROCE'S JAZZ BAR (802 Fifth Avenue, at F Street; (619) 233-4355), is a top club for traditional jazz, while adjoining **CROCE'S TOP HAT** leans toward the blues; both are run by late musician Jim Croce's widow, and his son A. J. occasionally performs . **PATRICK'S II** (428 F Street; 619/233-3077) is another enduring favorite for jazz and blues. The newer **JUKE JOINT CAFÉ** (327 Fourth Avenue; 619/232-7685) shows a lot of promise and very non-juke-joint elegance. The cooler-than-cool crowd frequents **BLUE TATTOO** (835 Fifth Avenue; 619/238-7191) and **E STREET ALLEY** (919 4th Avenue; 619/231-9200). Other hopping spots include **JIMMY LOVE'S** (672 Fifth Avenue; 619/595-0123) for the thirtysomething crowd, high-energy **CLUB 66** (901 Fifth Avenue; 619/234-4166); and **CASBAH** (2501 Kettner Boulevard; 619/232-4355), the best alternative club in town. **THE FLAME** (3780 Park Boulevard; 619/295-4163) caters mainly to lesbians, though guys get a token night; and gay men gravitate to **RICH'S** (1051 University Avenue; 619/497-4588).

In the beach areas, the **CANNIBAL BAR** (3999 Mission Boulevard, in the Catamaran Hotel, Mission Beach; 619/539-8650) is a mainstay, featuring local and name entertainment. **HUMPHREY'S BY THE BAY** (2241 Shelter Island Drive; 619/523-1010) is quite possibly the city's best live music club, hosting a variety of entertainment, including an outdoor series from May through October and featuring seat-grabbers such as Willie Nelson and Ray Charles.

For sheer comedy, choose the **COMEDY STORE** (916 Pearl Street, La Jolla; 858/454-9176). Big-name hotshots from Los Angeles as well as promising amateurs dish out chuckles at this club.

SPECTATOR SPORTS

Though the **SAN DIEGO PADRES** lost the 1998 World Series, the team still won a baseball stadium. The new venue will be built near the Gaslamp Quarter; until then, the "Pads" can be cheered at Qualcomm Stadium (9449 Friars Road, Mission Valley; 619/283-4494). The **SAN DIEGO**

CHARGERS also grab cheers at Qualcomm and the stadium is also the site of December's Holiday Bowl, the Western Athletic Conference championship football game.

FESTIVALS

The SAN DIEGO CREW CLASSIC is saluted at Mission Bay in April (619/488-0700). As befits its proximity to Mexico, San Diego celebrates CINCO DE MAYO throughout the county. On this side of the border, Old Town is one of the best spots to join the festivities. THE BLUE ANGELS and other aero-showoffs blast the skies at Miramar's Naval Air Show, usually held in late July (45249 Miramar Way, 619/577-1227). The U.S. OPEN SANDCASTLE COMPETITION (619/424-6663), a July event in Imperial Beach, is one of the country's largest, attracting old pros and little kids. Balboa Park's Museum of Man (1350 El Prado, 619/239-2001) is transformed into a fabulously frightening HOUSE OF HORRORS at Halloween. The two-day CHRISTMAS ON EL PRADO in Balboa Park (619/239-0512) is a festive beginning to the holiday season, with a candlelight procession, entertainment, food stalls, and free evening admission to the park's museums. Another holiday kickoff is El Cajon's MOTHER GOOSE PARADE (619/444-8712), held the weekend before Thanksgiving. More than 200 floats are featured in this 50-plus-year-old event. The SAN DIEGO HARBOR PARADE OF LIGHTS, on two December weekends, is a dazzling display of decorated boats sailing from Shelter Island to Seaport Village. The HOLIDAY BOWL (San Diego State University, PO Box 601400, San Diego, CA 92160; 619/283-5808) parade and football game in late December is a traffic- and work-stopper. For more information on annual events contact the SAN DIEGO CONVENTION & VISITORS BUREAU (401 B Street, Suite 1400, San Diego 92101; 619/232-3101; www.sandiego.org).

RESTAURANTS

Athens Market Taverna / ★★

109 WEST F ST, SAN DIEGO; 619/234-1955

 This Greek restaurant is a favorite with lawyers and other downtown professionals for lunch, dinner, and after-work cocktails; their well-heeled, well-dressed demeanor goes nicely with the understated, elegant white linen tablecloths and napkins, tiny candles, and dried flowers gracing each table. Owner Mary Pappas has been cooking up sublime Greek food downtown since 1974, and her devoted clientele followed her from her first location at Fourth Avenue and E Street to the current digs just south of Horton Plaza. Among the most succulent dishes is the fall-off-the-bone baked lemon chicken, served with rice pilaf, roasted potato wedge, vegetable, and soup or salad. The lentil soup is zesty, though the egg-lemon soup is almost too subtle, and the salad greens at last visit were gasping for oxygen. Still, there's something so chic yet comfortable about Athens Market Taverna that occasional wilted lettuce is almost instantly forgiven. *$$; AE, DC, DIS, MC, V; no checks; lunch, dinner Mon–Sat, dinner Sun; full bar; reservations recommended; at Rancho Carmel Dr.* &

Azzura Point / ★★★⯪

4000 CORONADO BAY RD (LOEWS CORONADO BAY RESORT), CORONADO; 619/424-4477

A strong contender for best restaurant in San Diego, this dining room at the Loews Coronado Bay Resort is a star. A multimillion-dollar renovation turned the harbor-view restaurant into a vision of safari chic that perfectly reflects the resort atmosphere. Service is polished and knowledgeable, the wine list extensive (and expensive). Chef de cuisine Michael Stebner and his talented staff consistently turn out fantastic dishes incorporating Pacific Rim, classic French, and Mediterranean flavors. Pristinely fresh fish and shellfish imported from around the world always sparkle; particular standouts are the oysters splashed with sake vinaigrette, the lobster risotto, and France's rare *loup de mer*. Nightly prix fixe dinners offer multicourse tasting menus that are a signature of this dining room and a fine way to sample the cuisine. Save room for dessert—a melted chocolate truffle cake makes you feel like you've won the Lotto. *$$$; AE, MC, V; no checks; dinner Tues–Sun; full bar; reservations recommended; off Silver Strand Hwy.* &

Bali Authentic Indonesian / ★★

7660 FAY AVE, LA JOLLA; 858/454-4540

San Diego's first (and only) Indonesian restaurant is a charmer, from the gracious servers to the fascinating cuisine. Settle into the two-level dining room filled with Balinese artifacts and prepare to be delighted by a beautifully presented meal. You'll quickly learn why Indonesia earned the name Spice Islands: predominant flavors include ginger, nutmeg, lemongrass, cinnamon, and a variety of chilies. For starters, try the fiery tamarind soup or the *lemper*, a blend of chicken, sticky rice, and assorted spices cooked in a banana leaf. Then move on to any of the entrees that sound intriguing; we haven't found a loser in the bunch. Need a recommendation? Ask the batik-clad staff, or try the tofu curry, the pork with ginger, the chicken saté, or one of the rijsttafel combinations. The latter, a feast of various dishes and condiments, is a fun and instructive way to sample the best of Indonesian cooking all at once. *$$; AE, DC, DIS, MC, V; no checks; lunch Fri–Sun, dinner every day; beer and wine; reservations recommended; at Kline St.* &

Bayou Bar and Grill / ★★

329 MARKET ST, SAN DIEGO; 619/696-8747

Bringing a little bit of Bourbon Street to Market Street—that's what San Diego's best Cajun restaurant is about. Between the Dixieland jazz (including live performances for New Year's Eve and Mardi Gras), the Big Easy posters, and the huge selection of chili sauces for sale, it's easy to imagine yourself in the French Quarter. The Southern cooking delivers authentic punch as well, generating lots of requests for the jambalaya, shrimp po'boy, fiery blackened fish, and soft-shell crab. Save a little room for dessert because the place is famous for a chilled peanut butter mousse pie and a bourbon-spiked bread pudding. In addition to the bar area and dining rooms, there's patio seating on the sidewalk fronting Market Street, a favorite vantage point on busy weekend nights. If you're in town during Mardi Gras season, this is the place to be for hearty partying and hurricanes that go down smooth and cold. *$$; AE, CB, DC, DIS, MC, V; no checks; lunch, dinner every day; full bar; reservations recommended; bayoubar@aol.com; between Third and Fourth Sts.* &

Belgian Lion / ★★★⯪

2265 BACON ST, OCEAN BEACH; 619/223-2700

Chef/owner Don Coulon is the heart and soul of this exquisite French restaurant, which he runs with several members of his family. A star on the local scene for more than 15 years, the Belgian Lion continues to wow critics, longtime customers, and first-time visitors with a mix of traditional and contemporary fare. There's not a disappointing dish on the menu, but over the years the following have become true classics: salmon sauced with sorrel, hearty cassoulet, chicken Normande with apples and turnip soufflé. Lacy curtains, old-fashioned decor, a cozy bar, and flattering lighting make this a favorite choice for couples; larger groups can be accommodated in a separate dining room with advance notice. Be sure to spend some time perusing the wine list, which includes rarely seen imports and many little-known California treasures chosen by the chef, a committed connoisseur. The small staff treats repeat visitors practically like family, and while entrees average at least $20, the personal service and Old World ambience make the Belgian Lion one of our special occasion faves. *$$$; AE, DC, DIS, MC, V; no checks; dinner Thurs–Sat; beer and wine; reservations recommended; corner of Bacon St and W Point Loma Ave.*

Bella Luna / ★★

748 5TH AVE, SAN DIEGO; 619/239-3222

Downtown's Gaslamp Quarter offers a staggering number of trattorias, but those in the know keep going back to this eye-catching Italian restaurant whose name means "beautiful moon." The dining room is one of the Gaslamp's most striking; the ceiling evokes blue sky and clouds and has dozens of artworks celebrating the moon. There's also seating at the bar and on the sidewalk patio, a prime vantage point for Fifth Avenue people-watching. The tempting menu is strong on appetizers, with five different carpaccios (try the smoked duck with truffle oil) and a particularly nice salad of arugula, radicchio, and shaved Parmesan. Main courses of note include the veal saltimbocca, tagliatelle with salmon and leeks, penne with eggplant, and risottos that change with the season. Along with a decent wine selection, the restaurant serves six varieties of grappa and a number of fine aged tequilas. Service is skilled, and the restaurant has a distinctively European cachet that sets it apart from the crowd. *$$; AE, DC, MC, V; no checks; lunch Mon–Fri, dinner every day; full bar; reservations recommended; between F and G Sts.*

Bombay / ★★

3975 5TH AVE, HILLCREST; 619/298-3155

This Indian restaurant is a pleasing place to pass the time over lunch or dinner, especially if you sit near the trickling indoor fountain or on the sheltered outdoor patio. It's a peaceful refuge from bustling Fifth Avenue, with unobtrusive service and calming earth-toned decor. The wide-ranging menu is designed to please just about everyone. Top selections for carnivores are the excellent lamb stews (the red-hot vindaloo with ginger is a standout) and the moist tandoori-style chicken prepared in a real tandoor oven. Vegetarians will be delighted with a choice of more than 20 meat-free dishes, especially the curries and the delicious puree of fresh spinach. And everyone should love the breads, especially a garlicky naan that's just right for sopping up any last bits of sauce. The best deal here is a luncheon buffet for around $8; it's all-you-can-eat and includes basmati rice, various stews and curries, condiments, soups, and that terrific tandoori chicken. *$$; AE, DIS, MC, V; no checks; lunch, dinner every day; beer and wine, reservations recommended; between University Ave and Washington St.* &

Cafe Athena / ★

1846 GARNET AVE, PACIFIC BEACH; 858/274-1140

Service has always been the Achilles heel of this comfy, casual Greek eatery in one of Pacific Beach's wood-shingled strip malls, but the food makes up for it. Locals in casual clothes amble in to eat and converse, not to see and be seen. The restaurant's interior, although architecturally uninspired, is gladdened by oil paintings of the Greek isles crowding the walls. In addition to satisfying dishes such as lemon chicken soup (a bit chunky with lots of rice) and cinnamon-laced moussaka with a side of rice pilaf, there are some memorable house specialties. Try the Shrimp Scorpio: shrimp grilled and then baked in a spicy sauce of garlic, olive oil, parsley, and tomatoes. Spinach pastitsio is another house specialty;

it's a creamy casserole of penne pasta, spinach, and bechamel sauce. For an appetizer, split an order of four delicately flavored bourekia, fried rolls of filo stuffed with flavorful ground lamb, onion, and pine nuts. The hummus, tzatziki, and taramasalata are all inspired. There's a brisk business in takeout and catering service too. *$; AE, CB, DC, DIS, MC, V; no checks; lunch, dinner every day; beer and wine; reservations recommended for groups of six or more; at Lamont in Pacific Plaza II.* ⟵

Cafe Japengo / ★★
8960 UNIVERSITY CENTER LN, LA JOLLA; 858/450-3355

Owned by the adjacent Hyatt Regency La Jolla, Cafe Japengo is one of the most stylish and sophisticated restaurants in San Diego County, catering to the unabashedly trendy who relish attitude along with their order. The decor is a marvelous combination of industrial chic, Asian design, and California cliché—exposed-duct ceilings, Japanese-pebble flooring, Chinese paper lanterns, bamboo and birds of paradise, an exhibition kitchen, and showpiece sushi bar. The menu is well-coordinated with the environment—an eclectic blend of Asian inspiration and North and South American influences. Dinners include imaginative miso marinated halibut over Israeli couscous (with straw mushrooms, soy mirin, and crispy sweet potato), tamarind-honey glazed swordfish (with citrus black bean sauce, wok-mixed vegetables, and crispy leeks), grilled beef filet on garlic-chili mashed potatoes (with Chinese broccoli, cipolline onions, and black bean demi-glace), and ten-ingredient wok-fried rice. And for dessert? What else but warm gingerbread. *$$$; AE, DC, DIS, MC, V; no checks; lunch Mon–Fri, dinner every day; full bar; reservations required; at La Jolla Village Dr.* ⟵

Café Sevilla / ★★
555 4TH AVE, SAN DIEGO; 619/233-5979

After a long, hard day, downtown office workers unwind at this Spanish tapas bar in the Gaslamp district, and empty bar stools are a rarity after 5pm. The ambience is the main draw. Bullfight posters and oil paintings of Andalusian beauties surround the mirrored bar, where two bartenders dispense plates of Spanish olives stuffed with anchovies and glasses of Spanish and domestic wine. Although you can make a dinner of such tapas as tortilla española, fried calamari, or mushrooms in white wine garlic sauce at either of the two bars (serenaded by live flamenco guitar after 9:30pm), you might head to the dining room, El Patio Andaluz, which is dressed up like a courtyard from southern Spain. Wrought-iron grills and potted geraniums decorate make-believe windows, and a black light brings out a ceiling full of stars. The most popular dish here is traditional paella valenciana—seafood, sausage, and chicken in saffron rice—but you can also get seafood-only and vegetarian versions. Some of the desserts (all made on the premises) really do shine, like the sinful crema catalana, a chocolate espresso crème brûlée topped with whipped cream, with a bottom layer of chocolate chips. In the downstairs Club Sevilla, there's a different brand of live Latino music nightly, with samba and lambada lessons, Spanish rock, salsa, and on Fridays and Saturdays, a so-so flamenco dinner show for $35. *$$; AE, DC, DIS, MC, V; no checks; dinner every day; full bar; reservations recommended; sevilla@ cafesevilla.com; www.cafesevilla.com; between Market and Island Sts.* &

Chez Loma / ★★

1132 LOMA AVE, CORONADO; 619/435-0661

Before you even enter this restaurant, you'll be charmed by the handsome Victorian house and old-money elegance of the Coronado neighborhood. Inside, chef Ken Irvine's graceful mix of classic and updated French cuisine is sure to impress. The small menu emphasizes seasonal seafood and usually includes stellar preparations of duck, salmon, and filet mignon (including a signature steak in a heady blue cheese sauce). The servers here are particularly well-trained—always available when needed, but never intrusive. Add a carefully chosen wine list, romantic enclosed patio, and very fair prices for the quality, and you've got one of Coronado's most delightful eateries. It's an especially good choice for couples celebrating anniversaries. Although children are welcome, this is one of the more grown-up-feeling establishments in town. *$$; AE, DC, DIS, MC, V; no checks; dinner every day, brunch Sun; full bar; reservations recommended; at Orange Ave.*

Chilango's Mexico City Grill / ★★

142 UNIVERSITY AVE, HILLCREST; 619/294-8646

Some of the most interesting and authentic Mexican fare in San Diego is served here in the heart of Hillcrest. The restaurant is small and so are the prices, but the flavors are big, bold, and irresistible. Bring an asbestos palate for the super-spicy chicken-tortilla soup, a particular favorite here (for something milder, choose the black bean porridge). Move on to entrees such as roasted chicken, distinctively flavored with citrus juice and achiote paste; huaraches (thick corn tortillas topped with pork, salsa, and Mexican cheese); and chilaquiles, the comfort-food casserole fashioned from tortillas, chicken, onion, and cilantro. Need a palate quencher? Sample the fresh fruit salad laced with lime juice and cilantro, and you'll never touch fruit cocktail again. *$; cash only; lunch, dinner every day; no alcohol; no reservations; at Third St.*

Dobson's Bar & Restaurant / ★★★

956 BROADWAY CIRCLE, SAN DIEGO; 619/231-6771

One of San Diego's classiest watering holes, Dobson's has a big-city ambience and a clientele to match. Downstairs, the local mover-and-shaker crowd congregates at the polished bar for well-made martinis and smart conversation. Upstairs, a smallish dining room offers marvelous American and French cuisine. Specialties of the house include a rich-as-sin mussel bisque flavored with lobster stock and crowned with puff pastry, sautéed sweetbreads with a texture "like buttah," fresh fish specials, and rack of lamb. For lunch, try the Greek salad or the soup du jour, along with several refills of the warm house sourdough. This is a popular place for pre-theater dining and a good destination for a business lunch or dinner. The favored tables are upstairs overlooking the ever-bustling bar (where you can also dine). For a romantic evening, request the tiny upstairs alcove that's perfect for two. *$$; AE, CB, DC, MC, V; no checks; lunch Mon–Fri, dinner Mon–Sat; full bar; reservations recommended; off Broadway between First and Third Aves.*

El Indio Shop / ★★

409 F ST, SAN DIEGO; 619/239-8151
3695 INDIA ST, MIDDLETOWN; 619/299-0333
In San Diego, the name El Indio is pretty much synonymous with Mexican food. Just about everyone in town knows this little shop, which has built a reputation on tortilla chips, fresh salsa, beef taquitos, and combo plates. The chili-dusted tortilla chips and freshly prepared corn or flour tortillas are favorite souvenirs—locals regularly mail these as care packages to less-fortunate East Coast dwellers. In a nod to the times, a vegetarian menu was added a few years ago, offering surprisingly tasty items

such as mashed potato tacos and vegetarian tamales. At the Middletown location, you can dine inside or across the street on a patio in the shadow of Interstate 5. The downtown location offers a more urban setting in the busy Gaslamp Quarter. To order, head for the counter, then wait until your number is called. Be prepared at lunch: some days it seems as though everyone in town is lined up and ready to place their order. Catering is available too—many a local wedding reception has featured El Indio selections—and many items on the menu are available refrigerated or frozen for bulk orders. *$; MC, V; checks OK; breakfast, lunch, dinner every day; beer and wine; no reservations; at Fourth St.* ὃ

Fairouz Restaurant & Gallery / ★

3166 MIDWAY DR #102, MIDWAY; 619/225-0308
Fairouz is an oasis of fine Greek and Lebanese cuisine and contemporary art in the wasteland of car washes and strip joints that line Midway Drive. Dark blue carpet and wood-grain Formica tables provide a simple backdrop for owner Ibrahim Al Nashashibi's stylized acrylic paintings, which completely fill two dining rooms. Al Nashashibi runs the restaurant with his Moroccan wife Hasida; his sister Sawzia does the cooking. Lovers of Greek food will recognize their favorites, including a very lemony avgolemono (chicken and rice soup), admirable tabbouleh, hummus, tzatziki, and gyros. It's hard to resist the daily lunch and dinner buffets:

both are excellent values for carnivores or vegetarians, and a big hit with kids. The problem is, even if you try just half of the offerings in small portions, you come away significantly stuffed. Buffets consist of lots of salad ingredients, hot and cold potatoes, saffron rice, moussaka, lamb meat balls, and much more—in addition to the foods already mentioned. If humanly possible, save room for a dessert of rice pudding with rose water. Fairouz also caters. *$; AE, DC, DIS, MC, V; no checks; lunch, dinner every day; beer and wine; no reservations; at Rosencrans St.* &

Filippi's Pizza Grotto / ★

1747 INDIA ST, SAN DIEGO (AND BRANCHES); 619/232-5094

Mom and Pop are long gone, but seven sisters and brothers run this string of dependable Italian restaurants, situated all over San Diego. The original is in Little Italy and is the only one with a store. (That's how Filippi's began.) To enter, customers pass in single file past cases of cheese, sliced meats, a barrel of salted and filleted cod, breads from three bakeries, oils, vinegars, and every kind of pasta imaginable. The fragrance is overwhelmingly parmesan. The restaurant itself is huge, with an open kitchen and pizza oven, grotto-dark and busy-noisy. Tables are covered with red checkered cloths; Chianti bottles (hundreds, maybe thousands) hang from the rafters. The same theme prevails in other Filippi's locations in Pacific Beach and outlying neighborhoods. Specialties are lasagne, pizza, ravioli, spaghetti, hot sausage (made on the premises), and a variety of sandwiches on freshly crisp buns. Servings are ample; most diners leave with leftovers. Customers are clearly regulars, addressed by name by waitresses who seem to have been there forever. *$; AE, DC, DIS, MC, V; no checks; lunch, dinner every day; beer and wine; no reservations; between Dane and Fir Sts.* &

Fish Market Restaurant / ★★★
Top of the Market / ★★

750 N HARBOR DR, SAN DIEGO; 619/232-3474

The panoramic views of San Diego Bay are as much an attraction as the huge menu of fresh catches at the Fish Market Restaurant and its upstairs, upscale sister, Top of the Market. Downstairs you'll find a full-service bar, a busy oyster bar, a counter displaying fresh fish to go, and the friendly, casual Fish Market Restaurant. Be prepared to wait for a table (have a drink in the bar or visit the oyster bar for an appetizer). Seating overlooks the bay; the best tables are the ones on the outdoor patio, directly over the water. The menu features a huge selection of fresh-caught seafood prepared grilled, Cajun style, or fried, according to your preference. Fish is served with a side of rice or au gratin potatoes (a sinfully delicious choice) and steaming hot sourdough bread. For the money and bustling ambience, the downstairs restaurant is the better bet. Upstairs, the more formal Top of the Market serves more exotic fresh seafood with more refined presentation and service and price tags to match. The list of offerings is astounding; you can tour the seven seas with Norwegian salmon, Alaskan halibut, New Zealand mussels, and Chilean sea bass, all flown in daily. The linen and candlelight setting is sublimely soothing; window tables present a romantic view of twinkling lights on boats floating in the bay. The wine list is excellent; servers will assist in matching grape and sea flavors. Save this one for a special night. *$$$; AE, CB, DC, DIS, MC, V; no checks; lunch, dinner every day; full bar; reservations recommended for large groups; at Broadway and the end of Pacific Coast Hwy.* &

George's at the Cove / ★★☆

1250 PROSPECT ST, LA JOLLA; 858/454-4244

This popular restaurant on La Jolla's chic Prospect Street has been making local top-10 dining lists for more than a decade. Without a doubt, the three-level property has one of the finest views in the city—a panorama of La Jolla Cove and miles of Pacific coast. But unlike many a view restaurant in town, George's offers some terrific eating as well. The formal downstairs dining room is best for inventive fresh fish dishes that incorporate the flavors of California, France, and the Pacific Rim. The must-have starter is a smoked chicken and broccoli soup that's probably the most-requested recipe in the county (and yes, they'll share it). Follow that with the likes of crab cakes with shiitake "hash browns," diver-harvested scallops partnered with caramelized cauliflower, or local mussels roasted at high heat for a bold, smoky flavor. Upstairs, in the bar (a top destination for singles) and on the rooftop terrace, the menu is a lower-priced affair that features excellent seafood salads, a gourmet meat loaf sandwich, very good focaccia, and splendid desserts. Two more reasons to drop by: the ever-changing collection of contemporary art in the main dining rooms, and owner George Hauer's thoughtfully chosen wine list. Note: Reservations aren't accepted on the upstairs terrace, which is open daily for lunch and dinner, but the open-air setting and throngs of swell-looking diners make it worth the wait. *$$$; AE, DC, DIS, MC, V; no checks; lunch Mon–Sat, dinner every day; full bar; reservations recommended downstairs; www.georgesatthecove.com; at Torrey Pines Rd.* &

Jasmine / ★★☆

4609 CONVOY ST, KEARNY MESA; 858/268-0888

With seating for 800 diners, Jasmine at first glance might resemble a vast Chinese food factory. But don't be scared away. This handsome eatery specializing in Cantonese cooking manages to couple high quality with sheer quantity. Dim sum is served every day of the week, with the crowds peaking on Saturday and Sunday when the selection is at its most staggering. From sticky rice steamed in a lotus leaf to crispy chicken feet and barbecued pork, everybody's favorites show up on the fully laden carts.

Dinner entrees include steamed fresh fish pulled live from large tanks just minutes before it hits your plate, excellent prawns the size of small lobsters, a marvelous shellfish stir-fry, and top-notch Peking duck. The place is equally popular with businesspeople and large families. While it's often packed, the skilled servers handle everyone with speed and aplomb. *$$;* *AE, MC, V; no checks; lunch, dinner every day; full bar; reservations recommended; at Bagget St.*

Kaiserhof / ★★

2253 SUNSET CLIFFS BLVD, OCEAN BEACH; 619/224-0606

German food is done to perfection at this unpretentious biergarten just an oom-pah-pah from the beach. From authentic Wiener schnitzel to oh-so-tender beef rouladen to a dozen or so hearty side dishes, everything here is worthy of Oktoberfest in the Old Country. Portions are ridiculously large, and you may notice a waddle in your walk after a dinner that includes a choice of soup or salad, two side dishes, and plenty of bread. Of course, a number of German beers are available on tap, which makes up for a decided lack of wine selections. Best seating is in the dining room with the fireplace or on the shaded patio, depending on the weather. Customers range from fresh-faced young couples on first dates to white-haired regulars who've been Kaiserhof fans for decades. *$$; AE, CB, DC, DIS, MC, V; no checks; lunch, dinner every day; full bar; reservations recommended; at W Point Loma Blvd.* &

Karl Strauss Brewery & Grill / ★★

9675 SCRANTON RD, SORRENTO VALLEY (AND BRANCHES); 858/587-2739

Part of a locally founded chain that's become wildly popular over the last decade, this casual brewery-restaurant is set in a deceptively elegant Japanese garden. Half the fun of visiting here is winding along the paths and through the greenery to the koi pond and inviting deck; the other is knocking back well-made ales (along with an impressive selection of wines by the glass) and chowing down on filling traditional bar fare. Specialties of the house include plump, spicy sausages, well-made burgers, sandwiches from Philly-style steak to portobello mushroom, filet mignon, and grilled salmon. Given the sizeable business crowd that populates Sorrento Valley and the nearby Golden Triangle area, this can be heaven for yuppie singles, especially during happy hour. Keep in mind that the restaurant is closed on Saturdays, when it's often booked for wedding receptions and corporate parties. *$$; MC, V; no checks; lunch, dinner Sun–Fri (closed Sat for private parties); beer and wine; reservations recommended; at Miramesa Blvd.*

Kemo Sabe / ★★☆

3958 5TH AVE, HILLCREST; 619/220-6802

Forget any references to the Lone Ranger. In this part of town, Kemo Sabe simply means Wow, referring equally to this eatery's spicy fusion fare and the chic, confident decor. From the metal-inlaid tables to the intricate ironworks inspired by primitive Native American art, the look is smashing indeed. The faint of palate need not drop by; chef Deborah Scott's cuisine is fashioned from the fiery personalities of Thailand, Mexico, and the American Southwest. Typical dishes include a grilled fish napoleon layered with pesto, goat cheese, and grilled vegetables; Asian-style dim sum served as a platter for two; and a grilled skirt steak that ought to be served with a fire extinguisher. A good selection of food-friendly wines and bold microbrew beers accompanies the food with style, and service is hip and accommodating. The location in a happening part of Hillcrest (near the Hillcrest Cinemas, one of the best movie theaters in town) keeps Kemo Sabe hopping; make reservations if you're looking to dine on the weekends. *$$; AE, DIS, MC, V; no checks; lunch, dinner every day; full bar; reservations recommended; between University Ave and Washington St.* &

Laurel Restaurant & Bar / ★★★

505 LAUREL ST, SAN DIEGO; 619/239-2222

Laurel is so lovely and sophisticated you might think you've strolled into some chic new spot in San Francisco or New York. After you've valet-parked, make an entrance down the staircase into the main dining room and adjacent bar. Be graceful; this is the kind of place where heads turn each time the door is opened. While it's true that many come to Laurel simply for the panache of pricey furnishings, flattering light, and exquisite martinis, many more are drawn by the memorable fare. Chef Doug Organ, who also oversees the kitchen at the WineSellar & Brasserie, keeps palates entertained with an ever-changing mix of Mediterranean, North African, Provençal, and classic French cuisine. Organ is especially well-known for his rustic Provençal chicken stewed in a pot with a flurry of fragrant herbs and his masterful duck confit with silken meat and crackly skin. Lamb and Moroccan spices, long-simmered osso buco, and roasted wild boar are all favorites on his oft-changing menu. An outstanding wine list offers many an unfamiliar bottle from various regions of France, although the list by the glass is somewhat lacking. Service is generally quite good, but it's the genial bartenders who really set the standard for Laurel's staff. Maybe that's why so many regulars drop by for a quick bite at the bar. *$$$; AE, DC, DIS, MC, V; no checks; dinner every day; full bar; reservations recommended; at Fifth Ave.*

The Marine Room / ★★★☆

2000 SPINDRIFT DR, LA JOLLA; 858/459-7222

Between the unparalleled oceanfront location, the special-occasion ambience, and the talents of executive chef Bernard Guillas, the Marine Room is a true original. Descend the staircase into this dining room built right on the sand, and you'll see why generations of San Diegans come here for romantic evenings of dining and dancing. The north and south dining rooms offer unrestricted views of the coastline; the central bar has the cozy buzz of locals relaxing over the week's gossip with a gin and tonic. Light colored decor and crisp white linens create an airy, open feel. The cuisine came into its own when chef Guillas arrived on the scene a few years ago; today, a formerly good restaurant is outstanding. The French native infuses his brand of Mediterranean/Pacific Rim/California fare with imaginative flavors, from sambuca and fresh lavender to candied shallots and crunchy greens from the sea. Halibut, foie gras, ahi, and sweetbreads are some of the standouts on the menu, which changes according to the season and the chef's whims. Recent highlights have been the halibut poached in pinot Noir, the dry-aged strip steak with truffle-based potatoes, and the goose liver paired with preserved cherries and cognac. Be sure to check out the restaurant's dramatic High Tide Breakfasts during the winter, complete with a luxurious buffet and waves misting the windows. Since the dining room is connected to the La Jolla Beach and Tennis Club, you'll see some casually clad folks here, but it's really much more fun to dress to the nines, make an entrance, and get the other diners wondering which Who's Who you're listed in. *$$$; AE, CB, DC, DIS, MC, V; no checks; lunch, dinner every day, brunch Sun; full bar; reservations recommended; www.marineroom.com; at Torrey Pines Rd.*

MiXX / ★★☆

3671 5TH AVE, HILLCREST; 619/299-6499

One of San Diego's most exciting eateries, trendy MiXX is a place where innumerable culinary influences and ingredients blossom into a nightly kaleidoscope of flavors. The kitchen's goal, as stated on the menu, is "cuisine with no ethnic boundaries." That would explain the bold mix of southwestern, Pacific Rim, traditional French, Vietnamese, and fusion cooking that attracts a steady stream of customers to this lively, dinner-only establishment. Daily specials featuring lamb, pork tenderloin, or fish are always worth a try, but don't ignore the regular lineup: a French burnt walnut salad, peppered seared ahi, and duck ravioli helped make MiXX an instant hit on the local dining scene. The two-level restaurant offers a trio of seating options: the piano bar downstairs, a very see-and-be-seen dining room on the second level, and a plant-filled patio offering a bit more privacy at the back. In addition to the good-looking clientele, talented chefs, and skilled servers, MiXX is known as a showcase for contemporary art—much of it available for sale. *$$; AE, CB, DC, DIS, MC, V; no checks; dinner every day; full bar; reservations recommended; at Pennsylvania Ave.* &

Montanas / ★★

1421 UNIVERSITY AVE, HILLCREST; 619/297-0722

Ever since its splashy appearance on the dining scene some years back, Montanas has been packing 'em in with a sassy blend of spicy cooking, sleek environs, très cool crowd, and contemporary art. Business types often crowd the dining room during lunch, while an eclectic mix of young and old clad in anything from khaki pants to spandex keep the room busy right up to closing time. The appealing menu handles classic American cuisine with style, updating standards like grilled chicken and skirt steak with the flavors of the Southwest. Standout dishes include chili made with wild game or venison; barbecued ribs; a citrus-dressed salad tossed with pinenuts, perfectly ripe strawberries, and blackberries; and a silky chocolate caramel tart. Large parties can reserve a semiprivate room lined with wine bottles; prime seating for couples or foursomes is in the front booths overlooking the sidewalk. Often noisy and always interesting, Montanas is a great stop for a single perfectly made martini or an entire meal. *$$; AE, DC, DIS, MC, V; no checks; lunch Mon–Fri, dinner every day; full bar; reservations recommended; at Richmond St.* &

Morton's of Chicago / ★★★

285 J ST (HARBOR CLUB), SAN DIEGO; 619/696-3369

Welcome to the land of expense-account dinners, prime midwestern beef, expertly shaken martinis, and baked potatoes almost the size of footballs. Morton's offers steak house dining at its best, which means all the wood-paneled ambience and waiterly ceremony you can handle. The crowd is much less formal, however; this national chain draws a mix of Hawaiian-shirted tourists, name-tagged conventioneers, and others dressed in everything from Gap to Gucci. Steaks, vegetables, and other items (including outsized live lobsters) are presented for your approval at the table before being turned into some truly top-notch all-American fare. Black bean soup and Caesar salad are the appetizers of choice; then it's a toss-up between the New York strip, the double-thick lamb chops, or the lightly breaded Veal Sicilian as your main course. Portions are enormous, but you'll still want to indulge in one of the fabulous dessert soufflés or the Godiva chocolate truffle cake that takes the current rage for warm, gooey, melted-center desserts to new heights. A pricey but well-chosen wine list offers top California cabernets and double magnums of premium champagnes. Be ready to spend some money, and prepare for a splendid evening of excess. *$$$; AE, DC, MC, V; no checks; dinner every day; full bar; reservations recommended; www.mortons.com; between Second and Third Aves.* &

Nick's at the Beach / ★★
809 THOMAS ST, PACIFIC BEACH; 619/270-1730

Nick's is really two restaurants in one, both of them fun. On the first floor, a small bar area and spacious dining room offer a wide variety of well-priced, well-prepared meals ranging from meat loaf to Cajun gumbo. We're certain that the mussels steamed with tomatillos and lime juice take top honors here, but the competition is stiff from Nick's Caesar salad, the quesadilla stuffed with garlic mashed potatoes, the well-seasoned crab cakes, and the fresh fish specials. The seafood pasta dressed with feta cheese and basil is also a special treat. Upstairs, a young crowd parties with a CD jukebox, four pool tables, lots of TVs, and a terrific late-night menu served daily till 1am. A recent remodel has added an ocean-view patio upstairs, while creating a needed bit of soundproofing and intimacy in the main dining room below. In addition to a stellar collection of beers on tap, the wine list offers lots of selections by both glass and bottle at user-friendly prices. No one under 21 is allowed upstairs. *$; AE, DIS, MC, V; no checks; lunch, dinner every day (bar menu until 1am); full bar; reservations recommended; at Mission Blvd.* &

Olé Madrid / ★☆
755 5TH AVE, SAN DIEGO; 619/557-0146

One of the Gaslamp Quarter's most enduring clubs, Olé Madrid attracts an A-list crowd arriving late on Friday and Saturday to drink and dance the night away. On weekends, this is truly the home of the young and the restless. But although the sangria here is fabulous, the music cutting-edge, and the young male bartenders downright sexy, Olé Madrid manages to be a pretty good Spanish restaurant as well. Tapas range from basics like manchego cheese and chorizo sausage to garlicky grilled shrimp and chicken croquettes. Main dishes include well-made paellas and grilled fish and meats, and the wine list features some noteworthy Spanish reds. The bar and dining rooms at this three-level hangout are attractive, with enormous flower arrangements, velvet curtains creating private spaces, and curving stairways. On balmy nights, the sidewalk patio offers a front-row view of the passing scene and the less fortunate in line waiting to get in. *$$; AE, MC, V; no checks; lunch Saturday, dinner Tues–Sun; full bar; reservations recommended; at F St.* &

On the Border / ★
1770 CAMINO DE LA REINA, MISSION VALLEY; 619/209-3700

Sure, the Tex-Mex food at this bustling Mission Valley restaurant is somewhat gringo-ized—when's the last time you saw a sizzling fajita salad south of the border? But the faux-rustic space complete with fireplace is casual and comfy, and the place is spacious enough that you could drop in practically any time sans reservations and not have to wait. Order the luncheon special of tortilla soup garnished with avocado plus a quesadilla, or the well-made carnitas with extra-tender pork, and you'll be a happy compadre indeed. Enchiladas and tamales are other crowd-pleasers, as are the honey-drizzled sopapillas made with deep-fried, puffy dough (they taste much lighter than they sound). The chicken fajitas tend to arrive looking a bit singed, and the chips and salsa are pretty pedestrian, but overall, this is one of the better dining destinations in the Valley. Thirsty? Check out the selection of tequilas, as well as assorted margaritas and potent Acapulco rum punch. *$$; AE, DIS, MC, V; no checks; lunch, dinner every day; full bar; reservations recommended; at Mission Center Dr.* &

Ortega's / ★★

4888 NEWPORT AVE, OCEAN BEACH; 619/222-4205
Neighborhood Mexican restaurants abound in San Diego; this small cafe with barely a dozen tables is a local favorite. The Ortega family comes from Puebla, one of Mexico's culinary capitals, and they've created the perfect homeland ambience by including much of the extended family in the operation. The family specializes in steamed tamales, which are served at a sidewalk stand during street fairs and farmer's bazaars. Sons and cousins work at an open grill by the front door, letting the savory smells of marinated pork, spiced shrimp, and corn tortillas tempt passersby. Regulars show up during off hours to feast on huevos rancheros drenched in salsa verde and melted cheese, enchiladas topped with mole (a blend of a dozen or more spices guaranteed to challenge the palate), and the best tacos al pastor (corn tortillas filled with grilled pork) this side of Tijuana. Specials include fresh tuna, calamari, or dorado and those incomparable tamales. *$; AE, DIS, MC, V; no checks; breakfast, lunch, dinner every day; beer only; no reservations; at Cable St.*

Piatti / ★★

2182 AVENIDA DE LA PLAYA, LA JOLLA; 858/454-1589
The fashionable neighborhood of La Jolla Shores makes the perfect setting for this ever-trendy Italian restaurant where air-kissing has developed into an art form. Dressed-up socialites, wealthy vacationers, casually clad regulars, and cell-phone-toting businessfolk keep the place hopping at lunch and dinner, and the bar and dining rooms can be cacophonous. Repeat visitors seeking a little peace and quiet ask to sit in the walled-in patio reminiscent of a Tuscan courtyard. Dominated by an enormous tree and loads of greenery, it's a charming spot to savor a Pinot Grigio or Barolo from the wine list. Consistent best sellers include the fancy wood-fired pizzas, roasted chicken, risotto, vegetable lasagne, and beautiful salads. And for an appetizer, the garlicky bruschetta heaped with tomatoes and basil chiffonade can't be beat—it's one of the best versions in town. To fit in with the crowd, keep one eye on your plate, the

other constantly surveying the room to see who's doing what with whom. *$$; AE, DC, MC, V; no checks; lunch, dinner every day; full bar; reservations recommended; at La Jolla Shore Dr.* &

The Prince of Wales Grill / ★★☆

1500 ORANGE AVE (HOTEL DEL CORONADO), CORONADO; 619/522-8819
Recently remodeled with plenty of art deco glamour, The Prince of Wales Grill takes its name from the Duke of Windsor, who, legend has it, rendezvoused with Wallis Simpson at the hotel in 1920. Decorated in warm, rich golds, the dining room offers tables and booths (reserve a booth for privacy), and a predinner visit to the piano bar calls for a martini to get you in the right mood. While a tie isn't mandatory, it certainly isn't out of place and makes for a nice change of pace in laid-back San Diego. This is the place to come for the special celebration—or just to revel in the good life for an evening. Like the decor, the updated menu offers a nod to tradition with rich dishes like lamb chops, yet caters to lighter, contemporary tastes with pastas and fresh seafood. A wonderful wine selection complements the menu and impeccable service. *$$$; AE, CB, DC, DIS, MC, V; no checks; dinner every day; full bar; reservations recommended; on Coronado Island.* &

Red Sails Inn / ★★☆

2614 SHELTER ISLAND DR, POINT LOMA; 619/223-3030
OK, so the decor is some of the oddest in town, complete with stuffed crabs and fish mounted on the walls and a vintage diving suit that looks left over from Halloween. Just don't let that or the humble 50s-esque setting sway you from trying some of San Diego's best old-fashioned seafood at decidedly old-fashioned prices. You won't find any fancy stuff, but the kitchen does a good job with grilled swordfish, mahimahi, monkfish, and sea bass for under $20 a plate. That includes soup or salad and a baked potato on the side. In addition to the two spacious dining rooms, which include a fireplace and harbor view along with those mounted fish, there's a delightful patio right on the water of San Diego Bay. Cheerful servers and basic breakfast and lunch items such as pancakes and tuna sandwiches make this a favorite of locals on the weekends. A huge fountain, boats coming and going, and lots of slumming seagulls keep kids entertained while you eat. *$$; AE, DC, MC, V; no checks; breakfast, lunch, dinner every day; full bar; reservations recommended; 3 blocks off Scott St.*

Roppongi Restaurant, Bar, and Cafe / ★☆

875 PROSPECT ST, LA JOLLA; 858/551-5252
Local restaurateur Sami Ladeki, founder of the hugely popular, family-friendly Sammy's Woodfired Pizza chain, has gone upmarket with this flashy La Jolla endeavor. It's a sight to behold, from the expensive

bric-a-brac to the spectacular aquarium with Day-Glo tropical fish. And the requisitely trendy menu, colored with influences from cutting-edge Pacific Rim to classic Americana, has plenty to dazzle as well—as long as you stick to the appetizers and skip the so-so entrees. The key to dining at Roppongi is to graze, tapas-style, through the list of superbly made starters. A multilayered crab napoleon; skewered scallops, plump and pretty as South Pacific pearls; fiery kung pao calamari; pot stickers filled with shrimp; and more—each is an exquisite, if expensive, little treat. The open dining room includes booth and table seating, as well as a semiprivate dining room for large parties. Out front, a raised fire pit keeps diners comfortable on the coolest evenings. Service ranges from adept to iffy, and the wine list is overpriced, but those top-notch tapas keep us coming back. *$$$; AE, DIS, MC, V; no checks; lunch, dinner every day; full bar; reservations recommended; at Fay St.* &

Saffron Noodles and Saté / ★★☆

3737 INDIA ST, MIDDLETOWN; 619/574-7737
Nobody has done more to introduce San Diegans to the pleasures of Thai cuisine than owner/chef Su-Mei Yu, who founded the tiny original Saffron next door (still a favorite takeout joint). Today, she's expanded her original rotisserie chicken shop into a full-scale noodle house, with dozens of choices that explore a range of styles from mild to incendiary. Classic noodle dishes such as pad thai and spicy noodles are done well, but it's the exotic daily specials flavored with pickled vegetables or fried shallots and the silken curries that are the true stars of this aromatic show. In addition to the artful food, the restaurant features works by glass sculptor Dale Chihuly and painter Italo Scanga. The place is a feast for the eyes as well as the palate, and the low prices make it an affordable treat. *$; MC, V; no checks; lunch, dinner every day; beer and wine; no reservations; at Washington St.* &

Sally's / ★★

I MARKET PL, SAN DIEGO; 619/687-6080
With a prime location in Seaport Village overlooking the harbor and Coronado, Sally's would probably draw plenty of business for the view alone. Between the outdoor tables lining the bayside boardwalk and the great vantage points in the bar, this is one of the prime places in town to watch the world go by. But Sally's doesn't depend solely on its looks; the seafood served up with Mediterranean and Cal-Cuisine influences can be inviting as well. Fresh oysters are a house specialty, and we've found their fresh, salty goodness is further enhanced by one of the frosty Bombay Sapphire martinis prepared by the resident mixologists. Main-dish salads topped with grilled fish or chicken are top sellers for good reason, as are seared scallops, spicy crab cakes, and linguine heaped with sweet, flavorful rock shrimp. Along with the patio seating and comfortable booths in

the dining room, a chef's table in the kitchen may be reserved in advance for up to a dozen diners, who get to watch the staff whip up their custom-designed meal. *$$; AE, CB, DC, DIS, MC, V; no checks; lunch, dinner every day; full bar; reservations recommended; at Harbor Dr.*

Sammy's California Woodfired Pizza / ★★

565 PEARL ST, LA JOLLA (AND BRANCHES); 858/259-6600

San Diego has never been the same since Sami Ladeki brought wood-fired pizza to town. Savor varieties such as LaDou's Barbeque Chicken (with cilantro, smoked Gouda, and red onion), Artichokes (with tomato sauce, mozzarella, and gorgonzola cheese), or Smoked Duck Sausage (with spinach, Roma tomatoes, garlic, and smoked Gouda). Other mouth-watering offerings include Norwegian salmon fillet, grilled chicken salad, and some exquisite pasta dishes (the Spinach Ricotta Tortelloni in cream sauce with wild mushrooms is an artery-clogging trip to heaven). The open kitchen lets you keep a close eye on your order. A full take-out menu is offered. *$; AE, DC, MC, V; no checks; breakfast, lunch, dinner every day; full bar; no reservations; sammys@connectnet.com; www.sammys pizza.com; at Del Mar Heights.* &

Shakespeare Pub and Grille / ★

3701 INDIA ST, MIDDLETOWN; 619/299-0230

The most authentic British pub in all of San Diego, the Shakespeare (or "Shakey's" to the regulars) draws a crowd of expats in search of a bit o' Britain. Families come with the kids in tow for Sunday dinner, while lads gather at other times of the week to catch soccer matches on the telly. Indoors at the wooden bar, British brews dominate the tap—sample the likes of Boddington's and Fuller's, among others, by the half- and full pint. On a sunny afternoon, the outdoor deck overlooking the airport and bay is a fine spot to while away a few hours. A full menu is available too, featuring bangers and mash, shepherd's pie and, of course, chips (french fries), best enjoyed smothered with malt vinegar and salt. Sunday lunch is a feast of roast beef, but in a nod to its American patrons, the management has added fish tacos to the menu. Check with the waitresses for the daily beer specials. Insiders like to welcome the new year at Shakey's, a time when kilted bagpipers march around at 4pm (midnight in England). Not to be missed. *$; AE, MC, V; no checks; lunch, dinner every day; full bar; no reservations; at Washington St.* &

The Sky Room / ★★★☆

1132 PROSPECT ST (LA VALENCIA HOTEL), LA JOLLA; 858/454-0771

Saying La Valencia's The Sky Room is a romantic place to dine is like calling Placido Domingo a pretty good singer. This ocean-view dining room atop La Jolla's venerable pink palace of a hotel is *the* place in town to pop the question (whatever it might be), celebrate an important birthday or anniversary, or simply treat yourself to an evening of elegance and pomp. Gorgeous flower arrangements, tuxedo-clad servers, Wedgwood china, and long-stemmed roses for the ladies provide a feeling of old-world elegance and a lovely showcase for distinctly well-prepared California and French cuisine turned out by a cadre of experienced sous chefs. Selections range from contemporary (free-range chicken with morels, a trio of grilled Gulf fish with fruit relishes) to classic (delicate smoked salmon paired with julienned cucumber, cream of mushroom soup). If they're offering the filet mignon finished with a Merlot demiglace, it's a must have. So is the dessert plate, a selection of sweets that generally includes tidbits of tiramisu, cookies, and sublime chocolate truffles. An extensive wine list is particularly strong in California cabernet and chardonnay, but high rollers will also find plenty of premium French labels, including vintage champagnes. The courtly waiters and helpful sommelier, along with the rarefied ambience, leave you feeling like royalty. Stop by the piano bar in the lobby after dinner for a nightcap of good music in one of La Jolla's loveliest rooms. *$$$; AE, CB, DC, DIS, MC, V; no checks; dinner every day; full bar; reservations required; at Herschel St.* &

Spices Thai Cafe / ★★☆

3810 VALLEY CENTRE DR, STE 903, SORRENTO VALLEY; 858/259-0889

Locals tried valiantly to keep Spices a sort of unofficial secret, but word spread rapidly and now the place is almost always packed. Nonetheless, this soothing dining room decked out in pastel paint, black lacquer, and fresh flowers still feels like a calm oasis. A bad meal here is unheard of, the service is gracious, and even the large lunch and dinner crowds don't diminish the serene vibes. Starters range from Thai spring rolls to dumplings, calamari, tempura, and satés. The list of entrees is long and thought-provoking, including myriad curries, vegetables, noodle and rice dishes (prepared with or without meat and fish), and seafood. House specialties include Sizzling Lemon Grass Chicken, Choo-Chee Duck, and Pattaya Pineapple (pineapple stuffed with chicken, shrimp, and cashew nuts in special house sauce). All dishes are individually prepared, MSG is a no-no, and you can regulate the spiciness by using the restaurant's 1-to-10 scale (10 is for fire-breathing dragons). The lunch specials are a terrific value, with soup of the day, tossed salad, spring roll, fried wonton, steamed rice, and choice of entree thrown into one very inexpensive package. Go after the power lunchers return to their cubicles. *$$; AE, DC, DIS, MC, V; no checks; lunch, dinner every day; beer and wine; reservations recommended; at El Camino Real.* &

St. James Bar at Triangles / ★★

4370 LA JOLLA VILLAGE DR, LA JOLLA; 858/453-6650

One of the classiest restaurants in this singles-bar-heavy neighborhood, St. James tends to attract a well-dressed, sophisticated crowd that takes food and wine quite seriously. The elegant dining room practically glows with subtle lighting, gleaming wood, and a general air of well-being, and it's stylish without being fussy. The varied menu offers something for just about everyone, and a well-chosen wine list ventures far beyond chardonnay and cabernet, with plenty of selections by the bottle or glass. Many patrons choose to eat right at the bar, either at the counter or the nearby tables; for more privacy, request one of the spacious booths in the dining room. In addition to a snazzy mussel bisque (topped with a puff pastry crust and spiked with sherry, if you like), the restaurant is known for deftly grilled salmon and rack of lamb, and main-dish salads topped variously with goat cheese, marinated chicken, or roasted vegetables. During happy hour (4–7pm, Monday through Friday), the bar offers appetizers for half price, along with numerous wine specials by the glass. *$$; AE, CB, MC, V; no checks; lunch Mon–Fri, dinner Mon–Sat; full bar; reservations recommended; at Genessee Ave.* &

Thee Bungalow / ★★☆

4996 W POINT LOMA BLVD, OCEAN BEACH; 619/224-2884

For over 25 years, this family-run restaurant in a converted bungalow home has kept a faithful clientele while attracting new fans all the time. Some diners stick with classics that have been on the menu since the beginning: roast duck garnished with green peppercorns or à l'orange, sea bass served in a luscious seafood sauce, and rack of lamb. Others are attracted by chef/owner Ed Moore's newer creations, which include superb steamed mussels, black-pepper-crusted salmon, and handsome grilled halibut. Since you get soup or salad with your entree (we adore the smoked tomato soup and the tarragon-dressed house salad), you don't need to order a starter. But if you're extra ravenous, do start with the simple cream-sauced tortellini. And wrap up the evening with a crackle-topped crème brûlée, a Bungalow specialty. The lengthy wine list earns praise for both depth of selection and excellent prices, and the restaurant regularly hosts reasonably priced, heavily attended wine dinners that are some of the liveliest around. Although the service and menu are a tad on the formal side, the setting is casual and comfy. Show up in jeans or in jewels—the good people of Thee Bungalow will welcome you just the same. *$$; AE, DC, DIS, MC, V; no checks; dinner every day; full bar; reservations recommended; bungalow@adnc.com; www. theebungalow.com; at Bacon St.* &

Trattoria Acqua / ★★★

1298 PROSPECT ST, LA JOLLA; 858/454-0709

Opened in 1994, Trattoria Acqua is one of San Diego's best-known, best-regarded dining destinations. Part of the notoriety is due to a stunning setting; this indoor/outdoor restaurant, located in the Coast Walk building, is nestled into a La Jolla Cove hillside with ocean views that won't quit. But pretty views are a nickel a dozen in this seaside town; Acqua stands apart for actually delivering high-quality food and service too. The Mediterranean-influenced menu roams gracefully from Tuscany to Provence to Tangiers, with stops along the way for excellent designer pizzas, a variety of antipasti and salads, about a dozen pastas, and lots of grilled fish and meats. Start your meal with the complimentary spicy hummus dip while you peruse the lengthy wine list, where notable names from California and Italy are sold at most reasonable prices. Must-have dishes are the grilled portobello mushroom or bruschetta for starters; among the pastas, the lobster ravioli, penne Piemontese, or rigatoni with eggplant; and for main dishes, the veal shank or herb-crusted halibut. Prime seating is on the patio or one of the inside tables with a view of the water (reserve these well in advance). Validated parking is available in the garage under the building, or angle for a spot on busy Prospect Street. *$$; AE, MC, V; no checks; lunch, dinner every day; full bar; reservations recommended; at Torrey Pines Rd.* ♿

Trattoria Mama Anna / ★★

655 5TH AVE, SAN DIEGO; 619/235-8144

Downtown's Gaslamp Quarter is awash with Italian trattorias. Mama Anna's is not the glitziest, but it's certainly among the very best. All the dishes are prepared fresh, including the addictive fresh bread served with extra-virgin olive oil and balsamic vinegar for dipping. At lunchtime, focaccia sandwiches come with a green salad and are big enough to share with a friend. Our favorite: thin focaccia stuffed with goat cheese, basil, and sliced tomatoes. The pasta dishes are equally delicate and delicious. The restaurant has a nice bar stocked with Italian beers and wines. In addition to the large dining room, there is a small patio out front from which you can watch passersby on Fifth Avenue; the walls are adorned with photographs of the notables who have dined here. Let the trendies flock to the more expensive Italian restaurants up the street—those who know go to Mama's. *$$; AE, DIS, MC, V; no checks; lunch, dinner every day; beer and wine; reservations recommended for dinner; between Mission St and G St.* ♿

Tutto Mare Ristorante / ★★☆

4365 EXECUTIVE DR, LA JOLLA; 858/597-1188

The name means, basically, "everything from the sea," and that's what the menu at this glossy Golden Triangle destination is all about. The fish fest starts with the appetizers: a delicate lobster salad with baby lettuces, deep-fried calamari, and slivers of salmon flavored with grappa, to name just a few. Next come pastas, many of them starring fish or shellfish (pasta stuffed with smoked trout is a standout, but the penne with duck sausage is no slouch either). Entrees include grilled chicken and New York steaks; grilled sea scallops, their sweetness highlighted by tiny artichokes; boutique pizzas topped with clams and shrimp; and the best pasta in the neighborhood: Maine lobster in a feisty tomato sauce. There's a well-selected wine list and a full bar for appropriate libations. A well-dressed business crowd tends to frequent Tutto Mare at lunch (prime seating on nice days is on the enclosed terrace), and many of the same people come back for dinner. The ambience is stylish without being snobbish, with a sleek, contemporary look softened by displays of fresh ingredients like colorful handmade pastas hung to dry. Leave the little ones at home; Tutto Mare is meant for dates and power dinners. *$$; AE, DC, MC, V; no checks; lunch Mon–Fri, dinner every day; full bar; reservations recommended; at Genessee Ave.*

The Venetian / ★

3663 VOLTAIRE ST, LOMA PORTAL; 619/223-8197

Most of the peninsula's residents agree that The Venetian, near Point Loma High School, has the best thin-crust pizza in the city. First-generation Sicilian-American Vince Giacalone opened the business in 1965 as a small family pizza parlor. After years on Canon Street in Point Loma, he opened this second location, now run by sons Joe and Frank. (The original location, sold in 1972, is now called Old Venice.) Point Lomans and Obecians who ate here as kids now tuck their own offspring into the booths lining the walls of the original dining room, or head for the peaceful covered patio in the back, with potted shrubs dusted in tiny white lights. If you're not in a pizza mood (unthinkable!), try the tasty seafood pasta: shrimp, clams, scallops, and calamari in a tomato-based sauce over linguine. *$; AE, DC, DIS, MC, V; no checks; lunch Mon–Fri, dinner every day; full bar; no reservations; at Chatsworth St.* &

Via Italia Trattoria / ★★☆

4705-A CLAIREMONT DR, CLAIREMONT; 858/274-9732

A chorus of *buona seras* greets customers who enter this Italian gem tucked into an otherwise unremarkable mall. The accents are authentic (the entire staff is Italian), and so is the cooking, much of it based on regional specialties rarely seen in San Diego. While the thin-crusted, wood-fired pizzas are certainly a fine reason to visit, the nightly specials set this little dining room apart. Look for venison simmered in brandy, polenta flavored with truffle oil, bread-spinach dumplings (called *strozzapretti*) in a lush porcini sauce, and a memorable dessert pairing mascarpone cheese and fresh berries run under the broiler. On the regular menu, the stewed Italian sausage, Gorgonzola-topped greens, and penne with pancetta and vodka lead an eclectic parade that mixes the familiar with the unusual. While the restaurant is small and plainly decorated, candles glow on every table and the service is warm and sincere, making otherwise informal meals feel like special occasions. It's smart to make reservations for dinner, as the nearby movie theater draws plenty of pre- and post-show diners. *$$; AE, MC, V; no checks; lunch, dinner every day; beer and wine; reservations recommended; at Clairemont Mesa Blvd.* &

LODGINGS

Balboa Park Inn / ★★☆

3402 PARK BLVD, SAN DIEGO; 619/298-0823 OR 800/938-8181

If you want to stay near the urban Eden of Balboa Park yet close to downtown, check out funky Balboa Park Inn. Located on the edge of the park, the inn has 26 rooms in a series of pink adobe Mission-style buildings. Be sure to ask for detailed room descriptions, or check out the Web site, since all rooms and suites are individually decorated. Some are truly charming, though others veer toward kitsch. Some are definitely for grown-ups on a romantic play date, while others are ideal for small families. If you prefer rooms in tasteful, soft pastels, ask for the Monet suite or the Las Palomas suite, which boasts a roomy private balcony overlooking the park and a cozy glass-enclosed sunroom. Go all the way and ask about the specialty suites. The Tara suite has a *Gone With the Wind* theme (though you may or may not appreciate the portrait of Vivien Leigh as Scarlett O'Hara staring down at you), while you can get jungle-funky in the Tarzan-themed *Greystoke* suite. Some rooms have working fireplaces, and many have whirlpool tubs. Rates include continental breakfast for two, delivered to your room. *$$; AE, DC, DIS, MC, V; checks OK (2 weeks in advance); info@BalboaParkInn.com; www.balboa parkinn.com; at Upas St.*

The Bed & Breakfast Inn of La Jolla / ★★★

7753 DRAPER AVE, LA JOLLA; 858/456-2066 OR 800/582-2466

 It's easy to miss the ivy-covered entrance to this pleasant hideaway just a few blocks from the busy thoroughfares of Girard Avenue and Prospect Street. Designed by architect Irving Gill in 1913 as a private home, it's a historic treasure once occupied by John Philip Sousa in the '20s. Kate

Sessions, San Diego's grande dame of horticulture, designed the original gardens. Today, the 16 rooms offer guests a taste of genteel living. You'll find plenty of nice touches—fresh flowers, sherry, and fruit in the rooms, antiques and original artworks that lend the air of a private home. The first-floor Holiday Room is a romantic retreat with a four-poster bed and working fireplace. If you want a view of the water, reserve the Irving Gill Penthouse Suite, which has a private deck. The upstairs Peacock Room has a private balcony for sunbathing—you'll feel like you're at an elegant Côte d'Azur pension. Breakfast of homemade granola, crepes, quiche, and the like is served on Royal Albert bone china in the dining room or by the fountain on the patio. *$$; AE, MC, V; no checks; bed+breakfast@innlajolla.com; www.innlajolla.com; off Prospect Ave.*

Crystal Pier Hotel / ★★

4500 OCEAN BLVD, PACIFIC BEACH; 858/483-6983
Drive your car across the boardwalk and onto the pier. Park in front of a blue-and-white country cottage with flowers abloom beneath shuttered windows. Open the front door; gaze across the living room and kitchen to your back porch perched over the sea. Check out the bedroom; lie flat on your back atop a patchwork quilt. Feel the surge of the surf and sense the white noise of water and wind. Return to the hotel's office and request another night or more. The 26 Crystal Pier cottages are claimed months in advance by families from Arizona to Canada who set out barbecue grills, fill the fridge, and hang their beach towels over lounge chairs and wood railings. The scene is more peaceful during the off seasons, when couples and singles claim the cottages as private escapes. Winter nights are particularly exciting when the surf is high and the air has a salty chill. One longs for a fireplace to complete the ambience; sadly, there aren't any. The boardwalk scene is just a few steps away if you want to grab a great meal, rent a bike or boogie board, or mingle with humanity. After all, you'll be over the water from dark to dawn, sleeping above the sea. *$$; AE, MC, V; no checks; at Mission Blvd.*

Dana Inn / ★

1710 W MISSION BAY DR, MISSION BAY; 619/222-6440 OR 800/445-3339
Among the overpriced resorts at Mission Bay, this simple hotel stands out as a family-friendly and affordable hangout. The 196 rooms are spread about the property in two-story wood buildings facing parking lots, the bay, and the pool. Sensible rather than picturesque, the rooms all have small refrigerators, coffeemakers, and single or double beds; the wood-veneer and plastic furniture is designed to withstand sandy bodies and wet towels. All family members stay entertained with shuffleboard and tennis courts; two pools; bike, skate, and water-sports rentals; and all the parks and playgrounds on the bay. Sea World sits just across the water, providing free entertainment with the nighttime fireworks exploding

overhead. The coffee shop does a decent job with basic breakfasts and sandwiches. *$$; AE, MC, V; no checks; at Dana Landing Rd.*

El Cordova Hotel / ★★

1351 ORANGE AVE, CORONADO; 619/435-4131 OR 800/229-2032
In a beach town dominated by grand resorts, El Cordova Hotel is an affordable alternative. The salmon adobe building presiding over Coronado's bustling Orange Avenue is redolent of California in the 1930s. The airy, terra-cotta-tiled lobby sets just the right tone with a melodious fountain, intricate tile work, rustic carved-wood furnishings, and wrought-iron decorative touches. The inn's 36 rooms were recently redone, but still have a simple decor with carved wood furniture and Mexican tiles. Most rooms are accessed from the lush inner courtyard. We have a couple of quibbles, though. Noise is a factor, emanating from both busy Orange Avenue and the patio tables of Miguel's Cocina, which occupies El Cordova's courtyard. The inn also has a dinky pool, so plan to hit the beach instead. *$$; AE, MC, V; no checks; at Adella St.*

Embassy Suites San Diego Bay / ★★

610 PACIFIC HWY, SAN DIEGO; 619/239-2400 OR 800/EMBASSY
Families and conventioneers alike are enamored with this chain's sensible layout; the 337 suites all have separate living rooms, kitchenettes, and desk space outside the bedrooms. Though the rooms face a sky-high atrium, noise here is not a drawback; instead, the lively conversation from the lobby draws guests down to the complimentary breakfast buffet. Though the hotel lacks individuality, it more than makes up for that with its location, within steps of Seaport Village and the Gaslamp Quarter. Advance bookings are essential, no matter what time of year. *$$$; AE, DC, MC, V; checks OK; at Harbor Dr.* ᨑ

Glorietta Bay Inn / ★★

1630 GLORIETTA BLVD, CORONADO; 619/435-3101 OR 800/283-9383
John Spreckels, the sugar baron fond of all things grand and glorious for his vision of Coronado, hired architect Harrison Albright to design his family mansion on a sloping lawn facing the bay in 1908. The mansion now houses 11 of the hotel's rooms; the rest are in less glamorous (and less expensive) buildings with balconies and gardens above the bay. The original house is a wonder of polished wood, brass, glass, swooping marble stairways, and eye-boggling antiques. The rooms are the perfect beginning for a tour through Coronado's history. *$$; AE, DC, MC, V; checks OK; at Orange Ave.* ᨑ

The Grande Colonial / ★

910 PROSPECT ST, LA JOLLA; 858/454-2181 OR 800/832-5525, 800/826-1278 IN CA

In operation since 1913, the Grande Colonial (formerly the Colonial Inn) is overshadowed by its fancier neighbors, though it has a loyal following. The lobby and reception area have been freshly renovated, but this four-story, low-key Victorian-style establishment still offers traditional decor with original touches, antique furnishings, rich tapestries, an open fireplace, and flowers everywhere. A small pool area sits outside the lobby, and the beach is just a block away. All 75 guest rooms are scheduled for complete renovation by press time, including new furnishings, fabrics, and fresh paint. Most have ocean or village views. Putnam's Restaurant is a snazzy upmarket bistro and a popular gathering spot for local movers and shakers. Valet and overnight parking are available for a fee. *$$$; AE, DC, MC, V; checks OK; at Jenner St.* ♿

Heritage Park Inn / ★★

2470 HERITAGE PARK ROW, OLD TOWN; 619/299-6832 OR 800/995-2470

Nestled in a cluster of lovingly restored Victorian homes overlooking Old Town, Heritage Park Inn is true to its elegant, old-time roots. Twelve rooms are contained in two historic homes—the circa 1889 Christian House and the Italianate Bushyhead House. With a formal Victorian parlor (where classic films are screened every evening) and period antiques and stained-glass windows throughout, the inn transports guests back to San Diego's early days. It doesn't take long to slow your pace—maybe sit for a spell in one of the wicker rockers on the veranda. We recommend the romantic Turret Room, high in a tower overlooking the gardens, or the Garret, with its own secret staircase. For more luxury, reserve one of the three rooms in Bushyhead House, with whirlpool tubs for two. Rates include a gourmet breakfast, served by candlelight in the dining room, plus a filling afternoon tea of finger sandwiches and sweet goodies. The location is a plus too. You're a short stroll from Old Town's shops and restaurants and the trolley stop for rides to downtown or Mission Valley. *$$$; AE, DC, DIS, MC, V; checks OK; innkeeper@heritageparkinn. com; www.heritageparkinn.com; at the corner of Juan and Harney Sts.*

Hilton La Jolla Torrey Pines / ★★★

10950 N TORREY PINES RD, LA JOLLA; 858/558-1500 OR 800/762-6160

We blinked one day and the Sheraton Grande Torrey Pines had suddenly metamorphosed into a Hilton. Designed to blend into the existing palisades, this Mediterranean white glory sits on the 18th hole of the championship Torrey Pines Golf Course, looking out to the blue Pacific beyond. Two lobby areas are positioned on either side of the entry—one with a large, glass-enclosed fireplace, the other offering cozy seating and a grand piano—and both overlook the enticing pool area. Downstairs, the Torreyana Grille serves excellent seasonal fare in a large, light-filled dining room fitted with fountains, foliage, art, sculpture, an exhibition kitchen, and copper-topped bar. All 394 rooms feature private balconies or patios and many have ocean and golf course views. The decor is sophisticated yet understated, with contemporary furnishings and fabrics in muted tones. Every room offers personalized butler service wherein your own man Friday can be summoned for tasks like shoe shines and fax retrieval, and a business center is on the property. Cavort in the on-site exercise room and on the three tennis courts, or pay a pittance for entry to the adjacent Shiley Sports and Health Center with its mind-boggling array of toning and training facilities. *$$$; AE, CB, DC, DIS, JCB, MC, V; checks OK; www.lajollatorreypines.hilton.com; at Science Park Rd.* &

Horton Grand Hotel / ★★

311 ISLAND AVE, SAN DIEGO; 619/544-1886 OR 800/542-1886

Offering a nice antidote to downtown's cookie-cutter convention hotels, the Horton Grand Hotel is a touch of Victorian-era gentility in the heart of the historic Gaslamp Quarter. Composed of two historic Victorian hotels rescued from demolition, the Horton Grand has quite a colorful history. Wyatt Earp slept here when he lived in San Diego, and the management named the hotel's restaurant in honor of Ida Bailey, a notorious turn-of-the-century madam whose bordello once occupied this site. Outside, the hotel is a fantasy of blue-and-white gingerbread. Inside, all 108 rooms are individually decorated with period antiques, lace curtains, and working gas fireplaces. But we'll bet Wyatt Earp never had a microwave or a hair dryer. For more space, request one of the 600-square-foot minisuites. Sunday brunch at the Horton Grand is a sumptuous affair; for smaller appetites, make reservations for English afternoon or high tea served on Thursday, Friday, and Saturday afternoons. While the hotel has plenty of its own quirky charm, its location is the real bonus. You can live it up at the Gaslamp's many clubs and bars, then stroll or catch a pedicab back to the hotel. *$$$; AE, DC, DIS, MC, V; checks OK; info@hortongrand.com; www.hortongrand.com; at Fourth Ave.*

Hotel Del Coronado / ★★★☆

1500 ORANGE AVE, CORONADO; 619/435-6611 OR 800/HOTEL-DEL

"The Del" presides over Coronado—indeed, over San Diego—like the grand empress she is. Opened in 1888, this sprawling, white-frame Victorian confection of red-roofed turrets, stained glass, and crown-shaped chandeliers is a National Historic Landmark and much-beloved hub of local activity. The hotel has hosted just about every dignitary and celebrity to roll through town, including 14 U.S. presidents. It also played a starring role—alongside Marilyn Monroe, Jack Lemmon, and Tony Curtis—in *Some Like It Hot*. With all this history, the public areas can

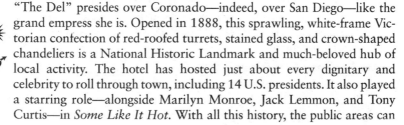

get overwhelmed with sightseers, hotel guests, and conventioneers. Still, if you like the bustling activity of a full-service resort, with its scheduled activities, shopping arcade, and such, The Del should fit the bill. Rooms in the original building are scheduled for some renovations, including installation of air conditioning as part of a five-year, $50 million restoration project. Rooms in the original building have a classic Victorian theme. For more privacy, look to the newer Ocean Tower. Its spacious, comfortable rooms overlook the Pacific or the bay, and have been decorated like country cottages in shades of blue and green, with wicker chairs and chintz fabrics; the tower has its own pool and a nice stretch of beach. The intimate Prince of Wales Grill (see Restaurants chapter) has a jazzy 1930s-inspired decor; the menu was recently revamped with a Continental-California theme. In addition, the entire hotel is being restored to enhance the views of the sea. Though the grill's menu will remain the same, it will soon have an outdoor terrace. *$$$; AE, DC, DIS, MC, V; checks OK; www.hoteldel.com; on Coronado Island.*

Hyatt Regency La Jolla / ★★★

3777 LA JOLLA VILLAGE DR, GOLDEN TRIANGLE; 858/552-1234 OR 800/233-1234

Though its name includes "La Jolla," this Hyatt is actually in the Golden Triangle area, just off Interstate 5, about 10 minutes drive from La Jolla village and 20 minutes from the airport. Housed within the Aventine mixed-use complex of office towers, a health club, and several restaurants, architect Michael Graves' postmodern design has managed to delight locals and visitors alike. Rome meets Southern California is the theme throughout the 16-story property, with a two-level balcony, square marble columns, plush velvet seating groups, and a plethora of amenities. Four diverse restaurants are located in the complex, including Cafe Japengo (see Restaurants chapter), one of the coolest, slickest dining spots in town. Michael's Lounge, adjacent to the main lobby, offers a clubby ambience for cocktails, billiards, satellite TV, and those de rigueur cigars, while an espresso bar serves coffee drinks. All 400 guest rooms are extra-spacious, with high-end yet homey furnishings, down comforters, and round-the-clock room service. Business and Regency Club floors offer a variety of extra perks, including complete office workstations. Unwind in the pool, on two lighted tennis courts, or in the 32,000-square-foot Sporting Club, with its array of exercise equipment and facilities. *$$$; AE, CB, DC, DIS, JCB, MC, V; checks OK; www.hyatt. com; at Lebon.* &

Hyatt Regency San Diego / ★★

1 MARKET PL, SAN DIEGO; 619/232-1234 OR 800/233-1234

Local wags call this bayside tower "the screwdriver," thanks to its sleek obelisk shape narrowing to angular points. The Skidmore, Owings &

Merrill architectural firm won the task of designing an 875-room hotel on a tiny lot wedged into the jam-packed waterfront; they succeeded by carving out gardens and pedestrian walkways past shops and restaurants, and put the pool on the third story overlooking the sails drifting under Coronado Bay Bridge. The rooms are undersize and the hallways noisy when conventioneers return from partying. The restaurants and bars are often packed with downtown workers and tourists. *$$$$; AE, DC, DIS, JCB, MC, V; checks OK; at Harbor Dr.* &

La Valencia Hotel / ★★★

1132 PROSPECT ST, LA JOLLA; 858/454-0771 OR 800/451-0772
To many residents and visitors, La Valencia Hotel *is* La Jolla. The Mediterranean-style "Pink Lady" has reigned over Prospect Street since 1926. And it's always been a hub of activity for well-heeled guests and local bigwigs. The hotel's 100 rooms and suites are individually decorated and have been "refreshed" over the last few years. Some have a green floral motif; others boast a beachy blue-and-white seashell theme. Naturally, rooms with million-dollar views of La Jolla Cove are the most desirable. "La V" is delightfully old-fashioned in that its public spaces are well trafficked, which gives the place a pleasant hum of activity. Every afternoon, the Mediterranean Room patio is filled with ladies who lunch, and the recently restored Whaling Bar is once again a favorite local hangout. At sunset, head to La Sala Lounge, sink into a sofa, and enjoy the view while you're serenaded by a pianist. Be sure to check out the hand-painted ceiling overhead. *$$$; AE, DC, DIS, MC, V; checks OK; info@lavalencia.com; www.lavalencia.com; at Herschel St.*

Loews Coronado Bay Resort / ★★★★

4000 CORONADO BAY RD, CORONADO; 619/424-4000 OR 800/81-LOEWS
At first, it seems strange to choose this isolated resort for a San Diego stay. Far removed from the bustle of downtown, the self-contained compound sprawls beside the west side of San Diego Bay at the southern end of Coronado. The neighboring Coronado Cays housing complex is an enclave of pricey homes on private canals; Silver Strand State Beach is right across the street. Why leave when you're stranded in paradise?

That's exactly what many guests think, especially San Diegans and frequent visitors on short escapes. The resort's Azzura Point restaurant consistently rates among the top five restaurants in the county; the Market Cafe facing the marina serves the most spectacular brunch this side of Hawaii. Energized souls sign up at Action Sports for sailboats, paddleboats, and all kinds of bikes for self-guided tours; lovers drift under the setting sun in gondolas stocked with champagne. The 438 rooms and suites all have water views and balconies; especially fine ones sit at the tip of the resort facing the 80-slip marina, where floating travelers throw casual cocktail parties on their prows. The rooms leave nothing to be desired. Kids get rubber ducks and bubbles in the giant bathtubs—although first they have to kick out the grown-ups. Chairs, couches, and beds are all comfy; it's hard to leave them for the padded pool chairs—though the idea of Häagen-Dazs bars sold poolside is enticing. Leave if you must; shuttles run regularly to downtown's Horton Plaza, and driving nearly anywhere is a breeze (literally, as you soar atop the arcing Coronado Bay Bridge to the mainland). *$$$; AE, DC, MC, V; checks OK; www.loewshotels.com; off Silver Strand Hwy.* &

Paradise Point Resort / ★★☆

1404 W VACATION RD, MISSION BAY; 858/274-4630 OR 800/334-2626
Originally opened by a Hollywood producer in the 1960s as Vacation Village South Seas Paradise, this sprawling 44-acre resort has gone through several transformations. New ownership and considerable renovations have only enhanced the private island setting in Mission Bay. The 462 rooms and suites are housed in single-level buildings with private patios, refrigerators, and coffeemakers. All are being gradually refurbished with dark patterned carpeting (to hide the marks of sandy feet), red, white, and blue linens, and marble baths. Guests are kept ultra- busy with the six swimming pools, 18-hole putting course, tennis courts, croquet lawns, and volleyball nets on the sand. The marina offers sailboat, Hobie Cat, and powerboat rentals; the activities center provides bikes for those wishing to cruise the bay on land. Restaurants include the ever-popular Barefoot Bar on the sand, along with the upscale Dockside dining room and the casual Village Cafe. The summer months bring Kids Kamp, filled with activities. You can easily stay put for days, but if the itch to wander attacks, Mission Beach, Sea World, Old Town, and other attractions are just a few minutes away. *$$$; AE, MC, V; no checks; www.paradisepoint.com; at Ingraham St.*

San Diego Hilton Beach and Tennis Resort / ★★

1775 E MISSION BAY DR, MISSION BAY; 619/276-4010 OR 800/221-2424
Craving action and adventure with massage and spa treatments on the side? You belong at this swath of beach, bike paths, lawns, and private terraces beside Mission Bay. Hotel facilities include several swimming pools, tennis courts, fitness center, and equipment rentals for nearly every water or land sport you can imagine. The 357 tropical-style rooms and suites, with tables and chairs for group snacks and games (or laptops if you must), are scattered through Mediterranean-style low-rise buildings (complete with terraces and balconies) beside the bay and one eight-story building facing Interstate 5. Rollerbladers whiz by from dawn to dusk, following trails for miles along the bay. Kites of every shape float in the sky. Multigenerational families celebrate weddings, birthdays, and sunny Sundays with elaborate picnics all around the hotel, and visitors are

completely immersed in the SoCal scene. *$$$; AE, DC, MC, V; checks OK; between Clairemont and Sea World Drs.* &

San Diego Marriott Hotel & Marina / ★★☆

333 W HARBOR DR, SAN DIEGO; 619/234-1500 OR 800/228-9290

Twin mirrored towers reflect the cityscape and San Diego Bay backdrop at the grandest hotel beside San Diego's Convention Center. Despite its 1,355 rooms, all with spectacular views, this place doesn't overwhelm its guests. Instead, it calms them with a central tropical lagoon replete with waterfalls and swimming pools. The marina shelters 446 of the most handsome yachts and sailboats this side of Newport Beach; guests sleeping aboard their seaworthy homes can order room service delivered on deck. The rooms and suites are geared more to business travelers than to vacationers, with fax and modem ports, desks, two-line phones, and coffeemakers. The regular rooms are small and have a disconcerting mix of plaid and floral fabrics, and the hallways are noisy when merry conventioneers return from their revelries. Suites on the Concierge Levels are larger and more serene. The Marriott is nearly always filled with corporate hotshots commandeering the best digs for their convention bigwigs. Book far in advance of your trip. *$$$$; AE, DC, MC, V; checks OK; at Front St.* &

ABOVE IT ALL

When the traffic jams are in full swing, it's a perfect time to take to the skies. Colorful **hot air balloons** lift off from Del Mar for dusk and dawn panoramas of the rising or setting sun, the Pacific Ocean, the backcountry, and the far-away-from-it-all freeway congestion below. Floats last about an hour, and are followed by champagne or other celebratory refreshments. Balloon companies include California Dreamin' (760/438-9550), and Skysurfer Balloon Company (858/481-6800). **Torrey Pines Glider Port** (2800 Torrey Pines Scenic Drive), poised on the cliffs 300 feet above the Pacific, affords hang gliders one of the most exquisite jumping-off-the-edge spots in the world. Lessons as well as tandem rides are available from the on-site **Hang Gliding Center** (858/452-9858). Live out wartime or *Out of Africa* fantasies in vintage aircraft with open cockpits— where the term "backseat driver" takes on new meaning: **Barnstorm Biplane Adventures** (760/438-7680) takes off from Carlsbad's McClellan-Palomar Airport for 20-minute to one-hour scenic or mock-combat flights. For a **whirlybird** tour of the coast, sign on with Corporate Helicopters of San Diego (619/291-4356).

U. S. Grant Hotel / ★★☆

326 BROADWAY, SAN DIEGO; 619/ 232-3121 OR 800/237-5029

Ulysses S. Grant Jr. thought of San Diego as a grand spot for a monument to his more famous dad, and commissioned Harrison Albright to design an Italian Renaissance palace in the heart of downtown. The hotel opened in 1910 amid much fanfare; after all, how many urban inns could boast a saltwater swimming pool and ladies' billiard hall amid marble pillars? Fortunes rose and fell in this hotel over the decades. It seems anyone who purchased the property felt like the poor offspring of a British duke saddled with the family mansion. The 340 rooms and suites are visions of far nobler times, with two-poster beds, Victorian chairs, and fireplaces (in some suites). Still, the lobby and bar are popular gathering spots for San Diegans, and the restaurant is a treasured landmark. *$$$; AE, DC, MC, V; checks OK; at Fourth Ave.* &

Del Mar

Famous since the 1930s as a haunt for celebrities who came to play the ponies, this seaside town still draws mega crowds each summer to the Del Mar Fairgrounds, both for the horse racing and for the gigantic **DEL MAR FAIR** (Interstate 5 at Via de la Valle; 619/755-1161). **DEL MAR PLAZA** (at the corner of Camino del Mar and 15th Streets; 619/792-1555) has such trendy shops and restaurants that it's even managed to put La Jolla on the back burner. Bluff-front **TORREY PINES STATE RESERVE** is a 1,750-acre natural habitat for the rare Torrey pine tree (North Torrey Pines Road, between Del Mar and La Jolla; 619/755-2063). For more information, contact the **GREATER DEL MAR CHAMBER OF COMMERCE** (1104 Camino del Mar, Suite 214; 619/755-4844).

RESTAURANTS

Bully's North / ★★☆

1404 CAMINO DEL MAR, DEL MAR; 858/755-1660

Though the atmosphere is not quite the same since California's no-smoking law went into effect (some places are just meant to have clouds), Bully's still exudes plenty of character (and characters). Del Mar residents and the summer racetrack crowd have been patronizing this dark and clubby restaurant with its deep red booths since the 1960s—making it their preferred haunt for a meat fix. The full- or half-cut prime rib, filet mignon, New York, porterhouse, and prime top sirloin steaks are renowned among local meat lovers (the prime rib is hand-selected USDA Choice, prime-grade Midwestern, corn-fed aged beef). Both top sirloin and prime rib can be ordered as a combo plate with lobster, crab leg, or shrimp, and every meal comes with soup or salad and baked potato, French fries, rice pilaf, or Spanish rice. Other favorites include the steadfast Bully Burger, French dip, New York steak sandwich, and baby back ribs. Non-bovine eaters can select from various seafood or chicken dishes, or daily specials that might feature fresh sea bass or halibut. The bar is a local institution, particularly during summer. *$$; AE, DC, MC, V; local checks only; breakfast, lunch, dinner every day; full bar; no reservations; at 15th St.* &

Cilantro's / ★★⯪

3702 VIA DE LA VALLE, DEL MAR; 858/259-8777
Cilantro's popularity has yet to diminish, even though other "Southwest-oriented" establishments have sprung up nearby (including Epazote, under the same ownership). Coastal dwellers and visiting celebs—as well as the horsey set—gather at this surprisingly unpretentious restaurant with its warm, inviting dining room and very cool bar. The menu offers a crowd-pleasing selection of spit-roasted and grilled meats and fish. Delicious dishes include seafood enchiladas (shrimp, crab, scallops, and Swiss chard with roasted tomato sauce and sautéed seasonal vegetables) and Cilantro's fajitas (fresh flour tortillas, black beans, guacamole, and spicy carrots, with a choice of steak, chicken, or shrimp). The tapas menu offers creative (and less costly) mini-meals. The benign-sounding tricolored tortilla chips are such a treat that consummate homemaker Martha Stewart requested the recipe from chef Tim Sullivan. Whatever you eat, try to save room for the house dessert—profiteroles stuffed with Häagen-Dazs cappuccino ice cream and drizzled with caramel sauce. *$$; AE, DC, MC, V; no checks; lunch, dinner every day; full bar; reservations accepted; www.cilantros.com; at Camino Real.* &

Epazote / ★★

1555 CAMINO DEL MAR, DEL MAR; 858/259-9966
Like Cilantro's, its sibling up the road, Epazote features southwestern decor and cuisine with an ocean view. The dining room is bright, light, and chic, though most diners clamor for seats on the patio-with-a-view. The vast assortment of tapas grabs top honors, and the wait staff doesn't sniff at those who make a meal out of green corn tamales with lime cream, Dungeness crab corn cakes with chipotle aioli and tropical fruit salsa, coconut curry shrimp with guava barbecue sauce, or Navajo flatbread pizza. Favorite entrees include sesame-honey seared ahi with plantains and ginger-chili sauce, turkey and wild mushroom enchiladas with apricot-melon chutney and Swiss chard, and spit-roasted chicken with chipotle aioli, roasted garlic and peppers, and mashed potatoes. The bar is a happening spot at sunset, and live jazz is featured every Wednesday night. *$$; AE, DC, MC, V; no checks; lunch, dinner every day, brunch Sun; full bar; reservations recommended; www.epazote.com; at 15th St.* &

Il Fornaio / ★★

1555 CAMINO DEL MAR, DEL MAR; 858/755-8876

When Il Fornaio opened its doors in the newly established Del Mar Plaza, this outpost of the popular California chain instantly became the hottest table in town for the upwardly mobile crowd, even rousting uppity La Jollans from their enclave. Reservations for dinner were backlogged for weeks, and it seemed nothing short of a miracle to garner a seat on the coveted ocean-view patio. The place still attracts crowds, though some of the excitement has worn off. The elegantly designed dining room is an instant transport to Italy with plenty of Carrara marble, terra-cotta flooring, vaulted ceilings, hand-painted trompe l'oeil friezes, and an open oven where meats and signature breads are baked to perfection (breads, pastries, and all food items are available for takeout). Most of the pasta dishes are excellent (ravioli di verdura al funghi is filled with Swiss chard, pine nuts, basil, parmesan, mixed mushrooms, and marinara), and the pizzas are fabulous (try pizza quattro stagioni with prosciutto cotto, asparagus, artichokes, and mushrooms). Other specialties include well-executed renditions of veal, steaks, chicken, and lamb. For dessert, the tiramisu is a must. For two weeks, every month of the year, the menu and wine list focus on a different region—enabling you to eat your way through Italy, from Trentino–Alto Adige all the way to Sicily. The chic bar is a favorite hangout for the beautiful people. *$$; AE, DC, MC, V; no checks; lunch, dinner every day, brunch Sun; full bar; reservations recommended; www.ilfornaio.com; at 15th St.* &

Pacifica Del Mar / ★★

1555 CAMINO DEL MAR, DEL MAR; 858/792-0476

"Pacific Rim" may be a term that's getting a little tired, but the concept remains fresh and exciting at this ocean-view restaurant in Del Mar. Given the proximity to the sea, it's only fitting that seafood dominates the extensive menu. The signature kimchi shrimp appetizer, served in an oversize martini glass, is one of the best items here. But don't rule out the likes of wok-seared catfish, ginger-marinated salmon, seafood pastas, and imaginative sandwiches, as well as some truly inspired Sunday brunch dishes. The dining room is pretty, but the real treat here is a seat on the patio. Don't just drop by for the food; the list of martinis and wines by the glass here is impressive, and the singles scene in the eye-catching bar is legendary. Troll here on a Friday night and you might end up with the catch of the day. And no, we don't mean catfish. *$$; AE, CB, DC, DIS, MC, V; no checks; lunch, dinner every day, brunch Sun; full bar; reservations recommended; kipp@pacificadelmar.com; www.pacifica delmar.com; at 15th St.* &

Taste of Thai / ★★☆

15770 SAN ANDREAS RD, DEL MAR; 858/793-9695
This former bank building behind the Flower Hill Mall is now the prettiest Thai restaurant in town. The whimsically decorated dining room is a visual feast, with squiggly cardboard lamps, colorful walls, and intricate tiled floors. Above, star-shaped cutouts in the ceiling change hue with the indirect lighting behind them. As for the fare, it's every bit as appealing as the setting. The lengthy menu ranges from the usual curries, soups, and appetizers to a number of stir-fries and grilled meats. Curries are particular standouts—try the panang version for a sweet 'n' spicy epiphany on what curry is all about. Seafood, noodles, and grilled or steamed fish are handled adeptly as well. A small wine list offers some spice-friendly selections like gewürztraminer at very reasonable prices. In addition to the two main dining rooms, there's a heated patio and a tiny bar where you can wait for to-go orders. *$$; AE, MC, V; no checks; lunch, dinner every day; beer and wine; reservations recommended; at Via de la Valle.* &

LODGINGS

L'Auberge Del Mar / ★★★

1540 CAMINO DEL MAR, DEL MAR; 858/259-1515 OR 800/505-9043
This deluxe 120-room resort may be right on Del Mar's main drag, but you'll find ample privacy for any rendezvous. Small and wonderful, L'Auberge has all the elements of a great getaway. Rooms are decorated in an upscale Provençal theme, and all have a private balcony or patio. Bring your swimsuit, because the inn has two pools—one for lounging, another for lap swimming—and the beach is a short stroll away. There are also tennis courts, a small but well-equipped fitness room, and a terrific little spa where you'll want to indulge in a treatment or two. L'Auberge's central location means you can explore Del Mar's shops and restaurants on foot. The only drawback: it's so close to the beach, yet doesn't offer much in the way of an ocean view. For the most privacy, request a top-floor corner room from which you can gaze at the treetops and get a glimpse of the Pacific. *$$$; AE, DC, DIS, MC, V; checks OK; at 15th St.*

Les Artistes / ★☆

944 CAMINO DEL MAR, DEL MAR; 858/755-4646
Don't let the Old Village Motel sign fool you. After extensive renovations in 1993, this rambling, pink adobe inn just south of Del Mar's main drag was transformed into a little treasure. True to its name, Les Artistes' 12 rooms are filled with unique touches. Behind the magenta bougainvillea, purple wisteria, and gurgling fountains out front, rooms boast creative

tile work and prints, object d' art, and original paintings to fit the room's theme. Seven "designer" rooms are larger than standard accommodations, and each is decorated to commemorate a different artist. The Diego Rivera room is a large upstairs unit with an ocean view and cozy, rustic Mexican decor. Similarly, with its wood beams and white stucco walls, the spacious Georgia O'Keeffe room befits its namesake. Other choices include the cowboy-inspired Remington room, the art-deco Erte room, and the South Pacific flair of the Gauguin. The hotel is walking distance from Del Mar's hopping restaurants and shops, yet set far back enough from busy Camino Del Mar that you'll enjoy some peace and privacy. If you like your accommodations on the bohemian side, you'll appreciate Les Artistes' offbeat charm. *$$; AE, DIS, MC, V; no checks; at 10th St.*

Solana Beach

RESTAURANTS

Cafe Zinc / ★★

132 S CEDROS AVE, SOLANA BEACH; 858/793-5436
The first eatery to set up shop in the Cedros Design District was destined to be a hit just by virtue of location. The fact that the food is terrific is a happy bonus. Though several tables are positioned indoors, dining is mainly alfresco on the people-watching front patio, the sunny side area, or the reclusive rear yard (where tables teeter precariously atop gravel). Breakfast items run from simple bagels and muffins to oatmeal with sour cherry and nut topping and frittata with cucumber salsa; ever-comforting fruit crisp or bread pudding are available on weekends. Lunch entrees, salad samplers, and specialty soups change daily, and all creations are meatless. Good bets are the vegetarian Zinc burger and the colorful mixed vegetable sandwich (pain rustique bread filled with thinly sliced fennel, aioli, red and green bell peppers, radish, celery, arugula, hard-boiled egg, olive tapenade, and vinaigrette). Personal pizzas are nouvelle hard-liners with pesto, Mexican, or southwestern toppings. *$; No credit cards; checks OK; breakfast, lunch every day; no alcohol; no reservations; at Lomas Santa Fe Ave.* ᕍ

Fidel's / ★

607 VALLEY AVE, SOLANA BEACH; 858/755-5292
Unlike the more stalwart Tony's Jacal next door, Fidel's has a touristy feel and real appeal to anyone who wants Mexican-party ambience without crossing the border. The sprawl of dining rooms, bars, and patios, combined with Mexican tile, dangling piñatas, and norteño music, all contribute to the atmosphere. Accordingly, the place is a frenzied melange of first dates, celebratory groups, families, and fair and racetrack goers, not

counting the buoyant students and surfers who show up for happy hour and the cheap taco bar. Standard Mexican favorites top the menu and nachos remain the appetizer of choice. Specialties include various renditions of chiles rellenos, carne and chicken asada, tortas, and tostadas. For something different, try nopales (nopal cactus in a spicy tomato and chile serrano sauce, topped with Monterey Jack cheese), or pescado ranchero (grilled dorado, topped with semispicy ranchero sauce). Burgers and fries are at the ready for kids, and logo T-shirts and baseball caps are for sale. *$; MC, V; no checks; breakfast, lunch, dinner every day; full bar; reservations recommended for 8 or more; at Genevieve St.*

Pamplemousse Grille / ★★☆

514 VIA DE LA VALLE, SOLANA BEACH; 858/792-9090

High rollers, socialites, businessfolk, and trophy spouses abound at this stylish bistro across from the Del Mar racetrack. While many are no doubt drawn by the ambience—a chic, sophisticated take on country French with beautiful people in every corner—others undoubtedly come for the imaginative fare. The food isn't always Triple Crown material, but the kitchen delivers artfully garnished, creatively conceived variations on nouvelle American and classic French cuisine. The foie gras usually served as a special is always outstanding, as are the grilled fish specials prepared with your choice of a half dozen sauces. Salads and side dishes make fine use of the vegetables from Chino's produce farm (favored by chefs from L.A. and S.F.) just down the road, and desserts—especially the semibaked, melting chocolate truffle cake or the trio of three crème brûlées—are always worth an extra hour on the StairMaster. Pamplemousse is particularly busy during the racing season (linger in the bar and you might get a hot tip), but the prosperous mood and society gossip stay in the air year-round. *$$$; AE, CB, DC, DIS, MC, V; checks OK; lunch Wed–Fri, dinner Tues–Sun; full bar; reservations recommended; at Jimmy Durante Blvd.* ᕕ

Tony's Jacal / ★★☆

621 VALLEY AVE, SOLANA BEACH; 858/755-2274

Family-owned and operated since 1946, Tony's Jacal has obviously been doing everything right. Even if you overlook the autographed photos of celebrity diners, you can't miss the long lines—up to an hour on weekends and during Del Mar's racing season. Hang out at the bar with a margarita while listening for your name to be sung out over the loudspeaker. A waitress in blue ruffles will show you to an aqua-upholstered booth in a cavernous room with wood paneling, open beams, Mexican knick-knacks, and half-moon-shaped stained-glass windows, or to a table on the outdoor patio with small pond, gurgly waterfall, and flowering plants. Customary Mexican combination plates fill a big chunk of the menu, featuring pork and turkey along with the ubiquitous chicken.

Special entrees include chili con carne, steak ranchero, and chicken mole, and the *platillos speciales* include various enchiladas, carnitas, tortas, quesadillas, and carne asada. *$; AE, MC, V; no checks; lunch Mon–Sat, dinner Wed–Mon; full bar; reservations recommended for 10 or more; at Genevieve St.* &

T's Cafe / ★★☆

271 N HWY 101, SOLANA BEACH; 858/755-7642
Locals have had a love affair with Mr. T's (as it's more commonly referred to) since it opened in 1978. Tucked unobtrusively as it is into one side of Solana Beach's rather uninteresting boardwalk, you'd never guess that lurking within are a spacious dining room with cozy bar area and small private function room (local artists' groups have staged Wednesday morn-ing breakfasts here for years). The woodsy feel and large open fireplace (blazing during the rare Southern California drizzle or foggy chill) lull

patrons into dreams of Montana mountain lodges as they linger a salty breath away from the Pacific, enjoying enormous omelets with king crab, homemade chili, and roasted turkey, as well as various scrambles, Bene-dicts, bagels, pancakes, waffles, and potato skillet dishes. Although break-fasts are the claim to fame here (and are served until closing), the lunch menu offers a lengthy assortment of deli and veggie sandwiches, burgers, soups, and New York steak sandwiches. *$; AE, MC, V; no checks; breakfast, lunch every day; full bar; reservations accepted for 6 or more; at Lomas Santa Fe Ave.* &

Cardiff

RESTAURANTS

Ki's / ★

2591 S COAST HWY 101, CARDIFF; 760/436-5236
Up until a few years ago, Ki's was just another hole-in-the-wall health-food cafe, where local surfers and the organic crowd congregated for smoothies, wheat grass juice, and Ki burgers. Making its move down the road to a decidedly more visible coastal location, Ki's has managed to up the ambience and the menu considerably, while holding prices way down. Both indoor and patio seating are plentiful, though the best seats in the house are at the long bar facing the ocean. Grab a New Age mag-azine from the stack near the door, place your order at the counter, then find a seat and await your meal. Organic fruits, veggies, and grains are incorporated into the mostly low-fat dishes, though cholesterol-laden eggs, avocados, and nuts are visible on the menu. The sizeable chicken or salmon salads combine baby greens, roasted red bell peppers, toma-toes, and cucumbers, topped with either a grilled chicken breast or salmon

fillet and orange-basil vinaigrette. Veggie lasagne remains a perennial favorite, and Mexican stand-bys such as burritos, tostadas, and fish tacos have been improved with whole wheat tortillas, organic rice, and lard-free beans. The fruit smoothies are filling, delicious, and healthy. *$; AE, MC, V; checks OK; breakfast, lunch, dinner every day; beer and wine; reservations recommended for dinner; at Chesterfield Ave.* &

Rancho Santa Fe

RESTAURANTS

Delicias / ★★★☆

6106 PASEO DELICIAS, RANCHO SANTA FE; 858/756-8000
Named for the tony street that runs through Rancho Santa Fe's chic village center, Delicias is definitely a celebrity on the San Diego county dining scent. For one thing, it's drop-dead gorgeous, and not a single designer touch has been neglected. Spectacular flower arangements punctuate the bar and adjacent dining room, which is bedecked with intricate tapestries. The place even has miniature footstools for ladies' purses, so that Vuitton bag never has to be slung over a chair. The visibly affluent, well-groomed clientele comes as much for the scene as the cuisine, and you'd better not walk in unless you're dressed to impress and ready to turn heads. The cuisine defies easy description, but tends to be a well-balanced mix of new California and classic French. The kitchen has a winning way with fish, and regulars here have learned that you can never go wrong with any of the seafood specials. Swordfish, salmon, escolar, and ahi make regular appearances, generally grilled and served with anything from tropical fruit salsa to polenta to garlic- or truffle-mashed potatoes. Hearty risottos are another specialty, and if they're serving the over-sized veal chop, go for it. Desserts are simpler than the rest of the menu, with homey selections like apple bread pudding or chocolate baby cakes. Prime seating is at the bar near the entrance, at the edges of the grand dining room, or in the flower-filled patio near the wood-burning fireplace. Definitely a place for those with Dom Perignon tastes and titanium credit cards, this gorgeous restaurant is a delicious find indeed. *$$$; AE, CB, DC, DIS, MC, V; no checks; lunch Wed–Sat, dinner Tues–Sat; full bar; reservations recommended; at La Grande.* &

Mille Fleurs / ★★★★

6009 PASEO DELICIAS, RANCHO SANTA FE; 858/756-3085

Possibly the most rarefied and romantic of all San Diego restaurants, Mille Fleurs manages to combine a fabulously lush atmosphere with spectacular cuisine. Tucked into a quiet courtyard in the heart of Rancho Santa Fe's little village, Mille Fleurs attracts with a seductive whisper rather than a flashy wink. Much of its allure is due to the winning team of Bertrand Hug, the legendary host/proprietor who never seems to forget a face, and Martin Woesle, the stunningly talented chef who's a stickler for using only the very finest ingredients. The cuisine leans toward updated French, with typical dishes including truffle-oil-dressed salads made from a variety of organic greens, sautéed sweetbreads, artful duck creations, and game specials such as venison and quail. One might start with delicate cream of parsley soup, fragrant as a patch of herbs, followed by sautéed soft-shell crab nestled on a salsa of local white corn and tiny tomatoes. Entree choices vary, but Woesle's best creations include venison medallions punched up with a juniper berry marinade, stuffed quail sauced with red currants, and monkfish flown in from France—and tastier than lobster. For dessert, there's a selection of imported cheese—surprisingly hard to find as a finale in this area—as well as pastries and sorbets often based on the season's best local fruit. Wine selections are limited only by your pocketbook, as Mille Fleurs offers one of the most impressive lists in town. The sophisticated service, understated Mediterranean decor, and welcoming piano bar all serve to show that gastronomically speaking, at least, money *can* buy happiness. *$$$; AE, CB, DC, MC, V; no checks; lunch Mon–Fri, dinner every day; full bar; reservations recommended; milfleurs@aol.com; www.millefleurs. com; on the corner of Avenida Acacias.*

Rancho Valencia Resort / ★★★⯪

5921 VALENCIA CIRCLE, RANCHO SANTA FE; 858/756-1123
Rancho Valencia, in the new-money enclave of Rancho Santa Fe known as Fairbanks Ranch, is far enough off the usual restaurant rows to feel like a secret destination. It could easily have been custom-built for lovers, boasting a secluded and exclusive setting in a world-class tennis resort. The dining room is at once rustic and upscale, and although it's spacious, there's a definite intimacy to the place. Glowing fireplaces, artful flower arrangements, high-beamed ceilings, and highly polished service all compliment the meals and add an air of effortless sophistication. Don't rush through a meal here. Instead, bask in the country club ambience while lingering over a well-chosen wine list and a menu inspired by France, California, and the Mediterranean. A number of notable chefs have passed through the kitchen here, each leaving a trademark dish or two. The cuisine is consistently well-prepared, with top honors going to the golden squash ravioli flavored with sage, pancetta-wrapped monkfish, and a quickly sautéed foie gras that could hold its own in a French kitchen. For dessert, choose the perfectly caramelized tarte tatin. After dinner, take a stroll through the bougainvillea-bedecked courtyards. If you'd like to stay at the resort, call well in advance to book one of the private casitas here. Yes, it will cost a small fortune, but this verdant retreat is worth the extra

green. $$$; AE, DC, MC, V; no checks; breakfast, lunch, dinner every day; full bar; reservations recommended; at Rancho Valencia Rd. ᕔ

LODGINGS

The Inn at Rancho Santa Fe / ★★

5951 LINEA DEL CIELO, RANCHO SANTA FE; 858/756-1131 OR 800/654-2928

In the heart of Rancho Santa Fe's tony but low-key village, The Inn at Rancho Santa Fe is an unassuming charmer that doesn't rush to embrace every trend. Eighty-seven rooms are spread throughout a cluster of white adobe buildings and cottages, surrounded by carefully manicured grounds. The inn's cool, wood-beamed main building was designed in 1923 by Lillian Rice, the architect responsible for Rancho Santa Fe's genteel Spanish-Colonial look. All rooms are individually decorated with gingham couches and Windsor chairs in a retro-1940s take on American Colonial. The result is a homey, unpretentious feel. About half the rooms have wood-burning fireplaces—a nice touch to chase away the evening chill. For extra privacy, request one of the garden cottages with a private patio. Still, you'll want to hang out on a chaise longue by the pool or borrow equipment for a rousing round of croquet on the front lawn. You could check in and never leave the premises—decent, if traditional, fare is served in the Vintage Room and the Library restaurants—but boutiques and more interesting restaurants are just a short stroll away. If you want to put in some time at the beach, the inn conveniently maintains a private day cottage on the sand in nearby Del Mar. $$$; AE, DC, MC, V; no checks; at Lomas Santa Fe off I-5.

Rancho Valencia Resort / ★★★⯪

5921 VALENCIA CIRCLE, RANCHO SANTA FE; 858/756-1123 OR 800/548-3664

You never know whom you might see on the tennis court or in the dining room at this deluxe hideaway—maybe Bill Gates and his family or Bob and Dolores Hope. They're among the well-heeled regulars who come for the resort's first-rate pampering. The 43 suites here are no bargain, but the staff certainly knows how to treat all guests like royalty. The smaller Del Mar suites are each a roomy 850 square feet of airy, Mediterranean elegance—terra-cotta floors, fireplaces, custom-made furnishings, and spacious private patios. The one-bedroom Rancho Santa Fe suites offer even more room to relax. Days here have a civilized start: a tray with fresh-squeezed orange juice, morning newspaper, and a rosebud is left just outside your door. Couples should ask about the one-night "Romantic Getaway." It includes lodging, a bottle of bubbly, a candlelit dinner and breakfast served in the room, plus in-room, one-hour massage for both. The resort's only drawback: while the 18 tennis courts and first-rate teaching staff make this a dream escape for tennis buffs, golfers

371

must find fairways off-property. *$$$; AE, CB, DC, MC, V; checks OK; www.ranchovalencia.com; at Rancho Valencia Rd.*

Rancho Bernardo

RESTAURANTS

El Bizcocho / ★★★

17550 BERNARDO OAKS DR (RANCHO BERNARDO INN), RANCHO BERNARDO; 858/675-8500

One of the most consistent dining rooms in the county, El Bizcocho charms diners with artful service, gifted chefs, and understated elegance. The spacious room evokes an upmarket country inn, with fireplace, well-spaced tables, and a view of the carefully groomed golf course. Updated French cuisine has always been a signature here, with classics like escargot topped with puff pastry and quickly seared foie gras sharing billing with more innovative creations. Depending on the season, these inventions could be fingertip-sized scallops arranged on ravioli and drizzled with vanilla, or a napoleon of lobster and caviar amid layers of phyllo. Fresh fish is treated with special reverence, so don't miss the roasted monkfish or sautéed John Dory. Roasted free-range chicken and braised duckling paired with fresh fruit are other standouts. Order the dessert soufflés at the beginning of a meal, and they'll arrive airy and perfect, right on schedule, just as you're ready for espresso. Waiters are personable yet professional and the wine list is superb, with several hundred top-notch brands from California and France from which to choose. An adjoining bar often features live piano music, providing an extra touch of class to this stately hacienda. Sunday brunch is an elegant affair, worth an extra night's stay at the hotel so you can take a proper siesta afterward. *$$$; AE, CB, DC, DIS, MC, V; checks OK; dinner every day, brunch Sun; full bar; reservations recommended; www.ranchobernardoinn.com; off the I5 Fwy/Rancho Bernardo Rd.* &

LODGINGS

Rancho Bernardo Inn / ★★★

17550 BERNARDO OAKS DR, RANCHO BERNARDO; 858/675-8400 OR 800/770-7482

Gourmands, golfers, business bigwigs, and vacationing families all feel at home in this hacienda-style inn set amid rolling fairways and clear valley air. Sculptures, fountains, and flowers mark the entrance to the lobby, where hand-painted tiles, hardwood beams, and blazing fireplaces evoke early California style at its most gracious. The best of the 288 rooms and suites have living room fireplaces, bedroom whirlpool tubs, and patios the size of an urban backyard. The rest are comfortable, though it's best to ask for a view of the grounds or distant mountain peaks. Guests in the know make time for at least one dinner and Sunday brunch at El Bizcocho, one of the county's finest restaurants (see Restaurants above). They can always work off the calories at the inn's championship golf course (along with four others in the neighborhood), 12 tennis courts, and fitness center, or vegetate beside the two pools, both so ensconced in flowering bushes and trees they feel like country lakes. The Wild Animal Park, several wineries, and the mountains and desert are all nearby, and San Diego is just a 25-minute drive south. *$$$; AE, DC, DIS, MC, V; no checks; off the 15 Fwy/Rancho Bernardo Rd.*

Encinitas

RESTAURANTS

Vigilucci's / ★★☆

505 S HWY 101, ENCINITAS; 760/942-7332
When Roberto Vigilucci opened his Italian restaurant in 1993, he not only brought his delectable hometown Milano recipes to North County, but also managed to turn one corner of an innocuous intersection into an elegant and intimate haven. Most afternoons and evenings the place is swamped with the well heeled looking to be well fed. Tables swathed in crisp linens and topped with fresh flowers are laden with gnocchi al gorgonzola e nocchi (potato dumplings with gorgonzola cheese sauce and walnuts), pollo alla florentina (chicken breast stuffed with spinach and ricotta cheese in a creamy white sauce), and saltimbocca alla romana (veal scaloppini topped with prosciutto, sage, and mozzarella in white wine sauce). Portions are large, and all entrees come with fresh vegetables and spaghetti aglio e olio. Lunch specials are quite reasonable, and the wine list is extraordinary, from $15 bottles of California chardonnay to a 1990 Château Lafite Rothschild (going for a whopping $900). Vigilucci's chef has changed recently but the charming all-Italian staff remains much the same, offering unpretentious and welcoming service. *$$; AE, DIS, MC, V; no checks; lunch Mon–Fri, dinner every day; beer and wine; reservations accepted for 4 or more; at D St.* &

When in Rome / ★★☆

1108 1ST ST, ENCINITAS; 760/944-1771
Restaurateurs Joe and Rosemary Ragone run this fine Italian restaurant the old-fashioned way, by doing just about everything themselves. They grow many of their own herbs, do much of the cooking, choose produce and meats with finicky precision, and even prepare their own breads and desserts. The results show in the perfect tomato and basil salad, the

falling-off-the-bone osso buco, a velveteen fusilli with vodka, and each of the nightly fish specials. If they're serving halibut, mussels, or salmon, you're in for a particular treat. Desserts rate an equal rave, especially Rosemary's tiramisu, crème brûlée, and fluffy fresh fruit mousses. The spacious restaurant offers an especially cozy dining room with a fireplace, as well as a covered patio complete with bar and piano next to a larger room that's good for private parties. All in all, a visit to When in Rome means spending the evening in the company of very talented, very gracious people who make you want to return. *$$$; AE, MC, V; no checks; dinner every day; full bar; reservations recommended; at J St.* &

Leucadia

RESTAURANTS

La Especial Norte / ★★

664 N HWY 101, LEUCADIA; 760/942-1040

It's hard to believe that this downscale joint, stashed along funky Leucadia's main drag, could be such a wild favorite with locals. Owner Angel Salazar swears he does not advertise. Still, word of mouth brings a steady flow of surfers, seniors, blue-collar workers, young professionals, families, and couples to this tired-looking dining room with institutional-like furnishings, hard booths, and decor consisting of several rickety gumball machines. The service is maddeningly slow—almost nonexistent—yet no one seems to mind as they wait for combo plates, tacos, or the Mexican soups that steal the show: chicken, tortilla, bean, hot shrimp cocktail, tlalpeño, albóndigas, eggplant caldo, and caldo de pescado, among others. Salazar tags his Caldo 7 Mares (shrimp, fish, clams, octopus, black mussels, crab legs, and scallops) the "king of all soups," promising that after downing a bowl, "today will be the first day of the rest of your life, sí Señor." Maybe so, but be prepared to wait almost a lifetime for that bowl to arrive. *$; MC, V; no checks; breakfast, lunch, dinner every day; full bar; no reservations; at Leucadia Blvd.* &

Carlsbad

Named for Europe's Karlsbad spa because of similar waters (the long-defunct wells, restored and re-drilled, now indeed operate as an elegant spa), this coastal community is rapidly becoming famous as the home of **LEGOLAND** theme park (1 Lego Drive, off Interstate 5, at Cannon Road; 760/918-5346), the Danish-made monument to its famous interconnecting blocks, with amusement rides, boats, cars, a maze, a tower, shops, and eateries. **FOUR SEASONS RESORT AVIARA** draws **GOLFERS** to the Arnold Palmer–designed course, and **LA COSTA RESORT AND SPA** is the site of February's Andersen Consulting Match Play Championships and August's Toshiba Tennis Classic. Carlsbad's "village," along Carlsbad Village Drive east of the coast, is filled with shops, cafes, and restaurants; State Street on both sides of Carlsbad Village Drive is a popular prowl for antique hunters. For more information, contact the **CARLSBAD CONVENTION & VISITORS BUREAU** (400 Carlsbad Village Drive; 760/434-6093).

RESTAURANTS

Bellefleur Winery & Restaurant / ★★

5610 PASEO DEL NORTE, CARLSBAD; 760/603-1919
Looking somewhat like a beautiful fish out of water, this upscale restaurant/bar anchors one end of an outlet store mall (the Carlsbad Company Stores) just off Interstate 5. It's a welcome presence among the fast food joints, the discount shoe stores, and the displays of last year's fashions. Inside the villa-esque building, soaring ceilings and graceful architecture provide a chic showcase for often innovative American cuisine, ranging from roasted poblano chili appetizers to a marvelous chocolate peanut butter torte. Other standout dishes are a quickly seared sea bass, and red-meat specials such as hanger steak and baby back ribs. An in-house bakery provides exceptional breads, and a petite gift shop offers wine paraphernalia and other souvenirs. At lunch, the place has a casual feeling; a dressier, older crowd shows up at night. Some customers may enjoy the wines sold under the Bellefleur label, but discerning drinkers will want to shell out some extra dough for the better-known California brands on the list. *$$$; AE, DIS, MC, V; no checks; lunch, dinner every day; beer and wine; reservations recommended; at Car Country Dr.* &

LODGINGS

Four Seasons Resort Aviara / ★★★★

7100 FOUR SEASONS PT, CARLSBAD; 760/603-6800 OR 800/332-7100
 Yes, the Four Seasons is sleek, swank, and serene. But we love it best for its beds, which feel like fluffy clouds. The mattresses are plenty firm, and the smooth, ironed sheets, puffy white duvets, and pillows cushion weary bodies in womb-like comfort. Soft green walls, understated furnishings (including a large desk with comfortable chair), perfect lighting, marble baths with soaking tubs, huge closets, and a wet bar with coffee machine make it hard to leave the room, though it is nice to settle on the private balcony's cushioned deck chairs for sunset cocktails. There are plenty of other diversions in this 331-room hotel overlooking Batiquitos Lagoon and the ocean. Floral arrangements rival the artwork in the public spaces.

The spa is filled with sensory delights from gentle chamomile scrubs to lavender wraps and will also send a masseuse to your room for pampering. The Jose Eber Salon is the perfect place to primp for dinner at Vivace, where Chef Pascal Vignau presents culinary wonders in a Mediterranean-style, ocean-view dining room. A to-die-for brunch (with a separate serving table overflowing with treats for kids) is displayed at the California Bistro; afternoon tea is graciously presented in the flower-filled Lobby Lounge. Golfers rave about the Arnold Palmer-designed Aviara Golf Course that sprawls over 180 acres of canyons and lagoons. Tennis buffs head for the six lighted courses; swimmers delight in a seemingly endless pool. Special programs include a jazz series on summer nights. You don't really need to know about nearby attractions—most guests refuse to leave the grounds. *$$$; AE, DC, DIS, JCB, MC, V; checks OK; www. fourseasons.com; at Aviara Pkwy.* ♿

Escondido

The biggest draw in this north San Diego area is **WILD ANIMAL PARK** (15500 San Pasqual Valley Road; 760/747-8702), which allows visitors to ogle more than 3,000 animals, including elephants, tigers, rhinos, and several endangered species. The animals roam (at least semi-freely) through their natural habitat. Monorails take visitors on 50-minute rides, hovering over areas that mimic Asia and Africa, and animal shows are scheduled daily.

Julian

Still rustic after all these years, this 1880s mining town is a favorite day-trip destination for San Diegans. The best time of year is fall, when visitors devour **APPLE PIES** at the local bakeries that line the highway from Julian to Santa Ysabel, or take the chill off with hot cider. Fewer people come in spring, when exquisite wildflowers take over the hillsides and meadows, and in winter months, which often bring snow. Interesting explorations include the **EAGLE MINING COMPANY**, an authentic gold mine (end of C Street; 760/765-0036); the **PIONEER CEMETERY**, with miners' graves (off A Street); and the **ANTIQUE AND COLLECTIBLE SHOPS** on and around Main Street. Don't leave town without sipping a soda at the fountain in the old-fashioned Julian Drug Store (2134 Main Street; 760/765-0332). Another mandatory stop near Julian is Dudley's Bakery (30218 Highway 78, Santa Ysabel; 760/765-0488), where people have been lining up for decades to buy twenty or so varieties of freshly baked bread. For more information, contact the **JULIAN CHAMBER OF COMMERCE** (2133 Main Street; 760/765-1857).

LODGINGS

The Artists' Loft / ★★

4811 PINE RIDGE AVE, JULIAN; 760/765-0765

For those weary of country-kitschy B&Bs, the Artists' Loft is a breath of fresh air. Owner-artists Nanessence and Chuck Kimball's serene 11-acre oasis outside the town of Julian is just the place to kick back and listen to the wind rustle through the manzanita trees. Two rooms in the main house are decorated with carefully chosen rustic antiques, Persian rugs, eclectic objets d'art and, of course, the Kimballs' own artwork. The Manzanita Room is a cozy retreat, complete with a working antique parlor stove to chase away the evening chill. The Gallery Room is a spacious, cheerful, yellow-hued hideaway. For added privacy, reserve one of the two separate cabins. The Cabin at Strawberry Hill, named for the wild strawberries that surround it, was hand-built by the Kimballs. You can't miss its delightful blue-tin roof. Inside, it boasts every comfort—an inviting couch, a wood-burning stove, a king-size bed, and a fully equipped kitchen. The cabin's huge screened porch is a special treat on warm summer evenings. The Kimballs' latest acquisition is the 70-year-old Big Cat Cabin, named for a mountain lion that hides nearby. They've lavishly remodeled this one-bedroom gem, which features a massive stone fireplace, fully equipped kitchen with countertops made of local oak, and a bathroom with a wood-paneled shower and a vintage cast-iron tub. You'll drift to sleep in an antique Balinese wedding bed, and the bedroom's screened study area is the ideal spot to curl up with a book or start working on that novel you always meant to write. *$$; MC, V; checks OK; www.artistsloft.com; at Pine Ridge Wy.*

Orchard Hill Country Inn / ★★★

2502 WASHINGTON ST, JULIAN; 760/765-1700 OR 800/716-7242

Upscale and elegant, Orchard Hill Country Inn offers an ideal combination of privacy and proximity to Julian's shops and restaurants. The inn opened in 1994 and is a loving reproduction of a California Craftsman lodge. There are 10 delightful rooms in the main lodge—all decorated with genteel country flair—but the best rooms are the 12 cottage suites. Each is named for an apple variety and has its own theme. You can delight in the soft, feminine pinks of the Sweet Bough cottage or relax among the warm plaids of McIntosh. The Cortland suite is a romantic refuge of blue toile fabric. Some rooms have a fireplace and/or whirlpool tub. Owners Pat and Darrell Staube attend to every detail—room amenities include a half-bottle of local merlot, a mason jar filled with fresh-baked oatmeal cookies, and luxuriously soft robes. They also thoughtfully provide magazines, board games, and a terrific video library of classic movies. While you'll be reluctant to venture away from your room, the inn's four acres have plenty of private benches and hammocks—perfect for dozing with a book or gazing at the stars. *$$$; AE, MC, V; checks OK; www. orchardhill.com; at Main St.*

Anza-Borrego Desert State Park

About 600,000 acres make up Anza-Borrego Desert State Park's ethereal landscape of sandstone canyons, dry lake beds, granite mountains, waterfalls, hidden springs, palm groves, bighorn sheep, hundreds of desert plants, and—each spring—a breathtaking explosion of flowers. The tiny town of Borrego Springs provides basic services, while **LA CASA DEL ZORRO** resort offers sheer luxury. For more information, contact **ANZA-BORREGO DESERT STATE PARK** (PO Box 299, Borrego Springs, CA 92004; 760/767-5311), or stop in at the **VISITOR INFORMATION CENTER** (622 Palm Canyon Drive; 760/767-5311). Get the update on blooms by calling the **WILDFLOWER HOTLINE** (760/767-4684).

Borrego Springs

LODGINGS

Borrego Valley Inn / ★★

405 PALM CANYON DR, BORREGO SPRINGS; 760/767-0311
Borrego Valley Inn's low-slung, Santa Fe–style adobe buildings are right at home in the Anza–Borrego Desert. Appropriately, the inn's 14 rooms are done in an unfussy, southwestern look with cool, terra-cotta-tiled floors, rough-hewn pine furnishings, and vibrant Indian fabrics. Most rooms also have fireplaces, kitchenettes, and private patios, making them a casual and warm place to unwind after a day exploring the desert's trails and oases. If it's hot out, you can always cool off in your choice of two pools and spas. In fact, either is a great spot from which to watch the sun set behind the Vallecito Mountains. In the evening, check out the stars through the inn's telescope. Room rates include a hearty breakfast buffet of granola, baked goodies, and locally grown citrus fruit. *$$; AE, CB, DIS, MC, V; checks OK; www.borregovalleyinn.com; at Hwy S22 at the 18-mile marker.*

La Casa del Zorro / ★★☆

3845 YAQUI PASS RD, BORREGO SPRINGS; 760/767-5323 OR 800/824-1884
There's no need to suffer and sweat in the desert. Instead, book a room or casita at this lush oasis buried in date palms set against a mountain backdrop. The casitas, with one to four bedrooms, are spread about in clusters throughout the 42-acre property. Some have fireplaces and private pools; all have kitchen facilities and living and dining rooms. Families book large casitas for reunions; couples hide out in one-bedroom settings with private hot tubs. Two-story white buildings with tiled roofs house the large, lodgelike guest rooms, most with fireplaces (the desert gets mighty chilly on winter nights). Several pools, one reserved for adult use only, are scattered about the gardens, and a river flows over boulders between the buildings. Prices are high in the restaurant, but you can get lots of touring tips from the staff. Big-name jazz groups play on summer weekends. Tours of the desert are available, in jeeps or on foot. Visit in spring when ocotillo plants thrust spires of red blossoms into the sky. *$$$; AE, DC, DIS, MC, V; no checks; www. lacasadelzorro.com; at State Rd 3 (S3).* &

LOW DESERT

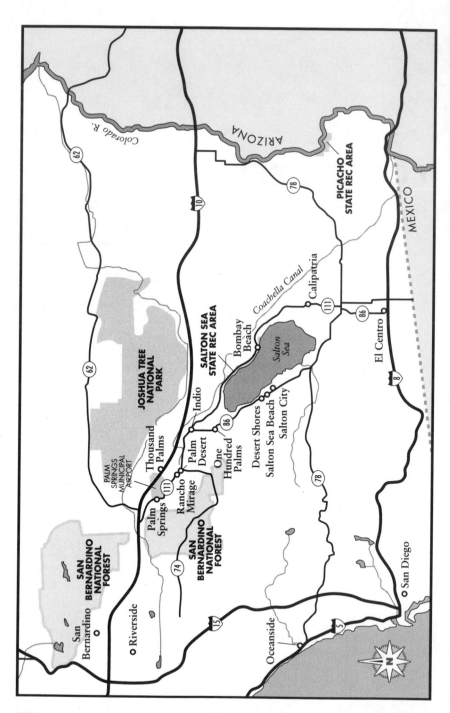

LOW DESERT

With its searing temperatures, soaring mountains, and a landlocked sea almost 230 feet below sea level, the low desert, which encompasses the Coachella Valley and Salton Basin, remains a place of baffling, exciting incongruities. On one hand, humans have made every effort to turn much of the long, level valley's sand and rock into a vast necklace of emerald-green golf courses surrounded by resorts and new residential colonies. Despite this, nature continues to hold the winning hand here and do what she pleases. Flash floods roar off the mountain flanks and tumble through washes that otherwise might stay bone-dry for years. Dead-calm mornings turn into afternoons riven by moaning winds, often powerful enough to knock a bejeweled Palm Desert matron right out of her stiletto heels.

In geologic nomenclature, the entire area is called the Salton Basin, the Salton Trough, or sometimes the Salton Sink. It stretches from San Gorgonio Pass near Palm Springs to the Salton Sea and beyond, fanning out over the U.S.–Mexico border and eventually disappearing into the Gulf of California. Although these low-down names may sound clumsy, they aptly describe an entire region that was lowered (in some places as much as 230 feet below sea level) over millions of years by earth movement along the San Andreas fault. Simultaneously, the San Andreas helped lift the Sink's adjacent mountains to 10,000 feet or more. Snow-capped in winter, these ranges, the San Jacinto and San Gorgonio, tower over the region like an Alps on Mars. Jumbled and hostile, they rise along the south side of Highway 111 in Palm Springs, Rancho Mirage, Palm Desert, and Indian Wells. Once you climb above about 5,000 feet, the summits soften under a cloak of pine and fir trees. Palm Springs' famed tramway whisks you from the valley floor into this forest, where the air is far cooler and the desert seems a continent away rather than a few miles below. Even with this cool escape, and enough air-conditioning in every car and building to frost your earlobes, the valley clears out from June through September, as 110-degrees-plus temperatures become breathtakingly common.

Naturally, the desert's heat is also why everyone loves the Big Sink, especially in The Season (winter and spring), when days stay in the 70s but nights are chilly enough for you to light a fire in your resort cottage's living room. Golf is nearly perfect here in winter, and almost a hundred courses now dot the landscape. Tennis, too: you can hear the racquet-on-ball thwocks emanating from every hotel and country-club grounds. Swimming pools, considered by tourists and residents alike to be an essential element of existence, host the bronzed, the bored, and the beautiful.

No trip to the Low Desert can be complete without a taste of all worlds, from the wilderness of a hidden palm canyon to the glitzy shopping gulch known as El Paseo in the city of Palm Desert. Visitors can golf in the morning, take a Jeep trek in the afternoon, and then savor fine French cuisine by candlelight in an open courtyard in the evening. Nothing is too improbable.

The valley first gained fame in the early 1900s as a sanitarium for wheezing asthmatics and tuberculosis victims who made their way here on doctors' orders to breathe the clean, dry air. The Hollywood set arrived in the 1920s and never really left. Frank Sinatra, Dean Martin, and Sammy Davis Jr. enlivened the 1950s and 1960s. Busts followed booms, but through it all the mountains watched in purple majesty. And the air— well, the air here, warm and dry as sable, just feels so very, very good.

ACCESS AND INFORMATION

PALM SPRINGS INTERNATIONAL AIRPORT (3400 E Tahquitz Canyon Way; 760/323-8161) is served from major cities around the U.S. by Alaska, American, American Eagle, United, United Express, America West Express, and U.S. Airways Express. However, many airlines offer far less frequent service during the hot "out of season" months (June, July, August, and September). **CAR RENTALS** (Avis, Budget, Dollar, Hertz, National) are available in Palm Springs at the airport or directly through the Valley resorts.

Most travelers touring the Low Desert approach via car on **INTER-STATE 10** from the Riverside/San Bernardino area. The final changeover of coastal plain to inland desert occurs as you pass through San Gorgonio Pass (famed for its weird forests of giant electricity-generating windmills). Immediately after the pass, with Mount San Gorgonio (elevation 11,499) to the north and Mount San Jacinto (elevation 10,804) to the south, Highway 111 splits off southward from the interstate, enters typical desert scenery of sand, rock, and scrub, and soon becomes a multilane boulevard (with traffic lights) that strings along from one desert resort community to the next—Palm Springs, Rancho Mirage, Palm Desert, Indian Wells, and Indio. At Indio, a traveler can continue south to see the immense Salton Sea and its birdlife; or rejoin Interstate 10 via Auto Center Drive. Interstate 10 continues east to enter Arizona at Blythe and is the primary route to Phoenix.

The Salton Sea area is close to Anza-Borrego Desert State Park, and travelers can make a giant loop tour of Southern California's deserts by going west from Salton Sea on Highway S22 into Anza-Borrego, south briefly to Highway 78, west to Highway 79, north to Aguanga and Highway 371, and east to Highway 74, which descends back into Palm Desert. Another route "over the hill" (and out of the desert) is State Route 74, also known as the Pines-to-Palms Highway. Route 74 enters the San Bernardino National Forest and leads to the mountain town of

LOW DESERT THREE-DAY TOUR

DAY ONE. Spend the morning browsing the shops and galleries along South Palm Canyon Drive in **downtown Palm Springs.** Don't miss the **Village Green Heritage Center**, where you'll get a sense of the city's early history. Duck in for lunch at **Las Casuelas Terraza**, then drive a few blocks into the old "Tennis Club district" to check into your room at **Korakia Pensione.** After a swim and a nap, drive 6 miles northwest of Palm Springs to catch the **Palm Springs Aerial Tramway**, on which you'll ascend almost 6,000 feet up the mountainside to Mountain Station. Stay long enough to enjoy the view and have a light snack on the aerie-like terrace. Return to your room for a freshen-up, then walk to dinner at nearby **St. James at the Vineyard**.

DAY TWO. Rise early, take your time with coffee and continental breakfast in Korakia's courtyard, then drive about a half hour "down valley" on Highway 111 to Palm Desert. Breakfast fans might want to stop at **Keedy's Fountain & Grill** for huevos rancheros. Next learn which plants and critters call the desert home with a visit in the cool of midmorning to nearby **Living Desert** (closed in summer). Backtrack to downtown Palm Desert for a big salad and a smoothie at casual and lively **Native Foods**. Spend a few hours poking into all the elegant shops and galleries along **El Paseo.** Head north from Palm Desert to the **Coachella Valley Preserve**, which is open until sunset. Venture out in the evening on foot for drinks and dinner at **Kaiser Grille**, followed by a live performance at either the Annenberg Theater in the Palm Springs Desert Museum or the historic **Plaza Theatre.**

DAY THREE. Spend the morning playing golf on one of the Coachella Valley's nearly one hundred golf courses, then return to your lodgings for one last swim and checkout. If you've worked up an appetite, try the Elvis burger at **The Burger Factory** in Palm Springs, then stroll through the spiny world of **Moorten Botanical Gardens**. You'll also have time in the afternoon for a visit to **Palm Springs Desert Museum,** where art and natural history cohabitate in a splendid building against the mountainside. If a special milestone (especially a romantic one) needs celebrating, wind up the day with a champagne toast at **Le Vallauris,** followed by a candlelit dinner on the patio.

Idyllwild. It also facilitates a return to Los Angeles or San Diego via Interstate 15.

Keep abreast of the area's highway conditions by calling the California Highway Patrol at 909/849-5646. High winds often kick up sand in open areas outside of cities, causing poor visibility, dangerous conditions for big rigs and recreational vehicles, and, at the very least, damaged auto finishes.

AMTRAK's Sunset Limited goes through the Coachella Valley as it crosses the country between Los Angeles and Miami, but no longer stops in Indio. The closest stop is San Bernardino station, 60 miles northwest of Palm Springs (1170 W Third Street; 909/884-1307). Amtrak BUS SERVICE arrives at and departs from San Bernardino and Palm Springs. Call 800/USA-RAIL for schedules and fare information.

Palm Springs

In a letter to a friend in 1914, the widow of famed author Robert Louis Stevenson wrote, "There is . . . a climate of extraordinary purity and dryness, and almost no rain or wind. Wonderful cures . . . have taken place here . . . if I had only known of Palm Springs in my Louis's time!" In those early days, weak-lunged patients gathered in tents amidst the palm groves, and there was no notion that the city of today—a place of glamour, golf, and dozens of restaurants, all grilling New York steaks and pouring big healthy shots of Johnnie Walker Red Label—might ever exist.

The first big boom hit in the 1920s. Bungalow courts and small motels sprang up, along with a few larger resorts. The Hollywood crowd swept in to vacation in the glorious, dry winter heat, arriving in automobiles that could negotiate the improving road system linking L.A. to such a formerly remote location. Some of these old lodgings remain, as do others from subsequent booms in the 1950s and 1960s, when Sinatra, Hope, President Eisenhower, Liz Taylor, and a host of other big names kept P.S. in the limelight. But by the 1980s Palm Springs was dying, and its reputation had taken a serious drubbing from wild Spring Break weeks, when thousands of students arrived to party. Most of the fine stores abandoned downtown (Palm Desert became the new mecca for shopping and galleries), leaving it to the T-shirt and curio shops.

Today Palm Springs is "hot, hot, hot!" as *Vanity Fair* magazine trumpeted in their June 1999 issue. The celebrities are back. Hipsters have discovered Palm Springs as an enclave of 1950s architecture, much of it by internationally acclaimed Southern California design masters like Richard Neutra and R. M. Schindler.

As you tour Palm Springs and the surrounding region's major attractions and other communities, keep the notion of "down-valley" in mind: residents think of Palm Springs as being at the head of the Coachella Valley, and other desert communities to the southeast are all down-valley from here. A big chunk (32,000 acres) of Palm Springs is owned by the AGUA CALIENTE INDIANS; the entrance to their reservation and three spectacular palm canyons open to hikers is 4 miles south of Palm Springs on S Palm Canyon Drive (760/325-3400). ANDREAS, MURRAY, and PALM CANYONS offer huge granite formations, water-polished rock, rushing streams and quiet pools, and *Washingtonia* palms—the hardy survivors from 10,000-plus years ago, when the climate here was much wetter. The **PALM SPRINGS AERIAL TRAMWAY** (760/325-1391) takes you high into **MOUNT SAN JACINTO STATE PARK** (760/659-2607) from its station on Tramway Road off Highway 111. The park features 54 miles of **HIKING** and **BACKPACKING TRAILS** in summer, and a more modest set of **CROSS-COUNTRY SKIING** and **SNOWSHOEING TRAILS** in winter when snow blankets the area (air temperatures at the top are often as much as 40 degrees lower than at the valley floor). You can **RENT EQUIPMENT** at the tram station's Nordic Ski Center (760/327-6002) when you arrive at the top. A ride-and-dine option includes a sunset dinner at the tram's mountaintop restaurant, followed by a spectacular descent beneath a night sky so dark and clear the Milky Way really does look like spilled milk. In town, **MOORTEN BOTANICAL GARDENS** (1701 S Palm Canyon Drive; 760/327-6555) houses over 3,000 varieties of desert plants (cactus

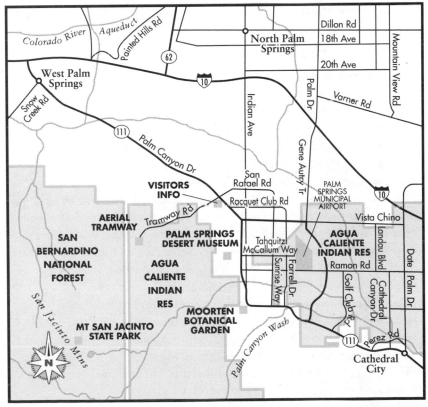

lovers, rejoice). Paintings, sculpture, and Native American artifacts as well as the natural sciences are showcased in the big-city-sophisticated **PALM SPRINGS DESERT MUSEUM** (101 Museum Drive; 760/325-0189 or 760/325-7186), which rests in a deep well of landscaped sculpture gardens set up against the mountainside. The Annenberg Theater on the museum's ground floor hosts concerts, drama, film, and dance.

The **GALLERY, SHOPPING, AND RESTAURANT SCENE** along S Palm Canyon Drive, which runs north–south between Amado Road and Ramon Road, saw a dramatic turnaround in the late 1990s. Don't miss Thursday night here, when the street closes to car traffic and artists and other vendors set up booths for a huge open-air market. Relatively new **SHOPPING DEVELOPMENTS** on S Palm Canyon that shouldn't be missed include the Vineyard (corner of Baristo Road and Palm Springs Promenade). Winning the award for Oddest Element amidst this hubbub has to be **VILLAGE GREEN HERITAGE CENTER** (221 S Palm Canyon Drive; 760/323-8297). Operated by the Palm Springs Historical Society, the Heritage Center surrounds a minipark with its array of several old buildings, including the McCallum Adobe (1884) and "Miss Cornelia's Little

THOSE WONDERFUL "MOP TOPS"

Stand on the floor of the Coachella Valley with your feet firmly planted on a sidewalk in Palm Springs. Look south toward the San Jacinto Mountains. Forbidding, no? A massive pile of crushed rock, barely able to sustain life? True, and not so true, for no plant symbolizes the opportune nature of desert flora more than the noble native fan palm (*Washingtonia filifera*) found in the many folded canyons of the San Jacinto and Santa Rosa Mountains. Here, usually hidden from view to everyone but hikers, the palms send down their thirsty roots toward subterranean year-round springs.

In winter these same canyons come to life with roaring freshets. And out on the desert floor, a few oases such as Thousand Palms also sustain these rustling 50-foot-tall trees. As you walk among them, look closely for the many inhabitants of and visitors to these wildlife "condominiums"—especially tree frogs, and birds such as hooded orioles. Some palms wear "skirts" of dead fronds down much of their trunk length. If a palm is naked, it was probably the victim of sparks from a campfire or vandalism.

To experience a few classic palm groves, consider a hike to Murray Canyon on the Agua Caliente Indian Reservation. To get there, go south on Highway 111 from downtown Palm Springs following signs to Indian Canyons. Pay a small fee at the reservation's entry station, and continue on to Andreas Canyon, where you can park and hike less than a mile into Murray Canyon. Within the reservation, you can also visit Palm Canyon, where about 3,000 palms line a 7-mile stretch of canyon.

House," made of railroad ties. Interiors are faithfully redone, and a modestly priced ticket also gains you admission to a museum of Palm Springs history. The historic **PLAZA THEATRE** (128 S Indian Canyon Drive; 760/327-0225) hosts the long-running *Fabulous Palm Springs Follies* from November through May. Depending on their age, patrons think the show is either swell or pure blue-haired camp.

Toward the mountains, the **HERITAGE DISTRICT** (called by locals "the tennis club district") features a concentration of small hotels, inns, and bed and breakfasts, many of them with a retro feeling. Visitors staying in this neighborhood can walk to Palm Canyon Drive, or stroll in the other direction toward the mountains and pick up a hiking trail that rambles over the wild desert mountainside.

Other outdoor activity options include **HOT-AIR BALLOONING** with Dream Flights (launch sites vary; 760/321-5154) and **TOURING THE WINDMILL FARMS** with Wind Farm Tours, Inc. (62-950 20th Avenue; 760/251-1997). Desert Adventures (760/324-JEEP or 888/440-JEEP) offers **JEEP AND HIKING TOURS** of surrounding desert lands to see remote canyons, wildflowers, and geological wonders. And outside town, the **PALM SPRINGS AIR MUSEUM** (745 N Gene Autry Trail; 760/778-6262) takes advantage of the dry desert air to preserve some of the world's last examples of still-operable World War II aircraft, including the famous *Flying Fortress* with its ball turret nose.

For an overview of Palm Springs area events and activities, contact the **VISITOR INFORMATION CENTER** (2781 N Palm Canyon Drive, at the north edge of the city, just south of the turnoff to the aerial tramway; 760/778-8418 or 800/347-7746, www.Palm-Springs.org).

RESTAURANTS

The Burger Factory / ★

333 S INDIAN CANYON DR, PALM SPRINGS; 760/322-7678

Chat to a customer seated next to you at the counter in this 1960s-feeling burger joint and you might discover he's driven down from Hollywood for the day—and for the burger. The mainstay menu item here is the Kong—a massive one-pound flattened softball of ground beef char-grilled and hugged by lettuce, tomato, onion, Thousand Island dressing, pickle, and a big bun. Their Hunk-Uh-Hunk-Of-Burning-Love/Elvis Burger stacks ground beef, ham, pastrami, bacon, and grilled onions between slices of grilled sourdough bread. The Great Balls of Fire/Jerry Lee Lewis Burger is nearly aflame with three different hot sauces and jalapeño peppers in addition to the usual burger accoutrements. Decor here reflects owner Louise Reymer's penchant for Elvis-this and Elvis-that, as well as pictures of celebrity customers such as rapper/actor Ice Cube. Turkey burgers and veggie burgers are also excellent. The really cool thing about the Burger Factory? Its hours: it stays open until 4am Friday and Saturday nights. *$; No credit cards; no checks; lunch, dinner every day; beer and wine; reservations not necessary; www.burger factory.com; nearest cross streets Baristo Rd and Ramon Rd.* &

Kaiser Grille / ★★

205 S PALM CANYON DR, PALM SPRINGS; 760/323-1003
74225 HWY 111, PALM DESERT; 760/779-1988
You won't find wiener schnitzel at Kaiser Grille. Named for owner Kaiser Morcus, the restaurant exemplifies a new energy and spirit in the Coachella Valley that makes some of the more *haute* valley restaurants seem stuffy. Here the clientele is a little more bare-shouldered, the collars a little more open, and the laughter a little louder than in the clubbier valley restaurants where geriatric decorum rules the evening. At the downtown Palm Springs location, two open-air dining terraces jut into the sidewalk like the prows of twin ships. During blast-furnace summer months, micromisters up in the metal-finned roofline cool diners with their wispy fog. At night, diners see (and are seen by) a constant parade of passers-by, but the food commands center stage. Prime rib arrives in a thick fork-tender slab (it can also be ordered blackened, Cajun style). Fish lovers have the unusual option of a "mixed grill" showcasing three different filets. Sauces are rich, and often based on a classic beurre blanc flavored with either mango or local citrus juices. Grilled steak is a specialty, served with heaps of fresh steamed vegetables and mashed potatoes. The only thing better than sitting outside is sitting inside, where you can see the activity in the huge open kitchen. There is a second location in Palm Desert. *$$; AE, DC, DIS, MC, V; no checks; dinner every day; full bar; reservations recommended; corner of Arenas Rd.* &

Las Casuelas Terraza / ★

222 S PALM CANYON DR, PALM SPRINGS (AND BRANCHES); 760/325-2794
Started in 1958 by Florencio and Mary Delgado, Las Casuelas has been a downtown Palm Springs institution virtually from the beginning. President Dwight Eisenhower was a regular customer, fueling up on Mary's tamales after his golf rounds. Liz Taylor, George Montgomery, Bob Hope, and Dinah Shore all plunked down for big combination plates of enchiladas, tacos, and burritos. The liveliest of their three locations, Las Casuelas Terraza draws its energy off the heavy foot traffic of Palm Canyon Drive. A big palapa-fringed bar and patio opens to the street, and live music pumps out from here as strongly as the straight shots of aged tequilas. If you love black beans Oaxacan style you'll enjoy the black bean "pizza" (really a tostada) with chicken. Unfortunately, Las Casuelas in general seems to have succumbed to too many tourist requests for mildness and offers few dishes that capture a sense of authenticity or innovation. (One of the burrito styles is a rather odd bland

packet loaded with diced potatoes and celery.) So why come here? For the Spanish Colonial decor, the crowd, the indoor-outdoor feel, the music, and the great location. Additional locations at Las Casuelas The Original, 368 N Palm Canyon Drive, Palm Springs; 760/325-3213, and Las Casuelas Nuevas, 70-050 Highway 111, Rancho Mirage; 760/328-8844. *$$; AE, DC, DIS, MC, V; no checks; lunch, dinner every day; full bar; reservations recommended; at Arenas Rd.* &

Le Vallauris / ★★★

385 W TAHQUITZ CANYON WY, PALM SPRINGS; 760/325-5059 OR 888/525-5852

Named for the small town in the south of France where Picasso took to making pottery later in life, Le Vallauris successfully combines uncompromising elegance with the informality of dining alfresco. The restaurant occupies an historic ranch-style house not far from the hubbub of Palm Canyon Drive (but seemingly a world apart), its ficus-shaded exterior seeming almost too understated—except for the covey of valet-parked Rollses and Mercedeses. Step through the door, however, and you're in a magical setting of indoor and outdoor spaces. The patio capitalizes on Palm Springs' fabulous winter weather. Outdoor tables are set with linens and fine china, and with stars overhead, cool night air, and candles aglow you sense that this is indeed a special dining space. Interior rooms are equally pleasing, with draped alcoves and fine paintings. Belgian-born owner Paul Bruggeman earned his stars operating St. Germain on Melrose Avenue in Los Angeles (the site now occupied by equally famed Patina), and the menu, overseen by executive chef Jean-Paul Lair, reflects Bruggeman's love of what he calls "contemporary French/Mediterranean" cuisine—with some Southwest overtones befitting his 40 years in Southern California. The menu is an extravagant journey. One can start with beluga caviar, or terrine of foie gras, or light, crisp crab cakes with whole-grain mustard sauce. Lamb lovers will yield willingly to a perfectly roasted rack, well seasoned in the classic manner with garlic and thyme, or, at lunch, to the more adventuresome marinated grilled lamb loin with sesame sauce. The veal chop with pommes soufflés is one of Southern California's best. The fish here, either seared or sautéed, accompanied by inventive sauces such as a citrus dressing or red chili sauce, is so buttery and fresh it seems the ocean must be nearly next door. *$$$; AE, DC, DIS, MC, V; checks OK; lunch, dinner every day, brunch Sun; full bar; reservations recommended; vallauris@aol. com; www.levallauris.com; from Palm Canyon Dr go 3 blocks toward the mountains on W Tahquitz Canyon Wy.* &

St. James at the Vineyard / ★★★

265 S PALM CANYON DR, PALM SPRINGS; 760/320-8041

Palm Springs's most interesting dinner menu fuses Pacific Rim, French, Indian Ocean, and American steak house cuisines in a unique style born of owner James Offord's love of travel. Although Offord has now turned over the kitchen to chef Johannes Bacher, the two are on the same page when it comes to delicious combinations. An endive, Asian pear, watercress, and grape salad will begin a meal on a perfect cool note if outside temperatures are soaring. But whatever the season, St. James turns up the heat with its well-known curries, including their standard-bearers—chicken, shrimp, or vegetable—as well as special ones like an ostrich and Chinese long bean curry served over steamed jasmine rice. Presentations are wonderful Jackson Pollock–like scatters of color. Other entrees include a stir-fried lobster tail over couscous (very pricey), a grilled lamb rack with vanilla-infused reduction, or a fabulous Bouillabaisse Burmese that immerses a bounty of seafood in a sauce enlivened with ginger, pineapple, lime juice, lotus root, and cardamom. After all these flavors you'll probably be too exhausted for dessert. Service is attentive but unhurried; feel free to enjoy a meal that will last several hours. The bar, featuring almost a hundred folk art masks on the walls, is downtown's most sophisticated watering hole, and the restaurant's wine list boasts a *Wine Spectator* Award of Excellence. *$$$; AE, DC, DIS, MC, V; no checks; dinner every day in high season, Tues–Sun in June, Thurs–Sun in July and Aug; full bar; reservations recommended; www.st-james. com; in the rear of the Vineyard shopping center.* &

LODGINGS

Coyote Inn / ★★

234 S PATENCIO RD, PALM SPRINGS; 760/327-0304 OR 888/334-0633

Within walking distance of downtown Palm Springs, the Coyote Inn has all the feel of a half-century-old classic little Spanish courtyard inn—except that the spotless little Coyote is virtually brand new. The walled and gated enclave shelters only seven tile-roofed suites, each with full kitchen (including dishwasher), library, small dining table, sitting area, fireplace, and comfortable, firm beds. Rooms all look out on the courtyard and pool, so the inn has a great sense of community (which can be a bit of a downside, however, if you're looking for privacy or anonymity.) From the pool, you look straight up at the mountains, making this one of Palm Springs's best lodgings in which to enjoy the beauty of the desert. A hidden garden spa is great for a before-bed soak. *$$; AE, DC, MC, V; no checks; www.springs.gardeninns.com; from Palm Canyon Dr (Hwy 111), take Arenas Rd towards the mountains and turn left on Patencio Rd.*

Korakia Pensione / ★★★

257 S PATENCIO RD, PALM SPRINGS; 760/864-6411
Located on a quiet side street within walking distance of downtown, Korakia immediately transports a visitor to a Moroccan oasis. Scottish artist Gordon Courts built the white-walled, wedding cake–like house in 1924 as a retreat and salon for his many artistic and intellectual friends. A fantasy then, it remains a grand stage set today. (A Mediterranean villa directly across the street with cocoa-brown walls, tile roof, and palm-fringed eaves has also joined the Korakia ensemble.) Current owner Doug Smith virtually invented the term "restorative designer" with his knack for making every room wildly hip; he lives in each room, waiting for his muse, before remodeling. Decor may include giant hand-carved four-poster beds draped in mosquito netting, campaign furniture, and African and Balinese influences. Smith travels the world frequently, and his inn has become a visual journal of his jaunts. Numerous fireplaces lend a magical warmth on cold winter nights. Continental breakfast is served in the walled entry patio to the full-throated accompaniment of 15 lovebirds and parakeets. Kitchenettes for light cooking are stocked with Häagen-Dazs ice cream, baguettes, and Brie, leaving one to ponder, What more does one need? *$$$–$$$$; no credit cards; checks OK; closed July 15–Labor Day; from Palm Canyon Dr (Hwy 111) take Arenas Rd 4 blocks west to S Patencio Rd, then left.* &

The Willows Historic Palm Springs Inn / ★★★☆

412 W TAHQUITZ CANYON WY, PALM SPRINGS; 760/320-0771
Everything glorious about Palm Springs's past—its history as a glamorous getaway, intellectual haven, nature sanctuary, and rejuvenative spa—lives on at The Willows. The eight-room inn was built in 1927 as a private estate. New York attorney and multimillionaire Samuel Untermyer bought it soon thereafter and massaged it into elegant perfection. Today the house steps up a hillside above old Palm Springs, its Tuscan-yellow walls, red-tile roofs, and multiple terraces tango-ing in and out of a grove of tall palms, fringed willows, and the stone mountainside itself. Owners Tracy Conrad and Paul Marut, both emergency-room doctors with a penchant for architectural triage, purchased the house in 1994. According to Conrad, it was but a forlorn husk of its days when Albert Einstein spent weeks visiting Untermyer, when Clark Gable and Carole Lombard hid away for a honeymoon, and when in the 1950s, Marion Davies, mistress of William Randolph Hearst, owned it and converted the only kitchen to a bar. Today every surface and every furnishing has been restored, from door hinges to flagstones. Rooms are large and tastefully furnished with fine antiques. Each terrace reveals a view of gardens and the ragged curtain of mountains beyond. A 50-foot waterfall burbles down the mountainside into the breakfast patio. The inn's full-time staff

serves a glorious breakfast (the bread pudding with walnut and berry sauce is heaven, accompanied by scrambled eggs with chèvre and chives) and keeps the service intuitively unintrusive without being stuffy. No visitors roam the grounds (although many ask). At twilight, as the desert cools, guests gather in an open veranda room beneath a Moroccan-arched ceiling to sip wine and enjoy hors d'oeuvres. At bedtime (after a day of swimming and reading), the crisp cotton sheets welcome your tanned skin, and the open terrace doors to your room admit the hushed twitters of birds settling in for a night in the palms. As are you. *$$$$; AE, DC, DIS, MC, V; checks OK; www.thewillowspalmsprings.com; 2 blocks toward mountains off Palm Canyon Dr (Hwy 111), across from Le Vallauris.*

Desert Hot Springs

LODGINGS

Two Bunch Palms / ★★

67-425 TWO BUNCH PALMS TRAIL, DESERT HOT SPRINGS; 760/329-8791
Water is precious enough in the desert, but when it rises—full of minerals—at a temperature of 148 degrees from deep in the earth into an oasis of palm trees, you have the makings of a classic hot springs spa. Only guests have access to the almost 60 acres of landscaped grounds. Accommodations are 45 casitas scattered throughout the lawns, linked by pathways and furnished with antiques and rattan. The property is exceedingly quiet and private. You can choose either a simple resort stay or an immersion in the spa's full program of massage treatments, sauna, mudbaths, and body wrap treatments. Serenity is the watchword here; in the mineral hot springs, even conversations among guests are kept to a whisper. And what springs! Landscaped for a grotto effect, the pools are rock-lined, rambling organic forms nestled amidst the palm trunks for an absolutely magical experience. Resort or spa packages can include meals, treatments, and even "romance" treatments, which feature side-by-side massages, Roman tub baths by candlelight, and private mud- and sun-baskings on a sundeck. Nude sunbathing is encouraged in special private "sun bins." When guests want a bit more activity, they can play tennis (two courts), work out in the exercise pool, walk trails around the property, or ride a bicycle. The Casino Dining Room features "Living Essence Cuisine," and although the name is somewhat egregious, the low-fat, "strictly fresh" fare is excellent. Curiously, the restaurant has a full bar and good selection of wines, so alcohol didn't make the no-no list. Meals are included in rate packages, and a two-night minimum is required. *$$$–$$$$; AE,*

MC, V; no checks; www.twobunchpalms.com; left off I-10's Desert Hot Springs exit 5 miles north to Two Bunch Palms Trail. &

Indian Wells

LODGINGS

Renaissance Esmeralda Resort / ★★★

44-400 INDIAN WELLS LANE, INDIAN WELLS; 760/773-4444 OR 800/552-4386
Taking its architectural cue from the surrounding peaks, Renaissance Esmeralda is a series of mountainous, but dramatically modern and stylish, buildings organized around a central courtyard shaded by stately Canary Island palms. The courtyard's centerpiece is an immense pool complete with a sandy beach that actually slopes into the water. The 560 rooms and suites amidst seven-story buildings are some of the largest in the valley. All have private balconies and are decorated in schemes of mauve that echoes the mountains' hues at sunset. Deluxe rooms include corner arrangements with windows on two walls, but one of the pair is behind a disconcerting grid that's part of the exterior ornamentation. Ask for a room with a view of the mountains to the west, or at the very least to the north or south; east side rooms have a much less interesting vista. Esmeralda's soaring atrium lobby is too huge to be friendly, and the decor is unabashedly ritzy. But with two 18-hole championship golf courses designed by Ted Robinson, extensive health club and spa services, four tennis courts, and in-room coffee and newspaper every morning, no one's complaining. Sirocco restaurant, featuring Mediterranean cuisine, is one of the prettiest spaces for dining in the desert. Overall service at Esmeralda is polished and worldly, as befits a hotel that hosts major corporate functions. On the other hand, the place can feel too businesslike for the vacationing family—despite its sandy beach. *$$$$; AE, DC, DIS, JCB, MC, V; no checks; www.renaissancehotels.com; located off Hwy 111.* &

Rancho Mirage

LODGINGS

Rancho Las Palmas Marriott Resort & Spa / ★★

41000 BOB HOPE DR, RANCHO MIRAGE; 760/568-2727 OR 800/458-8786

Desert resorts often weave golf holes close to their wings of rooms, but few do it as boldly as Rancho Las Palmas. Here two of the 27 Ted Robinson–designed holes plunge right into the very center of the resort compound, water hazards and all, their greens almost at the feet of diners or sunbathers. Rancho Las Palmas's main lobby, restaurant, and conference buildings, as well as its 450 low-rise rooms and 22 suites, are comfortably spaced across a wide area. Nothing feels crowded here. Appealing tile roofs give everything a hacienda feeling, and hundreds of lanky palm trees dot the grounds. A 25-court tennis club completes the sporting scene, as well as several pools and Tortuga Island, a 6,000-square-foot water playground with slide and pop jets for family fun. More languid luxury is offered at the 20,000-square-foot European-style health spa, which features 26 treatment rooms, saunas, steam, hydrotherapy, two fitness centers, and an outdoor pool with underwater music. While activity is generally geared toward the out-of-doors, the recently remodeled and refurbished rooms, with French doors opening onto private balconies, television armoires, and Mission-style furnishings, provide a serene setting for moments of rest. Mediterranean-style fine dining is featured each evening at Madeira, while Pablo's Restaurant and Tapas Bar is open all day, serving American food as well as Spanish specialties. Fresca's in the hotel spa offers light, guilt-free cuisine. Alas, like several other large resorts built out on the flat desert plain in the Coachella Valley, Rancho Las Palmas turns inward and doesn't offer a great sense of place: it's just not close enough to the mountains. But it creates its own self-contained world, and families can stay here for days without feeling the need to go anywhere else. *$$$; AE, DC, DIS, MC, V; checks OK; www.marriott.com/marriott/pspca; near corner of Hwy 111 and Bob Hope Dr.* ⅋

Ritz-Carlton Rancho Mirage / ★★★★

68-900 FRANK SINATRA DR, RANCHO MIRAGE; 760/321-8282 OR 800/241-3333

The only major resort hotel in the Coachella Valley region that's actually *in* the spectacular mountains, the uber-luxurious Ritz-Carlton is perched high above Highway 111. In contrast to the towering mountains, the hotel's architecture is linear, modern, and horizontal—a broad U open to the view. A bronze statue of a bighorn sheep greets you in the porte cochère, but inside all evidence of the desert's natural world vanishes; you're in a French country palace with gleaming marble floors, French antiques, baroque paintings, and long halls. The elegant guest rooms (240 of them, arranged in three-story wings) all have private balconies with views of the pool, mountains, or valley—or all three. Accommodations are spacious, with elegant stone finishes, fabrics, and crisp linens. A "club" floor offers added amenities: a private lounge, personal concierge, and complimentary food and beverage services during the day. The Ritz's swimming pool is one of the best in the desert: viewed from the hotel's main balcony, it looks like a David Hockney painting lined with blue and white cabanas near a canyon edge. Tennis players are well served at the Ritz, with ten courts and one clay to choose from. Croquet is also available on a permanent grass court on the east side. The fitness and beauty spa on site offers over 30 different treatments. Or if it's a simple soak you want, the outdoor hydro-spa has the best view in the Valley: it perches on the very rim of the hotel property. The hotel's restaurants are often booked solid, not only because of their excellence but also due to a tendency for guests to "stay in" rather than roam the tawdry Valley below. The Mirada features Southwestern cuisine, the Cafe offers Continental, and the Dining Room, which is closed June through October, elegantly explores French/Mediterranean. Service at the Ritz can be particularly stiff but is always first-rate. *$$$$; AE, DC, DIS, MC, V; checks OK; www.ritzcarlton.com; from I-10, take Date Palm Dr south to Hwy 111, go left to Frank Sinatra Dr, then right.* &

The Westin Mission Hills Resort / ★★★

71-333 DINAH SHORE DR, RANCHO MIRAGE; 760/328-5955 OR 800/937-8461
Of the Valley's many resorts built in the 1980s and 1990s in the flat desert neighborhoods north of Highway 111, the Westin ranks at the top for artful elegance without glitz. Its architecture recalls a Moroccan palace, so it seems to fit the desert clime perfectly. Long, open arcades stretch in several directions from the central shopping and lobby plaza. Sounds of splashing children draw you toward an oasislike pool where a 60-foot water slide springs from a minimountain (two other pools indulge adults only). Surrounded by the Mission Hills Country Club courses, one designed by Pete Dye and the other by Gary Player, the Westin caters to serious golfers and tennis players, but also gives the read-a-book guest quiet balconies and restful rooms. (A unique angled arrangement of the large, comfortable beds lets you gaze out the window at distant mountains.) Two restaurants celebrate indoor-outdoor dining during the high season when cooler winter temperatures prevail: Bella Vista (California cuisine) and La Concha (contemporary American). Children under 18 stay free, and numerous camplike programs and babysitters keep them busy. Service here can be exceptionally friendly, and the clientele seems more relaxed than at many other resorts closer to in-town nightlife. *$$$$; AE, DC, DIS, MC, V; no checks; ranch@westin.com; www.westin. com; at Bob Hope Dr.* &

Palm Desert

Shoppers, take heart: you've found the equivalent of Beverly Hills's Rodeo Drive transplanted to the desert. Palm Desert's **EL PASEO** boasts almost a hundred boutiques, gift and antique shops, and galleries and restaurants of the highest quality. Simply to walk up one side of the divided street and down the other gives you about a mile of nonstop window-shopping and browsing. **MCCALLUM THEATRE FOR THE PERFORMING ARTS** (in the Bob

Hope Cultural Center on the campus of College of the Desert, 73-000 Fred Waring Drive; 760/346-6505) hosts touring big-name entertainers and Broadway shows. The best attraction in town, without question, is the zoo and botanical garden named **THE LIVING DESERT** (about 4 miles south of Hwy 111 at 47-900 Portola Avenue; 760/346-5694). Look for directional signs in town and along Highway 74 (the Pines-To-Palms Highway leading into the mountains). Budget two or three hours to tour this fascinating collection of gardens and more than 130 animal species, including bighorn sheep gamboling over their own mountainside and a mountain lion in a realistic stone grotto.

RESTAURANTS

The Daily Grill / ★

73-061 EL PASEO, PALM DESERT; 760/779-9911
Heaps of hot, salty shoestring fries obscure your superb bacon, lettuce, and tomato sandwich. Sips from a rich, amber pint of cold Anchor Steam beer chill your desert-parched throat. You could be in San Francisco, but you're not. Soon you'll step back outside into the unmistakable heat of the low desert, but for now you and other diners in the busy lunchtime crowd are ensconced within mahogany walls and served by a white-aproned waitstaff. That's the plus side of the Daily Grill. And the minus side? That very same sense of tradition: the Grill's formula has been transplanted to Palm Desert by marketing types who've also opened several other branches around the Southland. It feels slick and planned. Yet though such formulaic restaurants never give you a sense of spontaneity, they can still offer up a good meal. Dinners range from large, savory char-broiled burgers, chicken pot pies, and broiled half chickens to more complex dishes such as chicken Marsala or broiled shrimp pomodoro with angel hair pasta. Although the place isn't open for breakfast, an early lunch here offers breakfast items such as a Joe's Special (egg, spinach, onion, and hamburger scramble), eggs Benedict, bacon and eggs, and an omelet filled with Cobb ingredients. *$; AE, DC, DIS, MC, V; no checks; lunch, dinner every day, brunch Sun; full bar; reservations not necessary; www.dailygrill.com; from Hwy 111, turn south on Monterey Ave and drive 1 block.* &

Jillian's / ★★★

74-155 EL PASEO, PALM DESERT; 760/776-8242

Beauty without pretension makes Jillian's a real find amidst desert resort bistros that cater to the well-heeled crowd. The decor here is elegantly rustic, with cottage-y dining rooms, doors, windows, and porches that open up to a magical center court where palms lit with twinkle lights seem like pillars holding up the night sky. Proprietors Jay and June

Trubee are well known in the desert for starting Cunard's in La Quinta (now the La Quinta Grill) in 1986 for the Cunard family. They moved on to open Jillian's in 1994, and to this day Jay does the honors in the kitchen. He trained at the Culinary Institute in Hyde Park, and his style is robust Americana, but with a strong emphasis on homemade pastas. All are made fresh daily and include such favorites as cannelloni—delicate tubes filled with four imported cheeses and served with a tomato-tinted cream sauce. Rack of lamb is another tour de force: a Colorado rack crusted with seasoned breadcrumbs and served with a demi-glace scented with home-grown rosemary. Whitefish Dijonnaise arrives on a bed of mashed potatoes beneath a Pomeray-mustard hollandaise. Desserts are made on the premises (as are all breads). Jay's Hawaiian cheesecake has been featured in *Gourmet* magazine; its macadamia nut crust provides a little crunch beneath a creamy filling, pineapple topping, and fresh raspberry sauce. *$$$; AE, DC, MC, V; local checks only; dinner every day in season, closed Jun–early Oct; full bar; reservations recommended; jillians@local.net; near Larrea St.* &

Jovanna's / ★★☆

74063 HWY 111, PALM DESERT; 760/568-1315
Jovanna Cruz is everywhere: in the kitchen, at the front door, on the outdoor dining porch, in the back room. In her small, narrow restaurant—very much like a New York Italian eatery, where space is so tight the waitstaff brush past each other back to back—Jovanna fills the space like the outgoing, hearty Philadelphian she is. She earned her chef's stripes at her parents' 1,800-meal-a-night restaurant in Acapulco, often putting in 18-hour days. Her pasta dishes are delicious, generous mountains of flavor, especially a chicken edifice of sautéed chicken tenders in a creamy basil sauce topped with bay shrimp and served over a bed of pasta. Osso buco is always on the menu, and her lamb in marsala sauce served over risotto or pasta merits mopping the plate with more bread to get every last rich drop. Cap your meal with one of her seasonal crème brûlées: eggnog during the holidays, orange liqueur in spring, toasted coconut in summer, pumpkin in fall. At press time she is changing her menu to give more emphasis to California-Italian bistro cuisine, but she promises to keep many of the old favorites. *$$; AE, MC, V; no checks; dinner Wed–Sun (Wed–Sat in Aug); full bar; reservations recommended; near Portola Ave on the south side of Hwy 111.* &

Keedy's Fountain & Grill / ★

73633 HWY 111, PALM DESERT; 760/346-6492

Also known as "Keedy's Fix," this classic cafe and its burgers haven't changed an iota since Bob Keedy established the joint in 1957. When he threatened to close the place in 1987 and retire, locals Bob and Patty Downs stepped in, bought it, and kept almost everything the same. They

DESERT FORE!

Nowhere on earth do so many golf courses (almost 100) cluster in such close proximity as in California's low desert. The improbability of the setting may well be its main attraction: lush fairways nestling amidst sun-scorched sand and rock, while a purple curtain of mountains rises like a silent playing partner watching your every drive. The experience can be intensely artificial, yet oddly naturalistic and satisfying at the same time.

Serious golfers don't care much about analyzing their addiction, however. They want answers: Who designed the course? What is its slope rating and reputation among players? What pro tournaments has it hosted? When can I get on? And how much will a round cost?

In Palm Springs and other resort cities, that last element can add up fast. Most greens fees run in the $100-and-up range during the cooler winter and spring seasons. Fees over $200 per round are not unheard of. At the same time, you can still get on numerous public courses for $50 or less. A course's name tells you little about its exclusivity or openness. Many "clubs" are open to the public—essentially public courses. Resorts often have their own courses, and guests have priority.

To sort out some of the mystery, visiting golfers often either turn to their hotel concierge (most concierges have "ins" with various nearby courses for tee times) or contact booking agencies directly. For a list of current, reliable agencies, contact Palm Springs Visitors Information Center (2781 North Palm Canyon Drive; 800/347-7746). They also have information on "passbooks" offering multiple-course discounts, PGA tournament schedules (if you enjoy being a spectator), and even golf guides who speak Japanese.

haven't even replaced the Formica on the counter, where 40-plus years of plates being slid in front of customers has all but worn the color off. You know the menu: classic American breakfast and lunch standards like omelets, BLTs, burgers, and patty melts. But a little bit of Mexico sneaks in. Try a menudo and tortillas special, spicy carne asada, or any of the classic enchilada-taco combos. Breakfast boasts more than a bit of Mex, too, with huevos rancheros, chorizo and eggs, and machaca (shredded beef and eggs). The heart-attack classic is still great: a triple-decker burger with bacon, along with a milk shake from the fountain. On your way out, take some time to look over the magazine photo collages on the wall. Americana—you gotta love it. *$; AE, DIS, MC, V; no checks; breakfast, lunch every day; no alcohol; reservations not accepted; just off the south side of Hwy 111.* &

Native Foods / ★★☆

73-890 EL PASEO, PALM DESERT; 760/836-9396

1775 E PALM CANYON DR, PALM SPRINGS; 760/416-0070

Native Foods feeds on the energy of co-owner Tanya Petrovna and her passion for vegetarian cooking with an international slant. The Bali Burger may sound like just another veggie patty, but Tanya makes it from scratch, then enlivens it with caramelized onions and guacamole (you can also order it blackened Cajun style). Big salads come out of the kitchen like baskets full of produce from a garden. Most unusual is the Jamaican Jerk Steak salad, a seitan "steak" (a vegetarian alternative to meat) over jasmine rice and romaine with flamed banana salsa. Tacos are another specialty, and they've gained fame among locals whose visiting friends are convinced that the tasty soy-based filling must be ground beef. Dinner entrees are hearty and require a few more trenching tools than ten fingers: try the baked yam topped with steamed vegetables, or I Love Lucy's Lasagna, whose pasta layers burst with squash, tofu, roasted eggplant and peppers, garlic cloves, spinach, and mushrooms. Decor is as much fun as the food: giant African-motif masks cover the walls. The crowd is hip, healthy, and every age from toddling to tottering. For dessert, tofu-based creamy dressing over carrot cake gets its zest from oranges, and Elephant's Revenge combines chocolate, coconut, and peanut butter in a rich, cinnamon-spiced cake. There is a second location in Palm Springs. *$; no credit cards; checks OK; lunch, dinner Mon–Sat; no alcohol; reservations not accepted; www.palmsprings.com/health/nativefoods; a few steps off El Paseo near San Luis Rey Ave.* &

La Quinta

Here's a glimpse of the old days in the Coachella Valley, but it's disappearing fast under a tide of new houses and golf courses. Still not much more than a village, La Quinta nestles in a "cove" (local parlance for a flat area of desert surrounded by mountains). Nights are dark here: local ordinances forbid bright lights so that residents can better enjoy the stars and the sense of living in the country. Home of historic La Quinta Resort, the village also hosts the annual outdoor **LA QUINTA ARTS FESTIVAL** (760/564-1244) each March, a four-day gatherings of artists selling their latest works. **SCULPTURELAND** (57-325 Madison Street; 760/564-6464) is a private arts park, owned by a local artist, that displays works from around the world for sale or lease; you can tour the grounds for a modest entry fee.

RESTAURANTS

Adobe Grill / ★★

49-499 EISENHOWER DR, LA QUINTA; 760/564-5725

Located upstairs above the hotel's famed fountain, Adobe Grill's dining patio seems almost to press against the velvet night sky. But seating accommodations aside, the menu here has long been a wonderful alternative to the steak-steak-steak mantra of other desert chefs. Adobe Grill has an elegant, inventive, and also quite traditional touch with Mexican cuisine. Sure, you can order a combination plate (wonderful tamales, enchiladas, tacos, etc.), but it's in the mysterious mole sauce that the Aztecan authenticity really shines. Seafood is a highlight, especially the halibut in a maple pecan crust with orange butter sauce. What's Mexican about it? It arrives with *fideo*, a Mexican pasta like angel hair or vermicelli where the thin strands are deep fried for about a minute before being doused with chicken stock, tomatoes, and herbs, then simmered until tender. *Caldo de marisco,* their bouillabaisse with a Southwest flavor, and *ceviche de mariscos marinera,* also showcase Mexico's love of seafood. Don't miss the margaritas here; the largest comes in a huge handblown glass filled with 1800 tequila, orange liqueur, and fresh lime and lemon juice. As you sip, wondering how you'll ever walk out across the tile floor, your eyes will wander to the open beam ceiling, Guadalajara-made glass art, and the passing dessert tray filled with orange custard flan, sopapillas dripping with honey, and lemon tarts with prickly pear sorbet. You're not in Kansas anymore, Toto. *$$; AE, DIS, MC, V; no checks; lunch, dinner daily; full bar; reservations recommended; www.laquintaresort.com; from Hwy 111, take Washington St south and turn right on Eisenhower Dr.* &

La Quinta Grill / ★★

78045 CALLE CADIZ, LA QUINTA; 760/564-4443

Arriving at La Quinta Grill will test your faith. The parking lot is bare desert sand. The building has all the architectural profile of a Texas roadhouse. But beyond the front door, you enter a big-city environment where soft tunes from a piano player float around a dark burgundy room, tasteful nudes gambol in gilt-framed paintings, and tablecloths are crisp and white. So popular in winter you may wait two hours unless you have a reservation, La Quinta Grill (formerly named Cunard's) draws a clientele hungry for its wonderful chicken Marsala or its popular scampi in a parsley-butter-white-wine-lemon sauce. Pasta dishes, like the grilled Italian sausage tossed with generous chunks of fresh tomato, fresh basil, white wine, and shaved Parmesan, are redolent of garlic and big enough for two. Service is friendly and efficient. La Quinta Grill offers big portions and a nice atmosphere for prices about 25 percent less than if they were located "up canyon" (closer to Palm Springs). The only drawback here is the bread: a pitiful, bland substance that could please only a denture-wearer. *$$; AE, DC, DIS, MC, V; no checks; dinner every day; full bar; reservations recommended; from Hwy 111 go south on Washington St to 52nd Ave, right to Avenidas Bermudas, right to Calle Cadiz.* &

LODGINGS

La Quinta Resort & Club / ★★★

49-499 EISENHOWER DR, LA QUINTA; 760/564-4111 OR 800/598-3828
The valley's second-oldest resort (it dates back to 1926) is the very definition of the classic Palm Springs–area experience. Set against a towering mountain backdrop, it boasts rambling oasislike grounds and subdued elegance, with a Hollywood Golden Era feel of the 1920s and 1930s (Mary Pickford was a frequent guest). To this day, no other resort in the desert approaches its grand sense of place and its understated charm. Originally a cluster of 56 tile-roofed guest casitas widely spaced on lawns, the resort has grown into a large town-size complex of golf courses, tennis club, new rooms, bungalows, ballrooms, and spa—yet without losing intimacy. From the moment you drive down the long entry road between towering columnar cypresses, you feel as though you're entering a Spanish village. The casitas are almost severe in their white-walled simplicity, with thick walls, small windows, and simple furnishings, but color abounds outside, where billows of bougainvillea spill over the rooftops. Almost all have a porch for sitting in the deep shade and listening to the mariachi music float over from an evening meal at Adobe Grill. Three fine restaurants make it possible to never leave the grounds: Montañas (elegant Mediterranean), Morgans (cafe) and Adobe Grill (regional Mexican cuisine with muchas margaritas). With plenty of programs for the kids (Camp La Quinta), golf and tennis, and a new 23,000-square-foot spa that includes a large fitness center—with yoga and other more meditative and spa treatments ranging from the golfer's massage to open-air showers, warm-stone therapy, and an outdoor aromatherapy tub—La Quinta continues to attract entire families generation after generation. *$$$; AE, DC, DIS, MC, V; checks OK; www.laquintaresort. com; from Hwy 111, take Washington St south and turn right on Eisenhower Dr.* &

Indio

Like a big county fair, the **NATIONAL DATE FESTIVAL** takes over Desert ExpoCentre (46-350 Arabia Street; 760/863-8247) every February for 10 days. Concerts and classic carnie rides are joined by exhibit halls crammed with fruits, vegetables, art exhibits, industrial arts, fossilized blue-ribbon pies—you know, all that great fair bric-a-brac. More of a blue-collar community than its resort brethren just up-valley, the city still has a thriving date palm industry, and several outlets sell date products and the famous "date shakes," including **SHIELDS DATE GARDEN** (80-225 Hwy 111; 760/347-0996 or 800/414-2555).

Thousand Palms

With all the golf courses and houses checkerboarding the valley along Highway 111, visitors who love the natural desert are hard pressed to find a patch of open habitat. But at **COACHELLA VALLEY PRESERVE** (5½ miles east on Ramon Road, then north 2½ miles north on 1000 Palm Canyon Road; 760/343-1234), you can tour 21,000 acres of relatively undisturbed "original desert." A highlight is the oasis area, where the Visitor Center, constructed of palm trunks set vertically in rows, is a wonder. This oasis is a lush grove of native, shaggy-trunked *Washingtonia* palms—the same palms usually found deep in desert canyons.

Calipatria and Salton Sea

In satellite photos, Salton Sea is a glistening, 35-mile-long-by-15-mile-wide ocean-blue mirror right in the middle of southeastern California's Colorado Desert. As large as it is, this "sea" didn't exist until a monumental engineering accident occurred. In 1905 the levee of an irrigation canal that channeled water from the Colorado River to Imperial Valley fields broke, and for 16 months the river gushed into the Salton Sink—a geographical bathtub with no drain. Today the sea is a refuge for migrating wildfowl and seabirds. Salton Sea is also popular with thousands of trailer- and tent-camping vacationers who flock to the region in winter to bask in 75-degree weather, spot birds through binoculars, catch scads of fish, and count shooting stars in skies of black velvet. The **INTERNATIONAL BIRD FESTIVAL** (760/344-5FLY) here takes place annually over a weekend in mid-February, with a focus on the National Wildlife Refuge northwest of Calipatria on Sinclair Road, 35 miles north of Interstate 8. For birding updates, call 760/348-5278. In Calipatria, a flagpole rises 184 feet above a modest city park. If that's not odd enough, note that its top ball is exactly at sea level.

HIGH DESERT

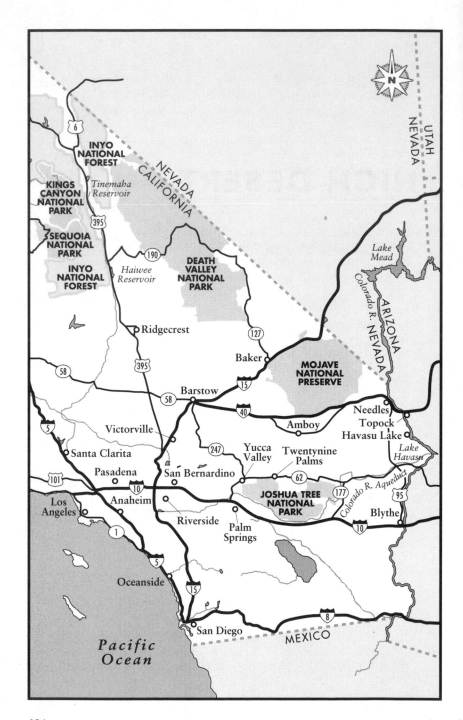

HIGH DESERT

In the land of the Joshua tree, three things are certain: it will get infernally hot, it will snow, and these spiky leafed, multiarmed trees will survive summer's griddle heat and stoically weather winter's occasional snow flurries and icy winds. The range of Joshua trees encompasses much of the Mojave Desert, from the upthrust hills and plateaus protected by Joshua Tree National Park (in dramatic contrast with the nearby glittering carpet of lights better known as Palm Springs) to the new Mojave National Preserve situated in the fork between Interstate 15 and Interstate 40 east of Barstow.

Consider the Joshua tree an indicator species for the area this chapter explores. The abundance of these plants (which are actually a species of yucca) throughout the region, as well as the area's many other scenic attractions, prompted Congress to upgrade Joshua Tree and Death Valley to national park status in 1994 and to declare the eastern Mojave a national preserve. The region, like the Joshua tree, embodies characteristics of improbable hardiness and range. Visitors willing to log some long, hard miles on interstates and backroads will discover—through the windshield, on a day hike, or especially from the rim of a slumbering desert volcano—that the high desert is a celebration of immensity, of emptiness, of quiet so intense you can hear your heart beating.

In **JOSHUA TREE NATIONAL PARK**, wind-smoothed boulders pile up like clusters of weird grapes. Rock climbers from around the world swarm here each winter, their chalked hands searching for fissures left by eons of harsh weather. Less acrobatic travelers seek out the park's boulder-garden trails, hike to hidden year-round ponds (known as "tanks" in desert parlance), and revel at the view of stunning wildflowers and occasional rare desert tortoises nibbling the spring blooms.

Only a half day's drive away in **MOJAVE NATIONAL PRESERVE**, strong winds deposit their plunder from an ancient dry riverbed into mountainous **KELSO DUNES**. Here the loose sand "sings" when your footfalls disturb it. Nearby, jagged granite and volcanic mountain ranges protrude from the land like sharp-toothed rakes. **MITCHELL CAVERNS**, a limestone cave high on a mountainside, hides the fossilized remains of Pleistocene sloths. And an enormously thick lava flow exposes its bubbly flanks in a series of narrow chasms called, aptly enough, Hole-in-the-Wall.

Skip this area in favor of pushing on to Las Vegas? Or think that Death Valley will be enough desert for one trip? Do so at your spiritual peril, for you'll miss what many consider the most sublimely beautiful desert region California has to offer.

ACCESS AND INFORMATION

You won't want to be without a car or recreation vehicle here: no buses or passenger trains serve this remote region. Towns are scarce, but the communities of **JOSHUA TREE** and **TWENTYNINE PALMS** are somewhat bustling because of tourist traffic from the neighboring national park. They also serve families and servicemen at the Marine Corps Air Ground Combat Center in Twentynine Palms. Interstate 10 provides access for most travelers heading for **MOJAVE NATIONAL PRESERVE** as well as **JOSHUA TREE NATIONAL PARK** from the Los Angeles area. Travelers going north to Mojave branch off on Interstate 15 at Fontana. Those continuing east to Palm Springs and Joshua Tree follow Interstate 15 to Highway 62, which leads to the northern entrances to the park at the communities of Joshua Tree and Twentynine Palms. Or continue on Interstate 15 past Indio and enter the park via Cottonwood Springs Road. From areas south of Los Angeles, access is much the same; make your way via any number of interstates to 15, or from San Diego, follow 15 all the way. Travelers heading for the high desert from the San Joaquin Valley and Bakersfield can simply head east over Tehachapi on Highway 58 to bypass the Los Angeles metropolis altogether.

MOJAVE NATIONAL PRESERVE lies between Interstate 15 on the north (the route to Las Vegas) and Interstate 40 on the south. Look at a map and you'll see why its nickname, "the Lonely Triangle," is catching on (the triangle's eastern boundary is north–south Highway 95). Within the preserve, however, only one primary north–south route, Kelbaker Road, splits the region between the interstates. Many roads in the preserve are unpaved, but most routes between major attractions such as **CIMA DOME, KELSO**, and **HOLE-IN-THE-WALL** are well graded and passable by passenger cars. Inquire locally regarding road conditions if you're visiting immediately after a major winter storm. You can also call ahead to **MOJAVE DESERT INFORMATION CENTER** in Baker (72157 Baker Boulevard, under the 134-foot-tall thermometer; 760/733-4040). For trip-planning information, write them (PO Box 241, Baker, CA 92309).

All **AUTOMOBILE TRAVEL** in desert regions can be potentially challenging and sometimes dangerous. Cars should be newly serviced (pay special attention to radiator hoses and fan belts) and in reliable condition. You won't find any gas stations inside the preserve, so fill your tank in Barstow or Baker before you leave the interstates, and keep an eye on the gauge and road map so you have enough fuel to make it to your next fill-up. Carry several gallons of drinking water per person. In the event of a breakdown, stay with the car and wait for help (cars are easier to find than people). Don't venture off main routes unless you are an experienced desert wanderer, and even then don't travel alone—a companion car can be essential for minor emergencies such as pulling you free from

HIGH DESERT THREE-DAY TOUR

DAY ONE: (Note: This itinerary and its activities are geared for late fall or spring, which is when we recommend you visit the region.) After picking up picnic supplies in **Joshua Tree**, head south on Park Boulevard, which becomes the 35-mile loop road through **Joshua Tree National Park**. Stop at **Hidden Valley Campground** to watch rock-climbing activity. Don't miss the ranger-led tours of **Desert Queen Ranch**. Two miles northeast of Hidden Valley, be sure to stretch your legs on the **Barker Dam Trail**—the rocks in this region are especially spectacular. Stop for the night at **Roughley Manor Bed & Breakfast Inn** just outside the park in Twentynine Palms and sleep in—but not until after you've ventured out for a big dinner at **Twentynine Palms Inn**.

DAY TWO: Rise early, fill the ice chest with cold drinks and lunch items at a grocery store or deli in Twentynine Palms, then drive north on Amboy Road over Sheep Hole Pass and down into **Amboy**, a remnant of the days when Route 66 passed right through here. Pull on your hiking boots and climb to the top of **Amboy Crater** before 10am for a view of its long-inactive lava flows. Continue north on Kelbaker Road, leaving pavement to continue on a well-graded road just after you enter Mojave National Preserve near Interstate 40. Stop at the **Kelso Dunes** for a picnic lunch (there are no restaurants or stores anywhere in the preserve) and a brief hike before driving to **Baker** for dinner at **The Mad Greek** and a night's lodging at **Bun Boy Motel**.

DAY THREE: From Baker drive east on Interstate 15 to Cima Road, then south to reenter **Mojave National Preserve**. Turn east on Cedar Canyon Road (unpaved), then south on Black Canyon Road for a visit to famed **Hole-in-the-Wall's lava flows**, as well as a stop at **Providence Mountains State Recreation Area** and **Mitchell Caverns**, where you descend into a limestone cave. Leave the preserve via Essex Road and hit Interstate 40 for the long drive back to Barstow . . . and civilization.

soft sand or going for help if your car conks out. A buddy system isn't necessary in the more popular areas covered below, however. Best times to travel are in the shoulder seasons—late fall and spring, when temperatures are generally below 80°F. Winter weather means cool, usually clear days and freezing nights, and when a storm blows through there can even be snow flurries. Be prepared with a warm jacket, pants, and hat, but dress in layers so you can peel down on sunny days. This is also true for spring, when the likelihood of 75-degrees-plus days is good, but nights are still cold and odd storms can surprise you. Spring means great weather and wildflowers, making it the most popular time to visit the preserve. From April to October (or later), temperatures vault into the nineties and above. Your clothing strategy shifts to heat protection: wide-brimmed hats, lightweight shirts and pants, and sunblock. Drinking water at 15-minute intervals or less becomes critically important: drink as much as two gallons a day if you're out and about in the heat. If all this sounds alarming, here's one more note of concern: the hospital nearest to the Mojave National Preserve is in Needles.

Morongo Valley

The town, located near the western beginning of State Scenic Highway 62 north of Interstate 10, is hardly noticeable—desert residents keep to themselves in small houses off the highway. But **BIG MORONGO CANYON PRESERVE** (11055 East Drive, off Highway 62; 760/363-7190) is worth a look if you're a bird-watcher. You may see a vermilion flycatcher or a beautiful blue grosbeak, and a flash of red might well be a summer tanager. Experts consider this one of the 10 best bird-watching spots in all of California, for 293 species have been seen here. Water seeps from the fault-tortured mountains to create a lush marsh crossed and skirted by trails, including a boardwalk that plunges through a veritable tunnel of greenery.

Joshua Tree National Park

Joshua Tree first gained protection in 1936 as a national monument. The region had remained fairly pristine, well protected by its remote location and harsh climate. Miners and homesteaders had been nibbling at the region's acreage for over 50 years without much impact on the natural scenery. A few hardy souls settled amidst the jumbled rocks, able to survive by finding natural dams or building their own tiny reservoirs. Others clustered, as Native Americans did before them, around the region's handful of oases, especially **OASES OF MARA** at what is now the park's northeastern entrance point. Fortunately for "JT" (as rock climbers and other frequent visitors now call it), the desert was too rugged, too dry, too spiny, and too rocky to attract much interest beyond that shown by adventuresome sightseers. Drawn to the beauty of its balding rocks, awkward-looking trees, and fascinating mix of flora from both low desert (the Colorado, below 3,000 feet) and the high desert (the Mojave), they wandered here then for the same reasons that now draw visitors from around the world.

Recently the park has seen increased visitor interest. JT gained the added cachet of national park status in 1994 with the passage of the Desert Protection Act, and the popularity of **ROCK CLIMBING** here has caused its legions of winter visitors to soar to the point that it can be difficult to find a campsite during the cooler season, November through May.

The Protection Act brought more to Joshua Tree than a new name. Wilderness acreage expanded to 630,000 acres, bringing the total park acreage to 794,000, or about 1,237 square miles (about the same size as Yosemite National Park). Despite its vastness, the park has a road system so simple and limited (about 100 paved miles connecting three main entry points) that you can drive it in a single day or less. Unfortunately, virtually all park visitors are on or near these few roads, especially in spring (March and April), when the wildflowers bloom.

Don't get the idea that Joshua Tree is a queue of cars, however. Its remote location and harsh weather extremes will always assure some elbow room, even along Park Boulevard where it skirts Wonderland of Rocks. Visitors must pay $10 per vehicle admission at one of three entry points: West Entrance Station near the town of Joshua Tree, North Entrance Station on Utah Trail near Twentynine Palms, and the Cottonwood Spring entry 22 miles east of Indio.

A one-day drive will take you past miles of interesting **ROCK FORMATIONS**, many swarming with rock climbers. Hikers enjoy the **BARKER DAM TRAIL** near **HIDDEN VALLEY CAMPGROUND**, an easy path through boulders that leads to a rockbound pool built at the turn of the century. The **DESERT QUEEN RANCH** (760/367-5555) offers ranger-led tours for a small fee. Make plans to join one by inquiring at park entrance stations or calling the above number. The Ranch is now a fascinating ghost town–like ruin that showcases the incredible ingenuity and resourcefulness of Bill Keys as he raised his family here in the early 1900s.

CAMPING has become so popular at Joshua Tree, because of all the winter rock climbing activity, that it can be difficult to get a site. Be sure to contact **JOSHUA TREE NATIONAL PARK** (74485 National Park Drive, Twentynine Palms, CA 92277 by mail, or phone 800/365-2267 or 760/367-5500) in advance for park information. Most camping in the park is first come, first served, but you may reserve a spot at Indian Cove, Black Rock, and Cottonwood. There are no accommodations inside the park, nor can you buy food, gasoline, or any other supplies.

Twentynine Palms

The last town on Highway 62 before the road plunges eastward across empty desert, Twentynine Palms is best known as the easternmost gateway to Joshua Tree National Park. It's here that you'll find the park's **OASIS VISITORS CENTER** (74485 National Park Drive, corner of Utah Trail before you enter the park; 760/367-5500), which received all-new interpretive exhibits in late 1999. Because Joshua Tree is often the first national park many visitors see as they begin a trip through the Southwest from Los Angeles, Oasis Visitors Center now has a "gateway" **INTERACTIVE EXHIBIT** that introduces Grand Canyon, Bryce Canyon,

Zion, and other Southwestern parks. While in Twentynine Palms, keep an eye out for the town's 13-and-growing wall-scale outdoor **MURALS**, each featuring a historic moment from the area's past. Lovers of desert paintings should stop at the **TWENTYNINE PALMS ARTISTS GUILD ART GALLERY** (74055 Cottonwood Drive; 760/367-7819), located next door to Twentynine Palms Inn.

LODGINGS

Best Western Gardens Inn & Suites / ★

71487 TWENTYNINE PALMS HWY, TWENTYNINE PALMS; 760/367-9141 OR 800/528-1234
Set against the boulder-strewn mountains of Joshua Tree National Park, this fairly standard motor inn is by far the nicest chain-affiliated lodging near the park's eastern entrance. Its guests are everyone from military individuals and families on business at the nearby base to national park visitors to many foreign tourists (especially from Germany). Its location lends travelers a great sense of "being there" in a desert landscape, even though it's plunked on the same long stretch of Highway 62 that's scattered with an anonymous collection of mini-malls, gas marts, and other encrustations doing their best to spoil a designated California State Scenic Highway. Organized around a good-sized swimming pool (heated year-round), the dusky-colored inn lines up 84 rooms in one- and two-story buildings. Twelve suites have efficiency kitchens for whipping together a simple meal after a day spent exploring Joshua Tree. The nicely furnished king-bed suites (some with murals of desert scenes) also have queen-size sofa beds, while one two-room suite and two minisuites include hot tubs. Ask for a room with a view of the mountains to the south, and do make a point of dropping into the outdoor Jacuzzi, which is great for evening star-watching. The included continental breakfast includes pastries, locally baked bread, and a full range of cereals, fruit, juices, and coffee. *$$; AE, DC, DIS, MC, V; no checks; www.bestwestern. com; at west end of town.* &

Roughley Manor Bed & Breakfast Inn / ★★

74744 JOE DAVIS RD, TWENTYNINE PALMS; 760/367-3238
In 1924 desert pioneers Elizabeth and Bill Campbell turned a once-primitive campsite next to a hand-dug well into an elegant two-story, stone-walled mansion. Today, a rustling oasis of mature fan palms, rose gardens, and trickling fountains surrounds the product of their years of toil. Located near the northeast edge of what is now Joshua Tree National Park, Roughley Manor has aged well (as stone is wont to do), and innkeepers Jan and Gary Peters couldn't be a better fit to carry on the original owner's dream. The two-story main house has a "great room" downstairs—a huge living room almost entirely paneled and

trimmed with hardwood wainscoting and moldings. The grandest accommodations are the Campbell and Magnolia rooms upstairs, each with fireplace and four-poster or canopy bed, and deep-set windows that look out into the treetops and surrounding desert landscape. There are five rooms in the stone main house and two in the stone "museum house," plus a wood-frame cottage and a small farmhouse. All are air-conditioned. Jan Peters's interior designs are tasteful, classical New England, with a merciful lack of stuffed bears and knickknacks. Her husband Gary seems never without a project, and the place is immaculate right down to the raked sandy yard (no lawns) with its comfortable, upholstered outdoor furniture set in the shade. Guests get a hearty breakfast of fresh fruit, toast, and twice-baked potatoes topped with eggs, bacon, and cheese (among other menus). The Peterses also set out desserts, coffee, and tea each evening. Evenings here are perfect for a soak in the hot tub under a sky peppered with stars. $–$$; MC, V; checks OK; themanor@cci-29palms.com; www.virtual29.com/themanor; off Hwy 111 off of Utah Trail (yellow blinking light at east end of town).

Twentynine Palms Inn / ★★

73950 INN AVE, TWENTYNINE PALMS; 760/367-3505
Rustic, sparsely landscaped, with dirt roads between the bungalows, the Inn captures the essence of an old-time California desert stay. This historic cluster of cottages, which sprawls over 35 acres, has been operated by the same family since 1928. It's the quintessential hideaway for stressed-out film industry types, European travelers, lizard-skinned desert oldsters, and just about everyone else. Built beside the Oasis of Mara, a rare natural source of open water in the high desert, the Inn offers bungalow rooms in the 1929 "old Adobe" section with sun patios (great for nude sunbathing) and fireplaces. Wood-frame cottages Gold Park and Faultline were moved here in 1928. Larger lodgings include several houses and cabins; well-known local painter Irene Charlton occu-pied one, La Querencia, for many years, and her artworks now decorate the walls. Interiors are rustic yet comfortable, with swamp coolers (rather than colder, but more humid, air conditioners) keeping them reasonably comfortable in summer. Bird-watching, swimming, and tours of the Inn's large organic vegetable garden are the major activities here. Many guests tour nearby Joshua Tree National Park (no lodging is located closer to the park), or just hunker down in the 100-plus heat if they visit in summer. Adjacent to the pool, the restaurant serves the best meals in the area. All seasonal vegetables come from the inn's year-round garden. The menu favors a hearty continental approach to grilled steaks, seafood, and chicken, and the bar blends up some of the best margaritas this side of Palm Springs. $–$$; AE, DC, DIS, MC, V (and all European cards); checks OK; info@29palmsinn.com; www.29palmsinn.com; off National Park Dr, about a quarter mile to Inn Ave. &

Amboy

Once a bustling stop on Route 66 for overheated cars and travelers braving the Mojave, Amboy suffered "bypass surgery" back in the 1970s when Interstate 40 pushed through. Located about 17 miles south of the interstate (as the crow flies), Amboy still attracts Route 66 (now known as National Trails Highway) aficionados, many of them European tourists eager to see creaky desert towns like this one. How creaky? Think of the movie *Bagdad Cafe*. The film was actually shot farther west on Route 66, in Newberry Springs, but no matter: the desert sun bleaches and the wind batters anything man builds out here until buildings crumple into anonymous—but starkly appealing—relics that all look identical.

AMBOY CRATER rises 285 feet from the desert's frying-pan flats like a burnt souffle. After the first eruption about 6,000 years ago, subsequent eruptions up until 500 years ago spewed lava in a south-southwest fan that covers 24 square miles. You can hike to the top via a trail that leads from the south side of National Trails Highway 2 miles west of Amboy. Wear sturdy boots for the steep trail, and allow a few hours: you'll probably linger at the top enjoying the view.

Baker

Smack in the middle of the East Mojave, 60 miles east of Barstow and 150 miles west of Las Vegas, little Baker sustains itself on hungry and sleepy drivers from Interstate 15. Most travelers know the town as the southern gateway to Death Valley via Highway 127 and the location of the **MOJAVE DESERT INFORMATION CENTER** (72157 Baker Boulevard, beneath the tall thermometer; 760/733-4040). Its sharp staff help thousands plan their forays into surrounding desert lands.

RESTAURANTS

The Mad Greek
72112 BAKER BLVD, BAKER; 760/733-4354
Its exterior plastered with signs like "Something for Everybody," "Special Bone-In Ham," and "Parking for Greeks Only," The Mad Greek may be the desert's most eclectic restaurant. The signs, of course, hope to pull in auto travelers headed for the more familiar menu at a nearby Denny's. Unless you have your heart set on a Grand Slam, however, you'll enjoy the Greek's food: sizzling shish kabob, eggplant salads, hummus, baklava, and their most popular item, gyros (spicy thin slices of lamb or beef tucked into pita bread with tzatziki sauce). They also have Amer-

ican hamburgers and sandwiches. The Mad Greek is justifiably well known for its milk shakes made with fresh strawberries. They'll even mix you up a margarita if you want one. *$; AE, DIS, MC ,V; no checks; breakfast, lunch, dinner every day; full bar; reservations not necessary; Kelbaker Road exit at Baker Blvd.* &

LODGINGS

Bun Boy Motel

72155 BAKER BLVD, BAKER; 760/733-4363

Popular with European travelers on their way to Death Valley as well as gamblers heading for Vegas (or returning, in victory or in defeat), Bun Boy is one of those classic little American motels (20 rooms, one story) from the days before the nationwide chains. Rooms are clean, inexpensive, and plain. There's no pool, but you can go across the street to swim at Wills Fargo, which belongs to the same owners. The name Bun Boy comes from the affiliated 24-hour cafe next door. *$; AE, DIS, MC, V; no checks; Baker Blvd exit from I-15 north.*

Wills Fargo Motel

72252 BAKER BLVD, BAKER; 760/733-4477

Talk to Bakerites and they'll tell you this is the "new" motel in town. It has a small wing that was added back in the early '90s, bringing the total number of rooms to 30. Rates differ slightly between the two sections, primarily because the older wing has queen beds and showers only, while the new has king beds and tubs/showers. (You're livin' now!) But it's essential to know about this basic, clean place to stay, for Baker's motels fill up fast on weekends. Most important, Wills Fargo (named for an owner named Will) has—drum roll, please—a 10-foot-deep pool. Baker gets hot, hot, hot every summer, and this little oasis can be a godsend. *$; AE, DC, DIS, MC, V; no checks; Baker Blvd exit from I-15.* ❧

Needles and Topock

Needles is a welcome sight. The cool, willow-lined Colorado River flows through this fried but friendly little town, whispering under the bridge on Harbor Avenue. To the southeast on the Arizona side, the Needles, a ragged mountain range cresting at 2,353-foot Powell Peak, pokes at hard blue sky.

Founded in 1883, Needles owes its existence to the railroad, highway travelers, and a nearby farming community to the north along the Arizona side. As the easternmost end of Southern California desert exploration, it offers a decidedly un-desert attraction: **CANOEING** through nearby Topock Gorge for a day. The gorge, part of **HAVASU NATIONAL WILDLIFE REFUGE**, begins at the Interstate 40. Canoeists meet outfitters on the river at **MOABI REGIONAL PARK** (locals call it Park Moabi; 11 miles southeast of Needles; 760/326-3831), then paddle downriver beneath a steel-strut bridge into a wild region of reddish cliffs, hidden coves, rush-lined backwaters, and a pictograph rock or two. The pickup point is on the Arizona side off Highway 95 at Castle Rock, north of Lake Havasu City (home of London Bridge and English Village). Contact **JERKWATER CANOE AND KAYAK COMPANY** (800/421-7803; www.jerkwater.com) for rental and guided-trip information.

The fictional Joad family camped for a while in Needles on their way west along "the Mother Road"—Route 66—in Steinbeck's *The Grapes of Wrath*. Here they debated how to get across the desert in their overloaded jalopies. "Gonna go 'crost her at night,'" says Ruthie, "... we get the livin' Jesus burned outa us if we go in daylight." We hope your car is in better shape than theirs.

MOJAVE DESERT INFORMATION CENTER (the National Park Service; 707 W Broadway; 760/326-6322) can help with local information, as can **NEEDLES CHAMBER OF COMMERCE** (100 G Street; 760/326-2050). **NEEDLES MUSEUM** (on the city park at 929 Front Street; 760/326-5678) will fill you in on local history. They're currently trying to restore the old block-long Harvey House hotel and restaurant nearby, which served Santa Fe Railroad passengers before the days of the interstates. The two-story cement building, noted for its many columns, has been vacant for about a decade.

Blythe

Situated on the California side where Interstate 10 crosses the Colorado River, Blythe marks the beginning of the lower desert. From here south to Yuma, the Colorado River flows more slowly, and surrounding desert lands lie nearly at sea level except for occasional small mountain ranges that tend to run northwest to southeast. For the traveler, Blythe is best known as the gateway to giant prehistoric **INDIAN INTAGLIOS** that sprawl across the desert 15 miles north of Interstate 5 on the west side of Highway 95. Now fenced off to protect them from foot and off-road traffic, the intaglios were unknown to modern man until first glimpsed from an airplane. As soon as the first pilot flew over, word spread that a huge four-legged animal, a human figure 160 feet long, and a spiral design had been inscribed in the desert landscape. You'll get some idea of the shapes and scope of the work by walking around, but you'll wish for an observation tower or a hot-air balloon ride.

Mojave National Preserve

Most travelers enter the preserve from Interstate 40 via Kelbaker Road and head straight north on the road to Kelso. Suitable for passenger cars, the wide graded road cuts through the Granite Mountains and descends into a wide valley on the west side of the Providence scarp (in winter, the Providences are occasionally snowcapped). Virtually a secret 20 years ago, the **KELSO DUNES** are now the Eastern Mojave's main attraction (if getting a few dozen visitors a day warrants being called "main"). A hikers' paradise, the area has long been protected from motorized vehicles. The terminus of the **MOJAVE SINK** is a vast catch basin for swirling sand lifted by winds and deposited here against the Providence wall.

These dunes "sing," but don't expect an aria. On a still day, sand dislodged by your footsteps slips like a great tongue of molasses down the dune face, and a chantlike hum can be heard. Nearby **KELSO DEPOT** was once a busy Union Pacific Railroad way point, with a Spanish-revival station grand enough for any major city (you could still get a lemonade and a slice of pie here in the early 1970s). Now it should reopen sometime after 2001 at the park's main visitors center and museum. From Kelso, you have a decision to make: Kelbaker Road to the northwest passes through incredible **LAVA FLOWS** and **CINDER CONES**. Kelso-Cima Road heads northeast through the world's largest **JOSHUA TREE FOREST**, which covers Cima Dome, a gently rounded igneous formation called a batholith. The Cima region's 75-square-mile bubble of once-molten rock is so big that humans seem more like ants exploring the top of the Houston Astrodome. Don't expect to see anything like the granite domes of

Yosemite. Mojave travelers commonly drive through and say "Where is it?" for about 20 miles—and never find it because they're actually on it.

Cima Dome has an overstory of Joshua trees in such abundance that if the desert can be said to have a forest, this is it. From the Cima area, return to Interstate 40 via Mid-Hills Campground, Hole-in-the-Wall, and Mitchell Caverns. From the Kelso-Cima Road, take Cedar Canyon Road east to Black Canyon Road, then go south on Black Canyon to Mid-Hills and Hole-in-the-Wall. The two developed campgrounds within the preserve are at **MID-HILLS** (30 miles northwest of Interstate 40 via Essex and Black Canyon Roads) and **HOLE-IN-THE-WALL** (20 miles northwest of Interstate 40 via same roads). Neither has a street address or a phone. Hole-in-the-Wall does have a visitor center (760/928-2572), which is staffed on weekends only and not at all during summer. Mid-Hills is a high area, prone to occasional snowfalls as winter storms sweep over the Providence Range. Always travel in this area with plenty of water, warm clothing in winter, and a close eye on the weather. Travelers have been known to spend the night in a blizzard (they happen once or twice a year), only to hike the following day in a T-shirt at Kelso Dunes. If time is short, save most of it for Hole-in-the-Wall, a good jumping-off point for an overnight backpacking trip or a day hike into the open desert of the **WILD HORSE CANYON** area and some scrambling amongst the cave-pocked **LAVA FLOWS** and staunchly upright **RHYOLITE MONOLITHS** nearby. One memorable experience is the short climb down a narrow slot canyon via several iron rings bolted into the rock. Further south off Essex Road, **PROVIDENCE MOUNTAINS STATE RECREATION AREA** (760/928-2586) offers a mountainside campground and **MITCHELL CAVERNS** (760/928-2586), a must-stop for anyone with an interest in underground mysteries (and cool cave temperatures in summer). Ranger-led cavern tours focus not only on the caves' geological origins, but also the site's long use by Chimehuevi tribesmen—as well as a few Pleistocene epoch critters.

Ridgecrest

If you're interested in petroglyphs, some of them dating back 3,000 years, you'll find over 100,000 ancient rock art drawings in Little Petroglyph Canyon on the China Lake Naval Weapons Center. One catch: most of the base is off limits to visitors. Fortunately, **MATURANGO MUSEUM** (100 E Flores Avenue; 760/375-6900) offers special docent-led tours up the canyon. Scraped into the dark desert "varnish" of sunburnt rocks, the artwork fairly dances in the shimmering desert sun. Other attractions near Ridgecrest include Fossil Falls, a now-dry, water-sculpted chasm that once linked several massive lakes of the Pleistocene epoch; Pinnacles National Natural Landmark, tufa spires created by geothermal springs

STAR WATCHING: THE AGELESS DESERT PASTIME

Desert travelers, especially in the remote Mojave Desert region where "light pollution" from cities is virtually nonexistent, often forget to bring one simple item that makes any desert trip more enjoyable: a star chart. Out here you'll see stars as you may never have seen them before—so many that you may have trouble recognizing even familiar, simple constellations as they swim through a truly milky Milky Way.

Many charts show horizon latitude; this can vary in North America, from latitude 30° at St. Augustine, Florida, for example, to latitude 50° for Medicine Hat, Alberta, Canada. For the Mojave, you'll want to reference latitude 35°. Otherwise you'll be looking for stars, especially in the southernmost and northernmost regions of the sky, that may be below your horizon. Most of the sky, however, is the same.

Some experienced desert travelers bring a folding chaise longue or lightweight cot so they can lie on their backs and watch the show. Look for planets traveling through the zodiac constellations along a line known as the ecliptic (shown on star charts). But note that you won't find planets themselves on any star charts because they wander. Five are usually visible to the naked eye: Venus (the brightest, on the western horizon at sunset or the eastern horizon at sunrise), Jupiter, Mars, Saturn, and Mercury.

Although summer heat is intense, some star watchers enjoy the desert night sky most in the month of August, the time of the Perseid meteors—so named because they occur in the region of sky occupied by the constellation Perseus (near Cassiopeia) after midnight. These showers can get intense, with little zips of light crossing the velvet blackness so frequently you'll soon quit exclaiming, "Look, there's a shooting star!" Set your alarm clock and enjoy the show.

in the depths of now-dry Searles Lake; the Randsburg and Johannesburg mining districts, where a few antique shops nestle in the midst of hundreds of abandoned mines; and the deeply eroded, color-banded cliffs and canyons of Red Rock Canyon State Park. For information on all these areas, contact Ridgecrest Visitors Bureau (760/375-8202 or 800/847-4830).

Death Valley

Something perversely fascinating about being in one of the hottest places on earth—not to mention its sinister name—has drawn tourists here since 1927, when the Furnace Creek Inn first opened. There's more to Death Valley than the thermometer's bulb-busting acrobatics, however. Stretching for about 110 miles along the California–Nevada border, Death Valley's boundaries contain 11,000-foot peaks, alkali flats, pinyon

WHERE DID ALL THE LAKES GO?

Coyote, Leech, Lost, Owl, Cuddleback, Searles, Cronese, Soda, Broadwell, Cadiz—the list goes on and on. All were lakes. Now all are broad, shimmering white flats of the utmost aridity—seemingly the California desert at its driest. Could there really have been water here?

There certainly was, sometimes to a depth of several hundred feet. Look closely at the hills and mountainsides surrounding many of the High Desert's dry lake beds and you'll see phantom "wave terraces"—the telltale shoreline of the ancient lake at its fullest. Most of these lakes filled toward the end of the Pleistocene epoch, a time when the ice cap had crept south well into what is now the United States. As the ice began to recede, melting waters drained southward across Nevada and Eastern California, pouring into the Salton Trough and the Gulf of California.

Searles Dry Lake off Highway 178 (20 miles east of Ridgecrest) is one of the most interesting of these phantoms, for here the Trona Pinnacles (now protected as Pinnacles National Natural Landmark) rise from the flats like misshapen "drip style" sand castles. Each pinnacle was formed between 10,000 and 100,000 years ago when underwater hot springs deposited calcium-rich groundwater into a lake of carbonate brine. The resulting columnar blobs of tufa (cemented in part by colonies of blue-green algae) grew to heights of 100 feet or more. When the waters receded, the rocklike spires remained. A half-mile trail takes you through some of the most interesting formations.

woodlands, rocky, narrow slot canyons, sand dunes, and an 8,000-foot-thick deposit of sediment forming the valley floor. The sediments arrived here via streams and rivers from much of the east side of the Sierra Nevada as well as western Nevada. Some have been exposed by erosion to resemble the folds and crevices of a massive multicolored mushroom.

Death Valley lay beneath a lake 600 feet deep during the Ice Age (the Pleistocene epoch). Today the only water here sneaks in via hot springs working their way up through the baking crust. Some small ponds host the rare desert pupfish, an evolutionary marvel descended from a diminutive species trapped as the giant lake dried up. Pupfish have adapted to super-salty water and temperatures as high as 111°F. In other areas, a strong flow is enough to irrigate a golf course and the grounds of the famed Furnace Creek Inn and nearby Furnace Creek Ranch.

A National Monument from 1933 to 1994 and now a National Park, Death Valley slowly saw the profile of its human visitors "evolve" as well—from pioneers and miners, who saw the area as nothing more than a source of borax, copper, gold, and other plunder-worthy metals, to a gradually increasing stream of tourists from around the world. Most arrive in winter, when glorious temperatures in the 60s and 70s are conducive to exploring the park's many natural attractions. The park does get visitors in summer, despite midday readings in the 120-plus range. At those temperatures, however, you can only stand outside your air-conditioned automobile or hotel room for a few minutes and gasp—like a pupfish out of water.

Plan to spend at least two days seeing the park. Start with detailed information regarding routes and safety precautions from **DEATH VALLEY NATIONAL PARK VISITOR CENTER** (Death Valley National Park, Death Valley, CA 92328; 760/786-2331). Note that without advance reservations, campsites and lodgings can be very difficult to procure during winter. The Death Valley area does have a small store (at Furnace Creek Ranch) and four service stations (at Furnace Creek Ranch, Stovepipe Wells, Scotty's Castle, and Beatty, Nevada).

Many of Death Valley's attractions are of the scenic-vista sort. **SCOTTY'S CASTLE**, built in 1924 by Chicago tycoon Albert Johnson at a cost of $2.5 million and now administered by Grapevine Ranger Station (760/786-2313), is a must-see. This Moorish mansion with its four towers opens daily for tours of its rooms (the grounds are open for self-guided touring). The Valley's famed **SAND DUNES** are 8 miles east of Stovepipe Wells via Highway 190. The oddest spot may well be Race-track Valley, a mud flat 29 miles from the last paved road via a graded dirt road. Pushed by howling winds, rocks (some too large for a man to lift) move across the surface when it's been made slick by rain or ice, leaving long, mysterious tracks. Then the surface bakes dry again, and visitors arrive to scratch their heads and wonder.

LODGINGS

Furnace Creek Inn / ★★☆

ON HWY 190, 1 MILE SOUTH OF VISITOR CENTER, DEATH VALLEY; 760/786-2345 OR 800/236-7916

Seen against the violet-hued backdrop of Death Valley's surrounding mountain ranges, the Mediterranean/Arabian style Furnace Creek Inn rises three to four stories up a slight hillside. Few resorts seem so suited to their location: the inn's tile-roofed wings sprawl horizontally, linked by arched loggias built of hand-laid desert stone and shaded a bit by scattered towering palms. Opened in 1927 (after a first life as quarters for borax miners), the inn has seen several remodelings over the years. Significant upgrades were made in the 1990s to the dining room—and to its prices, which now hover in the very expensive range. The 66 rooms range from small to quite large, and many, but not all, have been redecorated. Even a trip to your room is a memorable experience: the natural hillside forms one side of some of the corridors. Although the inn has lost a bit of its Art Deco feel, this venerable hotel still offers the historic ambience you might expect from a grand national park lodge. Remember, it can be too hot here in summer even to brave a trip to the pool. In winter, the Inn is so popular with foreign travelers that it can be booked solid weeks in advance. *$$$$ winter, $$$ summer; AE, DIS, MC, V; in-state checks OK; www.furnacecreekresort.com; Hwy 127 to Shoshone, to Death Valley junction, then left on Hwy 190 into the park.* &

Furnace Creek Ranch / ★

ON HWY 190, 1 MILE SOUTH OF VISITOR CENTER, DEATH VALLEY; 760/786-2345 OR 800/236-7916

Operated by the same owners as Furnace Creek Inn, the Ranch offers a low-cost alternative to the Inn's outright luxury. Once a working alfalfa ranch that harvested as many as nine crops a year to feed the borax-mine livestock (those 20-mule teams got hungry!), the spread now hosts two-story motellike units (224) with indoor and outdoor corridors, cabins (27), a spring-fed swimming pool, a golf course, a museum of mining history, a small grocery and camping goods store, horseback riding, and even an airstrip if you care to fly here in your own plane. A coffee shop and cafeteria/restaurant stay open all day, making this a low-cost home base for a few days spent exploring the park. The swimming pool is its most attractive feature: a steady supply from underground hot springs keeps it topped up with 85-degree water. Locals call this their "cold water supply"—there's no way to get anything cooler. *$$; AE, DIS, MC, V; in-state checks OK; www.furnacecreekresort.com; Hwy 127 to Shoshone, to Death Valley junction, then left on Hwy 190 into the park.*

INLAND EMPIRE

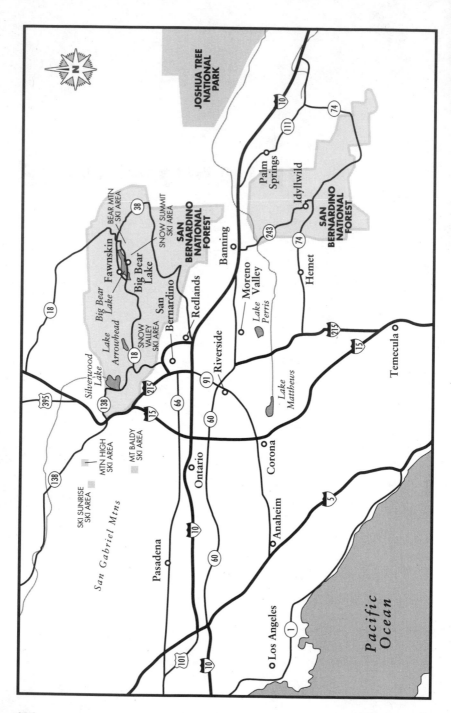

INLAND EMPIRE

For a generation or two, it *was* an empire. Groves covered the land with golden-fruited trees that yielded equally golden bank accounts for growers. The orange-growing boom, centered around Riverside and Redlands, brought a prosperity that briefly made Riverside the highest-per-capita-income city in the United States. Cross-country rail lines joined San Bernardino and Riverside Counties with the East Coast, and refrigeration technology brought California oranges to Eastern Seaboard tables in a matter of days.

Today Riverside and Redlands are known for their glorious civic and private architecture from the turn of the century, but the orange boom has been replaced by new housing sprawl. And after generations of terrible smog, the Inland Empire, as it came to be known from those glory years, is finally emerging from a long, hazy bad dream of being all but forgotten except by those who live here. Years of stringent automobile-pollution control measures have reduced smog dramatically—although it takes only one drive into the mountains and a view of the inversion layer to realize that the haze is still a fact of life most days. If you want the great views of snowcapped mountains above orange groves that inspired the early crate-label artists, come in winter or spring right after a storm.

Consisting of the western areas of Riverside and San Bernardino Counties (as well as part of eastern Los Angeles County), the Inland Empire embraces 28,000 square miles in the heart of Southern California. The area's population in the year 2005 is expected to range between 3.6 and 4.0 million. Its charm lies in the traveler's discovery of grand residential streets, old restaurants, classic hotels and train stations, and the surrounding mountains—the San Bernardinos and the San Jacintos. Both ranges separate the Inland Empire from the desert. Two mountain passes carry travelers eastward across the peaks: Cajon Pass on Interstate 15 and San Gorgonio Pass on Interstate 10. Incredibly to people not familiar with Southern California, the region's two highest peaks, San Gorgonio (11,499 feet) and San Jacinto (10,804 feet), are true alpine giants that would not be out of place in the Sierra Nevada or Rocky Mountains.

ACCESS AND INFORMATION

ONTARIO INTERNATIONAL AIRPORT (south of Interstate 10 between Haven and Vineyard; 909/937-2700) is served by nine commercial airlines connecting to every major U.S. city via nonstop or continuing service. **CAR RENTALS** at the airport include Alamo, Avis, Budget, Dollar, and National, while Enterprise and Thrifty are nearby. **AMTRAK'S**

(800/872-7245) service linking Chicago to Southern California stops in San Bernardino at 1170 W Third Street. **METROLINK**'s (909/808-5465) mass transit rail service links the Inland Empire to surrounding metro regions. Riverside's **GREYHOUND** bus station (800/231-2222) is at 3911 University Avenue. Redlands also has a depot (802 W Cotton Avenue).

From Los Angeles, motorists take Interstate 10 east to enter San Bernardino County via the city of Pomona. Interstate 10 continues east over San Gorgonio Pass to Palm Springs (see the Low Desert chapter). From San Diego, travelers enter Riverside County via Interstate 15 as it passes northward through Temecula and its burgeoning wine region. Interstate 15 skirts the western edge of San Bernardino County, bypassing the cities of Riverside and San Bernardino, before leaving the Inland Empire region over Cajon Pass near Victorville.

Motorists reach the **SAN JACINTO MOUNTAINS** and the **IDYLLWILD** resort area by going east from Interstate 15 on Highway 74 through Hemet to Highway 243 and the final tortuously curved climb into the pines (total distance about 40 miles). Idyllwild has no ski resorts, so you don't have to worry about ski traffic. You can also reach Idyllwild from Interstate 10: at Banning, take Highway 243 south about 25 miles into the heart of the mountains.

For information about Inland Empire tourist destinations, contact the **INLAND EMPIRE TOURISM COUNCIL** (c/o Inland Empire Economic Partnership, 301 E Vanderbilt Way, Suite 100, San Bernardino 92408; 909/890-1090; www.ieep.com/ietc).

Idyllwild

Gateway to San Jacinto State Park, this small resort town fills up each weekend with flatlanders who want a breath of crisp alpine air, a whiff of pines, a stay in a homey bed-and-breakfast inn, and perhaps a challenging day hike or overnight backpacking trip into the wilderness. In town, you'll find numerous small curio and gift shops oriented to the tourist trade, as well as several fine galleries. If you enjoy picnicking head up to Humber Park at the northeastern end of Fern Valley Road. Hikers use densely forested Humber Park as their jump-off point for either a day hike up Devil's Slide Trail (great views) or longer expeditions toward the summit of **MOUNT SAN JACINTO** (elevation 10,804 feet), **TAHQUITZ PEAK** (Southern California's premier rock-climbing site for long-pitch climbs on vertical granite faces), and the beautiful backpacker campsites in **TAHQUITZ MEADOW.**

The **IDYLLWILD CHAMBER OF COMMERCE** (54295 Village Center Drive, downstairs from the Idyllwild *Town Crier*; 888/659-3259; www. idyllwild. org) can help with trip planning. For backcountry permits and

INLAND EMPIRE THREE-DAY TOUR

While the Inland Empire is generally not a preferred California destination, should you find yourself in the area for a few days, there are plenty of areas worth exploring.

DAY ONE. Drive to **Riverside** for a morning of antique shopping in the downtown mall area on Mission Inn Avenue, or a little poking around the old Craftsman-house-dominated neighborhoods at the base of Mount Rubidoux and Little Rubidoux. Check in to the **Mission Inn** and get an immediate feel for this architectural fantasyland by taking a guided tour. Spend the afternoon relaxing by the pool before dining that evening at the inn, either in the courtyard **Mission Inn Restaurant** or inside in the swankier **Duane's Prime Steaks & Seafood**.

DAY TWO. Rise with the sun for a brisk hike up **Mount Rubidoux.** Return to the inn for breakfast in the courtyard, then take Interstate 215 north to Interstate 10 and go east to the **San Bernardino County Museum**. After a tour, drive further east on Interstate 10 to Yucaipa Boulevard. Go east to the Oak Glen Road loop through apple country, stopping for a piece of fresh apple pie at any of the apple stands and gift shops. Return to Riverside for dinner at **Table for Two**, or **Gay and Larry's** if you feel like Mexican food, before a nightcap back at the inn and a soak in the courtyard spa before bed.

DAY THREE. A long day awaits. Start off with breakfast at the inn, then check out and drive southwest on Highway 91 to the **California Citrus State Historic Park** for a brief tour. Return to Highway 91, continue southwest to Interstate 15, and drive south to **Temecula**. Spend the day touring **wineries**, stopping for lunch at **Cafe Champagne**, before checking into the **Temecula Creek Inn** for the night and dining at **Temet Grill**.

information, stop in at the **IDYLLWILD RANGER STATION** (San Jacinto Ranger District; 909/659-2117; corner Highway 243 and Upper Pine Crest in the village). For information on **ROCK CLIMBING** instruction and guide services, drop by Nomad Ventures (54415 N Circle Drive; 909/659-4853).

RESTAURANTS

Gastrognome / ★★

54381 RIDGEVIEW DR, IDYLLWILD; 909/659-5055

Locals and regulars call this place "the Gnome," and it's cozy enough for any forest creature. Gastrognome combines hearty fare and fine dining to suit mountain appetites quickened by a day on the trails high above town. Set in the pine forest that swathes most of Idyllwild, the restaurant has a rustic-chic vibe, from the floor-to-ceiling wine rack made of stacked clay pipe to the polished copper panels and brick and wood walls. Come in on a chilly night and you'll find a roaring blaze in the fireplace beneath a spectacular landscape painting. Dinner features tasty skewered shrimp brushed with mustard sauce and broiled to pink perfection. Other seafood choices include equally simple versions of broiled salmon, halibut, and lobster. Meat eaters choose rack of lamb, or tournedos of beef capped with mushrooms and béarnaise. Lunch takes an informal tack (the Gnome offers one of the better hamburgers in town) and can be eaten on either of two decks outside. *$$; AE, DC, DIS, MC, V; no checks, lunch Mon–Sat, dinner every day, brunch Sun; full bar; reservations recommended; www.thegnome.com; turn off Hwy 243 at Texaco and go 1 block.* &

LODGINGS

Idyllwild Inn / ★

54300 VILLAGE CENTER DR, IDYLLWILD; 888/659-2552
Idyllwild Inn, family-owned since 1909, scatters its 15 cabins through an open pine forest like a gracious little Tyrolean village. Families love it here, and although the inn doesn't have a pool, the tots' playground is a good substitute. Cabins are neat, with a simple mountain decor; each has a wood-burning fireplace, kitchen, and deck. Some were built as early as 1909, others in the 1930s, and the newest—the duplexes—in the 1980s, although it's obvious all have been constantly maintained and upgraded. The bustle of Idyllwild is literally outside the front gate, but once you're inside this compound you really feel you're in a mountain town. At some point, asphalt drives were put in so you can drive right to your cabin, and unfortunately they tend to dominate the setting a bit; when you reserve, ask to be on the side farthest from the entrance. *$–$$; DIS, MC, V; checks OK; www.idyllwildinn.com; from Hwy 243, turn at Texaco station on to Ridgeview Rd and go 2 blocks to Village Center.* &

Strawberry Creek Inn / ★★

26370 HWY 243, IDYLLWILD; 909/659-3202 OR 800/262-8969
One of the first bed-and-breakfast inns in the region and long one of the best, Strawberry Creek has a location just far enough outside town (about ¼ mile) to grant it the peace and quiet mountain visitors seek. Yes, there is a Strawberry Creek, and a walking path leads along it all the way into town. The inn was fashioned by owners Diana Dugan and Jim Goff from a large, shingled cabin that was built in 1941. Five rooms in the main cabin put you closest to the large living room/recreation room/library downstairs—the true heart of the house and a great place to gather around a fire on chilly days. Four rooms out back on the "courtyard" are newer but feel a bit less cozy, and there's a small single cabin close to the creek. Decor elements include a range of window seats, antique bed frames, wood-burning fireplaces, and skylights; all rooms

have private baths. A full breakfast is served out on a big glassed-in porch. Smoking is prohibited. *$–$$; DIS, MC, V; checks OK; www. strawberrycreekinn.com; ¼ mile south of the village.* &

Redlands

A treasure trove of Southern California's architectural heritage, this orange-growing town remains one of the best stops in California for anyone with an interest in **EARLY 1900S BUILDINGS**, especially Mission Revival style. From the moment you enter town on Orange Street heading south from Interstate 10, you sense the city's grandeur. An open-loggia train station on Orange just south of Pearl is a pillared temple to rail travel. Downtown Redlands has been tastefully redone (read "malled") with brick-pattern streets and circular intersections, and has enjoyed a mild renaissance. In the residential neighborhoods, don't miss **HOLT HOUSE** (405 W Olive Avenue), **BURRAGE HOUSE** (1205 Crescent Avenue), and **MOREY HOUSE** (140 Terracina Boulevard), the last of which is perhaps the most photographed Victorian in Southern California. This is also the location of the **SAN BERNARDINO COUNTY**

ON THE TRAIL OF GRAND PUBLIC ARCHITECTURE

Railroad barons of the late 1800s and early 1900s saw themselves as modern-day Greeks of a new Golden Age. Fittingly, they built a legacy of temple-like buildings across the Inland Empire. Venture into most towns built along a rail line in San Bernardino and Riverside Counties, and chances are good that you'll find a spectacular bit of train-station architecture. Styles range from brick Queen Anne (in Perris, south of Riverside), to the classical Greek temple of Redlands, to Riverside's "Hopi" Southwest style, to San Bernardino's huge Mission Revival pile. Some have fallen into disuse. Others have been adapted as restaurants. And a few still function as—surprise—railroad stations!

Other chunks of grand architectural styling to look for in every town include the public libraries. Redlands has a spectacular example, certainly one of the finest in the state. Keep an eye out, also, for civic buildings and churches. (Best church examples include the red Arizona sandstone First Unitarian in Riverside (at the corner of Seventh and Lemon) and Trinity Episcopal Church in Redlands (at 419 South Fourth Street).

Where did all the money to build, build, build come from? Agriculture, especially citrus, was the lifeblood of this temperate area. The rich reaped enormous profits from winter crops as the rest of the country waited for spring. In its southern realm at least, California's state moniker—"The Golden State"—came to signify oranges as much as it did the nuggets once found in a miner's pan.

MUSEUM (2024 Orange Tree Lane; 888/BIRDEGG), which depicts the region's heritage and natural history with three floors of exhibits on anthropology, archaeology, history, birds, mammals, reptiles, fossils, and fine arts.

RESTAURANTS

Joe Greensleeves / ★★☆

220 N ORANGE ST, REDLANDS; 909/792-6969

Gourmets in any city would love to have Joe Greensleeves just around the corner, so finding it in Redlands makes it all the more special. Chef Umberto Orlando fashions a changing menu that intrigues the culinary adventurer who wants to try ostrich, bison, elk, boar, venison, or any of several other farm-raised game dishes. At the same time, anyone who loves osso buco, or pasta, or simply a good steak, will find plenty of options. Orlando grills meats over an orangewood fire. Portions are extremely generous: bison, for example, is a thick but tender cut smothered in sautéed mushrooms and accompanied by a colorful medley of baby squash, spinach, and oven-baked rosemary potatoes. Orlando's osso buco is served amidst a mountain of saffron-scented risotto. Vegetarians haven't been forgotten—everything here is cooked to order (and may take a while), so the chef is willing to make some off-the-menu dishes on request. Few diners have room for dessert, but the cart creaks to your table with tortes, cheesecake, and other temptations. Decor includes a full-size classic wooden sailboat hull cut in half and attached to one brick wall of the narrow historic building. Look closely at the ceiling near the fireplace: it's composed of thousands of wine corks, for the wine list is another strong point of the restaurant, and Joe Greensleeves has won numerous *Wine Spectator* awards. The crowd is spirited and obviously enjoying themselves, making this a "romantic" place in a celebratory rather than a muted, wine-and-candles way. You'll clink glasses and enjoy the show not only from watching the open kitchen but simply by being part of the happy buzz. *$$$; AE, MC, V; local checks only; lunch Tues–Fri, dinner Tues–Sun; beer and wine; reservations recommended; from I-10 east, exit Orange St and go right, or from I-10 west exit 6th St and go south to Redlands Blvd, then right on Orange St.* &

Banning

RESTAURANTS

San Gorgonio Inn / ★

150 E RAMSEY ST, BANNING; 909/849-3448
You know there'll be a slice of canned beet atop the salad. You just know. But that's one of the charms of the old San Gorgonio Inn, where elements of this historic restaurant-and-stagecoach-stop building date back to 1883. The restaurant sprawls through several rooms behind diamond-paned arched windows that frame views of San Gorgonio Peak. Prices are fantastically low. A dark, smoky bar in the back does a lively business with the older crowd, most of them puffing away despite California's smoking ban. There's a touch of Greek to the place: one pasta dish features mizithra cheese, bread slices are cut from a circular sesame seed–sprinkled loaf, and dinner salads can be had with a Greek dressing. Dinners come with salad or soup, bread, mashed or baked potato, and dessert (cherry Jell-O was one of the choices on our visit). None of this ordinariness should dissuade you from pulling off the interstate when you're hungry, however. Chicken and fish dishes from the grill arrive at the table too hot to eat, the baked potatoes are perfect, and the cherry Jell-O . . . well, that's perfect, too, right down to its spritz of cream and its chromed champagne glass–style dish. We just have to whisper that a dinner for two here of prime rib and chicken cost well under $20. Shhh. *$; AE, DIS, MC, V; no checks; lunch, dinner every day; full bar; reservations accepted weekends for four or more only; dalz1@aol.com; exit 8th St., north to Ramsey, east 5 blocks to restaurant.* &

Big Bear

Despite its popularity with travelers anxious to escape the pace of city life in the Los Angeles basin, Big Bear will puzzle and probably appall the first-time visitor seeking mountain respite. No one "minded the store" here when it came to sensible town planning, sign control, or any other environmental concern over the last 75 years. Consequently, the south shore of this large lake has grown into a hodgepodge of crowded-together tourist ventures that rivals South Lake Tahoe in tackiness—all that's missing are a few casinos. Private cabins nestle off Highway 18, but unless you own one (or rent one), we can't recommend spending your precious vacation time on the south side. The **NORTH SIDE** of Big Bear is another matter. Far less populated, it has only one "town"—the cross-roads of Fawnskin. A new **DISCOVERY CENTER** (¼ mile west of Big Bear Ranger Station on Highway 38, 41397 N Shore Drive; 909/866-3437), operated by San Bernardino National Forest, provides any number of suggestions for hikes, Jeep treks, horseback rides, fishing, and visits to volunteer-staffed lookouts atop nearby peaks. It's also the western terminus of a bike trail along the lake edge back toward Big Bear City. This is also a good place to pick up an Adventure Pass, which must be displayed on any car parked at a National Forest trailhead. For **WINTER ROAD CONDITIONS** in the mountains, call **CALTRANS** (800/427-7623).

LODGINGS

Gold Mountain Manor / ★★

1117 ANITA AVE, BIG BEAR CITY; 909/585-6997
To call it a "log mansion" might be a stretch, but this big 1928 log house has good bones and a strong architectural pedigree. In these parts, contractor Guy Maltby was known for his rustic structures, including the famed Peter Pan Woodland Club, a Roaring '20s lodge that was all the rage with the well-to-do crowd from L.A. The Peter Pan went up in smoke long ago, but Gold Mountain Manor displays Maltby's penchant for building fine Adirondack-style cabins in the San Bernardinos. The best feature here is the front porch, a shady retreat looking across a front lawn set with pines. The living room with its hulking stone fireplace feels right on a snowy night. The rooms range from the very large Ted Ducey Suite with wood stove next to a private Jacuzzi, Mission tile, glassed-in-porch-turned-bedroom, and pioneer/Indian motif, to the Lucky Baldwin, a red-and-black-flannel-themed retreat. All six rooms have private baths. Full breakfast is served in a big downstairs front room, and beverages and hors d'oeuvres, as well as all the homemade oatmeal cookies you can eat, appear in the afternoon. One drawback is Gold Mountain's location: although it's on the quieter north side of the lake in a pine forest, the historic lodge has been surrounded by neighboring cabins of far more pedestrian scale. Secluded it's not. Still, this is your chance to experience log house living at its grandest. *$$; AE, DC, MC, V; no checks; www. bigbear.com/goldmtn; ½ block above N Shore Dr and 2 blocks west of Greenway St.*

Windy Point Inn / ★★★

39015 N SHORE DR, FAWNSKIN; 909/866-2746
No inn in the San Bernardino Mountains has a better view than Windy Point. This elegant, modern private-residence-turned-B&B has such a spectacular setting you'll be tempted to stay in your room all day—luxuriating in front of a fire, soaking in the two-person tub (most guest bathrooms have them), or sliding open a door to the breezes and just gazing over the sparkling expanse of Big Bear Lake. Decor is modern but not stark, thanks to the owners' varied collection of art and sculpture. Fur-

nishings are equally eclectic, but without any sense of hodgepodge: this is an inn with a bit of Zen to it. Decks off many of the rooms almost hang over the lake. Although it's located on the main route around the lake, Windy Point feels utterly secluded because it takes in a good 300-degree view of open water and distant peaks. Innkeepers Val and Kent Kessler are friendly and hard-working, and breakfast is a treat, especially their poached eggs and ginger pancakes. *$$$; AE, DIS, MC, V; checks OK with credit-card guarantee; off Hwy 330.*

Lake Arrowhead

The drive "up the hill" on Highway 18 to this crystalline blue lake in the pines is worth the trip alone (the lake is 90 minutes from Los Angeles). Roadway engineers conquered the mountainside's precipitous flanks with a series of close-to-the-ground bridges, making the route look like a toboggan run. At the summit, follow Rim of the World Drive toward Lake Arrowhead, a stretch with views of Orange County's Saddleback Mountain rising from a white sea of coastal cloud cover like a breaching whale. Most travelers to Arrowhead go past the Blue Jay turnoff and take Highway 173 to descend into the forested bowl containing the lake and **LAKE ARROWHEAD VILLAGE.** (Take note of the Blue Jay turnoff, however, for that's where you'll find most of the area's nontourist stores and services, which can be indispensable to anyone renting a cabin with a kitchen.)

Most tourist activity centers around Lake Arrowhead Village, a shop-and-restaurant complex that borders a south cove of the lake. Entering the Village, you're immediately confronted by garish real estate signs (the hills are alive with the sound of . . . carpenters' saws) and, on the weekends, too many cars prowling for too few parking spaces. But don't dismiss Lake Arrowhead completely: this is a stunning lake, and the twisting residential roads yield some interesting lodging possibilities at out-of-the-way bed and breakfasts. A street map is essential if you venture off the lakefront by car into these neighborhood streets that are as "tangled as angleworms in a bait can," as mystery writer Raymond Chandler might have put it (he featured Lake Arrowhead in his novel *Lady of the Lake*). You can pick up a free detailed map at Holiday Realty (291 Highway 173, on the right as you enter the village; 909/337-6122).

Walking along the lakefront promenade in the village is pleasant, but to see the area's beautiful private lakefront homes, you'll need to take to the water. Two interesting **TOUR BOATS** ply the lake. The *Arrowhead Queen* encloses passengers in a Victorian riverboat-style white salon, and the *Lake Arrowhead Princess* is a Hackercraft wood runabout with deep seats set inside a sleek aerodynamic mahogany-planked hull and deck. Purchase tickets at Leroy's Sports (909/336-6992), dockside.

RESTAURANTS

Belgian Waffle Works / ★★

28200 HWY 189, SUITE E140 (DOCKSIDE), LAKE ARROWHEAD VILLAGE; 909/337-5222

Even the wait here is pleasant. Crowds of hungry diners line the benches overlooking Lake Arrowhead, watching the classic motor launches come and go from neighboring docks. Once inside, you can dig into one of 15 different styles of waffles, from the classic thick Belgian sugar-dusted favorite to exotica such as a Brussels Belgian stuffed with ham, Swiss cheese, and turkey and fried Monte Cristo style. Many of these variations are a complete sugar rush: piles of strawberries, bananas, spiced apples, peach Melba, and whipped cream conspire to turn the most innocent breakfast into dessert. Owners Bob and Mary Baker pride themselves on the crispiness of their waffles, and for a long time, they've been tinkering with the batter recipe in search of ever-lighter confections. Your only disappointment might be the thin and rather tasteless "maple" syrup. Eggs, bacon, and omelets are also available. Lunch fare includes a wide variety of sandwiches, fish and chips (called a "Belgian Basket" here), and a strong selection of heart-healthy salads (to prepare you for a waffle dessert, no doubt). Waffles are served all day, so feel free to segue from breakfast to lunch without missing a caloric beat. A seat on the large outdoor patio is worth the extra wait on a sunny day, unless the wind's kicked up across the lake. *$; MC, V; checks OK; breakfast, lunch every day; beer and wine; reservations accepted for 6 or more; thebww@ aol.com; on the waterfront promenade opposite the tour boat docks.* &

LODGINGS

Arrowhead Saddleback Inn / ★

300 HWY 173, LAKE ARROWHEAD; 909/336-3571 OR 800/858-3334

Now totally renovated, the Saddleback began life in 1917 as the Raven Hotel. Restoration and expansion have been tasteful, maintaining the ambience of a small mountain cluster of peaked-roof cabins with stone foundations, set in a grove of giant pines and shaggy cedars. Decor in the cabins' small sitting rooms is a tasteful blend of Laura Ashley wallpaper and fabrics, comfortable upholstered chairs and sofas, and framed vintage prints, and every cabin has a fireplace. Unfortunately, Saddleback Inn lies close to the main road, and some of the cabins are too near the parking areas of a convenience store, but back in the grove you'll gain the mountain feel you're seeking, especially if you request one of the cabins numbered 25 through 28. The Altitude restaurant and a full bar are adjacent to the lobby of the main building, which also houses 10 guestrooms. *$–$$ weekday, $$–$$$$ weekend; AE, DC, DIS, MC, V; checks*

OK 10 days in advance; www.lakearrowhead.com/saddleback; at junction Hwy 189 and Hwy 173 near Lake Arrowhead Village.

The Carriage House Bed & Breakfast / ★★

472 EMERALD DR, LAKE ARROWHEAD; 909/336-1400

One of the most meticulously maintained B&Bs in Southern California, this small three-guest-room inn perches on a hillside in a quiet residential neighborhood in the pines. It also offers an important unseen bonus: the owners provide their guests with day passes to a Lake Arrowhead beach club that has the area's only sandy beach for swimming and sunbathing. (All of the lake shore is privately owned and otherwise hemmed in by docks and speedboats.) Carriage House encourages guests to enjoy the outdoors and lake views (mostly glimpses through the trees) from several comfortable decks and patios under the pines or from a big hammock. The house's complete remodel was done by owners Johan and Lee Karstens, who live in a separate house next door. The best room is the Brougham: its king-size bed divides the space like a mountain range of fine linens, and the claw-footed tub in a rose-pink and white bathroom sits under a narrow skylight in a slanting roof for cloud or moon viewing. The other two rooms are equally appealing—one with a window seat, the other with a small deck facing the lake. Overall, the decor scheme is country, with a goodly number of stuffed critters and dolls, but the Carriage House's meticulous order and upkeep keep the clutter at bay. At breakfast, the coffee is fresh-ground and strong, and the meal's good enough to keep you going until well after lunch. *$–$$; AE, MC, V; checks OK; www.lakearrowhead.com/carriagehouse; from Lake Arrowhead Village, drive counterclockwise around the lake 2.2 miles on Hwy 173 to Emerald Dr and turn right.*

Chateau Du Lac Bed and Breakfast / ★

911 HOSPITAL RD, LAKE ARROWHEAD; 909/337-6488 OR 800/601-8722

You won't find a more spectacular overlook of Lake Arrowhead than the one from this inn's huge downstairs common rooms—or from the ultimate suite, the Lakeview, at the very top of the house. Lakeview may well be Arrowhead's most romantic place to spend the night, with Jacuzzi tub, private entrance, fireplace, and balcony overlooking the lake. Almost the equal of the Lakeview Suite, the Loft Suite lets you sleep under a steeply peaked and dormer-windowed ceiling; its bathroom with Jacuzzi tub is particularly spacious. The house's modern architectural style frames views with tall expanses of glass, but wood-paneled interiors help it feel warm (exterior upkeep is not immaculate here, but the interiors are neat and beautifully furnished). Like many inns, Du Lac has been invaded by teddy bears and dolls, but the house is big enough to keep the cuteness in check (translation: husbands won't be put off). Innkeepers Jody and Oscar Wilson serve not only a good breakfast (eggs or quiche, muffins, croissants, fruit, and so on) but an afternoon tea as well. When the sun cooperates, they serve breakfast on a deck just off the kitchen, part of which extends into a hillside gazebo. *$$–$$$$; AE, DC, DIS, MC, V; checks OK; from Lake Arrowhead Village, go 3 miles on Hwy 173 to Hospital Rd and turn right.*

Rose Gables Victorian Bed & Breakfast / ★★

29024 MAMMOTH DR, LAKE ARROWHEAD; 909/336-9892

Leave it to the English to create the most pristine Victorian-themed inn in Lake Arrowhead. In their "retirement," owners Meryl and Don Jacks have created a four-room inn from a former single-family house high on a hilltop overlooking the mountains and desert. Only half of this duo— Meryl—is truly English, and Don is quick to give her all the credit for Rose Gables' extraordinary decor of English antiques, wallpaper, and plenty of creative touches that have guests asking "How'd you do that?" The walls in the living room, for example, appear to be papered, but the illusion was created by Meryl with a unique painting technique. The top room here is Pearls and Lace, with a step-up king bed, fireplace in both bedroom and bathroom, big tub, and forest view. All rooms come with his-and-hers cotton robes. Meryl's cooking is first-rate, and her hors d'oeuvres are generous enough to make some guests decide to skip dinner in town. Breakfast centers around her delicious waffles with fresh fruit, or omelets, or fresh-baked quiche. Menu requests are welcome. The Jacks also have a unique "return" policy: second-time guests are rewarded with a late-afternoon cruise aboard the Jacks' "party barge" to an island where all aboard enjoy an alfresco cocktail party. *$$; MC, V; checks OK; from Hwy 173 on northeast edge of the lake, turn right on Yosemite Dr, right on Yellowstone Dr, right on Banff Dr, and right on Mammoth Dr.*

Riverside

Entrepreneurs planted the first Washington navel orange trees here in 1875, and Riverside basked in agricultural prosperity for the next 80 years. But smog, sprawling housing, and commercial land development after World War II whittled Riverside's appeal to a nubbin of its former grandeur, and by the '60s and '70s even its crowning glory, the Mission Inn, had fallen into disrepair. Today both the town and the inn are showing signs of a full recovery.

A guided tour of the **MISSION INN** (3696 Main Street; 909/781-8241 or 909/784-0300, ext. 5035) is essential to the Riverside experience. Tours last almost 1½ hours and ramble through most of the public areas and up to the topmost parapets. Before you sign up, be sure to task whether you'll be able to see the inside of the chapel. It's often closed on

RIVERSIDE WINERIES

J. FILIPPI WINERY: Visit on a winter day when the snowcapped San Bernardinos loom as a backdrop, and you'll see how this historic winery recalls a day when vineyards covered thousands of acres of Southern California. Don't expect anything too scenic nowadays, however; the tasting room is set in the middle of a business/railroad/agricultural district. The modern world has pretty much surrounded the dream of Italian winemaker Giovanni Filippi, who planted his first vineyard in 1922. (The family also purchased Thomas Winery in Rancho Cucamonga, California's oldest winery, back in the '60s.) Today's wines are pressed from grapes all over the state, as well as the local valley. Award-winning wines include zinfandels, grenaches, cabernets, and Chiantis. The winery is located at 12467 Baseline Road, Rancho Cucamonga; 909/899-5755. Another tasting room is a 15-minute drive west in Ontario-Guasti. To get there, exit Baseline Road, turn right (west) and go about ¾ mile to the winery (2803 E Guasti Road; 909/390-6998).

GALLEANO WINERY: Many of the vines here are 90-plus years old, so if you have a taste for "old grape" wines, Galleano is worth a pilgrimage. Traditional European winemaking techniques prevail here, including head pruning, and no herbicides or pesticides are used. Grapes are dry farmed (not irrigated), yielding intense fruity flavor. The winery is open for touring, and a tasting room occupies an old house. Bring a picnic and enjoy some wine in their picnic area near a small menagerie of ducks, pheasants, pigs, goats, and donkeys that will keep the kids interested. Galleano is in Mira Loma, which is approximately 1 mile southeast of the Interstate 15 and Highway 60 junction. From Highway 60, take Etiwanda Road south to Riverside Drive, go west to Wineville Road, and turn south to the winery (4231 Wineville Road; 909/685-5376).

weekends because of weddings, and you'll be disappointed at missing the gilded Mexican altar and the Tiffany stained-glass windows and mosaic work—high points of the tour.

To get the best feel for what life was like here during the glory days, walk to the top of boulder-studded **MOUNT RUBIDOUX** (1,339 feet) via a pedestrians-only road-and-trails system that begins at 9th Street and Mount Rubidoux Drive. On the way up you'll pass a romantic stone watchtower financed by Mission Inn developer Frank Miller. Standing beneath the Father Serra Cross at the summit, you look almost straight down at the Santa Ana River to the west side, and downtown to the east. **LITTLE RUBIDOUX**, the hill opposite Mount Rubidoux just to the north side of Buena Vista Drive, is a fascinating neighborhood of Craftsman houses; follow the stone wall around it via Indian Hill Road to view several classic mansions.

Downtown Riverside surrounding the Mission Inn has been revamped with a pedestrian-only mall along Main Street. One of the best photography museums in the country, **UCR/CALIFORNIA MUSEUM OF PHOTOGRAPHY** (3824 Main Street; 909/784-3686), houses contemporary photography exhibits as well as a permanent collection of equipment and prints that will delight any photo buff. Further down Main Street, don't miss the **RIVERSIDE COUNTY COURT HOUSE** (4050 Main Street; 909/955-5536), a beautifully restored temple of justice with a vaulted main hall that copied the Petit Palais of the 1900 Paris Exposition; this is one of the finest Beaux Arts buildings in America. For more information, visit the Riverside Visitor's Center (3660 Mission Inn Avenue; 909/684-4636). Not far from downtown, **CALIFORNIA CITRUS STATE HISTORIC PARK** (Van Buren Boulevard at Dufferin Avenue; 909/780-6222) preserves some old navel orange groves and a historic irrigation canal, recalling Riverside's early days, when even Queen Victoria was known to have peeled its famous fruit.

RESTAURANTS

Duane's Prime Steaks & Seafood / ★★

3649 MISSION INN AVE, RIVERSIDE; 909/341-6767
Steps from the Mission Inn's courtyard restaurant (see review, below), its other restaurant, Duane's, is a completely indoor experience. Big chairs, big tables, big paintings, and big portions are the theme here. Arched windows and Rapunzel balconies flank the room, and a wonderful Old West painting of a cavalry skirmish dominates the end wall (look closely, and read the plaque, for the artwork tells a fascinating tale). A classic steak-and-prime-rib eatery, Duane's has become the best place in town to come for a no-holds-barred, let's-start-with-a-Scotch-on-the-rocks kind of meal. Duane's lives on the excellent reputation of its beef, and it doesn't disappoint. Steaks are flash-cooked, leaving the insides tender, rare, and juicy. The wine list is extensive. Although the two kitchen lines are separate, executive chef Gary Palm's two in-hotel restaurants share similar menu themes and have become the standard bearers for Riverside fine dining, with a harmonious marriage of historic decor and attentive cooking. *$$$; AE, DC, DIS, MC, V; no checks; lunch Mon-Fri, dinner every day; full bar; reservations recommended; www.missioninn.com; exit Mission Ave off Hwy 91 and go west.* &

Gay and Larry's / ★★

5556 MISSION BLVD, RIVERSIDE; 909/684-0645
Angelenos escaping to Palm Springs via Highway 60 first fell in love with the Mexican food at Gay and Larry's over 55 years ago. The place has a classic roadhouse feel, complete with dirt parking lot (except for handi-

capped vehicles) and surrounding tire repair shops and run-down squalid houses. Here the "combination plate" is a steaming, heart-stopping heap of enchiladas, chiles rellenos, tacos, or burritos, with refried beans and rice, all swimming in a pond of brick-red sauce on an oven-heated pewter canoe. Oddly, Gay and Larry's charges for chips—but they're brought with ceremony on a thick crockery plate in your waitress's oven-mitted paw. Draft beer, 40 ounces of it, costs only a five-spot. *$; no credit cards; local checks OK; lunch, dinner every day; beer only; reservations not necessary; from Hwy 60, exit Rubidoux Blvd and go south to Mission Blvd, then left.* &

Mission Inn Restaurant / ★★

3649 MISSION INN AVE, RIVERSIDE; 909/341-6767

Old-timers in Riverside still call this "the Spanish Dining Room," and they're a little ticked off at the Mission Inn's latest owner for changing the name to something as generic as "Restaurant." But, blessedly, everything else remains the same. Step into the courtyard and you enter a Moroccan desert keep. Giant lanterns of cast concrete top—believe it or not—flying buttresses above you. Tier upon tier of windows rise on every side, most arched, many with the Inn's famed "rain cross" bell-symbol motif in leaded glass. In the center, a massive tile fountain guarded by three Mayan-motif mutant-frog sculptures splashes happily, while the lighted dome of a miniature Vatican seems to float in the gathering darkness at dinnertime. Caesar salad is a perfectly tart and salty start to a hearty meal of lamb shank, osso buco style (it arrives steaming in the night air, with spears of asparagus propped about like green soldiers). A double pork chop with excellent garlic mashed potatoes is almost too much to eat. Prime rib or filet of beef are delicious and tender, while lighter choices such as spinach fettuccine with grilled shrimp, Maui onions, and thyme, or seared salmon with red-wine pasta or opal-basil pasta are equally satisfying. Service is attentive. *$$; AE, DC, DIS, MC, V; no checks; breakfast, lunch, dinner every day; full bar; reservations recommended; www.missioninn.com; exit Mission Ave off Hwy 91 and go west.* &

Table for Two / ★★

3600 CENTRAL AVE, SUITE I, RIVERSIDE; 909/683-3648

This small, sophisticated, and quite immaculate restaurant is located in the kind of building you'd expect to find occupied by an insurance office. Once inside, though, you're surprised by modern, arty decor and the wonderful spicy smells of a Thai kitchen at its best. Dishes are presented with an artful eye for color here, with sprays of thinly sliced vegetables piled high like pick-up sticks. Big white bistro-style plates turn the food into art, and bookshelves filled with wine bottles line the walls. This brilliant feast for the eye is matched by equally vibrant flavors. An unusual ground chicken and shrimp salad with grilled Japanese eggplant, onion, and green onion is bathed in a light vinegar dressing. Salads are reminiscent of flower arrangements. Entrees include stir-fry standards like cashew chicken, but this version is made with a roasted curry paste. Coconut shows up frequently, particularly in the soups and curries that dominate the menu. The neighborhood crowd here includes families, young couples, and retired professors from the nearby university—all loyal devotees of Table for Two's artful creativity. *$; MC, V; no checks; lunch, dinner ever day; beer and wine; reservations not necessary; exit Central Ave off Hwy 91 and go west.* &

LODGINGS

The Mission Inn / ★★★

3649 MISSION INN AVE, RIVERSIDE; 909/784-0300 OR 800/843-7755
A National Historic Landmark built in stages between 1902 and 1931 by hotelier Frank Miller, the Mission Inn began life as a two-story adobe home and gradually evolved into one of the West's grandest resort hotels. Architect Arthur B. Benton played off Miller's love of the dramatic, and the Mission Inn developed into a fantastical conglomeration of architectural themes—all hand-crafted by an army of artisans who made the Inn part church, part castle, part Mission-style. The finest of the 235 lodgings are located high up along "Spanish Row" or flanking an upper patio (numbers 420 through 431). If cost is no object, this "suites" region of the huge structure is the place to stay. Each room is different, and some have extraordinary architectural elements such as 13-foot-tall arched leaded windows, coffered ceilings, and window seats, plus balconies, patios, views, and fine furnishings and fabrics. Even the more modest rooms have a sense of drama, beginning with the hallways themselves— which were built wide enough to handle the enormous steamer trunks of guests arriving to spend much of the winter. Bonuses include a good-sized pool as well as a hydro-spa, set in a spectacular courtyard beside the front entry walk and gardens. The Mission Inn Restaurant and Duane's Prime Steaks & Seafood are located within the hotel (see reviews in Restaurants, above). In all, this is a classic monument hotel that must be experienced at least once in one's traveling life. *$$–$$$$; AE, DC, DIS, MC, V; checks OK; www.missioninn.com; exit Mission Ave off Hwy 91 and go west.* &

Rancho Cucamonga

LODGINGS

Christmas House Bed & Breakfast Inn / ★

9240 ARCHIBALD AVE, RANCHO CUCAMONGA; 909/980-6450

The Christmas House received its odd moniker long ago from neighbors who saw it aglow each holiday season with incredible decorations—the first two families to own it loved celebrations. After falling into disrepair after World War II, the house was purchased in 1983 and restored to pristine Victorian perfection, achieving historical landmark status from the city. Furnished in period antiques, the main house's four guest accommodations recall a genteel time of parlors and fainting couches. A two-room suite named Celebration offers fireplaces in both parlor and bedroom and an antique mahogany canopy bed draped in lace. The Carriage House in back contains two units, each with an elegant English garden theme. Elizabeth's Room here has an antique iron bed, a cabbage-rose duvet and starched white linens, and green wicker. Best of all, its shower is outside in a secluded atrium where you can soap up while watching the clouds go by. A full breakfast is served in the grand fine dining room or in your room. The cook uses fresh grapefruit from the yard's trees for juice, and the garden's herbs are abundant. Eggs Elegante is a guest favorite, a baked dish made with Jack cheese, nine herbs from the garden, sausage, and cherry tomatoes and served with a buttered croissant. *$–$$$; AE, DIS, MC, V; checks OK; take Archibald Ave north from I-10 to just north of 6th St.*

Temecula

Located where Riverside County meets San Diego County, the fertile Temecula Valley has attracted settlers for at least a thousand years, from Luiseño Indians to today's winemakers and suburbanites. Rainbow Gap, a pass in the coastal mountains to the west, lets a cooling breeze from the Pacific Ocean sneak in each afternoon, blowing away smog and helping offset hot temperatures. These maritime breezes often bring coastal fog to the edge of the Valley—hence its name, a Luiseño word meaning "sun shining through fine mist." The climate is ideal for growing grapes, and commercial growers began planting grapes in earnest here in the 1960s. Unfortunately, the fine weather has also attracted developers who seem determined to crust the land with housing subdivisions and chain stores. Today you drive east on Rancho California Road for about 4 miles through new communities before you reach the pleasant, open wine-growing countryside.

TEMECULA WINERIES

Temecula boasts 15 wineries, some of them competitive with the best in California. Most grow their own grapes, all have tasting rooms open to the public. Take Rancho California Road east from Interstate 15 for only 4 miles to where the strip malls and housing sprawl abruptly give way to rolling hills dressed in mustard flowers, vineyards, and citrus orchards. Most of the wineries are clustered along the next few miles, with signs directing where to turn off, while Filsinger and Keyways hang back on side roads that branch off farther east on Rancho California Road. Not surprisingly, Temecula's three oldest wineries (Callaway, Cilurzo, and Mount Palomar) are its standouts, but a few others are gaining notoriety. Expect crowds on weekends, especially Saturdays.

BAILY VINEYARD & WINERY: Phil and Carol Baily opened their winery in 1986. They are best known for their white wines, especially the gold medal Rieslings. Tastings daily 10am to 5pm. Located at 33833 Rancho California Road; 909/676-9463; www.baily.com.

CALLAWAY VINEYARD & WINERY: Temecula's largest, oldest, and best-known winery produces a very good chardonnay. Public tours daily. The Wine Terrace Cafe affords sweeping views from its outdoor patio, serving lunch Thursday through Sunday and dinner on Fridays and Saturdays. Tastings daily 10am to 5pm. Located at 32720 Rancho California Road; 909/676-4001 or 800/472-2377; www.callawaywine.com.

CILURZO VINYARD & WINERY: Vincenzo Cilurzo planted Temecula's first commercial vineyard in 1968 when he moved to the valley with his wife, Audrey. Their estate-grown petite sirah has been a consistent award-winner, and their merlots are also excellent. Don't miss this friendly, family-run winery with its tame peacocks and hand-painted signs. Tastings daily 10am to 5pm. Located at 41220 Calle Contento; 909/676-5250.

CLOS DU MURIEL VINEYARDS & WINERY: Clos du Muriel buys most of its grapes elsewhere and sells its wine only by order or on the premises. Tastings daily 10am to 5pm. Located at 33410 Rancho California Road; 909/676-5400 or 877/676-5400; www.closdumurielwinery.com.

FILSINGER VINEYARDS & WINERY: This family-owned winery makes a Temecula champagne, and it's one of the few wineries in California to grow and produce gewürztraminer. The tasting room is open on Fridays, Saturdays, and Sundays only. Located at 30905 De Portola Road; 909/302-6363.

HART WINERY: Truly a collector's find is tiny Hart Winery, which frequently outclasses many of California's biggest players at major wine competitions. Former schoolteacher Joe Hart specializes in dry, full-bodied reds and premium Mediterranean varietals. The tasting room in this cute little barnlike structure is open daily 10am to 5pm. Located at 41300 Avenida Biona; 909/676-6300 or 877/638-8788.

KEYWAYS VINEYARD: Carl Key operates a one-man operation at a handsome

Mediterranean-style building on 28 beautiful, vine-laden acres. Key prides himself on his red zinfandel, which can be tasted along with other varietals on Fridays, Saturdays, and Sundays, or by appointment. Located at 37338 De Portola Road; 909/302-7888.

MAURICE CARRIE WINERY: Maurice and Budd Van Rockel opened this giant, neo-Victorian California ranch manor and antique barn in 1986. The visitor-oriented establishment sells souvenirs and offers free tasting of its wines, which include some of the sweeter varietals and are available daily 10am to 5pm. Located at 34225 Rancho California Road; 909/676-1711 or 800/716-1711.

MOUNT PALOMAR WINERY: With its hilltop views, sunny orchards, soft grass, and shaded tables, Mount Palomar provides the ideal spot for a picnic. One of the valley's three original operations, it made its mark with riesling, exceptional dessert wines, and some lesser-known Italian varietals such as cortese and sangiovese. Tastings daily 10am to 5pm. Located at 33820 Rancho California Road; 909/676-5047 or 800/854-5177; www.mountpalomar.com.

SANTA MARGARITA WINERY: Temecula's smallest winery specializes in cabernet sauvignon, which they always age five years before release. Sitting on a quiet ridge well off the highway, the tasting room is open on weekends only or by appointment. Located at 33490 Madera de la Playa; 909/676-4431.

STUART CELLARS: Opened in 1998, this is Temecula's newest winery. Marshall Stuart, who studied viticulture and enology at UC Davis, already makes a fine vintage port. The tasting room is open daily from 10am to 5pm. Located at 33515 Rancho California Road; 909/676-6414 or 888/260-0870; www.stuartcellars.com

TEMECULA CREST WINERY: This hilltop winery, featuring a strikingly beautiful Old West structure of stained redwood, is noted for its estate-grown whites; riesling and sauvignon blanc are big hits and they can be sampled in the tasting room, which is open Monday through Friday from noon to 5pm, Saturday and Sunday 10am to 5pm. Located at 40620 Calle Contento; 909/676-8231.

THORNTON WINERY: Although this faux chateau feels more like a grandly financed marketing concept than a winery, their sparkling wines, formerly bottled under the Culbertson label, have won many awards. Try them at the tasting room, open daily from 11am to 4:30pm. Located at 32575 Rancho California Road; 909/699-0099 or 800/966-0099; www.thornton.com.

VAN ROEKEL VINEYARDS & WINERY: Budd and Maurice Van Roekel, who operate the Maurice Carrie Winery next door, purchased this facility with the intention of producing more carefully developed premium wines. They feature award-winning fumé blancs and syrahs, as well as gewürztraminer, mourvèdre, and others. Tastings daily 10am to 5pm. Located at 34567 Rancho California Road; 909/699-6961.

A brief drive west from the freeway on the same road brings you to the rapidly growing town's Front Street. Here Old West–style false storefronts and a few historic buildings provide a notion of the good old days. **OLD TOWN TEMECULA** was originally a stop along the Butterfield Overland Stage route in the 1850s. Shop here for **ANTIQUES**, indulge in a messy burger at any number of greasy spoons, or catch a tour in Otto Baron's Model T Ford (drop by 41915 4th Street, call 909/694-8746, or page 909/506-8249). Old Town features many well-preserved **ORIGINAL BUILDINGS**, like the Temecula Mercantile, built from local bricks in 1891, or the 1882 Welty Hotel on Main Street. But perhaps more interesting are the unrestored private homes lining side streets. Copies of Bob and Bea Taylor's "Old Town Walking Tour Map" can be found at most local businesses.

If you prefer to leave the planning to someone else, jump aboard one of Destination Temecula's (909/695-1232 or 800/584-8162; www.destem. com) daily tours of Old Town and the wine country. For a more athletic approach, Gravity Activated Sports (800/985-4427; www.gasports.com) offers a **TEMECULA WINE COUNTRY BICYCLE TOUR**. Or take their Palomar Plunge, a 16-mile descent on bicycles (you'll need to turn the pedals only a few times) over a 5,000-foot drop in elevation from the top of nearby pine-covered Palomar Mountain. For an airborne adventure, take in the Temecula sunrise from a **HOT-AIR BALLOON** flown by A Grape Escape Balloon Adventure (800/965-2122; www.agrapeescape.com). For visitors' guides and maps, stop by **TEMECULA VALLEY CHAMBER OF COMMERCE** (27450 Ynez Road, Suite 104, in Town Center Plaza; 909/676-5090; www.temecula.org).

RESTAURANTS

Baily Wine Country Cafe / ★★

27644 YNEZ RD, TEMECULA; 909/676-9567
Even though it's in a mall next to a supermarket, not out among vineyards as its appellation might suggest, Baily Wine Country Cafe is true to its name in spirit. Fine local wines, tasteful lighting, gracious service, and excellent California-continental cuisine make it easy to forget you've left the wineries behind. Phil and Carol Baily (who also own Baily Vineyard & Winery) created this upscale but casual restaurant with the intention of providing visitors an affordable fine dining experience to complement their vintages. Oenophiles will appreciate the cafe's wine list, which features the largest selection of Temecula wines in the world (70). The cooking of chefs Christopher Baily and Dana Ludwig is excellent, whether you choose the freshly made crab cakes, the chicken schnitzel in lemon-caper wine sauce, the grilled filet mignon topped with sauce bordelaise, or the blackened scallop and shrimp pasta. If you're on your way

to the wineries, stop in and the restaurant will make you a picnic lunch to go. *$$; AE, DC, DIS, MC, V; no checks; lunch, dinner every day; beer and wine; reservations recommended; baily@baily.com; www.baily. com; Exit I-15 at Rancho California Rd and go east to Ynez Rd.* &

Cafe Champagne / ★★

32575 RANCHO CALIFORNIA RD, TEMECULA; 909/699-0088

You can't miss the herb garden as you walk into Thornton Winery's Cafe Champagne perched on a north-facing terrace. It's located within steps of the open-plan kitchen so that the snips of rosemary, thyme, oregano, and other herbs can immediately make their way into the chef's Mediterranean-inspired infusions, rubs, and marinades. Diners seated in the courtyard can watch line cooks chopping vigorously, preparing executive chef Steve Pickell's wine-complementary menu. Calamari sautéed in garlic, lemon, shallots, dill, and Thornton brut arrives for a simple, fragrant beginning to the meal. It's followed, perhaps, by a Cafe Champagne Salad composed of fresh greens, spiced pecans, golden raisins, Gorgonzola, and champagne vinaigrette. Entrees such as pistachio-crusted Colorado rack of lamb, Pacific prawns or sea scallops in black fettuccine, and grilled pheasant breast roll out of ovens, off rotisseries, or off the wood-fired grill. Service by a young collegiate waitstaff is friendly, and the setting, especially on a warm afternoon or evening in summer, is conducive to hours of relaxed dining. *$$$; AE, DC, DIS, MC, V; no checks; lunch every day, dinner Tues-Sun, brunch Sun; wine only; reservations recommended; 4 miles east of I-15 from Rancho California Rd exit.* &

Temet Grill / ★★

44501 RAINBOW CANYON RD, TEMECULA; 909/587-1465

Set just a short walk from its companion hotel, the Temecula Creek Inn (see review in Lodgings, below), the Temet Grill glows at night like a small lantern in the woods. Inside, a snapping oak fire often blazes in the stone fireplace in the bar/lounge just off the main dining room. Decor in the cathedral-ceiled dining room follows a Native American motif: framed arrows, baskets, and other traditional craft objects hang on the walls, while huge iron chandeliers float like blazing campfires overhead. An entire wall of windows overlooks the golf course and valley—there isn't a bad seat in the house. The menu is equally inspired, featuring chef Stephane Baloy's herb-crusted Norwegian salmon with saffron risotto and tomato-basil beurre blanc; excellent beef, such as a New York cut in green peppercorn sauce; and a rich veal scallopine with Marsala and porcini risotto. Vegetarians will love the delicate, smoky flavor of roasted-vegetable ravioli served in a basil pesto cream sauce along with sautéed spinach. For breakfast, try the burrito of avocado, green chile, scrambled eggs, salsa, and black beans. Lunches are strong on salads, especially Asian chicken salad with ginger and plum vinaigrette. *$$; AE,*

DIS, MC, V; no checks; breakfast, lunch, dinner every day; full bar; reservations recommended; www.jcresorts.com; east on Pala from Hwy 79 exit on I-15. &

LODGINGS

Loma Vista Bed & Breakfast / ★★

33350 LA SERENA WAY, TEMECULA; 909/676-7047
Guests are greeted by a shy and gentle teddy bear–like golden retriever/chow mix, aptly named Bear, who belongs to Walt and Sheila Kurczynski, the caretakers of this 11-year-old Spanish Mission–style villa. From its high perch on a hill cloaked in fragrant orange trees in the middle of the wine country, Loma Vista Bed & Breakfast takes full advantage of the Temecula Valley's refreshing afternoon breezes and vine-quilted scenery. Not only do all six rooms command panoramic vistas, but most of them include private balconies. The rooms, each named for a wine varietal, are artfully decorated, from the rich cherry-wood of Merlot to the Southwestern desert hues of Sauvignon Blanc. All are air-conditioned (but who needs it, with that delightful breeze?), and all have private baths. Guests mingle at a complimentary three-course champagne breakfast each morning and informal wine tastings in the evenings. *$$; MC, V; checks OK; 5 miles east of I-15 just off Rancho California Rd.*

Temecula Creek Inn / ★★★

44501 RAINBOW CANYON RD, TEMECULA; 909/694-1000 OR 800/962-7335
Draped like a green velvet blanket across a mountainside of oaks, boulders and streams, Temecula Creek Inn and its golf resort rest above the Temecula Valley like a golfer's vision of paradise. Few courses and settings in Southern California are this naturally beautiful—the oaks and the soaring red-tailed hawks will remind you of Ojai or Northern California. The Inn itself is a series of two-story, tree-shaded, shingled wings set along a knoll above the course's opening holes. Operated by JC Resorts, which also owns the Surf 'n' Sand in Laguna Beach and the Rancho Bernardo Inn (about 45 minutes' drive to the south), Temecula Creek has 80 rooms that feature oversize furniture, Southwest-motif fabrics, and large, firm beds. Even though the pool is a bit small and the outdoor corridors leading to the rooms are showing some age, the Inn is still an upscale yet informal country resort for golfing couples and weekend vacationers, without the pomp or the stratospheric prices. It's like a good sports car without a walnut-veneer dashboard. *$$–$$$; AE, DC, DIS, MC, V; no checks; www.jcresorts.com; east on Pala Rd from the Hwy 79 exit on I-15.* &

SAN JOAQUIN VALLEY & SOUTHERN SIERRA NEVADA

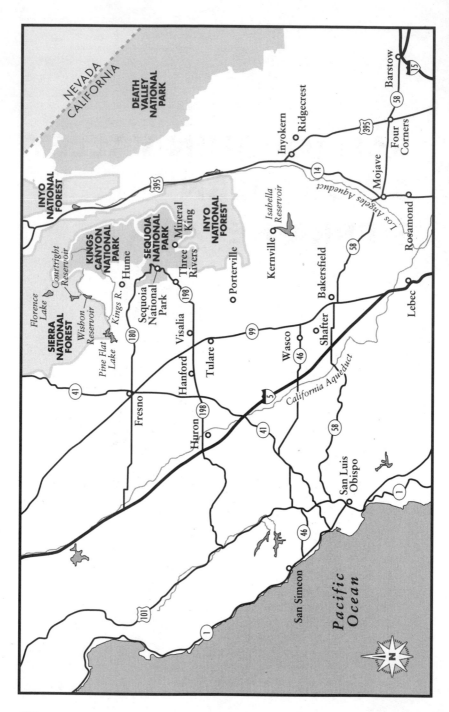

SAN JOAQUIN VALLEY & SOUTHERN SIERRA NEVADA

Once an arm of a vast inland sea 500 miles long and approximately 40 miles wide, the San Joaquin Valley now makes up the southern half of the Central Valley, which runs north–south down the middle of the state. The valley draws its name from the San Joaquin River, which flows from the Sierra Nevada above Fresno into the great Sacramento River delta and eventually out to sea through San Francisco Bay. The verdant region is surrounded by some of the state's largest mountain ranges: the Sierra Nevada to the east, the Tehachapis to the south, and the Diablo and Temblor coastal ranges to the west. The Spanish names Diablo ("devil") and Temblor ("earthquake") both refer to the presence of the devastating San Andreas Fault that is their geological mother.

Much to the delight of its residents, this lush and rural valley remains low-key. The tourist industry hasn't infiltrated the area the way it has other parts of the state, and the valley is predominantly known as one of the world's most productive farming regions. Its fertility is greatly due to the ancient sediments laid down here, where the former mud can be thousands of feet thick. Meanwhile, deep sedimentary rock produces natural gas and oil—which explains the grasshopper-like oil pumps that line the roadsides surrounding Bakersfield.

Valley towns such as Visalia and Bakersfield prosper, growing cotton, grapes, almonds, pistachios, roses, and a wide array of other crops. Because a cruise-control journey down Interstate 5 (the fastest way by far to traverse the state by automobile) misses much of the San Joaquin Valley's agricultural history, Highway 99, which runs north to south further inland, justifiably attracts travelers with more time on their hands. It is along this route that the valley that gained wrenching fame in John Steinbeck's *The Grapes of Wrath* becomes more accessible. Amidst the plight of Depression-era workers, Steinbeck also saw a place where blossoming groves spread like "fragrant pink and white waters in a shallow sea" and the land "quickens with produce" each spring. Though Steinbeck's observations still hold true, this is also a route that will satisfy any visitor's love for turn-of-the-century architecture, old family-run restaurants—and one of the valley's popular pastimes, antiquing. Many of the valley towns boast some of the state's finest civic architecture from the late 1800s and early 1900s, as well as grand old Victorian and Craftsman houses.

Farther inland from Highway 99, a side trip into the Sierra Nevada to Sequoia and Kings Canyon National Parks highlights the famous "big trees" of the Giant Forest Village area as well as the immense, glacier-carved canyon of the Kings River at Cedar Grove. Back-country day hiking, backpacking, and horse-packing opportunities abound in these gateways to the wilderness. The area, because of its high crest of "fourteener" peaks (those 14,000 or more feet high, culminating in Mount Whitney at 14,494 feet), was a favorite of early explorers Joseph LeConte and John Muir. Muir called the Sierra Nevada "the range of light," and on a clear day its snowy crest is a gleaming beacon visible not only from mountain parks and roads but from the San Joaquin Valley itself.

ACCESS AND INFORMATION

From the north, two **MAJOR HIGHWAYS**, Interstate 5 and Highway 99, provide access from San Francisco and Sacramento. From the south, Interstate 5 ascends the long grade over the "Grapevine" above Los Angeles and drops down into the valley before splitting at Highway 99, which continues northward to Bakersfield. Los Angeles-to-Bakersfield distance is 112 miles; from San Francisco to Bakersfield is about 300 miles. From either direction, Interstate 5 is your faster route for reaching valley destinations, even if you do have to travel as much as 35 miles west-to-east between Interstate 5 and cities located along Highway 99.

A tour of the San Joaquin Valley between Hanford or Visalia and Bakersfield can begin where Highway 198 crosses the valley from Coalinga, passes through Hanford and Visalia, and ascends the western foothills of the Sierra Nevada before entering Sequoia National Park. Highway 198 is also a link to U.S. 101 south of King City.

Dense, low-lying ground fog (known locally as "tule fog") is a grave concern to drivers when it settles over any San Joaquin Valley road or highway. Interstate 5, because it skirts the hills slightly above the valley, is less prone to dense fog, but it, too, can be socked in. If you're caught in a fog, take the first exit immediately and wait it out at a coffee shop, motel, turnout, or rest stop. Do not attempt to drive; horrendous multiple-vehicle accidents are not uncommon under such conditions.

The most central **AIRPORT** is Fresno Yosemite International Airport (5175 E Clinton Avenue; 559/498-4095), which is serviced by more that 14 airlines, including American Continental, Delta, and United. Nearby Bakersfield's Meadows Field (1401 Skyway Drive; 661/393-7990) is served by America West, American, American Eagle, and United Express. **AMTRAK** (15th and F Streets; 800/872-7245) services Bakersfield, Wasco, and Hanford. **GREYHOUND** (1820 18th Street; 800/231-2222) offers many routes and many stops, with main depots at Bakersfield and Visalia.

Fresno

Fresno dates back to 1872, when the town was founded as a water stop for the Southern Pacific Railroad. After the Gold Rush, many unsuccessful

SAN JOAQUIN VALLEY & SOUTHERN SIERRA NEVADA
THREE-DAY TOUR

DAY ONE. Enjoy an eye-opening café mocha or fruit frappé at **Art Works** in **Hanford**, then explore the **historic buildings** in and around Civic Center Park. Don't miss having lunch and the town's signature sundae at **Superior Dairy Products Company**, a little-changed creamery and fountain that's been in business since 1929. After lunch, head east on Highway 198 to **Visalia**, checking in at historic **Spalding House B&B** in time to enjoy the rosy sunset sky from its huge front porch. For dinner, make reservations at The **Vintage Press Restaurant**.

DAY TWO. After breakfast, drive east through **Three Rivers** to **Giant Forest** and stroll through **Sequoia National Park**'s ancient groves of *Sequoia gigantea*. If you had extra days, you'd continue on to Kings Canyon, but to keep moving you'll need to backtrack to Three Rivers, where you can spend the night deep in the trees at **Sequoia Village Inn** and dine overlooking the river at the **Gateway**.

DAY THREE. Get an early start for the drive to **Bakersfield** south via Highway 65, a scenic route through historic **Porterville**, where history buffs should make a quick stop at **Zalud House** and **Porterville Historical Museum**. Arrive in Bakersfield for a late lunch at **Happy Jack's Pie 'n' Burger** before spending the afternoon browsing for **antiques** downtown and along H Street. Spend the night at **Four Points Sheraton**, and don't miss trying a massive **Basque dinner** at one of the city's several restaurants that have been serving the community since the turn of the century. Or, if you're a country music fan, make dinner reservations at **Buck Owens' Crystal Palace** and honky-tonk the night away.

miners turned to agriculture to make a living. Today, farming remains the region's leading business, with more than 250 commercial crops grown annually.

However, the town itself is an endless stretch of strip malls, apartment complexes, and ranch-style homes. Just about every chain store and fast-food restaurant known to man can be found along its streets. Downtown, with its conglomeration of government buildings, may be the only part of Fresno with buildings more than four stories high, but on weekends and evenings it becomes a virtual ghost town.

One place where you will find activity—and a bit of history as well— is Fresno's TOWER DISTRICT. Built around the restored Tower Theater, a 1939 Art Deco movie house that was renovated in 1990, this trendy neighborhood is teeming with stylish restaurants, theaters such as Roger Rocka's Dinner Theater (1226 N Wishon Avenue; 559/266-9494) and the

Second Space Theater (928 E Olive Avenue; 559/266-0660), and lively watering holes such as Avalon Billiard Club (1064 N Fulton Avenue; 559/495-0852). The Tower Theater (815 E Olive Avenue; 559/485-9050) itself, with its Carvarts glass etchings and Italian terrazzo foyer, hosts concerts by performers like George Winston and Diana Krall.

History buffs can tour the elegant homes of several of Fresno's founders, like the **KEARNEY MANSION MUSEUM** (7160 W Kearney Boulevard; 559/441-0862) or the **MEUX HOME MUSEUM** (1007 R Street; 559/233-8007). Those who want to take a pleasant stroll outdoors can head to the **CHAFFE ZOOLOGICAL GARDENS**, set in Roeding Park (894 W Belmont Avenue; 559/498-2671). With more than 600 mammals, birds, and reptiles, this local zoo boasts a tropical rain forest exhibit and reptile house. The park offers picnic areas, lakes, tennis courts, and recreational areas for kids.

The **FRESNO FAIRGROUNDS** (1121 Chance Avenue; 559/650-3247; www.fresnofair.com) is home of the annual Big Fresno Fair each October, but it offers more than just that event: other events include live and satellite horseracing, the AgFRESNO agricultural show in November, and home and garden shows in spring and summer. For more about the Fresno area, contact the **FRESNO CITY & COUNTY CONVENTION AND VISITORS BUREAU** (808 M Street, Fresno, CA 93721; 559/233-0836 or 800/788-0836; www.fresno-online.com/cvb; tourfresno@aol.com). **FRESNO-YOSEMITE INTERNATIONAL AIRPORT** (5175 E Clinton Avenue; 559/498-4095) is served by more than a dozen commercial airlines, including United, Alaska, and Reno Air.

RESTAURANTS

The Daily Planet / ★★

1211 W WISHON AVE, FRESNO; 559/266-4259
Mahogany paneling, velvet drapes, Art Deco wall sconces, and a period mural on the ceiling take diners back to an era long past in this alluring eatery situated next to the historic Tower Theater. The menu, atmosphere, and bar also reflect the decadence of an earlier time, before we discovered cholesterol and the adverse effects of smoking and drinking. Here, as the faint strains of a piano player echo over the crowd, patrons swill cocktails like the Daily Planet's signature Stockholm 75 (citrus vodka, lemon juice, and champagne), sip Glenmorangie's single malt, smoke cigars, and sup on entrees with fat-gram counts in the triple digits. Start with oyster shooters with a zesty chipotle cream sauce, a bowl of fresh corn bisque with basil, or shrimp *spiedini*, tender skewered shrimp and prosciutto glazed with a tangy balsamic vinaigrette. For the main course, the hearty rack of lamb with a light basil-honey marinade and the homey pot roast with creamy garlic mashed potatoes take comfort food

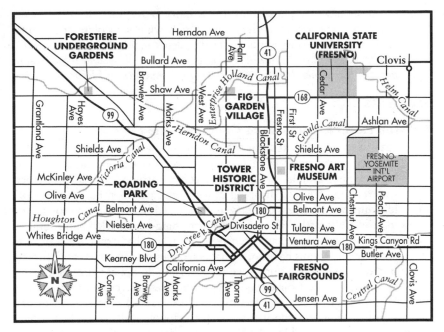

to new levels. If you can't decide what to order, go with the prix-fixe menu, which changes every three weeks to make the most of seasonal ingredients. Be sure, however, to save room for the decadent chocolate praline taco stuffed with white chocolate mousse and fresh fruit, or the chocolate apricot torte served with a rich brandy whipped cream. *$$$; MC, V; local checks only; lunch Mon–Fri, dinner every day; full bar; reservations recommended; www.tower2000.com; corner of Olive Ave.* &

Echo Restaurant / ★★☆

609 E OLIVE AVE, FRESNO; 559/442-3246

Opened in 1995, this charming French-California eatery changes its menu daily to make the most of chef Tim Woods's daily shopping trips to local farms and ranches in the neighboring San Joaquin Valley. Once he has selected the freshest seasonal ingredients possible, Woods returns to the kitchen to create such specialties as grilled Madera County quail marinated in Dijon mustard and herbs, creamy summer squash and garlic soup, savory roasted pork loin with a fennel-seed-and-black-pepper crust, and succulent grilled filet of Harris Ranch beef with apple-wood-smoked bacon and rosemary. Enjoy a glass of wine from the restaurant's impressive wine list, lauded with an award of excellence from *Wine Spectator,* sink into the comfy Frank Lloyd Wright–designed chairs at your white linen–covered table, and watch the action in the open kitchen—it's all a part of the dining experience here. Chocolate lovers shouldn't skip a slice of dense, moist bittersweet chocolate cake, but McGuinness strawberries with a rich white chocolate cream and champagne also score points on the decadence scale. *$$$; AE, DIS, MC, V; checks OK; lunch Mon–Fri, dinner every day; beer and wine; reservations recommended; www.echomenu.com; corner of Echo St.* &

LODGINGS

Radisson Hotel & Conference Center Fresno / ★★
2233 VENTURA ST, FRESNO; 559/268-1000 OR 800/333-3333
Just across the street from Fresno Convention Center, this 321-room hotel is built around an eight-story central atrium, with a three-story waterfall and faux ivy dripping down from each floor. Formerly a Holiday Inn, the place was extensively remodeled when Radisson took over in early 1999, with upgrades to the furnishings, remodeled bathrooms, a new fitness center, and an extensive game room that would keep any kid entertained. Rooms have coffeemakers, dataports, and irons and ironing boards, while deluxe suites give travelers an additional living room area to spread out in. Conventioneers and business travelers appreciate the hotel's extensive banquet facilities and 18 meeting rooms. A small but well-kept indoor/outdoor pool and whirlpool, a gift shop, and a full-service hair salon add to the hotel's list of amenities. The spacious lobby boasts the International Cafe for a quick, convenient meal and the Atrium Lounge, where guests can savor a cocktail and enjoy live piano music nightly. A complimentary shuttle transports guests to and from Fresno Yosemite International Airport. *$$; AE, DC, DIS, JCB, MC, V; checks OK; www.radisson.com/fresnoca; between Van Ness Ave and M St.* &

The San Joaquin Suite Hotel / ★★
1309 W SHAW AVE, FRESNO; 559/25-1309 OR 800/775-1309
This three-story apartment-complex-turned-all-suites-hotel boasts one-, two-, and three-bedroom suites all overlooking an immaculately kept garden courtyard with rosebushes, an Italian fountain, and a small pool and Jacuzzi. With six different floor plans (three of which include a full kitchen), the spacious suites are individually decorated and run the gamut in style—from Art Deco Moderne to austere Oriental. Even the smallest, the Squire, features a separate living room, bedroom, and huge bathroom, with such homey extras as full-length mirror, coffeemaker, medicine cabinet, and tons of closet space. Though there's no restaurant, room service is available from neighboring Applebee's. A complimentary continental breakfast is served in a nondescript nook off the lobby each morning, featuring fruit, bagels, cereal, coffee, and juices. In the evenings, sodas and juices are offered along with such happy-hour fare as meat-

balls, cheese and crackers, and crudités. *$$; AE, DC, DIS, MC, V; checks OK; sjh@fresno-online.com; www.fresno-online.com/sjh/index. html; west of Palm Ave.* &

Coalinga

RESTAURANTS

Harris Ranch Kitchen / Fountain Court Grill / ★★

24505 W DORRIS AVE (HWY 198), COALINGA; 559/935-0717 OR 800/942-2333
Fine dining next to an interstate in the middle of nowhere? It's possible here. California travelers who remember the Nut Tree near Vacaville will recognize the concept. The Harris family came to the Central Valley in the early 1900s, growing all manner of crops before they expanded into beef production. Located side by side in a sprawling hacienda-style building, these two restaurants showcase aged, choice beef raised under a stringent USDA-certified "residue avoidance" program. Like some steakhouses in Texas, whose menu word count approaches Proustian proportions and where every nuance of "how you want it" is explored in depth, Harris gives you plenty of decision-making to do. "Medium" has a "pink center" (nothing new), while "medium-rare" is distinguished by a "red, warm center." In addition to the beans and salads, side dishes typically include comfort fare such as mashed or baked potatoes and steamed broccoli. Dinner rolls are fresh and warm from an oven, not rendered rubbery by a microwave. The Ranch Kitchen is friendly and informal. One of its best introductions to the distinctive aged and flavorful Harris-raised beef is Jack's Favorite, an 8-ounce New York served atop two slices of grilled garlic-butter sourdough bread. Spinach salads are especially fresh, and the ranch-style beans are smoky and rich, although a bit toothy. Dinners in the Fountain Court Grill offer larger portions and larger prices to boot, but the soothing, clubby atmosphere is a welcome respite after a long day on the road. *$ (Ranch Kitchen); $$ (Fountain Court Grill); AE, DC, MC, V; no checks; breakfast, lunch, dinner every day (Ranch Kitchen); dinner every day (Grill); full bar; reservations recommended (Grill only); www.harrisranch.com; exit 198 East from I-5.* &

LODGINGS

Harris Ranch Inn / ★★

24485 W DORRIS AVE (HWY 198), COALINGA; 559/935-0717 OR 800/942-2333
Driving the valley in summer heat, you might come to believe that heaven is a big, cool, sparkling-clear swimming pool, and few are better than the

multilane 25-meter Olympic-style pool at Harris Ranch. Serious and casual swimmers alike enjoy this oversize antidote to the puddles at most motels. The hotel, with 123 rooms and suites in a cluster of two-story buildings, continues the tile-roofed hacienda theme of the famous Harris Ranch Kitchen nearby (see review, above). Spacious rooms with small balconies surround the pool. Those facing inward feature a country-garden decor that's pleasant although not inspired; outward-facing rooms offer hacienda-style interiors. Suites are furnished with a small table, two chairs, a sofa, and a comfortable rattan chair with ottoman; beds are nicely firm. Weary travelers from Interstate 5 who've decided to cut the trip in two with a good meal and a good night's sleep find that the hotel is well off the interstate and blessedly quiet. Pilots are welcome to use the 2,800-foot airstrip: there's no tie-down fee, and a free shuttle will take you to your room or to the restaurant. $; AE, DC, DIS, MC, V; checks OK; www.harrisranch.com; exit 198 East from I-5. &

Hanford

Visitors to Sequoia National Park learned Hanford's secret over 75 years ago. This small valley city, located halfway between Interstate 5 and Highway 99, has a prosperous charm exemplified in a classic downtown built around a shaded courthouse square. The local economy of Hanford, established in 1887 by the Southern Pacific, was originally based on the railroad, crops, and dairies. But as auto travel became the preferred means of reaching the valley and Sierra Nevada, Hanford languished. Even Highway 198 now bypasses the town by a half mile. Oddly enough, from the 1950s to the 1980s it was best known for its improbably huge, popular continental/Chinese restaurant, IMPERIAL DYNASTY—which is still open, although a bit quieter nowadays.

Today Hanford easily warrants an overnight stay. Many visitors arrive by train from the San Francisco Bay area via AMTRAK (200 Santa Fe Avenue; 800/872-7245). Pick up tour information at HANFORD VISITOR AGENCY (200 Santa Fe Avenue; 800/722-1114 or 559/582-5024), inside the 1898 railroad station.

Courthouse Square's magnificent COUNTY OF KINGS COURTHOUSE (on 8th Street between Irwin and Douty Streets), built in 1896, is worth a visit (note the see-through cast iron stairs inside), although it's occupied by businesses these days. The jail building next door (113 Court Street; 559/582-9741), built in 1898, has a castlelike tower and a great arched stone entry; it's now a restaurant known as the Bastille, where the decor is the main attraction. Other buildings of interest around the square include the CIVIC AUDITORIUM (in Civic Center Park, 400 N Douty Street), dating back to 1924; the former post office (218 Douty Street), built in 1914; and the **FOX THEATRE** (Irwin and 8th Streets; 559/584-7423), a 1929 Spanish colonial temple for the early talkies, which now hosts concerts and special events. In short, Hanford is a treasure box of civic architecture. Residential streets fan out through equally historic neighborhoods, although these have seen more incursion by the modern world. For the best look at the area's history, visit the stone **HANFORD CARNEGIE MUSEUM** (109 E 8th Street; 559/584-1367). Architecture scholars consider this 1905 structure the finest example of a Carnegie-built free public library in the state.

Thirsty doing all that meandering around the square? If you don't fancy a milk shake at **SUPERIOR DAIRY PRODUCTS COMPANY**, one of the world's great soda fountains, wander a few blocks from the square to **ART WORKS** (120 W Sixth Street; 559/583-8790), in the 1893 Arcade Building facing the railroad tracks; this hip little gallery and coffeehouse is a fine place to shop for enticing, inexpensive gifts. In the **CHINA ALLEY** district you can see a Taoist temple (a National Register of Historic Places site), an herb company, and a hand laundry that all date from the turn of the century, when Hanford's population of Chinese railroad laborers and their families was one of the state's largest. Tour appointment information is available from the Hanford Visitor Agency.

RESTAURANTS

Imperial Dynasty / ★★☆

2 CHINA ALLEY, HANFORD; 559/582-0087
Located in a windowless brick building on an historic Chinatown alley, Imperial Dynasty traces its roots back to 1883, when the Wing family first began serving meals in town. Over the years the menu evolved from Chinese to continental, with steak, seafood, and even escargots sharing the bill of fare. One seems caught in a time warp here: the back page of the menu features a photocopy of an award won in 1960 for "Best Dinner," bestowed by the Wine and Food Society of Pasadena. Clearly the passage of time has slowed here, where honors are treated like royal decrees that never lose their weight. Twin dining rooms up front feature pagoda-like roofs sheltering a wondrous art collection; a jade-museum room downstairs is used mostly for parties. After an appetizer of *escargots à la bourguignonne* (in Dijon mustard, Chablis, and butter sauce) or *fonds d' artichauts Monselet* (five small artichoke hearts and about ten oysters doing laps in a steamy pool of lemony butter), you'll think France has fully taken over the kitchen. Then comes a navy bean soup. Then a hot little patty of egg foo yung beneath a salty onion sauce. The eclecticism continues, with a huge serving of lamb shanks, perhaps, for an entree. You begin to realize that Imperial Dynasty embraces the big portion/multicourse ethic as strenuously as the Basque restaurants of other

valley towns. Overall, this restaurant is very 1960s; it was undoubtedly worthy of its acclaim at a time when American tastes were just warming up to Europe, but now it's noteworthy mostly for its longevity, grand history, and odd location. And, yes, for its excellent service by a grandmotherly Chinese waitress. *$$; AE, MC, V; checks OK; dinner Tues–Sun; full bar; reservations recommended; at Green St.*

Superior Dairy Products Company / ★★

325 N DOUTY ST, HANFORD; 559/582-0481

Take a seat at the counter in this 1929 fountain to watch fountain queen Ruby turn out one gargantuan shake or sundae after another, each topped with an Everest of whipped cream from a chrome nozzle leading to some hidden, endless reservoir. Superior has a movie-set feel, but it's all real and unaffected, from the pressed-tin ceiling right down to the black-and-chrome napkin holders. Waitresses wearing hot-pink shirts move efficiently from booths to counter and back, pitching the popular tri-tip combo (beef sliced and served on a split buttered-and-grilled French roll) or the other satisfyingly simple sandwiches that read like a throwback to your parents' or grandparents' eras: liverwurst, deviled egg, Swiss cheese, ham, tuna. The homemade ice cream is as spectacular as the setting. Served in huge quantities, fresh and creamy, it's rich and irresistible enough to seize up your arteries on the spot. As you eat, watch the world drift by through big picture windows overlooking Hanford's courthouse and jail—a classic small-town valley experience. *$; no credit cards; local checks only; lunch, dinner every day; no alcohol; reservations not accepted; corner of Ninth on Civic Center Park.* &

Visalia

Islands of trees rise above oceans of tilled earth around Visalia, an urban center set in a busy agricultural landscape. Located on the eastern edge of the valley, this gateway city to Sequoia National Park has a mild, warm climate that attracted early settlers because it promised abundant crops as well as good health. Boosters once touted its "pure air"; that's not quite as true today, but on a clear morning after a winter storm, the ragged scarp of the Sierra Nevada—rising like a white wave of granite surf—seems close indeed.

Located about 11 miles off Highway 99, Visalia is often bypassed by travelers. To make matters worse, Highway 198 running through town thoroughly cuts the city in two. But pull off, and you'll be rewarded with the discovery of a vintage downtown, historic houses turned inns, and some of the best dining in the valley.

While in the downtown area, take note of the 1,200-seat 1928 **VISALIA FOX THEATRE** at Main and Encina Streets. Like the Fox Theatre in Hanford, its Spanish colonial style evokes a massive Andalusian wedding cake with hints of Moorish influence—perfect for a Hoot Gibson or Errol Flynn movie. An old sign that says "The Coolest Spot In Town" dates back to the days when that claim referred to temperature, not degree of hipness. On a hot day you, too, may want to experience the "cool breezes of the Alaska air-washer." Movies, concerts, and special events will soon take place here again; after a period of decline, the Fox is being restored through a community-wide fundraising effort. Several Main Street restaurants and businesses are also part of the street's comeback. **ANTIQUE SHOPPING** can be rewarding in Visalia. Two worthy venues are the Showcase Mall (26644 S Mooney Boulevard; 559/685-1125) and Carriage House Antique Mall (1584 E Mineral King Avenue; 559/635-8818).

Once blanketed by oak trees, Visalia has preserved its original landscape in **MOONEY GROVE PARK** (5 miles south of Visalia off Highway 63 at 27000 S Mooney Boulevard; 559/733-6796), and has preserved some of its buildings as well in the park's requisite **PIONEER VILLAGE**, including an unusual cast-iron facade from an 1873 Masonic and Odd Fellows Hall. Don't miss the log-built boathouse set on the edge of a quiet, mirrored lake. **TULARE COUNTY MOONEY GROVE MUSEUM** (2700 S Mooney Boulevard; 559/733-6616) has a classic selection of historical artifacts.

One real oddity in the region is **RIATA RANCH**, "Home of the Cowboy Girls." When they're not touring the world giving trick-riding demonstrations, these young sprites (horse-riding gymnasts, really) train here on magnificent Appaloosas and Paints. Tour buses and other groups stop in for an occasional dinner show (barbecue fare by a local caterer) when the girls are in town. Individuals tourists can also attend by calling 559/594-4288 for directions and reservations.

RESTAURANTS

Mearle's College Drive-In / ★

604 S MOONEY BLVD, VISALIA; 559/734-4447
Patsy Cline is crooning "I Fall to Pieces" on the jukebox, the grill's sizzlin', and a tall, cold, curvaceous glass of Coke just arrived at your table. Welcome to Mearle's, where the 1940s and 1950s are alive and well. This basically unchanged vestige of drive-in culture opened in 1940, and three generations of Visalians have celebrated dates, grad nights, and weddings with its famous hamburgers. Today Mearle's fry cook still fills a bun just fine—classic air-bread, drippy melted cheese, pickles, lettuce, onion, tomato—with heaps of French fries on the side. Try the Chili Size to sample their fresh-made chili, and don't miss indulging in an old-fashioned fountain milk shake or a "mud slide" sundae. During summer, classic-car owners gather here on the last Saturday night of every month.

Lamentably, Mearle's no longer has carhops, the metal awning over the parking places looks like it's about to fall down, and the bathroom will remind you of an old gas station on Route 66. But hey, if you want new, there's a McDonald's down the street. *$; AE, DIS, MC, V; local checks only; breakfast, lunch, dinner every day; no alcohol; reservations not necessary; College of Sequoias exit off Hwy 198.*

The Vintage Press Restaurant / ★★★

216 N WILLIS ST, VISALIA; 559/733-3033
How fitting that one of the oldest towns in the Central Valley should have a restaurant steeped in history, art objects, and antiques. A love of fine California cuisine has brought Valleyites in from a 100-mile-plus radius since 1966 for every special occasion. Vintage Press fairly squeezes a rich, comforting ambience from its setting: a homelike suite of dining rooms and lounges that includes a large, flower-bowered outdoor patio. Owner John Vartanian and family (including chefs/sons David and Greg) pour all their efforts into finding the freshest ingredients, and local growers pull their trucks in each morning with just-picked lettuces and other row crops. Local mushroom foragers and cheesemakers contribute to the famous puff pastry wild mushroom appetizer (sautéed with cognac) and the good slab of white cheddar that's laid over a thick, sizzling lunchtime hamburger. Popular dinner entrees include a savory, garlic-fragrant rack of lamb in a red wine sauce and what is perhaps the restaurant's best-known showcase dish: bacon-wrapped certified Angus filet mignon with mushroom duxelles in a cabernet-shallot sauce spiral. For dessert it's hard to pass up a pecan tart with house-made cinnamon ice cream, or the chocolate Grand Marnier cake. An award-winning wine list includes over 900 selections from a 9,000-bottle cellar, fairly priced, with many "wines of the month" offered at the top of the list so you don't have to feel overwhelmed. Don't miss the "Hole in the Wall" saloon bar where you can sample one of over 60 single-malt Scotches. Or the 300-square-foot 1910 oil painting of cherubs and angels in a bevy of clouds. By the end of a meal, you'll have experienced the Valley's best version of culinary heaven. *$$$; AE, DC, MC, V; checks OK; lunch, dinner every day, brunch Sun; full bar; reservations recommended; thevintagepress@ thegrid.net; near Center St in downtown Old Visalia.* &

LODGINGS

Ben Maddox House / ★★☆

601 N ENCINA ST, VISALIA; 559/739-0721
 Sleep inside a sequoia tree? Only in a sense: carpenters built Ben Maddox House in 1876 out of lumber cut from the "big tree" sequoia groves in the Sierra Nevada. Ben Maddox was part owner of the Mt. Whitney

Power Co., which brought the first electricity to the Valley. He and other citizens also spearheaded efforts to preserve the redwoods, riding on horseback into the mountains with a delegation from Washington, D.C. Today this stately yellow Victorian with its white-columned portico and four guest bedrooms is a sweet reminder of his local contributions. Some guests prefer the spacious Ben Maddox bedroom with its large Italian marble bathroom. Others may choose the Rose Room for its floral motif and its more private location at the side of the house. In summer, a swimming pool offers a cool escape from valley heat. Another big attraction is owner Diane Muro's cooking. Unlike most B&B hosts, she lets guests choose from a full breakfast menu. Be sure to ask for her homemade jams—a bitter-cherry tree out front provides a mother lode of fruit each year. On warm mornings you can take breakfast outdoors on a deck. *$; AE, DIS, MC, V; checks OK; www.benmaddox.com; 5 blocks north of Main St at Race St.* &

The Spalding House Bed & Breakfast Inn / ★★☆

631 N ENCINA ST, VISALIA; 559/739-7877
Few houses in California boast a porch as grand as Spalding House's. The mansion's wide, low-roofed outdoor "room" sweeps down one side facing east (toward the snowcapped Sierra Nevada, visible on a clear day) and offers guests a seat in a Craftsman-style swing. A fine example of Colonial Revival style, built in 1901, Spalding House was a lumberman's dream home. The public rooms still give evidence of a gracious ease that once cosseted a prominent family. The three guest rooms are sedate and of the period: no wild wallpaper or "theme rooms" here. What you will find is accommodations tastefully decorated with antiques, white linens, and gauzy curtains. One touch of whimsy is in the Aviary Room, where a beautiful little sitting porch has been fashioned from what once was a colorful tiled aviary. The Cutler Suite was once a sleeping porch, and the Spalding Suite has a large sitting area off the bedroom. Owners Wayne and Peggy Davidson are gracious hosts, and Wayne cooks a great complimentary breakfast in the house's vast kitchen. *$; AE, MC, V; checks OK; 6 blocks north of downtown at Grove.*

Three Rivers

More than just a place to gas up the car before heading into Sequoia National Park, Three Rivers has long attracted artists, writers, and other free spirits. A group called the Kaweah Colony settled here in 1885 (six years after the town's founding), hoping to create an egalitarian, self-sustaining community based on harvesting timber from the giant redwoods nearby. For six years they met with some success, but the shift in public mood toward preservation of the mountains' scenic resources (rather than more plundering) doomed the Kaweahans' venture. Now with a population of about 3,000, Three Rivers has become a resort town at the confluence of the north, middle, and south forks of the Kaweah River. It's a good place to stretch your legs and spend the night, for lodging, always limited in national parks, is quite possibly unavailable if you venture into Sequoia-Kings without a hotel reservation. Three Rivers' lodgings, on the other hand, are numerous and vary from comfortable bed and breakfasts to sizable chain motels. **ART GALLERIES** and shops in town are few, but you might stop in at Gallery 198 (42268 Sierra Drive; 559/561-4716), featuring glass, ceramics, wood, and unusual copper baskets. Spring wildflowers are another attraction, and in early May the **RED BUD ARTS AND CRAFTS FESTIVAL** (at the Lions Club Roping Arena on N Fork Drive, about 1.5 miles up-canyon from Highway 198) celebrates their return before the 90-plus temperatures of summer—and the waves of park-bound tourists—arrive once more. A business association called the **RESERVATION CENTER** (559/561-0410) can provide you with local event and lodging information.

RESTAURANTS

The Gateway / ★★☆

45978 SIERRA DR, THREE RIVERS; 559/561-4133

It's hard to be far from water in the Sierra foothills below Sequoia-Kings, but the land still seems parched and thirsty until you get to higher elevations. Built on the gurgling Kaweah, a river fed by melting snow, with panoramic views of the canyon from both its open-air veranda and dining room, the Gateway straddles this world between wet and dry, hot and cold, especially if you have an icy beer in one hand and a juicy rib in the other. Along with the view, ribs made the Gateway famous. A rack of baby-back pork glistens in a glaze of beery-spicy tomato sauce before making a heavenly mess of your chin, fingers, and napkin—a "mountain man" kind of experience if there ever was one. Their fork-tender charbroiled filet mignon (cut on the premises) is one of the best in the mountains, and a lobster and steak dinner will make you think you're back in the big city (with both its fine steakhouse quality and its price). The Gateway makes its own salad dressings, and offers alternative fare such as fish so you don't have to feel like you're in a den of carnivores. While you're dining, you might be lucky enough to glimpse bears down along the river. *$$; AE, DC, DIS, MC, V; no checks; breakfast Sat–Sun, lunch, dinner Tues–Sun (closed Tues in winter); full bar; reservations recommended; 6 miles east of Three Rivers on Hwy 198.*

LODGINGS

Buckeye Tree Lodge / ★

46000 SIERRA DR, THREE RIVERS; 559/561-5900

Although the Buckeye definitely has an up-in-the-mountains feel, you're only at 1,300 feet. During the spring, the Kaweah River, which runs right beside the nicely landscaped 2-acre property, rages along through its canyon like an angry white horse. By summer it's calmed down and taken on lazy-stream status, perfect for sitting on a boulder and dangling your toes, or casting a line in search of trout. Twelve rooms in the main lodge are clean and plain. White is the predominant scheme for everything from walls to spreads—a refreshing break from the aggressively "country" theme of most mountain lodgings. The two-story lodge features verandas that double as walkways to the rooms, so each unit's deck is somewhat communal. Escape instead to the pool, which is large and well sited in the sun, or to the lawns and walks shaded by oaks. The Lodge's most interesting accommodation is the Redbud Cottage, a small house with a king bedroom, a half-bedroom with twin bed, and a living room with sofa sleeper, plus a kitchen and a wood-burning fireplace to take the chill off those cool mountain nights. *$–$$; AE, CB, DC, DIS, MC, V; no checks; info@buckeyetree.com; www.buckeyetree.com; 6 miles NE of town on Hwy 198 (½ mile from park entrance).*

Sequoia Village Inn / ★

45971 SIERRA DR (HWY 198), THREE RIVERS; 559/561-3652

Innkeeper Curt Nutter is well known in these parts as an inveterate hiker, and he'll bend your ear about the best places to tramp in the Sierra Nevada. In addition to being a walking guidebook, he runs a neat and quiet little inn in a deep canyon adjacent to historic Pumpkin Hollow Bridge. The first cabins here were built in the 1940s to house park rangers, so they have a little more room than do most typical tourist cabins or motel rooms. The decor is homey, and much of the clientele is families looking for a quiet retreat after a day spent in the national park. Smallest accommodations still have a queen bed, while two new large chalet-style cabins are for families or groups: one sleeps 9, the other 12. Both chalets have a California Craftsman style and boast views up the canyon. Amenities include pool and hot tub, French roast coffee, and popcorn (microwave in room). On clear nights Nutter will occasionally bring out a big reflecting telescope for some stargazing. *$; AE, DIS, JCB, MC, V; California checks OK; 5 miles past Three Rivers, take immediate left after Pumpkin Hollow Bridge.*

Mineral King

Driving to historic Mineral King isn't easy, but it's the only way to get there unless you're a backpacker. A narrow (mostly one-lane), 25-mile-long road snakes into the valley, climbing from Highway 198 near Three Rivers into the high country of Silver City until it dead-ends against the Great Western Divide. Along the way you'll be comin' round the mountain 698 times (sometimes blindly). Navigate this stretch slowly—take an hour or longer if you really want to play it safe—and enjoy the scenery, which ranges from oak woodland to giant sequoia groves. By the time you emerge at Silver City, the valley is classic Sierra high country, with great stands of pine and fir beneath towering snow-laden granite peaks and bowl-shaped cirques.

A failed silver-mining region after the 1870s, Mineral King drifted quietly along until it almost became a ski resort in the early 1970s. After a pitched court battle between environmental interests and a private developer (ol' Walt Disney himself), President Carter signed over 12,600 acres of Mineral King U.S.F.S.-administered wilderness to Sequoia National Park in 1978. The valley floor, however, is definitely not wilderness. Privately owned rustic cabins and a cabin resort/cafe/general store may eventually be phased out, but for now they help create an ideal destination for those who love being near enough to alpine high country to explore it on day hikes, yet return to a snug cabin each night.

Favored destinations for hikers include several lakes tucked high on the south face of the canyon. Best known are **WHITE CHIEF LAKE** and **EAGLE LAKE**, both about 4 miles in, one way—a long, steep day hike, or a more leisurely overnight backpacking trip. The trail to White Chief crosses one of the Sierra Nevada's most unusual natural features: here extensive marble veins course through the mountainside, hollowed by streams into low-roofed caverns (best explored by experienced spelunkers only). The White Chief trail passes right by one **OLD MINE TUNNEL**, however, that leads straight into the mountain. Unlike most dangerous remnant workings around the West, where the risk of cave-in or getting lost is alarmingly real, the White Chief shaft has been left open by rangers so that hikers can safely take a short walk into the darkness. Overnight trips in the backcountry require a permit, and it's often best to obtain one in advance because trailhead quotas can be limited during the short summer season. Write Sequoia National Park (Ash Mountain Headquarters, Three Rivers, CA 93271; 559/565-3341 or 559/565-3768). For campsite reservations in the valley, call 800/365-2267. The road into Mineral King closes each winter, usually from the first snow (November) through the end of May.

RESTAURANTS

Silver City Restaurant / ★★

NORTH SIDE, MINERAL KING RD; 559/561-3223 SUMMER; 805/528-2730 WINTER

Five mornings a week, almost 30 pies come out of the kitchen here. Hot, flaky, bubbling with berries or apples, or cool and deliciously layered with a chocolate-walnut cream, they've been known to make backpackers cut a trip short just to get back to this kind of "civilization." Pies aren't all this homey little cafe is loved for, however. Breakfasts are a platteresque repast of "secret recipe" hotcakes, two eggs any way you like 'em, home-fried potatoes (from scratch), bacon, and a side of fruit.

 Lunches are best known for the quarter-pound Mountain Burger or the Kaweah Jack—bacon, avocado, and Jack cheese captured between two slices of buttered sourdough and grilled until the innards are a blissful, molten mess. Dinner fare is the same as lunch, with the addition of well-loved specials on Friday and Saturday nights such as vegetarian spinach lasagne or chicken breasts in lemon and mushroom sauce with rice pilaf. Rolls and breads are homemade (when the pies aren't hogging all the oven space). *$; MC, V; checks OK; breakfast, lunch, dinner Thurs–Mon, limited service (pies and beverages only) Tues–Wed; no alcohol; reservations not necessary; silvercity@thegrid.net; www.silvercityresort.com; 21 miles up Mineral King Rd from Hwy 198.*

LODGINGS

Silver City Mountain Resort / ★★

NORTH SIDE, MINERAL KING RD; 559/561-3223 SUMMER; 805/528-2730 WINTER

Once there were dozens of rustic cabin and tent-cabin resorts like this one in the Sierra Nevada. Now Silver City has become one of the last nostalgic holdouts in a busier world where travelers usually demand large full baths and electricity. That's right, these cabins and "chalets" have no power other than kerosene and propane. Many of Silver City's accommodations, however, still qualify as downright luxurious in these parts. They range from tiny 12-foot-by-12-foot sleeper cabins, adorned with knotty pine paneling, an upholstered easy chair or couch, and a kitchen table, on up to fully stocked chalets, which might have a queen bed and are so popular they should be reserved about six months in advance for holidays and weekends. Most have nicely stocked kitchenettes so you can prepare your own meals (the resort's restaurant is open only five days a week), and all have housekeeping, providing the ultimate luxury in the mountains: cool, clean sheets and pillowcases. At night you'll warm your cabin with a wood stove after sitting out front around a campfire and counting stars with other travelers who share your love of a simpler inn experience. *$–$$; MC, V; checks OK; silvercity@thegrid.net; www. silvercityresort.com; 21 miles up Mineral King Rd from Hwy 198.*

Sequoia and Kings Canyon National Parks

Kings Canyon is the northernmost park; Sequoia lies just south of it. An automobile traveler gets only a small taste of these parks. For the most part, these are backcountry parks.

Named for its large stands of trees, **SEQUOIA NATIONAL PARK** is best approached from Visalia via Lemon Cove and Three Rivers, a route that follows the robust Kaweah River as it drains off the Great Western Divide. Ash Mountain Entrance is not far past Three Rivers. Be sure your gas tank is over half full before leaving Three Rivers: at press time no gas was for sale in the national parks. The **FOOTHILLS VISITOR CENTER** (559/565-3341), at a 1,700-foot elevation, will acquaint you with both parks' main features and help you assay the campsite situation if you don't already have a reservation.

The 38-mile highway from Ash Mountain through Sequoia to the Kings Canyon National Park boundary is known as Generals Highway. Passable most of the year, in winter the highway may require chains or be closed for several days after a storm.

Be prepared for hot weather in summer, as well as occasional delays as road crews work to repair the historic road—an ongoing process much needed in recent years after damaging winter storms. Four of the five largest trees thrive in **GIANT FOREST**. Most of these Methuselahs are between 1,800 and 2,700 years old, about 250 feet tall, and close to 100 feet in circumference (picture a tree's base wide enough to block a two-lane street!). Continuing on to **KINGS CANYON NATIONAL PARK**, you pass through **GRANT GROVE**, site of the "Nation's Christmas Tree" (General Grant Tree). From Grant Grove, Highway 180 threads 30 miles northeast into the Grand Canyon of the south fork of the Kings River and a park site known as **CEDAR GROVE**. This road is closed in winter (and with it, the entire valley).

Cedar Grove and the Grand Canyon area, where summer temperatures may climb into the 90s, are well-forested, with granite sentinels rising high on all sides. **CEDAR GROVE VISITOR CENTER** (559/565-3793) and a permit station at Road's End (6 miles east of Cedar Grove Village) can help out with information and permits. One small hotel, **CEDAR GROVE LODGE** (559/335-5500) offers overnight accommodations along with a cafe.

To learn more about backpacking or horse packing in the parks' wilderness, or to join a guided trip, call the information numbers given above for help in hooking up with a reputable guide service. Additional information about Sequoia and Kings Canyon is available on the parks' web page at www.nps.gov/seki.

LODGINGS

Grant Grove Village / ★★

ON HWY 180, KINGS CANYON NATIONAL PARK; 559/335-5500

After many years of the status quo, accommodations at Kings Canyon National Park changed dramatically for the millennium with the expansion of Grant Grove Village. The Village's new John Muir Lodge, operated by park concessionaire Sequoia Kings Canyon Park Services Company, offers 30 rooms and 6 suites in a woodsy two-story building hidden in the forest behind the village. (This concessionaire also operates the clean, basic lodge deep in Kings Canyon called Cedar Grove Lodge; reservations can be made via the same number above.) One of the challenges along the year-round highway through the big trees of Kings Canyon used to be winter lodging: most of this resort's tent-style, "rustic" or "bath cabin" Meadow Camp cabins had to be closed during snowy months. Now the new John Muir Lodge hosts year-round visitors in hotel-style comfort. Deluxe rooms come with private baths and are priced well over $100—a far cry from some of Grant Grove Village's classic tent cabins, which still go for about $35 a night. Many guests here are weeklong visitors; some have been coming for generations. Those who like a more rustic experience often choose the Meadow Camp cabins. Those equipped with baths rent for just under $100. Others have no running water, no bath, and no heat other than a wood stove and are priced accordingly: about $50. Snow closes the road from Grant Grove Village into Kings Canyon each winter. *$–$$; DIS, MC, V; checks OK; www.sequoia/kingscanyon.com; 65 miles east of Fresno on Hwy 180.* &

Wuksachi Village & Lodge / ★★

64740 WUKSACHI WAY IN LODGEPOLE, SEQUOIA NATIONAL PARK; 559/565-4070 OR 888/252-5757

Wuksachi Village & Lodge, brand-new at press time, features 102 hotel-style rooms ranging from economy to deluxe. Rooms are thoughtfully flexible in furnishings and layout: most have two queen beds and a queen-size sofa bed, so you can really fit in a crowd. Many of your fellow visitors will be spending at least several days here, so a friendly, community feel soon develops as you see familiar faces. Overall, the Lodge has an upscale feeling, nicely decorated with Native American motifs, Mission-style furniture, and stonework in the public areas. A crackling fire in a wood stove greets you in the lobby. Steps away, the Lodge's restaurant has a "walk-in" fireplace. Other than a pizza place in Lodgepole, this Wuksachi eatery is the only casual, sit-down dining option around. *$$; AE, DIS, MC, V; checks OK; 30 miles from Ash Mountain park entrance.* &

Tulare

Two big fires in the late 1800s destroyed most of Tulare's early heritage. Today the town is justly famous for hosting the **CALIFORNIA FARM SHOW** (4450 S Laspina Street, next to Highway 99, 2.5 miles south of downtown), one of the world's biggest and best international fairs showcasing agricultural equipment. Each February the newest, most sophisticated farm machinery is displayed for three days in a tent city so extensive you ride a small people-mover to see it all. Nonprofit community groups fire up their barbecues and vie to see who grills the best marinated tri-tip beef, which is then hacked into delicious slices and piled on buns. At press time, construction was under way on the new **CALIFORNIA FARM EQUIPMENT MUSEUM/LEARNING CENTER** (4450 S Laspina Street; 559/688-1030), an agricultural history museum adjacent to the Farm Show site that features live steam demonstrations. For information about the California Farm Show, antique tractor shows, and other events, call 800/999-9186.

Porterville

Life in Porterville centers on farming, cattle, and citrus ranching. It's proximity to the Sierra Nevada also makes it, like Visalia, a last-chance stop for camping food, supplies, and fishing gear if you want a wide selection and flatland prices. The city still has some charm, but unfortunately many of downtown's buildings fell prey to the "modernizing" mania of the 1950s. You won't find many vestiges of the days when it was a stop for the Butterfield Overland Mail Company, but the town celebrates a **JACKASS MAIL RUN** (559/784-9202) each April, when mule teams ride to Springville and join a festival.

PORTERVILLE HISTORICAL MUSEUM (North D Street, in the town's sprawling Mission Revival Santa Fe train station; 559/784-2053) has grown into one of the valley's best artifact collections. The 1918 building showcases antique farm equipment, as well as priceless Yokut Indian baskets. Stop in here for information on just about anything regarding Porterville from the local volunteers who run the office. Also helpful is the **PORTERVILLE CHAMBER OF COMMERCE** (36 W Cleveland Avenue; 559/784-7502).

The **ZALUD HOUSE** (on a narrow side street at the southwest corner of Morton and Hockett; 559/782-7461), built in 1891, is still completely original and open to the public. The last surviving family member, Pearle, donated all Zalud family furnishings and memorabilia to the city of

Porterville. Now listed in the National Register of Places, the Victorian-style house, which is operated as a museum by the city, has dizzyingly steep front-hall stairs and a wonderful Second-Empire mansard roof. The Zaluds were one of the first families in the valley to have electricity, and curators proudly point out the unique early light bulbs that were found in the house's once-deep piles of ephemera and junk. Juicy scandal rocked the family over a half century ago: ask a tour guide about the chair with the bullet hole.

Allensworth

Black American Colonel Allen Allensworth envisioned a township free of segregation and prejudice. In 1908 he purchased this farmland site and moved here with numerous followers. The town grew quickly, soon merited its own railroad stop, and prospered culturally and socially. Momentum slowed with Allensworth's untimely death in 1914, however, and by the 1940s the town was all but abandoned. The state declared it an historic park in 1976. Today only a few buildings remain on a site that's mournful but well kept. One structure, Allensworth's own house, stands as a rare, almost-perfect example of an early Sears-Roebuck mail-order house (with clever factory-made joinery). The park is 32 miles south of Hanford on Highway 43; the ranger's office can be reached at 805/849-3433.

Wasco/Shafter

Located along Highway 43 not far from Bakersfield, these two quiet farming towns may be best known for their settings amidst thousands of acres of roses. Over 50 million roses are grown here—almost 46 varieties, with more developed every year. Growers' sheds and offices are not generally open to the public, but **WASCO'S FESTIVAL OF ROSES** each September takes over **BARKER PARK** (on Poso Drive 7 blocks west of Highway 43), which is also the site of a rose garden. For information call the **CHAMBER OF COMMERCE AND AGRICULTURE** (805/758-2746). Shafter also has a "blink and you'll miss it" quality, but the **GREEN HOTEL** (1913) at 530 James Street is a well-restored example of a Craftsman-era lodging house. Tours and overnight lodging can be arranged in advance; call 805/746-1913.

TRAILS OF THE BASQUE SHEEPHERDERS

Hiking deep in a side canyon of the Sierra Nevada, you come across evidence of their passing. Perhaps a rusted kettle. Or even their names. Some immortalized themselves with florid script lightly carved into the growing bark of aspen trees, names like Arrieta and Carrica. It's still possible to find such names preserved in the living bark, and even an occasional date such as 1904—or earlier.

Who were they?

Basque sheepherders. They immigrated as young men from the western end of the Pyrenees to herd sheep in the United States, especially during the years from the 1850s (the California Gold Rush) to about 1960. Most came just after the turn of the century. With them they brought one of Europe's oldest (and most mysterious) cultures, eventually setting up colonies throughout California, Nevada, and on up into Idaho. The camp life was hard, lonely, nomadic. Town beckoned, and eventually the days of the West's open range were gone.

Today you can still experience their proud role in the West's history, especially in the southern half of the Central Valley, but the opportunity is fading. Older family members keep the Old Country ways alive by holding grand festivals at which strong men toss 250-pound weights or play pelote (handball), and beautiful, dark-haired girls dance in swirling red dresses and black-aproned vests. Everyone tries a swig or two from the *bota*—a kidney-shaped leather bag held at arms' length to squirt a thin stream of acrid red wine directly into pursed lips (or all over an amateur's shirt!). Some bakeries in towns like Bakersfield still turn out distinctive "sheepherders' bread"—the high-domed round loaves that herders originally baked in cast iron pots buried in coals.

And always the lamb sizzles over a white-hot bed of coals, lovingly turned and brushed with a garlicky marinade by men in red berets. Accompanying the lamb are side dishes such as beans with ham or chorizos, hot sauce (not unlike a fresh salsa), salad, pasta dishes, pig's feet, and sliced beef tongue. Many Basque "family style" restaurants are still located in the very hotels that once housed single men who were between jobs out on that lonely range.

Once in a rare while, if you look across an open field along California's Interstate 5 around Kettleman City and spot a herd of sheep, you may see a sheepherder's trademark home: the curious canvas-sided (or more often, bent-plywood-sided) wagon on wheels. A few are still around, but a way of life—a lonely life that helped feed the West—is all but gone.

Bakersfield

Bakersfield is a tough, gritty city with a soft heart. Just when you think it consists of nothing more than a confusing tangle of streets and railroad tracks, industrial districts and a still-struggling (but greatly revitalized) downtown, you stumble upon a pocket of vibrancy—and, most important, authenticity—that's missing in many cities. And the further east you get from Highway 99 into downtown, the better it gets.

Named for early landowner Colonel Thomas Baker and incorporated in 1873, Bakersfield thrives on oil, natural gas, cotton, and other agriculture. However, when it comes to leisure, residents love good food and antiques—and the city has plenty of both. Drive by a city park on the weekend and your nose may well lead you to a **BASQUE BARBECUE** where an entire lamb, redolent of its garlic marinade, turns slowly on a spit above a white-hot oak fire. Poke around downtown, or on 19th Street east of Chester, or on H Street between Brundage Lane and California Avenue, and you'll find great **ANTIQUE SHOPS** and emporiums. Bakersfield must be the Valley's storehouse of knickknacks: whatever disappeared from your grandmother's attic seems to have ended up here. Most items are reasonably priced, and it's not uncommon for a charter busload of antique hunters to arrive from Los Angeles for a look around. Downtown's **FIVE AND DIME ANTIQUE MALL** (1400 19th Street, at K Street; 661/323-8048) took over an old Woolworth building some time ago; its luncheonette area hasn't changed a whit since the 1940s, and it's still open if you want a Coke and a grilled cheese sandwich. As they say in the collectibles business: It's mint! The two best **ANTIQUE MALLS** are Great American (625 19th Street; 661/322-1776) and Central Park Antique Mall (701 19th Street; 661/633-1143); you can easily budget a couple hours for each. On H Street, shopowners have taken over about two long blocks of Craftsman-era bungalows and turned them into tea shops and one Martha Stewartesque haven after another. One of the best is Grandma's Trunk (1115 H Street; 661/323-2730); be sure to work your way through the house all the way to the back garden and garage. Cottage Gardens (30 H Street; 661/322-6254), which would make the Mad Hatter envious, is run by Diane Strickland, who sells hundreds of antique bone china cups and saucers along with her dried herbs.

For even more history, visit **KERN COUNTY MUSEUM AND PIONEER VILLAGE** (3801 Chester Avenue, at 36th Street; 661/861-2132), a cluster of vintage and architecturally significant houses on a site in the fairgrounds. In all, about 50 original buildings have been moved here from other parts of the city and county. For general tourist information visit or call the **BAKERSFIELD CHAMBER OF COMMERCE** (1725 I Street; 661/327-4421) or the **CONVENTION & TOURISM BUREAU** (1325 P Street; 661/325-5051).

BASEBALL fans who've grown tired of the Big League hustle of big ticket prices and Grand Canyon–scale stadiums should attend a game at Sam Lynn Ball Park (4009 Chester, next to the Kern County Museum; 661/322-1363). Here the Bakersfield Blaze, a Class A farm team of the San Francisco Giants, battles other up-and-coming ball players April through August. Tickets are $3 to $5 at the ballpark ticket office—that'll take you back!

Several of the town's best RESTAURANTS are located near the original train station, in the vicinity of E 21st Street and Baker Street (the old Southern Pacific line). Basques gathered here in the early 1900s before heading out for sheep camps as far away as the Owens Valley in the eastern Sierra, and they continue to gather here today. You'll still hear Basque spoken at the area's famed Basque bars and family-style restaurants such as the NORIEGA HOTEL or the WOOL GROWERS RESTAURANT (see below). Although this neighborhood can feel a little deserted and spooky at night, don't shy away; popular restaurants have their own well-lighted parking lots, and incidents are rare.

RESTAURANTS

Bill Lee's Bamboo Chopsticks / ★

1203 18TH ST, BAKERSFIELD; 661/324-9441

Bring a big appetite to Bill Lee's, an institution in Bakersfield since 1938. The decor here is postmodern sophisticated and spacious, with an entry foyer guarded by a terra-cotta tomb warrior statue and beautiful carved-wood panels in the dining rooms. Portions are huge and inexpensive. Dinner often begins with a bowl of won ton soup loaded with slices of cured pork, vegetables, and plump dumplings (although on a recent visit the broth was not quite hot enough and the dumplings a little tough). Fried rice and various chow meins can feed a hungry family for little more than $5 each, while more sophisticated dishes such as a delicious shrimp Cantonese in a garlic–black bean sauce are still priced well under $10. As each dish stacks up in the middle of your table atop odd little stainless steel toadstool-shaped stands, you'll find yourself wondering why you ordered so much. To take some home, of course. *$; AE, DC, DIS, MC, V; checks OK; lunch, dinner daily; full bar; reservations recommended; comments@ billlees.com; www.billlees.com; from 99N, off the Chester exit on 178E.* &

The Bistro / ★★

5101 CALIFORNIA AVE, BAKERSFIELD; 661/323-3905

Can the best "fine dining" in Bakersfield possibly be located in a hotel? Many locals think it can, and the Bistro, in the Four Points Hotel by Sheraton, makes a strong run at proving it. Geared for the well-heeled oil executive and business-traveler crowd, the Bistro has also won the hearts of Bakersfield residents, who treat it like their own high-end club whenever it's time for a graduation or anniversary dinner. Designed by a San Francisco firm imported expressly to give it a big-city look, the room greets you as you walk in with an elegant display of mahogany paneling and trim in the big high-back bar area. In the main rooms the style becomes a bit lighter, with cedar trim and plenty of glass display cases showing a superb collection of contemporary Native American craft pieces. In short, the Bistro feels good, and despite the Valley's generally casual tone, you'll feel good here too, in a nice dress or a sport coat for dinner. Chef Mike Kelly, presiding over the line since the early 1990s, changes the menu seasonally, often incorporating traditional continental themes with plenty of Pacific Rim interlopers. A favorite starter is the tempura artichoke hearts drizzled with a honey-mustard sauce. Entrees may include sea bass peanut crust that cracks open to reveal a steamy, fragrant filet. Oven-fried prawns wrapped in sweet crab-meat sizzle in lemon-garlic butter. Rack of lamb, baked with a tamarind barbecue sauce, pays tribute to Basques and their love of a good leg or chop. Meat lovers relish their chateaubriand, a massive, succulent cut that is typical of the Bistro's un-dainty portions. Entrees include soup or salad, helping to keep the prices a pleasant surprise for this quality and quantity. For dessert, their crème brûlée just might be the best north of the Tehachapis. At lunchtime, big salads like the Cobb or the crackling chicken are first-rate. *$$; AE, DC, MC, V; no checks; breakfast, lunch, dinner every day; full bar; reservations recommended; www.fourpoints.com; take California Ave exit off Hwy 99 and head southwest.* &

Buck Owens' Crystal Palace / ★★

2800 BUCK OWENS BLVD, BAKERSFIELD; 661/328-7500

"They're going to put me in the movies" sings Buck as he steps to the mike on the Crystal Palace's porchlike stage. The country music and television (*Hee-Haw*) legend, still belting them out at age 70, often takes the stage here Friday and Saturday nights to let the crowd know this is his joint and he's there to have as much fun as they are. Fashioned after a Wild West town whose false storefronts surround the stage as in an Elizabethan theatre, Crystal Palace is a great honky-tonk—without some of the honkier elements like cigarette smoke, tossed beer bottles, and chicken-wire between the performers and the crowd. In fact, you can feel comfortable bringing your young 'uns and your grandma here. Buck's kitchen serves hearty, well-prepared burger-and-potato skins-type fare, plus more upscale selections such as Buck's Cowboy Steak, a 32-ounce mesquite-grilled extravaganza; shrimp kabobs, or catfish broiled with Cajun spices. The cold beer arrives in mugs big enough to dunk a softball. But the heart of the experience is Buck or the other acts on stage: great music seven nights a week, exemplifying the days when Owens and

Merle Haggard put Bakersfield on the country music map. *$; AE, MC, V; no checks; dinner every day; full bar; reservations recommended on weekends; crystalpalace@atg.com; www.buckowens.com; Buck Owens Blvd exit off Hwy 99.* &

Happy Jack's Pie 'n' Burger / ★

1800 20TH ST, BAKERSFIELD; 661/323-1661

Waiting for your burger, your eye drifts to a photo of the local high school's Driller Wrestling Team. An elderly lady next to you, surely a regular customer, says sadly to no one in particular, "It's nice to know that life's eternal." Ennui settles in like a low-lying tule fog. And then it arrives: the best hamburger in the valley. At Happy Jack's, the fry guy constructs a burger so carefully he could almost be a food stylist for some Ansel Adams of food photography. Stacked high, perhaps with a spicy Anaheim green chile and Russian dressing joining the usual tomato-lettuce-onion tucked inside, a Happy Jack burger needs its white jacket of tissue paper just to keep it all together. No french fries sully the simplicity of Happy Jack's menu—they're not available, probably because the chef's too busy attempting perfection at one thing and one thing only. Desserts feature the unforgettable "Rudy"—a peanut butter and chocolate cream pie with a thin, very flaky crust. Not big. Just good—real good. Full and happy, you take one last look backward, look at this bizarre little place with its varnished wood siding as you totter into the blazing heat of downtown Bakersfield. *$; no credit cards; no checks; lunch, dinner, Mon–Fri; no alcohol; reservations not necessary; behind the Fox Theatre, downtown.*

Luigi's / ★★

725 E 19TH ST, BAKERSFIELD; 661/322-0926

Bakersfield's Italian community (and seemingly everyone else in town) has been piling into this noisy storefront since 1911, when it started as a small grocery that also served fresh pasta, stews, and minestrone. Today this crowded, informal deli, bar, and dining hall hosts a brief but lively lunch hour at picnic-style tables covered with red-checkered cloths. The Luigi sandwich is a hefty engineering feat of dry salami, cotto salami, mortadella, provolone, Swiss, mustard, Luigi's special sandwich sauce, lettuce, and onion. Pasta bolognese features a rich sauce recipe that has been in the family (and made fresh daily) since 1911, when Emilia Lemucchi first lovingly stirred up a batch. Team photos from over 50 years of local high school football, baseball, and other sports cover the walls. Two of the waitresses in the front room have worked side by side for over 20 years; regular patrons look forward to their quick wit and a friendly shoulder rub when they tie on a customer's pasta bib. Lunch specials include a different pasta daily, baked stuffed chicken breast, baby back ribs with rigatoni pasta, and a special New York steak on Fridays.

$; AE, MC, V; checks OK; lunch Tues–Sat; full bar; reservations not necessary; near railroad tracks just south of E Truxton Ave. ₺

Noriega Hotel / ★★

525 SUMNER ST, BAKERSFIELD; 661/322-8419
Founded by Faustino Noriega in 1893 and taken over by the Elizalde family in 1931, Noriega's still honors its boardinghouse traditions and proudly proclaims itself *Eskualdunen Etchea*—"the Basque People's House." Step through the door of this historic hotel before 7pm and you may think you've come to the wrong place. In classic Basque fashion, the front room is a large and lively bar, but there's no dining room in sight. Promptly at 7pm the bar clears, and everyone goes into the back room for dinner. Noriega's serves hearty fixed-price family-style meals, and dinner courses arrive in unending waves: salad, soup, beans, pickled tongue, cottage cheese (a unique garlicky mixture that is almost like a dip), salsa, pasta (often spaghetti), two entrees for everybody (that's right, two!), hot, greasy french fries, vegetables, a chunk of blue cheese just before dessert, and ice cream or flan. The beef stew and baked chicken are excellent, but the roast leg of lamb with garlic, which is served on Friday nights, is the hands-down winner with long-time customers. What makes this place different from other Basque restaurants? Better-than-average cooking and the variety of courses. Red wine—jug variety, but almost perversely tart and delicious—arrives at the table in a screw-top bottle. They decant it, no doubt, from some vast tank in the back room. For real Basque tradition, this is the place. *$; no credit cards; checks OK; breakfast, lunch, dinner Tues–Sun; full bar; reservations recommended; near Baker St.* ₺

24th St Cafe / ★★

1415 24TH ST, BAKERSFIELD; 661/323-8801
So crowded on a weekend morning that dozens of people sit in chairs on the sidewalk sipping coffee while they wait, 24th St deserves its popularity. Breakfast sweeps you away like some long-lost lover; you just can't remember when you've had one this good. The extensive menu has all sorts of creative yet somehow fundamentally right dishes such as a grilled sourdough egg sandwich, layered with melted Swiss cheese, ham, chopped jalapeño pepper, grilled and lightly caramelized red onion, one fried egg over easy, mayo, and mustard. Homemade hash comes to the table with a thin, spectacularly well browned crust and steaming insides. Pancakes are big and light. Scrambles include sautéed scallops with scrambled eggs, green onions, and garlic. The wide-ranging menu also includes fresh trout, pan-fried or poached with eggs. Full yet? While breakfast is served all day, lunch is equally well prepared with such selections as a tri-tip sandwich with corn and pinto beans, chili, or meatloaf. Service is efficient and friendly. Decor is a mix of antique bicycles, toys, and other collectibles: a diner look, yet very "today." No one who's in

Bakersfield for more than half a day should miss this place. *$; no credit cards; checks OK; breakfast, lunch daily; beer and wine; reservations not accepted; at 24th St (aka Hwy 178) and K St.* &

Wool Growers Restaurant / ★★

620 E 19TH ST, BAKERSFIELD; 661/327-9584

Bakersfield has many good Basque restaurants, so it's almost a disservice to the community to pick one over the other. Perhaps loyal Basques make the rounds from one to the next. If that's the case, there must be a lot of Basques in Bakersfield, for Wool Growers is jammed on weekend nights. Owned by Jenny Maitia, Wool Growers has been redecorated in recent years; consequently, it doesn't feel quite as authentic as some others (Pyrenees Cafe at 601 Sumner, for example, where the dark, long barroom still echoes with the voices of men speaking in their native tongue

while tossing down glasses of Picon punch). Wool Growers has become civilized, but that's a good thing. You can bring your skittish Auntie Doris here and she'll love it. Dinners run the gamut: plenty of bread, pickled beef tongue, steaming hot soup (we had a hearty spicy cabbage that turned absolutely sublime with a good dollop of the house salsa), salad, pasta, entrees (such as lamb chops, oxtail stew, or scampi), vegetables, mounds of french fries. These all come in wondrously large, hot, fresh helpings from a huge kitchen at the back of the main room, served family style at your party's own booth or table. *$; AE, DIS, MC, V; no checks; lunch, dinner, Mon–Sat; full bar; reservations recommended; just before Baker Ave.* &

LODGINGS

Four Points Hotel by Sheraton / ★★

5101 CALIFORNIA AVE, BAKERSFIELD; 661/325-9700

Think again if your image of Bakersfield is still one of a sleepy little farm and railroad town. Big Oil spurred much of Bakersfield's recent growth, and industry executives from around the country pour in here weekly to visit various corporate headquarters. In response to this gusher of business travelers, Sheraton has built one of the most sophisticated yet unpretentious hotels in the Central Valley. Six two-story wings cluster around a lushly landscaped courtyard full of fountains, streams, and ponds, as well as a near-Olympic-length pool with a trellis-shaded seating area cooled by misters. Of the 197 rooms, 58 have patios adjacent to the courtyard. Rooms are furnished with cherry-wood pieces in a continental style or in a lighter, whitewashed look with peach-colored draperies. All rooms have at least three telephones, all with dataports, and the 27-inch televisions are larger than those in most homes. A full buffet breakfast in the restaurant, the Bistro (see review in Restaurants, above), is included with all room rates over a certain very-reasonable price point; lower-priced rooms still get a continental breakfast. *$–$$; AE, CB, DIS, MC, V; checks OK; www.fourpoints.com; take California Ave exit off Hwy 99 and go SW.* &

Kernville

At only 2,650 feet above sea level in the Sierra Nevada foothills east of Bakersfield, Kernville has a pleasant identity crisis. On one hand, it's definitely a mountain resort town set in Sequoia National Forest—but where are the forests? On the other hand, because of its location on the fringe of high desert, it seems hot, open, and distinctly un-alpine. The small (population 1,656) but lively resort town hides in a canyon created by sun-baked hillsides, clad with oak and chaparral, that fold around the mighty (and ice-cold) **KERN RIVER**. The Kern flows right through the heart of town, so you're never far from its murmuring voice. When you want the murmur of pine forests, you must drive up the Kern River Canyon until the great pines seem to walk down from the ridges and greet you.

As the Kern drops steeply down its rocky bed, it creates an almost ideal whitewater "garden" of rapids and riffles, making this region Southern California's **RIVER-RUNNING** capital. One of the favorite training spots for kayakers runs right through town. If you're new to the sport you'll get a close-up look by stopping at **RIVERSIDE PARK** in the heart of Kernville, immediately downriver from the bridge. Here you can spread a picnic blanket on acres of shaded lawn and watch the whitewater experts strut their stuff, their tiny craft darting in and out of danger like needle-bodied water birds. Beginners anxious to give it a try have come to the right place: **WHITEWATER TOURING** companies offer kayak rentals and instruction. River rafters who enjoy floating in inflatable rafts bob down a popular stretch of rapids just upstream from town. Here you can navigate through gentle rock gardens that still have a pretty decent whoop-de-do factor. Local companies offer everything from one-hour to overnight trips. One reputable operator in town who combines mountain biking and river rafting packages for visitors is Mountain & River Adventures (11113 Kernville Rd; 800/861-6553 and 760/376-6553). Other activities in the area include **HIKING, HORSEBACK RIDING, CAMPING, FISHING**, and several **FESTIVALS**, the largest of which is Whiskey Flat Days, a long weekend in February with parades, whisker-growing contests, food, and crafts booths. For more information on local events, contact the **CHAMBER OF COMMERCE** (11447 Kernville Road, at Sierra Way; 760/376-2629). To learn more about local history through Gold Rush and early ranching artifacts and Native American baskets and implements, visit **KERN RIVER VALLEY HISTORICAL MUSEUM** (49 Big Blue Road Street; 760/376-6683).

LODGINGS

Kern River Inn Bed and Breakfast / ★★

119 KERN RIVER DR, KERNVILLE; 800/986-4382

This six-room lodge built in 1991 near the banks of the Kern River has as solid a reputation for its food as for its homey, prim architectural style that easily fools most passersby into thinking that it was constructed 70 years ago. The sweet surroundings begin with roses lining the white picket fence and a huge, welcoming front porch. Inside rooms are named for local events and places, such as Movie Street, which refers to the false storefronts that once lined Old Kernville. Decor isn't overbearing or stage set–like, however. The Piute Room, for example, has a simple South-western decor with a wood-burning fireplace, while the Whiskey Flat room is rustic, with a stone fireplace. The Inn's largest rooms are Green-horn and Big Blue, both with country oak furniture, king beds, whirlpool tubs, and bay windows with river and mountain views. (Big Blue's name doesn't refer to innkeeper Jack Prestwich's former life as a software engineer for IBM; it was the name of the region's largest gold mine.) Best views of the river can be enjoyed from the Whitewater and Whiskey Flat rooms. Because this inn was built specifically as a B&B, rooms and baths are large, private, and modern. Guests are usually in their places promptly each morning at the big table in the dining room awaiting the arrival of Carita Prestwich's wonderful baked apple pancakes—gravity-defying creations that puff like hot-air balloons and curl up on their edges—served right out of the oven, laden with fresh strawberries in season. *$; AE, DC, MC, V; checks OK; kernriverinn@lightspeed.net; downtown across from Riverside Park.* ₲

Fairview

RESTAURANTS

McNally's Restaurant / ★

ON MTN HWY 99, FAIRVIEW; 760/376-2430

Steak lovers follow the Kern River deep into the mountains to find McNally's, part of a motel/grocery store/campground resort complex on the river. Steaks here are huge: a "regular" filet mignon runs 16 ounces, and a "large" a whopping 24. Porterhouses come in two sizes: 24- and 40-ounce. You'd have to be a professional wrestler to down these portions, but loyal diners don't seem to mind (they tote home their leftovers, or share dinners). Steaks are fried on the grill (none of that sissy mesquite stuff) and develop a wonderful seared flavor. Seafood's also on the menu, meekly taking a back seat to all the beef but good just the same. The scallops au gratin are rich and delicious. McNally's cuts their own beef

GOING FOR THE GOLD

On the verdant hillsides that flank the Central Valley, you'd expect those brilliant greens in spring. But there! What is that huge patch of gold in the distance? Or those brushstrokes of blue, like fragments of fallen sky?

In the hills rimming California's great valley, wildflower watching is still a popular spring-drive activity, despite the loss of most wild acreage to farming and ranching. Gone are the days when naturalist John Muir strode the region in 1868 and remarked, "When I walked, more than a hundred flowers touched my feet, at every step closing above them, as if wading in water . . . go where I would, east or west, north or south, I still plashed and rippled in flower-gems."

But you'll still find incredible floral color displays in nature preserves and even on rangeland: cattle ranching is not at all incompatible with the growth of native wildflowers, as long as the cattle range freely over a wide area. Best time to look is March through April. Best places? Two are highly regarded by sightseers and native plant authorities alike: Carrizo Plain and Antelope Valley.

To reach Carrizo Plain, go west from Buttonwillow and Interstate 5 on Highway 58 toward San Luis Obispo and the coast. After about 50 miles you'll enter an area called the Carrizo Plain—the rift zone of the San Andreas fault. Turn south on Soda Lake Road and go 18 miles to the Guy L. Goodwin Education Center (805/475-2131), open Thursday through Sunday, offering guided tours on weekends in April and May. From here you can head south on 22 miles of graded gravel road into a paradise of flowers and wildlife.

To reach Antelope Valley, go southeast from Bakersfield on Highway 58 over Tehachapi Summit (4,064 feet). You'll see plenty of roadside bloom along the way. Then go south on Highway 14 to the Antelope Valley California Poppy Preserve, open mid-March through mid-May for hiking and picnicking. Contact California State Parks (805/724-1180) for a status report on the year's bloom cycle. For Information regarding the California Poppy Festival each April in Lancaster, call (805)723-6000.

(procured from the same purveyor for over 30 years), makes their own dressings and desserts (a creamy cheesecake), and accompanies every meal with a relish dish, plenty of rolls, and a salad or their famed black bean soup, rich and dark. Don't expect any pretension here, but there's a magic to standing on the porch outside overlooking the river, cocktail in hand, waiting for your table—and the inevitable over-indulgence to come. $$; MC, V; *local checks only; dinner every day April–Oct, Fri–Sun Nov–March; full bar; reservations not necessary; 15 miles upriver from Kernville on Mtn Hwy 99, 15 miles north of Kernville.* &

Lebec

A famous (and infamous) stretch of Interstate 5 nicknamed "the Grapevine" connects Bakersfield to the Los Angeles metropolis. This radiator-scorching stretch, especially the grade from Wheeler Ridge up to Tejon Pass and Fort Tejon State Historic Park if you're southbound, sends many a car to the roadside with a bubbling boil-over. Turn off your air conditioner in summer to lessen the chances of your engine over-heating during the 3,700-foot gain. Snow also wreaks some havoc here—yet another hazard of this twisting 40-mile-long roadway.

One welcome rest stop is **FORT TEJON STATE HISTORIC PARK** (805/248-6692), a reconstructed Army post (established in 1854) that often hosts encampments and mock battles staged by Civil War–reenactment buffs.

The area gained international fame as the site of conceptual sculptor Christo's 1991 *Umbrellas* project. Hundreds of huge yellow parasols sprouted on the virgin hillsides during the event, attracting tens of thousands of backroad tourists until one umbrella toppled in high winds (common in the pass) and fatally injured an art lover—certainly one of the few cases in history when someone has been killed by an artwork.

Each April the hillsides are awash with California poppies, which open and close in sunlight and passing clouds. Spiked blooms of purple-blue lupine also line roadsides in patches so extensive that it looks almost as though pieces of sky have fallen on the hillsides. One fine backroad driving loop, best taken in springtime when the blooms are at their peak, is a daylong tour from Interstate 5 west on Highway 166 to Maricopa, then south through the folded foothills of the Tehachapis to the junction with Klipstein Canyon Road leading through Bitter Creek National Wildlife Refuge. Continue on to Mt. Pinos via Potrero Valley (on your map, you'll spot these roads as the obvious loop route that dances along Kern County's southern border). Mt. Pinos also attracts cross-country skiers each winter. Rejoin Interstate 5 via Cuddy Valley Road, which becomes Frazier Mountain Park Road.

Los Angeles Area: Restaurants by Neighborhood

LOS ANGELES

BEL-AIR
The Restaurant at
Hotel Bel-Air

BRENTWOOD
Peppone
Vincenti Ristorante

BEVERLY HILLS
The Belvedere
Crustacean
The Dining Room at
the Regent Beverly
Wilshire
Gardens
Ginza Sushi-Ko
The Grill on the Alley
Il Cielo
Kate Mantilini
Lawry's The Prime Rib
Matsuhisa
Mr. Chow
Nic's & The Martini
Lounge
Nouveau Cafe Blanc
Ruth's Chris Steak
House
Spago Beverly Hills

BEVERLY GLEN
Four Oaks

BOYLE HEIGHTS
La Serenata de
Garibaldi

**CENTRAL LOS
ANGELES**
Authentic Cafe
Boxer
Campanile
Flora Kitchen
The Ivy
The Little Door
Locanda Veneta
Mimosa
Sonora Cafe
Tahiti

CENTURY CITY
La Cachette

CHINATOWN
Yang Chow

CULVER CITY
Versailles

DOWNTOWN
Bernard's
Cafe Pinot
Cicada
Indochine
Pacific Dining Car
Seoul Jung

HOLLYWOOD
Cafe des Artistes
Citrus
Jitlada
Les Deux Cafe
Musso & Frank's Grill
Off Vine
Patina
Pinot Hollywood
Spago Hollywood
Zankou Chicken

LOS FELIZ
Katsu

MALIBU
Granita

MARINA DEL REY
Cafe del Rey

PACIFIC PALISADES
The Beach House

SANTA MONICA
Border Grill
Chez Mimi
Chinois on Main
The Hump
The Ivy at the Shore
JiRaffe
Lavande
Michael's
One Pico
Pacific Dining Car
Remi
Rix
Röckenwagner
Valentino

VENICE
Chaya Venice
Joe's
72 Market Street

WEST HOLLYWOOD
Ago
Alto Palato
Arnie Morton's of
Chicago
Chaya Brasserie
Dan Tana's
Dar Maghreb
Diaghilev
Jozu
La Boheme
Le Colonial
Le Dome
L'Orangerie
Lucques
Morton's
Orso
The Palm

GREATER
LOS ANGELES

SOUTH CENTRAL
Harold & Belle's
Inn at 657

HUNTINGTON PARK
Avila's El Ranchito

WHITTIER
Dattilo Restaurant

DOWNEY
Sambi
Szechwan

SOUTH GATE
La Barca Jalisco

GARDENA
Tsukiji

BELLFLOWER
Café Camellia
Johnny Rebs'
Marino's

SAN FERNANDO VALLEY

BURBANK
Cafe N'Awlins

CALABASAS
Saddle Peak Lodge

ENCINO
Delmonico's Seafood
Grille

GLENDALE
Cinnabar
Fresco Ristorante

NORTH HOLLYWOOD
Barsac Brasserie
Ca' del Sole

SHERMAN OAKS
Café Bizou
Joe Joe's
Mistral Brasserie
Paul's Cafe
Posto

STUDIO CITY
Bistro Garden at
Coldwater
Pinot Bistro
Sushi Nozawa

TARZANA
Kushiyu

TOPANGA CANYON
Inn of the Seventh Ray

VAN NUYS
Dr. Hogly Wogly's Tyler
Texas BBQ

SAN GABRIEL VALLEY

ARCADIA
The Derby

CLAREMONT
Aruffo's Italian Cuisine
Harvard Square Cafe
Heroes Bar and Grill

COVINA
Hayakawa

MONROVIA
Devon
La Parisienne

MONTEREY PARK
Harbor Village
Lake Spring
Ocean Star

PASADENA
Arirang
Arroyo Chop House
Bistro 45
Buca di Beppo
Cafe Santorini
Celestino
Clearwater Seafood
Crocodile Cafe
DeLacey's Club 41
Derek's
The Grill at the
Ritz-Carlton
Huntington Hotel
& Spa
Houston's
Il Fornaio
Kingston Cafe
Kuala Lumpur
Market City Caffe
Marston's
McCormick & Schmick's
Mi Piace
Parkway Grill
Pinot Restaurant &
Martini Bar
The Raymond
Shiro
Twin Palms
Xiomara and Oye!
Yang Chow
Yujean Kang's

PICO RIVERA
Dal Rae Steak House

SAN GABRIEL
El Emperador Maya
Tung Lai Shun Islamic
Restaurant

SAN MARINO
Julienne

SOUTH BEACHES

HERMOSA BEACH
The Bottle Inn
Club Sushi

LONG BEACH
Belmont Brewing
Company
Delius
Lasher's
The Madison Restaurant
& Bar
Shenandoah Cafe

MANHATTAN BEACH
Anacapa Restaurant
Cafe Pierre
Fonz's Restaurant
Good Stuff

PLAYA DEL REY
Caffe Pinguini
Inn at Playa del Rey

REDONDO BEACH
Chez Melange
Kincaid's Bay House

SAN PEDRO
Papadakis Taverna

TORRANCE
Depot

CATALINA ISLAND

The Channel House
Clubhouse Bar & Grille
El Galleon

San Diego: Restaurants by Neighborhood

CLAIREMONT
Via Italia Trattoria

CORONADO
Azzura Point
Chez Loma
The Prince of Wales Grill

DOWNTOWN
Athens Market Taverna
Bayou Bar and Grill
Bella Luna
Café Sevilla
Dobson's Bar &
  Restaurant
El Indio Shop
Filippi's Pizza Grotto
Fish Market Restautant
Laurel Restaurant & Bar
Morton's of Chicago
Olé Madrid
Sally's
Top of the Market
Trattoria Mama Anna

HILLCREST
Bombay
Chilango's Mexico City
  Grill
Kemo Sabe
MiXX
Montanas

KEARNY MESA
Jasmine

LA JOLLA
Bali Authentic
  Indonesian
Cafe Japengo
George's at the Cove
The Marine Room
Piatti
Roppongi Restaurant,
  Bar, and Cafe
Sammy's California
  Woodfired Pizza
The Sky Room
St. James Bar at Triangles
Trattoria Acqua
Tutto Mare Ristorante

LOMA PORTAL
The Venetian

MIDDLETOWN
El Indio Shop
Saffron Noodles and Saté
Shakespeare Pub and
  Grille

MIDWAY
Fairouz Restaurant &
  Gallery

MISSION VALLEY
On the Border

OCEAN BEACH
Belgian Lion
Kaiserhof
Ortega's
Thee Bungalow

PACIFIC BEACH
Cafe Athena
Nick's at the Beach

POINT LOMA
Red Sails Inn

SORRENTO VALLEY
Karl Strauss Brewery &
  Grill
Spices Thai Cafe

Index

We Stand By Our Reviews

Sasquatch Books is proud of *Southern California Best Places*. Our editors and contributors go to great lengths and expense to see that all of the restaurant and lodging reviews are as accurate, up-to-date, and honest as possible. If we have disappointed you, please accept our apologies; however, if a recommendation in this 1st edition of *Southern California Best Places* has seriously misled you, Sasquatch Books would like to refund your purchase price. To receive your refund:

1. Tell us where and when you purchased your book and return the book and the book-purchase receipt to the address below.
2. Enclose the original restaurant or lodging receipt from the establishment in question, including date of visit.
3. Write a full explanation of your stay or meal and how *Southern California Best Places* misled you.
4. Include your name, address, and phone number.

Refund is valid only while this 1st edition of *Southern California Best Places* is in print. If the ownership, management, or chef has changed since publication, Sasquatch Books cannot be held responsible. Tax and postage on the returned book is your responsibility. Please allow six to eight weeks for processing.

Please address to Satisfaction Guaranteed, *Southern California Best Places*, and send to:
Sasquatch Books
615 Second Avenue, Suite 260
Seattle, WA 98104

Southern California Best Places Report Form

Based on my personal experience, I wish to nominate the following restaurant, place of lodging, shop, nightclub, sight, or other as a "Best Place"; or confirm/correct/disagree with the current review.

_____

_____

_____

_____

(Please include address and telephone number of establishment, if convenient.)

REPORT

Please describe food, service, style, comfort, value, date of visit, and other aspects of your experience; continue on another piece of paper if necessary.

_____

_____

_____

_____

_____

_____

_____

I am not concerned, directly or indirectly, with the management or ownership of this establishment.

_____

SIGNED

_____

ADDRESS

_____

_____

PHONE   **DATE**

Please address to Southern California Best Places and send to:
SASQUATCH BOOKS
615 SECOND AVENUE, SUITE 260
SEATTLE, WA 98104
Feel free to email feedback as well: **BOOKS@SASQUATCHBOOKS.COM**